Grounded Law

Comparative Research on State and Non-State Justice in Multiple Societies

Published by

Wildfire
Publishing House

Manufactured in the UK
www.wildfirepublishinghouse.com

Grounded Law

Comparative Research on State and Non-State Justice in Multiple Societies

Chukwunọnso Okafọ, Ph.D.; B.L.
Professor of Law
University of Nigeria

Grounded Law: Comparative Research on State and Non-State Justice in Multiple Societies

Copyright © 2012 by
Chukwunọnso Okafọ

ISBN 978-978-923-376-2

Published by:

 *Wildfire*
Publishing House

The Wildfire Publishing House publishes prestigious premium-class books you can be proud of. For information please visit:
www.wildfirepublishinghouse.com

Printed in the United Kingdom. All wood product components used in the manufacture of this book are Forest Stewardship Council™ (FSC®) Mixed Credit. FSC® C084699

For my wife, Ezinwanne,
and children, Chinedu, Chidozie, and Chukwunọnso II,
with love

Contents

Part A
Challenges of Law 26

Part B
Politics of Law and Its Enforcement 150

Part C
Criminal Responsibility, Sanction, Environmental Crime Analysis 254

Part D
Case Studies of Alternative Law, Justice, and Social Control
382

Foreword

A society such as a modern State simpliciter is an abstraction. On that score, there is little complication about it. However, a modern society is typically very complex. A major factor constituting a society (State), its makeup, and tendencies is the aggregate of its peoples who naturally manifest diverse idiosyncrasies. In recognition of the diversity, and to provide clearer definitions of acceptable and unacceptable conducts by the citizens, every human society takes steps to state in various forms what is expected of the members in assorted situations and circumstances. The definitions (including customs, traditions, and laws) serve to minimize conflicts and deviations from a society's behavior norms; the definitions also help to unify the citizens in their expectations and obligations to one another. Thus, standardized behaviors are what make a society tick. Consequently, different human societies in diverse climes have since the formation of the societies designed patterns to accommodate and sanction tendencies that respectively agree or disagree with societal norms. This is necessary to consistently remind violators and the generality of the citizens of the society's expectations.

However, colonialism in its wake in various parts of the world has brought about dislocations in the behavior patterns of colonized peoples, leading in most instances to culture shock. In every colonized society, each colonizing power has imposed its mode of conduct as the fit and proper standard. In numerous instances, the colonizer has gone so far as to condemn pre-existing, broadly accepted, well-understood, effective, efficient, and sensible behaviors by criminalizing them. It does not matter to the colonialists that a behavior labeled as criminal may not be so amongst the colonized people. Since the prerogative of a conqueror is usually to re-write the worldview of a conquered people, colonialism has imposed its laws, championing them as superior to the customs, traditions, and laws that have existed over millennia in the subjugated territories. A major consequence of this colonial impunity is behavioral dislocation among colonized peoples.

As an example, the English common law, which was imposed in British colonies, postulated (and for the most part still insists) that the only customs, i.e. indigenous laws of the colonized peoples, *which should exist pari pasu with the English jurisprudence,* are those that are not "repugnant to natural justice, equity and good conscience". Meanwhile, colonial culture determines the yardstick for measuring this test. Indigenous laws that fail the test are seen and treated as "barbarous".

Interestingly, indigenous laws have survived up to this day, notwithstanding centuries of the "acceptance" and application of the laws of colonization. But it is more interesting from the African perspective that the African concept of criminal law, unlike its European counterpart, is restitutional, compensatory, and reconciliatory. Today this African jurisprudence is packaged as original research work in the name of "restorative justice" by modern Western legal thinkers. I remember Professor Reid of the School of Oriental and African Studies, University of London, who was my informal academic adviser while I was a research student at London School of Economics, telling me in 1982 that common law criminal jurisprudence has failed to solve the crime problem. He stated further that the African concept of reconciliatory criminal justice might well be developed towards finding a solution to criminal behavior. I believe that Professor Reid's assessment is correct, especially for those societies on which the common law criminal jurisprudence was imposed.

It is against this background that I welcome *Grounded Law* as an excellent contribution to this area of legal knowledge. The name *Grounded Law* is very apt; it shows the fundamental nature of indigenous laws in pre-colonial, colonial, and post-colonial societies. The indigenous laws have remained grounded in the cultures of the different peoples of post-colonial countries, showing that no matter the circumstances, indigenous laws are part-and-parcel of the citizens' lives, passed from one generation to another, enabling their existentialism since the remotest of antiquity.

I am very pleased with this excellent work, *Grounded Law*, especially as it addresses the indigenous laws of different societies and their roles in the law and justice of a modern State. In particular, I am proud of this book's author/editor, Professor Chukwunọnso Okafọ, who was my student in the Faculty of Law, University of Nigeria, in the middle 1980s. *Grounded Law* is a must-read for all lovers of legal knowledge. It is a source book for legal scholars, students of law, as well as policy makers in government who may wish to utilize the ideas and suggestions in the book for the improvement of society.

George O. S. Amadi, Ph.D.; B.L.
Professor of Law
University of Nigeria
Enugu, Nigeria

Preface

Increasingly, the limitations inundating official (that is, State or governmental) law and justice systems in various parts of the world are becoming obvious. There are numerous accounts detailing the inability of so many official systems to effectively and efficiently regulate behaviors and manage criminal and civil grievances, conflicts, and disputes among their citizens. This is particularly glaring in relatively recent postcolonies in which the social dislocations brought by colonization are fresh. Thus, it seems apposite to look closely at ways to designate appropriate methods and elements of unofficial (that is, non-State or non-governmental) law and justice for improved social control in a modern society.

In this connection, the body of the indigenous laws, customs, and traditions of a society is relevant. However, hitherto, *customary law, native law, aboriginal law,* or *indigenous law* (also called *custom, tradition,* etc.) has been used pejoratively to imply that the original law of a colonized society is inherently inferior to the law of the colonizer. For avoidance of doubt, Western societies (Europe and America) are the colonizers, while the other parts of the world, especially Africa, are the colonized. The negativity conjured up in the uses of the derogatory terms is widely known, but unjustified. There is no credible or rational foundation for the view that the original law of a society, which law probably dates back millennia, is inferior to the law of a colonizing power. Therefore, to correct the misconception and properly reflect the value of the homegrown legal philosophies, systems, processes, and practices of former colonies, such as those in Africa, this book offers the name *Grounded Law* to replace *Customary Law, Native Law, Indigenous Law,* and similar labels (see also Okafọ, 2009, pp. 7-8). *Grounded Law* reflects the homegrown quality of the original law of a society as distinct from the foreign law applied to the society, such as that imposed on Africa through colonization.

With contributions from various experts, *GROUNDED LAW: Comparative Research on State and Non-State Justice in Multiple Societies* presents original research on many countries and societies. The book analyzes a variety of unofficial as well as official law, justice, and social control systems and processes used in many societies around the world. It scrutinizes the vital law and justice need the unofficial processes serve in a modern State. Each society's unofficial processes are analyzed relative to some of the widely known and used official processes found in the relevant country. For example, in considering the contributions of Nigeria's unofficial law and justice, the common law of England as adopted for

Nigeria is relevant. For Cameroon, the Germanic and French legal codes, as well as the English common law, are relevant because of Cameroon's mixed colonial experience. The colonial encounters of Nigeria and Cameroon, respectively, differ and these have significantly influenced the law and justice systems of the two countries.

Thus, the historical circumstances of each country are unique and are considered accordingly in analyzing the relevant law and justice. The countries studied and addressed in this book include Cameroon, China (Hong Kong), Eritrea, Ethiopia, Kenya, Mali, Nigeria, Philippines, Singapore, Somalia, Tanzania, Tunisia, Uganda, and United States of America. Other countries, such as Britain, Congo, France, Germany, Ghana, and South Africa, are cited wherever relevant throughout the book to illustrate a point. However, with necessary situational adjustments to accommodate differences in environments, the reader will find that most of the legal/justice processes and issues discussed in this book apply to societies beyond those listed here. In addition, as appropriate throughout the book, the discussions in the various chapters offer comparative analyses of law, justice, and social control issues between or among countries.

Each study presented in GROUNDED LAW demonstrates the complex workings of alternative (unofficial, non-State, or non-governmental) law and justice and the critical need they serve in various societies. These analyses highlight the need to expand the meaning of "law" beyond its parochial sphere as a government-imposed or government-sanctioned phenomenon. Based on the various research and analyses presented in the book, a strong case is made that in spite of the philosophical disputations over the meaning of "law" (see examples: Austin, 1832/1998; Kelsen, 1945; Fuller, 1958; Hart, 1958; Hart, 1961/1997; Ratnapala, 2009; Bederman, 2010), it is reasonable to conclude that the concept cannot justifiably be constrained to the statements and actions of the State and its officials. Because of the crucial roles they play in managing criminal and civil cases and justice delivery generally, traditional and community institutions – most of whose statements and actions predate those of the modern State – cannot be discounted in determining the "law" of a State.

GROUNDED LAW is separated into four Parts and twenty Chapters. Part A (Challenges of Law) is made up of Chapters 1-5, which dwell on the role of law and alternative forms of control in doing justice. Part B (Politics of Law and Its Enforcement) consists of Chapters 6-10. The chapters examine forms of governmental and non-governmental policing along with the political implications of law enforcement. Chapters 11-15 constitute Part C (Criminal Responsibility, Sanction, Environmental Crime Analysis), which addresses criminal penalty, modifications of sanctions, corruption, and environmental influences on various forms of criminal behavior. And, Part D (Case Studies of Alternative Law, Justice, and Social Control) is made up of Chapters 16-20, which present and analyze the African jurisprudence vis-à-vis Euro-American jurisprudence. The Part D chapters also critique the interactions of State and non-State institutions and processes in the formulation, application, and enforcement of formal and informal laws in such countries as Cameroon, Nigeria, and the Philippines.

A study of the chapters will further clarify the relevant issues for the reader. However, now, suffice it to state that Part A (Challenges of Law) examines the challenges *to* and *of* law in a modern State. The challenges *to* law are the factors, conditions, obstacles, and other actions and inactions that oppose, question, or otherwise threaten the official law of a State and take away from its capacity to effectively and efficiently regulate the citizens to whom the law applies. Challenges *to* law emanate mainly from outside the law; the challenges derive from the environment in which the law operates in line with a society's dynamics. On the other hand, the challenges *of* law derive from the inherent quality of law to regulate relationships and adjudicate disagreements with validity, reliability, fairness, and in line with the other elements of the rule of law (see Chapter 1). In a nutshell, with challenges *to* law, the law is challenged, confronted, or opposed, whereas regarding challenges *of* law, the law challenges or sets the proper behavior standard. Perception is particularly important in considering challenges *to* law. Thus, for example, citizens' perception of the capacity of the law applicable to them informs their decision to challenge or not challenge the law. The citizens' perception and decision may be formed irrespective of the inherent quality of the law. That is, the perception and decision may not accurately reflect the law's quality.

In particular, several of the chapters in this book explain and illustrate challenges *to* and *of* the rule of law in modern States. Various studies show how in many modern States the citizens resort to alternative law and justice systems and processes to manage grievances, conflicts, and disputes. The cases are of civil as well as criminal types. Alleged crimes managed in the various societies range from some of the simplest (or least serious), such as simple assault and petty theft, to some of the most difficult (or most serious), including terrorism and murder. A challenge to a modern State's official law and justice system (which presumably was instituted to enthrone and/or maintain "the rule of law") is a challenge to the rule of law in the society, at least from the perspective of the official, State law. This challenge brings to the fore the fact that the modern State cannot by itself (that is, without contributions from the traditional, community, and other non-State institutions and processes in the country) effectively and efficiently maintain a just and legally stable society.

Finally, *GROUNDED LAW* is an excellent resource for scholars, students, practitioners, and policy makers in many fields of learning, including law, criminology, criminal justice, sociology, political science, government, and public policy. A great value of the book lies in the fact that the chapters are based on contributions by experts who understand the respective subjects very well and have performed original research on them, in the relevant countries. The increasing demands in many parts of the world for more relevant, effective, and efficient systems and processes of law, justice, and social control substantiate the importance of this book as it provides alternatives to the official systems and processes. As indicated, the book offers multiple illustrations of the workings of the unofficial systems and processes in varied settings across the world. The book contains many examples of State and non-State collaboration for improved law, justice, and social control. In particular, university and law school teachers, researchers, practitioners, students, and policy makers will benefit a great deal from this book because of its capacity to bring to the forefront hitherto unknown (or lesser-known) but effective and efficient law and justice systems and processes.

References

Austin, John (1832/1998) *The Province of Jurisprudence Determined*. Sudbury, Massachusetts, USA: Dartmouth Publishing.

Bederman, David J. (2010) *Custom as a Source of Law*. New York, NY, USA: Cambridge University Press.

Fuller, L. (1958) "Positivism and Fidelity to Law," 71 *Harvard Law Review*, p. 630.

Hart, H. L. A. (1958) "Legal Positivism and the Separation of Law and Morals," 71 *Harvard Law Review*, p. 598.

Hart, H. L. A. (1961/1997) *The Concept of Law*. Oxford, Britain: Oxford University Press.

Kelsen, Hans (1945) *General Theory of Law and State*. Cambridge, Massachusetts, USA: Harvard University Press.

Okafọ, Nọnso (2009) *Reconstructing Law and Justice in a Postcolony*. Surrey, England and Burlington, USA: Ashgate Publishing.

Ratnapala, Suri (2009) *Jurisprudence*. Melbourne, Australia: Cambridge University Press.

Chukwunọnso Okafọ, Ph.D.; B.L.
Professor of Law
University of Nigeria
2012

Acknowledgments

In many ways and to various degrees, several people contributed to the lengthy, rigorous, and taxing process that led to this book. I would be remiss if I did not mention their respective inputs. In particular, the following three groups of people deserve to be named here. One group is the staff of Wildfire Publishing House led by Wildfire Divine-Favour, the Chief Communications Architect. I am proud of their professionalism and commitment to original and innovative ideas. The second group is made up of the colleagues with whom I engaged in numerous exchanges of ideas, presentations, and roundtable discussions at professional conferences and other avenues over the years. In some instances, the interactions helped to clarify some of the issues and ideas presented in some areas of this book. These colleagues include Professor Timothy Austin (Ph.D.), Dr. Oko Elechi (Ph.D.), Professor Ihekwoaba Onwudiwe (Ph.D.), Professor James Opolot (Ph.D.), Dr. Simon Ortuanya (SJD), Professor Susan Smith-Cunnien (Ph.D.), and Dr. Victoria Time (Ph.D.). The third group consists of those who contributed materials for this book. These are the colleagues named in the second group, along with Dr. Smart Otu (Ph.D.), Caroline Time (LL.B.), and Ph.D. Candidates Sikiru Asifatu and Kingsley Ejiogu.

Thanks to all.

List of Abbreviations
(LAW REPORTS)

AC – Appeal Cases
All NLR – All Nigeria Law Report
CCHCJ – Certified Copy of High Court Judgment (Lagos)
Cr. App. R. – Criminal Appeal Report
Cr. L. J. – Criminal Law Journal
KB – King's Bench
NMLR – Nigerian Monthly Law Report
NRNLR – Northern Region of Nigeria Law Report
NWLR – Nigerian Weekly Law Report
QB – Queens Bench
SCNLR – Supreme Court of Nigeria Law Report
US – United States Supreme Court Cases
WACA – West African Court of Appeal
WLR – Weekly Law Report
WNLR – Western Nigeria Law Report

Part A

CHALLENGES OF LAW

In this Part

Chapter 1

The Rule of Law: Characteristics, Alternative Models, and the Challenges of Application in Society

Chukwunọnso Okafọ
University of Nigeria

Introduction

"Adịghị eke ikpe na ọnụ otu onye" (Igbo, Nigeria proverb. English language translation: A case is not decided based on one person's story).

"The rule of law is better than that of any individual" (Aristotle).

"An equal application of law to every condition of man is fundamental" (Thomas Jefferson, former President of the United States of America).

What does "the rule of law" mean? At the outset, it is necessary to mention that this concept is broadly understood and interpreted. Like "law" (Hart, 1961/1997), "the rule of law" has defied a standard definition. Rather, numerous legal scholars, jurists, philosophers, as well as average citizens have contributed to the present understanding of the rule of law. By addressing various aspects of the concept, the numerous thoughts have contributed to a *checklist* of the characteristics that would qualify a law and justice system as one based on the rule of law. Therefore, the rule of law encompasses a wide variety of law and justice elements.

In addition, an appropriate interpretation of the rule of law requires accommodations to be made for differences in the circumstances of societies, groups, and persons, as well as other relevant variations. Further, a rule of law discussion includes the official and unofficial responses to the various environmental factors found in the place under consideration. Thus, although reasonable people will (and do) agree on some of the elements of the rule of law, the same reasonable people may (and often do) disagree on some other elements. Even where an element of the rule of law is generally understood and accepted, the methods of applying and enforcing the element to specific groups, persons, and circumstances are sometimes subjects of disagreement.

A corollary of the foregoing is that "the rule of law" idea has long been a contentious subject among countries and societies, such that one country's idea of furthering the rule of law is another country's evidence of imposition of a foreign or external idea. These disagreements breed suspicion and resistance. Nowhere are these disagreements more evident than in the relationship between the Western World and Africa. With these in mind, this chapter explores and analyzes the elements of the rule of law. It is recognized that the concepts may apply differently between dissimilar populations. Also, the chapter points out that the rule of law is one of the models of justice and social control. Further, the difficulties of applying the rule of law are examined. Because of the particular challenges accompanying the application of the concept to the unstable, so-called developing countries, such as those of Africa, much of this chapter references several relevant rule of law situations to illustrate the difficulties and frustrations.

In examining the elements of the rule of law, it seems necessary to distinguish between the "conceptual" and "applied" characters of the model. The distinction, although loose and in some cases somewhat arbitrary, is aimed at identifying and explaining the ingredients of the rule of law, as well as demonstrating how they could be applied for justice and social control in sample settings. Thus, the distinctive elements are provided mainly to clarify the constituents of "the rule of law".

"The Rule of Law": Conceptualization

As indicated in the Introduction section, the rule of law model has been expressed in innumerable ways by countless legal and social philosophers. Aristotle's and Thomas Jefferson's respective interpretations (cited at the beginning of this chapter) are only two of such expressions. The various definitions/interpretations of the rule of law tend to emphasize different aspects of the concept. For examples, while Jefferson's definition emphasizes the need to apply law equally to the citizens and other subjects, Aristotle, in his interpretation, emphasizes the supremacy of law – that law ought to be above all the citizens and subjects, as well as on top of all other models for justice and social control. There are numerous other definitions/interpretations of the rule of law, each with its emphasis area.

Consequently, to understand the rule of law completely, we need to consider and appreciate its various components or elements. In this connection, efforts should be made to, as much as possible, emphasize the various components equally. No part of "the rule of law" is more important than another part. A de-emphasis of an aspect of the justice and social control model is likely to diminish the proper authority of law, thus compromising the understanding of the concept. True, to ensure clarity, the different components of the rule of law are identified and explained in this chapter. Nevertheless, a comprehensive appreciation of the model requires the reader to study all the various elements and consider them holistically.

All reasonable interpretations of the rule of law must hinge on the existence of a set of laws that applies in specified circumstances – a place, time, human subjects, subject matters, etc. Such interpretations also must rest on the equality of all persons and groups in the relevant society, before the applicable laws. The expectation then is that, based on the laws, all the parties ought to be recognized as equals and treated as such in the determination of their relationships, rights, and obligations. Based on the rule of law characteristic of equality before the law, the parties to a case and other stakeholders have an opportunity to enjoy fairness in the hearing and determination of the issues that concern them. The foregoing notions of the rule of law seem to be generally well understood. Nonetheless, endless battles have been and continue to be waged over the accurate meaning of "the rule of law".

Despite the absence of a universally accepted *definition*, the rule of law idea (that is, the reasoning that the law of a society should rule or regulate relationships, activities, rights, and obligations in the society) is a genius human invention. Once it became necessary for one human being to co-exist and routinely interact with another human being, an objective mechanism for managing grievances, conflicts, and disputes became critically important. The human society needed to evolve such a system. It is an inevitable truth that wherever two or three are gathered, there are bound to be conflicts. And, neither of the parties to a grievance, conflict, or dispute can reasonably be expected to satisfactorily play two opposing roles at the same time: interested party and impartial arbiter. No human being, however pure his (or her) heart, can always or routinely judge fairly an issue in which he has interest. Thus, the inevitability of the rule of law became clear as human relationships began, developed, and diversified. Of all human inventions, the rule of law ranks as one of the most important assurances against systemic unfairness and eventual society's failure. The rule of law, if properly practiced, gives the citizens confidence in their society. This justice and social control model appropriately grounds and stabilizes a society. In turn, this will foster cohesion, faith, and support for the society and its leadership.

However, the rule of law is by no means the only model for justice and social control. Despite the crucial need for the rule of law, the other models (such as custom, tradition, culture, and religion) contribute to justice and social control in every society. In some societies, several or all of the alternative models, particularly custom and tradition, contribute greatly to justice and social control. But, to appreciate the importance and suitability of the rule of law for a just and progressive society, one should consider the alternatives to the rule of law. Among the decipherable alternative justice and social control models, the rule of law appears to be the fairest and most sustainable, especially if the goal is to build and maintain a credible society for the present time and long into the future, in which the citizens and outsiders will be free within the parameters of the law. The alternative models for justice and social control include "the rule of personality", "the rule of community", "the rule of custom/tradition", "the rule of experts", "the rule of religion", etc.

Rather than have a society based exclusively on one *rule* or the other, all or some of the *rules* may be found in a society at the same time. Many of the provisions of "the rule of religion" may co-exist with the provisions of "the rule of law", for instance. Moreover, in some respects, the different rules overlap. Thus, for instance in a society, differentiating between religious rules and customary rules may be difficult, if not impossible. Further, a rule of religion will become a rule of law provision once the law incorporates the former such as through formal legislative action. Similarly, a custom or tradition, notwithstanding questions about its "law" quality (Hart, 1961/1997; Bederman, 2010), will become a component of the rule of law once a legislature formally enacts the custom or tradition or it is adopted through an official judicial decision.

Each of the alternatives to the rule of law is designed to achieve justice and social control by means of a set standard, defined, sustained, and applied by a specific person or group in society. Thus, justice and social control in a society where any of the alternative models applies is based on a person's or group's norms and idea of justice. The standard is not the norm of the society in general. Instead, it is specific to a person or subgroup of the society. The idiosyncratic and narrow nature of each of the alternative models should concern every reasonable member of an affected society. This is because each model is liable to produce uncertain, inconsistent, and narrowly defined principles and applications in the justice and social control process. On the other hand, the rule of law leads to justice and social control based on a society's reasonable and broad-based laws. These laws reflect the generality of the citizens of the affected society. Consequently, the rule of a dictatorship (individual or small, unelected and unaccountable group), however benevolent or functional, cannot qualify as the rule of law. Nonetheless, it is acknowledged that in a limited circumstance, such as the next few paragraphs demonstrate, a dictatorship may be a necessary step to the rule of law in a society.

To be sure, in general, a dictatorship does not qualify as a rule of law. But, even if the rule of a dictatorship does not *immediately* qualify for the rule of law, a strong argument can be made that a society may actually need a benevolent and functional, even if unaccountable, dictatorship for a short period of time. In the interim period, the dictatorial leadership can take fundamental steps to establish (or re-establish) the institutions of the State, such as the law and justice system, to make them effective and efficient. Thereafter, the State institutions can take over and run as they should for the benefit of the majority of the citizens. Such short, targeted dictatorship may be justified as a necessary step toward building a system based on the rule of law. The brief dictatorship envisaged in this thesis is clearly premised on the understanding that public leadership is far more about the character and achievements of the leaders than about their brand name. Thus, even a "dictatorship" can be organized and managed for public good. This seems acceptable, provided that it is meant, implemented, and serves as an interim measure.

The case of Ghana under the former military Head of State, Jerry Rawlings, offers a strong argument in support of a brief, targeted dictatorship where it is justified. Prior to Rawlings' emergence as Ghanaian dictatorial leader, the country was on the verge of collapse, mainly due to unbridled corruption and gross incompetence among the leaders. Many Ghanaians sought economic and political refuge in Nigeria and other West African countries as well as other parts of the world. Rawlings set out to rescue his country. He did so by staging a *coup d'état*, rounding up and executing the key leaders who had almost succeeded in destroying the Ghanaian nation. Through several reforms, he soon put Ghana on the paths to infrastructural and economic recovery, as well as substantial electoral reform. Today, Ghana is one of the most successful countries on the African continent. Their economy is doing so well that many Nigerian companies and businessmen have relocated from the unpleasant Nigerian environment to Ghana.

The country's electoral system is one of the most transparent and strongest in Africa. In short, today's Ghana is very different from its pre-Rawlings (dictatorship) era. Relative to other African countries, including Nigeria, the rule of law is strongly entrenched in Ghana. But, without Rawlings' dictatorial intervention, Ghana might have ceased to exist as a nation, or at least been significantly diminished.

Pre-Rawlings Ghana was a *failing*, if not a *failed*, State. Consequently, it seemed justified for Rawlings' dictatorship to intervene and rectify the fundamental errors in the State's structure, organization, and conducts. A common thread among the States that have failed is the absence of the rule of law. In every such instance, the citizens of a failed State have lost confidence in their State and its ability to regulate and treat the citizens fairly. Consequently, the citizens take the laws into their own hands. By taking the laws into their own hands, the citizens deny the State's crucial supervisory authority and oversight function. Somalia, Sudan, Zimbabwe, as well as Afghanistan, and Iraq during the insurgent-plagued United States occupation (particularly the 2003-2009 period) are frequently cited as instances of *failed* States. See generally *The Fund for Peace*'s "Failed States Index 2009". Besides the specific absence of the rule of law, a *failed* State lacks several other qualities. More broadly, a *failed* State is often typified by economic, political, and social failures. Thus, a *failed* State is discerned by the following criteria:
   (a) Absence of physical control of the country or of the monopoly on the legitimate use of physical force in the country;
   (b) Attrition of legitimate authority to make shared decisions;
   (c) Incapability to provide reasonable public services; and
   (d) Powerlessness to interact with other nations as a complete member of the international community (see generally "Failed States Index 2009").

In considering the rule of law, *failed* States should be distinguished from their *failing* counterparts. Nigeria and Burma are at least *failing* States. A number of factors characterize a *failing* State, among which are:
   (a) inexistence of, or extensively degraded, public services;
   (b) severe economic decline; and
   (c) pervasive criminal behavior, bribery, and corruption.

These three categories of factors accurately define contemporary Nigeria. The country's public services either do not exist or are unreliable. As much as 70% of the country's 150 million citizens are reputed to live below the poverty line. Official and unofficial crimes, bribery, and corruption have eaten so deeply into the Nigerian society that it is practically impossible to get something of significance done without participating in the illegal activities (as either an offender or a victim). By a reasonable measure, Nigeria is at least a failing State. Thus, in the country, the rule of law (or what is left of it) is on the verge of disappearing as the dominant regulator and determinant of justice, relationships, and responsibilities among the citizens.

Overall, considering the alternative models of justice and social control, and to prevent or correct the *failed* and *failing* State characteristics, the rule of law model should be preferred. A major advantage of the rule of law model over many of the alternatives is that the rule of law offers a strong basis for broad-based consensus and legitimacy among the diverse citizens of a modern State. In the long run, a diverse State is built, sustained, and thrives because the citizens view and relate to the State as a joint venture in which all the citizens have more or less equal stakes. Thus, each citizen regards his or her survival, improvement, and long-term interest as intertwined with those of the State. And so, a citizen is far more likely to work for the sustenance of a State that observes the rule of law than another that follows the idiosyncratic rule of personality (or any of the other narrow alternatives to the rule of law).

Although one of many models of justice and social control, the rule of law (or some of its elements) can be found in most modern as well as pre-modern societies. Apparently, in recognition of the seeming universality and importance of the rule of law, every modern State lays some claim to "the rule of law" – each State somehow justifies or attempts to justify the rules that apply to its citizens and their affairs. In addition, each State invests significantly in the system, methods, and procedures for defining, identifying, applying, and executing the relationships, rights, and obligations of the citizens. The invocation and application of the rule of law in a society throws up the specific principles that guide the society. Sometimes, the principles found in a society are unique to that society and not easily reproducible in another society. However, more often than not, a principle of the rule of law found in one society has an identifiable equivalent in another society. This evidences the seeming universal nature of the rule of law. The apparent wide appeal of the rule of law derives from the fact that its principles are sensible, reasonable, and fair for justice and social control.

Take the example of the Igbo (Nigeria) proverb: "Adịghị eke ikpe na ọnụ otu onye" (English language translation: "A case is not decided based on one person's story").[1] This principle of justice and social control stipulates that a judge or other arbiter should not render a verdict or conclude a case unless and until both (or all) sides to the issue have been heard. "Both (or all) sides" encompasses the parties directly involved in a case as well as the other stakeholders. Often, the stakeholders (other than the parties) in a case have valuable information that would assist the judge to reach the legally sound and just decision in the case. Every reasonable effort should be made to accommodate these stakeholders in the decision process. Thus, besides the Plaintiff and Defendant in a civil case (or Prosecutor and Accused in a criminal case), factual and expert witnesses ought to be counted as some of the "sides" to a case. Also, close relatives of a victim are included, such as when they are needed to give impact statements to the court before the latter determines the sentence to be imposed on a convict. In receiving relevant information from

---

[1] The Latin maxim "Audi alteram partem" ("Let the other party be heard") is an equivalent expression.

the sides to a case, the hearing opportunity granted to each side ought to be reasonable and fair relative to the opportunities allowed for each of the other sides.

By the "Adịghị eke ikpe na ọnụ otu onye" principle, the Igbos believe that hearing only one side to a grievance, conflict, or dispute and deciding it on the basis of that hearing alone, inevitably prejudices and disadvantages the sides that are unheard. Similarly, granting unequal hearing opportunities to the parties and stakeholders is unjust because the process likely puts a side to the case at a disadvantage. Hearing from all the sides to a case before deciding it is not just an ideal; such hearing establishes the proper foundation for a just decision. Thus, the process serves two main purposes, as follows. One, the comprehensive procedure allows the judge to consider all the stories, arguments, and counter-arguments in the case. The procedure enhances the quality of justice by ensuring that the judge is apprised of all the relevant facts and circumstances of the grievance, conflict, or dispute before rendering a decision. Two, involving all the parties reassures them and gives them a sense of belonging in the process. In this circumstance, it is clear that the *procedure* for justice can be a valuable tool for quality social control, perhaps as much as the *substantive* judgment. A process that appropriately accommodates all the sides to a case (parties and other stakeholders) enhances the efficacy of the *substantive* judgment because, having been reasonably involved in the procedure leading to the decision, the parties and others are more likely to accept and comply with the court's judgment, even if they disagree with its substance. Thus, it comes to this: The procedural and substantive aspects of justice reflect on and reinforce each other.

In "Adịghị eke ikpe na ọnụ otu onye", the Igbos recognize that one of the easiest things to do is to accuse another person of something or lay a claim against him or her. The harder thing is to prove that accusation or claim. The difficulty of proving an accusation or claim is further compounded when the accused person and other witnesses are given reasonable opportunities to challenge the allegation. Thus, considering the elements of the rule of law, including the requirement that a case is to be heard and decided by an independent judiciary through an open, fair, and objective procedure, this Igbo principle significantly furthers justice and social control. Therefore, the Igbo principle is a key component of the rule of law. The principle is well founded and applicable in other societies as well.

In the same way that the rule of law (such as the "Adịghị eke ikpe na ọnụ otu onye" principle illustrates) is valuable to justice and social control in Igbo, most modern States regard it as an indispensable component of a properly grounded and functioning society. For the reason of the concept's universal appeal or relevance and applicability, and to underscore the importance of the idea in both concept and practice, the United Nations Organization (UN) has studied and published extensively on the rule of law. The UN, being a worldwide organization, has through its publications and initiatives, sought to guide a universal understanding, application, and use of the rule of law. The UN guide (reproduced below) is particularly valuable because it identifies and addresses the rule of law on multiple levels: General Rule of Law; International Rule of Law; National Level; and Human Rights (see "UN Rule of Law Guidance and Policy Material", 2010).

The UN's rule of law standards are couched by the following topics and subtopics ("UN Rule of Law Guidance and Policy Material", 2010):

1.   *General Rule of Law*, which contains information on such issues as the United Nations Development Program's reports on global partnership for development; the other issues addressed by the General Rule of Law include: empowering people and institutions; reports on strengthening and coordinating UN rule of law activities; enhancing global rule of law assistance; various dialogues with Member States on the role of the rule of law in the achievement of national and international goals; etc.

2.   *International Rule of Law,* including: multilateral treaties and related materials; international standards and principles; UN Charter related issues; and Security Council resolutions and statements.

3.   *National Level,* which comprises: constitution-making; transitional justice; access to justice; corruption and transnational organized crime; criminal justice; security institutions; justice for children; gender justice; and legal pluralism (restorative justice approaches, alternative dispute resolution, informal justice, and security mechanisms).

4.   *Human Rights*, comprising: fact-finding and commissions of inquiry; legal system monitoring; national human rights institutions; and internally displaced persons (IDPs).

The broad-based topics enumerated by the UN mean that a (UN Member) country's justice and social control system, if it is to be accepted as based on the rule of law, is required to address the various topics, at the identified levels. Thus, the characteristics of the rule of law named and discussed in this chapter ought to apply at all the levels, and to all the topics. "Rule of law" at one level or in one subject area without the rule of law in the others is not sufficient to describe the affected society as one based on the rule of law.

In addition to the identified levels for the rule of law, the UN has provided a comprehensive definition of the concept to accommodate the various issues arising at the various levels identified above. Specifically, the UN has defined "the rule of law" for universal use. In presenting the UN definition below, I highlight the key elements of the concept by identifying each element with italics and a number in brackets [ ]. Altogether, the italics and brackets show the fifteen important elements of the rule of law in the UN's definition, as follows:

For the United Nations, the rule of law refers to a principle
of governance in which all persons, institutions and entities,

public and private, including the State itself, are *accountable to laws*[1] that are *publicly promulgated*[2], *equally enforced*[3] and *independently adjudicated*[4], and which are *consistent with international human rights norms and standards*[5]. It requires, as well, *measures to ensure adherence to the principles of supremacy of law*[6], *equality before the law*[7], *accountability to the law*[8], *fairness in the application of the law*[9], *separation of powers*[10], *participation in decision-making*[11], *legal certainty*[12], *avoidance of arbitrariness*[13] and *procedural and legal transparency*[14, 15] ("The Rule of Law and Transitional Justice in Conflict and Post-Conflict Societies: Report of the Secretary-General", 2004).[2]

It may be valuable to mention that the UN's definition, although provided in the context of "transitional justice in conflict and post-conflict societies", is applicable to other societies as well. A careful study of the identified elements reveals the thoroughness of the UN definition. If followed, the definition will serve a society well in creating and maintaining the rule of law in its jurisdiction. Again, in every effort to apply the rule of law principles to a population or matter, the peculiarities of the parties and circumstances should be considered to the extent that reasonableness permits.

Now, the following question is important. Does "the rule of law" idea extend to the form (process) and substance (contents; specific provisions) of a law? The short answer is "yes". As the UN definition of the rule of law shows, understanding the concept and its application begins with a consideration of the source(s) of a law sought to be applied. In considering "the rule of law" concept, it is tempting to overlook the law making process and concentrate instead on the law's interpretation and application. Laws that regulate human relationships in a society are either made contemporaneously with those relationships or discovered (from the past or other society). However a law comes into being, it is vital to consider the law's origin and the process by which the law came into being, as factors in establishing or denying its credibility as a legitimate means of social control. I now proceed to offer a more detailed response to the question concerning the process followed in making a law.

As stated, "making" a law includes enacting a new law as well as amending or otherwise modifying an existing law. It also extends to receiving a law made and used by a previous generation of the same society where it is intended to be applied in the present. Further, law making encompasses borrowing a law made in another jurisdiction for that other society – for a present or past generation. In considering whether a specific law complies with the rule of law standard, the precise manner (process) by which the relevant law was made is pertinent. The extent, if at all, to

---

[2] Italics, brackets, and numbers added.

which the process complies with the requisite procedural ingredients of the rule of law is of great value in evaluating the legitimacy of the law sought to be used.

Granted that whatever the origin of a law, an important issue is whether or not the law (substantively and procedurally) *rules*. That is, does the law control or govern the allocation and enforcement of relationships, rights, and obligations among the interested parties? The rule of law standard is that the law should *rule*. Otherwise, the situation is that a model of justice and social control other than the rule of law *rules*. However, the importance of the process for making a law lies in the fact that the capacity of the law to *rule* does not exist independently of the process by which the law came into being in society. Thus, law's capacity to rule or regulate relationships, rights, and obligations in a society significantly depends on how the law came into being (along with the legitimacy it enjoys among the citizens).

As shown in the preceding paragraphs and by the UN's definition of the rule of law, the process for making laws is relevant and important to a complete and proper appreciation of the rule of law situation in a society. This is because the fairness essence of law requires that the parties (citizens) to whom a law is to be applied must have a credible part in the formulation as well as the implementation of the law. If not, the citizens are liable to reject or ignore the law. A few words are needed here to explain citizens' *credible role in law making*. *Direct citizen participation* (by every citizen) in law making is the purest form of citizen involvement in law making. However, that would be impossible or unrealistic, considering the size of a modern society. Thus, indirect citizen participation is the second best option. *Indirect citizen participation* is viable and it can be credible. This channel allows the citizens to contribute (through representatives) their views to the formulation of the laws that govern their affairs.

Modern States' representative democracies, such as the presidential system of the United States of America, the British and Japanese parliamentary cum monarchical systems, and the Indian parliamentary system, among others, allow the citizens to participate indirectly in making the laws that govern them. Note that the form of law making that will satisfy the rule of law does not depend on the label placed on a government system, such as when a State claims to be practicing "democracy" or to be a "democratic" State (example, Nigeria 1999-present – see below). Where the citizens participate directly in law making, the rule of law requirement is satisfied. However, as already noted, direct participation is often impossible or too difficult because the number of citizens in a society (State) is too large to be managed directly. The remaining option is for the citizens to participate indirectly through their elected representatives. For the citizens to truly participate indirectly in law making, the process for electing the representatives must be widely accepted as genuine, beyond reproach, and reflective of the electorate's choices. A thoroughly or reputedly flawed electoral process cannot produce genuine representatives of the people.

Representatives produced by a flawed electoral process are usurpers. They are at best an illegitimate legislature. The laws that result from an illegitimate legislature do not qualify as proper laws of the legislature of a rule of law-based society. "Proper laws of the legislature of a rule of law-based society" are expected to comply with the characteristics of the rule of law, including the recognition and enforcement of the rights of the citizens to participate genuinely and fully, directly or through their freely chosen representatives, in making the laws that govern the citizens. Similarly, the laws of the illegitimate legislature cannot be a credible basis for establishing the rule of law. Where the laws of a society are made by a legislature that lacks the genuine and free consent of the citizens, the laws lack the authority to be the foundation for creating and strengthening the rule of law in that society. Therefore, even if the rule of law is sought to be installed in an otherwise disordered society, if the legislature is illegitimate or otherwise lacks credibility, its laws are thus bereft of the proper grounding for the rule of law.

It is quite fitting to cite Nigeria here as an example of an advertised "democracy" that is in truth undemocratic. The country's undemocratic character, in turn, undermines the rule of law. Nigeria's undemocratic personality stems from the widely known and acknowledged fact that since 1999, when Nigeria allegedly returned to democracy, no credible election has been held in the country. Thieving politicians consistently steal the citizens' rights to choose their leaders through credible, periodic elections. The 1999 elections exercise, which ushered in the return to "democracy" in the country, was fatally flawed in significant ways. The failings include the following two. One, the *Constitution of the Federal Republic of Nigeria, 1999* that was supposed to set the road map for elections and the subsequent government turned out to be a contraption by a few elite military and military-backed civilians over the other millions of Nigerians. The Constitution was not even released to Nigerians until after the 1999 elections had taken place. Moreover, the citizens were not allowed the opportunity to decide (such as through a constitutional assembly of elected representatives) the contents of the Constitution. It is hard to imagine that such a document could be anything other than a device to advance the narrow interests of a few powerful persons over the interests of the vast majority of the citizens.

Two, the 1999 elections were marred by widespread fraud. Many ordinary Nigerians as well as home and foreign elections monitors verified this. Numerous voters were so intimidated that they could not vote or voted for candidates other than those they preferred. In addition, votes were suppressed, ballot boxes were stuffed with votes illegally, results were forged, there were significant violent encounters before and during the voting, etc. Nonetheless, many Nigerians and foreign watchers were willing to endure these ills as a price to pay for instituting democracy in the country after many years of military dictatorship. The expectation was that the subsequent elections would be better organized and implemented to improve the country's profile among its citizens and in the international community. Regrettably, the processes and results of the subsequent elections of 2003 and 2007, respectively, have overwhelmingly belied the optimism that democracy would soon become the norm in Nigeria. So bad have things unfolded that the 2003 elections exercise was worse than that of 1999.

As if the 2003 elections were not bad enough, Maurice Iwu's (Nigeria's elections commission chairman) 2007 "elections" have since proved to be the worst in the country's history. In fact, many indigenous and foreign observers have concluded, with justification, that the 2007 exercise is the worst election ever in Africa, perhaps in the modern world. The vastness and depth of the crime called the 2007 elections becomes particularly clear and mind-boggling when one considers the enormous waste of national human and material resources and the infamy the exercise produced. After wasting billions of Naira, Maurice Iwu, with impunity, presided over the manufacture of fictitious and illogical "elections results" that bore minimal, if any, resemblance to the Nigerian citizens' preferences. Iwu's machinations ensured that the ruling PDP political party retained its corrupt and debasing stranglehold on Nigerians.

Thus, it is not surprising that many of the results of the 2007 elections have since been voided by the courts (see Ezekwere, 2008; "Nigeria Court Annuls 11th State Governor Election", 2008; "Nigerian State Election Overturned for Fraud", 2008; "Nigerian Court Annuls Southwest State Governor Vote", 2009). More than three and one-half years after the 2007 elections, the courts are still annulling some of the results. For the annulment of the Ekiti state governorship election, see "Maurice Iwu, Ayoka Adebayo Slammed As Court Declares Fayemi Ekiti Governor"

Maurice Iwu, Ayoka Adebayo Slammed as Court Declares Fayemi Ekiti Governor" (2010); Adeyemi, et al. (2010); Ndujihe and Akinyemi (2010); Odebode and Oni (2010); and Olanrewaju (2010). Regarding Delta state, see Aliu, et al. (2010), Amokeodo, et al. (2010), and Aziken, et al. (2010). Other results continue to be challenged in the courts. Thus, the current Nigerian "democratic" State does not qualify as one based on the rule of law.

Individuals and groups that posit "the rule of law" to regulate human behaviors should appreciate the need to properly and accurately identify, define, and apply the concept to situational issues, places, times, and parties. Thus, satisfying the rule of law standard in any given circumstance depends broadly on the definitions provided by the relevant laws and the applications of the laws to extant grievances, conflicts, and disputes. It is acknowledged that the rule of law is difficult to apply to real grievances, conflicts, and disputes, in real circumstances. However, the appropriateness of an application goes a long way in telling the parties and observers in any case, that the rule of law does or does not hold sway in their society. By its handling of the rule of law, a society shall be known as either a place in which the law is supreme or an environment in which the whims and caprices of other narrow interests dominate, such as in the rule of personality.

The following section examines in detail the elements of the rule of law, especially as they apply to postcolonies that are more recent.

Fundamental Notes on the Rule of Law: Application and Challenges

The foregoing discussion demonstrates that an available and strong rule of law is important for a stable society. The need for a strong rule of law is even more critical in an unstable society. The UN's definition and other policy positions on various aspects of the rule of law support this view. Recent or relatively new postcolonies tend to be less stable than older postcolonies. Newer postcolonies, such as Nigeria and most African countries, provide obvious examples of countries lacking acceptable standards of order based on democratic, just, and fair laws. For reasons that seem obvious, it is more challenging to achieve and sustain the rule of law in a more recent postcolony than in a longer established and ordered society. The increased difficulty stems mainly from the numerous entrenched parochial interests and mutual suspicions that trigger and fuel competitions for limited "national" resources. In this environment, protecting one's narrow group interest is generally viewed as superior to advancing the national goal of cohesion and advancement. Thus, even national laws are applied and enforced with a view to achieving narrow individual and group advantages.

To extend the rule of law discussion, it seems necessary at this juncture to itemize and further explain the key elements of the concept. In doing so, where necessary, I will cite an example to buttress a point. However, care should be taken to avoid painting all "more recent postcolonies" as unorganized, disorganized, or unordered. None of the nomenclatures necessarily fits all recent postcolonies, in much the same way it would be misleading to argue that all older postcolonies are organized and ordered. Rather, the organizational condition and arrangement vary from one society to another due to multiple factors. This section's emphasis on the special needs of the more recent postcolonies flows from the significant and prevailing anomie that the citizens of the more recent postcolonies, such as Nigeria, endure in various aspects of their lives. By contrast, citizens of the older postcolonies, such as the USA, Canada, and Australia have succeeded in resolving or otherwise managing many, if not most, of the dislocations that remain as common features of the more recent postcolonies.

As we examine in greater depth the "the rule of law" and its application to specific environments, the several key elements of the concept are discernible from diverse definitions/interpretations. This chapter provides some of the definitions/interpretations. Considering the various theses, for the rule of law model of justice and social control to prevail in a society, all of the following elements have to be recognized and properly accounted for.

(1) Law making is the province of the legislature

In a society, such as a modern State, where the rule of law prevails, elected representatives of the citizens (the Legislature) make laws for the State. Proper law making requires full deliberation before a legislative enactment. The legislators should carefully weigh a proposed law, considering all its components and consequences. It is important for the legislators to identify and explain the effects of the nascent law on the society in general. They should also take note of the relationship between the proposed law and existing laws. As appropriate, the legislators should invite and receive inputs from the other citizens in the process of making a law. Like the authority to make law, the authority to change or amend existing law should be vested in the legislature or in such other body as the legislature delegates.

It is acknowledged that, along with the legislature, there are various sources of laws in a society. Besides laws made by the legislature, laws emanate from customs and traditions (Okafọ, 2009; Bederman, 2010). Also, in military dictatorships, such as Nigeria and many other countries have experienced, the dictator makes laws through decrees and edicts with little, if any, regard for the rule of law. The rule of law is subjugated to the whims and caprices of the dictator in a military regime (Ibekwe, 1993). Thankfully, military administrations are an aberration, not the norm. Further, even in a society governed by the rule of law, the executive arm of government makes laws in limited situations, usually consistent with the guidelines given by the legislature. In addition, the judiciary often makes laws through judicial interpretations. This is especially so in those "hard cases" where the law does not (sufficiently) regulate the issues that a court is asked to decide (Hart, 1961/1997, p. 272). However, see Hart (1961/1997, pp. 272-276) for the contrary view that the judiciary should limit its functions to interpretation and application of the law, not law making. In the final analysis, where the executive or the judiciary makes any law at all, this should be limited and closely monitored. The legislature should be the highest law making authority in a modern State governed by the rule of law.

(2) Legislation ought to be prospective; it should not be retrospective

In making laws, a legislature is to be guided by the past, present, and future experiences and needs of its society. However, the laws emanating from the legislature should aim at regulating and correcting behaviors *going forward*. This means that although inevitably and deservedly a legislature makes laws based on its determination that existing and past events show that a law is necessary to address a social problem or issue, a law cannot be made to *go back* to regulate activities that were unregulated when they took place. The proper procedure is to make a law, inform the citizens that the law is in place and will become effective on "X" date, to prevent or respond to specified behavior. Consequently, all contraventions of the law from the "X" date will make the violator liable under the law. The *principle of legality*, which requires all laws to be clear, ascertainable, and non-retrospective, like *legal formalism*, shares the *rule of law* expectation of prospective instead of retrospective law.

Moreover, to enact a law to *go back* and regulate previously unregulated behavior could amount to specifically targeting particular individuals or group. A law that goes back and targets specific persons or group would be retroactive as well as discriminatory. The legislation would amount to oppression and witch-hunting by the State. On a related issue, a law that targets a person or small group in society may be focused on a *personal* (or *private*) *problem*. A (good) law, by definition, is enacted to address a *social problem*, rather than a personal problem. Thus, a good law deals with a general or broad-based issue in society. Finally, a just law in a society based on the rule of law adequately informs the citizens of the expectations of the law well in advance before law violators are required to account for their disobedience.

(3) Law as stated or defined regulates relationships, rights, and duties

In a society in which the rule of law prevails, the statement of the law determines the procedural and substantive decisions on grievances, conflicts, and disputes. Typically, the legal statements and definitions are written. This is to increase verifiability and minimize ambiguity. In those situations where applicable laws, such as customary laws, are unwritten, they are verified through case law and evidence. However, the provisions of the law, not the preferences of a ruler or other influential interested party, shall determine a party's entitlements and obligations. The stated or defined law is above everyone and everything in a society where the rule of law applies. The law is supreme.

A clear statement or definition makes a law reasonably certain and ascertainable. The main reason for this is law's public character. Also, equally importantly, law should be certain and ascertainable because vague and/ or undiscoverable law compromises the citizens' rights. When a person is unable to reasonably identify and verify in advance the legal standards by which his or her behavior will be judged, the person's rights have been violated or at least compromised. In the circumstance, the State is the violator or compromiser because it is the State's responsibility to ensure that its citizens are reasonably well informed about what the law expects from them.

Writing is an effective means of stating or defining laws. However, the specific language medium used to write a law is relevant. The proper standard is that law should be written in the citizens' language – the language that most, if not all, the citizens speak and write fluently. If, on the other hand, in a society law is written in a language that most citizens do not speak or write (or the citizens lack fluency in the language), it would be very difficult to convince a prudent observer that the law is verifiable to the citizens. Similarly, a prudent observer would regard the law as ambiguous to the people, thus leading to the conclusion that the citizens do not sufficiently understand their law. Unfortunately, many postcolonies, especially those of Africa (example, Nigeria) have retained with little or no modification the colonial languages imposed upon the respective postcolonies. Consequently, their laws are typically written in foreign (usually European) languages even though most of the African countries' citizens speak and/or write minimal, if any, of the applicable foreign languages (see Okafọ, 2009, pp. 57, 135-136, 186-188).

However, while recognizing the certainty and verifiability qualities of law, a system predicated on the rule of law should make allowance for changing aspects of the law that are at variance with the common expectations of the population. The process for making the law of a society, as well as that for changing it, should include free and open participation by average citizens, directly or through elected representatives. If the citizens are not meaningfully involved in the making or changing process, the resulting law will lack credibility. That, in turn, will negatively affect the law's efficacy.

(4) Law as applied goes a long way in determining the rule of law

This element qualifies the rule of law element (3) above. The rule of law element (4) highlights the difference between the *statement* or *definition* of a law and its *application* to specific grievances, conflicts, and disputes. Whereas the *statement* or *definition* of a law makes it easier to identify and access the law for understanding and interpretation, the *application* of the law focuses on using the law to appropriately address the subject matter and parties in a case. In line with the rule of law, the main concern of law application is the actual use to which the law is put to determine relationships, rights, and duties. The focus is on the appropriate use of law for justice and social control. The various conditions of persons subject to the law (the parties' and other affected citizens' circumstances) are to be taken into consideration.

Thus, appropriately applying a law sometimes requires a judge to be creative, within legally allowed limits, to ensure that justice is done, even if the *statement* or *definition* of the law would produce a contrary result. In this sense, the application of law within the standards of the rule of law incorporates judicial discretion. Judicial discretion allows – even encourages – a judge to exercise reasonable flexibility in judging. Thus, if the circumstances of a case permit, and to ensure that justice is achieved, a judge may *individualize* the case and the decision thereon. Such *individualization* can be evidence of relative informality in a judicial proceeding (see Okereafọezeke, 1996; 2002, particularly pp. 31, 38, and 203). However, as mentioned earlier, see Hart (1961/1997, pp. 272-276) for the view against judicial discretion. By this opposing idea, the judiciary should limit its functions to the interpretation and application of the law, not law making. Nonetheless, law as applied to individual cases goes a long way in determining whether the rule of law subsists in a given society.

Note, however, that in the final analysis the *rule of law* (along with the *principle of legality* and *legal formalism*), among other things, requires law to be ascertainable and non-retrospective. Even in spite of allowances for justified adjustments in law during the administration of justice, this basic requirement of certain and non-retrospective law remains critical to the three related concepts.

(5) The law restricts discretions

To be sure, while allowing and encouraging judges to *individualize* cases and judicial decisions [see the rule of law element (4) above], the rule of law places limitations on the discretions that judges may exercise and how those discretions may be exercised. Although discretion is an indispensable component of justice, the rule of law delineates the substance and form of the discretion. Consequently, the rule of law excludes unchecked discretion. Rather, restraints are necessary to control the substance as well as the form of discretion. *Controlled discretion* is necessary to avoid or respond to judicial abuses. Law is not to be adjusted to serve an illegal or otherwise illegitimate purpose. *Uncontrolled discretion* would allow illegal and illegitimate exercises of discretion.

(6) Citizens are equal before the law

Equality of citizens before the law is a fundamental characteristic of the rule of law. This means that: (i) there is one law for all; (ii) the law is to be applied to all; and (iii) the law is to be applied equally. However, this rule of law requirement admits of important exceptions, such as through lawful and reasonable exercises of discretion. As I noted earlier [see the rule of law element (4)], discretionary exercise of judicial authority allows reasonable and justifiable accommodations to be made in the application of the law to individual cases, to ensure that justice is done. Thus, by the rule of law element (6), short of legal and justified adjustments in specific cases for the purpose of achieving justice, the law ought to be applied equally to all citizens. Equal application means that the law sees and treats every person subject to it in the same way regardless of varying conditions, such as prestige, title, office, influence, or other difference. Failure to apply the law equally to all in a society leads to the conclusion that the rule of law is absent or at least compromised.

Perhaps as much as any other rule of law element, equality (or lack thereof) of the citizens before the law is easy to recognize. As an example, lack of equality before the law in Nigeria is widely acknowledged. The absence of equality before the law illustrates the lack of the rule of law in the country. Nigeria is notorious for its official declarations (through the Constitution and other laws) that the citizens are equal before the law. However, the realities of law interpretation, application, and enforcement are that there are at least two sets of laws in the country: one set of laws for the privileged, rich, and influential citizens, and the other set of laws for the rest of the citizens. The citizens in the first category are significantly fewer in number than the rest of the population. The remaining citizens are in the overwhelming majority but possess minimal, if any, authority or power in the society. However, the few advantaged Nigerians possess and use their authority and power illegally and immorally, to promote their narrow interests and dominate the rest of the population. The illegal activities of the privileged Nigerians subvert the rule of law because those activities violate the legal declarations of citizen equality.

Anele (2010) thoroughly and succinctly describes the form and depth of the rule of law problem in Nigeria, thus:

> ... irrespective of constitutional provisions that guarantee equality of all [Nigerian] citizens, and the facile pronouncements of judges and law teachers to that effect, in reality there are two sets of laws operating side-by-side in the country. The first set applies to the anonymous "common man," the down trodden, the ordinary Nigerian distant from the centres of power as Pluto is distant from the sun. Under this very law, a man who stole a goat will have one of his arms amputated; if he sole (sic) a million he will be in prison for up to ten years. The other set applies to "sacred cows," the oppressors, the big men and thick madams who run things in Nigeria. This group includes top politicians, former heads of state and governors, high ranking members of the business elite, well-heeled clergymen and women etc. Under this law former military dictators, kleptomaniac bank executives and failed politicians who misappropriated billions of naira are not only free to "enjoy" their stinking wealth, they even have

the audacity to contest elections! A big man or thick madam who stole billions can return a small part of what he or she had stolen, enter into plea bargain with the relevant authorities and go home to mock the stupid system. At any rate, going by what have been happening since the EFCC [Economic and Financial Crimes Commission] was created, Nigerians know that when a prominent and well-connected person commits an offense no matter how serious, the worst punishment he or she might receive is two years imprisonment. This is the reality of inverted justice in our nation: it is the major reason why the ogre of corruption is spreading its tentacles to all aspects of our national life (p. 2).

In sum, the rule of law problem in Nigeria is not for want of legal provisions guaranteeing citizen equality. The problem derives from the lack of proper and equal interpretations, applications, and enforcements of the existing laws among all the citizens.[3]

(7) In adjudications, the law follows time-honored standards and procedures

If the law is to be the basis for adjudging cases and allocating rights and responsibilities to the parties, the provision of a law, its interpretation, and application to cases should be clear and as consistent as possible over time. This means that two identical (or similar) cases, governed by identical (or similar) laws, within the same geographical jurisdiction, ought to be adjudged similarly even where they are separated by time. That is, judicial precedent is to be observed. To be sure, no two cases have the same facts. Therefore, similarity of facts will suffice in this consideration. If identical (or similar) cases are treated similarly, we can speak of consistency of the law.

Borrowing from the Latin *stare decisis* (the binding force of precedent), the rule of law requirement that similar cases be treated similarly means that a party to a case (or his lawyer-representative) can legally rely on a decision in a similar previous case to persuade the court to decide the present case similarly. And, in line with the precedent rule, the court will be expected to accept the binding precedent and decide the present case as persuaded, unless a distinction can be made between the present and previous cases. Factual difference is an important basis for distinguishing a present case from a previous case. On an invocation of the doctrine of precedent, a judge or opposing party may distinguish between a

---

[3] Negotiated justice (plea bargain) as a prominent example of legal deviations from the equality-before-the-law principle is examined in-depth in Chapter 11.

present case and a previous case by showing that there is no factual basis to decide both cases similarly. Thus, the previous case would not apply to the present. Also, a decision based on an established precedent may be overruled by the same or a higher court. This can take place where, for example, the overruling tribunal finds that the previous decision, even if it was itself based on precedent, had been reached erroneously. The importance of precedent cannot be overstated. If the rule of law is to prevail in a society, the citizens deserve reasonable certainty as to the position of the law, on grounds of the courts' decisions in previous cases.

However, to be sure, there are various exceptions to *stare decisis*. In sum, where *stare decisis* is raised to ensure that a previous court decision binds a court in a subsequent case, the subsequent court may, depending on the facts and the law, decide on the *stare decisis* principle in any of the following ways:

(a) Accept the previous decision and decide the subsequent case accordingly. Therefore, the previous decision binds the subsequent case, and lives on.

(b) Reverse the previous decision. This means that the previous decision ceases to have effect.

(c) Overrule the previous decision. In this situation, a higher court decides in a later case that the earlier case was wrongly decided.

(d) Refuse to follow the previous decision. This means that a subsequent court, which lacks the authority to overrule the previous decision, but is also not bound by the decision, refuses to abide by it.

(e) Distinguish the previous decision from the present case. Such distinction means that the previous decision is denied authority over the subsequent case. A previous case is distinguished from the subsequent case either because the two cases differ in their facts or because the law in the former case is too narrow to apply to and decide the issues in the subsequent case.

(f) Explain the previous decision. Rather than accept and apply a previous decision as it is, the judge in a subsequent case may first interpret or clarify the previous decision. Thereafter, the judge applies or distinguishes the previous decision. The consequence then is that the previous decision is modified to suit the subsequent case.

Another important component of the rule of law element (7) is the need for courts to follow established procedures in deciding cases. A modern judicial process includes *civil procedure* as well as *criminal procedure*. These procedures are typically in writing, again to ensure objectivity and clarity, and minimize ambiguity. A judicial decision based on the rule of law has to comply with the applicable procedure. Otherwise, such a decision would be capricious and likely to be overturned on appeal. A court's *civil procedure* or *criminal procedure*, as the case may be, is what makes a judicial process certain, and removes undue exercises of discretion.

(8) An independent and open judiciary is essential

An open, free, self-reliant, and self-governing judiciary is a vital component of a justice system based on the rule of law. If, on the other hand, the judiciary of a society were controlled by, or dependent on, another person or institution, the rule of law would be compromised. The importance of an independent and open judiciary is predicated on the following essentials. One, officials of the judiciary need to be free to consider and decide law and justice issues that are brought before them without being beholden to a person or group. Two, parties to a case in the judiciary, as well as the general citizenry, ought to be confident that judicial officials are detached from the other organs and powers of the State, and are capable of independently hearing and deciding the issues brought to the judiciary without external control. And, three, an effective way to demonstrate that a society's judiciary is independent and open is to ensure that the judicial process is readily accessible to the citizens. In addition, the proceedings of the judiciary are to be conducted in the public domain, rather than in secrecy. However, it is reasonable to make exceptions to the public-trial standard in those rare cases of credible threats to the survival or security of the State or its citizens. The rule of law element (8) recognizes the importance of earning and retaining the confidence of the parties to a case as well as the other citizens in a society based on laws. If the citizens lose confidence in their judiciary, then the law loses its capacity to rule in that society. That would be the end of the society's rule of law.

Nevertheless, for the most part, an *independent judiciary* is an illusion. It is a key component of ideal law and justice. An *independent judiciary* is unreal. At best, it is a goal to be pursued, but it may never be achieved. In essence, no society has an independent judiciary. As far as is foreseeable, considering the multiplicity of interests and the competition for authority, power, and limited resources in a society, no population can have an independent judiciary. This is because *independence* portends complete separation from all other persons and groups in society or even within the constituent arms of government. In practice, it is impossible for the judiciary of a society to divest itself of *all* controls and influences by the other arms and agencies of the society's government. In fact, it is undesirable for such a complete separation to take place or exist. Instead, the judiciary, as well as the other departments and organs of a State, should be subjected to oversight to prevent or correct illegal conducts and abusive exercises of authorities and powers. Absent such oversight, the society runs the risk of a dictatorial judiciary, which will feel empowered to issue orders to all other organs, departments, and citizens, without being obligated to explain its actions and omissions. Consequently, the *independent judiciary* that the rule of law envisages is of a moderated form. This means that the judiciary of a justice system based on the rule of law should exist and function as an organ of the State, in some ways subject and answerable to appropriate organs and authorities in the State. Similarly, other State organs and authorities answer to the judiciary. The mutual obligations provide for checks and balances. That is precisely why in Nigeria (despite its questionable rule of law credentials), the President, who is the leader of the Executive arm of government, appoints the Chief Justice and Justices of the Supreme Court of Nigeria (the highest court in the Judicial arm). The President makes the appointments on the recommendation of the National Judicial Council and subject to the Senate's confirmation (Section 231 of the *Constitution of the Federal Republic of Nigeria, 1999*). Also, two-thirds majority of the Legislature at the federal level have to address the President before a Chief Justice can be removed from office (for a Justice to be removed, the National Judicial Council would have to recommend to the President) (Section 292). As further illustration of the checks and balances involving the judiciary, the Judicial arm hears and decides the constitutionality of Legislative and Executive acts and omissions as well as the rights and obligations arising therefrom. The United States of America is similarly structured (see the *Constitution of the United States of America*).

Thus, to function effectively, the rule of law needs an environment in which the arms, departments, and organs of the State are balanced and interdependent, rather than an environment of complete judicial separation from the other segments of the State. In the final analysis, an *independent judiciary* for the rule of law means that the constitution and other laws creating and empowering the judiciary allow it (along with its officials and agents) ample authority, power, and protections to carry out judicial duties without fear of harm or liability.

(9) Law is fundamental in society

For the avoidance of doubt, law is the basis for establishing, organizing, and managing all the organs, institutions, agencies, and programs of a society based on the rule of law. The constitution and the other laws of such a society provide the legal foundations for the organs, institutions, etc. This means that no organ, institution, or other entity can be created, financed, or maintained by the State unless the constitution or law authorizes the entity's creation and sustenance. Thus, the policies and programs of the society's government are predicated on the rule of law, rather than the personality of the prevailing ruler or other consideration. This increases the likelihood that a program or policy predicated on the rule of law will survive the leader that authored it. Also, the role of law in a society based on the rule of law is to delineate the authorities and powers of the different departments, organs, agencies, and officials of the society. Based on the legal demarcations, conflicts in official businesses are minimized. Where a conflict arises, the law is the objective basis for resolving the disagreement. This rule of law element recognizes the fundamental character of law in a society. The law helps the society to avoid an unpredictable environment for the citizens and outside observers.

(10) Law should be justifiable on grounds of morality

This means that a law's positive statement and its application as such do not suffice for the law to be a legitimate component of the rule of law. Positive law is the passed, promulgated, or adopted ("posited") law in a society. It is made up of the written rules and regulations laid down by the government or its authorized constituent, which rule or regulation is an expressed written command of the government. See Austin's (1832/1998) "command theory". The character, content, or quality of the positive law is irrelevant. Thus, its goodness or morality is immaterial so long as the law came into being through the prescribed law making process (see Austin, 1832/1998; Kelsen, 1945; Fuller, 1958; Hart, 1958).

However, it seems that in general but especially for the purposes of the rule of law, the character, content, quality, goodness, and morality of a law are worthy of consideration. Even if it is clear and easy to understand, a *positive* law may lack sufficient credibility to be a component of the rule of law if the law's provisions are morally unjustifiable. A law issuing from a dictator that disregards or does not account for the welfare, interests, preferences, or aspirations of the generality of the citizens detracts from the rule of law. Thus, the quality of a law is relevant to the rule of law. The "law" that the rule of law model envisages is that law which accords with the proper moral standard that the relevant society and reasonable persons expect. The "law" in the rule of law must not offend the reasonable person's sense of good, fair, and just law. In this connection then the statement of the law alone, or its strict interpretation and application, is not enough to qualify a law as a credible component of the rule of law. More is expected of a law seeking to qualify as a component of the rule of law. Such law ought to be consistent with and further the best interests of the general citizenry to which it applies.

Thus, law that oppresses a majority of its citizen-subjects while serving the narrow interests of the influential elite members of the society is not good enough as a constituent of the rule of law. Indeed, if the law of a society is at variance with the society's general morals, and oppresses the majority of the citizens, it is expected that the law will soon lose its authority and capacity for justice and social control. To be sustained over time, the law of a society must reflect enough of the population's moral standard that the citizens would consent to and follow the law. However, since a society's morals change over time, it is unreasonable to expect the society's law to reflect all such changes. Rather, to become stable and continue as a credible justice and social control instrument, the law of a society must be reasonably in line with the general citizenry's moral standard.

It is noteworthy that sometimes the moral standard of the majority in a society may not be beyond reproach. Just because the majority of the members of a society hold a particular moral standard does not mean that it is a "good" enough standard to regulate all persons in the society. To be applied to all the members of a society, the moral standard of the majority in the society has to satisfy an important condition. The proper test of a society's broad-based moral standard is whether it extends "minimal protections and benefits to all within [its] scope" (Hart, 1961/1997, p. 200). If not, then although it is a standard held by the majority, it is not a proper moral standard. Such was the situation in the Slavery and Racial Discrimination eras in the USA. In both times, the official laws of the majority European (White) population approved of the immoral behaviors (that is, enslavement and racial subjugation, respectively) towards Africans.

In the final analysis, law's aim ought to be more than citizen control. Law should do more than control the citizens by all means. A good law aims to advance the legitimate interests of the citizens while regulating the citizens' behaviors. In this connection, Nonet and Selznick's (2001) analysis of law as potentially a "progressive" instrument is relevant. According to Nonet and Selznick (2001; see also Okafọ, 2006), the least progressive type of law is *repressive law*, followed by *autonomous law*, and finally the most progressive *responsive law*. Accordingly, of the three options, *responsive law* seems to be the most justifiable law form on grounds of morality. Therefore, *responsive law* most accords with the aspirations of the rule of law.

Taken together, the various rule of law theses lead to the conclusion that, for the rule of law model of justice and social control to prevail in a society, the ten elements identified and explained above have to be satisfactorily accounted for and represented. The following section expands on the foregoing discussion of the rule of law elements.

Further Discussion on the Application and Challenges of the Rule of Law

The identified elements of the rule of law (see the section on "Fundamental Notes on the Rule of Law: Application and Challenges") encompass the concept's *form* as well as its *substance*. In emphasizing form, the rule of law may be viewed as an official statement of the law in a society regardless of the fairness of the law itself. On the other hand, substantively, law goes beyond the issuing of a statement and looks to the character or quality of the statement to determine (based on its fairness or justness) whether or not it is good enough to rule over the citizens. It seems more reasonable to define "the rule of law" in line with the substantive paradigm. Law is meant to regulate human behavior. It is not just a mechanical abstraction. Therefore, all the identified ingredients of the rule of law are crucial for understanding the idea, and they all have to be taken into account in the application of the concept to a society.

In deciding whether the rule of law applies to a society, it is important to contemplate whether the society is peaceful. Peace or peaceful coexistence is a key purpose of law (Okafọ, 2007). The central focus of the rule of law in a society is to establish and maintain peace founded on legitimate order, among the citizen-subjects as well as between them and outsiders. Establishing and maintaining peace in a society is a major challenge for the rule of law model, especially because of the many ideals and interests the rule of law has to balance. Examples: The rule of law is required to protect the rights of the citizens of a society and satisfy their safety expectations against criminals while at the same time enforcing the rights of criminal suspects. Similarly, the rule of law requires justice officials to follow the law, always, and equally, while also mandating the officials to exercise discretion to achieve justice in individual cases. In spite of the challenge that establishing and maintaining peace poses for the rule of law, peace remains a worthy rule of law ideal. The difficulties notwithstanding, peace can be achieved for a society in which the rule of law standard described in this chapter is allowed to regulate law and justice.

A law system that lacks focus on the peace essential lacks a core quality of the rule of law. Peace stems from avoiding anomie (normlessness – a condition in which the proper norms or governing standards of conduct do not exist, have disappeared, or have become so weakened that they are incapable of regulating behaviors and relationships in the society) and enthroning credible, effective, and efficient norms. Peace results from proper interpretation, application, and enforcement of credible laws in society. Peace avoids jungle living and its survival-of-the-fittest mentality. Ordered, undisturbed, and serene coexistence are essential for the progress of a society.

The rule of law is arguably the most credible guarantor of lasting order and security in a society. Order or security predicated on the rule of personality, rule of religion, or other less desirable justice and social control model is bound to be short-lived. Likewise, order or security imposed by a dictatorial, high-handed regime, such as a military junta or other illegitimate group, is artificial and will soon collapse because it lacks the citizens' consent and support. To the extent that the citizens were not legitimately involved in the formulation of their society's laws and/or their laws' applications, the citizens are unlikely to identify with those laws. Such a situation significantly undermines the society's progress. Therefore, the rule of law is crucial to the survival and advancement of a society.

As indicated earlier, the challenge of creating and maintaining an ordered society based on the rule of law is higher in more recent postcolonies than in their older counterparts. Consistent with the elements of the rule of law identified in the previous section, true, meaningful, and lasting peace in a society, such as the rule of law envisages, can only be established and maintained where a *fair, reasonable, certain*, and *verifiable* interpersonal and inter-group standard prevails. These criteria, along with others identified elsewhere in this chapter, constitute the foundation for the rule of law.

Fairness connotes evenhandedness – in both process and substance. A peacemaker or peace guarantor (the lawgiver as well as the given law and the process for its giving, application, and enforcement) must be fair and reasonable to the citizens. As mentioned while outlining the rule of law elements (3) and (4), the process followed to decide relationships and allocate rights, privileges, and responsibilities must be equally applied to the parties and other interested persons and the process must be generally viewed as equal. Perception is an important component of determining whether a process is fair. In addition, the results of law applications to comparable situations should be closely matched, else the substantive component of the rule of law may be lacking. Unreasonable or inexplicable variations in the substance of applications of the law between otherwise identical or similar situations will inevitably raise suspicions of favoritism, incompetence, or both.

However, applications of the law that fail to fully and accurately consider and incorporate the facts of each case should be adjudged as unreasonable. *Unreasonableness* can be found in the process of law making or its interpretation, application, or enforcement. At any of those points in a justice system, an unreasonable action or omission denies the rule of law quality or, at a minimum, it interferes with a citizen's ability to accept that a system of law is predicated on the rule of law. A law that is unduly harsh in imposing penalties for its violation is both unreasonable and unfair. Its excesses divest the law of the ideal humaneness and relevance that would properly ground a legal provision rooted in the rule of law.

The *certainty* attribute of law [see the rule of law element (3)] refers to law's stability – in definition, interpretation, application, and enforcement – in society. Uniformity in a system of laws assures the citizens that their actions and omissions will be treated fairly without fail regardless of an individual case. Of course, as pointed out, however *certain* a law is, a measure of variations is inevitable. Such variations are necessary to accommodate the unique circumstances of each case. Nevertheless, where a *certain* law is varied, such variation ought to be reasonable and fully justified. Otherwise, it would appear to be an alteration made contrary to the expectations of the rule of law at the whim or caprice of an interested or influential person. Thus, *certainty* imposes on the lawgiver, interpreter, and enforcer the duty to consistently follow known, available, and relevant principles of law in the management of grievances, conflicts, and disputes. This is the way to create a stable and peaceful society.

Also, *certainty* means that the law giver (legislature), law interpreter (judiciary), and law enforcer (police and other law enforcement agencies), while observing the certainty of law – in form (process) and substance (content), are required to appreciate and incorporate *flexibility* in the quest for justice. As such, and as mentioned earlier in outlining the rule of law elements, a relevant official should focus on doing justice in circumstances that confront him/her, even if an otherwise *certain* principle of law would have to be modified through exercise of discretion to achieve justice.

"Justice", notwithstanding its varied definitions, interpretations, and connotations, necessarily evokes a fair *process* and *result* for the stakeholders (parties, community, State, etc.). It is doubtful that an unfair process can lead to a fair result. Thus, both the process and the result have to be considered to determine whether justice is present in a given case. Justice officials should remind themselves and one another to be fair, and to be seen to be so, in carrying out their duties. This is in spite of the rule of law element that requires laws to be certain and consistent over time [see the rule of law element (3)]. However, in every justice system, laws, their interpretations, applications, and enforcements are often modified or adjusted through exercises of discretion. A closer examination of discretion in law and justice reveals its value to the rule of law.

What is discretion in law and justice? What are the proper parameters for applying discretion within the strictures of *certainty* in the rule of law? Discretion in a justice system is "a situation in which an official has latitude to make authoritative choices not necessarily specified within the source of authority which governs his decision making" (Atkins and Pogrebin, 1981). In the specific area of criminal justice, the agents and exercises of discretion are identifiable, thus:

> In criminal justice organizations staff have broad discretionary powers to invoke the criminal process or to send a suspect or offender on to the next stage. For police, the power is to arrest or not to arrest. Prosecutors exercise broad discretion in the charging decision, and judges have wide latitude in managing the judicial process and in sentencing. In corrections, probation officers, prison staff, and parole officials exercise discretion over program placement, penalties for rule infractions, and release (Stojkovic, Kalinich, and Klofas, 2003, p. 309).

To illustrate the pervasiveness of judicial discretion, civil as well as criminal court judges have and exercise significant latitude in interpreting and applying laws even in spite of *stare decisis*. Often, the exercise of discretion goes beyond adjusting the law to do justice in a case (individualization). The higher level of judicial discretion involves *judicial law making*, in which a judge devises or formulates a legal principle to address an aspect of a case before the court because the legislature has not provided a law for the issue. To the extent that no legal system is capable of anticipating and creating specific legislative provisions to address all possible issues in a society, *judicial law making* seems inevitable and necessary, provided that it is done prudently. However, it has been challenged as *ultra vires* judicial authority and dangerous for a free society where law making is the province of the elected representatives of the people (see generally Hart, 1961/1997, pp. 272-276).

In addition to the police, prosecutors, judges, and corrections personnel, many other officials exercise various forms of discretion in their day-to-day functions in the course of justice. It is necessary to bear in mind that besides government justice officials, there are numerous private sector members and agencies that contribute to the justice process. Often, their roles are invaluable to the police, prosecutor, defense attorney, judge, corrections personnel, etc. Example: a private security organization that protects its employer's life and property or a community watch group that secures the community because the official police cannot be in every location to prevent or stop a crime is contributing immensely to the course of law and justice. And, in doing so, each of the private contributors inevitably exercises discretion.

As important as discretion is in a justice system, there is an important argument against it. Some critics view an exercise of discretion as evidence of lack of control. They take the position that discretion amounts to "decision making unfettered by constraints of law or policy" (Gottfredson and Gottfredson, 1980, p. 350). To the extent that discretion extinguishes or dilutes law's capacity to control a justice official's decisions and conducts at all times, discretion raises concern. For example, discretion allows a police officer to decide whether or not to arrest a crime suspect. This important decision – which "controls the gate to the entire criminal justice system" (Stojkovic, Kalinich, and Klofas, 2003, p. 310) – depends on the (reasonable) assumptions of the police officer. Moreover, discretion can lead to illegitimate and corrupt behavior by a justice official due to the lack of specificity in the relevant laws. Consequently, supervisory authorities in the justice system, such as among the courts, have taken steps to counter possible abuses of discretion. A major step is the requirement that every exercise of discretion must be *reasonable*. This means that the decision must be such that a prudent person similarly situated as the decision maker would make. There must be verifiable facts and other circumstances that support the decision. A decision maker's preference is not necessarily reasonable. For a preferred decision to be reasonable, the facts leading to the decision and its other circumstances must support the decision. In a hierarchical court structure, for example, a superior court is authorized to assess and pronounce on the reasonableness of an inferior court's exercise of discretion.

However, notwithstanding the drawbacks of discretion, it is an inevitable and useful tool in a justice system. In reality, it is impossible to manage many similar cases similarly. Even similar cases are likely to be different in important respects. The differences may be within the facts of the cases or due to relevant events in the larger society. If justice is to be done, and seen to have been done, the applicable differences ought to be recognized and addressed to the extent possible and reasonable. Moreover, overall, a justice system is dynamic. This means that it evolves and changes over time. Thus, the system often makes changes to the substance of the laws and justice as well as the relevant procedures. As such, a justice system makes various adjustments in the course of making, interpreting, applying, and enforcing laws to cases. Many of the changes are minor – these adjustments are made merely to accommodate specific details arising from the circumstances that the law or lawgiver did not foresee. Sometimes, however, significant changes are called for to ensure that justice is achieved. However, as indicated earlier in this manuscript, it is important to note that a call for *flexibility* (minor or significant) in a justice process cannot be an excuse for whimsical or capricious conduct or other kind of abuse by a justice official.

Discretion should be employed and used only to the extent reasonably necessary and clearly discernible to the average citizen. The test is whether a reasonable person similarly situated, as the official that exercised the discretion, and armed with the facts of the case at issue and its circumstances, would manage the case in the same or similar manner as the official has managed it. If "yes", the exercise of discretion is consistent with the rule of law. If, on the other hand, the answer is "no", then the show of flexibility amounts to an abuse of the process and/or substance of the rule of law. Moreover, an acceptable form of flexibility would show that the justice official exercises discretion similarly. That is, the official consistently handles similar cases similarly, rather than making inconsistent changes to a law that is certain. In addition, a justice official's handling of a case is expected to be consistent with the official actions and omissions of peer justice officials as well as the directives by superior justice organs (such as a court order) and superior officials.

Consistent with the rule of law element 3 identified earlier in this chapter, the *verifiability* of law captures the need for available objective evidence that a law exists and complies with the rule of law standards, in both form and substance. Such evidence can be written or otherwise documented, or it may be oral such as where oral tradition is used to convey the circumstances of a law and examples of its interpretation, application, and enforcement. I recognize that written or otherwise documented evidence is preferable due to its relative ease of proof. However, credible oral evidence, such as from an authoritative witness or expert on a law or relevant subject matter, is no less useful in establishing a law. Whether evidence is documented or oral, the important feature in relying on it to demonstrate this rule of law quality is that the evidence conveys the historical circumstances of the enactment of the relevant law and/or instances of the law's uses in fairly and properly managing grievances, conflicts, and disputes.

Periodically published law reports offer classic examples of the sources for verifying the laws of a society. Similarly, of course, criminal and civil law codes in a society are credible sources of verification. Furthermore, case law (even if the decisions are not published) demonstrates the process and substance of the relevant judiciary's interpretation of the law considered in each case. Beyond that, in criminal cases, the enforcement of each decision is up to other agencies of the State, such as the custodial authorities (police, corrections, prisons, jails, etc.). For civil case decisions, the courts and the parties, with the assistance of State agencies as needed, enforce the judiciary's decisions.

However, writing has significantly improved the capacity of the justice system to keep track of its past legal position and, as much as possible, bring it in line with the present. Accordingly, the justice system is properly equipped to verify the existing position of the law. This allows the system to prudently chart the future direction of the law, thus providing a strong foundation for the rule of law in society. In those societies where accurate records of law making, interpretation, application, and enforcement are created and maintained, the verifiability of a law in the context of the rule of law is easier to establish.

In addition to being *fair, reasonable, certain*, and *verifiable*, a good law ought to be *perceived* positively. The views of the immediate parties to a case, their relatives and other citizens, as well as outside observers are important to building and managing a rule of law-based society. The perception that a law enjoys is based in part on the law's moral standing [see the earlier discussion of the rule of law element (10)]. It is necessary that both the citizen-subjects of a law as well as its non-subject (foreign) observers perceive the law and its system positively. The points of views of the citizens and observers go long ways in creating and/or authenticating the credibility of a law and its system. Without positive feedbacks from the relevant stakeholders, a society is likely to be regarded as oppressive, insensitive, and unfair to its citizens and others with whom it deals.

Perception is formed based on the diverse elements of a society's rule of law or lack thereof. In line with the rule of law elements identified earlier in this chapter, the ingredients that contribute to the positive or negative perception of a law and its system include the following: one, the quality of the law making process; two, the contents of each law; and three, the law's ability to satisfactorily attend to the needs of the citizens (law's effectiveness) (Okafọ, 2009). A fourth ingredient is the law's goodness relative to those of comparative societies. Thus, international law and justice standards as stipulated by various organizations for their respective member-States, such as those of the United Nations Organization,[4] Economic Community of West African States, African Union, European Union, Organization of American States, Association of Southeast Asian Nations, etc.,

---

[4] Earlier in this chapter, I quoted and examined in some depth the UN's definition and categories of "the rule of law".

are relevant. In the present era of interdependency, every State depends on the cooperation of others to succeed in international and various national engagements. A negative label on a State (that it does not follow the rule of law standard) will likely harm its chances to prosecute many local and foreign economic, political, cultural, and other interests. Therefore, it is expected that, to avoid being perceived negatively and isolated from the rest of the international community, member-States of various international organizations, such as the UN, will make efforts to comply with the respective rule of law standards that apply to them.

Spanning the length and breadth of a rule of law-based justice system are the roles and influences of the lawgiver, law interpreter, and law enforcer. These officers of the law and their respective justice organs are in fact agents of peacemaking and peace guarantee. The roles of the various officers and their agencies are unquestionably critical for the survival and progress of their society. On behalf of the society's government, these agencies have the task of working daily to ensure peace in the society. The individuals and groups that carry out assignments for and on behalf of these agencies – along with the leadership of the entire country and its subdivisions – need to comply with proper and established procedures, rules, and regulations, if they are going to succeed in their rule of law responsibility concerning peace. Consequently, it is important for the peacemaker or peace guarantor and the constituent parts to scrupulously abide by the laid down rules and procedures for dealing with issues that come up in the society.

As indicated above, *certainty* of law requires a leader or justice official to avoid changing the rules, procedures, or legal standard to achieve a specific (illegitimate) end. Accordingly, it is to be noted that abiding by the established procedures, rules, and regulations to achieve the rule of law in a society means that the peacemaker or peace guarantor avoids favoritism or bias (in favor of self, relative, friend, associate, etc.). In a society where the rule of law prevails, even the leader is subject to the law. Neither the leader nor other citizen is favored over others. Favoritism equals the absence of *equality* of all before the law [see the rule of law element (6)]. Any form of favoritism, whether of self or other, substantially jeopardizes the rule of law standard in society. Favoring one side to an issue necessarily means denying another side of that to which it is otherwise entitled.

Further, a society with *certainty* of law appreciates and works hard to avoid all forms of favoritism and their consequences. In particular, favoritism has far-reaching consequences for law and justice. Favoritism, bias, nepotism, and related forms of behavior in a society work against the success of the society. By definitions, the identified forms of behavior emphasize compromising high quality and standard among the citizens. Thus, a society predicated significantly on the identified negative forms of behavior is doomed to remain mediocre at best. As tempting and perhaps logical as it is to cut corners and assist oneself, relative, friend, or other associate (contrary to the rule of law), persons and groups charged with the responsibility to establish and maintain the rule of law in a society owe a higher duty to the society as a collective entity. It ought to be clear, especially to the leaders and justice officials in the society, that there is an overriding responsibility to treat all persons equally before the law regardless of their closeness to, or distance from, the leader or official. This will ensure a fair environment. A population in which people are treated fairly is expected to be peaceful.

To ensure peace in a society through the rule of law, it is primarily the duty of the leader to build and sustain the ingredients of peace among the citizens. How does a leader create and ensure peace in society? The best way to create and ensure societal peace, for instance in a modern State, is to devise and follow a fair system of laws to extract compliance from the citizens and reward them as they deserve, for their actions and inactions. Therefore, in a modern democratic State, such as Nigeria professes, good law, not the wishes and commands of a maximum ruler, is the foundation for peace. Good law (that is, fair, predictable and yet reasonably flexible, generally accepted, progressive law) evolves or is made for the general population or a substantial portion thereof, not a specific individual or small group. Good law is created to prescribe, protect, or proscribe a social (broad-based) behavior. Good law comes into being to prevent or correct a social, not private, problem.

Good law that can build and sustain peace must be transparent. Transparency is critical in the performance of all the functions in the justice system, including law making, law alteration, interpretation, application, and enforcement. In addition to transparency being a necessary ingredient of a fair and just law, transparency directly relates to law's ability to persuade or compel the citizens to comply. The complexity of "law" (Hart, 1961/1997) and its varied sources (Bederman, 2010) are recognized. The differences in the definitions and interpretations of law and its sources notwithstanding, the purposes of law seem clear. The objects of law in a society include standardizing behavior by (re)stating the society's expected behavior, and specifying the consequences for non-compliance with the law as well as the processes for determining relationships, disagreements, and consequences.

The national responsibility of upholding the rule of law should trump narrow personal and other sectional advantages even in the face of significant personal gain. Living up to the national duty is a true test of patriotism and faithfulness to the rule of law. Primarily, the best immediate and long-term interests of the country should always guide the leader or other official in such a circumstance. It is no doubt a difficult responsibility to satisfy, especially in those societies, such as recent postcolonies – example Nigeria, where kinship, ethnic, regional, and other familial ties remain strong. It ought to be acknowledged that the ancestral ties in these postcolonies often lend themselves to positive uses. However, in those situations where they are misused to impede national cohesion and the creation and maintenance of a universal rule of law standard for the country, they should be identified and addressed as obstacles to the enthronement of a just modern society.

The stories of many countries, such as Nigeria, where nepotism is more or less a national ideology tell of State-sanctioned mediocrity. This occurs when an official law or other policy requires, mandates, or encourages discrimination or favoritism on factors such as ethnic, regional, or similar considerations. Inevitably, such a law or policy puts excellence at a disadvantage. Even if it was unintended, the Nigerian Constitutional "federal character" requirement in appointments to all manner of offices (Section 171 of the Nigerian Constitution) has the effect of favoring some Nigerians on such grounds as ethnicity, over others. This is especially so because typically, to succeed in any of those offices, a person occupying it has to possess significant expertise or knowledge of the tasks to be performed by the officeholder. It is difficult to understand how a citizen's ethnic grouping adds to or takes away from Nigeria's developmental needs. Instead, the Constitutional requirement seems to create an unequal environment for the citizens, which will lead to the country's regression. Thus, the absence of equality among the citizens in the various pursuits compromises the rule of law.

It follows that to avoid favoritism or inequality in a society, its laws should be designed to extract behaviors that accord with the society's legal standard, from all the citizens. Such behaviors, in turn, will lead to an ordered and peaceful society. Law (and its legal system) is only as good as its capacity to extract compliance. Regardless of its length and breath, or its "superior" claim, every law (and legal system) suffers many lacunas. The gaps mean that no law is capable of compelling full compliance by all the citizens. This is despite the fact that laws generally stipulate punishments and penalties (criminal law) and denial of legal approval, such as in the case of a contract entered into contrary to law (civil law) (Hart, 1961/1997). Law's compelling power need not be based on threat of violence or other sanction. Rather, law's compelling influence predicates far more on the effectiveness of each citizen's self-control. Indeed, maximum social control in a society derives from the citizens' conviction, belief in, and exercise of free will in favor of (individual) self-control. Maximum social control will be present in a society where the citizens conduct themselves in ways that are consistent with the statements of the law, even if the official system is incapable of detecting and punishing law violators. It is trite that law alone (without other social control means, such as custom, tradition, culture, religion, etc.) is inadequate for effective and efficient social control in a society. Therefore, a good law, to be effective, needs wide acceptance by the citizens.

The foregoing leads to a major point in this chapter, as follows. For the law of a society to enjoy wide acceptance, the leaders and justice officials must avoid steps that would undermine the integrity or independence of the law. I recognize that such steps can be found in a "democracy" as much as in a "dictatorship". Thus, a credible assessment of the leaders' and justice officials' actions and omissions, not the label used to describe their government, will reveal whether or not a relevant conduct undermines the integrity or independence of the law. Apart from changing the law as necessary, which, as I mentioned earlier in this chapter, is the province of the legislature [see the rule of law element (1)], *selective enforcement* of law is another threat to the rule of law. Selective enforcement refers to the action or omission of a leader or justice official who picks and chooses which law (including statutes, judicial decisions, other court orders, etc.) or aspect thereof to prosecute, apply, or enforce, against whom, to what extent, when, where, etc. A leader or justice official that indulges in selective enforcement is faithful to some provisions of the law but not to others.

But, a leader or justice official in a society based on the rule of law ought not to take advantage of the aspects of a law that he or she likes nor suppress those portions of the law that are not so appealing. A leader or official who selectively complies with preferred aspects of a law is fundamentally dishonest and untrustworthy. No excuse can be made that such a person is merely complying with those aspects of the law that are good. An honest leader or official would follow the laid down legal procedures and work to change a bad law instead of taking selfish advantage of the bad law. In the post-military "democratic" governments of Nigeria (1999-present), especially in the President Olusegun Obasanjo era, selective adherence to the rule of law is rife. The government, its agencies, and privileged associates choose the aspects of the law they would uphold. As an example of selective compliance with the rule of law, the Attorney-General and Minister of Justice (A-G) in Obasanjo's presidential tenure, Bayo Ojo, notoriously arrogated to himself the authority to certify court judgments before they could be enforced.

Thus, in an effort to maintain an unearned advantage over the ruling PDP's (political party) enemies, A-G Ojo resorted to reviewing court judgments and orders to determine whether or not they should be enforced. Of course, as expected, he rejected those judgments and orders that interfered with PDP's dominance. It bears emphasizing that the Nigerian justice system confers no such review authority on the A-G. Ojo's claim of a review power is unconstitutional. The Nigerian Constitution empowers the state and federal courts to decide cases brought before them (Chapter VII of the Constitution). The courts' decisions and orders are to be enforced by, or with the assistance of, the country's law enforcement. Ojo's illegal arrogation of a review power to himself was an abuse of the A-G's office. It was, in fact, a damning oddity in the history of the office in Nigeria. Where the government or the A-G disagrees with a court decision or order, the proper way to challenge the decision or order as well as strengthen the rule of law is to follow the stipulated appeal process. At the end of the process, the final decision binds the A-G and the government, and the decision should be enforced in full. Additionally, instead of ignoring unfavorable court decisions, the A-G and the government should work within the constitutional stipulations to amend those laws perceived as requiring amendments.

As demonstrated in this chapter, the rule of law model of justice and social control offers a great opportunity to create a just, stable, and progressive State. However, notwithstanding the advantages and possibilities of the rule of law, some of the alternative models, such as the rule of custom, the rule of tradition, and the rule of culture are capable of great contributions to building and sustaining a just, stable, and progressive society, if not single-handedly then as contributors along with other models. Earlier in this chapter, I made the point that law (or official law) lacks the capacity for justice and full social control of a society, unless other models contribute. In recognition of the inevitable and valuable cooperation between law and other means of social control, many of the chapters in this book examine the interactions between the law and other forms of justice and social control in respective research populations.

For avoidance of doubt, wherever it applies, (formal) law alone lacks the capability to provide the effective and efficient levels of social control desired for an ordered society. To do so, law has to be complemented by other forms of social control, including custom, tradition, culture, religion, etc. To one degree or the other, each of the alternative social control forms has unique ingredients and strengths to help in building and sustaining a law and order-based society. As an example, each of the various religions in Nigeria – as in other countries – goes a long way in checking the behaviors of its adherents. These checks are independent of the country's laws. This means that religious followers adhere to the rules of their respective religions whether or not the formal laws are relevant. Thus, a religious adherent may tailor his behavior in accordance with his religion even if he believes or suspects that the formal criminal justice authorities are incapable of identifying and/or punishing him for a criminal violation. Similarly, a tradition-minded Nigerian is likely to model his behavior in line with the relevant traditional standard, even if he is unlikely to be identified and sanctioned by the formal State criminal justice system. It is conceded that sometimes the requirements of religion, tradition, and other alternative social control forms are so sectional that they derogate from the standard of a modern, heterogeneous, law and order-based society. However, notwithstanding, these alternative forms of social control contribute positively in other ways. Their contributions are predicated mainly on the fact that they enjoy the confidence of many citizens who would otherwise disobey or avoid the formal law, perhaps for lack of trust for State institutions and personnel.

In view of the critical roles of the various forms of social control in a society, it is imperative to view, interpret, and apply "the rule of law" broadly. For this purpose, "the rule of law" should be regarded as a convenient expression that includes "the rule of custom", "the rule of tradition", "the rule of religion", etc. This means that the rule of law can neither sensibly nor logically be regarded as an idea based merely on Kelsenian pure legal principles.

Similarly, the rule of law transcends the Austinian command theory. The same goes for the other philosophical explanations of law. Well beyond the dictates of (formal) law, the rule of law embodies the relevant, verified (or verifiable), legitimate, and broadly accepted and used forms of social control in a society.

Consequently, the reader will find that throughout this book, numerous examples of the forms of social control used in many countries are presented and analyzed. The analyses make it evident that legitimate social control is much broader than narrowly defined (formal or government-sanctioned) "law". Thus, relevant, verified (or verifiable), legitimate, and broadly accepted and used customary law qualifies as a component of the rule of law, even if it does not issue from a sovereign authority or is unwritten. Similarly, the customary law remains a legitimate component of the rule of law even if the customary law's validity depends on the morality of its principles.

It comes to this. Considering that custom, tradition, religion, etc. are indispensable for effective and efficient social control of a modern State, these alternative social control forms are parts of the society's rule of law. In the final analysis, the rule of law in a modern State is grounded in the society's formal law as well as the relevant, verified (or verifiable), legitimate, and broadly accepted and used informal laws (custom, tradition, religion, etc.) that legitimately regulate relationships among the people. In such a situation, the society's rule of law, properly called, is *grounded* in the society.

Conclusion

The rule of law is one of several models of justice and social control available to a society. Alternative models to the rule of law include the rule of custom, the rule of tradition, the rule of personality, the rule of group, the rule of religion, the rule of experts, etc. The rule of law appears to be the most credible option. "The rule of law" connotes a variety of things, including the following. Law must be objectively verifiable. Writing is an effective way to accomplish this. The rule of law model is intended to subject every person in a society to the same legal standard. This means that similar grievances, conflicts, and disputes will be managed similarly. Where it is necessary to change the process and/or the result of a law, the change should be effected consistently across the board, without discrimination against any person. One of the manifestations of the rule of law in a society is the manner in which the law treats the leaders and other influential members of the society. If the law overly protects the leaders or is otherwise ineffectual in regulating the behaviors of the leaders relative to the generality of the citizens, it would be difficult to convince a reasonable citizen or other observer that the society observes the rule of law. In addition, a society based on the rule of law should recognize that a law bereft of morality is a bad law. Whether or not the rule of law exists in a society depends on the quality of the applicable law, not just the statement of the law.

The existence of the rule of law in a modern (diverse) society is fundamental to the society's sustainability and progress. The citizens' and others' perceptions of the society's law are critical. The procedures for law making, enforcement, interpretation, application, and execution significantly affect the citizens' and others' perceptions. Similarly, the substance of the law (its capacity to effectively and efficiently respond to the grievances, conflicts, and disputes in the society) strongly influence the citizens and other observers. Perceptions are relevant because of the need to carry the citizens and the other stakeholders along in law and order maintenance in society. If the stakeholders perceive the law applied to them as unjust, ineffective, inefficient, or imposed, they are less likely to accept or willingly follow the law. If, consequently, the citizens withhold support for their leaders and their social control efforts, it will be difficult to create and sustain peace and progress in the society.

The absence of meaningful and enduring peace as well as significant and steady progress in the more recent postcolonies, such as Nigeria, shows that for the most part, the rule of law is absent or significantly compromised in these societies. Where the rule of law is absent or compromised, there is an uneven playing field (inequality before the law). This condition leads to impunity by the leaders and other influential persons. "The rule of law" – the idea that law (good, just, progressive, generally accepted law), not a person or group, should regulate relationships, rights, and duties in a society – is generally lacking in Nigeria. This allows illegalities, transgressions, and other failures to take place, especially in official government businesses. Corrupt behaviors have eaten so deeply into the Nigerian society that most postcolonial Nigerian civilian and military leaders view themselves as the citizens' lords; thus, above the law. These personalities, rather than the law, rule.

The most dangerous aspect of the rule of personality, such as the Nigerian example, is that the rule of personality is too unpredictable to guarantee justice, meaningful social control, or stability. Rule of personality standards are subjective and vary with a change in the mood of the person in charge. In particular, the demise of the dominant person highlights the subjectivity and variations inherent in this form of social control. Often, when a different person takes over a society on the demise of its previous dominant leader, fundamental changes are made to suit the new persona. Finally, it seems undeniable that since the advent of human society, with its attendant interpersonal and inter-group interactions, which led to the building of the modern States, the idea that objective, widely accepted law, not a person's or few people's wishes, should regulate a society is one of the most important theses formulated. A society that lacks good law – and the stability and peace that the law produces – is unlikely to make significant progress.

However, we must not forget that law (formal law) is a limited form of social control. As such, it is incapable of regulating the affairs of a society by itself. To be effective and efficient in social control, this law needs contributions from the other social control forms, including custom, tradition, cultutre, religion, etc. Thus, it is legitimate to understand, interpret, and apply "the rule of law" as encompassing these various role playing institutions and their principles in a society's social control. In the circumstances, it would be accurate to describe the rule of law as the justice model *grounded* in the relevant society. The chapters in this book illustrate many forms of this grounding.

Finally, it must be reaffirmed, the idea that the rule of law should be grounded in the society to which it applies is sensible and credible. As a society's statement (or restatement) of the proper behavior standard in that population, a properly grounded rule of law should be able to effectively, efficiently, and fully regulate relationships in the society. However, at the most basic level, law is only as good as the character of the leaders, officials, and agents of law and justice. As an idea to be applied to facts, in real world circumstances, by powerful authority figures exercising all manner of discretion, the rule of law in a society will achieve justice only to the extent allowed by the authority figures. The training, knowledge, competency, philosophy, etc. of the leaders, officials, and agents, as well as the availability of resources, are important to the quality of justice emanating from a justice system. However, where law/justice leaders, officials, and agents of questionable character dominate a justice system, their actions and omissions are capable of nullifying the advantages offered by an abundance of resources and the other relevant criteria. This means that the character of a law/justice leader, official, or agent (legislator, Governor, President, Attorney-General, policeman, prosecutor, judge, prison staff, etc.) is fundamental to the rule of law. And, the character of such an authority figure is reflected in the level of self-control exercised by the person. For the rule of law in a society to properly regulate relationships and serve the citizenry, each law/justice leader, official, or agent must recognize and adhere to the proper level of self-control, that is, that level which innately instructs, cautions, or guides the authority figure on the proper behavior in each situation, regardless of whether or not the law is capable of detecting and/or sanctioning an offending figure. No legal system is capable of anticipating every issue that may arise. Similarly, no system can provide complete and unassailable physical presence to monitor, prevent, or react to every illegality. Consequently, the rule of law depends significantly on each State law/justice leader, official, or agent to regulate his conducts by utilizing the self-control mechanism, with which every rational human being is equipped.

In line with the foregoing, to a great extent, a rule of law based society depends on law/justice leaders, officials, and agents to do the right thing, consistent with the spirit as well as the statement of the law. Merely complying with the words of the law, while betraying its good intention, negates the rule of law. As an example, too often, authority figures in Nigeria are wont to thwart the rule of law for their convenience. Although the country has an abundance of legal restrictions, the weak enforcement mechanism facilitates the routine, short-sighted, and senseless repudiation of the rule of law. In this connection, the endless constitutional amendments in post-1999 Nigeria significantly irritate a discerning mind. Nigerian law makers and executive leaders should heed the following piece of advice: An abundance of laws does not a just society make. A just society requires faithful implementation of the good intentions of the law to serve the best interests of the citizenry, rather than those of the privileged few. Thus, when the late President Umaru Yar'Adua fell ill and travelled to Saudi Arabia for months for medical treatment without handing over power to his deputy, many Nigerians felt scandalized and betrayed by Yar'Adua's refusal or failure to comply with the law or even exercise self-control based on common sense. By his omission, the President jeopardized the stability and continued functioning of the Nigerian State. Even if the law at the time did not compel him to hand over the government, common sense should have guided him to conclude that he had obligation to ensure that Nigeria maintained order and strength at the highest level of government. Instead, he and his clique personalized the Nigerian State by retaining the presidential power that he was clearly incapable of exercising. Following the incident, many Nigerians called for a Constitutional amendment and the National Assembly took steps to modify the Constitution to require the President to hand over to his deputy if he is to travel outside Nigeria for more than twenty-one days or is otherwise unable to perform his duties in that period. Although the amendment appears to be a good correction to the Yar'Adua debacle, Professor G. O. S. Amadi aptly raised the following question in a conversation I had with him: Considering the astonishing impunity and mischief by Nigerian leaders and public officials who routinely avoid the good intent of the law for temporary selfish gains, what in the amended provision would stop a President lacking self-control from leaving Nigeria for twenty days, re-entering on the twenty-first day (thus giving an impression that he is performing his duties), and exiting from Nigeria again on the twenty-second day? In theory, the President (or Governor) can do this several times over while the citizens suffer. As absurd as this may sound, it is not far from realistic in Nigeria where public officials generally lack basic self-control. In the final analysis, in spite of a clear, noble, and good law, self-control is fundamental to a working and just society.

References

Adeyemi, Muyiwa, et al. (2010) "Fayemi Takes Charge In Ekiti Today," *The Guardian* (October 16); http://www.guardiannewsngr.com/index. php?option=com_content&view=article&id=26147:fayemi-takes-charge-in-ekiti-today&catid=1:national&Itemid=559; Internet.

Aliu, Alemma-Ozioruva, Seye Olumide, and Kodilinye Obiagwu (2010) "Court Sacks Uduaghan, Orders Fresh Poll in Delta," *The Guardian* (November 9); http://www.guardiannewsngr.com/index.php?option=com_content&view=article&id=28757:court; Internet.

Amokeodo, Tony, Mudiaga Affe, Simon Utebor, and Success Nwogu (2010) "Appeal Court Sacks Uduaghan," *PUNCH* (November 10); http://www.punchng.com/Articl.aspx?theartic=Art20101110461410; Internet.

Anele, Douglass (2010) "The Vicissitudes of Justice in Nigeria (1)," *Vanguard* (October 24); http://www.vanguardngr.com/2010/10/the-vicissitudes-of-justice-in-nigeria-1/; Internet.

Atkins, B. and M. Pogrebin (1981) *The Invisible Justice System: Discretion and the Law*. Cincinnati, Ohio, USA: Anderson.

Austin, John (1832/1998) *The Province of Jurisprudence Determined*. Sudbury, Massachusetts, USA: Dartmouth Publishing.

Aziken, Emmanuel, Clifford Ndujihe, Dapo Akinrefon, and Gbenga Oke (2010) "Court Nullifies Uduaghan's Election," *Vanguard* (November 9); http://www.vanguardngr.com/2010/11/court; Internet.

Bederman, David J. (2010) *Custom as a Source of Law*. New York, NY, USA: Cambridge University Press. *Constitution of the Federal Republic of Nigeria, 1999. Constitution of the United States of America*.

Ezekwere, Ijeoma (2008) "Sixth Nigerian State Election Overturned for Fraud," *REUTERS* (January 18); http://uk.reuters.com/article/dUKL1871187020080118; Internet. "Failed States Index 2009", *The Fund for Peace* (accessed October 19); http://www.fundforpeace.org/web/index.php?option=com_content&task=view&id=99&Itemid=140; Internet.

Fuller, L. (1958) "Positivism and Fidelity to Law", 71 *Harvard Law Review*, p. 630.

Gottfredson, M. R. and D. M. Gottfredson (1980) *Decisionmaking in Criminal Justice: Toward a Rational Exercise of Discretion*. Cambridge, Massachusetts, USA: Ballinger.

Hart, H. L. A. (1958) "Legal Positivism and the Separation of Law and Morals," 71 *Harvard Law Review*, p. 598.

Hart, H. L. A. (1961/1997) *The Concept of Law*. Oxford, Britain: Oxford University Press.

Ibekwe, George Chike (1993) *The Rule of Law: The Nigerian Experience – A Theoretical and Functional Analysis*. A Ph.D. in Law Thesis Submitted to the Faculty of Law, University of Nigeria; http://repository.unn.edu.ng/index.php/Law/View-category.html; Internet.

Kelsen, Hans (1945) *General Theory of Law and State*. Cambridge, Massachusetts, USA: Harvard University Press. "Maurice Iwu, Ayoka Adebayo Slammed As Court Declares Fayemi Ekiti Governor"

Maurice Iwu, Ayoka Adebayo Slammed as Court Declares Fayemi Ekiti Governor"

(2010) *Sahara Reporters* (October 15); Maurice Iwu, Ayoka Adebayo Slammed As Court Declares Fayemi Ekiti Governor Posted by site admin http://www.saharareporters.com/news-page/maurice-iwu-ayoka-adebayo-slammed-court; Internet.

Ndujihe, Clifford and Akinyemi, Demola (2010) "Ekiti: How Fayemi Became Governor," *Vanguard* (October 16); http://www.vanguardngr.com/2010/10/ekiti-how-fayemi-became-governor/; Internet.

"Nigeria Court Annuls 11th State Governor Election" (2008, July 25) (accessed October 8, 2010) *South African News*; http://www.polity.org.za/article/nigeria-court; Internet.

"Nigerian Court Annuls Southwest State Governor Vote" (2009) *REUTERS* (February 17); http://www.reuters.com/article/idUSLH17859; Internet.

"Nigerian State Election Overturned for Fraud" (2008, March 20) (accessed October 8, 2010); http://dalje.com/en-world/nigerian-state-election-overturned-for-fraud/133760; Internet.

Nonet, Philippe and Philip Selznick (2001) *Law & Society in Transition: Toward Responsive Law*, New Brunswick, USA: Transaction Publishers.

Odebode, Niyi and Ademola Oni (2010) "Kayode Fayemi: Tortuous Trek to Justice," *PUNCH* (October 16); http://www.punchng.com/Articl.aspx?theartic=Art 20101016435793; Internet.

Okafọ, Nọnso (2006) *Law & Society in Transition: Toward Responsive Law (Book Review)*, International Criminal Justice Review, Volume 16, Number 3, December, pp. 202-204.

Okafọ, Nọnso (2007) "Rule of Law, Political Leadership, and Nobel Peace Prize: Analysis of the Obasanjo Presidency 1999-2007," *NigeriaWorld* (January 12); http://nigeriaworld.com/articles/2007/jan/122.html; Internet. Article culled by the following newspapers:*SaharaReporters* and published as "Analysis of the OBJ's Presidency" (see http://www.saharareporters.com/da001.php?daid=204; Internet.

Daily Triumph and published as "Analysis of the OBJ's Presidency" (I; January 19, 2007) and (II; January 22, 2007) See I: http://www.triumphnewspapers.com/archive/DT19012007/ana19107.html; Internet. See II: http://www.triumphnewspapers.com/archive/DT22012007/any22107.html#; Internet.

Okafọ, Nọnso (2009) *Reconstructing Law and Justice in a Postcolony*. Surrey, England and Burlington, USA: Ashgate Publishing.

Okereafọezeke (Okafọ), Nonso (1996) *The Relationship Between Informal and Formal Strategies of Social Control: An Analysis of the Contemporary Methods of Dispute Processing Among the Igbos of Nigeria*. (Ph.D. Dissertation). UMI Number 9638581. Ann Arbor, Michigan, USA: University Microfilms.

Okereafọezeke (Okafọ), Nonso (2002) *Law and Justice in Post-British Nigeria: Conflicts and Interactions Between Native and Foreign Systems of Social Control in Igbo*. Westport, Connecticut, USA: Greenwood Press.

Olanrewaju, Layi (2010) "Appeal Court Sacks Oni, Declares Fayemi Duly Elected Governor", Daily Sun (October 16); http://www.sunnewsonline.com/webpages/news/national/2010/oct/16/national-16-10-2010-001.htm; Internet.

Stojkovic, Stan, et al. (2003) *Criminal Justice Organizations: Administration and Management*. Belmont, California, USA: Thomson Wadsworth.

"The Rule of Law and Transitional Justice in Conflict and Post-Conflict Societies: Report of the Secretary-General" (2004, August 23) *United Nations Organization*. See Report of the Secretary-General, http://www.unrol.org/files/2004%20report.pdf; Internet. See also http://www.un.org/en/ruleoflaw/index.shtml; Internet. See further http://ods-dds-ny.un.org/doc/UNDOC/GEN/N04/395/29/PDF/N0439529.pdf?OpenElement; Internet.

"UN Rule of Law Guidance and Policy Material" (2010) *United Nations Organization*; http://www.unrol.org/document_browse.aspx; Internet.

Chapter 2

Challenging "Law" and "Justice" Through Alternative Social Control[1]

Chukwunọnso Okafọ

University of Nigeria

[1]An earlier version of this chapter had been prepared for the African Journal of Criminology and Justice Studies.

Abstract

As should be expected, where the citizens of a society are unable to receive justice in the dominant legal system, they will seek out other avenues and processes to achieve justice. Moreover, for many citizens, the extremity of an alternative justice process is unlikely to dissuade their quest for fairness if the citizens regard the alternative as a viable means for justice. This article examines the alternative justice process demonstrated in Nigeria's Okija shrine incident in 2004. The incident provides the case study for this paper. Consistent with a string of previous studies, this article explains that on many law and justice subjects, the English colonial standards detract from the indigenous Nigerian standards in various communities. However, this paper is unique because it deduces that sometimes the divide between English law and indigenous Nigerian law yields extreme justice, such as happened in the Okija shrine incident. In particular, the article offers nine major explanations for the persistence of the Okija and similar shrines as case management avenues in various Nigerian communities. The paper concludes that as long as the official law and justice system fails to properly address the relevant subjects and satisfactorily accommodate germane indigenous Nigerian law and justice ideas and standards, extreme versions of justice, such as that found in the Okija incident, are likely to persist.

Introduction

Pluralism, Democracy, and Competition as Challenges to the Rule of Law in Society

Despite a declared unity and common democratic purpose in a modern State, the pre-existing factions and sometimes fractious relationships among the constituent groups typically remain long after such a declaration. Diverse ethnic, religious, social, cultural, and other sub-groups retain their identities, interests, and *modus operandi* for achieving their sectional goals and objectives. Often, these detract from or oppose the declared common national goals and objectives. Even criminal penalty may not be sufficient to dissuade the sectional interests because the promoters and participants are convinced in the rightness of their cause. Their loyalty is primarily to their respective communal groups. Consequently, the promoters and participants do what is needed to protect and advance the interests of their respective communities, ethnicities, religions, and other sub-populations, rather than champion the best interests of the nation.

As should be expected, communal, ethnic, religious, and other sectional interests in a State pose significant challenges to the State especially where it is working towards a united society with a common national purpose. Most of the States in Africa are of this kind because of their relatively recent colonial experiences. Although post-colonial States are found in all regions of the world, they are most prevalent in Africa since almost the entire continent was subjected to various colonial powers. The modern African States are filled with colonial relics, which pose a challenge to nation-building. Overall, the challenges in a modern State, such as in an African State, take various forms. Magnusson (2005) captures the tensions and disagreements within a modern State, especially a democratizing African State. The tensions and disagreements are between the State's (official) systems and processes, on the one hand, and those of its constituent groups (unofficial), on the other hand.

To clarify the issues as they relate to security, law enforcement, and the rule of law, Magnusson (2005) analyzes:

> ... the tensions between security and accountability in new African democracies. Even as democratizing states seek to extend the rule of law through a newly found legitimacy in the formal legal system, these efforts are often challenged, if not confounded, by 1) local communities seeking to provide a degree of security for themselves that the state is incapable of providing through its formal security services; 2) competing sub-national or transnational authorities seeking to protect their interests by financing private security forces that trespass the boundaries of public and private. While rebel, militia, and warlord organizations have been the subject of research on collapsing, failed, and rogue states, this paper [investigates] the security terrain of newly democratizing states (e.g. Benin, Nigeria, South Africa) and, in particular, the uneasy confrontations between, on the one hand, the state and its security and judicial institutions and, on the other hand, the informal security zones in which the state is either absent or competing for authority with local power-brokers.

Whatever form a disagreement between the State and its sub-groups takes, a major reason for sectional efforts by local communities, sub-national, and transnational authorities to provide security for themselves and their investments is that the State has demonstrably failed to meet the security needs of the stakeholders. Consequently, these groups, as well as other private citizens, engage in self-help efforts to secure themselves.[1]

Rule of law issues are most visible and perhaps most problematic where criminal responsibilities are concerned. It is to be expected that, more than the activities of the civil justice system, the activities of the criminal justice system of a society would give rise to concerns and questions about the rule of law and compliance therewith. This is because the criminal justice system, which exercises far-reaching legal authority, is empowered to take away a citizen's life, liberty, or property, as the case may be. The heightened concerns and questions regarding criminal justice may lead to greater efforts to meet the needs of a society's criminal justice system and its agencies. In recognition of this, a constitutional expert told a United States Embassy-organized conference on security that: "The biggest challenge to *establishing* the rule of law is criminal justice. Most of [the efforts of the justice system] go to promoting confidence in the three legs of the criminal justice tool: police, courts and prisons"[2] (*Stabroek News*, 2008).

Although the expert in *Stabroek News* (2008) referred specifically to the challenge of *establishing* the rule of law, many of the challenges to the rule of law in a society concern its *establishment*, while others concern its *sustainability*. Often, the difficulties of establishing or instituting the rule of law in a society differ from the impediments of maintaining the rule of law model. In particular, the obstacles to sustaining the rule of law change, sometimes rapidly, according to the dynamics in society.

Therefore, it is understandable that private citizens and groups in a society, concerned about the lives, liberties, and properties of their members under the criminal justice system, may take some overt and covert steps to challenge the official system with which the members disagree, such as by resorting to ethnic, religious, and other sub-group systems and processes.

Challenges to the State and its law and justice system and processes are to be expected, especially in a plural society. The pluralism of a modern State refers to the diversity of cultures, religions, languages, and other marked differences among the constituent groups in the State. The differences require accommodations to be made for the various competing constituencies in the State even while the society takes steps to build a united nation. Specifically in the law, justice, and social control matters of a State, compromises are necessary for maximum effectiveness and efficiency. Thus, Bugaje (1997) recognizes the important role of pluralism in creating and sustaining the rule of law in a modern State. The pluralism allows the many religious, cultural, political, and other groups in a modern State to believe and operate as they see fit. This gives each group a sense of belonging. However, it makes sense to legally circumscribe and expect

---

[1] Chapters 7 and 10 of this book examine the patterns of law enforcement in Africa in view of the disagreements and tensions between the State and the indigenous security models.

[2] Italics added for emphasis.

the diverse beliefs and sub-group activities to take place subject to broader State interests and within established legal standards. Consequently, as an example, an indigenous law and justice system that serves a Nigerian ethnic group should be able to regulate the affairs of the group's members provided that the system complies with the standard set by the State (preferably through a people's Constitution and representative legislature). If the indigenous law and justice system meets the Constitutional and other legal stipulations, the system should be regarded as operating within the rule of law.

Therefore, it seems straightforward that a rule of law-based system of a modern State has to involve and reflect its diverse cultures, religions, languages, and other relevant societal differences. This must be taken as a given for every modern State based on the rule of law. There appears to be international recognition for this point of view. For instance, in the area of law and international development, the rule of law is central since international assistance generally depends on the extent of legal safeguards in each receiving country. In this connection, the ability of a country's government to assure the international community on a rule of law-based, credible law and justice system, either by itself or in concert with private groups and organizations, is crucial. And so, there are generally two views, one view ("Rule of Law Orthodoxy") promotes the rule of law idea from the government's perspective, while the other view ("Legal Empowerment") emphasizes the citizens' perspective.

According to Golub (undated; accessed May 24, 2011), the Rule of Law Orthodoxy and the Legal Empowerment paradigms are relevant as follows:

> The field of international aid for law and development has been dominated by what some critics have come to call the "Rule of Law Orthodoxy." This orthodoxy has been mainly but not solely promulgated by the multilateral development banks. ROL Orthodoxy basically maintains that development can best be promoted through top-down assistance to government legal institutions, especially judiciaries. It is top-down in the sense that its projects usually are initiated by international donors and consultants working in cooperation with top jurists and justice ministry officials. ROL Orthodoxy mainly aims to improve laws and government legal institutions in ways that can make contracts, property, and domestic and foreign investment more secure. The thinking is that ROL orthodoxy in turn promotes such investment, which in turn increases jobs and other economic activity. ROL orthodoxy is not always the wrong approach. But the international community invests too much faith and resources in it. Its track record is questionable and it relies too much on the assumption

that even if its reforms are effective and worthwhile they will trickle down to benefit the poor. It is more of an ideology than an evidence-based strategy. It would be better to instead invest more in alternatives that take a more balanced approach (instead of being so top-down in nature) and that focus more directly on the disadvantaged. Many such alternatives can be summarized as legal empowerment: the use of legal services and capacity-building for the disadvantaged, often in combination with other development activities, to increase their control over their lives and to help alleviate poverty and improve governance. Legal empowerment, which usually is carried out by NGOs working in combination with partner populations, varies from country to country, issue to issue, sector to sector, and even community to community. It can involve diverse activities, including: paralegal development; training and other capacity-building for the disadvantaged; advocacy regarding the legal and justice-oriented decisions of local governments, ministries and other government offices that affect the rights and well-being of the poor; public interest litigation; policy and legislative advocacy; and working to make traditional, nonformal and formal dispute resolution processes fairer ….

Therefore, the Legal Empowerment perspective, which involves and reflects the relevant differences in a society, is essentially a challenge to the Rule of Law Orthodoxy. And the Legal Empowerment outlook may be preferred to the Rule of Law Orthodoxy. Moreover, there is strong evidence that a diverse approach is preferable because, according to Golub (undated; accessed May 24, 2011), "experience from around the world demonstrates that there are many roads to justice ... the fact is that there are many roads to justice". It is expected that the various paths to justice will accommodate and account for the diverse groups and other stakeholders in the law and justice of each country.

Degrees of Challenge to the Rule of Law

The "rule of law", as established in chapter 1, posits that all persons in a society – including a plural society – are subject to, and ruled by, the same legal standard. Accordingly, no one is treated preferentially, without legal justification. This is the way to build and sustain a fair, just, and lastingly progressive society. Building and upholding such a society requires the contributions of good law, custom, tradition, and other forms of social control (see Hart, 1997). Law (that is, official law) alone cannot achieve this condition. However, in the absence of fair, just, and lastingly progressive conditions, a society will be weak, teeter, and likely to fail due to internal failings (ineffective system due mainly to lack of citizens' support) as much as external weaknesses (low regard for the society by other societies that observe the rule of law) (Okafǫ, 2007). Thus, the rule of law is fundamental to a society. When the rule of law fails, as often happens in more recent postcolonies (that is, less developed countries), such as Nigeria, the official law and justice are challenged *through* and *by* alternative social control.

A society lacking the proper rule of law standard faces several present and future challenges. The capacity of the society to function optimally in the present is legitimately questionable mainly because of the wide dissatisfaction with which the citizens are likely to view it. The law and justice system of the society is likely to be both ineffective and inefficient because of its lack of proper and legitimate grounding among the citizens. In addition, the future of the society will be highly speculative. Its survivability will become an open question. The high level of unpredictability of the future direction and actions of the society will substantially compromise the society's present functioning and future. The present and future challenges will conspire to degrade the quality of the lives of the citizens of such a society. Life, at both the individual and group levels, will likely be bleak.

Thus, the social control challenges facing a society in which the rule of law is absent or prominently compromised are of two main kinds: individual (or personal) and institutional. Individual citizens and small groups of citizens in a society without the rule of law readily resort to alternative social control. These citizens challenge the official (governmental) law and justice system *through* (by means of isolated, individual cases, actions, and omissions within) the available alternatives. In addition, larger groups of citizens, such as communities, groups of communities, ethnicities, and regions of the affected country, in time, may use the alternative social control as a means to challenge the official system. As the challenges to the official law and justice system expand, the alternative system is constituted into a powerful, all encompassing institutional obstacle or challenge to the ineffective official system. Thus, the now large alternative social control becomes the alternative system that challenges (*by*) the official system.

In many instances, the challenges to an official law and justice system are *mild*. This means that those challenges are routine, not fundamentally threatening ways of expressing dissatisfaction with the prevailing rule of law shortcomings of the official system. Such mild challenges do not undermine the foundations of the official system. The regular challenges do not oppose the essential characteristics of the law and justice system. Rather, the challenges operate in ways that offer alternatives *within* the existing dominant official system. Examples include situations where citizens opt to manage their grievances, conflicts, and disputes informally according to their indigenous ways of life contrary to the stipulated official standards. Disputants are likely to choose an indigenous process where they derive greater satisfaction from the indigenous system than the official (likely foreign) system. However, these mild challenges do not significantly challenge (or threaten) the official law and justice system. As such, it is perfectly "normal" that official and unofficial law and justice systems coexist and the citizens routinely opt for one system or the other to manage grievances, conflicts, and disputes as the citizens see fit.

Beyond the *mild* forms of challenges that produce "normal" law and justice situations, there may be extreme challenges to the official law and justice of a society. Extreme challenges seek a system that will replace or operate outside the dominant official system. Whether a law and justice system experiences *mild* or *extreme* challenges may not be evident. In a revolutionary context where, for example, the protagonist declares intent to replace or significantly alter an existing law and justice system, we can see that an *extreme* challenge has occurred. However, in the majority of situations, such overt statement of change will not be provided. Thus, an observer needs to look for more subtle indicators of *mild* challenges or *extreme* challenges, as the case may be. The best way to understand a system as pursuing such an extreme stance is to recognize that the extreme objective may not be expressed or declared. Thus, it is to be understood as a subtlety discernible from the extent of the actions within the justice system as well as the circumstances surrounding it. In a previous work, I contrasted three levels of interactions between (and within) societies. Those forms of interactions (*Cooperative, Pluralistic, and Substitutive Interactions* – see Okereafọezeke, 2002, pp. 18-19) – are relevant for understanding the forms of challenges that could face a law and justice system.

The *Ogwugwu Isiula*, Ọkịja incident of 2004 seems to be an extreme challenge to official law and justice in Nigeria. There is substantial evidence that the judicial process applied in the shrine violates the country's official laws. The incident appears to detract from the standards of law and justice expected in a modern State. This paper analyzes the nature of the incident as well as the conditions that gave rise to it. The paper emphasizes that *Ogwugwu Isiula*, Ọkịja and similar tradition-based avenues for extreme justice subsist in Nigeria in part because of the shortcomings of the British-dominated, official justice system.

Extreme Challenge to the Rule of Law in a Modern State: A Nigerian Case Study

Ogwugwu Isiula, Ọkịja

In August 2004, the Nigeria Police Force (NPF) in Anambra State received a report of possible illegal activities at the Ogwugwu Isiula shrine in Ọkịja town of the state. The state Police Commissioner, Felix Ogbaudu, led a police team to the location. At the shrine and in the surrounding area, the police made some gruesome findings. They discovered dozens of headless bodies, skulls, and human corpses, along with a record of names – ostensibly, the names of individuals that patronized the shrine. The police and the Ọkịja residents were alarmed at the extreme nature of the findings, and the fact that the patrons list contained the names of notable Nigerians from within and outside the community.

Ordinarily, as a component of indigenous Igbo (Nigeria) law and justice, the Ogwugwu Isiula shrine is an avenue for case management. A person with a dispute has the option of taking the dispute to the shrine, through the shrine's priest and other officials, and asking the shrine to step in and adjudicate the case between the disputants. The guilty party risks punishment, ranging from a minor fine, substantial fine, to death, depending on the gravity of the dispute or offense. Thus, the existence of the Ogwugwu Isiula and similar shrines in Igbo and other parts of Nigeria is normal. Even in modern (postcolonial) Nigeria, the shrines and other indigenous avenues for case management subsist and play major roles in the management of cases (see Okereafọezeke, 1996; 2002).

For avoidance of doubt, shrines such as Ogwugwu Isiula and other similar indigenous case management avenues in Igbo, as in other parts of Nigeria, are widely used and are not all bad. This was precisely why the 1986 Winner of the Nobel Prize for Literature, Professor Wole Soyinka, an ardent believer in indigenous Nigerian religions and practices, cautioned the NPF in the wake of the Ọkịja incident to avoid using the incident as an excuse to intimidate, denigrate, or destroy traditional religions in the country. Similarly, Colonel Achuzia (retired), then Secretary-General of Ọhaneze Ndigbo, accused the NPF of using the Ọkịja incident as an excuse to scorn the Igbo and their culture. See also Asoegwu and Anoliefo (2004). Moreover, the list of patrons that the police obtained during their raid of Ogwugwu Isiula substantiates the wide use of the shrine. The list, containing hundreds of names, included the names of some public figures and high ranking government officials (see "Full, Authentic List of Patrons of Okija Shrine", 2004). In addition, Ọkịja-like incidents have occurred in some other parts of Nigeria. See as an example, Oyekola (2010) for the discovery of a replica of the

Ọkija shrine in Ido-Osun in Egbedore Local Government Area of Osun State.

However, the NPF's grouse with the Ọkija shrine is that, according to the police, the richest party in a dispute before the Ogwugwu Isiula is always guilty. The police have given the *modus operandi* of the shrine operators as follows. The representatives of the shrine track down the rich disputant in a case and put poison or charm in his or her motor vehicle to ensure that the wealthy disputant dies. Alternatively, according to the police, other rich parties are made to consume drink or some potion after which he or she dies. The police further state that the Ogwugwu Isiula shrine priests' leader is a named individual who, according to them, owns millions of Naira worth of property in Lagos. The implication is that the shrine is a means for moneymaking, rather than a just case management body.

Analyzing the Okija Incident and Similar Events

As mentioned, the Ọkija incident is not an isolated occurrence in Nigeria. It has been duplicated in various forms in other parts of the country. For many Nigerians, the continued existence and strength of the country's traditional justice and social control systems contradict the country's status as a "modern" state. The Ọkija incident may be cited as an example of the evils of traditional justice and social control (see Okafọ, 2005). Also, to many Nigerians and non-Nigerian observers, "outdated, heathen" indigenous-rooted social control is not expected to continue as a means of case management in modern Nigeria. But, there is strong evidence that traditional social control remains very popular among Nigerians. This form of social control is widely used. However, sometimes, the wide use leads to significant abuses, such as those that the Ọkija incident exemplifies.

Therefore, the question is: "Why do the Ọkija's (traditional courts, tribunals, and other tradition-based justice and social control organs and processes) exist and flourish in Nigeria?" The following sections of this article will answer this question. However, the fact that Nigeria's official *Criminal Code* criminalizes the type of traditional crime management that apparently occurred in the Ọkija incident makes this question particularly relevant. The Code defines some of the crimes alleged by the police in the case as having arisen from a "trial by ordeal", which is punishable under Sections 207-213 of the Code. In light of the *Criminal Code*'s criminalization of the traditional process, it seems reasonable to point out that the many Nigerians who persist in managing their civil and criminal cases through the deities must be doing so for compelling reasons. Thus, on close examination of the Ọkija incident and other similar cases, I have identified nine explanations for the continued recourse by the citizens to Ọkija's Ogwugwu Isiula shrine and similar deities in Igbo and other parts of Nigeria, for case management.

Why Do the Okija's Endure in Nigeria?

The Ọkịja case exemplifies extreme challenge to official law and justice in Nigeria because its judicial *modus operandi* violates the country's official criminal procedure. Also, the case contravenes Sections 207-213 of the substantive Nigerian *Criminal Code*. A careful consideration of the case (and similar occurrences) in Nigeria has led to the following nine factors as explanations for the continued relevance of this form of harsh tradition-based justice in the country. The nine variables are the rationales for the extreme challenge that the Ọkịja and similar cases pose to official law and justice in Nigeria.

The Relationship Between Nigerians and the English System

It is well documented that imperial Britain, through its colonial regime in Nigeria, imposed the English-based common law system of social control on Nigeria (Okereafọezeke, 1996; 2002; Okafọ, 2009). A consequence of the imposition is that the English law and justice system in Nigeria is widely regarded as groundless because in Nigeria it lacks the foundation that it enjoys in its native England. The English system is alien to Nigeria and Nigerians. In varying degrees, most Nigerians (including the so-called well-educated, modern Nigerians) have some appreciation for their indigenous cultures and traditions. These cultures and traditions are strikingly different from the English culture and tradition, on the basis of which the English common law evolved. The mere absence of consultation by imperial Britain before importing and imposing the English law and justice system on Nigeria is sufficient for Nigerians to reject the system or, at least, treat it with suspicion and trepidation. With little, if any, confidence in the English-style, British-imposed law and justice system and its officials (police, judges, prosecutors, prisons and corrections personnel, etc.), the average Nigerian has no significant choice but to depend on his/her indigenous system of justice and law.

The disparity between indigenous Nigerian cultures and traditions, on the one hand, and the English common law in Nigeria, on the other, is very wide. Many principles and rules of the common law contradict some widely held indigenous beliefs in Nigeria. These contradictions are found on many dispute subjects in the country, including matrimonial causes (marriage, divorce, inheritance, custody, etc.), land (ownership, lease, sale, use, mortgage, etc.), title and other types of inheritance. The use of the English language to write the English common law in Nigeria, as well as to process cases in the official law courts, is one of the greatest illustrations of the extent to which Nigerians are alienated by the official system. Most Nigerians neither speak nor write the English language, at least not the correct grammatical version.[3]

Nonetheless, the non-English speaking Nigerians continue to be subjected to foreign-based laws couched in English, in Nigeria. In all likelihood, the language difference interferes with these Nigerians' ability to follow the English-based laws. How can a citizen conform to, or challenge a law that he/she does not understand? In the circumstances, the State (through the Legislature) has denied the affected citizen the opportunity to know, understand, appreciate, comply with, and critic, the law. It is quite reasonable to surmise that Nigerians' alienation from the English law and justice system operating in Nigeria contributes to the citizens' preference for their traditional law and justice systems, even if sometimes, as the Ọkịja case study shows, the traditional systems result in extreme challenges to the State.

A Question of Effectiveness and Efficiency of English Law and Justice

The English law and justice in Igbo and other parts of Nigeria has an image problem. This means that many, perhaps most, Igbos and other Nigerians view the English system of law and justice, as introduced and practiced in Nigeria, as ineffective and inefficient for social control in the country. This is based in part on the fact that the English model of law and justice seems unable to satisfactorily manage grievances, conflicts, and disputes among Nigerians. Facts on the ground support this image of the English system. There are numerous cases that had been tried, decided, and, it seemed, concluded by Nigeria's official, English-style courts. However, the disputes festered long after they were supposedly settled. In many instances, these cases remain major subjects of contention and even violence years or decades after the official courts had decided upon the cases.

Land disputes (ownership, use, transfer, etc.) are prime candidates for these types of volatile matters. For many of these cases, there is no doubt that Nigeria's official, English-based common law system has been unable to identify and address the deep-seated issues between the parties and address them permanently. In some cases, mere perception that the English-based common law system is ineffective or inefficient suffices for Nigerians to be wary of managing their cases within the system. In social control, perception goes a long way to encouraging or discouraging compliance, as the case may

---

[3] Other than the correct English grammatical version, many Nigerians speak and understand Pidgin English. Pidgin or Broken English, widely spoken across Anglophone West Africa, merges English and indigenous language words and phrases to convey information. In Nigeria, many people that are unable to speak or understand correct English grammatical expressions communicate effectively in Pidgin English. However, Pidgin English is not recognized as a medium of communication in government business.

be. After all, social control is about complying or being influenced or made to comply; thus the complier's state of mind toward the guiding rules of conduct is important. The view that the English system in Nigeria is incapable of satisfactorily addressing certain disputed issues encourages the citizens to seek out other systems and methods of case management (Okereafọezeke, 1996; 2002).

Pride in Culture

Pride in indigenous Nigerian culture, such as an Igbo person's pride in his or her culture, also helps to explain the continued existence and apparent expansion of Nigeria's traditional social control and justice systems. As pointed out, the extreme nature of the Ogwugwu Isiula shrine incident in Ọkịja does not accurately represent the vast majority of the traditional systems and processes, which play crucial roles in case management and social control. Cultural pride is a significant variable in understanding and explaining the endurance of the tradition-based laws in Nigeria. Britain's colonial "Substitutive Interaction" agenda in Nigeria led to the imposition of the English common law system on Nigerians (Okereafọezeke, 2002, pp. 18-20; see also Okereafọezeke, 1996; Okafọ, 2009). This, in turn, fuels the rejection or cold reception that Nigerians give to the English system in Nigeria.

Culture is mainly bred within a society. It is true that inevitably, in time additional cultural elements are borrowed from other societies to complement the home-grown, fundamental characteristics of a society's culture. However, foreign culture that displaces or threatens to displace another culture is liable to be condemned or rejected. Therefore, a society's culture represents the society's history, experiences, failures, successes, and its other ways of doing things. In short, a society's culture is its essence. Culture, as a society's heart and soul, ties, or should tie, directly to its substantive and procedural law, justice, and social control statements and interpretations.

Hence, even with full recognition of globalization and the need for the right kind of interaction (that is, "Cooperative Interaction" or, at least, "Pluralistic Interaction" – see Okereafọezeke, 2002, pp. 18-20), "justice" and "law", like "crime", remain largely culture-specific. This means that justice, law, and crime are defined and understood in the context of each society. Inevitably, there are variations – sometimes fundamental variations – in understanding and interpreting justice, law, crime, etc. between societies. It is therefore quite natural and essential for Nigerians to remain proud of their indigenous law, justice, and social control. This is to be expected and important even in the face of erstwhile British-initiated and Nigerian officially-sustained efforts to destroy or emasculate the indigenous systems and processes. There is something to be said for Nigerians' desire and preference to be identified with, and to practice, a system that belongs to them naturally, rather than a system that belongs to the British. The sheer pride in

Nigeria's indigenous systems and processes helps to sustain interest in, and increase the uses of, the traditional mechanisms of law and justice.

Knowledge and Understanding of Other Systems and Processes

Another important factor that adds to the sustenance of the Ọkịja's in Igbo and other parts of Nigeria is the absence of, or limited, knowledge or understanding of other systems and methods of law, justice, and social control. The issue here is the lack of sufficient exposure to other world cultures and systems of social control and justice. Such exposure often occurs through education (formal and informal). An adult Nigerian that has spent all or virtually all of his or her life in a secluded village, where the Ogwugwu Isiula shrine is accepted as the highest judge, is not likely to contemplate or take steps to deviate from the person's obligations to the shrine. Thus, some of the chief priests, priests, servants, enforcers, and other agents that participate in, or patronize, the deities in Nigeria do so because these agents are trapped physically and psychologically by the circumstances in which they were born, were brought up, and live. These agents know no differently from their environment.

Assessing the Developmental Conditions for Law and Justice in Nigeria

As mentioned earlier in this article, some Nigerians and non-Nigerian observers readily regard the country's indigenous law, justice, and social control as outdated and heathen. They argue that the traditional model is consequently unfit for case management in a modern, developed or developing Nigeria. The suitability of indigenous law, justice, and social control ("customary law") for a modern State has been addressed in another work (Okafọ, 2009). In sum, the correct position is that customary law remains highly relevant in official law and justice, even in a modern State. Thus, the customary law of a society plays a crucial role in its social control, and should therefore be included in the society's official law and justice arrangement.

However, there is strong evidence that Nigeria lacks the basic characteristics of a developed or even developing nation. A hallmark of a developed (or developing), modern nation is that basic State institutions and infrastructure exist and they work. In such a State, there is a reasonable expectation that the institutions and infrastructure work for the benefit of the average citizen, not just the privileged few. Thus, the average citizen should be assured of effective and efficient public institutions, such as the legislature for law making, the police for security maintenance and law enforcement, and the courts for judging cases fairly. Also, infrastructure such as electricity, motorable roads, and clean water should be present and functioning reasonably well.

Unfortunately, contrary to the developmental expectations outlined in the preceding paragraph, in virtually every aspect, the institutions and infrastructure of the Nigerian State and its constituent authorities (State and Local governments) are poor and degrading. The institutions and infrastructure are below the minimally acceptable level for a modern society. The institutions and infrastructure are, in many cases, worse than they were under imperial British rule. The quality of the services expected from the institutions and infrastructure has practically disappeared, mainly because of immense corruption and incompetence among government officials at the Federal, State, and Local levels. While these officials trumpet religiosity and Godliness, there is abundant evidence that they do not seriously consider moral precepts in their conducts. Thus, the governments and their officials typically preach one thing while practicing something different.

The negative images witnessed around the country contradict official claims to development or modernism in contemporary Nigeria. In many parts of the country, there are no motorable roads. Often, the horrible conditions of the open spaces (or narrow paths) belie the "road" label placed on them. In the vast majority of circumstances, the deplorable conditions persist after the responsible authority (the Federal Government of Nigeria, state Government, or Local Government, as the case may be) has budgeted obscene amounts of money through annual and supplementary budgets to construct or rehabilitate the roads. However, as often happens, the lion share of the budgets is diverted to private accounts. In addition to the horrible road conditions, most parts of Nigeria have no (reliable) electricity supply, clean water, medical care, educational system at the primary, secondary, or tertiary level, etc. Rather than developed and modern policies and services, the overwhelming majority of Nigerians are subjected to the negative images of the official governments, their policies, and programs.

Official Nigerian policies and actions in two vital areas of the citizens' lives (petroleum products and education) will illustrate the dim view of governments as facilitators of development and modernism in the country. Since the inception of the present civilian era on May 29, 1999, the Olusegun Obasanjo/Atiku Abubakar and Umaru Yar'adua/Goodluck Jonathan regimes have increased the prices of petroleum products more than seven times. Each time, the increase is made without input or prior notice to Nigerians. Every increase is by about 30% over the previous price. What sort of "developed" or "modern" government ambushes its citizens and complicates their lives on such essential merchandise as petroleum products (used for cooking, lighting since there is no reliable public electricity supply, powering motor vehicles, etc.)? Regarding education, teaching, research, and service at the primary, secondary, and tertiary levels are routinely interrupted, sometimes for months at a time, due to incessant industrial actions by teachers, administrators, as well as students. Contemplating the future of the Nigerian youth and the country in the circumstances of the disruptions to teaching and learning is unsettling, to say the least.

Faced with the governments' role in creating the massive evidence against development and modernity, it is not surprising that many Nigerians reject official law and justice, or at least regard them suspiciously. Instead these Nigerians retreat to their kinship groups, highlight, and follow their indigenous cultures, religions, and traditions, including their traditional processes for law and justice. This is not to say that indigenous law and justice are antithetical to development or modernity. Rather, retreating to the traditional system signifies that, to achieve some certainty in a time of unpredictability, the citizens prefer a familiar system, such as the traditional law and justice system.

Mixed Signals by the Governments and Officials

Evidence shows that officials of Nigeria's governments at the various levels are some of the most prominent clients of the Igbo and other Nigerian deities. The officials patronize the shrines for various purposes, including material wealth, influence, political fortunes, and supernatural protection from real and perceived enemies. Apparently, the shrine patrons experience successes in their various pursuits, hence the continued allegiances to the deities. Also, the perception in the general public that the patrons of the deities are successful – especially in terms of increased wealth, influence, and protection – lend credence to the claim that the deities are potent. The wide belief in the strength and potency of the deities, in turn, draw more Nigerians to the idols.

However, by their conduct, government officials that patronize deities in Nigeria thereby contradict the official position of the governments. Officially, the various governments condemn and sometimes criminalize allegiances to deities (see as an example *Criminal Code* of Nigeria, Sections 207-213). In the circumstance, doing business with the deities and their agents is illegal. But the individual practices of influential government officials frequently belie this official position. Thus, it is common for a public official in Nigeria to publicly condemn illegal trials, rituals, and other activities involving deities, while privately participating in the same activities. It makes no difference that the condemned behavior contradicts official law and other policies. As mentioned earlier in this manuscript, the Nigeria Police Force (NPF) raid on the Okija shrine yielded a list of some of the shrine's patrons. The list showed that prominent, influential public figures in and out of governments were some of the deity's clients (see "Full, Authentic List of Patrons of Okija Shrine", 2004).

It is fitting to add the following. In the vast majority of cases, a public official patronizes deities contrary to the official's assumed "Christian" or

"Muslim" label. Ordinarily, a "Christian" or "Muslim" should not be involved in other idolatry practices, including patronizing deities for supernatural advantages. But in Nigeria, this is common because the patrons regard the deities, such as the Okija shrine, as sources of assured and quicker wealth, influence, etc. over their competitors. This is quite telling in a country where virtually every public official claims to be either a Christian or a Muslim. Not surprisingly, the chasm between the claims to "Christian" or "Muslim" label and actual conducts have created a situation where corruption and other official criminal behaviors enjoy "norm" status at all levels of government in Nigeria (Okafo, 2003).

The fact that Nigerian government officials patronize Igbo and other Nigerian deities is not bad in itself, and should not be regarded as such. There is nothing inherently wrong with participating in shrine activities. Rather, the emphasis ought to be on the morality and legality of specific shrine activities. Shrines of various forms are commonplace throughout the world. Some of the more famous shrine examples are the Christian churches, the Islamic mosques, and the Jewish synagogues. By political expediency, undeserved and unjustified influences, the three religions that the named shrines represent (Christianity, Islam, and Judaism, respectively) have been offered to the world as "the three great religions". But, there is nothing intrinsically great about any of the three religions. The greatness of a religion lies in its proper use to influence or regulate human behavior in a society and between societies. Political, economic, or social dominance does not a great religion make. In particular, a religion whose great political, economic, or social advantage was obtained violently, forcefully, corruptly, or otherwise dishonestly cannot be a great religion. In determining the greatness of a religion, the capacity of a given religion to offer human beings and groups the moral and ethical tools to relate with others, with pure hearts, ought to be accorded greater consideration. Thus, there is no credible reason that Nigerians should be discouraged from patronizing all Igbo (and other Nigerian) traditional religious shrines.

There is another significant way in which Nigeria's governments and their officials send mixed signals to the citizens. The official Local, State, and Federal governments continue to meddle in traditional community matters. These official, Western-style governments intrude in the traditional community affairs in a variety of ways. As examples, the official governments appoint, recognize, and sack the various communities' traditional rulers (such as "Eze", "Oba", or "Emir") more or less at will. The recent removal of the Deji of Akure, Ondo State (see Johnson, 2010; Sowole, 2010), offers a good illustration of how the official government can interfere in such a traditional institution.

Regardless of a justification for interfering in a traditional institution, such as removing the Deji for alleged public assault, the official meddling is really a form of blending indigenous with official (foreign), Western-style politics and government. But, interference by an official government is not the only way to redress a wrong in a traditional institution. In many instances, a traditional institution will have an in-built procedure for correcting such wrong. Where no such procedure is found, the institution is quite capable of creating a credible procedure with minimal, if any, interference by the official government. However, in view of the governments' officiousness, it must be asked: Why don't Nigeria's official governments take equal interest in unifying the indigenous with official, English-style law and justice to minimize the likelihood of another Ọkịja-like incident happening in the country? This question should be the basis for another research.

Desire for Quick, Inexpensive Justice

Justice in Nigeria's English-style official law and justice system is long, drawn-out, and expensive. This is well documented (see as examples, Okereafọezeke, 1996; 2002; Okafọ, 2009). Criminal, as well as civil, justice clientele (plaintiffs, defendants, victims, accused persons, witnesses, interested communities, etc.) incur great costs to achieve some justice in Nigeria's official system. The types of costs vary from money to time and reputation, among others (Okereafọezeke, 1996; 2002). On time cost, as an example, it is common for a criminal case to drag on for years, while a civil case can go on for decades.

Considering the long time needed for a trial, hearings, and multiple appeals, the average Nigerian cannot afford the attorney's fees and other expenses for conducting a case in the official court system. The prevailing harsh economic conditions exacerbate this citizens' inability. Those citizens that are able to afford the huge sums of money needed for official case processing, are only able to do so after making significant sacrifices. In this condition, it is not surprising that many Nigerians yearn for less expensive, faster avenues for justice. The country's indigenous tribunals and processes of law, justice, and social control, such as Ọkịja's *Ogwugwu Isiula* shrine, respond to this need. Relative to the English common law-based official justice system, the deities are widely regarded as quick and cheap dispensers of justice. This shapes the citizens' preference for the indigenous law and justice processes over the foreign, English-style process.

Financial and Material Gains

This is another strong reason why some Nigerians persist in, or begin, following the deities and similar traditional justice institutions. There are money and other forms of material gains to be acquired by creating or championing a deity and presenting it (sometimes, falsely) as having supernatural powers. In many instances, Nigerians in difficult situations, who are asked to accept such a deity with promised redemption from their difficulties, accept the offer. There is nothing unique about this condition in the Nigerian traditional environment. Cheaters and their victims are found in every institution of every society. Those who use religion to further their selfish interests and enrich themselves are regarded as false prophets. False prophets are common among Christians, Muslims, and other so-called major religions.

Similarly, among traditional Igbo and other Nigerian religious followers, there are bogus prophets. These "prophets" regard their religious endeavor as a business and thus exploit their clients for maximum profits. This is so because great opportunities exist for the false prophets to defraud unsuspecting citizens who, because of their ignorance and naivety, usually accept without question that any person with the "Christian" or "Muslim" label is an honest person. In an environment that accommodates all manner of "prophets" with little or no questions asked, false prophets of Nigeria's traditional religions find relative ease in appropriating their believers' material and financial belongings. Since it is this easy to enrich oneself by falsely claiming to be righteous, many dishonest people are encouraged to do so, through the Christian, Islamic, as well as Traditional religious shrines. That is what occurred in the Okija shrine incident in which, according to the Nigeria Police Force (NPF), the deity's leaders and officials enriched themselves at the expense of their clients.

Confused Attitudes to Deities, Traditional Religions, and Practices

Deities in Nigeria are generally respected and highly regarded, even by those that profess to be "Christians", "Muslims", or followers of other religions. On many important issues involving shrines, many Nigerians defer to the deities. Thus, it is not just the practitioners of the indigenous religions that hold the deities in high regard. Other Nigerians routinely appeal to the various deities for different degrees of interventions in the appellants' lives. As stated earlier in this article, such appeals are for various things, such as wealth or increased wealth, influence, political fortunes, and supernatural protection from (perceived) enemies. Of course, these Nigerians would not appeal and defer to the deities if they (the Nigerians) did not believe in, or fear, the deities. Because of the widespread use of the deities in Nigeria (by "Traditionalists" as well as "Christians" and "Muslims"), it is safe to state that many, perhaps most, contemporary Nigerians fundamentally believe in, and/or fear, the deities. This leads to the following: the average Nigerian – even if he/she flaunts another religious label – is convinced in the potency of the supernatural powers of the Nigerian deity.

The foregoing shows that Nigerians who reject the indigenous shrines somehow indirectly acknowledge that the shrines are potent. The attitudes of these citizens towards the deities and their followers belie the claim that the shrines are of no consequence. However, sometimes the negative attitudes of the opponents to the deities degenerate to violence against the followers of the indigenous religion. A December 2004 incident in Enugu State illustrates the religious extremism that Christians can visit on non-Christians in Nigeria. In the incident, Christian youths in Abor, Enugu State, took it upon themselves to destroy the traditional religious shrines in their community because, according to the youths, those who worship the deity are holding back the progress of the area (Edike, 2005). Contrast the warnings by Soyinka and Achuzia, respectively, against convenient, opportunistic attacks on traditional religions (referenced above). Ostensibly, the rampaging youth took the destructive action for two main reasons: to serve their God and further his will at all costs; and because if they failed to act as they did the deities would harm the community. This, in effect, acknowledges the potency of the destroyed deities, even while the same Christians sought to dismiss the deities as inconsequential.

Another important component of many Nigerians' confused relationship with traditional religions, deities, and indigenous practices is found in the celebration of traditional festivals and anniversaries. Every year, in communities across Nigeria, celebrations take place to mark many traditional beliefs. These celebrations are typically joyous occasions. New Yam Festival, New Farming Season, and New Masquerade Season are some of the celebrations that take place annually. Ordinarily, these should be celebrated by community members that hold only traditional beliefs. However, many people professing other beliefs, such as Christianity, Islam, etc., routinely and prominently participate in the celebrations. The non-traditionalists do not merely observe the traditional celebrations, they participate actively and fully in the festivities. This is symptomatic of the confounding attitude that the non-traditionalists have toward the traditional beliefs. On the one hand, the non-traditionalists reject (by word declaration) the traditional beliefs and practices, on the other hand, the non-traditionalists accept and participate in the relevant traditional celebrations. So, on this issue, it seems accurate to describe the average Nigerian as a dual-believer (a "Traditional-Christian" or "Traditional-Muslim", etc.).

The confused attitudes to deities also stem from lethargy by some citizens. Some people prefer not be bothered with the activities of traditional believers, except when traditional festivities are taking place. Such dismissive attitude toward the traditional religion ignores the indigenous way of life. By their attitude, the general citizenry fails to monitor the activities of the traditionalists. The Ọkija shrine incident and a number of other events around the country should convince the average person that such neglect can lead to significant abuses by the traditionalists. Whereas reasonable pressure from "Christians" and "Muslims" could have caused the traditionalists to observe human rights standards in their activities, ignoring the deities and the practices at these shrines is likely to lead to substantial violations.

In the midst of the enumerated confused attitudes towards deities, traditional religions, and practices among Nigerians, the traditional shrines thrive. And sometimes their protagonists misuse the deities in law and justice processing, as the Ọkịja case evidences.

Conclusion

Based on a study of Ọkịja *Ogwugwu Isiula* shrine incident in which the Nigeria Police Force discovered dozens of human dead bodies and other evidence of gross violations stemming from traditional judicial processes, this article has identified, analyzed, and illustrated nine variables that explain the continued and widespread uses of deities as traditional courts in parts of Nigeria. Besides Ọkịja's *Ogwugwu Isiula* shrine, the indigenous-based justice institutions in contemporary Nigeria are widely available. In the great majority of cases, the traditional institutions serve very useful social control needs. They successfully manage grievances, conflicts, and disputes among the citizens, even on issues that the official English-style courts and processes have no remedies (Okereafọezeke, 1996; 2002). This paper demonstrates that the uses of the traditional law and justice avenues are likely to continue and expand as long as the nine identified variables persist in Nigeria. The variables are factors that encourage and contribute to the citizens' decisions to use (as patrons or clients) the deities to achieve justice on disputed issues.

Thus, the traditional practices will not abate any time soon, nor should they fade away. These practices are borne out of the citizens' culture. For most Nigerians, their culture remains a strong source of identity. The citizens are unlikely to abandon their essential character, even in the postcolonial era. In the modern Nigerian State, most aspects of the culture ought to be reasonably encouraged and expanded for more effective and efficient law, justice, and social control (Okafọ, 2009). However, as demonstrated in this paper, in addition to culture, there are compelling religious, ethnic, and material reasons, as well as reasons of official ineffectiveness, inefficiency, citizens' pride, belief, fear, apathy, and limited resources for Nigerians to use the traditional courts. In many instances, the failures of the official foreign-based law and justice system and the extreme circumstances in which most Nigerians find themselves force or encourage the citizens to resort to long-standing indigenous customs and traditions to manage their cases.

References

Asoegwu, Jimmie and Anoliefo, Obi (2004) "The Ogwugwu Okija Fairy Tale," *VANGUARD*, http://web.archive.org/web/20040908195300/http://vanguardngr.com/articles/2002/columns/c208092004.html; Internet.

Bugaje, Usman (1997) "The Rule of Law and the Challenge of Pluralism." Paper presented to the workshop on the Rule of Law and the

Administration of Justice in Kano, Kano State, Nigeria, July 24-27. See at: http://www.webstar.co.uk/~ubugaje/pluralism7.html; Internet (accessed May 20, 2011).

Criminal Code Act (Nigeria).

Edike, Tony (2005) "Tension in Enugu as Youths Destroy Shrines," *VANGUARD*, January 5, http://allafrica.com/stories/200501050090.html; Internet.

"Full, Authentic List of Patrons of Okija Shrine" (2004, October 11), *BiafraNigeriaWorldNews*, http://news.biafranigeriaworld.com/archive/2004/oct/12/246.html; Internet.

Golub, Steve (undated) "Challenging the Rule of Law Orthodoxy: Many Roads to Justice," see at: http://cc.bingj.com/cache.aspx?q=challenging+rule+of+law&d=5011462526076017&mkt=en-US&setlang=en-US&w=8fd2ccc5,2b53dd35; Internet (accessed May 23, 2011). See also at: http://www.bing.com/search?q=challenging+rule+of+law&qs=n&sk=&x=0&y=0&first=11&FORM=PORE (accessed May 23, 2011).

Hart, H. L. A. (1997) *The Concept of Law*, Second Edition. New York, New York, USA: Oxford University Press.

Johnson, Dayo (2010) "Deji Deposed, Banished, Arrested," *VANGUARD* (June 10), http://www.vanguardngr.com/2010/06/10/deji-deposed-banished-arrested/; Internet.

Magnusson, Bruce A. (2005) "Whose Security? Challenging the Rule of Law, and the Dilemmas of Accountability in New African Democracies." Paper presented at the annual meeting of the International Studies Association, Hilton Hawaiian Village, Honolulu, Hawaii, USA, March 5. See at http://www.allacademic.com/meta/p70121_index.html; Internet (accessed May 22, 2011). See also at http://www.allacademic.com/meta/p_mla_apa_research_citation/0/7/0/1/2/p70121_index.html; Internet (accessed May 22, 2011).

Okafọ, Nọnso (2003) "Religious Labels and Conduct Norms in Government," *NigeriaWorld*, March 13, http://nigeriaworld.com/articles/2003/mar/132.html; Internet.

Okafọ, Nọnso (2005) "Foundations of Okija Justice," *NigeriaWorld*, March 1, http://nigeriaworld.com/articles/2005/mar/033.html; Internet.

Okafọ, Nọnso (2007) "Rule of Law, Political Leadership, and Nobel Peace Prize: Analysis of the Obasanjo Presidency 1999-2007," *NigeriaWorld* (January 12), http://nigeriaworld.com/articles/2007/jan/122.html; Internet. See also "Analysis of the OBJ's Presidency," *SaharaReporters*, http://www.saharareporters.com/da001.php?daid=204; Internet.

"Analysis of the OBJ's Presidency," *Daily Triumph*, http://www.triumphnewspapers.com/archive/DT19012007/ana19107.html; Internet. http://www.triumphnewspapers.com/archive/DT22012007/any22107.html#;

Internet.

Okafọ, Nọnso (2009) *Reconstructing Law and Justice in a Post-colony*. Surrey, England and Burlington, USA: Ashgate Publishing.

Okereafọezeke (Okafọ), Nọnso (1996) *The Relationship Between Informal and Formal Strategies of Social Control: An Analysis of the Contemporary Methods of Dispute Processing Among the Igbos of Nigeria*. (Ph.D. Dissertation). UMI Number 9638581. Ann Arbor, Michigan, USA: University Microfilms.

Okereafọezeke (Okafọ), Nọnso (2002) *Law and Justice in Post-British Nigeria: Conflicts and Interactions Between Native and Foreign Systems of Social Control in Igbo*. Westport, Connecticut, USA: Greenwood Press.

Oyekola, Tunde (2010, January 22) "S-H-O-C-K-E-R: Strange Shrine Found in Osun," *Nigerian Tribune*, http://www.tribune.com.ng/index.php/front-page-news/300-s-h-o-ck-e-r-strange-shrine-found-in-osun-leader-says-its-a-church-members-worship-only-at-night-founders-skeleton-many-skulls-found.html; Internet.

Sowole, James (2010) "Akure Monarch Deposed, Banished," *ThisDay*, June 11, http://allafrica.com/stories/201006110060.html; Internet.

Stabroek News (2008) "Criminal Justice Biggest Challenge to Rule of Law" (August 14). See at http://www.stabroeknews.com/2008/news/stories/08/14/criminal-justice-biggest-challenge-to-rule-of-law/; Internet (accessed May 23, 2011).

Chapter 3

Thinking About a Postcolonial Return to Indigenous Justice in Africa

Susan Smith-Cunnien
University of St. Thomas, USA

Introduction

It is often noted that the formal justice systems in most African nations today essentially retain the legal structures and practices imposed by the former colonial powers. These structures and practices no doubt derived from the social circumstances and values of the countries in which they were developed but there is little reason to believe that they reflect the social milieu of the populations on which they were imposed. Furthermore, the justice systems imposed on African colonies by various European powers were designed to dominate the local populations by reinforcing racial subjugation and supporting the exploitation of their labor and natural resources. Why, then, have African nations retained so much of these foreign justice systems? Why haven't African nations returned to the justice systems that existed prior to colonization?

To begin to answer these questions requires one to consider the following. First, some forms of indigenous justice have indeed continued fairly uninterrupted by the period of colonial domination. Second, what has been called customary law and customary justice was often a creation of colonialists to meet their own social control goals and at the same time often bolstered the standing of some groups over others. Third, the call for a return to indigenous justice today likewise sometimes appears to meet the needs of outsiders to African nations, including international financial institutions. Fourth, societies in African nations today are essentially different from what they were prior to colonization and an indigenous justice system that worked in the past is probably not completely suited to African societies today. And, lastly, new systems of justice need to be developed in line with the values and traditions that underlie African societies today. Each of these considerations will be discussed in this chapter. The purpose of this chapter is not to answer the question of why African nations have not returned to pre-colonial forms of justice, but to address the issues that must be considered before that question can be answered.

Most readers will recognize that, for the most part, these ideas have been widely discussed in various literatures. But those working in these different areas do not always converse. Those "working on the ground" in development work do not always connect their work to the more abstract considerations of sociologists of law and criminologists or postcolonial scholars. Likewise, those working in academic settings do not always link their ideas to the tasks of those working towards meeting the concrete needs of real people. In this chapter, I will attempt to link some of these discussions by offering both a critique of current thinking and suggestions for future directions in the efforts to create just societies. This will be done using Mali as the primary context for discussion in the final section, although knowledge gleaned from the experiences of other African nations will be considered as well.

The Continuation of Indigenous Justice

The various forms of the colonization of African nations always involved a reworking of the pre-existing legal systems and processes of the various groups living in the occupied lands. Among current scholars, this has been most often conceptualized as a "capture" of the legal system to promote the interests of the colonialists. Among the colonialists themselves, this was more often seen as the systematic "revamping" of the pre-existing legal systems to render them "modern" and in accordance with Western ideas of the rule of law. But in either case the changes in the legal systems were never complete, in the sense that they rarely permeated every area of a country (spatially speaking) and they never covered every area of behavior or every type of dispute (socially speaking). Instead, certain geographical areas – often those most distant from the colonial capital or those without resources of immediate interest to the colonialists – were sometimes left out of the sweeping administrative and legal changes or, at least, were affected only superficially by a rudimentary structure that existed in name but without much change in practice. Perhaps more commonly, colonialists enforced a more overarching change throughout the lands they occupied, with the jurisdiction of some matters – usually labor, tax and serious crime – firmly ensconced in the new courts and new procedures, and the jurisdiction of other matters – such as family, marriage and inheritance – either relegated first to Native Authority Courts and then new Customary Courts or left to be handled according to traditional practices. It is the latter that is the focus of this section.

Much has been written about the continuation of indigenous justice in many sub-Saharan African nations. To mention just a few from different parts of the continent as examples, Gibbs (1963) wrote about informal dispute settlement processes among the Kpelle of Liberia. More recently, Elechi (2006) provided a detailed description and analysis of indigenous justice in Afikpo, Nigeria. Mangokwana (2001) described and analyzed a traditional *lekgotla* operating in Ramakgopa in the Northern Province (now Limpopo) in South Africa in 1994.

While the particular procedures vary in each of these justice systems, all share what many African scholars describe as the typical and essential elements of indigenous African justice systems: a focus on restoring harmony in social relations. This restoration usually involves an acknowledgement of harm (sometimes on the part of all parties) and compensation for losses incurred. The process typically allows both the parties involved and members of the community – or at least the elders in a community – to present their views on how best to resolve the issue, and discussion typically continues until some semblance of a consensus has developed. Even in situations where a "headman" makes the final decision, the decision must be in accord with the discussion.

It is clear that these indigenous systems rarely disappeared completely during the time of colonization and thus are available for nations today to build upon and expand, should they choose to do so.

"Customary" Law and Justice in the Period of Colonization

Martin Chanock (1998) offers the clearest articulation of the idea that what became known as customary law in the colonial period were not simply the customary practices of an area codified in customary law. He provides substantial evidence in two British colonies that practices were altered in this codification process in ways that benefited certain groups and disadvantaged others. Many times it was particular ethnic groups who were advantaged or disadvantaged, but at other times it was particular social categories of people (based on gender or financial standing, for example) or even particular practices (such as matrilineal or patrilineal inheritance).

In the Luapula district of North Easter Rhodesia, for example, Chanock documents how the customary courts became embroiled in a conflict over marriage customs:

> The picture which emerges is by now familiar, a rigid and definite 'law' is being insisted upon by some in the fact of it being widely ignored by others. This was not a customary legal 'system' but a situation of conflict into which Chapman [the Assistant Native Commissioner] wanted the administration to step by insisting on one set of claims (the ignoring of which was 'rapidly increasing') and thus making marriage prerequisites strictly observed and divorce difficult (1998, p. 177).

The point here is not that there were not preexisting customs or laws. There were. But as with all customs and laws, there is some degree of change over time. Change in these cases had often been the result of colonial actions, and so it was occurring at perhaps an accelerated pace. For example, Chanock discusses the consequences of the movement of males to the city to secure currency with which to pay colonial taxes. This rendered a man unable to reside in the village of his future wife to provide services for the wife's family in the months leading up to the wedding. This in turn led to the increasing replacement of this custom with higher bridewealth payments, which in turn gave rise to greater concern with the disposal of these large payments upon a marriage's dissolution.

In this case, however, the discussion of the process and the change was not in the hands of traditional leaders or the people themselves. It was in the hands of colonial administrators. British administrators were oftentimes well aware that they were imposing a different standard (as with the repugnancy rule, for example). But sometimes they believed they were in fact codifying preexisting custom in accordance with local wishes, unaware of the varieties or complexities of traditions and codifying one particular practice out of a wide variety of acceptable practices. Colonial administrators likewise often missed more subtle issues. I will cite the following example from Chanock (1998, pp. 184-185) because it so clearly illustrates this lack of understanding on the part of colonial administrators.

While the Boma saw itself as finding out the customary rule with which to decide a case, the local perception of what was happening was different. Chief Mukobela was asked whether a son could sue for his mother's bridewealth if she refused marriage by inheritance. The exchange is recorded as follows:

> *Mukobela*: Today he will – because of the Europeans – but long ago he could not.
> *Court*: That is not so because we have made no such law. We have made no such laws about your manners we have followed your own customs.
> *Mukobela*: Some you follow – some you don't.
> *Court*: Explain.
> *Mukobela*: Long ago if your son married and you paid his dowry for him – and after a time [the son and his wife] parted – You the father would take back the dowry. But today if you so claim the official says – Not at all.

It is important to see what is at issue here. The court's perception is that it is administering the customary law, while Mukobela's is that it is standing in the way of parents' power.... The customary practice (i.e. the 'customary law') of pre-colonial times was elders' authority and control over marriages.

When newly independent African nations were constructing Constitutions, they often explicitly wanted to accord a formal role to the customary practices and laws of their citizens. But in doing so, they often actually formalized the adulterated customary law as it had been reformulated under colonial rule. This is one of the reasons that some argue for the elimination of customary courts (for example, see ACAT/Sid-Kivu (2006), although their call for the elimination of customary courts in the Democratic Republic of Congo is founded on other arguments as well).

As Bowd (2009, p. 48) notes in his discussion of whether or not Africa should retain its legal *status quo* or return to more traditional practices: "The [justice] structure and systems put in place during the colonial period were deliberately divisive, exclusionary and extractive." The question is, he says (2009, p. 48): "[Are] there other systems that could better meet those needs?" The following three sections address this question.

The Call for Traditional Law and Justice Today

Post-independence, many African nations retained a reference to customary law and/or customary courts in their new constitutions, continuing a version of the tradition of legal dualism started by the colonists. In South Africa, for example, the current constitution includes a section on Customary Law and Traditional leaders, and while the Constitution "trumps" customary law in all cases, the government formally recognizes the validity of customary law and procedures. In contrast, the Constitution of Mali, in effect since 1992, does not include any reference to customary or indigenous law. While Mali has a "unified" legal system formally, it would still be accurate to say that Mali is characterized by legal pluralism, sociologically speaking. Estimates of the percentage of legal action that takes place outside of the official justice system of Mali range from 60% (Nagel n.d.) to 90% (Feiertag, 2008).

It can be difficult to reconcile traditional justice with the democratic reforms often embraced by new constitutions. In South Africa, for example, the anti-discrimination thrust of the new (post-Apartheid) Constitution is strong and clear but customary law in South Africa is quite patriarchal and hence often sexist and ageist. The South African Law Commission (SALC) (2003) completed an investigation of traditional courts and the judicial functions of traditional leaders and proposed a bill clarifying these in light of the Constitution. It proposed a variety of measures to standardize procedures and jurisdiction and limit punishments. The bill did not make a specific proposal on the composition of the customary courts due to the disagreements on this matter (for examples, over whether members should be elected, whether the members had to be representative of the population, and over who should preside). Instead, the bill states that the courts should be composed in accordance with customary law, with "a proviso intended to ensure women's participation" (SALC, 2003, p. 8). The *Traditional Leadership and Governance Framework Amendment Act (No. 41 of 2003)* addresses the role of customary leaders and specifies that traditional leaders must "promote freedom, human dignity, and the achievement of non-sexism" and must "promote an efficient effective and fair system of administration of justice" (*Traditional Leadership and Governance Framework Amendment Act 2003*: Preamble).

Of course, the concern with sexism and ageism in indigenous justice is one that emerges from the Western focus on individual human rights. As Okafọ notes, African communities are more likely to focus on communal issues rather than individual rights. He notes (2009, p. 140):

> The applicable characteristics of communalism and individualism have served the respective societies for millennia. There is little reason to attempt to overthrow these essences. An overthrow attempt would breed societal dislocation and anomie. Thus, the proper approach is that a reconstructed law and justice system, in Nigeria for example, will, as much as necessary and possible, maintain communalism as a basic ingredient of the society. However, the new law and justice system will also recognize that one of the central tenets of fundamental human rights application and enforcement in a society is individualism.

Okafọ is optimistic about such a convergence: "With negotiation among the stakeholders, the proper balance can be achieved" (2009, p. 140). He offers several examples of how this could be done. Consider Igbo customary law, he says, under which females cannot own land and therefore cannot inherit, buy or sell land. While the law clearly discriminates against females, Okafọ says in practice a woman has the right to use family land and while she must ask permission from the male head of household to do so, the male is obligated to grant permission for any reasonable request. Ultimately, however, a male landowner must complete the land transactions. "Perhaps a reasonable way out of this conflict," he says, "is to enact a law that will continue to allow individually-owned and held lands to be transferrable by those individuals, males and females. Also, the law should provide for family and other group-owned lands to be transferrable by the group leader (preferably male or female), according to the applicable indigenous law" (Okafọ 2009, p. 138).

Mangokwana (2001), too, notes that some of the people in the *legkotla* that he studied in South Africa had complaints about its operation, including the exclusion and unequal treatment of women and youth, the failure of particular headmen to meet the needs of everyone in the community, and the requirement to join a burial society (which was seen as a violation of the right to choose). However, he also points out that the operation of the *lekgotla* has begun to change, in accordance with changes in ideas about equality and choice.

Other analysts are not so certain that changes will come. In his comments on the first 25 years of independence for most African countries, Michael Crowder, for example, suggested that the democratic dream envisioned for the future may really have been about a particular vision of democracy that will not fit Africa. He wrote in 1987 (p. 11): "I believe that historians will consider that contemporary judgments about the so called failure of Africa are really judgments made in terms of a Eurocentric dream for an independent Africa in which liberal democracy would be the norm, a dream that was shared only by a few elitist politicians..."

What is clear, however, is the push that African leaders have received from several major players in the international community to change their justice systems in accordance with this liberal democratic vision with its emphasis on individual rights and liberties. Additionally, the resources and assistance of smaller organizations have played a role in pushing this agenda. This is an extremely important point, because very poor nations, such as Mali, do not always appear to have the luxury of deciding how to develop the "reconstructed" law called for by Okafọ.

The United Nations Development Program (UNDP) has been urging nations of the world to take action to decrease poverty and increase various standards of living in poor nations since its inception in 1965. The Millennium Development Goals initiative is certainly one way the UN in general and the UNDP in particular have worked to support such changes and the World Bank has supported these goals as well. The World Bank's interest in poverty eradication relates at least in part to their interest in establishing robust economies with investment opportunities. However, since abandoning the stringent structural adjustment loan policies of the 1980s the Bank has begun to acknowledge the importance of approaching at least some problems from the perspective of those living in the society. The Poverty Reduction Strategy Paper (PRSP) approach of the World Bank and the IMF, where countries requesting the Bank's assistance must devise their own strategies and priorities for poverty reduction, requires the participation of various segments of the country to be involved in the creation of these priorities. While the process is not working equally well across all countries who have completed PRSPs (Cheru, 2006), it has resulted in some valuable outcomes.

Five years ago, the World Bank and the United Nations began another effort, one focusing on the legal empowerment of the poor. Then World Bank President Paul Wolfowitz said, "We cannot make headway in the fight against poverty without supporting equality before the law and the legal empowerment of the poor" (cited in Palacio, 2005/ rev. 2006, p. 3). This effort was seen to be different from the previous focus of World Bank justice sector activities, which concentrated on establishing civil legal structures – especially relating to land titling and contract enforcement – that would lead to stable investment environments. The more recent efforts focus on access to justice and have included projects on court reforms, legal services and legal aid, public awareness and education, less formal dispute resolution mechanisms, and increasing public sector accountability and have focused on some basic research (Maru, 2009). These World Bank studies have used qualitative research methods to get a more holistic understanding of how and why justice processes operate as they do in communities without access to formal justice processes (Manning, 2008; Sage, Menzies and Woolcock, 2009). Some of the findings are of great interest to sociologists, and will be discussed in the last section, even though the Bank's interest may ultimately still be "the likely possibilities and limits of local legal institutions in the promotion of economic outcomes" (Gauri, 2009, p. 5).

But the World Bank is also interested in promoting change as efficiently as possible. Some of its interest in looking at legal change at the local level stems from its recognition that change from the top down has not always worked. In nations where the State is "fragile", either economically or politically, or in nations where the State may be more directly part of what the Bank sees as the problem, there may be some advantage to pursuing other strategies for change. If the order created by indigenous justice systems can support the growth in local economic enterprises, this could be sufficient, from the Bank's perspective.

In any case, the funding for legal change has been channeled a little more toward the reforms noted above that are more likely to affect individual citizens as legal actors than previous government-oriented effort to develop the rule of law. In linking legal empowerment of the poor and poverty eradication, the Bank has also lined up its mission with the Human Rights-promoting NGOs who are also interested in developing the culture of the rule of law from the bottom up. My comments here are purely speculative, but it seems reasonable to ask whether a nation in financial straits is in a position to refuse assistance even if that nation does not wish to pursue the agendas implied in the rule of law-human rights alliance, particularly those fostering gender and age equality.

The Impossibility of a Complete Return to Indigenous Justice

Even if there were consensus among African leaders and citizens that a return to original (i.e. pre-colonial) forms of indigenous justice is desirable – which there is not – it is difficult to avoid the conclusion that such a return is not possible. From a sociological perspective, the classic works on changing societies elucidate how the social bases for cohesion are different and thus there are different bases for law (see, for example, Durkheim's classic work on mechanical and organic solidarity and how that is related to the evolution of legal systems (Durkheim, 1933).

A comprehensive examination of changes that were forced by the colonists would be too large an endeavor for a chapter such as this. But it is clear that the new patterns of labor migration and urbanization, for example, resulted in changes that cannot be undone. Whether forced off the land or forced to seek a monetary wage to pay colonial taxes or some other reason, many Africans left their traditional homelands for cities. These patterns have been in place for decades and cannot be undone. Among younger Africans, for example, it is not unusual to find increasing numbers who declare "I am from Accra" or "I am from Bamako," rather than refer to the original villages of their families. These young people have never lived in a village – nor have their parents before them or even two generations before them. While many maintain at least yearly travel to their original family homes, many others do not. The indigenous justice practices of these villages may thus be either unknown to these youth or be seen to hold no relevance for these youth.

On the other hand, the heterogeneity of cities, characterized by absence of agreed upon mechanisms of social control, lead many city-dwellers to create their own institutions for "ordering" their lives. This was especially true in countries such as South Africa where Black South Africans were purposely excluded from the protection of the dominant legal systems (while being subject to its oppression). These citizens, then as now, "live in the interstices of the state system, exploit their contradictions and inadequacies, and develop the spaces for survival and mutual support" as Wilkerson and Webster phrase it (cited in Nina and Schärf, 2001, p. 3). But this has been true in other countries as well. While the Bakassi Boys of Nigeria may not be the most pleasant example of this, Harnischfeger (2003) has demonstrated how this organization developed in the city of Aba to control the extortion problems market traders experienced in the absence of effective government social control.

Indeed, the absence of formal means of social control as one of the major factors leading to the development of popular means of control is an ongoing theme in the literature in the sociology of law. It thus complements the rationale for a return to some traditional justice systems proposed by international agencies discussed in the previous section.

Finally, the numerous concrete changes wrought by many colonists provide many tragic examples of changes that seem not to be able to be easily undone. Joko (2006), for example, describes the inability of the Bakweris to reclaim their ancestral lands in what is now Cameroon, or be compensated for those lands. The Bakweri people claim this land was taken from them by the Germans, then the English, and, then, eventually, the State of Cameroon. When the State-owned corporation that farmed the land was privatized, the land did not revert to the Bakweri people as they had hoped. Joko's point is that the traditional conception of land as belonging to a people – not individuals – that is known and recognized in indigenous law must also be learned and understood by the broader legal community. While this is no doubt true, learning about indigenous law will not solve a problem that has been created across decades of people acting on different premises. A just solution can probably be reached in this case, but it is not likely to be one that solely relies on traditional law; rather, it will also have to take into account the changes that have occurred in the intervening generations.

New Justice Systems for New Societies

African nations have seen numerous efforts to reclaim indigenous justice processes that may have continued in many rural areas of the continent, but lost their foothold with the rise of urbanization, colonial legal systems and colonial customary courts. Chabal and Daloz (1999) refer to the broader process of "re-traditionalization", by which they refer not so much to the "movement backwards" that the continent has taken in the eyes of some analysts but as the various reassertions of traditional identities (particularly ethnic identities) and beliefs (particularly relating to religion and witchcraft). However, I think by focusing on these particular examples of "re-traditionalization" – on traditions, which they see as best forgotten – Chabal and Daloz reveal some of the same biases as earlier generations of colonists. Chabal and Daloz's point of view misses the analytical point so clearly articulated by Chanock (1998, p. xi) "that custom is constantly recreated, reimagined, and reinvented." It is to these processes of change – which are as forward-looking as they are tied to tradition – that we now turn.

In the preface to the new printing of his book, Chanock reflects on how his original thesis on the colonial construction of customary law – and the continual recreation of custom – can be read today. He argues: "Africa's institutions could be alive to these processes, and could acknowledge now, as the colonial state could not, that there are many voices and dialogues involved. By hearing more than one voice, by avoiding the trap of essentializing and freezing culture, states could restore life to the realm of law and custom" (1998, p. xi). But is this necessarily a state project?

As Okereafọezeke (now Okafọ) notes (2001), it is essential that the new systems of justice develop from the ground up. A system in which customary law is designed, structured and imposed from the top down will be neither an acceptable nor an accepted system. In his more recent work, Okafọ reiterates this point (2009, p. 223) and explicates some of the principles that should guide the law and justice reconstruction. But he also notes that considerable changes at the corporate level – both private and public – will need to take place for the successful reconstruction of law and justice.

Gauri (2009) takes a more critical look at indigenous justice. He notes that in 11 of 34 cases described in World Bank studies, there is not a clear separation of the use of formal and informal legal systems. While Feiertag (2008) says that in Mali this usually means that people use traditional systems first and those who do not like the outcome all appeal the decision in the courts of the official legal system, Gauri points out, as have others, that in some countries the opposite occurs: people attempt to use the official legal system only to be rebuffed, alienated or discouraged at the request for a bribe and will then turn to the traditional system for relief. Elechi (2004; 2006) and Bowd (2009), among many others, point to the superiority of indigenous justice systems in avoiding these and other problems with the formal justice system for those who seek legal assistance.

But Gauri's (2009) analysis of informal justice is interesting because he is trying to figure out – for very practical purposes – what the World Bank has learned from its research on this over the years. This practical orientation is present in his discussion of the three ways in which informal legal systems differ from formal legal systems. First, like others, he notes that informal legal systems are more variable and flexible in both operation and substance. This could allow informal legal systems to adapt more quickly to changes in the social (and economic) contexts. Next, he notes that informal legal systems "are imbedded in cosmic and social significations" (p. 6). This means that the resolution of disputes are important for maintaining social, moral and even cosmic order and increases the investment of the community in a restorative outcome (hence, this contributes to stability). Finally, he notes that judicial authorities in informal legal systems are often the social, political and economic authorities in the community as well. He poses no positive or negative outcome of this but notes that it violates the principle of the separation of powers that is important in some societies.

Citing evidence from several past and recent studies funded by the Bank, Gauri (2009) concludes that informal legal systems do not seem to reduce inequality. Less powerful disputants were found to be less likely to have favorable outcomes in informal legal systems, just as was true in formal legal systems. In cases of criminal acts, particularly those involving youth, results from World Bank studies are a bit more positive, with satisfaction on the part of all parties in about half the cases (and satisfaction in most cases involving youth). Gauri also noted that local justice systems were ineffective as venues within which villagers could hold local leaders responsible for the provision of basic services or in which public actors (such as companies or government entities) could be held accountable for their actions. He concluded that local justice systems are better able "to support personal integrity rights than the positive liberties that are also constitutive of development as the expansion of freedom" (Gauri 2009, p. 26).

The findings offered by this review by Gauri are thought provoking, since he reviews many studies that show a negative side of indigenous justice systems in terms of their perpetuation of inequality in general, rather than focusing on the unequal legal standing of women and youth in particular. Additionally, his findings direct us to questions that social scientists need to address: Are there some types of indigenous justice processes that can be fairer for weaker disputants? Are there ways that indigenous justice processes can change to become fairer for weaker disputants? Alternatively, are there some kinds of cases – such as when there is a large status gap between the two disputants – that should not be informally adjudicated?

Finally, the criticisms of local justice systems presented by Gauri need to be considered in light of the many criticisms and inadequacies of the colonial-based formal justice systems in African nations today. Indigenous systems may not be perfect but in many cases, they provide superior experiences and outcomes for people seeking justice.

As African societies continue to develop as independent nations, it is hoped that their leaders and their citizens will build on the traditions and practices that created the strong communities and justice systems that have served and continue to serve these societies. As both Chanock (1998) and Okafọ (2009) point out, that does not mean doing things exactly as they were done in pre-colonial times. Traditions – in spite of what that term implies – are ever changing.

Justice Systems in Mali

The purpose of this final section is to illustrate how the dynamics discussed in this chapter have played themselves out in one nation, Mali. I will begin with descriptive information about the country to provide context for the reader unfamiliar with its recent history and experience.

Mali achieved independence from France in 1960, after an attempt to be part of a larger independent federation with Senegal failed after less than a year. The 8-year reign of Mali's socialist-leaning first president, Modibo Kéita, ended with a *coup d'état* led by General Moussa Traoré, who ruled for the next 23 years. After a national conference in 1991 to plan for the transition to a democratic form of government, Alpha Konaré was elected in 1992 and the current constitution came into effect on 25 February 1992. Konaré served for the two terms allowed by the Constitution and Mali underwent another peaceful regime change with the election and reelection of current president, Amadou Toumani Touré in 2002 and 2007, solidifying its reputation as a stable democracy.

Mali continues to be one of the poorest nations in sub-Saharan Africa. With a population of about 13 million, half of whom are under age 16, almost three-quarters of whom live on less that US $2 per day and 80% of whom work in the agricultural sector, it is easy to understand how assistance efforts could become focused on food and education. But the assistance efforts in Mali are as diverse as they are numerous, just as they are in most developing nations. The governments of Canada and France are particularly large donors but countries as varied as the Netherlands, Libya, South Africa and the U.S. are also involved in Mali. Non-governmental organizations (NGOs) from these and other nations as well as international NGOs abound. Less present are the religious-affiliated NGOs common in other areas of West Africa. Numerous Malian NGOs exist as well, perhaps as the result of recent efforts of external NGOs to foster the development of civil society. These many organizations and governments are focusing on everything from developing commodity value chains for mangoes and shea to promoting the well-being of women and children to promoting biodiversity and environmental sustainability, as well as promoting legal reform.

The changes in orientation of world financial institutions and development agencies that were noted earlier in this chapter are also reflected in the developed world's involvement in Mali. In the mid-1990s, USAID completed a series of assessments of the transition of Mali to the democracy propounded in its new constitution. While this assessment was broad-ranging, there was at least one area of particular relevance to this chapter's focus on indigenous justice. The USAID report was quite negative in its assessment of the rule of law and justice systems in Mali (Hobgood, 1995). The Constitution's emphasis on human rights and access to justice was not reflected in current practices, said the report, and the situation was seen as dire:

> As practiced by State and private actors alike, the generalized lack of an effective "rule of law culture" in Mali today represents nothing less than a major threat to the sustainability of the new democratic order. The courts are penuriously provisioned. Criminal and civil cases are backlogged. Citizens distrust the corrupted system and lack access to courts to resolve their problems. The lack of a "rule of law culture" and a justice system to undergird and nurture it may well constitute the greatest menace to the sustainability of Mali's democratic polity (Hobgood, 1995, Internet).

In 1998, a massive effort to improve Mali's justice system began with a national consultation and forum to articulate what reforms were needed. A ten-year Justice Development Program (PRODEJ) was started to reform the judiciary. Funded heavily by the Canadian International Development Agency (CIDA), the project accomplished much in terms of supporting the Malian governments' initiatives to increase communications among stakeholders through conferences, consultations, and forums. CIDA was also involved in building and revamping court infrastructures, information management systems, procedures for moving people and cases through the system, and advancing gender equity (see CIDA, 2010a; b). While acknowledging some of these accomplishments, Feiertag (2008, p. 17) argues that the top-down approach of PRODEJ limited what could be achieved, noting: "The program's success depended on the political will of the Ministry of Justice, which turned out to be one of the main weaknesses in the design of the programme."

In 2001, the Mali National Assembly passed a new penal code (Loi No. 01-

079 du 20 août 2001) and code of criminal procedure (Loi No. 01-080 du 20 août 2001) replacing laws which had been enacted in 1961 and 1962 respectively and had retained many of the repressive features of the colonial legal system. The new laws include many of the due process procedures common in Western criminal law. However, a recent assessment of the Malian criminal justice system by the African Human Security Initiative (AHSI) (AHSI, 2009a), under the direction of Barbara Chikwanha, indicates that actual practice often differs from that mandated in the new law. The AHSI (2009b) identifies numerous problems, including: understaffed agencies; poorly trained personnel; institutional and infrastructural problems; no statistics (and therefore no overview possible); provisions in the law are not followed; corruption; and money and gender can determine access to justice.

In her short summary of the Malian criminal justice system, Chikwanha notes: "Historically, those with French citizenship would appeal to modern law and the 'indigenous' people would resort to customary justice. This situation has not changed since decolonization" (Chikwanha, 2008, p. 2).

There is limited information on the variety of actual indigenous justice practices in Mali. Malejacq (2009, p. 1) notes that the indigenous law is recorded in the form of proverbs, tales, legends, adages, maxims, dictums, sayings, parables and songs still sung by griots. Nagel (n.d.) describes a peacemaking caste in Mali, the *jeliw*, to whom she refers as griots or bards. While griots are well known to the Western world as the recorders and keepers of history through their song, Nagel refers to *jeliw* as people who intervene to mediate disputes. She reports that a *jeli* may be either male or female, which differs from the traditional portrayal of griots. Citing Schulz (2001, pp. 152-153), Nagel says that *jeliw* are more common in rural areas than urban areas, where they may actually be paid to mediate a dispute. "Nevertheless, *jeliw* still have a lot of influence in modern Malian society and contribute to the resistance of Malians to utilize the French justice system to address grievances and offenses," says Nagel (2008, p. 7).

Today the 2006 Civil Code (Loi No. 06-023 du 28 juin 2006) allows for customary courts, where justices of the peace, along with two local assessors, knowledgeable in local custom and with voting rights, are authorized to decide a broad array of civil cases (AHSI, 2009a). In addition, the civil code recognizes "*Cadi*" justice in Tombouctou, Gao and Kidal. And, finally, the civil code allows for the chief, or other groups or neighborhoods to regulate civil matters in accordance with traditions (AHSI, 2009, pp. 61-62).

In criminal matters, the law does not allow for traditional justice practices in the broad manner allowed in civil matters. The 2001 Code of Criminal Procedure allows for penal mediation, but only in a very limited number of areas (Article 52). A 2006 decree (Décret No. 06-168/P-RM du 13 avril 2006) spells this out in a little more detail and says that penal mediation can be used in *contraventions* and délits, which are the lower two of the three levels of crime, except for cases of crimes against public good and sexual offenses (Article 5). The law covering the protection of juveniles also allows for limited penal mediation (AHSI, 2009a). While penal mediation is described as meeting many of the same restorative goals of indigenous justice, the procedure is formally organized by the office of the procureur. The AHSI report recommends the expansion of penal mediation[1] but this procedure seems sufficiently different from indigenous justice practices so that the need and preference for indigenous practices is likely to continue.

In 2005, a Malian NGO, Deme So, started pushing hard to establish the development of paralegals who could provide basic legal information about rights and processes to the majority of the Malian population who live in rural areas. In 2006, a national conference was held to develop a national curriculum for the training of paralegals in Mali; the curriculum was developed jointly but written by consultants at the Netherlands-based Center for International Legal Cooperation (CILC). These *"parajuristes,"* as they are called, do not work under the auspices of attorneys but are men and women who are trained in the basics of legal rights (including civil, land, human, women's, and children's rights), decentralization, the rule of law, access to justice administration, and the prevention, resolution and management of conflicts (CILC, 2006). The *parajuriste* program in Mali now operates under the leadership of the National Steering Committee for the Training of *Parajuristes* (CNPCP), in a framework suggested by CILC, with close cooperation with the Malian government and a number of Malian NGOs (CNPCP, 2009).

However, neither the penal mediators nor the *parajuristes* would appear to function in Malian society in the same way that indigenous justice functions. Writing about indigenous justice systems in Mali and Benin, Malejacq (2009, p. 1) explains:

> These rules and norms function to assure the survival of the groups, to protect the individual, to provide for the security of the community as well as to promote social integration by ensuring the active participation of different social actors in the daily functioning of the community.

Thus, as has been described elsewhere, the protection of the individual is indeed one of the purposes of indigenous justice in Mali, but it is only one among a number of other more collectively oriented functions.

In Mali, the rights of individuals are not seen in the same way as they are in Western societies. The Malian Constitution embraces the principle of equality

---

[1] The AHSI report (2009a) does not mention the 2006 decree expanding the application of penal mediation and detailing who can be a mediator. The full text of the decree is available Online through the Library of Congress' Global Legal Information Network (http://wwwglin.gov; Internet).

for all its citizens.[2] However, it is not at all clear how the principle of equality under the law can be applied when discriminatory practices are embraced by the population – and, indeed, are often not seen as discriminatory in the eyes of many Malians. As Chikwanha (2008, p. 2) observes, "The law is incongruent with the wishes and core values of the people since the latter's values have not changed." The widely publicized public protests over the new persons and family law passed by Mali's National Assembly last year illustrate this conundrum. The new law changed numerous aspects of family law, but particularly controversial was the change from the stipulation that wives were required to obey their husbands to the idea that spouses owe each other fidelity, protection, help and assistance.[3] Thousands protested the change and the president returned the law back to the National Assembly for reconsideration.

Mali is in the midst of a variety of changes in its criminal justice system, some of which, like the development of penal mediators and *parajuristes*, indicate perhaps a small but official move toward the more participatory and restorative practices of indigenous justice systems. Likewise, a story told by Nagel (2008, p. 70) also illustrates how Malians today are officially questioning the colonial justice structures that remain in their nation:

> On my research trip to Mali in 2002 ... a judge told me the following: "I used to be very tough on crime, sentencing every offender to long prison terms. One day my son was stopped on the street and told, 'Your father is a thief! He is stealing people.' Then I had a change of heart and I am now rethinking punishment." This judge is currently heard of the corrections system and is reflecting on the use of rehabilitation and demarcation. Interestingly, he attended the International Conference on Penal Abolition (ICOPA) in Toronto in 2001 to gather information from scholars and practitioners internationally on how to minimize the use of imprisonment as a corrective measure.

Mali, like many other African nations, may be starting to move forward by retrieving indigenous practices from their past. This may be easier for Mali than it will be for other African nations because these indigenous practices

---

[2] Article 2 of Title I of the Constitution of Mali reads: "All Malians are born and live free and equal in their rights and duties. Any discrimination based on social origin, color, language, race, sex, religion, or political opinion is prohibited." Translation by Jeffrey Craver for Constitution Finder (http://confinder.richmond.edu/admin/docs/Mali; Internet).

[3] Article 311 (page 53) of Loi No.09-038/AN-RM Portant Code des Personnes et de la Famille was translated by the author (as are all the following translations in the chapter). It reads in the original French: "Les époux se doivent mutuellement fidélité, protection, secours et assistance. Ils s'obligent à la communauté de vie sur la base de l'affection et du respect." (http://www.mj.gov.ml/contenu_documentation.aspx; Internet).

remain alive and well throughout much of the nation. But the French orientation and preference for centralized governmental systems still prevails in Mali, and that may make it more difficult to officially embrace the wide-ranging practices and substantive rulings that characterize Malian indigenous justice. Finally, the question of how to reconcile the Western push for human rights and retain the Malian values honoring men and the elderly over women and youth remains to be answered.

Conclusion

Malejacq (2009, p. 4) identifies a key problem for African nations today, thus: "Beyond the conflict between customary and formal justice is the matter of an eminently political problem. This question of 'measured (restrained) modernity' seems to have not yet been tackled head-on by either political actors... or by recognized traditional leaders."

While Malejacq is writing specifically about Mali and Benin, his comments are clearly more broadly applicable. In a world where incremental change in African nations could be allowed to proceed at a pace unfettered by outside forces and demands, perhaps this conversation could be deferred. In today's world — where NGOs, international financial institutions and external governments have their own agendas, which color their relations and financial assistance to African nations — this is an issue that, as Malejacq says, perhaps needs to be tackled "head-on."

Of course, in African tradition, tackling issues "head-on" means that stakeholders in this issue must talk and talk and talk and eventually, the path forward will become clearer. While Malejacq calls for a national conversation (2009, p. 4), the question of how any nation wishes to proceed with "measured modernity" is not one that can be answered *in toto*. The bottom-up approach suggests that individual villages and sociocultural groups need to begin to work through these issues themselves. Most African nations are comprised of many different sociocultural groups with different traditions, ideas, and practices and different ideas about whether or how to modernize. Thus, there is no reason to expect that these different entities will proceed either on the same path or at the same speed. But conversations need to occur, and as Natukunda-Togboa (2009, p. 3) recommends, both the government and development partners need to be encouraging "dynamic exchanges between the actors in these two modes of justice [customary and modern]."

Likewise, the issue of "measured modernity" is not one that can be answered once and for all. As has been noted at various points in this chapter, indigenous law and indigenous justice practices are always changing. Custom, as Chanock reminds us (1998, p. ix), "is constantly recreated, reimagined, and reinvented." It is in looking to both the futures they desire and the pasts that they embrace that Africans today will decide how to proceed.

References

ACAT/Sud-Kivu (Christian Action for the Abolition of Torture) (2006) "Customary Courts in the Congolese Judiciary System: A Reform for Better Administration of Justice." Open Society Institute, African Governance Monitoring and Advocacy Project. Retrieved 25 February 2010 (http://www.afrimap.org; Internet).

African Human Security Initiative (2009a) *Mali: Criminalité et Justice Criminelle*. Institute for Security Studies Monograph 162. Retrieved 17 November 2009 (http://issafrica.org; Internet).

African Human Security Initiative (2009b) "Pleins Projecteurs sur le Crime et la Justice Criminelle au Mali." Policy Brief Number 04, July 2009. Pretoria, South Africa: Institute for Security Studies. Retrieved 29 November 2009 (http://www.africanreview.org/frpays.php; Internet).

Bowd, Richard (2009) "Status Quo or Traditional Resurgence: What is Best for Africa's Criminal Justice Systems?" Pp. 35-55 in African Human Security Initiative (ed) *The Theory and Practice of Criminal Justice in Africa*. ISS Monograph 161. Institute for Security Studies. Retrieved 5 January 2010 (http://www.africanreview.org/docs/mono161.pdf; Internet).

Canadian International Development Agency (CIDA) (2010a) "Project Profile for Preparation of the Ten-Year Justice Development Program (PRODEJ)." Retrieved 6 March 2010 (http://www.acdi-cida.gc.ca; Internet).

Canadian International Development Agency (CIDA) (2010b) "Project Profile for Implementation of the Ten-Year Development Program (PRODEJ)." Retrieved 6 March 2010 (http://www.acdi-cida.gc.ca; Internet).

Center for International Legal Cooperation (CILC) (2006) *Curriculum National de Formation du Parajuriste au Mali*. Accessed 25 November 2009 (http://www.cnpcpmali.org/pdf/curriculum_national.pdf; Internet).

Chabal, Patrick and Jean-Pascal Daloz (1999) *Africa Works: Disorder as Political Instrument*. Oxford and Bloomington, Indiana: The International African Institute, Kings College, in association with James Currey and Indiana University Press.

Chanock, Martin (1998/1985) *Law, Custom and Social Order: The Colonial Experience in Malawi and Zambia*. Portsmouth, New Hampshire, USA: Heinemann.

Cheru, Fantu (2006) "Building and Supporting PRSPs in Africa: What Has Worked Well So Far? What Needs Changing?" *Third World Quarterly* 27(2):355-376.

Chikwanha, Annie Barbara (2008) "Mali Crime and Criminal Justice System

Dissemination Report." Presented 13 December 2008, Hotel Azalai Salaam, Bamako, Mali. Human Security Initiative. Retrieved 10 November 2009 (http://docstoc.com/docs/19786108/Mali-Crime-and-Criminal-Justice-System-Dissemination-report-13th; Internet).

CNPCP (2009) "Welcome to the Site of the CNPCP." Retrieved 10 November 2009 (http://cnpcpmali.org; Internet).

Crowder, Michael (1987) "Whose Dream Was It Anyway? Twenty-Five Years of African Independence," *African Affairs* 86 (342):7-24.

Durkheim, Emile (1933/1893) *The Division of Labor in Society*. New York: Free Press.

Elechi, O. Oko (2004) "Human Rights and the African Indigenous Justice System." Paper presented at the 18th International Conference of the International Society for the Reform of Criminal Law 8-12 August 2004. Montreal, Quebec, Canada.

Elechi, O. Oko (2006) *Doing Justice Without the State: The Afikpo (Ehugbo) Nigeria Model*. New York, NY, USA: Routledge.

Feiertag, Servaas (2008) "Guide to Legal Research in Mali." Globalex. New York: Hauser Global Law School Program, NYU School of Law. Retrieved 10 November 2009 (http://www.nyulawglobal.org/globalex/mali1.htm; Internet).

Gauri, Varun (2009) "How Do Local-Level Legal Institutions Promote Development? An Exploratory Essay." Justice and Development Working Paper Series. 6/2009. Washington, D.C., USA: World Bank. Retrieved 10 December 2009 (http://www-wds.worldbank.org; Internet).

Gibbs, Jr. James L. (1963) "The Kpelle Moot: A Therapeutic Model for the Informal Settlement of Disputes," *Africa* 33:1-10.

Harnischfeger, Johannes (2003) "The Bakassi Boys: Fighting Crime in Nigeria," *Journal of Modern African Studies* 41(1): 23-49.

Hobgood, Harlan (1995) "Governance in Democratic Mali: An Assessment of Transition and Consolidation and Guidelines for Near-Term Action." Edited, Revised Extracts from the Final Draft Report (7/94). Presented at a Workshop Hosted by the U.S. Agency for International Development, February 1995, Washington, DC., USA (Retrieved 10 November 2009) (http://pdf.usaid.gov.pdf_docs/PNABU032.pdf; Internet).

Joko, Michael (2006) "Access to Economic Justice in the Common Law Jurisdiction of Cameroon." Open Society Institute, African Governance Monitoring and Advocacy Project. Retrieved 25 February 2010 (http://www.afrimap.org; Internet).

Malejacq, Romain (2009) "Entre Tradition et Modernité: La Justice Coutumière au Bénin et au Mali." Policy Brief No. 12, October 2009. Pretoria, South Africa: Institute for Security Studies. Retrieved 29 November 2009 (http://www.africanreview.org/pubs/PBNo12Oct09.pdf; Internet).

Mangokwana, Andries Mphoto (2001) *"Makgotla* in Rural and Urban Contexts."
    Pp. 148-166 in *The Other Law: Non-State Ordering in South Africa.* Edited
    by W. Schärf and D. Nina. Lansdowne, South Africa: JUTA Law.
Manning, Ryann Elizabeth (2008) "Research Methodology: Justice for the
    Poor and Understanding Processes of Change in Local Governance."
    Washingon, DC., USA: World Bank. Retrieved 4 March 2010 (http://www-
    wds.worldbank.org; Internet).
Maru, Vivek (2009) "Access to Justice and Legal Empowerment: A Review of World
    Bank Practice." Justice and Development Working Paper Series. 9/2009.
    Washington, D.C.: The World Bank. Retrieved 10 December 2009 (http://
    www-wds.worldbank.org; Internet).
Nagel, Mechthild (2008) "I Write What I Like": African Prison Intellectuals and
    the Struggle for Freedom," *The Journal of Pan African Studies* 2(3): 68-80.
Nagel, Mechthild. n.d. "Gender, Incarceration and Peacemaking in Mali."
    Retrieved 10 November 2009 (http://www.einaudi.cornell.edu/files/
    calendar/3020/Nagel; Internet).
Natukunda-Togboa, Edith (2009) "Réform de la justice Criminelle au Bénin et au
    Mali: Une Riposte à l'Accroissement de la Criminalité?" Policy Brief No.
    10, September 2009. Pretoria, South Africa: Institute for Security Studies.
    Retreived 5 January 2010. (www.africanreview.org/pubs/PBNo10Sep09.
    pdf; Internet).
Okafọ, Nọnso (2009) *Reconstructing Law and Justice in a Postcolony.* Surrey,
    England and Burlington, USA: Ashgate Publishing.
Okereafọezeke (Okafọ), Nọnso (2001) "Judging the Enforceability of Nigeria's
    Native Laws, Customs, and Traditions in the Face of Official Controls."
    Paper presented at the Spring Meeting of the Southeastern Regional
    Seminar in African Studies 6 -7 April 2001. Northern Kentucky University,
    Highland Heights, Kentucky, USA.
Palacio, Ana (2005/revised 2006) "Legal Empowerment of the Poor: An Action
    Agenda for the World Bank." Washingon, DC., USA: The World Bank.
    Retrieved 4 March 2010 (http://www-wds.worldbank.org; Internet).
Sage, Caroline, Nicholas Menzies and Michael Woolcock (2009) "Taking the Rules
    of the Game Seriously: Mainstreaming Justice in Development, The World
    Bank's Justice for the Poor Program." Justice and Development Working
    Papers Series. Retrieved 10 December 2009 (http://www-wds.worldbank.
    org; Internet).
Schulz, Dorothea (2001) *Perpetuating the Politics of Praise.* Köln: Rudiger Koppe
    Verlag.
Shorter, Alyward (1977) "Concepts of Social Justice in Traditional Justice," *Pro
    Dialogo Bulletin* 12: 32-51. Retrieved 17 November 2009 (http://www.
    afrikaworld.net/afrel/atr-socijustice.htm; Internet).
South African Law Commission (2003) Report on Traditional Courts and the Judicial

Function of Traditional Leaders. Project 90. 21 January 2003. Retrieved 7 July 2004. (http://www.server.law.wits.ac.za/salc/report/pr90report.pdf; Internet).

Traditional Leadership and Governance Framework Amendment Act (No. 41 of 2003) (South Africa).

Chapter 4

Legal Pluralism and Harmonization of Laws: The Dilemma

Victoria Time
Old Dominion University, USA

Introduction

Legal pluralism represents a process whereby two or more systems of law exist in a given nation (Merry, 1988). This is frequently the case in postcolonial territories; but as Tie (2002, p. 885) points out "... modern nation states now routinely contain more than one legal system. The weaker versions of this claim refer to the manner in which formal legal proceedings frequently incorporate values and norms from subordinate systems of social regulation, such as indigenous customary law." In the context of post colonial territories especially those classified as developing nations, legal pluralism entails the transplant of foreign law to a developing nation that already has its customary laws in force (see Time, 2000). In many postcolonial societies, the introduction of foreign law involves just one system of law, but some countries like Cameroon present a peculiar occurrence where three systems of laws at one point were introduced to the country following its distinctive colonial history. First, the German civil code was introduced to Cameroon then Anglo common law, and Franco civil law was introduced.

Tie observes correctly that legal pluralism usually leads to a process whereby one system of law, more frequently, customary law is marginalized by the imposed law. Customary law, which hitherto governed legal proceedings, becomes the secondary rather than the primary controlling body of law (see for instance what happens in Cameroon, Sierra Leone, Brazil, and a host of other countries). The problem is more complicated when there is a multiplicity of customary laws in a country and they are interpreted as well as enforced differently from tribe to tribe, or from one part of the country to the other. Controlling crime and enforcing the law represent aspects by which governments regulate peoples' behavior. To give state action validity, such laws that control behavior should be harmonized and should be uniformly enforced. Such steps as Lombardo (1986) suggests is one dimension of "nation building," a gradual process of creating a "political society." Mindful of the fact that there are different functions of law, the discussion here relates to the dynamics of dispute resolution.

Relevant Issues and Responses

Several questions arise regarding conflict management, and they center around: (1) Which law should take prominence – acquired law or indigenous/customary law, and why? (2) When more than one system of law is introduced in a country, which one should govern?

Which Law should Take Prominence – Acquired Law or Indigenous/Customary Law, and Why?

Nation building in several parts of the world particularly Africa has in part comprised attempts at reconciling contradictions that stem from the existence of acquired laws and those indigenous to the land. While foreign law introduces values and doctrines that are sometimes absent in customary practices, it is evident that many indigenous people still prefer the primacy of traditional/customary laws over acquired/imposed laws (see Brillion, 1983; Lombardo, 1986; Austin, 1994, 1996; Thompson, 1996; Time, 2000; Okafo, 2009). As Brillion (1983, p. 3) notes:

> Research conducted in Ibadan and Abidjan shows that tribal justice—even today and even for major offenses—appeals to the majority of the native African population. Some experts argue that traditional forms of settlement are on the increase. Obviously, the new codes and administrative mechanisms are better suited to city dwellers than the rural majority population. Nevertheless, even in the cities, where the agglomeration of different ethnic groups necessitates the existence of a common law, the inefficiencies of the official criminal justice system contribute to the growth of primitive justice. Cases of tribal justice and lynchings are reportedly on the rise. This leads us to believe that modern justice is not only ill suited to traditional modes of thought but also incapable of dealing with the new criminality of the cities.

That customary law is still preferred by autochthonous groups is not unique to African societies. Collier (1973) reports that this is the case in rural areas in Mexico where only after attempts by the council of elders are deemed unsatisfactory is the case taken to formal courts where western laws are applied. As well, Tie (2002) observes that in New Zealand, aspects of customary laws are infused in criminal trials, and in the United States of America, traditional laws regulate land disputes among the Navajo Indians. Customs and traditions in part define a country's or a peoples' identity; as such most would be less inclined to efface their heritage even when some of their customs may seem repugnant and archaic. Customs are not read from any avenues of publication, people are simply born into them, they are unwritten rules (*lex non scripta*), they are conducts of behavior that people emulate, and seldom create ambiguity in interpretation. Preference for the pre-eminence of traditional laws is backed by the following advantages: expediency and satisfaction/effectiveness relating to dispute resolution.

Efficiency/Expediency: This relates to prompt disposition of cases. Since outcomes are informally arrived at in indigenous/customary law processes, they permit fast and economical processing. Customary laws and processes limit discord in the sense that their goal is not to castigate the wrongdoer but to adjust the aggrieved person to a position closely matching what he/she was prior to victimization. Certainly, crimes destabilize society, but what customary practices try to do is to mediate between the parties and find some conciliatory end to the issue – an end that reflects foregone practices as well as present community interests. The criminal justice system's functions are not only to punish and curb crimes. Their functions include establishing peace in the relevant community. However, traditional settings seem to advance this more by having those entrusted with mediating community issues meet together with the victim and perpetrator. Since incarceration is not a focus of traditional justice, the expense and resource waste associated with formal justice are minimized in customary dispute settlements. Overall, traditional law and dispute resolution are effective in that dispute resolution in the traditional sense accomplishes several objectives such as healing, reconciliation, and punishment, as well as refocusing the perpetrator on community values and expectations. This group conferencing format reminds the parties of community ideology, values, and responsibilities. At the end, defaulters for the most part do feel shamed and remorseful. Even if they are not written, traditional laws endure because of their efficacy and expediency.

Western or formal law does interrupt this customary process by introducing its own processes, and legal principles that regulate activities that also fall in the domain of indigenous law, and those that are presumed not contemplated by customary law. In this regard, for instance, crimes that stem from modern transactions and technology, such as banking, money laundering, cyber crimes, antitrust crimes, and others, at first glance may appear to be crimes that are suited for formal legal regulation. However, upon deeper introspection, traditional law employs the same reasoning as formal law thus making it possible to apply the same reasoning to complex and novel crimes not hitherto contemplated. Assuming even that formal law is better suited for more complex and contemporary crimes, it is not without its own shortcomings – every system of law or justice has its inadequacies (Okafọ, 2009, particularly chapter 1). As Tie (2002, p. 886) notes, "formal law routinely maximizes conflict between disputing parties in order to create a 'resolution'. It does so by defining the disputing parties in the black-and-white terms of guilt and innocence, a strategy that has the immediate effect of escalating differences between those parties."

As an example, Tie makes the point that handling domestic disputes informally mitigates an otherwise acrimonious outcome that would obtain in a formal court. When the indigenous mores and processes are examined, some especially those relating to matrimonial issues still carry with them vestiges of primitive times. Women in transitional societies are still considered chattels; consequently, their chances of getting favorable outcomes in hearings presided by traditional leaders or in customary courts are minuscule. Take the example of *Njang v. Njang* (1991). In the case, the Limbe customary court in Cameroon refused to grant a divorce at the request of Mrs. Njang who had demonstrated unequivocally the constant abuse she endured from her husband. The court reasoned that the couple had been married for a long time and as such, the marriage could not be dissolved. In essence, even when folkways are obnoxious, repugnant, and capricious, customary courts are still inclined to maintain the status quo. In *Njang v. Njang*, however, the Appeals Court righted the error of the customary court by applying common law. A divorce was granted on the following grounds: (a) the marriage had broken down irretrievably; (b) there was "uncontradicted evidence of cruelty by the defendant against the plaintiff;" and (c) the husband had constructively deserted his wife (Ngassa and Time, 1999, p. 141; Time, 2000, p. 27). In an earlier case of *Bih Ngwa v. Munifor* (1987), pursuant to tradition, the Njinteh customary court in Cameroon awarded Mr. Munfor 153,000 CFA ($306) as total amount he had spent on his wife for both a dowry and for her personal upkeep for the four years he was married to her. The traditional court reasoned that since the woman had called off the marriage she had to refund money to the equivalent of what the husband alleged to have spent on her throughout the duration of their marriage. The North West Court of Appeal quashed the decision and reasoning of the customary court on the premise that "the appellant rendered to respondent various services to which the respondent cannot afford a satisfactory compensation" (Ngassa and Time, 1999, p. 40).

However, the following questions remain, and they should be addressed to clarify the role of customary law in a modern society. How about issues involving jural persons but not persons in fact, such as corporations, universities, churches? Are customary courts equipped to adjudicate issues that may arise from these establishments? What if the issue concerns interpretation of the country's Constitution? How can folkways be applied under such a circumstance? To this, Tie (2002) makes the point that Constitutions act as mucilage of diverse cultures, and through them a healthy "national identity" is manifested. Following Tie's reasoning, Constitutions provide a popular medium for creating harmonious ways by which discord among "ethnic, social, and religious groups can be resolved" (Tie, 2002, p. 887). Given the new age of wireless communications, internet communications, transnational banking operations, and what have you, crimes that emanate from these intricate transactions may not fall under the purview of traditional laws.

The thesis here is that deference should be made to formal law in situations where traditional laws are unclear, capricious, obnoxious, repugnant, or unable to resolve complex internal issues, and those that arise from the myriad of activities and transactions brought by globalization.

When More Than One System of Acquired Law Obtains in a Country, Which One Should Govern?

Most post colonies received just one system of law from the colonizer. Cameroon and Canada present peculiar histories. Cameroon, a former colony of both England and France has a pluralistic legal system, common and civil law, and its own indigenous laws. Canada on the other hand has a dual system of law, English common law, and French civil law that obtains in Quebec and three territories of the country. The example in Canada is not as complicated, because common law is practiced throughout but for the one province and three territories that defer to civil law. The situation in Cameroon is more complicated in that traditional laws also permeate dispute resolution. In a simplistic fashion, the law of the place where the crime was committed (*lex loci delicti*) should govern, but things may be more intricate particularly when the disputants take their disputes to a traditional court.

Most countries in Africa, and that's the case in Cameroon, comprise several tribes, sometimes dozens of them, or hundreds even, and customs and dialects differ from one tribe to the other. Further complication may arise when the litigants are from different tribes and reside in a tribe other than that from which either of the litigants hails. To simplify this dilemma, the law of the place where the traditional court is (*lex fori*) prevails, but assessors from the tribes of the litigants have to be brought to court at the expense of the litigants. The role of the assessors is to interpret the customs of the litigants. Failure of assessors to appear in court nullifies any judgment in the traditional court. What the parties intended at the inception of their relationship may not be reflected in the verdict since the *lex fori* is likely to be employed. Harmonizing tradition is almost impossible, because of how different they are from tribe to tribe. Further, with in-migration, traditions get mixed-up, and it violates precepts of fairness to punish one for not comporting oneself to a tradition that is not one's and that may not be immediately understood. Not knowing the law or custom is hardly a defense, but this may become trite in the case of customs since customs are not scripted, and just being a sojourner in a place may not suffice to familiarize oneself with a custom. Further, since dialects abound just as there are tribes, and in rural areas most do not speak the official languages, suggesting that people should know the dialects of the several tribes is a little unrealistic.

Where there are two systems of formal law, such as in Cameroon where there are common law and civil law, harmonizing both may be successful in some circumstances and in others, suppressing or marginalizing one is really what obtains. Additionally, the system that is marginalized is usually the one that obtains among the minority segment of the society (see Time, 2000). In some odd sense, harmonization of laws within pluralistic systems of law does not come about through internal endeavors, rather it comes about following the adoption of international charters. Take for instance, the *African Charter on Human and Peoples' Rights*, which was adopted in Nairobi, Kenya on June 27, 1981 by forty-nine African countries, Cameroon included. On the one hand, the African Charter introduced a series of due process rights that were to be uniformly applied to litigants in the territories of the signatories of the Charter regardless of system of law. On the other hand, a 1996 treaty that harmonizes civil and commercial laws in sixteen francophone countries to which Cameroon is again a signatory completely ignores any common law considerations.

Conclusion

In order to arrive at a proper harmonization of laws, legal analysts have to sort out the reasons why a particular system of laws dominates, the scope of its dominance, and the extent to which people refrain from challenging the law. Similar issues need to be addressed in explaining why a system of law is marginalized, along with the extent to which its diminished authority is acceptable. Ultimately, laws that are identified as most reflective of the interests and rights of the people should be selected and then harmonized. However, harmonization is complicated, and it takes time to accomplish. That the process of harmonization is easy, is a fallacy especially when there are pluralistic laws and diverse tribal groups in a country, even if the country's constitution is relied upon to create harmony (Tie, 2002).

References

African Charter on Human and Peoples' Rights, 1981.

Austin, T. (1996) "Banana Justice in Moroland: Peacemaking in Mixed Muslim-Christian Towns in the Southern Philippines" in C. Field and C. Moore, *Comparative Criminal Justice: Traditional and Nontraditional Systems of Law and Control*. Prospect Heights, Illinois, USA: Waveland Press, pp. 270-92.

Brillion, Y. (1983) "Judicial Acculturation in Black Africa and its Effects on the Administration of Justice," *International Summaries*, No. NCJ 78583. Washington, D.C., USA.

Collier, J. F. (1973) *Law and Social Change in Zinacantan*. Palo Alto, California, USA:

Stanford University Press.

Lombardo, L. (1986) "Nation Building and Social Control: Observations from Ivory Coast and Tanzania," *International Journal of Comparative and Applied Criminal Justice*, Vol. 10, No.1, pp. 41-55.

Merry, S. (1988) "Legal Pluralism," *Law and Society Review*, Vol. 22, pp. 869-96.

Ngassa, V. and V. Time (1999) *Gender Law Report*. Vol. 1. Cameroon: Friedrich Ebert Stiftung.

Okafọ, N. (2009) *Reconstucting Law and Justice in a Postcolony*. Surrey, England and Burlington, USA: Ashgate Publishing.

Thompson, R. (1996) "Due Process and Legal Pluralism in Sierra Leone: The Challenge of Reconciling Contradictions in Laws and Cultures of a Developing Nation," in Fields, C. and Moore, R., *Comparative Criminal Justice: Traditional and Nontraditional Systems of Law and Control*, pp. 344-61, Prospect Heights, Illinois, USA: Waveland Press.

Tie, W. (2002) "Legal Pluralism," in Kritzer, *Legal Systems of the World: A Political, Social, and Cultural Encyclopedia*. Vol. 2, pp. 885-88, Santa Barbara, California: ABC-CLIO.

Time, V. (2000) "Legal Pluralism and Harmonization of Law: An Examination of the Process of Reception and Adoption of Both Civil Law and Common Law in Cameroon and their Coexistence with Indigenous Laws," *International Journal of Comparative and Applied Criminal Justice*, Vol. 24, No.1 & 2, pp.19-29.

Chapter 5

Beccaria in Mind: Nigeria and the Challenges of Criminal Justice Administration in the 21st Century

Simon Ortuanya
University of Nigeria

Introduction

> It is our considered opinion that the administration of justice in Nigeria lacks vision and leadership. It is indeed strange that there is not one document in which the policy trust on Justice sector reform of the Jonathan administration is to be found either at the relevant ministerial level or within the Presidency.[1]

Kayode Fayemi contested the governorship election in Ekiti State, South West Nigeria, on the 14th of April, 2009 on the platform of the Action Congress of Nigeria (ACN). He lost, according to the Independent National Electoral Commission (INEC) (the body charged with the responsibility of conducting elections in the country). Segun Oni, another contestant and candidate of the Peoples Democratic Party (PDP), was declared the winner of the governorship election. Fayemi challenged the result of the election, from the Electoral Tribunal up to the Court of Appeal. He was declared the winner by the Court of Appeal and sworn into office on the 16th of October, 2010, some three years and six months after the election took place and just five months to the end of the tenure of the unlawful Oni governorship.[2]

In Anambra State, South-East Nigeria, a similar scenario had played itself out. Chris Ngige of the PDP was declared Governor of Anambra State after the 2003 elections and was sworn into office. Peter Obi of the All Progressive Grand Alliance (APGA) went to court to challenge the election. The case lasted for three years before Obi was declared the winner. Obi was in office for barely one year when the 2007 election was conducted and Andy Uba of the PDP was declared the winner and sworn in as Governor. Again, Obi went to the Supreme Court for a judicial interpretation of when his term of office expired. The Supreme Court, in a landmark judgment, held that Obi's tenure started to run from the day he took oath of office.

At the time of writing this paper, the Sokoto State governorship election petition stemming from the 2007 general elections is yet to be concluded, just five months to a fresh round of elections in the country. Indeed, the Supreme Court in the Sokoto State governorship case was said to have arrested the judgment as the Court effectively prevented the Court of Appeal from delivering its judgment on the governorship election petition. Similar battles were fought in Edo State,[3]

---

[1] J. B. Dauda, SAN, President, Nigerian Bar Association, presenting the position of the Bar at a media briefing on the state of the administration of justice in Nigeria, on September 29, 2010.

[2] Toba Suleiman and Olawole Olaleye. "Fayemi: The Siege is Over". *Thisday* Vol. 15 No. 5656, Sunday, October 17, 2010, p. 1. See also: Simon Kolawole "Blessed are the Longsuffering" *Ibid*, p. 104; Louis Odion "Ekiti: Truth Always Finds a Way". *The Nation* Vol. 5 No. 1553, October 19, 2010, p. 11; Olatunji Dare "The Ekiti Restoration" *Ibid*, p. 64.

[3] In Edo State for instance, just in August 2010, the Court of Appeal nullified the election of the

Ondo State,[4] and Rivers State.[5]

Perhaps, Cesare Beccaria had Nigeria in mind in the 18th Century. Beccaria, an Italian, was trained as a Mathematician but was attracted to politics and economics. In his classic work, *On Crimes and Punishments* (1764), he highlighted the arbitrary and barbaric penal system of 18th century Europe. According to him, the criminal justice system was ill-defined as crime itself was vague and nonspecific and covered all manner of misbehavior. There was hardly any due process of law. Beccaria noted the injustices inherent in the administration of criminal justice. Typical of such inequity was the unusual privilege, which the nobility and the clergy enjoyed under the legal system. To him, the law was made by the powerful to protect their interest. And due to the chains that shackled criminal justice, he advocated for penal reforms in the administration of criminal justice. It is, therefore, from the window of Cesare Beccaria that we intend to look at the challenges of criminal justice administration in Nigeria in the 21st Century.

Conceptual Issues

The term "criminal justice system" encapsulates the following three important institutions and their activities: the police, the courts, and the prisons. The activities of these three range from prevention of crime to punishment of criminals. The concept of justice has been given a prime place because we believe that the sole aim of recourse to the courts is to get justice. And, considering the aphorism, "justice delayed is justice denied", in a situation where justice is deferred because of administrative and bureaucratic inadequacies, can we say that there is justice?

"Justice" is a universally held notion even though, as should be expected, the language medium used to express it differs from one society to another. In essence, everyone – old, middle age, or young – talks about justice. In every legal system, justice is a concept that is given a serious consideration. Thus, we make sentences such as 'it is just', 'it is right', 'it is not fair', and so on. These statements suggest that there is a particular standard expected in the treatment of people.

---

incumbent Governor, Emmanuel Uduaghan of the PDP upon a petition brought by Great Ogboru of the Democratic People's Party (DPP). The Court of Appeal ordered a rerun within ninety days, which was recently concluded. Expectedly, Uduaghan of the PDP won the rerun just three months to another round of general elections.

[4] In Ondo State, it took more than three years of litigation before the present Governor was declared winner of the election.

[5] In the case of Rivers State, Rotimi Amaechi fought up to the Supreme Court before he was declared the rightful candidate to fly the governorship flag of his party, the PDP. This was, indeed, after another candidate, Celestine Omehia, had contested the election under the same party and was returned as the winner of the election. Omehia was sworn in and was already in office as Governor for some months before the Supreme Court came down with the decision that he (Omehia) was not even the rightful candidate to stand for the election.

It is the notion of justice that directs our attention to the reasonableness of the rules, principles, and standards that are the components of the legal structure.

The *Longman Dictionary of Contemporary English*[6] defines justice as "fairness in the way people are treated". The same dictionary sees justice as "the system by which people are judged in courts of law and criminals are punished".[7] The first definition anticipates just distribution in dealing with people. The second meaning sees justice as a system adopted in courts by which people are judged. But we are still faced with the question, what is "fairness"? What is the yardstick for measuring what is fair? Does it automatically mean that justice has been done when an action is fair? The word "system" in the second definition does not seem to answer the question either. In that sense, justice may mean the judicial administration of law or equity; exercise of authority or power in maintenance of right, vindication of right by assignment of reward or punishment.

The word "justice", according to Rawls, a contemporary jurist, "is the first virtue of social institutions as truth is of systems of thought".[8] He aptly noted that in "...justice as fairness, the original position of equality corresponds to the state of nature in the traditional theory of social contract".[9] In social contract theory, justice as fairness simply means the observance of rights, duties, and obligations on the part of both the governor and the governed. In other words, the nature of the contract imposes rights, duties and obligations on the inhabitants of the society. A balance must be struck between guaranteeing the fundamental rights of citizens by the governor and the observance of duties and obligations by the governed. In criminal justice, therefore, the sum total of justice is equal to the fair application of rules, with the effect that "... laws should be fair and reasonable in themselves".[10]

Writing about justice with respect to criminal law, Denham opined:

> Justice is concerned with content. Laws should be fair and reasonable in themselves. It is not just a matter of applying the rules reasonably, whatever those rules might be, it is also about making society a fairer and more reasonable place in which to live. Such justice may be called distributive justice since it is about the distribution of obligations and opportunities in society.[11]

---

[6] *Longman Dictionary of Contemporary English* (Edinburgh: Pearson Education, 2001).

[7] *Ibid.*

[8] John Rawls, *A Theory of Justice* (Cambridge, Massachusetts, USA: The Belknap Press, 1971) p. 3.

[9] *Ibid*, p. 12.

[10] Abduh – Rahman Bello Dambazau, *Law and Criminality in Nigeria* (Ibadan, Nigeria: University Press, 1994) p. 12.

[11] P. Denham, *A Modern Introduction to Law* (London, England: Edward Arnold, 1983) p. 476.

The essence of a criminal justice system should be that justice is done in cases involving allegations of crimes, having the peculiar conditions of each society in mind. Thus, it is our opinion that for "justice" to be done, the peculiarities of a given State cannot be divorced completely.

Nature of the Criminal Justice System

According to Dambazau, Criminal Justice can be defined either as a legal process or as an academic discipline".[12] As a legal process, criminal justice involves the procedure of processing the person accused of committing crime from arrest to the final disposal of the case. As an academic discipline, its studies provide a thorough understanding of the criminal justice system in relation to the society.[13] And, in the words of Clare and Kramer:

> It is possible to view criminal justice as a sequence of decision-making stages. Through this system offenders are either passed on to the next stage or directed out of the system. This diversion may be due to any number of reasons such as lack of evidence or a desire to reduce the load on the system. Each subsequent stage of the process is dependent upon the previous stage for its elements; it is this dependence that best exemplifies the 'system' nature of criminal justice.[14]

The above is a clear description of the nature of the criminal justice system. Therefore, the criminal justice system is an entity with interrelationships of criminal justice elements comprising the *police*, *courts*, and *prisons*. These three elements work hand in hand but the system is enveloped by society. It is a limited system to the extent that the different agencies are linked "... through a process in which one agency's 'outputs' becomes the next agency's input".[15] Let us illustrate how the output of one agency becomes the input of another agency in the system. The output of the police for example is the arrest of offenders, which in turn, and based on the outcome of police investigation, becomes the input into the courts. Having been developed as the output of the prosecution and defense, the decided cases invariably become the output of the courts after conviction and sentencing.

---

[12] Abduh – Rahman Bello Dambazau, *Criminology and Criminal Justice* (Ibadan, Nigeria: Spectrum Books, 2nd ed., 2007) p. 174.

[13] *Ibid.*

[14] Pau K. Clare and John H. Kramer, *Introduction to American Corrections* (Boston, Massachusetts, USA: Holbrook Press) pp. 3-4.

[15] M. H. Moore, "The Legitimation of Criminal Justice Policies and Practices", in James Q. Wilson, et al., (eds), *Perspectives on Crime and Justice*, National Institute of Justice, Research Report, 1996-97 Lecture Series, vol. 1, Nov. 1997.

Thereafter, the conviction and sentencing become input for the prisons, and so on. We can then observe that at the beginning and the end of the system are the police and prison institutions or correctional facilities respectively.

Contemporary criminal law is of the view that everybody outside the system is presumed innocent. It is also noteworthy that an accused citizen who has entered the system is also presumed innocent until he is convicted by the court.[16] The aim of the system has been aptly summarized thus: it is to sustain the Rule of Law by preventing crime wherever possible, by detecting the culprit, when crimes are committed, by convicting the guilty and acquitting the innocent, and by giving proper effect to the sentence and orders, which are imposed. It must be pointed out that Nigerian criminal justice system is one exceedingly complex process that involves a large number of formal and informal agencies, but we are more concerned with the formal agencies that include, the police, the courts, and the prisons.

The police receive complaints about commission of offenses. They also detect offenses on their own. If the detection is successful, the suspect is arrested and then further investigation is made. The outcome determines whether the process will be continued or not. The criminal justice system will not move on to the next stage unless a *prima facie* case is established against the suspect. Where there is no evidence to rebut the suspect's innocence, the police set him free back into the society. However, it is a different ball game when the investigation proves otherwise. If this happens, he is charged to court and the bell for the next stage is chimed. The first stage is important because the decision of the policeman on the street is as important as the existence of the criminal justice system.

At the second stage, the police exercise their power of prosecution. They assist the court in making sure that evidence needed for justice is made available. This power of prosecution is exercised at both the Magistrate and High Courts. Conventionally, the police power of prosecution is confined to Magistrate Courts. The court is an impartial arbiter as the police prosecute cases and accused persons defend themselves. If the prosecution is successful, the guilt of the accused will be established. The court will then pass a proper sentence on him. According to Pound, the administration of justice revolves around the court system. A person who violates the criminal law is brought before the court and tried, and it is followed through with the disposition or judgment made by the court.[17] Before the conviction and sentencing of the accused person, he must have been given fair hearing by the court.[18]

---

[16] Section 36 (5) of the *Constitution of the Federal Republic of Nigeria*, 1999 as amended.

[17] Roscoe Pound, *Justice According to Law* (New Haven, Connecticut, USA: Yale University Press, 1952) pp. 89-91.

[18] Section 36, the *Constitution of the Federal Republic of Nigeria*, 1999 as amended; *Isiyaku Mohammed v. Kano N. A.* (1968) 1 All NLR 428; *Ajuwon v. Akanni* (1993) 9 NWLR (pt. 316) 182 S.C.

It is not in all cases that the court sentences a guilty person. In those exceptional circumstances, the convict is typically cautioned and discharged. Consequently, the convict moves straight from the court into the society. However, once he is sentenced he moves to the next stage: he is imprisoned or committed to a reformation (correctional center). The accused, depending on the discretion of the judge, can also be fined or committed to community service. In doing this, the severity of the case is taken into consideration. Capital punishment can also be imposed on him depending on the nature of the crime.

For an incarcerated convict, while in prison he undergoes another process for a specific period (he may also be serving for life). A school of thought[19] believes that the period of imprisonment is a time of reformation before the prisoner returns to society. However, if the prisoner was sentenced to death, reforming him for re-entry into society becomes perhaps a non-issue since, eventually, he will be executed. It is worthy of note that not all trials end in convictions. In this regard, the accused may be discharged on the merits of the case or acquitted in which case he is immediately pushed back into society. Furthermore, a *nolle prosequi* to stay proceedings may be entered by leave of the relevant Attorney-General at any time before judgment.[20]

As demonstrated in the foregoing, it is crucial that these three institutions – the police, the courts, and the prisons – have a cordial relationship for an effective dispensation of criminal justice.

Historical Perspectives

Colonial Britain had introduced in Nigeria the criminal justice described in the previous section. Decades after political independence, Nigeria retains some vestiges of colonial Britain. In some respects, the colonial evidence is particularly prominent. The Nigerian criminal justice system offers many such examples. Before their advent, Nigerians existed in various communities. Every community had rules regulating conduct in certain spheres and imposing sanctions for breach. In southern Nigeria, there were many rules prescribing sanctions for deviant conduct based on the family unit, extended family, village or groups of villages. In the northern part of the country, Islamic law dominated, although some communities retained their own criminal laws. There was a highly advanced Islamic law of crimes and there existed schools of jurists, notable among which was the Maliki School. Apart from Islamic law (which is also customary law), the chief characteristic of all

---

[19] The Classical School of Criminology – see Cesare Bonesana Beccaria (1738-1794) and Jeremy Bentham (1748-1832); see also Beccaria, *On Crimes and Punishment*, Henry Paulucci (Trans.), (New York, NY, USA: Bobbs-Merrill), p. 99.

[20] Section 174 of the Nigerian Constitution 1999 as amended.

customary criminal laws was that they were unwritten.[21]

One outstanding feature of English criminal justice is the accusatorial (or adversarial) procedure adopted in the prosecution of indicted persons within the system. "The adversarial method is one which gives the parties and their lawyers a great deal of control over the way in which facts are collected and presented".[22] The accusatorial system of criminal justice presumes that the accused is innocent until proven otherwise by his accuser. Thus, the best method to unravel the truth about the case in hand is to have a "contest" between the two parties involved – the State that champions the victim's case through the police and the prosecutor, and the accused who champions his own case or through someone else, such as a lawyer. The inquisitorial system can be contrasted with the accusatorial system, as follows. Unlike the accusatorial model, the inquisitorial system presumes that the accused is guilty until he (the accused) proves otherwise. This is the major difference between accusatorial and inquisitorial systems of criminal justice.

The presumption of innocence or guilt, as the case may be, affects the burden of proof in criminal cases. The general principle of the law of evidence states that he who asserts the affirmative must prove his assertion.[23] In an accusatorial system this burden, which is quite onerous, lies on the person (the prosecution) who complains against the accused. By discharging this burden, the prosecution will simultaneously be rebutting the presumption of innocence. In *Woolmington v. Director of Public Prosecution,*[24] this common law approach was given a judicial recognition. The kernel of that case is that the prosecution must prove every charge beyond every reasonable doubt.[25] In the inquisitorial system, because the accused is presumed guilty, he is required to not only rebut the assertion of his accuser but also, at the same time, prove that he did not commit the offence. In other words, he has the burden of proving his assertion that he is innocent. This system is prone to abuse due to the heaviness of the burden especially in less developed legal systems. This explains why the inquisitorial approach to criminal justice involved such methods of ascertaining innocence or guilt as trial by ordeal. This allowed the accused to be subjected to mental and/or physical torture. Sadly, torture as a means of extracting evidence from the accused is also part of the accusatorial system of criminal justice.

A bold step was taken in the Nigerian criminal justice system when in 1904

---

[21] C. O. Okonkwo (ed), *Introduction to Nigerian Law* (London, England: Sweet and Maxwell, 1980) pp. 41-42.

[22] John H. Farrah, et al., *Introduction to Legal Method* (London: Sweet and Maxwell, 1990, 3rd edn.) pp. 62-63.

[23] S. 135, *Evidence Act, Laws of the Federation,* 2004; *Murana Elemo & Ors v. Fasasi Omolade & Ors,* 1968 NMLR 359 at 361.

[24] (1935) AC 4621.

[25] The Nigerian case of *R. v. Basil Ranger Lawrence* (1932) II NLR 6 at 7 had earlier established the principle in *Woolmington.*

the Lugard administration introduced a *Criminal Code* into Northern Nigeria by proclamation. Following the unification of Nigeria in 1914, the code was extended to the whole country in 1916. The *Nigerian Criminal Code* was modelled after the *Queensland Criminal Code*, which was introduced into the state of Queensland, Australia in 1899.[26] It is important to state that due to the dynamism and peculiarity of Muslim Communities, the *Criminal Code* was replaced with the *Penal Code* in 1959. Professor Okonkwo captures the circumstances thus:

> The code which eventually emerged, the 1959 Penal Code law, to displace the Criminal Code was based on a code which had been working successfully in a Moslem Community, namely the code of the Sudan. It therefore has a strong link with English Law because the Sudanese Code was modeled on 1860 Indian Penal Code, which in turn owed much to a draft prepared almost entirely by Lord Macaulay. But of all the codes derived from English Law, the Indian Code exhibits considerable deviations from the common law. And the Northern Nigeria Penal Code goes further still. It represents, in fact, a compromise between the reformers and the traditionalists.[27]

Therefore, the Nigerian criminal law is dual in nature. In addition, criminal procedure in the country is not just governed by the Criminal Code; there is also the *Criminal Procedure Act*.[28] The Act was enacted in 1945 and was of general application throughout Nigeria. At the attainment of independence on 1 October, 1960, the Act ceased to be applicable to the whole of Nigeria, and its application was confined to the southern regions of the country. A *Criminal Procedure Code*[29] was enacted and it became the applicable law for the northern regions of the country.[30]

Apart from the Criminal Code and Penal Code, there are other statutes or enactments stipulating offenses in Nigeria.[31] The two Codes are just the principal enactments. The two Criminal Procedure Acts, i.e. for the southern states and the northern states, are also the principal enactments regulating criminal procedure

---

[26] C. O. Okonkwo and M. E. Naish, *Criminal Law in Nigeria* (Ibadan, Nigeria: Spectrum Books, 2nd edn, 1980) p. 5.

[27] *Ibid*, pp. 9-10.

[28] The *Criminal Procedure Act* is now CAP C41, *Laws of the Federation*, 2004.

[29] We now have *Criminal Procedure (Northern States) Act* as C42 in the *Laws of the Federation*, 2004.

[30] See Oluwatoyin Doherty, *Criminal Procedure in Nigeria: Law and Practice* (Gosport, Hants: Ashford Colour Press, 1999), pp. 19-20.

[31] For examples, the *Economic and Financial Crimes Commission Act*, Cap EI LFN, 2004; the *Corrupt Practices and Other Related Offences Act*, Cap 31 LFN 2004.

in Nigeria. There are other enactments on criminal procedure in the country. The *Constitution of the Federal Republic of Nigeria* is one of them. The Constitution, for instance in its Fundamental Human Rights provisions, stipulates many rights relating to criminal law and procedure. The relevant Constitutional provisions include the right to fair hearing, which is a *sine qua non* in any criminal trial.[32]

Except for tribunals, all courts in Nigeria try criminal and civil cases. This is unlike the situation in England where the courts are separated according to whether they try criminal or civil cases. In the southern part of Nigeria, there are Customary Courts charged with hearing and deciding criminal matters. The rules governing the procedure of Customary Courts in criminal matters are contained in the *Customary Courts Rules 1973*. There are also the Magistrate Courts. And Northern Nigeria historically has Upper Area Courts and Area Courts of different grades charged with trying criminal matters. Throughout the country, a High Court for each state, the Federal High Court, the Court of Appeal, and the Supreme Court have been established with various rules regulating criminal matters. The courts were established at different times in our history,[33] thus laying a foundation for our criminal justice system.

The origin of the Nigeria Police Force dates back to 1943 when the *Police Ordinance*[34] was promulgated and came into force on April 1 of that year. It was an ordinance to make provision for the organization, discipline, powers, and duties of the police. The *Police Act 1967*,[35] as subsequently amended, lays down the powers and duties of the Nigeria Police Force.

Regarding prisons, the British colonial regime in Nigeria, in order to handle the "outputs" of the courts as components of the criminal justice network, established prisons in principal towns of the country. More prisons have also been established in some other towns and cities since independence. The Nigerian *Prisons Act*[36] was enacted on 10 April, 1972 to make provisions for the administration of prisons and other matters ancillary thereto. Relatedly, the *Criminal Justice (Miscellaneous Provisions) Act* and the *Criminal Justice (Released from Custody) (Special Provisions) Act* were enacted in 1975 and 1977 respectively to support the criminal justice system.

---

[32] Part IV of the *Constitution of the Federal Republic of Nigeria 1999* deals with Fundamental Human Rights, and Section 36 of the Part guarantees fair hearing.

[33] The Court of Appeal was established as the Federal Court of Appeal on October 1, 1976; the Federal High Court was established as the Federal Revenue Court in 1973; the Supreme Court of Nigeria was established in 1963.

[34] The 1999 Constitution created the Nigeria Police Force under Section 214.

[35] The *Police Act* is now Cap P19, LFN 2004.

[36] Now Cap P 29, LFN, 2004.

Challenges Confronting Nigerian Criminal Justice

The challenges facing criminal justice administration in Nigeria are monumental. The number one challenge, it seems, is the complexity of the court procedures. There is the need to simplify the Nigerian court proceedings and even the law itself. It is essential to review the complexities in the law and rules governing the courts, as well as reform obscure or uncertain substantive laws. No less important is the need to explore the usage of alternative dispute resolution mechanisms, including in election matters. In addition, it is necessary to revisit the Nigerian adversarial environment where the questions of expense, delay, compromise, and fairness have low priority. Perhaps, more inquisitorial elements need to be introduced into the Nigerian criminal justice environment to redress the failure to progress cases sufficiently by the respective role-players.

The inadequacies of the Nigerian justice system are best appreciated when one recognizes the serious unjust conditions suffered by the clients of the system, especially its criminal justice component. For example, when one ponders how Kayode Fayemi could pursue justice for years regarding the 2007 Ekiti state governorship election, the picture becomes more sober. On a wider scale, the fact that there are numerous persons in Nigeria's prisons who have been awaiting trial – many for over 10 years – throws more light on the problems in the country's justice system. Indeed, at a recent meeting of prison workers, the Nigerian Prisons Service informed an alarmed audience that 50 percent of the awaiting trial population in Nigeria's prisons has been on remand for between 5 and 17 years without their cases being concluded.[37] Thus, there is an unacceptable number of awaiting trial inmates who have spent an unreasonable length of time in prison for mundane reasons. The reasons include missing case files and absence of prosecution witness or investigating officer. This unjust situation demands an urgent corrective measure.

For the awaiting trial population in Nigeria's prisons as well as other concerns, there are several options for rectifying the criminal justice challenges already identified in this chapter and the others listed and explained below. At this juncture, it seems necessary to describe the nature of a measure to address a challenge facing the system. First, there is a need for a service delivery agenda for the justice sector. Reform in the justice sector cannot exclusively be limited to interventions by government structures and institutions. It is important that civil society actively participates in the reform process. In order to enable civil society participation, there is the need for a clear policy statement of intent, which will form the basis of collaboration between the government and the citizens.

---

[37] Olawale Fapohunda, "Fayemi's Victory, Justice Administration's Low Point" *Thisday* Vol. 15 No. 5658, October 19, 2009, p. XI.

Second, the aforementioned policy should include a number of recurring justice sector concerns. A radical paradigm shift is imperative to transform the "Nigeria Police Force" into the "Nigeria Police Service." The ultimate objective of police reform in Nigeria must be a shift to a democratic structure where the police work primarily for public interest. Achieving police reform in Nigeria will require a wide range of reforms including replacing the outdated *Police Act* with a new legislation that reflects Nigeria's constitutional imperatives and entails a holistic review and redefinition of the role and function of the police as well as organizational restructuring aimed at making the police less militaristic.

The bold decision of the appeal court in the *Fayemi* case has once again placed the judiciary in the forefront of positive national discuss. It should be realized that in general the judicial system in Nigeria today is largely characterized by incessant delays and a backlog of cases in almost all the courts. This problem is compounded by insufficient remuneration of judicial officers and court personnel as well as limited facilities. The reality of the majority of state High Courts is that state governments habitually refuse to release funds required to finance capital expenditure. These factors, combined with a cumbersome, opaque, and outdated system of written trial procedures, have created a general atmosphere of limited confidence in the judicial process. A reform policy must include amendments of Section 81 (2) as well as Section 84 (4) (7) the Constitution of Nigeria. This should allow the recurrent and capital expenditures of both the federal and state judiciaries, in addition to the salaries and allowances of all judges of the lower courts and personnel staff thereof, to be charged to the Federation account.

Establishing an appropriate legal framework is important in achieving sustainable reforms in the justice sector. Law reform is essential to any justice sector policy. It is regrettable that not one justice sector bill has been passed in the National Assembly since 1999 (the year Nigeria returned to civilian, rather than military, government). A cursory look at the more than twelve administrations of justice bills presently awaiting passage by the National Assembly will indicate the unsatisfactory nature of this state of affairs. This is especially so when one imagines the impact that the Police Act Amendment Bill and the Evidence Act Amendment Bill are likely to have on the country's electoral justice system.

Increased and varied criminality, weak justice institutions, poor policing, and lack of confidence in the electoral justice system are all indicators of a failing justice system. A failed or failing justice system works against the consolidation of the democratic process in Nigeria and threatens the country's nascent democratic experiment. However, the development of a new justice system in the country – a system that is in line with the Nigerian Constitution and democratic values – will be a process not an event. Ordinarily, such a process will unfold gradually. But it is important for policymakers and justice sector actors to recognize that in the Nigerian situation change must be accelerated to keep up with the people's expectations.

The above is a bird's-eye view of the 21st century challenges of criminal justice administration in Nigeria. However, for the purposes of clarity, we shall itemize and further explain some of the societal and institutional difficulties as follows.

Under-funding and Inadequate Facilities

A visit to many of the courtrooms in Nigeria – courts of various categories and jurisdictional levels – will reveal the infrastructural dilapidation in the justice system. Modern facilities are lacking in the courts due mainly to lack of adequate funds to procure and maintain their needs. Stationeries, where available, are rationed; record books are no more available; courtrooms are inadequate. The basic needs to make the system function are either not available or grossly insufficient. Essential materials, including computers and copiers, that a 21st Century court needs to do thorough and quick work, are lacking. Judicial proceedings in the various courts (Magistrate and High Courts inclusive) are taken in long hand in very hot and humid atmosphere, typically without reliable electricity to power air conditioning. There are no conducive storage facilities to keep court records and exhibits. In some states, for example, magistrates sit in shifts due to insufficient courtrooms. No one seems to care that most of the criminal cases that found their ways into the court process end at the magistrate court level due, in part, to the extreme conditions to which the parties, particularly the accused, are subjected. It is not the duty of the courts to fund and provide facilities for their operation. The government (Executive and Legislature) should ensure that this important responsibility is discharged.

Poor Remuneration and Lack of Motivation

One can only expect and receive the best service from another who is satisfied, contented, and happy about his or her life situation. This should apply to all human beings irrespective of their profession, trade, or other responsibility. Thus, it ought not to surprise anyone that the living and working conditions of Nigerian judicial officers affect their motivation and productivity. By extension, the quality of justice derived from many of these officers is compromised. A person that is well paid, has good living quarters, adequate means of transportation, and maximum security is likely to give his best in the discharge of his duties. Unfortunately, many Nigerian magistrates in particular lack adequate conditions of service and motivation for the onerous responsibility they carry in the dispensation of criminal justice. According to a Senior Advocate of Nigeria, Yusuf O. Ali,

... the welfare of our magistrates leaves much to be attended to. Official quarters are becoming a rarity, official vehicles were things of the past, minimum security have been forgotten, the pay is left to the whims and caprice of the respective state governments. This has resulted in some Chief Magistrates in some states earning what magistrate grade II earns in some states.[38]

The prevailing inadequacies in the living and service conditions of many judicial officers notwithstanding, it must be conceded that there has been a marked improvement on the conditions of judges and justices of the superior courts, at least since 2000. However, the converse appears to be the case for magistrates. This is dangerous for our justice system. With particular regard to the criminal justice component, more than 80% of criminal cases that get to the court, end up before the magistrate courts.[39] Therefore, it is imperative that the magistrates who are burdened with the duty of hearing and deciding the majority of the criminal cases in the Nigerian courts are appropriately remunerated.

The Role of Lawyers and Judges

Another challenge facing Nigerian courts on a daily basis and delaying the criminal justice process is the activities of some lawyers and judges. The ethics of the legal profession enjoins lawyers to assist the court in the attainment of efficient and quick justice. In many instances, the rule is observed in the breach. The hard economic situation in the country has added to the malaise. Many unwholesome practices go on among lawyers before the courts. Touting and outright chicanery are common features of the practice of many lawyers before the courts. Many lawyers, who perceive that they have a bad case, rather than advise their clients properly, resort to unfair tactics including asking for unnecessary adjournments or continuances.

Thus, cases are too readily adjourned in Nigerian courts. Many adjournments are unjustified. Even where a lawyer requests adjournment, it is at the discretion of the court to adjourn a matter, and this discretionary power is invoked everyday in judicial proceedings.[40] In other words, the power of adjournments can be controlled by the courts especially when the requested continuances are frivolous and unreasonable. However, we have seen situations where judges were too quick to grant adjournments even when the relevant applications should have been rejected to expedite the judicial process. The

---

[38] Yusuf O. Ali, "Delay in the Administration of Justice of the Magistrate Court – Factors Responsible and Solution," *Nigerian Bar Journal*, Vol. 4, No. 2, April 2006, p. 36.

[39] *Ibid*, p. 20.

[40] See *Obomhense v. Erhahon* (1993) 7 NWLR (pt. 303) 22 SC; *E. D. Tsokwa & Sons Co. Ltd. v. C.F.A.O.* (1993) 5 NWLR (pt. 291) 120 CA.

interest of justice should have been paramount. Moreover, apart from legal counsel, judges themselves seek and take adjournments, in many cases because they are not ready themselves.

Whether a lawyer or judge is responsible for a frivolous continuance in a particular case, this leads to needless and unjust delays for the specific case as well as other cases that should have been given more attention. In the circumstances and consistent with the aphorism "Justice delayed is justice denied", criminal justice clients and other stakeholders do not receive the efficient and quick justice that they should have.

Archaic Laws and Rules

On many occasions, Nigerian justice administrators – magistrates, judges, and justices – are brought face to face with archaic laws and rules. The encounter is particularly challenging because the justice administrators are expected to interpret the provisions of the laws brought before them for examination. However, these administrators do not have the constitutional right to enact or amend laws. So, even though the judge feels that a law, a provision, or a rule should be changed or reviewed, he cannot do much. This is the situation even where a law or rule is obsolete and stands in the way of expeditious determination of cases. For example, the problem of *holding charges* still features in the criminal justice system. Also, the use of *first information reports* in the northern states of the country engenders some delays in criminal trials. Thus, some criminal justice rules should be abolished, but the judiciary cannot do that.

Inappropriate Appointments

Another problem evident in the Nigerian criminal justice system, particularly the courts, is the inappropriate appointment of some magistrates and judges. In too many situations, appointments of the judicial officers have been politicized and sometimes nepotism, sectionalism, and other such sentiments play prominent roles in the appointment process. In other words, professionalism and competence are sacrificed on the altar of favoritism. This definitely affects the quality of justice emanating from the courts. The downturn in the country's economy has led to a situation where some lawyers are appointed as magistrates or judges not because they desire to make a career of it but out of exigency. Many such appointees have no viable means of livelihood and they see a position on the Bench as a way to make a living. It is also apparent that many people who find themselves in the courts as magistrates or judges lack many of the basic qualities of an adjudicator, such as deep knowledge of the law, patience, independence, and impartiality.

Harsh Criminal Justice System

The administration of criminal justice as presently constituted in Nigeria is harsh and tends to be prejudicial against the poor and helpless members of the society. Indeed, the helpless condition of poor accused persons from the time of arrest until the conclusion of trial is disturbing. Under the country's criminal procedure, an accused is subjected to an intolerable hostility of the police and the court. The dehumanizing physical hardships he undergoes in the overcrowded jails as well as the overall unfriendly procedure does not speak well of the criminal justice system. This has contributed in no small measure to the prevalent negative image of the system and those who participate in it.[41]

Bribery and Corruption

The problem of corruption in Nigeria is cancerous and is an ill wind that blows nobody any good. Corruption has hit virtually all aspects of the Nigerian national life and unfortunately, the judiciary, which should be the custodian of justice, is not left out. A corrupt person is blind to the truth. His mind is diseased and he is incapable of doing justice in a case before him. Bribery and corruption are offenses against the Nigerian State. Both the *Criminal Code* (southern states) and the *Penal Code* (northern states) make bribery and corruption criminal offenses. Yet, there are many cases of bribery and corruption of key Nigerian officials at the various levels of government, including several serious allegations against judicial officers. For avoidance of doubt, a corrupt judge is a serious threat to his society.

Sometime ago, justices of Nigeria's apex court, Supreme Court of Nigeria, were accused of receiving thirteen Honda cars from the Honda Place (an automobile dealership company in Nigeria) with a view to tilting the scale of justice in the company's favor. Also, recent election petition decisions in Nigeria have raised the issue of justice in the country being purchasable by the highest bidder. Some of the bribery and corruption allegations are such that, due to their sources and the alleged offenders, no reasonable citizen can dismiss the allegations with a hand wave. For example, in early 2011, the President of the Court of Appeal, Ayo Salami, in a suit he filed against the Chief Justice of Nigeria – CJN, accused the CJN, Aloysius Katsina-Alu, of corruption. Justice Salami alleged that CJN Katsina-Alu exerted undue influence on Salami to constitute or reconstitute an election hearing panel of judges to achieve a certain judicial outcome in a Sokoto state election petition stemming from the infamous 2007 general elections. The fact that the allegations of wrongdoing involve the highest levels and personalities of the Nigerian judiciary is a source of major concern to justice stakeholders

---

[41] I. A. Ayua (ed.), *Law, Justice and the Nigerian Society* (Lagos, Nigeria: Nigerian Institute of Advanced Legal Studies, 1995) p. 5.

and all Nigerians. Thus, it is not surprising that there have been many calls for either the CJN or both the CJN and the Court of Appeal President to resign from their respective offices.[42] Further, interim orders and injunctions, especially as they relate to electoral disputes, appear to be given for a fee and depending on the depth of the pocket of the applicant. At the very minimum, these serious allegations against the Nigerian judiciary erode the average citizen's confidence and perception of the judiciary as fair, just, and a guarantor of justice.[43]

Absence of Judicial Independence

Another impediment to the dispensation of criminal justice in Nigeria is the dishonorable alliance between some judges and the executive arm of government. A learned author captured the situation as follows: "The unholy alliance between some judges and the executives gives room for suspicion. If the judiciary is perceived as another branch of the Executive then the principle of separation of powers is only a subterfuge for emasculation of citizens."[44] What the inappropriate alliance entails is that a judge in such a relationship will find himself obliged to give judgment in favor of his friend or partner in the executive arm of government thereby leading to injustice.

Overcriminalization

In Nigeria, incarceration is the predominant offender disposal method. Payment of fines is another means of punishment. Additionally, there is the death penalty in capital cases.[45] In spite of the alternatives, incarceration is the most common form of criminal punishment. However, the prison/jail conditions are deplorable. The circumstances in the institutions are often less than ideal. Moreover, incarceration is very expensive for the State. And, at the end of their terms, the inmates are worse than they were when they were sent to prisons/jails, which leads one to wonder whether justice has actually been served. In view of the overcriminalized Nigerian justice system, could a reasonable person actually conclude that the country's courts can effectively do justice, *a fortiori* criminal justice? The present legal environment in the country forecloses or

---

[42] See Lemmy Ughegbe, "Civil Society Groups Fault NJC Probe, Demand Resignation of Katsina-Alu, Salami," *The Guardian* (Nigeria), March 9, 2011.

[43] See Joseph Onyekwere, "A Corrupt Judiciary Means a State of Anarchy, Says Ezeobi," *The Guardian* (Nigeria), March 8, 2011.

[44] A. O. Aluko, "The Role of Judicial Officers in Ensuring Efficient Litigation" in Adedotun Oribokun (ed.,) *Contemporary Frontiers in Nigerian Law, Essays in Honour of the Hon. Justice Salihu Moolibbo Alfa Belgore, CJN* (Makurdi, Nigeria: Oracle Business, 2007) p. 117.

[45] Chapter 12 provides a detailed discussion of capital punishment, the need for a sanctions model to replace it, and offers a credible replacement accordingly.

greatly hampers the uses of alternative offender management processes to ensure justice. These alternatives are needed if the Nigerian courts will live up to their duties to do justice, particular in criminal cases. Thus, as an alternative to the expensive, generally ineffective, and sometimes inhumane practice of incarceration, we propose that as a way of dealing with the challenges of the Nigerian criminal justice system, the courts should be empowered to use offender disposal methods other than incarceration. Some of the relevant and useful disposal methods are as follows.[46]

Community service

Community service should be introduced into the Nigerian criminal justice system as a non-custodial means of handling offenders. This means that some offenders should be made to perform specified services to the community rather than be incarcerated. Typically, the services should be performed in the jurisdiction where the relevant offense was committed. Community service is an intermediate sanction: it is less severe than incarceration but more restrictive than probation.[47]

Lagos state has blazed the trail in this aspect of criminal justice administration reforms. Accordingly, the state enacted the *Lagos State Administration of Criminal Justice Law, 2007* to empower the courts.[48] The law identifies prison overcrowding as a major problem confronting the administration of criminal justice. The legislation contains provisions on community service as a new non-custodial means of treating offenders in the state. Its objective is to decongest the prisons by avoiding committal to prison of first-time offenders for minor offenses and to avoid mixing them with hardened criminals. Its other aim, among others, is to serve reformatory and different purposes.[49] Under the law, a court can impose community service on a person that commits an offense punishable with not more than 2 years imprisonment. The law also prescribes the community service activities to which a person may be committed, including: (a) Environmental sanitation; and (b) Assisting in the care of children and the elderly in government approved homes; or (c) Any other type of service which the court considers to have beneficial and salutary effect on the character of the offense. The court is empowered to proceed to order a custodial sentence where

---

[46] For more comprehensive examination of offender disposal/management alternatives for Nigerian criminal justice, see Nọnso Okafọ, *Reconstructing Law and Justice in a Postcolony* (Surrey, England and Burlington, USA: Ashgate Publishing, 2009) particularly pp. 193-208, 231-235.

[47] Steven M. Cox, et al., *The Criminal Justice Network* (Boston, Massachusetts, USA: McGraw-Hill, 1998) p. 246.

[48] See Olasupo Shasure, "Criminal Justice Administration Reforms in Lagos", *The Guardian*, June 10, 2008 p. 83.

[49] Sections 345 (1) and 350.

the terms of an order of community service are breached.

It is expected that by means of laws such as the Lagos state legislation, minor offenders and first-time offenders would be committed to community service instead of being blatantly slammed with imprisonment. Implementation of the Lagos state law in the state – and its replication in other parts of the country – will significantly improve the quality of the Nigerian criminal justice system.

Victim compensation and restitution

Victim compensation and restitution are mainly monetary sanctions imposed on convicts instead of imprisonment. However, the two concepts (*compensation* and *restitution*) differ in an important respect. Restitution binds the offender to pay the victim for the loss incurred, whereas in victim compensation schemes it is the government that recompenses crime victims.[50] The purpose of restitution is to make up for some of the victim's financial losses. Many times when offenses are committed, the law focuses on the accused and neglects the victim. For instance, in general, the criminal justice system is not designed to care very much about what happens to a rape victim. What of an armed robber that has used up a huge sum of money he snatched at gunpoint? If he is convicted and sentenced, what happens to the victim of the crime? In such circumstances, victim compensation can be useful. Victim compensation should be used to assuage the victims' losses and feelings. If an offender cannot restitute the victim, the government should do so. At present, crime victims are largely neglected in the Nigerian criminal justice system. This lacuna should be addressed without further delay.

Parole

Parole is a prisoner's conditional release under supervision after a portion of a custodial sentence has been served. The concept was introduced in the 1940s, about the same time as that of probation.[51] The public sometimes confuses parole and probation. Like probation, parole is a supervised, revocable (conditional) release. However, unlike probation, parole occurs after part of the original custodial sentence has already been served in prison or jail. Its success depends on the parolee. If he violates the conditions of his parole, he can be returned to prison or jail to serve the remainder of the original sentence.[52]

Therefore, parole is a tail-end measure available to prisoners who are ready to comply with the conditions prescribed. Typically, offenders earn parole

---

[50] Freda Adler, et al., *Criminal Justice* (Boston, Massachusetts, USA: McGraw-Hill, 1994) p. 453.

[51] *Ibid*, p. 445.

[52] Cox et al., *op. cit.*, p. 248.

through good conduct in prison. A prisoner who is allowed the parole privilege thus does not languish completely in prison but is given the opportunity to be released early into the general society, albeit with specified conditions to be useful to himself and the community. The Nigerian criminal justice system should adopt this disposal method, which has gained acceptance in other countries. Some prisoners actually show true repentance while incarcerated; they should be monitored and granted parole.

Probation

Probation is the conditional, supervised, and revocable release of an offender into the community in lieu of incarceration.[53] Through this process, a prison-bound convict is instead released into the community under the supervision of a trustworthy person, typically a criminal justice official ("probation officer"), and bound by specified conditions. The conditions may include court directives barring the convict from violating the law, leaving the court's geographic jurisdiction, as well as directing him to maintain employment.[54]

There are many important benefits of probation, and the Nigerian criminal justice system can gain from them. The benefits include the following three. (a) It is not all types of offenses that are serious enough to require incarceration. Therefore, probation in Nigeria would allow the courts to respond to cases appropriately rather than excessively through routine incarceration of offenders. (b) The probation option allows probationers to obtain and maintain employment and pay taxes thereby helping to grow the country's economy. (c) Probation allows offenders to (continue to) take care of their families and other dependants without becoming or imposing burdens on the State. Probation also makes it possible for the offenders to fulfill their social and other responsibilities to their communities. However, it must be added that probation is an alternative sentence for less serious crimes and it is a front-end measure imposed by the court. Instead of allowing the Nigerian prisons to remain hopelessly congested, policymakers in the legislature, executive, and judiciary should adopt probation as an offender disposal method. There is no reasonable ground for continuing to incarcerate minor offenders, especially in view of the sordid conditions of the prisons. However, for probation to work well, effective supervision of probationers is essential. This means that a probation policy should provide for the recruitment, training, and maintenance of a sufficient number of probation officers to ensure that this offender disposal option succeeds.

---

[53] *Ibid*, p. 246.

[54] Charles Lindner and Margaret Saverese, "The Evolution of Probation: University of Seattle and its Pioneering Role in Probation Work" in Freda Adler, et al., *Criminal Justice* (Boston, Massachusetts, USA: McGraw-hill, 1994) p. 438.

In sum, it is not in all cases that imprisonment, fine, or other more punitive criminal sanction is ideal. Perhaps, in recognition of this and in their bid to achieve justice, the United States criminal justice system uses the alternative offender disposal methods enumerated here. On its part, the Nigerian criminal justice system should become more robust and dynamic by providing for probation and other useful options. This is in the best interest of justice. To ensure fair and just treatment of offenders and to avoid overburdening the society, the Nigerian criminal justice system should be armed with alternative sentences. And these must be formalized, explored, and used as necessary.

Other Recommendations

Nigerian courts and other related institutions have made steady progress in the administration of criminal justice, but a lot is left undone. In the 21st century, the problems and challenges constraining the Nigerian system should be given more attention to ensure justice. In line with the discussions and suggestions already provided in this paper, the following recommendations, if implemented, should help to improve the quality of criminal justice in Nigeria. The recommendations are because justice is indispensable and prompt justice cannot be overemphasized. It is a fundamental constitutional requirement provided for in Section 36 (1) of the Nigerian Constitution 1999 that every litigant shall be entitled to a fair hearing within a reasonable time by a court or other tribunal established by law. A judge must therefore ensure that everything is done to give effect to this important provision of the constitution. It is axiomatic that justice delayed is justice denied. This saying is of utmost relevance in Nigeria, having regard to the general social, political, and economic circumstances, which could significantly affect the outcome of litigation. A judge should therefore accord priority attention to prompt and credible dispensation of justice.

In view of the above, we make the following additional recommendations for more effective, efficient, and just administration of criminal justice in 21st Century Nigeria.

1. An adjudicator (Magistrate, Judge, or Justice) is expected to know the law, which is the instrument for dispensing justice. Therefore, the adjudicator should be versed in the kinds of law to be administered in various situations. The adjudicator is expected to be especially learned in the law applicable within his jurisdiction. To ensure that the adjudicator possesses these qualities, he should be well trained in the law and experienced in the law's application to the society. Only professionals that meet these criteria should be appointed as adjudicators. Even then, an appointee should be required to continue to participate in on-the-job trainings for continuous improvement in the various aspects of the law

and its application to society.

2. The Nigerian Constitution vests judicial powers on the courts,[55] yet there is need for the independence of the adjudicator. This means that the adjudicator should decide a case before him in line with his own understanding of the law and facts, and governed by his conscience. He should therefore ensure that he is not blackmailed, coerced, intimidated nor in any other way influenced to decide a case in a particular way. Individual citizens, and indeed the government and other authorities should have no influence over courts' decisions. Thus, a situation as obtains in Nigeria, where judicial officers are appointed by the executive and ratified by the legislature cannot ensure full independence of the judiciary. The lawyers know one another and should be authorized to appoint suitable colleagues for ratification by the legislature. The executive should have no hand in it. This will check the current trend where discretion is unduly fettered or judgment influenced because of perceived "state's interest".

3. The courts and all persons involved in the administration of criminal justice should take deliberate and purposeful steps to discourage delay in the administration of justice. Accordingly, lawyers and judges should be made to account for their conducts that result in unnecessary delays. Counsel and parties in a case should ask for adjournment only when it is necessary and the court should not grant a long adjournment, unless it is necessary to do so and in the interest of justice. A judge should not grant every application for adjournment. Frivolous application for adjournment should not be granted. However, this is not to suggest, as revealed in *Ayua v. Gbaka*,[56] that a case must go on willy-nilly once it is fixed for hearing regardless of the reason advanced for applying for an adjournment by an absent litigant or his counsel. Rather, in every case, the court should consider the reason advanced for applying for an adjournment before issuing a ruling.

4. The adjudicator must be incorruptible. For proper dispensation of justice and a successful operation of the rule of law, a judge is expected to be incorruptible. A corrupt judicial officer is one who dishonestly uses his position to gain or award some unmerited advantage. The advantage could be monetary, promotion, sexual, or in any other form. A corrupt magistrate, judge, or justice is a morally bankrupt person. The justice system should include a credible process for detecting and dealing with corrupt judicial officers. This is important to ensure the confidence of the parties and the general citizenry in the justice system. Otherwise, the

---

[55] Section 6 of the *Constitution of the Federal Republic of Nigeria, 1999*.

[56] (1997) 7 NWLR (14514) 659, at p. 672.

parties and other citizens may resort to self-help methods for justice.

5. The courts should ensure that they sit on time and take little or no recess in the course of each day's hearing. During proceedings, magistrates, judges, and justices should only rise in very compelling circumstances. One of such compelling circumstances would be illness. A judicial officer rising for a frivolous reason, such as to see a visitor, is inappropriate and should not be entertained.

6. A magistrate, judge, or justice should intervene in a judicial proceeding (other than that over which he presides) only when it is necessary to do so, and in the overall interest of justice. Otherwise, a judicial officer has no business interfering or meddling in another court's proceedings because to do so will compromise the exalted and independent status of judicial officers in the administration of justice.

7. The governments at the state and federal levels have enormous responsibilities to ensure that the administration of justice in Nigeria is improved. They should therefore attend to the following:

   (a) An educated and aware citizenry is more likely to protect and champion the citizens' rights under the law. In recognition of the importance of education and citizen awareness in the justice system, the governments should critically address the problem of poverty and poor education standard in the country. For a long time, they have paid lip service to the issue of poverty eradication. Nigerians can be empowered through the provision of quality education at all levels of the educational sector. Teachers should be well trained and scholarship provided for indigent and gifted students. These will in turn positively affect the justice system.

   (b) The dearth of judicial officers in Nigeria is widely acknowledged. This leads to undue delays in judicial proceedings and the inability of the available judicial personnel to thoroughly address the issues in the cases they handle. Thus, there is the need to appoint more judicial and quasi-judicial personnel to the judiciary. This requires the improvement of the conditions of service for government-employed lawyers to attract skilled and experienced private practitioners for the government positions.

   (c) The state and federal governments, respectively, should provide the necessary infrastructure and other facilities like court buildings, stationery, and other things that are needed for smooth and efficient administration of justice.

   (d) Nepotism and favoritism should not be the yardstick for appointment of judicial officers. Honor, competence, and skill should be treated as important criteria for the appointment of magistrates, judges, and justices.

(e) To improve justice and the functions of the justice system, the judiciary should be well funded and judicial officers well motivated. This will ensure efficiency and effectiveness in the administration of justice.

(f) Specific mention should be made of the present method of recording evidence and judicial proceedings in long hand in Nigerian courts. As a matter of utmost urgency, the governments should provide for recording of judicial proceedings by mechanical devices, such as computers, as is done in more sophisticated legal systems. Recording in long hand causes significant delay in the proceedings as well as avoidable pain for the judicial officer. In this connection, the *imperative of computerization* in the 21st Century means that it is not only desirable but also mandatory to conduct judicial proceedings in computerized form that will stop the judicial officer from taking notes in long hand. So far, except for courts in Lagos state and a few other jurisdictions, manual typewriters are still used in Nigeria.[57] Moreover, very few litigation officers are computer literate. Some judges have had to retire from the bench five or more years earlier than the due date because of pain that impeded their ability to continue recording proceedings in long hand. This situation militates against effective litigation and justice.

Conclusion

Criminal justice is the process for determining whether or not an accused person is guilty as regards a crime he is alleged to have committed. In Nigeria, that process involves three agencies: the police, the court, and the prison. The agencies work complementarily towards the attainment of justice. Together, the agencies constitute a "system." The essence of the criminal justice system is the dispensation of justice. Accordingly, recourse to the court is predicated on a desire for justice. Thus, it is pertinent that justice be done to everybody who finds himself in the court. In this chapter, we have examined the criminal justice agencies in Nigeria particularly the courts, their circumstances, and efforts in the administration of criminal justice. It seems reasonable to state that justice provides (or should provide) a situation in which the various parties involved in a dispute get more or less what they deserve. An offshoot of this is that at the conclusion of each case, justice should be seen to have been done, not only by the person dispensing it, but also by the accused, the victim, as well as reasonable observers and citizens.

---

[57] C. J. Dakas, et al., "Impediments to the Speedy Dispensation of Criminal Justice in Nigeria and the Imperative of Urgent Remedial Act" *Jos Bar Journal*, Vol. 1 No. 1 (2005) p. 158.

The process of establishing the Nigerian State's criminal justice system started with the British colonial regime. Since Nigeria attained political independence in 1960, the various constitutions have empowered the courts to dispense justice. Therefore, constitutional backing is the backbone for the establishment of the various Nigerian courts, which dispense criminal justice. An overview of the activities of Nigerian courts from independence shows that they have made significant progress, especially in the area of constructing or reconstructing the country's jurisprudence. However, the problems and challenges facing the courts are enormous. These problems and challenges are a clog in the justice wheel, especially in the 21st Century. As the world progresses technologically, for example through increased use of computers in judicial proceedings, there is a need to provide the technological devices for faster and more thorough dispensation of justice in Nigerian courts. So far, Nigeria is lagging behind on this issue. The many technological aids that are commonplace in the courtrooms of many other countries are absent or grossly insufficient in Nigerian courts. Apart from technological concerns, the Nigerian judiciary ought to be active to be able to dispense justice. This is important since a passive judiciary wallowing in unnecessary conservatism is more prone to injustice. Therefore, alternative offender disposal (corrections) methods should be explored in Nigeria as it is done in other countries such as the USA and Canada. The alternative methods, including probation, parole, victim compensation, restitution, and community service, will obviate the need to resort to incarceration for virtually every crime.[58]

---

[58] Okafọ (2009) *op. cit.*, pp. 193-208, 231-235.Chukwunọnso Okafọ

Part B

POLITICS OF LAW AND ITS ENFORCEMENT

In this Part

Chapter 6

Failed Justice and Political Extremism: Discussing the Dilemma

Victoria Time
Old Dominion University, USA

Introduction

In the context of postcolonial societies, crime control is one of several ways in which governments attempt to assert their influence on the lives of citizens through established criminal justice agencies. The guidelines or laws and procedures that these formally created agencies have to adhere to are usually derivatives of those of the colonizers. As well, activities that are labeled criminal are reflections of the political and economic system from which those definitions are inherited. Societies in transition increasingly have to re-define the laws and crimes to suit their circumstances, or apply the laws and definitions in their entirety as in the colonial states. This dichotomy is unhealthy, and fuels the discussion of whether the measures applied by government are satisfactory, or if they are ill-suited to address the needs of the society. Further questions of what the proper place of formal laws are, in transitional societies ensue from the literature (Brillion, 1983; Lombardo, 1986; Nonet et al., 2001; Okafọ, 2009).

This doubt about the proper place of formal laws, and the ability of governments to effectively apply the rule of law, and to address the insurgence of criminal activities has given rise to a spate of mob justice in many of these post-colonial societies. Mob justice, individual vigilantism, or "collective violence" as Senechal de la Roche states is usually a "symptom of something else" (1996, p. 9). As a participant in mob violence in Limbe, Cameroon noted, jungle justice is "our own way of passing a vote of no-confidence in law enforcement officers and judicial authorities" (http://news.bbc.co.uk/2/hi/africa/5111106.stm.`Jungle justice sweeps Cameroon, August 13, 2006.

According to Nonet et al., in *repressive* systems:

> "Law is subordinated to power politics." The rules of law and the judges who apply them legitimate and serve the interests of the politically powerful, who personally are only weakly bound by legal contract. In political systems characterized by *autonomous* law, in contrast, "law is 'independent' of politics" and acts as a restraint on political power. This is the notion that underlies most contemporary understandings of the "rule of law." In a regime of autonomous law, the judiciary is institutionally separated from the realm of politics, it decides disputes and punishes violations solely by references to formally promulgated legal rules or precedents, which are applicable equally to all litigants, rich or poor, politically favored or socially denigrated. The government itself is bound by the legal rules (Nonet and Selznick, 2001, p. ix).

Post independence, governments in Africa and those in South America still face problems of establishing the rule of law, applying the law evenly to all, and establishing allegiance to established systems of justice. This is obvious in Cameroon, Ghana, Brazil, and a host of other post-colonies. Using Cameroon as foundation for the discussion, this treatise examines the bifurcation between formal law and justice, and mob justice. Three primary questions form the basis of this analysis. First, how are formal state institutions to apply the rule of the law? Second, what factors give impetus to mob justice? Third, what implications can be drawn from the dislodgment of formal criminal justice?

How are Formal State Institutions to Apply the Rule of Law?

Political institutions are designed to ensure the smooth running of society through a legitimate and fair process. Trusting justice administrators to enforce and apply the law requires that they do so by applying the rule of law, the rules of criminal procedure, and rules of evidence. Failures in this regard and ambiguities in exercising justice sometimes are viewed as "illegitimate coercion." As Reichel (2008, p. 15) states, "to understand a country's criminal justice system, we must understand its political one."

The political system of Cameroon is complex following its colonial history. During the German rule of Cameroon, which lasted until 1916, a dual court system existed: one system that catered to issues concerning Europeans, and the other that addressed matters relating to indigenous people with the application of traditional law under the auspices of the Germans. Following Article 9 of the League of Nations Mandates Agreement, both England and France established their respective laws in Cameroon. When a unitary government was set up in Cameroon in 1972, efforts began to unify the varied legal and political culture in the country. Ordinance No. 72/4 of the Constitution of 1972, and subsequent amendments established a unitary system of law, although Article 38 gave allowance for both English and French laws to still be applicable in Anglophone and Francophone Cameroon respectively as long as they were not anomalous to newly enacted laws (see Fombad, pp. 247-248, in Kritzer, 2002).

The president of the country has unilateral powers to make policy, appoint government officials from all professions and to summarily fire them. The president appoints judges of all court levels, as well as the Minister of Justice who supervises the judges. The National Assembly however has the responsibility of electing a nine-member panel of High Court Justices responsible for prosecuting high ranking government officials accused of treason, or other grave crimes against the state (Fombad, p. 248, in Kritzer, 2002). The president is the "Supreme Commander" of the Police, and reserves the right to dismiss corrupt police officers regardless of rank.

Cameroon is affiliated with a variety of international organizations, as well; it is a signatory to the Universal Declaration of Human Rights, the Charter of the United Nations, and the African Charter on Human and Peoples' Rights. In theory, Cameroon promotes freedom of speech, the banishment of torture, cruelty, any forms of human degradation, and to add gravitas to these commitments, these rights are inserted in the preamble of the constitution. By virtue of Article 65 of the Constitution, the preamble is part of the constitution.

How then is the justice system of a transitional state to operate?

At the core of each country's principles is the obligation to carry out justice on those who breach the laws of the State following a process that conforms to the rule of law. The laws of each country lie in the beliefs of its citizens about order and morality. The rule of law, as Zalman (2008) and Hall (1961) note, "lies in supporting institutions, procedures, and values." These institutions include law enforcement, the judiciary, and corrections; the rules of procedure require proper arrest, adjudication, and sanctioning of accused persons. The values include liberty, privacy, and equality. Liberty relates to people's ability to come and go without unwarranted interference by government, and should such freedom be interrupted as for example by an arrest, government must show just cause for the interference. Privacy denotes people's ability to enjoy the sanctity of their personal effects and homes without government meddling, and should there be need for disruption of one's peaceful enjoyment of one's home or property, there must be a need that tips in favor of government. Equality insinuates that the law be applied to all equally, and that the values advanced by law be applicable to all in a similar fashion. These are values espoused in all civilized societies, and by all legitimate governments.

In France for instance, from which francophone Cameroon inherited much of its laws, the rules of procedure require that the suspect be taken in for preliminary questioning. At this stage of the investigation the suspect can be held for twenty four hours without any formal charges filed, and this time frame can be extended should need be for further investigative procedures (Fairchild and Dammer, 2001; Hodgson, 2004). This in essence is an extended detention, but upon determining that there is probable cause that the suspect committed a crime, the suspect is placed under an arrest and formal charges are handed down. The judicial police, the procurator, and the examining magistrate are responsible thereon to conduct further investigation and to forward the case to the assize court to adjudicate the suspect should the facts of the case warrant that (see Fairchild and Dammer, 2001). Throughout the process, the judge maintains a pivotal role in the fact-gathering process; as well, the defendant and his attorney are involved in every stage of the investigation – a hallmark of the inquisitorial system (see Time, 2000, p. 21).

In England, Parliamentary Acts, the Magna Charter, the Bill of Rights, common law, doctrine of equity, and other legislations represent several of the laws that govern individual rights in the country. The rules of criminal procedure from England, which were transplanted to Anglophone Cameroon, include the adversarial process that imposes on the prosecutor the responsibility to prove the guilt of the defendant, a process that accords the defendant the right to confront those accusing him/her of a crime, and the right of the defendant to appeal a verdict. Before the criminal process against an accused person is put in motion, there must be a legitimate basis for an arrest; safeguards of the suspect's rights must be put in place. These English principles were impressed on Anglophone Cameroon following the 1955 Magistrate Court Law (see Time, 2000, p. 20) and stayed in force even after independence in 1961.

The police as autonomous entities in Britain have as their primary task to enforce the law and keep the peace. The French have the *police nationale* and the *gendermarie nationale* (a branch of the military) who are responsible for crime control and order maintenance. In Cameroon, the task of law enforcement lies on the police and the gendarmeries, a derivative method from France. The president and the minister of defense, as well as the head of police, control the police and the gendarmes. In 1999, the government introduced a different branch of crime control – the Light Intervention Battalion (BLI), although it did not become functional until recently (see Crime and Society, http://www-rohan.sdsu.edu/faculty/rwinslow/africa/cameroon.html; Internet). This battalion, which is more sophisticated in its training, is directly accountable to the president. However, despite its training, it is not immune from allegations of torture, false arrests and other human rights violations, just as the regular police and the gendarmes (see Crime and Society, http://www-rohan.sdsu.edu/faculty/rwinslow/africa/cameroon.html; Internet).

For avoidance of doubt, the Cameroonian police are supposed to comply with the law. Thus, they are to arrest only upon probable cause, and in circumstances where the arrest is not done while the crime is in progress, a warrant must be obtained prior to any searches and arrests. That this is the case is almost utopian because as report after report state, the Cameroonian police are unprofessional, brutish, and plagued by graft and avarice (see Irin News.org 2/7/2002/; 3/6/2006; Transparency International, 2007; 2008; news.bbc.co.uk/2/hi/Africa/7131637.stm; Crime and Society, http://www-rohan.sdsu.edu/faculty/rwinslow/africa/cameroon.html; Internet. Transparency International notes the following on justice in Cameroon, "the judiciary, police, customs service, and educational sector are rife with corruption…" (Irin News.org 2/7/2002). According to a report by Winslow, R. (2009), "…Security forces have committed numerous extrajudicial killings and are responsible for disappearances, some of which may have been motivated politically. They also have tortured, beaten, and otherwise abused detainees and prisoners, generally with impunity…." (Crime and Society, http://www-rohan.sdsu.edu/faculty/rwinslow/africa/cameroon.html; Internet).

The principles of due process and respect of human rights are applicable in every society, but may be applied variedly from nation to nation. Ingraham (1987, p. 17) states, "Nations may differ from one another in the manner of collecting evidence, the way they sift it, refine it, and evaluate it prior to trial, and the way they present it at trial, but they all have procedures to do these things." Given that most nations subscribe to the rule of law, what factors account for widespread vigilantism particularly in these transitional countries?

What Factors Give Rise to Widespread Vigilantism/Disrespect of Formal Laws (Mob Justice)?

A variety of factors is responsible for the widespread disregard of the law. In Cameroon, for instance, the factors include: (1) apathy towards the police and the judicial system – laissez faire attitude; (2) economic strife; and (3) population surge.

Apathy towards the Police and the Judicial System

Apathy towards law enforcement agents, such as the police and prosecutors, takes root when there is corruption, ineffectiveness, laissez-faire, and a complete dereliction of duties. Both formal and informal rules in transitional societies help place checks on peoples' behavior. Informal institutions of social control include schools, families, religious entities, peers, and neighbors. The forms of control emanating from the informal institutions are less challenging than those imposed by the police and the courts. This is so because in the informal institutions, the threat of loss of liberty or life does not hang over peoples' heads. Even when informal sanctions, such as restitution, are put in place by the elders in a community or by senior family members, on a person that contravenes community values, adequate methods of enforcing the sanctions are non-existent. Generally, there is an expectation of compliance; otherwise, the assumption is that shame will beset the violator. However, in the contemporary era, shame appears to have less value as an effective deterrent to criminality. Even in the villages where behavior that deviates from the norm is eschewed, shame plays very little role in correcting behavior. This is the case because deviance, including blue-collar crimes and white-collar crimes like bribery and corruption, is just a way of life from those at the top of government, to the pauper at a desolate neighborhood corner.

It is common in Cameroon to turn on the television and see line-ups of arrested armed robbers that include police officers as well as gendarmes. This author saw this on recent visits to Cameroon. In 2006, in Kumba, a town in the South West province of Cameroon, two men suspected of theft were dowsed with petrol and set on fire after tires were placed around their bodies. When asked why the deceased criminals were not handed over to the police instead of the residents taking justice into their hands, the response was:

> Take them to the police? You are not serious my man! As soon as you turn your back, the police will take money and free them, and before you know it they are drinking with you in the bar and threatening to deal with you."
> www.amren.com/mtnews/archives/2006/07/jungle_justice.php; Internet (retrieved June 18, 2011).

Police mistrust is a common attitude among the people, and Transparency International echoes that sentiment. In 2006, the U.S. State Department blamed the spike in "mob justice on the absence of an effective criminal prosecution system" www.amren.com/mtnews/archives/2006/07/jungle_justice.php; Internet (retrieved June 19, 2011).

In another case, a correspondent for the BBC in Cameroon noted that he asked a member of a mob that was about to burn a suspect alive in Limbe, Cameroon, to explain why the mob chose this form of justice. According to the correspondent, the mob member stated that the killings were "our own way of passing a vote of no-confidence in law enforcement officers and judicial authorities" http://news.bbc.co.uk/2/hi/africa/5111106.stm; Internet (retrieved June 19, 2011). The general belief is that in Cameroon, criminals can easily buy freedom simply by bribing the police. As a local told the BBC, "Immediately he [suspect] gives them [police] money, he will be freed" BBC News, Limbe, "Jungle Justice Sweeps Cameroon". In a stimulating piece by Mbom (2009), he poignantly surmises:

> Justice is giving each man what is his due. It is false to assume a culture of peace amidst a culture of blatant injustices. The failed judicial system in Cameroon is just an epitome of the failed culture of justice. Justice delayed is justice denied. One is better off settling issues outside of the court for criminals are better off amongst their peers the magistrates and legal

practitioners. How will civilians not resort to jungle justice and roast a thief for example? http://www.thefrontiertelegraph. com/?p=179; Internet (retrieved June 19, 2011).

Besides corruption that plagues the justice system, the absence of resources, including standard tools and equipment, also hampers the system's ability to be effective. In the area of criminal justice, there are hardly any updated criminal databases and basics such as computers, telephones, walkie/talkies, radios; and police cars are high-end luxuries that the overwhelming majority of police officers in the country do not have. It is common to see an arrestee in shackles walking for miles with an officer to get to the jail, or for a police officer to use his authority to have a cab driver transport for free the suspect and the officer to the police station. Pay is dismal and as a Cameroonian civil servant proclaimed, "wages were too low for them to be work-conscious" (see "Tardy Cameroon Workers Locked Out," 2005, BBC News Africa). Further, the number of police officers *vis-à-vis* civilians is woefully disproportionate. Such imbalance prevents effective policing.

As already indicated, the same is true for the judiciary. In accordance with the law, police are to refrain from arbitrary and discriminatory arrests and detentions, and the necessity for a more prompt review of one's detention is highly advocated in Anglophone Cameroon. Unfortunately, "such detention often is prolonged, due to the understaffed and mismanaged court system" (Crime and Society,

http://www-rohan.sdsu.edu/faculty/rwinslow/africa/cameroon.html; Internet). There is an absence of computers for managing court calendars and keeping abreast with pending cases. As well, there is an absence of data on the number of judicial employees in the country. Further, not to be overlooked is the fact that there is a shortage of judges because of limits placed on those who graduate from the National School of Administration and Magistracy (ENAM). Based on this limit, only twenty judges are to graduate per year from the school of magistracy (see Fombad, 2002, p. 251).

Economic Strife: Widespread Poverty

Structural theories such as anomie usually explain why economic crimes permeate the lower strata of society. In his strain theory, Merton (1938) explains why there is a high level of crime in the United States. Merton contends that the American society emphasizes the goal of financial success, but at the same time, enough legitimate means to attain this goal are not available. Consequently, persons striving to attain this goal but deprived of legitimate methods to do so, resort to deviance and criminality. Hence, not only are there high incidences of crime in the United States, also, certain segments of the society are more prone to commit crime because of deprivation. While it is difficult to discern the goals in place in Cameroon, like many countries that advance capitalist ideals, monetary success is emphasized directly or indirectly, hence, the views espoused by Merton can be applied to the situation in Cameroon. Many of those deprived of means to acquire wealth or riches through legitimate means (and most Cameroonians are because of the astronomical level of unemployment, and low wages), innovate ways to attain those goals, and that may explain the gargantuan increase of property offenses such as, pick pocketing, burglary, robbery, larceny, and auto theft.

Literature from Messner's and Rosenfeld's work titled *Crime and the American Dream*, also sheds light on why Cameroon is experiencing a colossal increase in crime. Social institutions are crucial in advancing the well-being of society. These social institutions include the economy, polity, family, and education. Ordinarily, these institutions foster the health of society. However, when proper checks or measures to stabilize them are not in place, anomic tendencies are experienced. The economy, as Messner and Rosenfeld discuss, "functions to satisfy the basic material requirements for human existence, such as the need for food, clothing, and shelter" (1994, p. 73). When much emphasis is placed on "monetary success," this emphasis, as Messner and Rosenfeld contend, supersedes other goals and thus becomes a way for gauging achievement.

One cannot say with certainty that monetary success is emphasized in Cameroon. For the most part, it is reasonable to contend that a huge segment of the Cameroonian population will be content at this point with a stable economy that provides prospects for upward mobility. With a faltering economy in Cameroon, and wealth and monetary rewards persistently in the hands of a few, the masses suffer from chronic deprivation. The citizens' responses to their plight are different: many conform, some retreat, and some others innovate means to sustain life. Abhorrent crimes like armed robbery, murder, grand larceny, auto theft, which were very sporadic a little over a decade ago, are now common occurrences in Cameroon. This phenomenon, coupled with an inept and corrupt criminal justice system, has precipitated individual and mob justice throughout the country.

The polity, according to Messner and Rosenfeld in their *Crime and the American Dream*, is "dependent on the economy for financial support. Governments must accordingly take care to cultivate and maintain an environment hospitable to investment" (1994, p. 81). The reverse is true in Cameroon. Mismanagement, fraud, and graft, plague political institutions in Cameroon. In 2005, about 500 officials in the Ministry of Finance were cited by the prime minister for mismanagement of funds and fraud by "either awarding themselves extra money or claiming salaries for non-existent workers" (bbc.co.uk, 2 March, 2005; Internet). Further, in early

2006, several high ranking civil servants were arrested for embezzlement, and as the *Cameroon Tribune* indicated, further arrests were imminent following the arrest on March 24, 2006 of a high ranking cabinet member at the Directorate General of the Douala Autonomous Port (www.Cameroon-tribune.net/Samedi 25 Mars 2006 Douala Police make Another Big Catch; Internet). If dominant institutions such as the finance ministry and ports authority fail to foster "the collective good" of society by ensuring a sound economy, it becomes a causal link to criminality not only among those within the institution, but among the masses. "In addition to the negative impact on the political front, corruption also affects a nation economically, damages the social fabric of a society, and can result in environmental degradation" (Reichel, 2005, p. 49 citing Transparency International, 2003b).

The aggregate impact of corruption and mismanagement of resources in Cameroon quite substantially exceeds that of street crimes. This assertion is not limited to the economic cost of crimes; rather, it encompasses deaths resulting from sub-standard medical care because of inadequate funding to hospitals, deaths resulting from profound suffering caused by unemployment, low wages, preventable diseases, and other hardships, which are a direct result of mismanagement of funds, graft, and apathy for the masses. In an article titled "Cameroon Corruption Hinders Aids Fight," the BBC expressed skepticism regarding use of funds allocated for HIV/AIDS testing and treatment in Cameroon. The BBC expressed profound doubts as to whether the $133m (68m pounds) allocated to fight HIV/AIDS in Cameroon would be put to proper use. Following investigations that revealed blatant mismanagement of the funds, BBC surmised thus: "Tackling AIDS cannot happen until a cure is found for Cameroon's second deadly virus – corruption" (http://news.bbc.co.uk/2/hi/africa/6198337.stm; Internet. Retrieved 1/6/2007).

It seems clear that the anomic conditions evident in Cameroon, including individual and group (mob) justice, stem from a convolution of issues, most of which are not directly connected with the reason for the individual and group spontaneous and macabre actions. As Senechal de la Roche observes:

> Collective violence directed at social inferiors and marginals is commonly not even regarded as sociologically meaningful in itself, but rather is characterized as a symptom of something else. It is not the punishment of deviant behavior, as its participants claim. Instead, it is, for example, an indirect byproduct of macrostructural disruptions or strains such as urbanization, unemployment, or competition—conditions that are said to frustrate or otherwise predispose individuals to aggressive behavior (1996, p. 9).

Population Surge, In-migration

Cameroonians have blamed the drastic rise in crime on the influx of refugees into the country. There is no official confirmation of this. Based on unofficial accounts from locals, the areas most highly hit by banditry and highway robberies are also the areas with the highest numbers of refugees. It is thus reasonable for locals to draw a nexus between the increased number of crimes and the presence of refugees – most of whom are not placed in shelters, and have to fend for themselves somehow. Foremost, jobs are scarce even for autochthonous people. Consequently, it is almost impossible for refugees to find even menial jobs.

Furthermore, migration breaks supportive ties. With no social ties in a new environment, coupled with little source of livelihood, frustration builds, and that may be disruptive to self-control and other forms of informal social control. In spite of their high literacy rate (which in developed countries would lead to most citizens having white-collar jobs), the majority of Cameroonians rely on subsistence farming for sustenance. Farming is done on one's own land, or on land owned by family members. Refugees, who own little or nothing, rely on the goodwill of the masses (who are themselves needy) for necessities, or on panhandling and scavenging in dumpsters, or on committing property offenses. On a couple of trips to Cameroon, first hand observations were made of refugees panhandling, much of the time aggressively, and getting whatever they could out of trash fields. It was common to see a refugee child being sent by the mother to pursue a passerby until the passerby surrendered money or food to the child.

The exact number of refugees in Cameroon is unknown. However, the United Nations Committee for Refugees and Immigrants places the number at approximately 25,000 in 2003, of whom 17,000 were from Nigeria, 4,000 from Congo Kinshasa (now known as the Democratic Republic of Congo), and over 4,000 from other African countries. The number of refugees indicated above does not comprise the approximated 40,000 Chadians in Cameroon at the end of 2003 (UN Commission for Refugees & Immigrants, 2005). These Chadians are not classified as refugees but as "refugee-like" because according to the U.N. Commission on Refugees, they have "integrated into local communities" and are "self-sufficient." Further, the U.N. Commission contends that "all refugees" in Cameroon are self-reliant since the U.N. High Commission for Refugees "operate[d] no refugee camps in Cameroon." The Commission also states that the Cameroonian Red Cross gives "education, health care, and financing for micro-projects" to the refugees, including 1,000 tons of food given to the refugees in 2003.

Given that corruption is pervasive in Cameroon (Transparency International, 2003; 2006; 2007), it is unlikely that without UN supervision, food and other supplies were given to the intended recipients. Moreover, with chronic poverty and joblessness, it is hard to conceive that most of the refugees in Cameroon are self-reliant. Further, to contradict the notion of self-sufficiency, it was reported that "almost a quarter of a million people in neglected northern Cameroon are faced with serious food shortages and more than US $1 million is still needed to ensure they all get emergency rations" (UN Food Programme, in United Nations - OCHA IRIN Africa News, 22 Sep. 2005, http://www.irinnews.org, 11/5/2005).

A majority of the refugees abound in the northern part of Cameroon. Subsistence farming and petty trade which go just a little way to maintain a healthy livelihood are relied on by the majority of the masses, and this would be true for those refugees who are industrious. As Bandura (1979, p.58) posits, "aversive conditions increase the probability that deviant patterns will arise." Even if these refugees were conformists prior to their displacement, following Bandura's reasoning, their now "thwarted strivings," "impoverished" and "discontented" states brought about by "privations" may explain their aggressiveness. However, Bandura also cautions that "most impoverished" persons do not turn to violence, only a few do. This holds true for the refugees in Cameroon. The preceding analysis suggests two things: either refugees are ruthless in their crimes as locals contend because they are in dire need, or both groups, that is, locals and refugees, are culpable. The latter contention seems more persuasive because both groups are needy, even if slightly less so for one.

The connection between crime and urbanization has received much attention since Shaw and McKay's 1942 treatise on the issue. They contend that even though conforming behavior is emphasized in urban areas, the proliferation of deviant and criminal "influences" are likely to trump orderly behavior, and non-conforming behavior becomes entrenched over time. Many authors have since elaborated on, and modified this theory. Stark (1987), for instance, asserts that since forces that control law abiding behavior are compromised in communities with loose social controls, the absence of interpersonal bonds breeds criminal tendencies. Others reason that urban areas plagued by increased mobility, indigence, and diverse groups, are suitable breeding places for criminal behavior (Bursik and Grasmick, 1992; Sampson and Groves, 1989; Smith and Jarjoura, 1989; Bursik, 1988). Further, Nomiya, Miller, and Hoffmann (2000, p. 4), explain that "we can conceive of migration patterns as a continuum running from positive to negative population growth, with both ends leading to social disruption."

The population of Cameroon has tripled since the 1980s, and it is now estimated at 19.5 million (UN, 2009) with the bigger towns and cities experiencing severe urban exodus. While there are divergent opinions on whether urbanization breeds criminal tendencies, in their study on Japan, Nomiya, et al. (2000, p. 6) contend that urban disorganization by itself cannot explain criminality, rather, crime in urban areas can be better explained by the multitude of opportunities available to manifest that behavior. In some societies, "ethnic or racial heterogeneity" may make urban areas more susceptible to crime, but in Japan, according to Nomiya, et al., other factors such as "population size, density, and in-migration" may provide the necessary opportunities for criminal behavior.

Following the UN Commission for Refugees, there are approximately 25,000 refugees and about 40,000 "refugee-like" persons living in Cameroon. The number of illegal immigrants living among the 16 million Cameroonians is a matter of speculation. Cameroon is comprised primarily of a youthful population given that the mortality age is 45 years. Most of these youths gravitate towards the big cities or towns in search of jobs or to hustle for a livelihood leaving behind in the rural areas, aging parents, and family members traditionally responsible for providing social network of support. Anonymity, lack of guardianship, and architectural patterns of houses that are either structurally untenable, or surrounded by high walls, which insulate a criminal from the view of neighbors or passers-by, exacerbate opportunities for home invasions, and other predatory crimes. Social ties are loose, community support is fragmented, and traditional conformist values have been compromised, thereby attenuating any formal or informal social controls. Groups of criminals band together, identify a target, stalk the target, and carry out their crimes.

This method of working in groups through successive periods of time, and in the same areas supports Shaw and McKay's premise that crime and delinquency can be "transmitted down" from generation to generation of criminals and delinquents in similar fashion like other social activities are transmitted. Hence, to a large extent, the application of theory does help us understand what is going on in Cameroon regarding blue-collar criminality. For the crimes that constitute corruption, such as bribery, misappropriation of funds, taking pay for work not done, or for deceased persons still on pay roll (see "Cameroon Tracks 'Ghost Workers'," http://news.bbc.co.uk/2/hi/africa/4785721.stm., retrieved June 18, 2011), the theories discussed above do not satisfactorily explain why other than greed. These crimes are perpetrated primarily by those who are relatively well to do as Cameroonians themselves attest (see "Cameroon Dances to Anti-graft Beat," http://news.bbc.co.uk/2/hi/Africa/7131637.stm, retrieved January 4, 2008). Poor people succumb to the culture of bribe-giving because much of the times it is the only way they can get some basic services, or get out of the scourges of the powerful.

What Implications Should be Drawn from the Dislodgment of Formal Criminal Justice?

What is Justice?

According to *Black's Law Dictionary*, justice is the "proper administration of laws" (Black, 1990, p. 864). For Robinson (2002), there are two disparate views of justice. As he explains, one view stems from a retributive stance. In this regard, crime victims consider justice as a square with the offender, as for example, when a defendant is incarcerated for the crime. The second view relates to leveling the scale of justice by being fair and unbiased through like treatment of similar offenders who commit similar crimes.

Following the retributive view of justice, those involved in individual and mob justice advocate that an offender should get his or her just desert. However, their justice is extreme, and the punishment they impose on the suspect often exceeds the harm caused by that suspect. After reviewing several newspaper accounts[1] on vigilantism in Cameroon, it is obvious that most of the incidents for which crime suspects are burned alive or are severely maimed stem from accusations or suspicions of property crimes. In any case, the value of the item at issue is typically so low that the relevant crime is considered a petty offense or misdemeanor. Only in a few circumstances are the crimes felonies. Hardly does an allegation against a suspect relate to a crime involving loss of life. Mensah (2005) observed this in Ghana, as did Sekhonyane and Louw (2002) in South Africa.

It is not unusual for an innocent person to be mistaken for a criminal. For instance, in one incident, a man was set on fire when a police officer saw him riding a bike that the officer erroneously thought was stolen. As well, it is common for thrill seekers to just raise a false alarm and then randomly target an innocent passerby (see http://news.bbc.co.uk/2/hi/africa/5111106.stm; Internet, retrieved August 13, 2006, 'Jungle justice' Sweeps Cameroon). Also, can it be retributive justice when a person who steals a bunch of bananas or 1000 francs cfa ($2) is lynched by a hostile mob? How can that be tooth for tooth, or eye for eye? Shouldn't the punishment fit the crime? Glaser (1997) opines that when the criminal justice system dispenses a punishment, there is less likelihood that private persons would administer disproportionate and barbaric punishments. Robinson (2002, p. 273) elaborates on this by stating that if private persons were left to inflict punishment, the bounds of their vengeance will vastly exceed that

---

[1] Newspapers constitute a source of vital information for this study because in Cameroon, there is a paucity of official records or data on vigilantism – and other criminal justice issues.

acceptable by law. In essence then as he explains,

> a single murder might lead to two more deaths—the death of the guilty offender and perhaps also the death of someone standing next to the offender when the victim's family opens fire. This in turn could lead to the desire for vengeance on the part of the offender's family and the family of the innocent bystander. Without state-controlled retribution, where would the cycle of vengeance and escalation end?

Certainly, a person who steals or who commits any crime should be punished, but to what extent and what purposes do punishments serve? Punishments should reflect their crimes, but as Samaha (2008, p. 15) observes "...it's difficult to translate abstract justice into concrete penalties. What are a rapist's just deserts? ...how many years in prison is robbery worth...?" While it is impossible to provide concrete responses to these questions, one thing stands at the forefront: punishment should be "fair and impartial" (Robinson, 2002, p. 273). To be fair, the punishment must not be drastically disproportionate, as well, the defendant should be able where applicable, to offer mitigation. A desperately destitute person who steals a loaf of bread to give to a malnourished child should be able to offer his privation as a mitigating factor. After all, in Cameroon and many developing countries, welfare programs that cater to the plight of the poor are non-existent. Individual and mob justice fail to consider this.

Further, the administration of punishment should be impartial. Vigilantes let their emotions take the better of them. A petty thief may meet the unfortunate end of death, but sometimes, a violent offender may escape with just treatable injuries. If Senechal de la Roche's conclusion that collective violence perpetrated on those of one's equal, or social inferior, is symptomatic of "something else" then the punishment inflicted by vigilantes to street criminals is meaningless. As the vigilante in Limbe, Cameroon blatantly acknowledged, mob lynching was the vigilantes' way of casting a "vote of no confidence" on the criminal justice system. This being the case, their anger, frustration, and savagery should be directed at the agents of the justice system. Sparing the criminal justice agents and targeting the pauper on the street or the petty offender serves no good.

According to Mill (1859), and Hart (1968), punishments should be imposed for the sole purpose of forestalling any harm to other people. Preventing or deterring future crimes may only be effective when the predicate reason for mob anger is addressed. If mob anger emanates from disgruntlement over the behavior of decadent politicians and inept criminal justice personnel, then targeting street criminals is really misplaced justice. Deterrence is premised on the point that punishing a criminal will prevent that criminal from committing further crimes (specific deterrence), and on a larger scope will scare the general population from committing crimes (general deterrence). Certainly, mob justice achieves the first. Once an alleged criminal is lynched, the ultimate deterrence would have been achieved. However, do individual and mob justice deter the rest of the community from engaging in crimes? Empirically, this is not known; and a clear fact is that the killing of a man on the street does not deter the politician or the police officer, prosecutor, or judge who is comfortably situated at an office or a police post, free from the scourge of public anger.

Further, that a criminal will be detected and caught by the mob is infrequent, and thus even when mob action may be brutal, the fact that many criminals go undetected by the mob stalls any visions of deterrence. What is obvious, as Beccaria (1776) states, is that:

> the certainty of punishment, even though it be moderate, will always make a stronger impression than the fear of one more severe if it is accompanied by the hope that one may escape that punishment, because men are more frightened by an evil which is inevitable even though minor in nature. Further, if the punishment be too severe for a crime, men will be led to commit further crimes in order to escape punishment for the crime…. It is essential that it be public, prompt, necessary, minimal in severity as possible under given circumstances, proportional to the crime, and prescribed by laws.

How Should Justice be Implemented?

Formal social control denotes that government can arrest and prosecute any law violators, and administer a fitting punishment upon conviction. The implication here is that the legitimacy of an arrest, as well as guilt and punishment, are determined pursuant to fair and objective guidelines. The Rule of Law or the Principle of Legality states that there cannot be a crime if the law has not defined a behavior as criminal; and there cannot be a punishment for a behavior, which the law has not prescribed (See Samaha, 2008, p. 20). This rule advances four values: (1) fairness: people should be given fair warning about what constitutes a crime; (2) liberty: peoples' freedoms should not be interrupted by an arrest if they had no way of knowing that their behavior constitutes a crime; (3) democracy: only those elected to make law should define what constitutes a crime; (4) equality: like criminals should be treated similarly by the justice system (Samaha, 2008, pp. 20-21).

Of particular relevance to this discussion are points 1, 3 and 4 in the preceding paragraph. With regard to points 1 and 3, in a democratic State or one striving to be democratic, to maintain some degree of stability, it is necessary that only those who have been elected through a democratic process be able to define clearly what behavior is criminal, and these definitions or laws should be made public so that people have prior notice of what the law expects of them. Further, the definition of crimes should be accompanied by a corresponding punishment for each crime. That, at least, is a first step of assuring that the masses, as well as law enforcement officers, do not arbitrarily pick up people for what they assume is a violation, and should anyone be arrested, the arrest should be premised on a legitimate reason. Point 4 is intended to curb any discriminatory practices where the agents of the law treat similar offenders who have committed similar offenses differently. To ensure a fair process, people who commit like offenses, in similar circumstances, should be processed in a similar fashion and should receive similar punishments.

See Chapter 1 of this book for more in-depth discussion of the rule of law, its elements, alternatives, and application.

However, the State should be the entity to impose punishments, and it should impose punishments that are not barbaric. It should impose punishments that reflect the current stage of civilization, and more importantly, that are consistent with the crime committed. If a crime is worthy of the punishment of death, then a practical method to carry out the death penalty should be employed. Punishments like "neck-lacing" (placing a car tire around a suspect's neck and setting the suspect on fire), or dowsing a suspect with gasoline and then setting the person ablaze that are utilized by vigilantes, are cruel and unusual, and should not be tolerated.

As a fair start, a suspect must be arrested only upon probable cause – a showing of facts that substantiate the occurrence of a crime, and that form a nexus between the crime and the suspect. If the suspect is not caught *flagrant delicto* committing the crime, then there should be a proper process of identifying the suspect. As Zalman (2008, p. 442), notes "eyewitness identification is the most important source of truth in most criminal cases and, ironically, the leading source of error that results in the conviction of innocent people." That this is the case is evident in Kumba, Cameroon where in 2006, a police inspector was sentenced to five years in prison for setting on fire a man who he mistakenly thought was a bicycle thief (see http://news.bbc.co.uk/2/hi/africa/5111106.stm, retrieved June 19, 2011).

Next, upon arrest, there should be an initial appearance or at the very least a preliminary hearing or an arraignment whereby the defendant is clearly informed of the charges and other rights that he/she has. Any of these proceedings tests the strength of the State's case against the defendant, and ensures that an innocent person is not bound for trial. Zalman (2008, p. 504) states: "the factual investigation of cases, and not the legal research or procedural filings, is the most important thing that prosecutors and defense lawyers do during the pretrial process." This process is not only emphasized by the adversarial process, it is the bedrock of the inquisitorial system. For the avoidance of doubt, vigilantes or those determined to engage in "self-help" justice do not bother to inquire into the truth. Whoever is identified as a culprit (even an innocent person), pays for a crime he did not commit or becomes a target for thrill seekers and idlers looking for something to relieve the stressors that plague their lives. In compliance with the rule of evidence, the onus to prove guilt lies with the prosecutor, but vigilantes deny the suspect this privilege.

For the prosecutor to be able to have a defendant found guilty, the prosecutor has to prove the elements of a crime, which include the guilty act (*actus reus*), the guilty mind (*mens rea*), concurrence, attendant circumstances, bad results. The prosecutor does not have to prove all of these elements in every crime, but the underlying requirement of a guilty act must be present to set the criminal process in motion. Proving the *mens rea* is crucial for many kinds of crimes because those who act purposefully (those who premeditate their crimes) are more culpable than those who act negligently. This said, a person who commits a strict liability offense (an activity that a statute outright prohibits, and for which the State is not required to determine a person's mindset), deserves the stated punishment for the crime. Make no illusion about proving the *mens rea*; without a confession, the prosecutor has to rely on circumstantial evidence, and the best way around this is to scrutinize the actions of the person and whatever else he or she may have to say.

Besides proving the elements of a crime, it is necessary for the sake of fairness to give the accused an opportunity to provide a defense if he/she has one, and for the accused person to establish that defense. A person who acts in self-defense should not be treated in the same way as the instigator. As well, when there is a mitigating circumstance, the court should take cognizance of that. Mitigating circumstances should not exonerate an accused, but under certain circumstances should reduce an accused person's punishment. Given any irregularities in a trial, and any disproportionate sentences meted, an accused should be able to appeal. These substantive and procedural factors should prevail in a court of law. However, vigilantes deny suspects of the benefits.

What Should be Done to Curb Chronic Poverty and Corruption in Cameroon?

With regard to the root causes of widespread vigilantism in Cameroon, which are apathy, economic strife, and surge in population, the following implications are drawn: How Africa's problems, and specifically how Cameroon's problems, can be solved remains daunting. Ayodele (2003) surmises that Africa should follow the following advice: "if you want something done well, do it yourself." He maintains that even though the Western world is sometimes blamed for Africa's tribulation, Africa to a large extent is instrumental to its own problems (see Arnold, 2001; Sender and Smith, 1986; Warren, 1980), and governments could reduce these problems by increasing economic growth, by doing away with policies that stifle trade.

Since the upsurge of crimes in Cameroon is partially blamed on a crippled economy, and absence of social programs, a starting point to curb crime in the country is to revamp the economy by introducing better trade policies within the country, and with other African and Western countries (see Kitching, 1987; 1982; 1980). High trade tariffs and very strict border laws with other African countries impede trade. It is thus necessary to decrease trade tariffs and taxes in order to increase trade. Berry (1991) has argued that perhaps less restricted market barriers may not be a suitable idea for "African social realities." However, this line of reasoning is rejected by those (see as examples: Musevini, 2000; Ayodele, 2003) who see semi-open or open markets as a pathway to better economic development in Africa.

African countries, Cameroon included, always rely on producing and exporting raw materials, and apparently have little initiative to figure out how to manufacture finished products from these raw materials. Consequently, when market prices for these raw materials fall because of over production, or if advanced technology makes these materials obsolete, the exporting country finds itself in a financial crisis. History has shown that reliance on specific products to vitalize the economy is bad economic foresight (see the examples of Libya, Gabon, Uganda, Democratic Republic of Congo/Zaire). Cameroon needs to get into the manufacturing of finished products, and into diversifying its economy. Only with a revitalized economy and a meaningful and sustained domestic investment can any other social programs, such as health care and better infrastructure, be instituted (see Kentor, 2001). Several decades ago when there was relative prosperity in Cameroon, there were also relatively fewer incidents of white collar as well as violent crimes; and hospitals were seemingly better equipped and better managed, and the roads even though bad were better maintained than they are today.

Like many other African countries, Cameroon relies on aid from the World Bank or from more developed countries. However, the aid money is hardly ever fully accounted for (see BBC commentary at http://news.bbc.co.uk/2/hi/africa/6198337.stm; Internet, retrieved June 18, 2011). In his assessment, in "Aid and its Consequences" to Africa, Arnold (2001, p. 121) presents a grim outlook of the perceived consequences, thus:

Two of the unfortunate consequences of these aid flows

to Africa have been first, the creation of huge debts that can never be repaid but whose servicing cripples the recipient economies; and second, possibly even worse than the legacy of debt, the parallel creation of aid dependence on the part of the recipients, an expectation that aid will always be forthcoming, that the world owes Africa permanent economic assistance.

In 2006, much of Cameroon's debt was set aside (see BBC article "Cameroon Sees $5 Billion Debt Erased by World Bank and International Monetary Fund" www.news.bbc.co.uk/2/hi/business/4964808.stm; Internet; retrieved October 28, 2007). There are little, if any, signs that the aid went to foster progress in the country. Further, the inability of Cameroon to repay the debt suggests that if at all the debt was put into public use whatever purpose the loan was directed towards never yielded any profit. Granted, sometimes investments do not thrive even under the best circumstances, but Cameroon has been notorious for chronic mismanagement of funds (http://news.bbc.co.uk/2/hi/africa/6198337.stm; Internet; retrieved June 19, 2011). With no profit, it is unfathomable how the debt can be repaid. The foregoing substantiates Arnold's assertion.

In advocating progress in Tanzania, Julius Nyerere advised that education "has to prepare our young people to play a dynamic and constructive part in the development of a society in which all members share fairly in the good or bad fortune of the group and in which progress is measured in terms of human well-being..." (1970, p. 239). Education, as he notes, is not limited to formal training in schools, but comprises one that instills a "sense of commitment" to promote growth and proper values in society. Even though Nyerere's ideas were espoused decades ago, they make as much sense now as they did then, and not only in Tanzania, but in Cameroon as well. Not only should formal education continue to be advocated, a curriculum that teaches values and ethics entailed in good citizenship should be incorporated in school courses as early as primary school.

In March 2007, an Anti-Corruption Commission was created in Cameroon, headed by the president of the country. This commission hopes to bring a stop to corruption through education via the radio, by circulating flyers that denounce graft, and by publishing the names of those found guilty of graft (http://news.bbc.co.uk/2/hi/africa/7131637.stm; Internet, retrieved June 18, 2011). Besides this, seminars or workshops should be routinely held to educate the public on the need to avoid bribery and corruption. The Cameroon Tribune, the most popular newspaper in the country, reported on Saturday, March 25, 2006 that the Commonwealth Secretariat in the country's capital, Yaounde, organized a three-day workshop, the purpose of which was to promote "the independence of justice" and fight against corruption in the judicial system." This comes after several persons in high positions, including politicians, judges, and other civil servants were exposed for engaging in colossal corrupt practices. However, sporadic workshops seem hopeless. If Cameroon's problems are to be solved, a change in attitude should not be a matter of occasional workshops attended by a few. Those workshops should be arranged frequently, and participants should include people of all works of life.

Formal education should be diversified to include vocational, technical, scientific, and intellectual trainings in different works of life. Musevini (2000) contends that Africans can be competitive in the world only if the populace becomes skilled. Further, jobs should be created to provide employment for these skilled workers, and pay and other incentives should be such as to curb the Diaspora of the skilled professionals.

Corruption and bribery persist because the benefits that accrue from the illegal behaviors supersede the cost of being caught for engaging in these crimes. In a simplistic fashion, one would suggest that the solution should be to raise the cost of criminal activity by punishing, or making the punishment more draconian, or opening up legitimate opportunities for the masses to attain a decent livelihood (see Lukestich and White, 1982). The problem is that agents of the criminal justice system in Cameroon are not immune from corruption. According to a BBC report of 12/7/2007 on Cameroon, "policemen still openly collect bribes from cab drivers who do not have valid documents or whose vehicles are not roadworthy, while bribery in the civil service remains the norm" (http://news.bbc.co.uk/2/hi/africa/7131637.stm; Internet, retrieved June 19, 2011). Who polices the police becomes a crucial question, and what sanctions should be meted on those found guilty of corrupt practices is contentious. Some Cameroonians are of the opinion that both incarceration and restitution must be imposed on embezzlers, while others are drawn towards incarceration alone (see http://news.bbc.co.uk/2/hi/africa/7131637.stm; Internet, retrieved June 18, 2011). While the president is concerned about the "cancer of corruption" in the country, the reality of lack of prison space does not escape his thoughts. Acknowledging all the reports he gets about corrupt citizens, the president concedes, "if I take them for their word, the prison will not be large enough to accommodate everybody...." (http://news.bbc.co.uk/2/hi/Africa/7131637.stm; Internet, retrieved January 4, 2008). It seems sensible that the government should implement methods of retrieving as much money or property as possible from embezzlers and those guilty of other practices of graft. For a country that does not have much to begin with, restitution must be mandatory.

Conclusion

The family in African societies is critical in ensuring conformity to the norms and values of each community. Two factors associated with family risks that are connected with criminality are economic adversity and weak family ties/ population mobility (see Phillips, et. al., 2006, p.677). Accordingly, several issues demand attention, perhaps by means of new or updated policies and programs, in parts of Africa. The disintegration of families should be halted by developing rural areas, and opening up job opportunities in those areas. Rural exodus should occur only because youths are looking for better jobs, or for ways to advance themselves in legitimate ways, but not simply because they are looking for "criminal gold mines" in the cities. Salaries or wages should be guaranteed each payday, and payment should be in full. Most people are still very active and productive at the age of fifty. It is thus economically unsound to retire people of that age. The words of Messner and Rosenfeld (1994, p. 109) appropriately serve as a conclusion to this expose, thus:

> The distinctive and powerful feature of the sociological paradigm is that it directs attention to the interconnections among social institutions. Because of these interconnections, piecemeal reforms are likely to be ineffective .... institutional reforms must go hand in hand with cultural change, because culture and institutional structure are themselves inextricably bound.

References

Abrahamsen, R. (2004) "Disciplining Democracy: Development Discourses and Good Governance in Africa," *International Journal of African History Studies*, Vol. 37, No. 3, pp. 557-579.

Adler, F. (1983) *Nations Not Obsessed With Crime*. Littleton, Colorado, USA: Fred B. Rothman.

Afrol News (2008) "7 Killed in Cameroon Protest." Retrieved February 26, 2008 from the World Wide Web: http://www.afrol.com/articles/28129; Internet.

Alden, C. and Le Pere G. (2004) "South Africa's Post Apartheid Foreign Policy: From Reconciliation to Ambiguity?" *Review of African Political Economy*, Vol. 31, No. 100, pp. 283-297.

American Renaissance News (2007) '"Jungle Justice" On The Rise In Cameroon,' Retrieved 2/12/2007 from the World Wide Web: http://www.amren.com/mtnews/archives/2006/07jungle_justice.php; Internet.

Appiahene-Gyamfi, J. (1998) "Violent Crime in Ghana: The Case of Robbery," *Journal of Criminal Justice*, Vol. 26, pp. 409-424.

Arnold, G. (2001) *A Guide to African Political and Economic Development*. Chicago, Illinois, USA: Fitzroy Dearborn.

Asuagbor, G. (1998) *Democratization and Modernization in a Multilingual*

Cameroon. Lewiston, New York, NY, USA: Edwin Mellen Press.

Ayodele, Thompson (2003) "Trade & development-Trade, Not Aid: What Africa Needs," *National Review*. Retrieved 7/27/2007 from the World Wide Webb: http://findarticles.com/p/articles/mi_m1282/is_17_55/ai_107223567; Internet.

Bandura, A. (1973) *Aggression: A Social Learning Analysis*. Englewood Cliffs, New Jersey, USA: Prentice Hall.

Bayart, J. (1989) *L'Etat en Afrique: La Politique du Ventre*. L'espace du Politique Series. Paris, France: Fayard.

BBC NEWS/Africa/Cameroon Corruption Hinders AIDS Fight (2007) Retrieved 1/6/2007 from the World Wide Web: http://news.bbc.co.uk/2/hi/africa/6198337.stm; Internet.

BBC News/Africa/Cameroon Dances to Anti-graft Beat (2007) Retrieved 1/4/2008 from the World Wide Web: http://news.bbc.co.uk/2/hi/africa/7131637.stm; Internet.

BBC News/Africa, "Cameroon Tracks 'Ghost Workers'" (2007) Retrieved 1/4/2008 from the World Wide Web: http://news.bbc.co.uk/2/hi/africa/4785721.stm; Internet.

BBC NEWS/Africa/Child Shot Dead in Cameroon Drama (2008) Retrieved 2/28/2008 from the World Web: http://newsvote.bbc.co.uk/mpapps/pagetools/print/news.bbc.co.uk/2/hi/Africa/7268861.stm; Internet.

BBC NEWS/Business/Cameroon Uncovers Salary Scandal (2005) Retrieved 2 March, 2005 from the World Wide Web: http://www.bbc.co.uk; Internet.

BBC NEWS/World/Africa/Country Profiles Cameroon (2005) Retrieved November 3, 2005 from the World Wide Web: http://www.news.bbc.co.uk; Internet.

BBC NEWS/World/Africa/Country profiles/country profile (2005) Retrieved 12 February, 2005 from the World Wide Web: http://www.bbc.co.uk; Internet.

BBC NEWS/World/Africa/Frustration Threatens Cameroon Calm (2004) Retrieved 7 January, 2004 from the World Wide Web: http://www.bbc.co.uk; Internet.

BBC News/World/Africa/Tardy Cameroon Workers Locked Out (2005) Retrieved 14 January, 2005 from the World Wide Web: http://bbc.co.uk; Internet.

Beccaria, C. (1776) Dei delitti e della pen. (On Crimes and Punishments), translated by Henry Paolucci, New York, NY, USA: The Liberal Arts Press, 1963.

Berg, B. (2005) *Qualitative Research Methods for the Social Sciences*. Boston, Massachusetts, USA and London, England: Allyn and Bacon.

Berry, S. (1991) *Copping with Confusion: African Farmers' Responses to Economic Instability in the 1970's and 1980's*. Unpublished manuscript, Johns Hopkins University, Baltimore, Maryland, USA.

Black, H. C. (1990) *Black's Law Dictionary*, 6th ed. Centennial Edition (1891-1991); St. Paul, Minnesota, USA: West Publishing.

Bursik, R. J. (1988) "Social Disorganization and Theories of Crime and Delinquency: Problems and Prospects," *Criminology*, 26:519-551.

Bursik, R. and H. Grasmick (1992) *Neighborhoods and Crime: The Dimensions of Effective Community Control*. Lexington, Massachusetts, USA: Lexington Books.

Cameroon Tribune: www.cameroon-tribune.net/Samedi 25 Mars 2006 Douala Police Make Another Big Catch, 3/25/2006.

Cameroon Tribune: www.cameroon-tribune.net/Samedi 25 Mars 2006 Toward a Judiciary Code of Conduct, 3/25/ 2006.

Crime and Society: A Comparative Criminological Tour of the World (Cameroon):http://www-rohan.sdsu.edu/faculty/rwinslow/africa/cameroon.html; Internet. Retrieved December 2010.

Cuffe, J. Cameroon Corruption Hinders AIDS Fight (2007) Retrieved 1/6/2007 from the World Wide Web: http://news.bbc.co.uk/2/hi/africa/6198337.stm; Internet.

Dicklitch, S. (2002) "Failed Democratic Transition in Cameroon: A Human Rights Explanation," *Human Rights Quarterly*, Vol. 24, NO. 1 February, pp. 152-176.

Eker, V. (1981) "On the Origins of Corruption: Irregular Incentives in Nigeria," *The Journal of Modern African Studies*, Vol. 19, No. 1 March, pp.173-182.

Fairchild, E. and H. Dammer (2001) *Comparative Criminal Justice Systems*. 2nd. Edition, Belmont, California, USA: Wadsworth/Thompson Learning.

Fombad, C. (2002) "Cameroon," in H. Kritzer, *Legal Systems of the World: A Political, Social, & Cultural Encyclopedia*. Vol. 1, Santa Barbara, Californis, USA: ABC-CLIO, pp. 245-252.

Gibson, J. (2002) "Truth, Justice, and Reconciliation: Judging the Fairness of Amnesty in South Africa," *American Journal of political Science*, Vol.46, No. 3, pp. 540-556.

Glaser, D. (1997) *Profitable Penalties: How to Cut Both Crime Rates and Costs*. Thousand Oaks, California, USA: Pine Forge Press.

Hall, J. (1961) *General Principles of Criminal Law*, 2nd ed. Indianapolis: Bobbs-Merrill.

Hart, H. (1968) *Punishment and Responsibility*. New York, NY, USA: Oxford University Press.

Hodgson, J. (2004) "The Detention and Interrogation of Suspects in Police Custody in France: A Comparative Account," *European Journal of Criminology, 1(2)*, 163-199.

Ingraham, B.L. (1987) *The Structure of Criminal Procedure: Laws and Practice of France, the Soviet Union, China, and the United States*. New York, NY, USA:

Greenwood Press.

Jeeves, A. (2004) "Assessing a Decade of Democracy in South Africa," *Canadian Journal of African Studies*, Vol. 38, No.3, pp. 505-520.

Kentor, J. (2001) "The Long Term Effects of Globalization on Income Inequality, Population Growth, and Economic Development," *Social Problems*. Vol. 48, No. 4, pp. 435-455.

Kitching, G. (1980) *Class and Economic Change in Kenya*. New Haven, Connecticut, USA: Yale University Press.

Kitching, G. (1982) *Development in Historical Perspective*. London, England: Methuen.

Kitching, G. (1987) "The Role of the National Bourgeoisie in the Current Phase of Capitalist Development," in Lubeck, 1987, pp. 27-55.

Konings, P. & F. Nyamnjoh (2003) *Negotiating an Anglophone Identity: A Study of the Politics of Recognition and Representation in Cameroon*. Leiden and Boston, Massachusetts, USA: Brill Afrika- Studiecentrum Series, No. 1.

Lubeck, P. (1992) "The Crisis of African Development: Conflicting Interpretations and Resolutions," *Annual Review of Sociology*: Vol. 18, pp. 519-540.

Luksetich, W. and White, M. (1982) *Crime and Public Policy: An Economic Approach*. Boston, Massachusetts, USA: Little, Brown, and Company.

Mbom, L. (2009) Jungle Justice. http://www.thefrontiertelegraph.com?p179; Internet. Retrieved 12/9/2009.

Mensah, A. (2005) "Vigilante Homicides in Contemporary Ghana," *Journal of Criminal Justice*, Vol. 33, Issue 5, September-October, pp.413-427.

Merton, R. (1938) "Social Structure and Anomie," *American Sociological Review* 3: 672-682.

Messner, S. and R. Rosenfeld (1994) *Crime and the American Dream*. Belmont, California, USA: Wadsworth Publishing.

Mill, J. (1859) *On Liberty*. Tokyo, Japan: Kenkyusha.

Musevini, Y. (2000) *What is Africa's Problem*? Minneapolis, Minnesota, USA: University of Minnesota Press.

New Anti-corruption Drive Leaves Many Skeptical (2006) Retrieved on 3/6/2006 from the World Wide Web: www.irinnews.org/report.asp?ReportID=51385 & Select Region=West_Africa Select; Internet.

Nomiya, D., Miller, A, and Hoffman, J. (2000) "Urbanization and Rural Depletion in Modern Japan: An Analysis of Crime and Suicide Patterns," *International Journal of Comparative and Applied Criminal Justice*, Spring. vol. 24, No.1 pp.1-18.

Nonet, P. and Kagan R. Selznick (2001) *Societies in Transition: Toward Responsive Law*. New Brunswick, New Jersey, USA: Transaction Publishers.

Nyerere, J. (1970) "Education for Self-reliance," in Cartey, W. & M. Kilson (Eds.), *The Africa Reader: Independent Africa* (pp. 237-255). New York, NY, USA:

Vintage Books.

Ocheje, P. (2001) "Law and Social Change: A Socio-Legal Analysis of Nigeria's Corrupt Practices and Other Related Offences 2000," *Journal of African Law*, Vol. 45, No. 2, pp. 173-195.

Okafọ, N. (2009) *Reconstructing Law and Justice in a Postcolony*. Surrey, England and Burlington, USA: Ashgate Publishing.

Phillips, S., A. Erkanli, G. Keeler, E. Costello, & A. Angold (2006) "Disentaling the High Risks: Parent Criminal Justice Involvement and Children's Exposure to Family Risks," *Criminology & Public Policy* Vol. 5, No. 4, pp. 677-702.

Reichel, P. (2005) *Comparative Criminal Justice Systems*. 4th Edition, Upper Saddle River, New Jersey: Pearson/Prentice Hall.

Reichel, P. (2008) *Comparative Criminal Justice Systems: A Topical Approach*. 5th. Edition. Upper Saddle River, New Jersey: Pearson/Prentice Hall.

Robinson, M. B. (2002) *Justice Blind? Ideals and Realities of American Criminal Justice*. Upper Saddle River, New Jersey: Prentice Hall.

Samaha, J. (2008) *Criminal Law* 9th ed. Belmont, California, USA: Thomson Learning.

Sampson, R. J., and B. W. Groves (1989) "Community Structure and Crime: Testing Social Disorganization Theory," *American Journal of Sociology*, 94: 774-802.

Sekhonyane, M. and Louw, A. (2002) *Violent Justice: Vigilantism and the State's Response*. Institute for Security Studies, Pretoria, South Africa.

Sender, J. and S. Smith (1986) *The Development of Capitalism in Africa*. London, England: Methuen.

Shaw, C. and H. McKay (1942) *Juvenile Delinquency and Urban Areas*. Chicago, Illinois, USA: University Press.

Smith, D. and R. Jarjoura (1989) "Household Characteristics, Neighborhood Composition and Victimization Risk," *Social Forces*, 68(2): 621-640.

Stark, R. (1987) "Deviant Places: A Theory of the Ecology of Crime," *Criminology*, 25: 893-909.

Takougeg, J. and M. Krieger (1998) *African State and Society in the 1990s: Cameroon's Political Crossroads*. Boulder, Colorado, USA: Westview Press.

Time, V. (2000) "Legal Pluralism and Harmonization of Law: An Examination of the Process of Reception and Adoption of both Civil and Common Law in Cameroon and their Coexistence with Indigenous Laws," *International Journal of Comparative and Applied Criminal Justice*, Vol. 24, No. 1, pp. 19-29.

Transparency International (2003) Corruption Surveys and Indexes. www.transparency.org/faq-corruption.html; Internet. Retrieved July 20, 2003.

Transparency International (2006) Corruption Surveys and Indexes. www.

transparency.org/faq-corruption.html; Internet. Retrieved May 5, 2006.

Transparency International (2007) Corruption Surveys and Indexes. www.transparency.org/faq-corruption.html; Internet. Retrieved September 10, 2007.

UN (2009) Country Data. www.undp.org/en/profiles/CMR/html. Retrieved October, 5, 2009. United Nations Food Programme, in United Nations-OCHA IRIN Africa News, 22 September 2005. Retrieved 11/5/2005 from the World Wide Web: http://www.irinnews.org..; Internet.

U.S. Committee for Refugees and Immigrants (2005) Retrieved 4 February 2005 from the World Wide Web: http:/www.refugeereports.org; Internet.

Warren, B. (1980) *Imperialism: Pioneer of Capitalism*. London, England: New Left Books.

Werlin, H. (1972 July) "The Roots of Corruption: The Ghanaian Experience," *The Journal of Modern African Studies*, Vol. 10, No. 2, pp. 247-266.

Werlin, H. (March 1973) "The Consequences of Corruption: The Ghanaian Experience," *Political Science Quarterly*, Vol. 88, No. 1, pp. 71-85.

Zalman, M. (2008) Criminal Procedure; Constitution and Society. 5th ed. Upper Saddle River, New Jersey, USA: Pearson/Prentice Hall.

Chapter 7

Law Enforcement in Postcolonial Africa: Interfacing Indigenous and English Policing in Nigeria[1]

Chukwunọnso Okafọ

University of Nigeria

[1]Reprinted by permission of the International Police Executive Symposium, from Working Paper Series, Number 7, May 2007.

Abstract

Most postcolonial African countries are faced with the challenge of reconciling different and often conflicting indigenous and foreign law enforcement systems. The lack of honest, genuine efforts by the postcolonial African State to manage and resolve the conflicts for the welfare of the generality of the citizens exacerbates the anomie engendered by the conflict situations. Nigeria, while not by any means the only postcolonial African State in this situation, typifies it. Successive Nigerian postcolonial governments have ignored, and often fought against, the country's normally effective, efficient, and widely used indigenous law enforcement and social control systems. The official governments' hostilities notwithstanding, the indigenous systems persist and are in general use throughout Nigeria. This article argues that law enforcement in postcolonial Nigeria should be redesigned to reflect the centrality of the indigenous systems in Nigerians' lives.

Introduction

Social control in postcolonial Nigeria, and most of Africa, is largely divisible into indigenous and foreign types. In the Nigerian example, the indigenous variety is rooted in various Nigerian traditions, customs, and indigenous laws (*Grounded Law*), while the foreign type is English in origin and bears the hallmarks of European culture. It is true that over the years the English social control system in Nigeria has taken on some local Nigerian coloration. Nonetheless, it remains fundamentally English and European. Thus, it is mostly alien to Nigerians. In the present Nigerian setup, the foreign system is expected to anticipate and regulate lives that are mainly alien to the system. The lifestyle of a Nigerian or other African seems fundamentally different from that of an English or other European. For this reason, the English social control system in Nigeria may be unsuitable to effectively regulate relationships in Nigeria.

The observation that the English-based law enforcement system may not sufficiently guarantee a stable postcolonial Nigeria appears to contradict the country's "modern" status. To many Nigerians and Africans, a postcolonial, modern nation should earnestly pursue social control consistent with the systems and techniques bequeathed to it by its ex-colonizer. According to this line of reasoning, Nigeria's modern social control has to fundamentally agree with the colonial era British system in Nigeria or its postcolonial version. In any case, this way of thinking argues further, social control in postcolonial Nigeria ought to be mostly, if not entirely, consistent with the imported British type. This is a rather curious and unfortunate line of reasoning. There is nothing universal about a European social control system. The English system, as an example, developed from the traditions, customs, and native practices (tribal laws) of England. Thus, the English system is perhaps best suited to regulate relationships among the English people, not among Nigerians.

The prevailing postcolonial setup in Nigeria allows dual social control systems (foreign and indigenous). However, successive Nigerian governments – like those of most African States – invest a great deal of resources in promoting foreign social control systems over the indigenous systems. But, since the foreign systems reflect foreign (usually European) norms rather than African norms, the average African experiences a confused (normless) condition in which the official governing rules of conduct differ from, and do not reflect, the indigenous expectations or practices. Such is the case in Nigeria (Okafọ, 2005, September 23).

Despite the African elites' and official governments' tendencies to advocate and promote European social control systems over their indigenous African counterparts, the African systems persist. In the Nigerian example, several factors account for this.

Factors Enabling Indigenous Social Control in a Modern African State

The prevalence and, many would argue, efficacy of indigenous social control in postcolonial African States is well established (see as examples: Nzimiro, 1972; Okereafọezeke, 1996; 2002; Elechi, 2006; Okafọ, 2009). With the Nigerian State example, this section of this article identifies and briefly examines the reasons grounding indigenous social control. Okafọ (2005, March 1), referring to the August 2004 Ọkịja incident (in which the Nigeria Police Force recovered dozens of human skulls and decaying bodies at the site of Ogwugwu Isiula, Ọkịja, a traditional Igbo shrine in Ọkịja town, Anambra State) as an example of traditional social control gone bad, asks:

> "Why do the Ọkịja's ... exist and flourish among us?" The fact that Nigeria's official *Criminal Code* criminalizes the type of traditional crime management that apparently occurred in the August 2004 Ọkịja incident makes this question particularly relevant. The *Code* defines this form of native-based crime management as a "trial by ordeal" punishable under sections 207-213. In view of this strong, negative official attitude toward this traditional process, those Nigerians that persist in managing their civil and criminal cases through the deities must be doing so for compelling reasons.

Okafọ (2005, March 1) goes on to identify several explanations for the continued existence and critical role of the Ọkịja's and other indigenous agencies of law and order in Nigeria (see also Okereafọezeke, 2006).

The following are five of the explanations (see Okafọ, 2005, March 1; Okereafọezeke, 2006). One, (Perceived) Ineffectiveness and Inefficiency of English Law and Justice: In the face of rising crimes, particularly violent personal and property crimes, many, perhaps most, Nigerians view the English system of law and justice in Nigeria as ineffective and inefficient for social control in the country. Two, Alienation From the British-Imposed, English System: The imposed English-based common law system of social control in Nigeria lacks the foundation that it enjoys in its native England. The common law in Nigeria is bereft of the cultural foundation it enjoys in England. Three, Pride in Culture: The continuation and expansion of Nigeria's indigenous social control systems partly derive from many Nigerians' natural human impulse to resist British "substitutive interaction" (Okereafọezeke, 2002, pp. 18-20) policies toward Nigeria. By these policies, colonial Britain sought to destroy, emasculate, or substitute Nigeria's indigenous systems and practices with their British versions. Four, Mounting Evidence Against a "Developing, Modern Nigeria": In virtually every respect, the institutions and infrastructure of the Nigerian State (electricity, roads, medical care, educational institutions, elections organization and supervision, etc.) have degraded substantially. Today, these institutions and infrastructure are, in most cases, far worse than they were under imperial British rule, mainly because of entrenched official corruption. The highly questionable and widely condemned 2007 Nigerian "elections" evince the immensity of official corruption in the country. Witnessing the images of the failures of the Nigerian State, the citizens understandably focus on their ethnic nations and indigenous systems to regulate relationships.[1] Five, Desire for Quick, Inexpensive Justice: Justice in Nigeria's English-based official system is too expensive, time consuming, and insensitive to the indigenous Nigerian culture. The country's indigenous social control mechanisms, on the other hand, appear to satisfy Nigerians' yearnings for quicker, less expensive, and culturally relevant justice and social order.

The five explanations offered in Okafọ (2005, March 1) for the continued and growing uses of indigenous social control in modern Nigeria support the view that the tradition will not die anytime soon. There are compelling religious, cultural, philosophical, ethnic, and material reasons, as well as reasons of official government ineffectiveness, inefficiency, citizens' pride, belief, fear, apathy, and limited resources for Nigerians to use their indigenous social controls, rather than the English-based system. The practice will likely continue and probably

---

[1] It should be added that the 2011 general elections, presided over by Attahiru Jega, appeared to substantially improve on the 2007 debacle, which Maurice Iwu led. Many voters as well as Nigerian and foreign election monitors and observers concluded that overall the 2011 elections were free and fair, and that the results reflected the votes cast in the process. However, time will tell whether or not the gains made in the 2011 elections will be sustained to convince the citizens to have a more positive view of the country.

expand as more people lose faith in the English-based system. As in other African countries, as long as the foregoing reasons persist in Nigeria, indigenous systems and practices of order maintenance and other social control will remain strong even in a "modern" Nigeria.

For more in-depth examination of the August 2004 Okija incident and the factors enabling indigenous social control in modern Nigeria, see Chapter 2.

With particular focus on law enforcement and based on the Nigerian example, the following sections of this article examine the role of indigenous systems in policing and order maintenance as well as the nature of the relationship between the indigenous systems and the official, European-based law enforcement systems.

Relationship Between Indigenous and Foreign Law Enforcement in Postcolonial Africa

Similar to other aspects of social control, justice, and law in indigenous Africa, there is strong evidence that the traditional mechanisms for security maintenance, crime prevention, and general law enforcement remain strikingly relevant in modern Africa. In pre-colonial Africa, the details of the mechanisms varied from one community to another. Nevertheless, the general theme was the furtherance of control, justice, and law in the African societies by using the applicable indigenous strategies and techniques. The indigenous strategies of control, justice, and law in each pre-colonial African society had grown out of the society's traditions, customs, and native laws. Some aspects of social control in contemporary Africa are similar to the pre-colonial practices.

In traditional Africa, security maintenance, crime prevention, and general law enforcement are based on each society's historical circumstances and desires. Thus, most members of each society willfully partake in programs and activities to prevent and control crimes and deviant behaviors. Community members, individually and collectively, play roles in each society's law enforcement efforts. Community members generally accept the group's methods and procedures for security maintenance, crime prevention, and general law enforcement. One of the main reasons for the wide acceptance and celebration of the indigenous methods and procedures is that the citizens tend to know their society's control, justice, and law personnel well. The citizens have a reasonable knowledge of each office holder's morals, values, and ethics. Since the citizens of an indigenous society have direct and indirect influences on their control, justice, and law personnel, persons whose morals, values, and/or ethics are at variance with the general societal standards are unlikely to occupy or remain in their assigned positions.

The security maintenance, crime prevention, and general law enforcement duties in a traditional African community devolve on various community institutions, groups, and members. The obligations fall on such community structural levels of government as the Family, the Extended Family, the Village, the Village Group, the Town, and the Community of Towns based on well understood geographical and subject matter jurisdictional considerations. At each government and administration level, there are provisions for security maintenance, crime prevention, and general law enforcement by the entire community acting together or, as is more often the case, through their elected or appointed representatives as well as by specialized agencies, such as the Age Grades. For instance, a Young Men's Age Grade among the Igbos of Nigeria may be charged with the responsibility of security maintenance and general law enforcement. Community members may mandate and expect the Young Men's Age Grade to use commonly sanctioned vigilantism to prevent crimes by identifying, apprehending, and processing persons suspected of committing crimes. The Age Grade's other responsibilities may include enforcement of judicial decisions, such as by means of *oriri iwu* (retrieving a fine) or *igba ekpe* (publicly shaming and humiliating a criminal) (Okereafọezeke, 1996; 2002). In addition, as in the pre-colonial era, the *mmanwụ* (masquerade) in postcolonial Igbo has, among other things, the task of law and order maintenance in some cases:[2]

> You also have the masquerade cult *mmanwụ* as a [traditional] government functionary. Much of the function of these masquerades is to effect obedience to the sanctions of the town on a culprit. These masquerades could invade a culprit's home, and seize all his belongings until the owner paid the stipulated fine for his crime, and again reclaimed his property by a further fine. This police action of the masquerades is generally referred to as *iri iwu*. Some masquerades, the clever one of the young boys, called *Iga*, also kept surveillance over the village streams during the dry season, to see that water wasn't misused (oral historical account by a witness, Noo Udala, aged c. 102 years, native of Ụmụaga, Agbaja, Igbo, quoted in Isichei, 1978, p. 74).[2]

Security maintenance, crime prevention, and general law enforcement in postcolonial Africa involve contests and struggles between indigenous and foreign (colonially imposed European) ideals (Okereafọezeke, 2002; 2006). The official governments of modern African countries have either adopted the colonially imposed European models or created such foreign ideals in the respective postcolonial countries. Whatever its form, the prevailing situation gives rise to

---

[2] Italics are in the original source.

many systemic conflicts between indigenous and foreign models of social control, justice, and law in Africa. For instance, the Nigeria Police Force (NPF),[3] which the British colonialists patterned for Nigeria after the alien British security and law enforcement models, lacks indigenous Nigerian foundation and is structurally and procedurally a stranger to Nigerians. Regardless, successive Nigerian governments since the country's independence have favored the imposed foreign model over the indigenous law enforcement systems. Thus, the Nigerian NPF – as its equivalent police organizations in most other contemporary African States – has officially assumed the security maintenance, crime prevention, and general law enforcement functions that the indigenous security systems performed in the pre-colonial era. As a result of African governments' official emphasis on the foreign models, these governments use a lot of human and material resources to pursue and apply to African conditions strategies that are designed for other (usually, European and American) conditions. The pursuit and application of the foreign strategies is mostly done without making honest efforts to respond to the African circumstances that differ substantially from those of the West (see Onyechi, 1975).

For several reasons, the security maintenance, crime prevention, and general law enforcement systems in postcolonial Africa, exemplified here by the Nigeria Police Force (NPF), are incapable of satisfying the security and law enforcement needs of the citizens. The origins of the foreign-styled systems should further inform the reader about the limited capabilities of these systems. For example, the NPF can be traced directly to the colonial era British West African Frontier Force (BWAFF), which the British created for their colonized populations in West Africa. Therefore, it is not surprising that both the BWAFF and the NPF follow largely the same structure, philosophy, and model as the British idea of public security and policing. As a result, the NPF can be identified as little more than a throwback to the period of Nigerians' subjugation to colonial Britain. The NPF is largely foreign to Nigeria's indigenous law enforcement systems and practices. Its foreign structure and mainly unquestionable powers over the citizens, among other factors, demonstrate the NPF's inconsistency with Nigerians' traditional models and forms of law enforcement and social control.

Several other factors compound the divide between Africa's official security and law enforcement systems, on the one hand, and the indigenous systems, on the other hand. These factors include unjustified unitary policing,

---

[3] Early in its tenure, the President Olusegun Obasanjo regime (1999-2007) stated that it wanted the "Nigeria Police Force" changed to "Nigeria Police" to de-emphasize the police use of force in its dealings with the citizens and promote cooperation between the police and the citizens. These would make the police more effective and efficient. It was an open question whether the name change would increase the effectiveness or efficiency of the country's official policing. In the years since the government's statement, insecurity of lives and properties in Nigeria, and general lawlessness, has deteriorated beyond their pre-1999 levels.

police corruption, and insufficient number of police officers and personnel. Corruption in African police organizations appears to be widespread. Apart from incidents of the police demanding and receiving bribes or "settlements" from sometimes equally corrupt citizens, many police officers and personnel actively participate in criminal activities. Sometimes in Nigeria, police officers plan and commit serious crimes, such as robbery and murder, against the citizens that the police are supposed to protect. Police officers alone may commit the crimes or the officers may commit the crimes in conspiracy with civilian criminals. A Nigerian case in which three policemen were tried and sentenced to death for the murders of defenseless traders is illustrative. The policemen, while on official duty, burned the commuting traders alive in the victims' motor vehicle and stole over one million Naira belonging to the victims. The victims were traveling to a wholesale market to purchase goods for resale (see "Three Policemen to Die for Setting Traders Ablaze", in *The Guardian*, April 3, 2001).

A case such as that of the three murderous police officers contributes a lot to the citizens' lack of trust in the official police. However, the lack of trust is not limited to Nigeria. Hammer (1993) reports that in one case in Kenya, a woman was robbed of jewelry worth fifty thousand dollars. She reported the crime at the local police station. To her consternation, she recognized that the police officer recording her report was wearing one of her stolen diamond rings! Could a crime victim in such a situation have faith in the police?

In Nigeria, the negative images of the country's official police undoubtedly lead many honest potential police officers to avoid the NPF by pursuing other careers. Thus, the negative police image leads to the exclusion of decent citizens from official policing. Consequently, less honest and less effective people generally staff Nigeria's official law enforcement system. I suspect that this is similar to the situation in many other African countries. The fact that many of these official police organizations employ far less than the number of officers and personnel needed to adequately police their countries worsens the situation.

Also of critical importance is the fact that most of the official governments in Africa run their police organizations as unitary agencies, often to be manipulated to serve the shortsighted interests of the prevailing regime, rather than as broad-based democratic institutions to be used to maintain public security, prevent crime, and generally enforce laws for the greater public good. While professing constitutional federalism, many African governments, such as Nigeria's, insist on rigidly unified official police. Such an organization, no matter how large, answers to one person. As in the colonial era, the unitary model makes it easier for the rulers to dominate and control their population.

If any objective Nigerian had an illusion about the quality of law enforcement by the NPF, that illusion should have disappeared after the so-called 2007 elections in the country. In the April 14 and 21, 2007 exercises, the trio of

President Olusegun Obasanjo leading the ruling PDP party, Maurice Iwu leading the Independent National Electoral Commission (INEC), and Sunday Ehindero leading the NPF participated in giving Nigerians one of the worst elections in postcolonial Africa, perhaps in the world. Nigerian and international elections observers expressed shock and unanimous condemnation of the exercise, with the European Union calling it a "charade". Weeks before the exercise, President Obasanjo had described the coming elections as "a do or die affair" for him and his party. A couple of days after his comment, the media pressed Obasanjo to clarify his earlier statement. He barefacedly repeated his hugely unpatriotic comment. True to his intolerant posture, the 2007 elections showed that he and his PDP lived up to his prophecy of "winning" at all costs.

The NPF and INEC roles in actualizing the Obasanjo script are shameful and damning. Ostensibly, the NPF directly or indirectly aided the ruling PDP and its agents in manipulating the 2007 elections and results for the PDP. In some instances, ballot papers were thumb printed and ballot boxes stuffed contrary to the elections procedure. Where the thumb printing could not be completed quickly, fictitious election results were written declaring PDP candidates the winners, regardless of the votes. The extent of the official corruption among the PDP, INEC, and the NPF was so brazen that the INEC felt comfortable in declaring the then PDP governorship candidate in Anambra State, Emmanuel Andrew Uba, as the winner, twice. The first time, the number of votes allocated to him was so high that the alleged votes exceeded the number of registered voters in the state; so that even if there had been 100% voting by the registered voters in the state (an impossibility), the allocated votes would have been higher. INEC Chairman Maurice Iwu and his hatchet men, realizing their stupidity in not being able to count and total figures, revised the numbers to present a second set of figures, which INEC considered more believable than the first. Based on either the first or the second set of numbers, the ruling PDP received undue advantage over the other political parties. The extent of the corruption involved in the elections was startling, and the IGP Sunday Ehindero NPF's willingness to serve the narrow ends of one political party at the expense of the majority of Nigerians was stunning.

Patterns of Indigenous Security Maintenance, Crime Prevention, and Other Law Enforcement

The following hypothesis guides the discussion in this section of this paper: "An unsatisfactory system of official security maintenance, crime prevention, and law enforcement in a modern African community will lead to an increase in a demand for alternative (unofficial, sometimes extra-legal) security and law enforcement systems and organizations aimed at addressing the citizens' desire for secure and ordered lives."[4] Instances of African countries in which the citizens generally yearn for alternatives to the official security and law enforcement systems abound. However, suffice it to cite Cameroon, Kenya, Nigeria, and South Africa as some of the countries that are popularly regarded as having ineffective official police forces and other official crime prevention structures. See Okereafọezeke (1996; 2002; 2003; 2006; Okafọ, 2009) for Nigerian examples. Some other examples are discussed below. Considering the utility of the indigenous systems in the prevailing circumstances, there is an incontrovertible need in many African countries for each government to recognize and promote the relevant indigenous systems of security maintenance, crime prevention, and general law enforcement.

Instances of unofficial, indigenous security and law enforcement systems and organizations abound in Africa. It seems that the generally held view that the official, Western-style systems and organizations are incapable of providing needed security and law enforcement has strengthened the indigenous systems. The other related reason for the re-emergence of the unofficial security and law enforcement organizations is that most citizens regard the official organizations as imposed, irrelevant, and different in forms and procedures from the citizens' traditional outlooks, convictions, practices, and beliefs. In Nigeria, for example, there are the more prominent *Bakassi Boys* of the Igbo, the *Hisha* of the Hausa/ Fulani, and the *Odu'a Peoples Congress* (*OPC*) of the Yoruba, among many other indigenous law enforcement and social control organizations. Each of the relevant state governments in Nigeria officially charges the Hisha, an Islam-based law enforcement organization, with the responsibility of enforcing the laws in the state's *shari'a*[5] system. Note that until about the middle of year 2000, the *Hisha* had no official legal backing in Nigeria. In fact, the form of the *shari'a* that the *Hisha* is now directed in many northern Nigerian states to enforce came into being in 2000/2001. The *Bakassi Boys* and the *OPC* are not as religious-based as the *Hisha*. Nonetheless, the *Bakassi Boys* and the *OPC* often use indigenous African religious beliefs and practices to insure the supernatural powers with which the organizations operate.

In the southeastern states of Nigeria where the *Bakassi Boys* operate, the organization is widely regarded as an effective public security and law enforcement group. The organization is, over and above the official Nigeria Police Force, the *de facto* guarantor of public security particularly in the Igbo area of the country. The *Bakassi Boys* are reputed to be so good that they are capable of identifying a criminal despite attempts to conceal his or her identity. The *Bakassi*

---

[4] A similar hypothesis regarding an unsatisfactory official judiciary is the basis for Chapter 2 (Challenging "Law" and "Justice" Through Alternative Social Control).

[5] Islam-based law and justice.

Boys move from one community to another fishing out suspected criminals (mainly perennial thieves, armed robbers, and murderers), arresting, and quickly judging and punishing the criminals. The punishment is typically death, which is applied swiftly by decapitating and burning the adjudged criminal. In my summer 2000-2006 field trips to Nigeria, most of the locals with whom I discussed the *Bakassi Boys'* operations expressed satisfaction with, and enthusiastic support for, the *Bakassi Boys'* crime-fighting activities. Most of the locals expressed confidence that the *Bakassi Boys* are able to accurately identify a criminal even among a large group of people, thus avoiding misidentification or punishment of an innocent person. To provide an update on this citizen's perspective, since 2006 I have travelled to Nigeria every year for research. The *Bakassi Boys* remain widely popular, particularly in the southeastern states. However, there have been several efforts by the NPF and the Nigerian government to abolish or limit the operations of the *Bakassi Boys*. As a result, the areas of operation of the *Bakassi Boys* have been substantially reduced.

The *Bakassi Boys*, the *Hisha*, and the *OPC* illustrate the large, coordinated, and well-organized indigenous organizations for security, crime prevention, and law enforcement in African societies. As indicated, these organizations, which were initially conceived as purely *unofficial, indigenous groups* for law enforcement, later assumed positions as *official, indigenous-based (or in the case of the Hisha, religious-based) groups*. Their new positions stemmed from the fact that the various official governments, through laws, formally recognized the different organizations, even though the organizations continue to operate based largely on indigenous ideals of social control, justice, and law. However, as I mentioned in the preceding paragraph, the Nigerian government, particularly at the federal level, strongly opposes the adoption of the *Bakassi Boys* and other indigenous law enforcement groups by various state governments in the country. The federal government under President Obasanjo (1999-2007) went so far as to use the NPF to intimidate, stifle, and break up the *Bakassi Boys*.

Apart from the large, coordinated, and well-organized indigenous law enforcement organizations found in many African countries, there are numerous other groups, such as neighborhood watch organizations or vigilante groups, found in most African communities. Again, these groups result from the ineffectiveness and inefficiency of the official law enforcement organizations.

In Nigeria, for example, the watch organizations or vigilante groups exist to help guarantee security, law, order, and stability to the citizens of each community. Generally, the groups are more active in the night than during the day. Usually, able-bodied young men of each community, supported financially and materially by the other community members, are charged with the task of securing the community and enforcing the law, often with the aids of small weapons, such as machetes, bows and arrows, spears, and some guns. The watchers often seek to limit access to parts of the community by erecting temporary, movable obstacles on the roads that would slow vehicular and human traffic. Whatever their limitations, the neighborhood watch groups (vigilante groups) are deliberate, coordinated efforts at control, justice, and law, even if these groups operate outside the official laws. Moreover, it seems that most citizens are satisfied with the groups' activities.

Other less organized local attempts at social control, justice, and law enforcement are plainly based on *mob action*. These are neither deliberate nor coordinated. Thus, they are typically *ad hoc* and often thoughtless. The persons who seek to enforce the law by this method may take some rash action before thinking through the issues involved. Example, if a person (innocent or guilty) is alleged at a public place in Nigeria, such as an open marketplace, to have stolen another's property, a mob may immediately take brutal action against the accused person, which action may result in death. It may later become apparent that the accused person was, in fact, innocent. By then, it would be too late for the accused. In addition to the obvious undesirability of this result, there are other legitimate concerns regarding indigenous (unofficial) law enforcement.

While recognizing that traditional policing, vigilantism, and mob action may be necessary and beneficial responses to official law enforcement failures, the potential for abuses of traditional policing, vigilantism, and mob action should be highlighted. One of the key features of indigenous law enforcement is its wide acceptance by the citizens. Members of a society to which traditional policing, etc. apply generally accept and participate in their indigenous system. In short, the community members own the indigenous system. As part owners of the system, it is very unlikely that any significant portion of the population will be excluded from the arrangement or its operation. Generally, decisions are made and enforced with members' knowledge and consent. However, as in every human system, there is a danger of abuse of a traditional law enforcement system. This is so particularly where the indigenous (unofficial) and the State (official) policing systems, rather than complement each other positively, collude to abuse the citizens. Anyanwu (2007) reports an example of this.

According to Anyanwu (2007), in a late night and early morning of early February 2007 gun- and machete-brandishing men of a local vigilante group terrorized the inhabitants of Okpoko community in Ogbaru Local Government Area of Anambra State, Nigeria. Community members interviewed for the report informed the reporter that the problem began when a group of people organized themselves, with the assistance of the Nigeria Police Force (NPF) in the area, and imposed the group as a vigilante force. The group imposed levies of 3,000 Naira each on the locals and forced them to pay against their will. Apparently, the levies were intended for funding the vigilante group to secure the community, except that, as the report shows, most community members opposed the arrangement. The vigilante group ignored the wishes of the community members as well as an official court judgment allegedly against the group. In fact, the vigilante group increased the levy amount and, with the active connivance of the NPF, used every (illegal) force at their disposal to force compliance. The spokesman of the community members who went to the Anambra State capital, Awka, and reported the matter to Governor Peter Obi, expressed the community's experiences and pleas to the governor, as follows:

> We have an ugly situation, people forced themselves on us as our vigilance group, while the majority of Okpoko said 'no.' They started extorting money from us and killing us in order to enforce the payment. They started brutalizing people, matcheting us, gunning us down and even the people they shot were taken in a bus to the Government House and the governor saw them. We want the group to be dissolved, we don't want them. We've even gone to court and court even ordered them to stop, still upon the injunction they continued, now the court gave judgment, they continued. The High Court in Onitsha had in its judgment on the matter ruled: "It is never the part of the functions of police to enforce contract, collect rates debts including levies imposed by individuals or group of individuals".

Responding to the complaints, Governor Obi assured the delegation that the Anambra State Government would immediately look into the issue and hold the suspects accountable. I speculate that the Okpoko community members rejected the vigilante group at issue in Anyanwu (2007) for reasons other than a general community opposition to all forms of vigilantism. More likely, the community rejected *this* vigilante group because of questions about the honesty or character of its leaders/members or for the group's deviant/illegal activities. However, it bears repeating that the errant vigilante group is able to defy the community members and continue with its illegal and unpopular activities because the official NPF supports the group.

In view of the NPF support for, and collusion with, the errant vigilante group and the governor's assurance (see Anyanwu, 2007), what realistically can the governor do? The governor of each of Nigeria's thirty-six states is often referred to as the "chief law officer" of the state. But a governor is helpless regarding police control and actions. The governor does not control the police and the police can, and do, ignore the governor's expressed wishes to secure his state. As long as the police comply with the Nigerian president's and Inspector-General of Police (IGP)'s orders and wishes, the police can carry on as they wish. This is so particularly where the governor and the president are political enemies. There are numerous examples in the Olusegun Obasanjo presidency (1999-2007) where Obasanjo, directly by action or indirectly by inaction, used the NPF as an instrument of oppression and opposition to governors perceived as enemies of the president. Some of the presidential abuses of police powers are criminal. Such was the case in July 2003 when Ralph Ige, Assistant Inspector-General of the NPF in charge of Anambra State, led the police and kidnapped Governor Chris Ngige of the state. The police, without legal authority to do so, informed Ngige that he was no longer the governor of the state. For hours, the police detained and prevented him from performing his duties. The police and their civilian co-conspirators purported to swear into office the deputy governor as governor of Anambra. There is no doubt that the police action was a *coup d'etat*, being a forceful, unconstitutional take-over of government. However, Ige, the other participating police personnel, and their civilian collaborators got away with their crimes because President Obasanjo approved of their actions: years after their illegal actions, the criminal suspects have not been charged with any crime. Thus is the overwhelming power of the President over the Governor of a Nigerian State.

However, traditional policing and mob action efforts at security and law enforcement in postcolonial African societies illustrate the ineffectiveness and inefficiency of the official security and law enforcement apparatuses. The unofficial, indigenous alternative systems and models of control, justice, law, security, and enforcement are established and maintained principally because the citizens of the communities where the models operate recognize and accept them as preferred alternatives to the official, Western-based models. The wide acceptance that the indigenous models enjoy over their Western-based counterparts strongly attests to the relevance and currency of the indigenous African systems of control, justice, and law even in the modern State. What is missing is the official State adoption of, and support for, the unofficial efforts to indigenize law enforcement and social control in postcolonial African societies.

Conclusion: Effective Policing of a Postcolony

This article identifies forms of law enforcement in postcolonial Africa. The two main varieties are official governmental and unofficial indigenous law enforcement. Further, the paper uses Nigeria to illustrate the nature of the interactions and relationships between official governmental and unofficial indigenous law enforcement. Overall, there is lack of coordination between the two principal avenues for law enforcement; they tend to operate with little or no effort to strengthen each other. The official governmental system – with the huge financial and other State resources at its disposal – shows little regard for the unofficial indigenous law enforcement. This is so despite the fact that the unofficial indigenous system plays an invaluable role in social control. It seems that the greatest law enforcement challenge facing most postcolonial African States is over-reliance on Western standards in attempts to address Africa's postcolonial social control needs.

The African writer, Ali Mazrui, once advised African countries to re-conceptualize "development" for their use. According to him, these countries should redefine development to suit their individual indigenous needs. A new definition would likely, and I submit should, differ from the European and North American (Western) meaning. The characteristics of Western "development" reflect Western history, belief, culture, and ideals. An African-based definition of "development" should be grounded in African history, tradition, lifestyle, and future. Even though there are likely to be common features of development between Africa and the West, the need to conceptualize and operationalize "development" for Africa's specific needs necessitates a divide between its African and Western meanings. Mazrui's counsel leads to the logical view that effective law enforcement in an African postcolony, such as Nigeria, requires the following. One, an official State understanding and acknowledgment of the current anomic (confused) social control condition in which the process of socializing the average Nigerian differs starkly from many aspects of the behavior standard imposed by the official English-style legal system. Two, honest efforts by State social control agencies to synthesize and blend the imported English-style law enforcement system to Nigeria's indigenous law enforcement systems widely available and applied in all parts of the country, while borrowing useful and relevant ideas from other African and world societies.

Okafọ (2005, September 23) argues that the social control process in Nigeria is in a condition of normlessness. This means that the governing rules of the Nigerian society are conflicting, confusing, and/or differ from the cultures and expectations of many, if not most, Nigerians. The average Nigerian is mostly socialized from birth in his or her cultural expectations and standards of behavior. These expectations and standards are typically rooted in the Nigerian's traditions, customs, and native laws. At a later stage in his or her life, the Nigerian is more prominently confronted with English-style rules and regulations that diverge from the previously learned indigenous norms. The resulting conflict situation creates an anomic condition with legitimate questions about the proper standard of behavior in the society. Okafọ (2005, September 23) recommends the following as ways out of this anomie:

> For a more effective and efficient social control in Nigeria, the official Local, State, and Federal governments, through their respective legislatures, should pass legislations adopting the country's native customs and traditions (customary law) as

the grundnorm (basic law), that is, the fundamental sources of Nigerian law. Formal adoptions (by legislations) of the native customs and traditions will strengthen the customs and traditions. Thereafter, other sources of laws, such as English law, will be used to supplement the basic Nigerian law. While urging the proper Nigerian authorities to reinforce the country's native customs and traditions over the English law, it is equally important to point out that unreasonable, unpopular, and outdated customs and traditions should be discarded and replaced with more progressive principles. Like every postcolonial society, Nigeria should strive to achieve a modern society that maintains a reasonable balance between the welfare and freedom of its citizens and the progress and orderliness of the State. Of course, the Nigerian Bar and Bench will be invaluable partners in these efforts to reengineer law and justice in the country and deemphasize English law.

The present chapter strongly re-asserts the above recommendations for Nigeria. For other African countries, the recommendations can be applied with necessary modifications to accommodate local circumstances.

In conclusion, effective and efficient policing of Nigeria or other African country requires primary emphasis on the country's homegrown laws, not foreign (European and American) laws re-enacted for Africa. Effective and efficient policing of Nigeria or other African country should be based primarily on the enforcement of laws and standards indigenous to the country through enforcement means home-grown in that country (*Grounded Law*). Where and to the extent appropriate, foreign laws, standards, and means of enforcement should only serve as opportunities to augment the indigenous-based system and processes.

References

Afigbo, Adiele E. (1972) *The Warrant Chiefs, Indirect Rule in Southeastern Nigeria 1891 – 1929*. London, England: Longman.

Anyanwu, Geoffrey (2007) "Tyranny of Vigilance Group: They Brutalise Residents Over Illegal Levies," *Daily Sun* (February 28), available at http://www.sunnewsonline.com/webpages/news/national/2007/feb/28/national-28-02-2007 ...; Internet.

Criminal Code (Laws of the Federation of Nigeria).

Elechi, Oko O. (2006) *Doing Justice Without the State: The Afikpo (Ehugbo) Nigeria Model*. New York, USA & London, England: Routledge.

Hammer, Joshua (1993) "Nairobbery," *The New Republic*, November 29, 11-14.

Isichei, Elizabeth (1976) *A History of the Igbo People*. New York, NY, USA: St. Martin's

Press.

Isichei, Elizabeth (1978) *Igbo Worlds: An Anthology of Oral Histories and Historical Descriptions*. Philadelphia, Pennsylvania, USA: Institute for the Study of Human Issues.

Johnson, Samuel (1921/1970) The History of the Yorubas: From the Earliest Times to the Beginning of the British Protectorate. Westport, Connecticut, USA: Negro Universities Press.

Nzimiro, Ikenna (1972) *Studies in Ibo Political Systems: Chieftaincy and Politics in Four Niger States*. Berkeley, California, USA: University of California Press.

Obi, S. N. C. (1963) *The Ibo Law of Property*. London, England: Butterworths.

Okafọ, Nọnso (2005, March 1) "Foundations of *Ọkija* Justice," *NigeriaWorld*, available at http://nigeriaworld.com/articles/2005/mar/033.html; Internet.

Okafọ, Nọnso (2005, September 23) "Customs and Traditions as Answer to a Normless Nigeria," *NigeriaWorld*, available at http://nigeriaworld.com/articles/2005/sep/232.html; Internet.

Okafọ, Nọnso (2006) "Legalism, Tradition, and Terrorism in Nigeria," *The International Journal of African Studies*, Volume 5.2, Winter, pp. 27-61.

Okafọ, Nọnso (2009) *Reconstructing Law and Justice in a Postcolony*. Surrey, England and Burlington, USA: Ashgate Publishing.

Okereafọezeke (Okafọ), Nọnso (1996) The Relationship Between Informal and Formal Strategies of Social Control: An Analysis of the Contemporary Methods of Dispute Processing Among the Igbos of Nigeria, UMI Number 9638581, Ann Arbor, Michigan, USA: University Microfilms.

Okereafọezeke (Okafọ), Nọnso (2002) *Law and Justice in Post-British Nigeria: Conflicts and Interactions Between Native and Foreign Systems of Social Control in Igbo*. Westport, Connecticut, USA: Greenwood Press.

Okereafọezeke (Okafọ), Nọnso (2003) "Traditional Social Control in an Ethnic Society: Law Enforcement in a Nigerian Community," *Police Practice & Research: An International Journal*, ISSN 1561-4263, Volume 4, Number 1 (March), pp. 21-33.

Onyechi, N. M. (1975) "A Problem of Assimilation or Dominance," in T. O. Elias, et al., eds., *African Indigenous Laws: Proceedings of Workshop (7-9 August, 1974)*. Enugu, Nigeria: The Government Printer.

Ottenberg, Simon (1971) *Leadership and Authority in an African Society: The Afikpo Village-Group*. Seattle, Washington, USA: University of Washington Press.

Proclamation No. 6 of 1900 (Laws of the Federation of Nigeria).

Thompson, Bankole R. (1996) "Due Process and Legal Pluralism in Sierra Leone: The Challenge of Reconciling Contradictions in the Laws and Cultures of a

Developing Nation," in C. B. Fields and R. H. Moore, Jr., eds., *Comparative Criminal Justice: Traditional and Nontraditional Systems of Law and Control*. Prospect Hills, Illinois, USA: Waveland Press.

"Three Policemen to Die for Setting Traders Ablaze," *The Guardian* (2001, April 3), available at http://www.ngrguardiannews.com/news2/nn817302.html; Internet.

Chapter 8

Strategies for Credible and Effective Crime Control in Nigeria[1]

Chukwunọnso Okafọ
University of Nigeria

---

[1] This condensed chapter contains the crime control recommendations, which I submitted to the Nigeria Police Force in 2009.

Introduction

Strategies for crime control in a country should continuously evolve to accommodate changing circumstances, ideas, and lessons learned. A country that fails to apply this approach to its law enforcement is likely to experience inefficient and ineffective crime control due mainly to its use of outdated crime control systems and strategies. Notwithstanding the need for evolving law enforcement, there are basic constants in a society's crime control effort. Specifically for policing and other forms of law enforcement, strict adherence to the constitution (or other *grundnorm*) as well as other relevant laws of the society has to be maintained. Also, whatever the changes made to a country's law enforcement, it is vital that only persons of integrity are employed and retained to enforce the law. And a credible mechanism has to be put in place and properly utilized to monitor and ensure that law enforcement personnel comply with the requisite legal and moral standards. Otherwise, the society's crime control effort is liable to fail or be compromised. The adherence-to-the-constitution-and-other-law standard, which is an aspect of the rule of law (see Chapter 1), as well as the need to hire and retain only persons with good character and credibility, equally apply to the other components of a society's crime management system: law making, judiciary, prison/jail (corrections), etc.

However, this Chapter 8 addresses the law enforcement constituent of the Nigerian criminal justice system. It is trite that the Nigerian law enforcement community, exemplified by the Nigeria Police Force (NPF), is burdened by a widespread negative image among Nigerians and non-Nigerians. Much of the negative image was earned through illegal and immoral behaviors by some police personnel (see examples of illegal/immoral police behaviors in Okafọ, 2009, pp. 143-161). On the other hand, there is no doubt that the police have performed well in some instances. But much of the commendable law enforcement work performed by the NPF is largely ignored or overshadowed by their bad conducts. Thus, the wide perception is that the NPF and law enforcement in Nigeria are corrupt, incompetent, and incapable of credible and effective crime control in the country. Numerous unsolved murders and other serious crimes in the country (including the yet-to-be-solved murder of the then Attorney-General of Nigeria, Bola Ige, in 2001) lend credence to the pervasive and strong view among Nigerians and non-Nigerians that the NPF in particular has failed to properly serve and protect the citizens.

In light of the Nigerian law enforcement reality and image, this Chapter succinctly offers specific steps to correct the failures and shortcomings of the NPF. The recommended actions are expected to aid significantly in establishing a credible and effective crime control organization in the country. Consistent with the key requirement that all law enforcement activities should adhere to the Nigerian Constitution and the other relevant laws, there is the need to enact credible, broad-based, and relevant substantive and procedural laws that can be used for effective and efficient crime control in contemporary Nigeria. To a reasonable extent, such laws already exist in the country. However, the proper utilization of the existing laws is lacking. To achieve credible and effective crime control in Nigeria, this Chapter examines specific actions that would lead to this outcome. In some instances, existing laws, institutions, and arrangements may be used to achieve the crime control objective. But, to ensure more effective and efficient crime control, the chapter recommends necessary modifications to the existing institutions and resources. Further, suggestions are offered for the establishment of new organizations, arrangements, and processes, as necessary.

Importance of the Citizen in Crime Control

As in every society, crime control in Nigeria is a function of both reality and perception. The way the citizens view the Nigeria Police Force (*imagined* crime control ability) may be as important as the *real* ability of the organization to control crime. This is because citizens who perceive their law enforcement agency negatively are unlikely to share vital information or otherwise cooperate with the agency in its activities. Therefore, to succeed, the Nigeria Police Force (NPF) ought to recognize and address its *real* as well as *perceived* crime control ability and the obstacles to effective and efficient performance. Because of their uniforms and other official paraphernalia, the NPF agents are perhaps the most visible justice officials. Understandably, other than undercover assignments, official law enforcement actions are normally performed in distinctive attire. It is common for less educated, less informed Nigerians to determine the severity of a breach of society's norm by the presence or absence of the police. In the eyes of the ordinary Nigerian, therefore, law enforcement by the NPF is the most critical component of the country's criminal justice system.

As a corollary, justice scholars, practitioners, and average citizens alike hold and readily offer strong and often fact-based opinions regarding the NPF's effectiveness, efficiency, responsibility to the citizens and communities, professionalism, ethics, etc. Often, substantiated and unsubstantiated police corruption stories spice the strong opinions. True or not, the NPF needs to understand and vigorously address the less-than-flattering image they now carry. The damning image of the NPF continues to seriously undermine the good law enforcement works of some of the officers and personnel of the organization, especially in international law enforcement assignments through such organizations as the United Nations, African Union, and ECOWAS. See as an example the 2009 United Nations award honoring the exemplary services of the NPF in international peacekeeping assignments: Ibulubo (2009); "UN Commends Nigeria Police for Peace Keeping Role" (2009).

Now, here is an important question. How can the NPF become more effective and efficient in crime control and at the same time respond better to the image problem from which it suffers? It must be acknowledged that the image problem of the NPF is likely to disappear once the agency's substantive performance shortcomings are addressed. As soon as the NPF performs its duties well, the citizens and outside observers are sure to view the agency favorably. Therefore, some of the recommendations in this paper deal with the image issue, while the majority of the recommendations target substantive law enforcement changes. In *Reconstructing Law and Justice in a Postcolony* (2009), I addressed in detail the necessary changes to re-design the law and justice system of a post-colony, such as Nigeria's. Such law and justice reconstruction will take a long time to plan and implement. Before (or as part of) a full-scale reconstruction of the Nigerian law and justice system, many positive changes can be made to Nigerian law enforcement. Therefore, suffice it here to identify and briefly explain the specific actions the NPF can take to immediately improve crime control in the country. Taking the recommended steps will substantially improve the effectiveness and efficiency of law enforcement in Nigeria.

Consistent with the theme of this book, the changes offered in this chapter for improved law enforcement in Nigeria will greatly involve Nigerians – beyond law enforcement officials – in the control of crime in their communities. The changes will extend, to a much greater extent than currently obtains, crime control to average Nigerians and their community (non-governmental) groups and institutions.

Changes Proposed for the NPF

Considering the current state of law enforcement – and criminal justice in general – in Nigeria, the following changes are necessary to significantly improve crime control in the country (see Okafọ, 2009 for further discussion of the needed law enforcement changes). As the chief crime control organization in Nigeria, the NPF is at the center of the analysis and recommendations in this chapter. This is not to say that the NPF necessarily has to perform all the crime control functions. Instead, it means that the organization has to lead the crime control efforts in the country, especially because it has far more resources (money, equipment, specially trained personnel, etc.) than any of the other official (governmental) as well as unofficial (non-governmental) crime control groups in the country.

However, in line with its central position as the leading crime control organization in Nigeria, the NPF has to periodically evaluate its performance and determine whether the recommendations contained in this chapter, once implemented, are working. If so, how can they be made to work better? If not, why not? What alterations can be made to ensure that the recommendations produce the desired results? Etc. Periodic evaluation of police work should include day-to-day monitoring and assessment of the organization's activities. Quite apart from an option to engage any other reputable group or agency to evaluate its work, the NPF will need a standing body of law enforcement stakeholders to monitor the activities of police personnel and officers. Thus, to gauge its progress on the implementation of the recommended changes, the NPF should constitute a group and process for overseeing their implementation. A permanent body will be needed to oversee (monitor) the implementation of the changes. To help explain the recommended changes and how they would work, I call the monitoring body, the "Law Enforcement Monitoring Group (LEMG)". The composition and task of the body are described later in this chapter.

Change 1: Create Information Sharing Channels Between Citizens and Police

The NPF should assure and continually re-assure citizens who witness crimes, or have information about planned crimes, that the citizens will be protected if they report such information to the police. The police organization should designate trusted officers with proven high police ethics to oversee this program and show that the NPF is seriously committed to protecting its citizen-informants. Encourage citizens to freely but responsibly use their now common cellular phones, e-mails, and other media to report suspected crimes and information about planned crimes, to designated police officers. An essential ingredient of this effort should include widely publicizing toll free phone numbers, e-mail addresses, paper mail postal addresses, etc. that citizens can use to inform the police.

An important element of the recommended information-sharing program is that the NPF needs to convince the citizens that crimes and indiscretions committed by the police will not be swept under the carpet. Thus, the NPF should emphasize citizens' strong interest and freedom to report police crimes and indiscretions anonymously, by creating and/or strengthening an "Internal Affairs Division" (IAD) in each police department or station across the country (several small police stations may be combined for the purposes of IAD monitoring). Each IAD should include credible police officers and personnel as well as credible average citizens from the relevant police jurisdiction. The IAD membership should include adult males, adult females, and youths. Again, the NPF should widely publicize toll free phone numbers, e-mail addresses, paper mail postal addresses, etc. that citizens can use to file complaints with the IAD. The IAD must thoroughly investigate and issue a report on every complaint filed with the division. The report should contain the IAD's findings, conclusion, and recommendation. It is expected that the police authorities will act on the report as appropriate. Where necessary, evidence of a crime should be handed over to the appropriate criminal investigation agency and the prosecutor for further action.

Change 2: Institute Cooperative Policing

This requires the NPF in each Nigerian community to invest substantially in the citizens by involving them as equal partners in a cooperative effort to control crime. This change means that each police station should focus strongly on the communities within its jurisdiction and work with the average citizens as equal stakeholders in law enforcement. It is safe to state that the average citizens of a community have at least as much stake in effective and efficient law enforcement as the NPF. Therefore, it is a useful idea for the police to work closely with the relevant organs, groups, and individuals in each community to improve law enforcement. An important way to enhance the implementation of this change is for the NPF to seek out and work with credible community groups and organizations probably through their leaders. Ensure the institution and use of periodic conferences, seminars, workshops, etc. between the police and the citizens. This would provide both sides with opportunities to be heard openly. And, every effort should be made to address the concerns and ideas derived from the police/citizen interactions.

Change 3: Entrench the Rule of Law as a Cardinal Principle of Law Enforcement

For effective and efficient law enforcement, it is crucial that police officers and personnel, at all times, understand, apply, and follow the rule of law in the performance of their duties. Such faithfulness to the rule of law makes it possible for the citizens to believe in their police and to support the police in their functions (see Chapter 1 for more detailed discussion of the rule of law). Thus, the NPF should ensure that each police officer has the minimum understanding of the laws needed to function effectively in a democratic Nigeria. To achieve this, the NPF should set up a mechanism for periodically teaching and assessing police knowledge and understanding of the basic provisions of the Constitution of Nigeria, the Police Act, and other key statutes regulating police functions. The level of police knowledge and understanding of the rule of law can be assessed periodically by an independent, licensed tester designated by the police to perform the task on behalf of the NPF. Many Nigerian universities and colleges have colleges/faculties (law, social sciences, etc.) and departments (criminology, sociology, political science, etc.) that the NPF can employ to teach the police personnel, administer and manage the test.

Change 4: Designate Universities and Colleges to Train and Assess Officers and Personnel

Beyond the rule of law issue (see Change 3), the NPF will do well to designate accredited Nigerian universities and colleges, by contracts, to offer short-term seminars, workshops, trainings, lectures, etc. for police officers and personnel. The program should emphasize the proper role of the police in a constitutional democratic society. Officers and personnel should be made to weigh and analyze the societal impacts of various police decisions, actions, and inactions on such persons and groups as the crime suspect, victim, suspect's family, victim's family, community, state, federation, other police officers and personnel, etc. The point of these emphasis areas is to teach the police about the interconnectedness of the Nigerian society. No longer should NPF officers and personnel regard their crimes and other indiscretions as isolated and far removed from the perpetrators. These conducts affect average Nigerians and the police perpetrators can identify with many of these victims, directly or indirectly.

It is expected that the training and assessment of officers and personnel would expose the police to the real consequences of their law enforcement decisions, actions, and omissions. Wherever necessary and appropriate, citizens at the receiving ends of police decisions, actions, and omissions should be cited or presented as part of the training and assessment. Naturally, this exercise implicates multiple social science subjects, including law, criminology, criminal justice, political science, sociology, anthropology, and religion. These should form parts of the training and assessment. Other non-social science subjects may be relevant and should be considered for inclusion on a case-by-case basis. This social sciences venture (Change 4) will help the police to appreciate the snowball effect of their conducts and hopefully encourage them to use this understanding to guide their decisions, actions, and inactions in the performance of police duties.

Change 5: Measure Police Performance

Besides educating police officers and personnel and assessing them on the rule of law, it is imperative to routinely measure, document, preserve, and use the job performance of each police employee, not only for promotion, but also for other forms of public recognition. This would allow police employees that meet or exceed the established law enforcement criteria to be recognized and rewarded accordingly, such as through citations, commendations, and other awards. Recognitions and rewards for employee performance, even if monetary gift is not included, go a long way in encouraging the recipients to maintain a high performance level. Thus, a certificate issued to a police employee for carrying out his or her duty well may be all that is needed to spur the employee to do more. Regarding the contents of a police job performance measure, these should include both objective and subjective materials since the police have to respond to all manner of issues in doing their duties. However, employees who fail to meet the minimum job performance criteria should be removed from the NPF for non-performance.

Change 6: Monitor Police Ethics

The ethical standard of a profession goes beyond the law applicable to that occupation. Ethics capture situations that, although not prohibited by law, give rise to concerns – sometimes grave concerns – on the part of reasonable members of the profession as well as other reasonable citizens. Thus, for every line of work, ethics are determined *internally* by the applicable standard within the profession (among the professionals) as well as *externally* by the reasonable view the generality of the citizens hold regarding the profession and its activities. The internal and external perspectives are important in determining the proper ethical standard in a profession. This is especially so with regard to police functions because law enforcement routinely involves life and death issues or matters of individual liberty, property rights, etc. As such, it is imperative that the police perform their duties in ways that are above suspicion. Police ethics require that police employees perform their functions legally and scrupulously and are seen by the public as having done so. Again, as mentioned earlier, the citizens' perception is critical in the interpretation of police work. In view of the foregoing and in appreciation of the need to establish and maintain proper police ethics in Nigeria, the NPF should mandate a trusted law enforcement monitoring group to emphasize this aspect of the police responsibilities. In recognition of the importance of police ethics in law enforcement, the NPF should use the data derived from the monitoring group's work to judge its employees.

Change 7: Ensure Continuous Training

In addition to the required trainings and follow-up trainings, some of which I have identified here, the NPF should provide police officers and personnel with many opportunities and encouragement to participate in relevant continuous trainings on their own. Such continuous trainings should include workshops, seminars, supervised independent studies, education toward university degree or other certificate, etc. The police should reward employees that verifiably participate in such activities. Reward options may include conference grant or stipend, positive citation, consideration in promotion evaluation, etc. It is reasonable to expect the continuous training opportunity to drive police officers and personnel to continue to search for and take advantage of avenues to improve their preparation and performance for crime control.

Change 8: Partner With the Private Sector to Provide Up-to-Date Equipment for Law Enforcement

To ensure that sufficient funds and equipment are available for law enforcement, the NPF should convince and co-opt private businesses, organizations, groups, and individuals to join in the efforts to properly equip, train, and otherwise support the police for more effective and efficient law enforcement. Other than life, the security of lives and properties is probably the most important issue for a citizen. Therefore, it is logical that private entities will join with the government to prevent and control crime because of the promise of increased and better security of lives and properties. It makes business as well as personal sense to spend a little more to protect oneself and property.

However, while asking private parties to assist with equipping the police, the police must use the funds realized in the process with utmost transparency and judiciousness. Many contributors to the Police Equipment Fund (PEF) have had bad experiences, including diversion and misuse of funds. Steps must be taken to avoid a repeat of those experiences. It is only then that private parties would invest willingly and confidently. It should be emphasized that where private citizens and groups contribute to public law enforcement, the government through the public police nonetheless remains primarily responsible for securing the citizens and their properties. One of the basic duties of a government is the safety of its citizens and their properties. Therefore, the Nigerian government and the NPF remain accountable on the issue of the security of the citizens' lives and properties even where private parties assist in the task.

Law Enforcement Monitoring Group (LEMG)

As indicated earlier in this chapter, the NPF should constitute and commission a group of professionals and charge the group with the task of coordinating and monitoring the implementation of the various elements of the law enforcement reforms advocated in this chapter. The following are the main ingredients of the proposed coordinating and monitoring group. A highly skilled Nigerian professional, with credibility in society and ethics, should be designated to direct the coordinating and monitoring group. The group (it may be called the Law Enforcement Monitoring Group – LEMG) should be led by a Director with membership drawn from Law, Criminal Justice, Criminology, Political Science, Sociology, Psychology, and other Social Sciences disciplines. To properly perform LEMG's task, the LEMG will need to work closely with capable and trusted colleagues and other citizens, even though those colleagues and citizens are not LEMG members. The Director and Members of LEMG should be distinguished Nigerian professionals whose work and commitment to reforming law and justice in the country have prepared them for the task ahead. There are many distinguished Nigerian professionals in the relevant fields who are willing and ready to serve Nigeria along this line. As one of these professionals, I know many who are quite disposed to doing so if called upon and given the opportunity to serve. LEMG should report periodically to the Inspector-General of Police (IGP) or such other authority as he directs. If the IGP desires, in addition to coordinating and monitoring the implementation of the tasks outlined in this paper, the LEMG should advise the IGP on other related matters as needed.

Conclusion

The essence of this chapter has been to provide in a succinct form the specific changes that should be made to law enforcement in Nigeria, especially with regard to the role of the Nigeria Police Force (NPF). At the heart of the recommendations is the undeniable fact that effective and efficient law enforcement for credible crime control in Nigeria depends on the official (governmental) and unofficial (non-governmental) agencies, groups, and individuals working together. The average citizen is an indispensable part of effective and efficient crime control. So far, Nigeria's official police agency (the NPF) has operated with little or no regard for this fact of proper social control. The NPF, acting alone, cannot effectively control crime in the country. Information sharing between the official and unofficial agencies and citizen groups is critical, so is the sharing of personnel, expertise, equipment, etc. between them. The bottom line is that there is the need for a rethink of the concept and mechanism for law enforcement in Nigeria. For the new policing regime to control crime effectively and efficiently, the law enforcement reorganization must acknowledge and properly use the immense contributions of the country's unofficial, community-based institutions, agencies, and personnel for crime control. Such proper use is unfortunately absent in the present law enforcement set up in the country.

References

Ibulubo, Tamunobarabi Gogo (2009) "UN Award Nigeria Police" *AfricaNews* (24 August), http://www.africanews.com/site/UN_award_Nigeria_police/list_messages/26567; Internet.

Okafọ, Nọnso (2009) *Reconstructing Law and Justice in a Postcolony*. Surrey, England and Burlington, USA: Ashgate Publishing.

"UN Commends Nigeria Police for Peace Keeping Role" (2009) *Africa Good News* (25 August), http://www.africagoodnews.com/brand-africa/changing-perceptions/852-un-commends-nigeria-police-for-peace-keeping-role.html; Internet.

Chapter 9

Dimensions of Terror Crimes in Africa and Policing Strategies for Control[1]

Ihekwoaba D. Onwudiwe
Texas Southern University, USA

---

[1] Significant portions of this chapter appeared in the *International Journal of African Studies* in 2006.

Abstract

This chapter analyzes global terrorism in the African context. The paper examines the meaning of State terrorism, the ideology of terrorism, and low-intensity warfare in Africa. Further, the article offers community policing and other strategies for counter-terrorism in Africa. The measures advocated for dealing with terror crimes demonstrate the need for broad-based responses to terrorism. Such diverse measures include State as well as non-State actors, agencies, organizations, personnel, and other resources. This comprehensive approach to fighting terrorism is consistent with the African communal spirit for addressing social problems.

Introduction

Defining Global Terrorism

Africa was shocked by the dual bombings of American embassies in Nairobi, Kenya, and Dar es Salaam, Tanzania that claimed hundreds of lives in 1998. Africa also witnessed the bombings of the USS Cole in Aden, Yemen in 2000, and the bombing of the Israeli-owned Paradise Hotel in Malindi, Kenya in 2002. These attacks illustrate how Africa is no longer immune from international terrorism. Thus, with an almost unanimous condemnation of the attacks on African soil, African leaders became conscious of terrorism. Among Sub-Saharan African States, there was also a virtual universal denunciation of the September 11, 2001 attacks on the United States. The incidents in Kenya and Tanzania coupled with the attacks on the World Trade Center in New York – which claimed, not only American lives, but also African lives – demonstrate the global nature of terrorism. There is, arguably, an understanding that the September 11 destruction of the World Trade Center twin towers in New York, United States and damage of the Pentagon (United States Defense Headquarters) in Arlington, Virginia, have stimulated international awareness of the scourge of international terrorism. Some terrorism experts have noted that the events in Africa epitomize the view that the attacks on the United States did not occur in isolation (see Kegley, 2003; Cilliers, 2003; White, 2006).

In an interdependent world, terrorism is borderless and at the same time localized. Technology and efficient communication systems, along with global commerce, have indeed changed the face of terrorism in Africa in particular, and the world in general. The modern-day style of terrorism invites a new definition of the phenomenon. Sub-national groups or clandestine agents have broadly defined terrorism as politically motivated violence perpetrated against noncombatant targets. A terrorist group is defined as a group that practices, or which has significant sub-groups which practice, terrorism. According to Georges-Abeyie and Hass (1982), the goal of terrorism is to terrorize. Regarding their objectives, terrorist acts are atrocious and create confusion among the general public. Terrorism is also a "menace to society," as it instills fear in the masses (Cilliers, 2003; Kegley, 2003; Georges-Abeyie and Hass, 1982). While there is no precise definition of terrorism (Schmid, 1983), which is due primarily to the political interests of the definers, it has become a pejorative term (Poland, 1988; Jenkins, 2003). Yasser Arafat informed the United Nations that nobody is a terrorist "who stands for a just cause" (Jenkins, 2003). His understanding of the meaning of the concept further complicates an acceptable universal definition. It must be underscored that, today, terrorism is primarily and intrinsically a global phenomenon that is enmeshed in the international character. Therefore, an accurate definition must include the two faces of terrorism: it must acknowledge the terror perpetrated by States as well as the violence by transnational and national groups.

In 1972, the United Nations Organization failed to reach an agreement on the definition of terrorism, primarily because its member States, due to their divergent concerns, could not identify with any single description. Western countries preferred an explanation that portrayed terrorism as acts of violence used by clandestine organizations to undermine the legitimate activities of established governments, while most developing nations favored a definition that included the suppression of individual freedoms by States (Georges-Abeyie and Hass, 1989). Indeed, the African nations that emerged from the crucible of colonial domination gained their independence through revolutionary and low-intensity warfare. Naturally, these African countries, countries of Latin America, as well as those of Asia would not accept definitions favored by the Western interests.

Generally, definitions of terrorism share one common element: politically motivated behavior. Such characterizations do not include violence for financial profit or religious motivation. Until recently, most definitions placed emphases on groups and group members, without focusing equally on individuals. That is because leaderless resistance today characterizes most terrorism, with cadre members operating in cells or alone (Kegley, 2003). Moreover, modern technology makes terror attacks easier. For example, individuals are now capable of planting viruses in computers, which destabilize the infrastructure of States (Kuhr and Hauer, 2001; Combs, 2003; Ellis, 2005). Even the mere availability of technologically advanced weapons to individual or group rogue hands may cause more disaster than the September 11, 2001 tragedy in the USA (Ellis, 2005). In the face of all these realities, Africa is threatened by the new faces of terrorism and needs an unsullied approach that might focus on defining terrorist acts, giving less emphasis to the motivation behind the acts. Terrorism therefore entails the vile actions of States, agents of States, local, transnational, émigré, and international groups or individuals that employ violence to kill, threaten, and intimidate world citizens by causing damage to society in the form of life or property based on certain religious, political, social, cultural, economic, or ideological belief.

The Nature of Terrorism in Africa

While the position deduced above may make theoretical and policy sense for African leaders in their cooperation with the United States to counter international terrorism since the September 11, 2001 attacks, the problem of terrorism in Africa stems mainly from internal civil unrest and spillover from regional wars. African rebel movements and opposition groups employ terrorist tactics in pursuit of their political, social, and economic goals. Martha Crenshaw (1994) asserts that terrorism in Africa stems from revolutionary pressures at home, regional battles, economic conflicts, and regime tyranny. In short, several aspects of conflict in Africa have led to armed insurgency and outbreaks of terrorism. It has been noted elsewhere that terrorism in Africa is rooted in the devastating colonial policies that expropriated African resources to the metropolis and obliterated or reversed the economies of the indigenous populations (Onwudiwe, 2001; Rodney, 1982). Following World War II, Britain and France lacked the will and power to control and defend their overseas colonies. The false promises of Britain to the Arabs and the Zionists were not the only peccadillo committed by the conquerors and their lackeys (White, 2006). Presently, as the only remaining world superpower, and as reflected in the Middle Eastern crisis and the al Qaeda network's perpetual hatred against the United States, the USA is constantly paying for Britain's unfulfilled promises.

African countries, like their Latin American counterparts, are still afflicted by the residual effects of colonialism and the current impacts of neo-colonial exploitation in the name of multinational corporations (Irogbe, 2005). The obvious result is the dependency of the indigenous economies, while the comprador bourgeoisie controls the wealth and resources of the indigenous population. It is the combination of the abject poverty of the masses, political instability, and the desperation of the newly formed nations that have led to the emergence of popular uprisings in the form of low-intensity warfare in Africa (Irogbe, 2005).

Undoubtedly, Irogbe (2005, p. 41) aptly observes, "globalization is economic terrorism ... the socio-economic and political structure of the peripheral countries are subordinated via globalization to foster the economic interest (the superstructure) of the metropolitan countries." Good examples include the Islamic nation of Algeria, a French colony that started a bloody struggle for independence in the 1950s (Simonsen and Spindlove, 2004), the Mau Mau struggle in Kenya, (Throup, 1985), and the sufferings of black people quarantined in Bantustans under the grand apartheid regime of terror (Onwudiwe, 2001; Olson-Raymer, 1996; Rich, 1984). The efforts of these clandestine groups to struggle against and overcome States' suppression were labeled terrorism. While the actions of the illegitimate governments were given a sanitized name, these underground groups became the outsiders. It is this type of analysis that makes it difficult to have a universal definition of terrorism.

Low-Intensity Warfare

The United States military defines low-intensity warfare in the following statement:

> [Low-intensity warfare is] a broad spectrum of military and paramilitary operations conducted in enemy-held, enemy-controlled, or politically sensitive territory. Unconventional warfare includes, but is not limited to, the interrelated fields of guerrilla warfare, evasion and escape, subversion, sabotage, and other operations of a low visibility, covert or clandestine nature. These interrelated aspects of unconventional warfare may be prosecuted singly or collectively by predominately indigenous personnel, usually supported and directed by (an) external source(s) during all conditions of war or peace (United States Department of Defense, 1984, p. 164).

This statement provides an important perspective for understanding low-intensity and other forms of unconventional warfare in Africa.

While the actions of guerrilla movements have been linked to terrorism in Latin America and Africa in the later part of the 20th Century, some experts have argued that guerrillas are not terrorists (Kossoy, 1976). Others have argued that since they have attacked government establishments, engaged in the burning of villages, wholesale massacre as in Rwanda, and assassination of political leaders, they may equally fit the terrorism label (see Hyams, 1974; Wilkinson, 1977; Georges-Abeyie and Hass, 1989). Any act that results in the killing of human beings through the exercise of violence that is entrenched in an ideology of destruction constitutes terrorism. In this sense, depending on who is doing the defining, guerrillas are terrorists. But a popular scholar asserts as follows:

> To claim that guerrilla [warfare] is necessarily coupled with terrorism is certainly grossly inaccurate. A number of important guerrilla movements steadily refused to resort to terrorism ... The fact is that most of the contemporary guerrilla movements either habitually, or at various stages of their activities, use terrorism, at least as a form of revolutionary tactics (Kossoy, 1976, p. 328).

The point to remember is that African guerrillas may resort to terrorism, but their actions were designed to fight the original violence of the oppressor since the State itself uses terrorism against the guerrillas and their supporters. This is true with the Mau Mau and the African National Congress (ANC). Guerrillas view themselves as soldiers under military discipline. Most guerrillas pride themselves as fighting for political and economic independence. They are usually equipped with military weapons, such as mortars, rocket launchers, heavy machine guns, and other light military supplies. External help usually supports them; they also maintain ties with the indigenous community. They are usually numbered in hundreds and thousands with regular support of the people. In conducting their warfare, guerrillas endeavor to abide by the rule of law that governs conventional military (White, 2006).

Terrorists, on the other hand, are relatively few in number (tens, or at most hundreds of members). Many terrorist groups do not have the support of the community. For example, Osama bin Laden is an outcast in his native Saudi Arabia, and even radical Islamic societies have condemned the September 11, 2001 attack against the United States. Terrorists typically operate in cells, and their actions are usually bombings, ambushes, assassinations, hijackings, and kidnappings. They are more willing than guerrillas to kill innocent citizens in large numbers (White, 2006; Combs, 2003). These distinctions are construed to draw a razor-sharp line between the actions of guerrillas in Africa and modern terrorists. The reality is that Africa is no longer immune from terrorism, and African low-intensity warfare may be bloodier than it has been in the past. Modern terrorist groups are more deadly than old guerrillas and lack human empathy and morality; their targets are innocent by-standers.

Africa has different brands of low-intensity warfare that falls within the parameters of nationalistic and ethnic terrorism. National and ethnic struggles still permeate certain areas in Africa and the world in general. Terrorism experts have historically examined nationalist terrorists within the same framework as past left-wing terrorist groups. Trundel (1996) doubts this approach, arguing instead that since the operations of ethnic terrorists have changed, the old perspectives are no longer in vogue, and will limit an understanding of the new face of ethnic lawlessness. Trundel is correct. Ethnic and nationalist terrorism are still a factor in the new global age, although they have less significance since the proliferation of jihadism. Additionally, Bynam (1998) insists that ethnic terrorism varies from terrorism perpetrated in the name of religion, ideology, or economic purpose. While noting the impact of religion on terrorism, Bynam acknowledges that ethnic terrorism has its own identity, even though the line between ethnic and religious violence is unclear in some instances. In order to support his thesis, Bynam listed evidence from the Liberation Tigers of Tamil Eelam (LTTE), the Kurdish Worker's Party (PKK), the Provisional Irish Republican Army (PIRA), and the Basque Nation and Liberty (ETA).

In Africa, I will include the Eritrean Liberation Front (ELF), a Muslim separatist group that was founded in 1958, and that seeks independence for Muslim Eritrea from Ethiopia to fit the same framework. Other nationalistic and ethnic groups in Africa include the Eritrean Liberation Army with a militant arm known as the Peoples Liberation Front, National Liberation Front (FLN), or Front de Liberation Nationale, which was founded in 1954 and was credited with bombings against French colonial rulers in Algeria; and Islamic Salvation Front (FIS), a fundamentalist Islamic Party in Algeria that won the annulled 1991 elections, which led to the killings of its members by the government. Throughout the 1990s, the FIS responded with armed attacks against Algerian officials. It has been reported that more than 100,000 people died before a cease-fire was declared in 1999 (Simonsen and Spindlove, 2004; White, 2006; United States Department of State, 2005).

Since Bynam (1998) omitted some of the groups in Africa, an expansion of his thesis would incorporate many other groups, such as the Secret Army Organization (OAS), which was basically a violent radical group of the French and other European settlers in Algeria that fought against native Algerian Nationalists and against independence for Algeria. The African National Congress (ANC) fits Bynam's criteria on nationalist groups; this organization fought to defeat apartheid and the minority regime in the Republic of South Africa. Indeed, in 1961, following the Sharpsville massacre of innocent black Africans, the ANC fought back, using both political and guerrilla methods. While the ANC maintained a military wing known as Umkhonto We Sizwe (Spear of the Nation), the guerrilla attacks, in most cases, avoided innocent civilians. Later, the ANC reversed this strategy and encouraged attacks on government facilities and civilian supporters of the terrorist regime (United States Department of State, 2005).

Other examples in Africa comprise the Mozambique National Resistance (MNR) or RENAMO. Formed in 1970, it was an organization sponsored by the apartheid regime in South Africa and the White government of Rhodesia, and charged with the authority to destabilize the Mozambican communist government and to fight FRELIMO, which supported the ANC. The Zimbabwe African People's Union (ZAPU) was founded in 1961 by Joshua Nkomo, who fought for black liberation against the White-run government of Rhodesia, but lost power to the Zimbabwe African National Union (ZANU) under the auspices of Robert Mugabe. There are many more ethnic and nationalist groups in Africa, however, the MAU MAU, which was formed in the early 1950s by the educated Kikuyu tribe in Kenya, is often one of only a few groups that is mentioned in the literature (White, 2006). The goal of the Mau Mau was the total removal of all Whites and those who supported the colonial British government. While the Mau Mau lost a battle against the British colonial forces in 1956, which led to a massive detention of tribesmen and killings, Britain granted independence to Kenya in 1963 under the Kenya African National Union (KANU), headed by Jomo Kenyata.

There is evidence of ethnic and nationalist movements in other nations of the continent, including Nigeria, Liberia, Sierra Leone, Rwanda, Burundi, the Democratic Republic of the Congo, and Sudan (Onwudiwe, 2005a; 2005b; 2005c). On this issue, Okafọ (2006) has recorded and analyzed the use of State and domestic terror in Nigeria, while Opolot (2008) pointed to the deranged terror Ugandans faced under Idi Amin. An ethnic terrorist strives to forge a national identity. Since the goal of violence is to maintain an idea for a long period of time and to mobilize support for it, I must underscore that violence plays a vital role in ethnic terrorism. In Nigeria, for example, where the Ijaw people of the oil-producing constituency of Nigeria are demanding equitable resource allocations, the existing formations of radicals may last for decades, fighting and demanding the same allocations. Where the government fails to heed their warnings, they are certain to employ violence against the oil companies' personnel and property, as well as against government establishments.

The goal is to instill fear in the people, which is a special tool found in the literature on terrorism. Bynam acknowledges that governments are limited in their response to ethnic exploitation of fear, because retaliation tactics may cause a backlash among citizens. Ethnic terrorists are unique because of their appeals to patriotism. Finally, they can easily hide and find safe havens among the communities they serve, making it difficult for successful security surveillance. An excellent example in another part of the world would be the Chechnya nationalists, who have eluded Russian military might (Simonsen and Spindlove, 2004). Although ethnic and nationalist terrorism are important for critical examinations, the most dangerous and common form of terrorism – terrorism from above (State sponsored violence) – has historically characterized Africa.

State Terrorism

I use the term "State terrorism" to refer to official or government-sponsored violence against its citizens or groups. Notable terrorism analysts have described this form of terrorism as the most dangerous type (Herman, 1983; Poland, 1988; Griset and Mahan, 2003). In Africa, it has radiated in political assassinations of government leaders and political opponents, as well as ethnic cleansing and genocide (Simonsen and Spindlove, 2004). Cilliers (2003, p. 101) notes that government sponsored terrorism is prevalent in Africa, and that the threat of terrorism in Africa "lies in a complex mixture and intermingling of sub-national and international terrorism." State terror has historically been associated with Africa, beginning with slavery and its associated ills and colonialism. These forms of official terror, used to expropriate human beings and minerals to the West, has been unique to Africa. Sidetracking from the havocs of slavery and colonialism as systems of terror-networks (Herman, 1983), this present work will examine terror used by African leaders against their fellow citizens.

Falk (2003) asserts that the state arrogates for itself an unconditional security rationale, a raison d'être that culminates in the use of violence and the construction of dangerous arsenals, such as nuclear weapons in war preparations.

In order to be able to survive a nuclear attack and rebellions, States have also often instituted spy agencies against their enemies without regard for the rule of law and individual liberties. Analogously, groups that wish for liberation believe that their nationalist aspirations are unconditional, thus the law does not bind them as well. This analysis, although not exactly the same, resembled an earlier scrutiny of the literature, where one author argued that, in order to justify the use of terrorism against African people, the former Republic of South Africa claimed legitimacy because of its Statehood. However, the South African laws that were used to achieve this objective were declared illegitimate, and the Republic was labeled a terrorist State without legitimacy (Onwudiwe, 2001).

State-sponsored terrorism is as old as military conflict. State-sponsored terrorism comes in different shades. At one extreme, States are known to have established death squads, whose main task is to fulfill the States' brutal objectives (White, 2006). States have also provided safe havens for terrorists to operate without supervision (Simonsen and Spindlove, 2004). A review of the literature indicates that States have been inclined to provide terrorists with the financial security they need to carry out their terrorist operations. Paz (2000) reports that government funds can be made available to terrorists overtly and circuitously through social, religious, or charitable channels.

Indeed, each year the United States Department of State provides a list of States that it says support terrorism. Of course, the US Department of State will not put a country on the list if the Department considers the country friendly to the USA. Thus, pursuing an agenda that differs from that of the USA is a sure step towards being listed by the Department of State as a sponsor of terrorism. At various times, African States, such as Sudan and Libya, have been put on the United States list. Other countries, such as North Korea (for supporting communism), Syria and Iran (for supporting resistance against Israel) are still part of the list because they believe in their divergent causes (Harik, 2004). However, the inconsistencies of the words and actions of the United States on terrorism are not lost on other countries and their citizens. In an article that appeared in *Foreign Affairs*, Hirsh (2002) claims that in general the international community is confused about the United States' approach to global terrorism. Hirsh believes that many nations feel that the United States has a double standard because it denounces terrorism when it is convenient, and overlooks it when it favors America's interests.

Regarding Africa, many analysts have aptly stated that political power often means that a person or group in power utilizes any means possible, such as the employment of terror tactics or measures, including genocide, in the furtherance of political staying power (Cilliers, 2003; White, 2006; Simonsen and Spindlove, 2004). Notable examples of modern-day terror tacticians in Africa who sustain themselves as undemocratic rulers of their various countries include Robert Mugabe of Zimbabwe, Paul Biya of Cameroon, Muammar Ghaddafi of Libya, Hosni

Mubarak of Egypt (until early 2011 when his citizens' protests forced him to leave office), and Laurent Gbagbo of Cote d'Ivoire. These despots preserve themselves in offices through a variety of terror means mainly against their citizens. Before proceeding, I must stress that Nelson Mandela, the illustrious former President of South Africa, set an excellent example for all current and aspiring leaders on the continent, by demonstrating that Africans are also capable of serving as leaders without occupying offices as life presidents or political tin gods.

Public documents abound about the terror tactics that have been used by African despots and rebels, some of whom were, and are, sponsored by governments to kill other citizens. While Europe has had its own share of ethnic butchery (Simonsen and Spindlove, 2004) – in Germany against Jews and the elimination of Bosnian Muslims – in Africa, Idi Amin might well have coined the term ethnic cleansing by the nature of his reign over Uganda from 1972 to 1979 (Hacker, 1976; Olson-Raymer, 1996). Ugandans, especially citizens outside of Amin's Lugbara ethnic group, fell to the sword of the Public Safety Unit and the Bureau of State Research that were established for the sole purpose of terrorizing and torturing citizens (Simonsen and Spindlove, 2004). Scholars and public evidence have not fully accounted for the number of Ugandan citizens killed during Idi Amin's reign of terror. However, it has been estimated that as many as 500,000 or more were exterminated (see Hacker, 1976; Olson-Raymer, 1996; Simonsen and Spindlove, 2004). A prominent terrorism expert has noted that Ugandans were the victims of the ruthless bureaucracy of State-sponsored terrorism of Colonel Idi Amin whose "... grotesquely irrational, bizarre actions seem to be the result of thought processes so disturbed that, in contrast with other terrorist dictators such as Hitler and Stalin, he would be considered deranged in any conceivable setting" (Hacker, 1976, p. 11).

Another striking example of genocide in Rwanda has been widely documented by various reports of Amnesty International (see Onwudiwe, 2005a; 2005b; 2005c; Combs, 2003). Based on published reports, in 1959, prior to gaining political independence from Belgium on July 1, 1962 (primarily due to Hutu political agitation), the majority Hutu ethnic group overthrew the Tutsi ruling king. Subsequently, thousands of Tutsis were murdered, forcing about 150,000 others to flee into neighboring countries. The children of these exiles later formed a rebel group, the Rwandan Patriotic Front (RPF), which started a civil war in 1990. The war exacerbated ethnic tensions and culminated in the 1994 genocide, which claimed the lives of about 800,000 Tutsis and moderate Hutus. However, the Tutsi rebels defeated the Hutu regime and ended the massacre in July 1994.

In West Africa, more than 200,000 Liberians were killed (Cilliers, 2003), and about a million others were displaced and fled into refugee camps in neighboring African countries. The Liberian crisis has been referred to as one of Africa's deadliest conflicts (Onwudiwe, 2005c; Cilliers, 2003). In the northwest section of the country, government troops and sub-government mercenaries were accountable for killing, torturing, and abusing civilians, raping women and girls, and kidnapping civilians for forced labor and combat. In such a disorganized society, the police were warped and were utilized for the contentment of the authorities for their own egotistical motives (Onwudiwe, 2005c). Cilliers (2003, p. 96) observes, "In his September 2003 report to the Security Council, the UN Secretary General noted that the Liberian conflict had unleashed armed groups and criminal gangs, which has destabilized the entire sub-region."

During the gloomy era in Liberia, individual rights were violated with utter impunity. Law enforcement officials employed punitive force to achieve their cruel objectives. Additionally, European law enforcement agencies insisted that preceding the al Qaeda network's attack against the United States on September 11, 2001, President Charles Taylor of Liberia was mixed up in diamonds dealings with some terrorist groups. The United Nations Special Court on Sierra Leone declared that Taylor was providing safety nets for terrorists from the Middle East. On the issue of harboring foreign terrorists, Liberia may not be alone since Africa in general may become a breeding ground for international terrorist organizations. Finally, Cilliers (2003) claimed that, systematically, both rebel groups and State paramilitary units involved in the conflict that ravaged Libera's economic engine used terror against innocent civilians.

Thus, the examples presented so far in this paper show that State repression against citizens occurs in various forms in many parts of the African continent. Briefly, based on published documents, about 300,000 citizens of Burundi were killed in conflicts between the government and Hutu militias and hundreds of thousands of others were uprooted from their homes (Simonsen and Spindlove, 2004). In the Democratic Republic of Congo, some 3 million people had lost their lives due to sporadic conflicts. Conflicts in Sudan had also claimed over two million lives, and thousands of people have been scattered in neighboring countries (Cilliers, 2003). Reports of ethnic massacres have also been reported in Nigeria and Sierra Leone. From the above evidence, it can be construed that State sanctioned terror is not only dangerous, but it has become part of the parcel of the African landscape. Undeniably, both terrorism from above (State terror) and below (revolutionary terrorism) in Africa must have some ideological foundations.

Ideology of Terrorism

Ideology is an important component that distinguishes one terrorist group from another and terrorists from non-terrorists (Newman and Lynch, 1987). Very often, however, the ideology of those who define terrorism and terrorists determines who will be seen as the terrorist and which behaviors will be labeled as terrorism. Thus, the term "ideology" has many meanings. Consequently, in this article, "ideology" is regarded as consisting of a system of thoughts possessed by certain individuals, or a set of principles espoused by political groups (White, 2006). Ideology does not emerge in a vacuum. It is shaped by structural factors (Perdue, 1989; Vetter and Perlstein, 1991). Ideas embody and arise from struggles for power and are characterized by experiences and history. Thus, according to Perdue (1989), the privileged groups in a divided world who gain more from the hierarchical order of that world often view the world differently from the dispossessed. Those in powerful positions have greater access to institutions such as education, media, and religion that shape beliefs. This means that States will have the greatest impact on determining beliefs about who is or is not a terrorist.

Mannheim (1968, pp. 55-59) differentiates between two forms of ideology: the "particular" and the "total". Particular ideology asserts that opposing groups share similar views for questioning truth. Total ideology, on the other hand, rejects motivation while concentrating on different intellectual universal thought systems. It focuses on relationships between social forces and worldviews with emphasis on those that favor the *status quo* and those that favor change. Mannheim (1968) views ideology as collective thought schemes held by world ruling class groups whose interest is to keep things the way they are. Mannheim (1968, p. 40) asserts that: "Ruling groups can in their thinking become so intensively interest-bound to a situation that they are simply no longer able to see certain facts, which would undermine their sense of domination."

In his analysis of Mannheim's ideological thesis, Perdue (1989, pp. 7-8) made the following observations:

> Utopian thinking for Mannheim represented an opposing constellation. Her total systems of thought are forged by oppressed groups interested in the transformation of social or global orders. From the utopian side the purpose of social thought is not simply to diagnose (much less legitimate) existing reality. It is rather to provide a rationally justifiable system of ideas to legitimate and direct change. Utopian thought thus means that oppressed groups selectively perceive only those elements in the situation, which tend to negate it.

Perdue (1989) stressed that the conflict over ideas about terrorism embrace and alter power relations, which may result in social change. National liberation movements accused of terrorism may limit the use of violence in order to achieve international recognition. And, Mannheim's (1968, pp. 55-59) "total ideology" further speaks to the State's use and control of ideology concerning terrorism.

In fact, when we speak of the ideology of terrorism, we cannot speak solely of the terrorist's own ideology. We must also investigate the ideology of those who label terrorism and terrorists. Arguably, definitions of terrorism and terrorists will reflect the ideology of those with the power to define. Consequently, the way in which terrorism is defined has a political-ideological dimension. During the 1960s when virtually all-African nations regained their political independence, many African leaders were described as terrorists by powerful core nations (Hutchinson, 1973; 1978). In short, some scholars saw political movements in Africa as manifestations of terrorism or as communism rather than nationalism. Jaffe (1985), for example, reported that leaders of the nationalist movements in Africa were labeled as communist-inspired agitators. Kwame Nkrumah, the late president of Ghana, was among many nationalist leaders in Africa who were charged with spreading socialism in West Africa (Ohaegbulam, 1977; Jaffe, 1985).

The point is that early Western analyses of Africa were defective in their treatment and definition of African nationalism. In fact, European scholars denied the reality of everything they studied in and about Africa and used Europe and European nationalism as their points of reference. The result is that mainstream writers, including early African scholars (in the colonial and beginning portion of the postcolonial eras), distorted African nationalism, its nature, and meaning (Fetter, 1979; Jaffe, 1985). Examples abound to show that the ideological war on nationalism has been historically linked to terrorism.

The Mau-Mau uprising against the British in Kenya and the Algerian FLN (Front de Liberation) that opposed French colonialism were both linked to terrorism (Hutchinson, 1978; Throup, 1985; Presley 1988). The Simba forces that fought the Belgian imperial rule in Congo were not immune from the ideological-terrorism linkage (Waggoner, 1980). Later, ZANU (Zimbabwe African National Union) and ZAPU (Zimbabwe African People's Union), which together ended minority colonial rule in Zimbabwe, were also labeled terrorists (Danaher, 1984). Similarly, the African National Congress that opposed the racist apartheid regime in South Africa had also been stigmatized (Danaher, 1984; Rich, 1984; Francis, 1986; Clifford-Vaughn, 1987; Goot, 1989; Mukonoweshuro, 1991; Olson-Raymer, 1996).

However, the use of the "terrorist" label to delegitimize groups in periphery nations fighting against colonial rule is not limited to Africa. Other national revolutionary movements in Latin America, Malaysia, and Burma have also been tagged as terrorists (Perdue, 1989). Scholars have identified three major types of revolutionary terrorism that political ideology commonly links to nationalist liberation movements. These include classical anarchism and nihilism, third world revolutionism, and new left ideologies of violence (White, 2006; Onwudiwe, 2001; Combs, 2003).

Many social activists have influenced revolutions in the so-called "Third World". These include Guevara, Debray, Marighela, and Fanon (Parry, 1976; Wilkinson, 1990). According to White (2006), ideologically driven terrorism emerged from anti-colonial reactions, which was rooted on the idea of the urban guerrilla and urban terrorism. Although various scholars have different interpretations of Frantz Fanon's works (see for examples: Forsythe, 1960; Martin, 1970; Blackley, 1974; Hansen, 1974; Wright, 1986; Sonnleitner, 1987; Simonsen and Spindlove, 2004; White, 2006), there is no doubt in the abundant literature that in its early beginning, Fanon's ideas intellectually championed the models of ideological terrorism. The works of Fanon demonstrated in his numerous books, are of significant interest. Fanon's books include *Black Skin, White Masks*; *A Dying Colonialism*; *Toward the African Revolution*; and *The Wretched of the Earth*. In his various works, Fanon encouraged his followers in Africa and elsewhere to denounce and abandon colonialism. He recommended the use of violence and believed that violence is psychologically beneficial. He insisted that the strains engendered by imperialism were the primary causes of mental disabilities in Algeria. According to Fanon, colonialism destroyed native cultures and replaced them with Western values. Therefore, he insisted that the decolonization of Western traditions was destined to be a violent process. Indeed, the Black Panthers in the USA, the FLN in Algeria, and other nationalist groups such as Latin American revolutionaries adopted Fanon's avant-garde philosophy (Moss, 1972; Parry, 1976; Wilkinson, 1990; White, 2006).

Argument for a Counter-Terrorism Strategy in Africa

While I have sketched the patterns of terrorism in Africa with emphasis on low-intensity warfare, State-sponsored terror, and the ideology of terrorism, Africa today faces a new brand of terrorism that is escalating after the World Trade Center (United States) bombings on September 11, 2001. Globalization has ushered in a form of terrorism as evidenced by the spread of jihadism and wahhabism in Africa (Schwartz, 2003; see also Simonsen and Spindlove, 2004). Terrorists do not confine themselves to their homelands. Instead, they move to conducive locations, even if in other countries, for their acts. As an example, Osama bin Laden found solace in Sudan even though he is a native of Saudi Arabia. When terrorists move to a location, they thereby place the innocent members of the population in danger. Bin Laden's use of the Sudan location for his terrorist acts resulted in the United States destroying a pharmaceutical establishment that produced needed medicine for average Sudanese.

Thus, depressed economies and failed States may provide hideouts for terrorism to thrive in Africa. In both the Sahel region and the Horn of Africa, if dysfunctional economies are unchecked, terrorism may as well find its way in those regions of Africa without restrictions. The dilemma posed by this reality must be a global concern. The nations of the world are now strongly interconnected with one another. No country, including the USA, possesses the intelligence and resources to fight terrorism alone. To defeat the devastation of terrorism, an international commitment, supported by nations of the world, must be emphasized. The global war on terrorism cannot be realized by placing emphasis on military might or the exportation of core values. Consequently, as we shall demonstrate below, community policing, with emphasis on civilian involvement in combating terrorism, may yield some positive results in a democratic system.

On a related issue, it has been observed that consumer capitalism and religious fundamentalism are both threats to the development of a democratic State. The best way to avert an explosion of terrorism worldwide is to encourage and sustain egalitarian principles around the world. According to Barber (1992), it will be a losing war against terrorism if core countries promote capitalism without democracy; it can only breed chaos and hostility. Furthermore, other terrorism experts seriously question the social, political, and economic conditions of many countries and insist that poverty and injustice are the root causes of terrorism (see Onwudiwe, 2001). While adherents and followers of al Qaeda, with their deep resentments of the USA, may not be deterred by helping depressed economies out of their economic woes, providing the citizens with opportunities for better quality of life may indeed deter some political and ideological terrorists around the world.

This *opportunity* view is vital if the global society is to slow and counter the tidal wave of terrorism in Africa. For example, in 2004 the Belfer Center for Science and International Affairs at the John F. Kennedy School of Government at Harvard University conducted a seminar entitled "Combating Terrorism in the Horn of Africa and Yemen." In a public report of the conference, West (2005, p. 1) asserts:

> Djibouti, Eritrea, Ethiopia, Kenya, Somalia, and the Sudan – the countries constituting the Horn of Africa – together with Yemen, are potential hostages to terrorism. Their largely unsecured territories provide a platform for terrorists, and their internal conflicts and weaknesses create potential breeding grounds for current and future anti-American terrorism.

The report indicates that in order for the United States to control terrorism in the Horn, it needs a comprehensive strategy that would involve various US foreign policy arms of the government as well as involvements of State agencies in Africa. The report also suggests that the US must work together with its allies to design a cohesive multilateral approach to tackle the problems that confront the region. Civil societies, local authorities, and international communities must be included in any US strategic initiatives to combat terrorism in the Horn.

The following is a summary of the conference participants' recommendations for preventing terrorism in Yemen and the Horn:

1.   Yemen and the countries in the Horn of Africa constitute a closely linked region, and an anti-terrorism policy must be implemented regionally as well as State-by-State.

2.   Combating terrorism in the Horn of Africa and Yemen is as much a medium-and long-term effort as it is a short-term one.

3.   A coherent, effective vision capable of joining American diplomatic and security initiatives is essential.

4.   Poverty, disaffection, and hopelessness do not directly cause terrorism, but provide an environment in which terrorists can be recruited and terrorism can thrive. United States civilian agencies must focus on strengthening governance and governmental capabilities, building and maintaining infrastructure, creating jobs, improving education, and attempting to support local efforts to embed the rule of law in countries in the region.

5.   The United States and the governments of the affected countries should reach out to Islamic communities throughout the region, and strive to reduce social and economic inequality between Islamic and non-Islamic populations in Ethiopia, Eritrea, and Kenya, where Muslims do not control governments.

6.   Helping Ethiopia and Eritrea to resolve their border dispute and to stand down from it is critical.

7.   Curbing the flow of small arms through the region is essential, as is extending and monitoring the arms embargo on Somalia and extending the embargo on arms transfers to the Sudan.

8.   The United States military efforts, including the successful mailed fist and velvet glove initiatives organized by the Combined Joint Task Force-Horn of Africa (CJTF-HOA), must be applauded and continued. The United States must continue to strengthen and support each country's security and counterterrorism capacities and encourage trans-regional cooperation.

9.   To improve the United States intelligence, analysis, and policy-making capabilities, more US personnel must be trained in the languages, history, religions, cultures, and peoples of the region (West, 2005, p. 2).

These counter-terrorism strategies in the Horn are not only beneficial to the United States, but also important for the Horn region. Furthermore, the strategies are applicable to other parts of Africa and the world and should be expanded to them. Africa, for example, is just as vulnerable as America is to international terrorism (Flynn, 2004). As mentioned earlier in this paper, terrorism is a global event and it affects all of us. However, in addition to the above proactive steps, governments around the globe must be encouraged to enact laws against State and revolutionary terrorism and to enter into international accords with one another. The United Nations Organization must also play pivotal roles by promoting international peace and security, human rights, and actively participate in helping member nations resolve breeding political, cultural, and economic conflicts.

Another important component of comprehensive counter-terrorism measures is that the international community should make efforts to educate nations about divergent religions. I have argued elsewhere (Onwudiwe, 2005d) against the demonization of Arabs and Muslims in the United States, especially after the horrific events of September 2001 that encouraged the enactment of the draconian United States Patriot Act against terrorism. While aspects of the law are necessary to protect the United States, innocent Arabs and Muslims must not be the targets of selective enforcement. Selective enforcement could result from a misunderstanding of a different religion. Thus, Schwartz (2003, p. ix) contends that Islam is viewed by most people in the West as a monolith, even though there are diverse views, interpretations, and practices of Islam as there are among the followers of Judaism and Christianity. While cautioning about the sudden rise of Islamophobic writers, Schwartz (p. xii) also notes that the "real source of our problem is the perversion of Islamic teachings by the fascistic Wahhabi cult that resides at the heart of the Saudi establishment, our putative friend in the region." This warning must be heeded, even with regard to other parts of the world.

Community Policing and the Use of Non/Less-Than-Lethal Force in Combating Terrorism

In efforts to fashion the best counter-terrorism strategy for Africa, experts recognize the rise of religious turbulence in Nigeria, Somalia, and other areas on the continent (Simonsen and Spindlove, 2004). In their responses, the various African governments have resorted to the use of the military to deal with terror crimes. However, it seems that in line with community policing, non/less than lethal force will be most effective in combating terrorist activities. Thus, in this section, the use of non/less than lethal force and other community policing strategies to combat terrorism in Africa is discussed. For every country or situation, the broad as well as unique circumstances must be recognized and appropriately considered to effectively address terrorism.

It has been noted that the global society today suffers from a common threat of localized terrorism that, indeed, threatens global security. The nature and distribution of security threats is *global* as well as *glocal* in nature. In Africa, for instance, one threat in one region correspondingly affects other regions. The current (2011) security problem in Libya stemming from the massive protests and armed struggle by ordinary Libyans against the illegitimate, cult-figure regime of Muammar Gaddafi, which has ruled Libya for almost 42 years, has become a local as well as glocal problem. Almost every country or region of the world is suffering the effects of the Libyan crisis. However, the poor countries are more threatened as these societies are neither properly equipped nor militarily ready for rescue missions of their citizens in Libya. The core societies, such as the United States, Britain, and France, have the means to protect their citizens in Libya and, if necessary, to evacuate them from the country. Overall, the use of force is central to combating terrorism. Nonetheless, other non/less than lethal force methods are necessary.

Recently, I participated in a working-group research exercise organized by the United States Defense Threat Reduction Agency, with divergent scholars and professionals in the field of security. Under the leadership of Perry and Borchard (2010) and their proficient colleagues, the group dialogue focused on "Improving African Security Through the Use of Non/Less-Than-Lethal Force: Challenges, Issues, and Approaches." The discussion was designed to address the following issues (Perry and Borchard, 2010, p. 14):

(a)   How might African and United States government perceptions of the na-ture of African security problems and the value of non/less-than-lethal force to address them differ? Are there different perceptions across all African States? How do these perceptual differences affect the potential success or failure of ef-forts to improve African security through non/less-than-lethal force?

(b)   What issues should be discussed when determining the contribution of United States government players to address African security problems through non/less-than-lethal approaches over the long-term? What role might the US Africa Command have over the long-term in supporting US engagement in this area? What are some alternative or additional approaches to US engagement in this area that might be used to address emerging African security problems?

(c)   What are some ways the United States government can collaborate with others (other State governments, non-government and/or international organiza-tions) to address this security challenge area? What issues might the US govern-ment need to address when considering these partnership opportunities?

Generally, according to the report (see Perry and Borchard, 2010, p. 10), the participants examined some of the challenges facing African security. The challenges include peacekeeping, small arms and light weapons proliferation, and security sector reform. In every case, the question of whether non/less-than-lethal means can be used to address the challenges is dependent on the context being discussed. No two African contexts are the same. While non/less-than-lethal force options may be useful in improving the security situation in those areas that are not affected by major violent conflict, such options may not be appropriate responses to other situations. Therefore, the particulars of each security situation, including the nature of the problem, the nature of security forces engaged in the situation (private security firms, police, military, or paramilitary), and the cultural/political influences on that situation, need to be well understood when determining the implications of non/less-than-lethal approaches to address them.

Also, the participants in the group dialogue asserted that discussions of non/less-than-lethal force options to address security problems should take place in the broader context of African military and police reform. However, it should not be assumed that introducing non/less-than-lethal force options into African security forces will change how the military and the police interact with one another, how they perceive security situations, or their overall patterns of behavior in addressing security issues. Lessons from places like Sierra Leone on how to effectively engage security problems and transform security forces might be applied to other African contexts. Although implementing community policing (CP) may be an approach to consider when reforming and developing police forces, it should not be assumed that CP will be beneficial in addressing all African security problems or be appropriate in all contexts. However, CP could be useful in helping police forces work with communities to identify security problems and focus more holistically on security problems. If such tactics are successful, force will not need to be employed. If they are not completely successful, non/less-than-lethal force options may be considered with lethal back-up. The effective development of a CP approach in any African context will require training, resources, and a sustained commitment from all groups involved.

Further, the participants considered some principles to follow for external engagement in Africa on military and police reform and non/less-than-lethal weapons issues. The participants stressed the importance of a long-term, sustained, and consistent engagement strategy on these matters. Training may be an important component of this engagement, but effective engagement will require a good understanding of the African context of interest, the security forces that are engaging in the area, and how non/less-than-lethal force issues are perceived. Expectations need to be managed. Any externally-provided training needs to be tailored to the particular context of interest, the needs of those receiving the training, and the availability of the relevant weapons. As a practical matter, the introduction of advanced non/less-than-lethal weapons may not only be inappropriate in certain contexts, it may also be an incendiary issue (Perry and Borchard, 2010, pp. 16-17).

Conclusion

Colonialism in Africa was imposed and sustained by imperial violence. In the several decades that the world has witnessed the retreat of colonial powers from the regions previously infected by the colonial syndrome, Africa has been a volatile continent.[1] The volatility is manifested in various ways, including ethnic grievances, conflicts, and disputes, wars, and terrorism. This paper addresses terrorism in Africa and the challenge of preventing or controlling it. The African Union, ECOWAS, and other regional organizations are making various efforts to control terrorism. However, State terror, which encourages death squad formations by desperate rulers who insist on holding on to power illegitimately, has to be recognized as a major part of terrorism in Africa even in the postcolonial era. The 2011 uprisings against the entrenched, undemocratic, and oppressive rulers in Tunisia, Egypt, and Libya demonstrate that the reality of globalization and the spread of democracy is working against the continuation of illegitimate rulers in Africa. Also, globalization means that African nations must work together, and with foreign (non-African) countries and organizations, to combat terrorism. Sometimes, armed responses are needed against terrorism. At other times, however, non/less-than-lethal options are more appropriate. To this end, community policing (CP), which would utilize extensive citizens' involvement in counter-terrorism efforts seems attractive. The CP option has the potential to provide the various African States' governments and agencies with in-depth information and ideas for more effective and efficient terrorism control. Overall, however, every population is different, so are the circumstances of every act of terrorism. Therefore, the policymaker as well as enforcer should avail themselves of all the relevant pieces of information and strategy and select the best option or combination of options to ensure the most effective and efficient responses to terrorism.

References

Amnesty International USA Annual Report-Africa (2005) Retrieved, October 19, 2005. See www.amnestyusa.org/annualreport/newssupdate.html; Internet.

Barber, B. R. (1992) "Jihad v. McWorld," *Atlantic Monthly*, 269(3), 53-65.

Bekcer, H. S. (1963) *Outsiders: Studies in the Sociology of Deviance.* New York, NY, USA: Free Press.

Blackey, R. (1974) "Fanon and Cabral: A Contrast in Theories of Revolution in Africa," *The Journal of Modern African Studies*, Vol. 12, No. 2, 191-209.

Byman, D. (1998) "The Logic of Ethnic Terrorism," *Studies in Conflict and Terrorism* 21, 149-169.

Cilliers, J. (2003) "Terrorism and Africa," *African Security Review* 12(4) 91-103.

Clifford-Vaughn, F. Moa (1987) "Terrorism and Insurgency in South Africa," *Journal of Social, Political and Economic Studies,* 12, 259-275.

---

[1] However, some Afro-optimists (see Onwudiwe, 2003) believe that Africa will once again regain its prominence in the world as the cradle of human existence.

Combs, Cindy C. (2003) *Terrorism in the Twenty-First Century*. New Jersey, USA: Prentice Hall.

Crenshaw, M. (1994) *Terrorism in Africa: The International Library of Terrorism*. New York, NY, USA: Macmillan.

Cushman, T. (2003) "Is Genocide Preventable? Some Theoretical Considerations," *Journal of Genocide Research*, 523-542.

Danaher, K. (1984) *In Whose Interest? A Guide to U.S./South African Relations*. Washington D.C., USA: Institute for Policy Studies.

Ellis, J. O. (2005) "Yesterday's News? The WMD Terrorism Threat Today," L. L. Snowden and B. C. Whitsel. eds. *Terrorism: Research, Readings, and Realities*. New Jersey, USA: Prentice Hall.

Falk, R. A. (2003) "A Dual Reality: Terrorism Against the State and Terrorism by the State," C. W. Kegley. *The Global Terrorism: Characteristics, Causes, Control*. New Jersey, USA: Prentice Hall, pp. 53-59.

Fanon, F. (1962) *The Wretched of the Earth*. New York, NY, USA: Grove Press.

Fanon, F. (1965) *A Dying Colonialism*. Translated by Haakon Chevalier, Introduction by Adolfo Gilly. New York, NY, USA: Grove Press.

Fanon, F. (1968a) *Black Skin, White Masks*. New York, NY, USA: Grove Press.

Fanon, F. (1968b) *The Wretched of the Earth*. New York, NY, USA: Grove Press.

Fanon, F. (1982) *The Wretched of the Earth*. New York, NY, USA: Grove Press.

Fetter, B. (1979) *Colonial Rule in Africa*. Madison, Wisconsin, USA: The University of Wisconsin Press.

Flynn, S. (2004) *America the Vulnerable: How our Government is Failing to Protect us from Terrorism*. New York, NY, USA: HarperCollins Publishers.

Forsythe, D. (1960) *Frantz Fanon – The Marx of the Third World*. Phylon, Vol. 34, No. 2, 160-170.

Francis, S. T. (1986) "Communism, Terrorism, and the African National Congress," *Journal of Social, Political, and Economic Studies*, 11, 55-71.

Georges-Abeyie, D. and Hass, L. (1982) "Propaganda by Deed: Defining Terrorism," *The Justice Reporter*, Vol. 2, No. 3 (May-June) 1-7.

Georges-Abeyie, D. and L. Hass (1989) "Propaganda by Deed: Defining Terrorism," *The Justice Reporter* 2: 1-7.

Goot, E. L. (1989) "Should South Africa Be Named a Terrorist State?" *Brooklyn Journal of International Law,* 15, 801-841.

Griset, P. L. and S. Mahan (2003) *Terrorism in Perspective*. Thousand Oaks, California, USA: Sage.

Hacker, F. J. (1976) *Crusaders, Criminals, Crazies*. New York, NY, USA: Norton.

Hansen, E. (1974) "Frantz Fanon: Portrait of a Revolutionary Intellectual," *Transition*, No. 46, 25-36.

Harik, J. P. (2004) *Hezbollah: The Changing Face of Terrorism*. London, England: I.

B. Taurus.

Herman, S. Edward (1983) *The Real Terror Network: Terrorism in Fact and Propaganda.* Boston, Massachusetts, USA: South End Press.

Hirsh, M. (2002) "Bush and the World," *Foreign Affairs* 81 (September/October): pp. 18-43.

Hutchinson, M. C. (1973) "The Concept of Revolutionary Terrorism," *Journal of Conflict Resolution* 6; 338-341.

Hutchinson, M. C. (1978) *Revolutionary Terrorism: The FLN in Algeria 1954-1962.* Stanford, California, USA: Hoover Institution Press.

Hyans, E. (1974) *Terrorists and Terrorism.* New York, NY, USA: St. Martin's Press.

Irogbe, K. (2005) "Globalization and the Development of Underdevelopment of the Third World," *Journal of Third World Studies*, Vol. XXII, No.1 41-68.

Jaffe, H. (1985) *A History of Africa.* London, England: Zed Books.

Jenkins, B. M. (2003) "International Terrorism: The Other World War," C. W. Kegley, *The Global Terrorism: Characteristics, Causes, Control.* New Jersey, USA: Prentice Hall, pp. 15-26.

Kegley, C. W. (2003) *The Global Terrorism: Characteristics, Causes, Control.* New Jersey, USA: Prentice Hall.

Kossoy, E. (1976) *Living with Guerrilla: Guerrilla as a Legal Problem and a Political Fact.* Geneva, Switzerland: Librarie, Droz.

Kuhr, S. and J. M. Hauer (2001) "The Threat of Biological Terrorism in the New Millennium," *American Behavioral Scientist*, Vol. 44, No. 6, 1032-1056.

Lynch, M. J. and B. W. Groves (1990) *A Primer in Radical Criminology.* New York, NY, USA: Harrow and Hesston.

Mannheim, K. (1968) *Ideology and Utopia.* London, England: Routledge and Kegan Paul.

Martin, T. (1970) "Rescuing Fanon from Critics," *African Studies Review*, Vol. 13, No. 3, 381-399.

Moss, R. (1972) *The Way for the Cities.* New York, NY, USA: Cowand, McCann and Geoghegan.

Mukonoweshuro, E. G. (1991) "The Basis of Structural Violence Between Verwoerd and the ANC: Profiles of Contemporary Repression, Deprivation, and Poverty in South Africa's Bantustans," *Social Justice* 18, 171-185.

Newman, G. R. and M. J. Lynch (1987) From Feuding to Terrorism: The Ideology of Vengeance," *Contemporary Crises* 11: 223-242.

Ohaegbulam, P. U. (1977) *Nationalism in Colonial and Post-Colonial Africa.* Washington, D.C., USA: University Press of America.

Okafǫ, Nǫnso (2006) "Legalism, Tradition, and Terrorism in Nigeria," *The International Journal of African Studies*, Vol. 5.2, Winter, pp. 27-61.

Olson-Raymer, G. (1996) *Terrorism: A Historical and Contemporary Perspective.*

New York, NY, USA: American Heritage.

Onwudiwe, E. (2003) "Introduction: A Context for Post-Colonial African Discourse," E. Onwudiwe and M. Ibelema, eds. *Afro-Optimism: Perspectives on African Advances*, pp. 3-20.

Onwudiwe, I. D. (2001) *The Globalization of Terrorism*. Andershort, England: Ashgate Publishing.

Onwudiwe, I. D. (2002) "Terrorism," *Encyclopedia of Prisons*. New York, NY, USA: Sage Publications.

Onwudiwe, I. D. (2005a) "Rwanda," *Encyclopedia of World Police*. New York, NY, USA: Routledge.

Onwudiwe, I. D. (2005b) "Democratic Republic of the Congo," *Encyclopedia of World Police*. New York, NY, USA: Routledge.

Onwudiwe, I. D. (2005c) "Liberia," *Encyclopedia of World Police*. New York, NY, USA: Routledge.

Onwudiwe, I. D. (2005d) "Defining Terrorism, Racial Profiling and the Demonization of Arabs and Muslims in the USA," *Community Safety Journal*, 1-11.

Opolot, J. S. E. (2008) *Police Administration in Africa: Toward Theory and Practice in the English-Speaking Countries*. Maryland, USA: University Press of America.

Parry, Albert (1976) *Terrorism: From Robespierre to Arafat*. New York, NY, USA: The Vanguard Press.

Paz, R. (2000) "Targeting Terrorist Financing in the Middle East," Paper Presented at the International Conference on Countering Terrorism through Enhanced International Cooperation, Mont Blanc, Italy. See at www.ict. org.i1/articles/artcledet,cfm?; Internet (Retrieved October 20, 2005).

Perdue, W. D. (1989) *Terrorism and the State: A Critique of Domination Through Fear*. New York, NY, USA: Praeger.

Perry, J. and J. Borchard (2010) "African Security Challenges: Now and Over the Horizon; Improving African Security Through the Use of Non/Less-Than-Lethal Force: Challenges, Issues and Approaches." May 2010, Working Group Discussion Report Number ASCO 2010-010, pp. 1-49. See at http://www.tsu.edu/PDFFiles/academics/public/news/African%20Security%20Challenges%20Now%20and%20Over%20the%20Horizon.pdf; Internet (Accessed March 25, 2011).

Poland, J. M. (1988) *Understanding Terrorism: Groups, Strategies, and Responses*. New Jersey, USA: Prentice Hall.

Presley, C. A. (1988) "The Mau Mau Rebellion: Kikuyu Women, and Social Change," *Canadian Journal of African Studies*, 22, 502-527.

Rich, P. (1984) "Insurgency, Terrorism and the Apartheid System in South Africa," *Political Studies*, 32, 68-85.

Rodney, W. (1982) *How Europe Underdeveloped Africa*. Washington D.C., USA: Howard University Press.

Schmid, A. P. (1983) *Political Terrorism: A Research Guide to Concepts, Theories, Data Bases and Literature*. Amsterdam, The Netherlands: North Roland Publishing Company.

Schwartz, S. (2003) *The Two Faces of Islam: Saudi Fundamentalism and Its Role in Terrorism*. New York, NY, USA: Anchor Books.

Simonsen, C. E. and J. R. Spindlove (2004) *Terrorism Today: The Past, The Players, The Future*. New Jersey, USA: Prentice Hall.

Sonnleitner, M. W. (1987) "Of Logic and Liberation: Frantz Fanon on Terrorism," *Journal of Black Studies,* Vol. 17, No. 3, 287-304.

The 9/11 Commission Report (2004). New York, NY, USA: W. W. Norton and Company.

Throup, D. W. (1985) "The Origins of Mau Mau," *African Affairs*, 84, 399-433.

Trundel, R. C., Jr. (1996) "Has Global Ethnic Conflict Superseded Cold War Ideology?" *Studies in Conflict and Terrorism* 19. 93-107.

United States Department of Defense, Joint Chiefs of Staff (1984) *Dictionary of Military and Associated Terms: Incorporating the NATO and IADB Dictionaries*. 1 April. Washington, D.C., USA: Department of Defense.

United States Department of State (2005) *Patterns of Global Terror Report*. Washington, D.C., USA: Department of State.

Vetter, H. J. and G. R. Perlstsin (1991) *Perspectives on Terrorism*. California, USA: Brooks/Cole Publishing Company.

Waggoner, F. E. (1980) *Dragon Rouge: The Rescue of Hostages in the Congo*. Washington D.C., USA: United States Government Printing Office.

West, D. L. (2005) "Combating Terrorism in the Horn of Africa and Yemen," *BCSIA, Harvard University*. See at http://belfercenter.ksg.harvard.edu/publication/2110/combating_terrorism_in_the_horn_of_africa_and_yemen.html; Internet (Retrieved April 1, 2011).

White, J. R. (2006) *Terrorism and Homeland Security*. Kentucky, USA: Thompson-Wadsworth.

Wilkinson, P. (1977) *Terrorism and the Liberal State*. London, England: McMillan.

Wright, D. (1986) "Fanon and Africa: A Retrospect," *The Journal of Modern African Studies*, Vol. 24, No. 4, 679-689.

Chapter 10

Vigilantism in East Africa

James Opolot
Texas Southern University, USA

Introduction

We start this chapter on the premise that if all the forces of justice are at work there is no room for vigilantism in any of the East African Community countries – Burundi, Kenya, Rwanda, Tanzania, and Uganda or elsewhere in the African continent. These forces include the resilient elements of the indigenous informal control, the police, the judiciary, and the political institutions. A loophole in any or more of the justice forces generates some form of vigilantism. This means that the greater the number of loopholes the more complex vigilantism becomes not only in nature and form, but also in patterns and impact, which triggers a variety of often undesirable responses.

- The media headlines on vigilantism in the East African Community and elsewhere in Africa have since the 1990s become common. The following examples from various media publications are noteworthy:
- "Kangaroo Courts Demand Government Action" (Morris, 2002:1).
- "Linking Judicial Inefficiency to Mob Justice, Vigilantism and Spiritual Justice?" (*The Statesman*, Monday, December 21, 2009:1).
- "Police Warn Against Vigilantism" (*Independent Online News*, 2009).
- "Guilty and Innocent Alike Fall Victim to 'Necklace' Justice by South African Mobs" (MacGregor, 2001).
- "Frustrated Kenyans Are Turning to Mob Justice to Control Crime" (*The Free Library*, 2009).
- "Armed Banditry, Sexual Violence Increasing" (*IRIN*, Monday, February 22, 2010).
- "Linking Judiciary Inefficiency to Mob Justice, Vigilantism and Spiritual Justice?" (*The Statesman*, July 30, 2007).
- "Vigilantism Caused by Failure of Justice" (*Independent Online News*, 2001).

"And occasionally crime ... represents a call for justice...", writes Chippendale (2000: 8).

Discussions about commonly cited crimes in Africa in general and the East African Community in particular often involve statistical trends and rates. Not so with underreported crimes such as vigilantism. The numbers serve as approximations of events in the real world. This makes reliance on narratives unavoidable.

The calls for the reform of the current justice institutions in Africa are not new. The early advocates did not necessarily share the body of concepts and terminology, nor empirical findings to construct a coherent reform thesis to the extent that their crises were diverse by discipline. For instance, Szabo (1971) cites some of the major obstacles to the utilization of the findings in criminological research in much of Africa during the late 1960s and early 1970s. Clinard and Abbott (1973) concur in the observation that "Administration of police, prison, and probation services, particularly the civil service bureaucracy, tend to maintain the status quo" (p. 287). Clinard and Abbott (1973) also assert that "It is particularly important in developing countries to have good research programs and to collect good statistical data to evaluate the ongoing programs" (p. 287).

Widespread Resurfacing of Vigilantism as a Problem

This resurfacing entails challenging developments and trends, problems, issues, changes, and calls for vision for change on the part of stakeholders. Since the 1990s virtually all the national institutions in East Africa have come under some kind of challenge for not staying relevant to the social, economic, political, and legal demands (Opolot, 2003; Baker et al., 2005; Warigi, 2005). "Criminal justice systems in many parts of Africa are teetering on the verge of collapse as their capacity to deliver justice effectively and speedily is challenged," states Robins (2009:4). His recommendation calls for accommodation of selected resilient elements of customer justice. Reinvention of governance, transparency, accountability, and the quest for social justice are some of the common themes in the public discourse.

The World Bank joined the ranks of the key stakeholders during the 1980s and the 1990s not only in advocating the crucial importance for safety, security, and access to justice for the poor, but also in funding selected pilot projects. This pro-poor justice stance is demonstrated in the work record of the United Kingdom-based Law and Development Partnership in Kenya. The record is outlined in the following summary of activities:

- Crime prevention – involving the community in tackling the causes of crime;
- A focus on especially vulnerable groups, such as women, children and the disabled – e.g. through training of police and magistrates, and of chiefs, etc. involved in dispensing customary justice;
- Community policing – involving co-operation between local police and the public at the village level;
- Police reform – development of improved management and of "customer service" ethos (that of a police "service" rather than a police "force");
- Dealing with corruption in the legal system, e.g. by taking measures to reduce the number of adjournments and thus rent-seeking opportunities in Magistrates Courts;
- Strengthening the quality of justice dispensed through customary systems – e.g. training for peripatetic paralegals and for chiefs dispensing

traditional justice;

- Strengthening the linkages between customary justice and the formal legal sector, e.g. allowing appeals from customary courts to the formal court system;
- Encouraging the use of alternative dispute resolution, e.g. by reforming the rules of procedure and providing training in techniques such as arbitration, conciliation, and mediation;
- Developing appropriate and cost-effective methods of enhancing access to justice for all. As an example, in developing Kenya's Legal Sector Reform Program, different forms of legal aid provision were considered – including training paralegals, providing advice centers, and a proposed scheme for pro bono provision from lawyers. Their respective effectiveness and cost efficiency were also considered;
- Developing alternatives to prison, such as community service, and developing humane and appropriate prison regimes, with a focus on rehabilitation (The Law and Development Partnership, p. 1).

The changes in the nature and forms of vigilantism present not only opportunities, but also challenges to all stakeholders of vigilantism in the East African Community. For example, the increasing locations of diverse vigilante activities cause the traditional reactive and bureaucratic policing tactics to be of limited utility. Thus, calls for innovative proactive strategies seem in order. That said, what emerges is the need for change in policy and action. Ortmeier and Meese III (2010) note: "The ability to respond and adapt to change in society, and to utilize change as a constructive force, increasingly makes the difference between success and failure" (p. 4).

What Does Vigilantism Have to Do With African Criminology?

What does the foregoing have to do with African criminology? The answer: A lot, to the extent that African criminology's scope of inquiry has been broadened to cover not only the traditional (or conventional) areas of inquiry, but also new, emerging ones. "Criminologists' interest in understanding the process of breaking a law or any other social norm is tied to understanding society's reaction to deviance," write Adler, Mueller, and Laufer (2010, p. 16). "The study of reactions to lawbreaking demonstrates that society has always tried to control or prevent norm-breaking," they add. Adler, Mueller, and Laufer (2010) also note, "Crime waves always carry with them calls for more law enforcement authority" (p. 20). Further, "Law enforcement authority naturally varies with the nature and size of the crime problems police must combat." This means that it is necessary to modify the traditional law enforcement approach, while introducing new ones.

East African Community criminologists of the post-independence era are not known for their studies of vigilantism from a theoretical as well as policy perspective. Nor have they fully utilized the literature on banditry during the pre-colonial and colonial eras. This gap is one of the reasons for writing this chapter. Selected studies of vigilantism, informal justice practices, piracy and terrorism, environmental crimes, organized crime, and technology-related crimes affirm the latter development (Ndagala, 1991; Opolot, 1995; Heald, 2005; Penergast, 2008; Warigi, 2005).

Scanty Criminological Research on Vigilantism

Mainstream criminology contains insufficient African criminological research on vigilantism. In the eyes of social anthropologists, vigilantism remains a marginalized area of study even by criminologists like Zimring (2003). The same is true of the literature on African criminology.

In Africa, foundations on the study of vigilantism, which came to be associated with banditry, date back to the days of social anthropology icons such as Bohannan (1957), Fortes and Evans-Pritchard (1940), Gluckman (1965), Schapera (1943), and Southal (1956). Their works have resurfaced through those of the new generation of social anthropologists (Abrahams, 1987; 1989; 1998; Bukurura, 1995; Fleisher, 2000a and b; Heald, 1986; 2006; 2007; Pratten and Sen; 2007). The notion of "old debates and modern settings" suggests new wine in old skins. As an example, Kane, Oloka-Onyango and Jejan-Cole (2006) have echoed this point. They recommend empirical surveys of the resilient elements of the traditional administration of justice.

Socio-Political Contents

Abstract statements about vigilantism in the East African Community (EAC) should never be examined in isolation. They must be juxtaposed against the socio-political contexts in which vigilantism occurs. Examples of these contexts include rural areas, urban areas, border places, markets, and trading centers. All the five countries in the EAC have conservation reserves and national parks catering to the tourist industry. The EAC is essentially the regional intergovernmental entity whose country members are Kenya, Tanzania, and Uganda as the founding countries and Burundi and Rwanda as new members. The Community's headquarters are located in Arusha, Tanzania. The EAC is organized along the lines of other regional organizations, such as the Economic Community of West African States (ECOWAS). However, the ECA is not only a geographical entity, but also a political one to the extent that there exists the EAC Parliament. Thus, the developments, trends, and message in this chapter have impact on all the EAC countries.

To better explain terrorism in East Africa, the patterns of political as well as economic stability of the relevant countries need to be briefly presented. Tanzania has been the most politically stable country since decolonization. Uganda went through ups and downs from the late 1960s through the 1980s. Burundi and Rwanda had their own shares of political instability particularly during the 1990s. Kenya had its own run of instability particularly following the 2007 elections. Sometimes, disagreements between member-States feed instability within a State. "In view of the sharp ideological differences between Tanzania and Kenya and the personal animosity between Nyerere and Idi Amin, it can be argued that the EAC might have stood a better chance of survival..." writes Tordoff (2002, p. 244).

However, within each member-country, several criminogenic conditions contribute to crimes. These conditions seem to be more widespread in the other four EAC countries (Burundi, Kenya, Rwanda, and Uganda) than in Tanzania. Berry, Curtis and Gibbs (2003) cite several common features between and among the African States such as those in the East African Community. They write that "Most states in Africa offer multiple opportunities and provide few constraints on criminal behavior, whether this behavior is displaced by traditional criminal organizations or by corrupt political elites" (p. 8). They add, "Nation-states in Africa are almost all multi-ethnic entities in which local populations affect at least only embryonic allegiance to the nation as opposed to clan, tribe, or kin." Such conditions contribute to political and other crimes in EAC countries.

Focus of the Chapter

This chapter represents the expansion of the African criminological idea. This is illustrated by focusing on a benignly neglected crime, namely vigilantism, in the literature. The chapter targets not only scholars, but also politicians, parliamentarians, policy-makers and practitioners in the formal justice systems as sources of the neglect. In other words, the importance of this chapter cannot be overemphasized. For example, it offers a powerful way to understand the broader implications of the collapsed and collapsing institutions of justice in Africa. Vigilantism is one consequence of the condition of justice as administered by the institutions in Africa.

However, in view of the ever changing boundaries between and among the traditional (or conventional) crimes and new (or non-conventional) ones, this chapter is framed around an emerging new thrust of African criminological thought and practice. The traditional crimes include adultery, assault, robbery, theft, murder, crimes against public order, embezzlement, treason, piracy, and prostitution. Their non-conventional counterparts are environmental crimes, human trafficking, organized crime, high tech-related crimes, drug-related crimes, and vigilantism. These categories are not mutually exclusive in that selected elements of one category may be intertwined with those of at least another category. For example, some elements of piracy are intertwined with those of organized crime and terrorism, such as in Somalia.

This chapter is therefore located in the ongoing wider discourse on the bold efforts to reinvent, restructure, transform, or reform the collapsed and collapsing justice institutions in Africa in general and East Africa in particular in the twenty-first century. An analysis of the responses to not only the nature and forms of vigilantism, but also its patterns and impact, serves as the stepping stone to the ultimate (re)construction of justice institutions based on multi-party democracy, rule of law, human rights, and the international standards and norms to which virtually all the African governments subscribe (see Okafọ, 2009).

Organization of the Chapter

As much as possible and necessary, the issues in this chapter are organized by the following countries: Kenya, Tanzania, Uganda, Burundi, and Rwanda. This arrangement is based on the structure of information and data sources. Constituting these sources are the relevant Internet sites, the print media, selected monographs, and government reports. The extent of coverage of the individual countries varies according to the availability of information and data. Consideration of the issues includes a presentation of strategies for prevention and control of vigilantism. Examples of these strategies include community policing, police task forces, restorative justice, and community courts.

Definitions of Vigilantism

The term "vigilantism" derives from Spanish and Latin usages. In the former case, the word vigilante carries the connotation of "watchman" or "guard," while the Latin concept of vigil simply means "awake" or "observant" according to several authoritative sources. Vigilantism is often equated with such terms as "street justice," "mob justice," "shadow of justice," "extra-judicial self-help," "taking the law into one's hands," "banditry vengeance," "community justice," "popular justice," "retaliation," or even simply as "a form of informal justice," or "lawlessness."

Vigilantism is not just a simple occasional phenomenon associated with mass crowds. In some ways, vigilantism represents plain talk or testimony of the silenced voices pursuant to unfair treatment by government officials, failure of national institutions, corruption and/or lack of access to social justice. The complexity of vigilantism necessarily leads in many directions; as such, it is entangled with interconnected factors. For example, the traditional concept of vigilantism was ethnic-based particularly in pastoral rural areas in which protection of herds of cattle, goats, and sheep was a dawning task for the elders and heads of clans. The concept of protection of community property now extends in the urban slum enclaves of ethnic residences where there exist little police activity, such as in Kenya and Uganda.

Pastoral and agro-pastoral areas of Uganda have since the pre-colonial era been known for banditry and the associated vigilantism. The Northeast border with Kenya around which the Karamojong pastoral people live is a case in point. Cocks (2006) notes, "The isolated, arid Karamoja region sandwiched between Kenya and war-torn northern Uganda has long suffered banditry and unrest at the hands of heavily armed cattle rustlers" (p. 1). Some parts of the Kenya-Tanzania borders have come to be known as sparsely populated stock raider corridors (Ndagala, 1991). The same is true of those in the Kenya-Uganda-Sudan borders. Referring to the events during the 1970s, Clinard and Abbott (1973) write that "use is being made of smuggled automatic rifles and submachine guns and even four-wheel drive vehicles, particularly along the borders between Kenya, Uganda, and the Sudan" (p. 47). The governments of Kenya, Tanzania, and Uganda gave deep thought at least in public about the seriousness of cattle raids. Cattle raids in the East African Community during the 1960s and 1970s were reminiscent of the cattle rusting in the frontiers era in the United States albeit under different socio-political contexts (Clinard and Abbott, 1973).

With variations in individual states, vigilantism increasingly came to take on a new life of itself across the East African Community. At the same time, new key stakeholders came on board to respond to it. At the dawn of the twenty-first century, occurrence of vigilantism came to be predicated on such elements as the following (Johnston, 1996):
- Negligible planning or preparation.
- Private representatives acting in an unpaid capacity.
- Activity carried out without the state's permission or support.
- Force is applied or threatened.
- A response to the real or seeming contravention of institutionalized norms.
- Aims to offer people the guarantee that well-known order will prevail.

Burundi and Rwanda are no strangers to vigilantism considering the widely publicized episodes of mass genocide in the 1990s. However, suffice at this stage for us to remind readers that in the twenty-first century the two States have been focused on reconciliation, peace-building, and peacekeeping programs among their respective peoples (Jooma, 2005, Rackley, 2004; IRIN, 2004; Arusha Peace and Reconstruction Agreement, 2000). Overall, the nature and forms of vigilantism in the five East African Community countries varies from one country to another. Table 1 summarizes vigilantism in Kenya. The identifying characteristics and methods of operation for the different gangs in Kenya are used to illustrate vigilante group activities in East Africa.

Table 1

Different Forms of Vigilantism in the East African Community: Classification of Vigilante Groups/Gangs in Kenya

GROUP/GANG	LOCATIONS OF ACTIVITIES	MOTIVES	MODUS OPERANDI
Bagdad Boys	Kibera (Kenya's largest slum)		Slingshots and Machetes
Chinkororo	Several districts in Nyanza Province	Guarding against cattle raids or rustling-community	
Kalenjn Warriors		Espirit de corps-passage from childhood to manhood - rite of passage	Circumcision
Mungiki	Central Province and slums of Nairobi	Defense of the Kikuyu in the Rift Valley; expulsion of Luos	Weapons (i.e. guns) and links with elite Kikuyu politicians
Mulungunipa Forest Group	Coastal district of Kwale	Causing chaos at the Coast	Machetes and knives
Taliban	Around Nairobi in public transport stations	Extortion against public transport operators	Slingshots and machetes
Sungusungu Groups	Kuria: Northern border of Kenya and Tanzania	Redefine political loyalties and establish a new consensus	Lynch mobs and kangaroo courts

The casualties of vigilantism vary from one ethnic group to another or even within the same ethnic group, from time to time. The explanations for the variations are based on such factors as economic activities (including pastoralism), weather changes (such as the onset of droughts), and types of offenses (example, cattle raids).

Factors Contributing to Vigilantism

While colonial and neo-colonial policies are central to the undesirable condition of law and justice in African countries, other interrelated considerations deserve identification and broader examination. Discerned from the literature are several major contributing factors to criminality in general and vigilantism in particular. Berry, Curtis, and Gibbs (2003) describe the criminogenic conditions in the East African Community thusly: "The countries of Eastern Africa offer all of the advantages to international criminals and terrorists mentioned in the general overview of Africa: weak state institutions, corrupt politicians and law enforcement personnel, porous borders, ethnic groups with ties in neighboring and foreign states" (pp. 13-14). Berry, Curtis, and Gibbs continue: "Corruption is particularly pervasive and entrenched in many African states." Some of the causal factors are based on the traditional African societies. The numerous conflicts between and among neighboring communities illustrate the traditional perspective. "Conflicts with pastoralists from other communities are common in the search for grazing land during the long dry seasons, whilst the herds constitute an easy and profitable target for rustlers," writes Baker (2004, p. 179).

It seems logical to attribute mob justice in East Africa to the general failure of official investigation, management, and prosecution of crime suspects. In the midst of the broad dissatisfaction among the citizens, they invent self-help methods to achieve the justice that, in their view, the State has failed to achieve. However, sometimes, the individual and group efforts to achieve justice lead to undesirable results. "Popular frustration over deficiencies in the investigation and prosecution of crime is generally blamed for the worrying rise in vigilante action," writes Morris (2002, p. 1). He adds, "Mob justice is challenging the government to redouble efforts to overcome a dangerous crisis of confidence in the justice system and offset the immediate appeal to public lynching and the savage results of kangaroo courts." However, he informs us, "Commentators are united in rejecting mob justice perpetrated by self-proclaimed protectors claiming to serve the community's interests, warning that, if left unchecked, it will undermine society."

Furthermore, official corruption is central to the rise of vigilantism in East Africa. Orengo (Monday, December 14, 2009) notes, "While the survey identifies the private sector as a key source of bribes, greasing hands to influence public policy, laws and regulations, the police in Kenya were highlighted as the key sources of bribe demands" (p. 1). Bruce Kyerere, President of the Uganda Law Society, was quoted in late 2009 as saying that "A ministerial policy statement for 2008-2009 presented to parliament by [the] Justice and Constitutional Minister ... says that more than 76 percent of cases filed in the courts had not been disposed off by the middle of this year" (Kyalimpa, p9, 2009, p. 1). Of the situation in Kenya,

Refworld (2002) notes, "Prosecutions of offending police officers are rare, and inquiries by human rights groups meet with little or no government response" (p. 1). On corruption on the part of the police and the judiciary in Uganda, one of the observers was quoted in late 2009 as stating: "They are all corrupt. When you go to the police they will ask for transport to investigate; the judges will want money to hear the cases. It is a waste of time and money" (Kyalimpa, p9, 2009, p. 3).

However, it is worthy of note that corruption is not limited to the State police and judiciary. Corrupt acts and omissions are found throughout the official justice system, as well as outside the system. Instances of the location of corruption at the grassroots level have been documented, for example among the Kuria in Tanzania. Heald (2007) notes, "The tentacles of the raiding system spread out from the thieves; laterally through kinship connection and vertically through their ability to bribe officials making it difficult to estimate the degree of involvement and equally difficult to counter" (p. 6). He adds, "The effective merging of the 'official' with the 'unofficial' system, as is usual with corruption on this scale, creates a powerful coalition of interests that it had seemed impossible to counter."

Thus, the form of policing in a society is relevant to a consideration of the contributing factors to vigilantism. In this connection, it is important to distinguish between the proactive and reactive policing models as they apply to the East African countries. The reactive policing model has been under fire particularly in Western countries since the 1980s. The grounds for its criticism are many and varied. Perhaps the most common criticism is that reactive policing gives the false rationale that the business of fighting crime is an exclusive monopoly of the police. Reactive policing gives little consideration to the roles of other stakeholders, such as civilian citizens, in law enforcement. A related false assumption rests on the use of force as a ready tool to bring about law and order on both short- and long-term bases. However, invariably force has limited capacity to compel compliance with the laws. On the other hand, proactive policing employs a wider circle of stakeholders, methods, and other resources for effective and efficient law enforcement. In addition, the locations of the police stations, like the locations of the courts, have been determined to impede access to justice for the masses living in rural areas (Clinard and Abbott, 1973; Opolot, 2002).

Another important contributing factor to vigilantism in East Africa can be found in the differences between pre-colonial and post-colonial law and justice in these countries. In many respects, the differences are fundamental and as such can pose major problems for effective and efficient justice in a country. Scholars identify the elements of the pre-colonial model of justice to include (a) accessibility; (b) public participation; (c) use of local vernaculars; (d) dispensation of justice in accordance with the local values, norms, beliefs, customs and traditions; (e) peaceful resolution of conflicts; (f) uncodified and unwritten laws;

and (g) relevance to the lifestyles of the villagers. Additional elements of pre-colonial law and justice include the following: (h) geographic proximity of the justice venue(s); (i) simplicity and familiarity with the justice process; (j) speedy (sometimes instantaneous) handling of cases; (k) citizens' sense of ownership of the proceedings through participation; and (l) flexibility through compromises relative to outcomes of proceedings.

On the other hand, the nature of law and justice in postcolonial East Africa is significantly different due to the colonial importation of foreign (European) law and justice models into the African societies. Several factors account for and illustrate the dissimilar take on present-day law and justice in East Africa. The factors include the following: (1) political manipulation of ethnic identities; (2) dependence of the petty bourgeoisie on access to the State and its resources; (3) ethnically targeted intimidation; (4) official downplaying of the efficacy of customary justice; (5) corrupt political leaders; (6) alliance between Christianity and corrupt political leaders; (7) complexity and high cost of judicial proceedings; (8) weak formal systems of justice; (9) lack of citizens' confidence in the formal systems of justice; (10) lack of resources, including operating budgets; (11) official impunity and corruption; (12) marginalization of customary law and justice to land issues, personal and marriage affairs; and (13) continuing tensions between certain elements of customary law systems and those of the formal justice systems, even on those issues identified in (12). The other ways in which law and justice in contemporary East Africa differ from the pre-colonial era include: (14) present-day direct or indirect participation of foreign and national stakeholders in the justice system of an African society; (15) State adherence to broader values of the rule of law, justice, and respect for human rights; (16) externally- and internally-induced justice reform which often leads to the imposition of alien conditions for granting funds for law and justice reform; and (17) the existence and operation of parallel informal justice and formal justice systems.

The numerous disagreements between indigenous-based and foreign-based law and justice in East Africa feed the confusion in the sub-region's law and justice. Consequently, official (governmental) and unofficial (non-governmental) policies and programs to advance justice and prevent vigilante activities are generally absent. For instance, in most East African Community countries national crime-prevention policies and programs and in particular youth programs, which would steer the youth away from terrorism and other crimes, are lacking (eTurboNews, 2009). Further, "Poor governance, insecurity, conflicts, poverty and economic disparities among and within countries of the region are providing opportunities for transnational organized crime" (eTurboNews, 2009). And, as the United Nations Organization (UN) observes, weak rule of law leaves East African Community countries as preys to organized crime. The criminal justice systems of the East African Community countries lack adequate resources and most of their prisons are overcrowded (UN News Center, 2009).

In view of the long list of factors contributing to largely ineffective and inefficient justice in the East African Community countries, it is not surprising that many citizens of these countries resort to self-help (vigilantism) to achieve justice. While vigilantism does not always equal injustice, it often means that the vigilante actors and their sponsors use inconsistent, unverified, and largely unregulated standards and methods to judge and execute judgments. In fact, sometimes, narrow, unjust interests devoid of just pursuits drive vigilante actors and sponsors. Such methods inevitably raise important questions in the minds of reasonable citizens of a modern society.

Prevention and Control of Vigilantism

The often unpredictable and unsettling nature of vigilantism in East Africa, as in other parts of the world, means that law and justice professionals as well as other stakeholders, should seriously consider ways to avoid or regulate its use in each country. Thus, what is the appropriate way to prevent or control vigilantism in East Africa? In view of the socio-economic, cultural, and other circumstances of the EAC countries reviewed in this chapter, preventing or controlling vigilantism in these countries requires the uses of multiple approaches. Consequently, the following strategies are recommended.

Decentralization of Dispute Settlement at the Grassroots Levels

Decentralization of case management and the locales for such actions is vital for fighting crime and vigilantism in the EAC countries. Decentralization of this form of decision-making was endorsed during the 1990s, thanks largely to the insistence of the World Bank and the International Monetary Fund. By the dawn of the twenty-first century, several countries had made names for themselves in implementing the idea of decentralizing the justice delivery process. Uganda is a case in point. The establishment of community service orders by the courts attests to this development. The other EAC countries have not lagged behind Uganda in significant ways. The decentralization practices contribute to rural poor masses' access to justice. These are citizens who for years have had difficulty in not only meeting transportation expenses to the formal State courts, but also in negotiating their way through the corrupt bureaucratic networks (Opolot, 2002).

There is increased use of community-based justice forums for conflict resolution in the rural areas of the EAC countries, especially the pastoral communities of each country. These forums are meant for outreach for justice beyond, in the words of Nyamu-Musembi (2003), "simply the police and judiciary" (p. 3). The forums are particularly expected to be useful in land disputes in Kenya, Tanzania, and Uganda per the discourses prior to Burundi and Rwanda joining the EAC. However, it is also acknowledged that there are hurdles to be encountered in decentralization. Thus, Nyamu-Musembi (2003) observes as follows:

> Measures to improve non-formal justice should be pursued alongside efforts to decentralize and streamline formal justice structures so that people are able to meaningfully choose remedies from the range of systems available. The fact of high usage of non-formal justice systems in rural areas does not automatically lead to the conclusion that those systems are the best; it could simply mean that they are the only ones available (p. 6).

Identifying a Means to Accomplish Goals: The Case for Community Policing

Community policing has increasingly gained ground in Africa since the 1990s. It is a vital networking tool that creates opportunities for proactive policing. Community policing requires meeting certain preconditions such as identifying police brokers and members of various communities to establish lines of communication for dialogue. When the lines of communication are established, what may follow are arrangements for face to face meetings to identify issues to be resolved through give and take.

In considering the necessary preparations to implement community policing in a society, both scholars and practitioners recognize that some well-conceived legwork is a necessary precondition for a meaningful implementation of community policing. This has been done in the five East African Community countries, to a greater or lesser extent. Additionally, it is important that key partners come on board to assist each country in its community policing efforts. For instance, in Tanzania, the United States Government has provided leadership. In its October 2007 press release, the US stated its active involvement in the Tanzanian program, thus:

> The United States Department of Justice International Training Assistance Programme (ICITAP), in an effort to continue the bilateral agreement to enhance the institutional capacities of the Government of Tanzania to carry out effective measures in the implementation of a comprehensive community policing programme, is conducting two one-week courses on community

policing for 110 participants from October 15-26, 2007.

Community policing remains essentially little understood by the police in the EAC countries. Therefore, community policing has minimum impact on the lives of the average people. Several factors account for the limited role of community policing programs in these countries. Four obstacles to the implementation of a community policing model in Northern Uganda illustrate the difficulties surrounding the idea in the EAC countries. The obstacles are: (1) general police ineffectiveness, or citizens' perception of police ineffectiveness, which works against the implementation of community policing; (2) significant underreporting of crimes, which shows citizens' unwillingness to cooperate with the police; (3) despite the assignment of a "community liaison officer" to each district in the North, there remains little opportunity for meaningful coalition-building or preventive outreach in partnership with each community; and (4) the lack of any legitimate policing in the North can also be linked to the breakdown in the rest of the country's criminal justice system.

In recognition of the difficulties of community policing and their negative impact on law enforcement in the EAC countries, Safeworld (2008) (a United Kingdom-based NGO) concludes as follows: "Whilst relations between the community and the police have improved since the inception of the community-based policing approaches, there is still some way to reverse the legacy of negative experiences and poor relations" (p. 17). Thus, significant attitudinal and policy and program changes are necessary to create and implement effective and efficient community policing in each of the EAC countries. In turn, this form of policing is expected to aid the law enforcement efforts in each country to prevent or control vigilantism.

Police Task Forces

Police task forces have the potential to contribute significantly to preventing or controlling vigilantism in East Africa. This recommendation is based on the experiences the EAC countries have accumulated in their previous joint task-force ventures. Since the 1990s, the practice of creating police task forces (or committees) for crime prevention and control has been common in East Africa. Perhaps the most celebrated example is the establishment in 1994 of what is commonly known as the Lusaka Task Force. It is a protocol or memorandum of understanding among several East African and Southern African countries along with the Democratic Republic of the Congo and Ethiopia. The countries joined forces in 1994 to reduce illegal trade involving endangered species. The East African countries participating in the 1994 protocol are Kenya, Tanzania, and Uganda. Their Southern African counterparts are South Africa, Lesotho, Zambia, and Swaziland, plus the Democratic Republic of the Congo, and Ethiopia. This is essentially a protocol that was arrived at in Lusaka, Zambia, on September 8, 1994. The named countries became signatories to the protocol. The countries committed themselves to reducing or cutting down illegal trade involving endangered species. The 1994 protocol (Lusaka Task Force) can serve as a model for a joint task force among the EAC countries to prevent of control vigilantism in the sub-region.

Use of Restorative Justice

In view of their different approaches to crime prevention and management, the application of restorative justice in the EAC countries is likely to aid efforts to prevent or control vigilantism. "Restorative justice", as a concept and practice, is gaining ground in the East African Community. It represents efforts to settle disputes in unofficial and informal settings or through such processes. As such, restorative justice is an alternative to the use of formal State courts, which decide cases based on the applicable laws, and allocate liabilities and sanctions accordingly. On the other hand, restorative justice is a justice framework that emphasizes moving away from the imposition of pain and harm. Rather, restorative justice redirects individual and community efforts to reparation and healing (Castellano and Gould, 2007; Brown, 2009). Restorative justice has been widely used in many parts of the world, albeit in various forms.

In line with the restorative justice formula, an Uganda journalist, Joshua Kyalimpa (2009) notes, "Overwhelmed by the number of unresolved cases, the judiciary is resorting to arbitration as an alternative to what they see as the cumbersome judicial system inherited from Great Britain" (p. 1). He adds, "During a workshop by the Justice, Law and Order sector, a consortium bringing together organizations working on access to judicial services, participants resolved to use arbitration to solve minor disputes." Also, Bruce Kyerere, President of the Uganda Law Society, makes a case for restorative justice, thus: "Under arbitration the parties agree to an arbitrator whose decision will be respected by both." He added, "It cuts the court process and eases the dogged judicial system" (Kyalimpa, 2009, p. 1). Thus, the use of restorative methods, rather than insistence on the full application of the formal law, has the potential to strengthen the justice system among the citizens. A strengthened justice system can only aid the fight against crime and vigilantism in the EAC countries.

Establishment of Community Courts

It seems that the time has come for community courts to be established in the urban as well as the rural areas of the EAC countries. Already, community courts are fairly common in the rural areas. These courts remain significant resilient elements of the traditional administration of justice in spite of challenging colonial and neocolonial policies that threaten to obliterate the traditional justice model. Urban community courts, if established, will be new social constructs in the EAC countries. However, community courts, in both rural and urban areas, are expected to play major roles in the justice system of each EAC country. The anticipated grassroots character of these courts will likely endear them to the average citizens. Confidence in the justice system is likely to rise. The courts will be more likely to address issues in ways that are consistent with their community standard and expectation.

Rwanda's gacaca courts constitute an impressive example of community courts that have been used successfully. Rwanda's gacaca courts are community forums for resolution of disputes, using selected resilient elements of the traditional model of justice. The word "gacaca" means "doing justice on the grass" – short grass. The gacaca courts are not only community courts to resolve petty offenses; they are also used to preside over some of the most serious crimes, such as allegations of genocide during the 1990s. The judges of the gacaca courts are not traditional elders, but trained lawyers. It seems that the constitution of the gacaca courts has produced the proper balance between knowledge of the law (formal law) and knowledge and sensitivity to the relevant community standard and expectation. For more on gacaca courts, see "Side by Side, With the Guilty, After Courts Send them Home" (New York Times, 2010), an award winning film on gacaca justice. Overall, the establishment of community courts in urban and rural areas should allow the citizens of each EAC country to participate in and identify with their judicial process. Such level of participation should be higher than what obtains in the formal, foreign-based courts in each country. Increased citizen participation is likely to reduce the urge for self-help responses to crimes, thus controlling vigilantism.

Conclusion

Vigilantism is a common, nagging phenomenon that symbolizes the dysfunctional institutions of justice in East Africa (Burundi, Kenya, Rwanda, Tanzania, and Uganda). Over the years, vigilantism in East Africa has changed in its form. However, there was a dearth of professional debate or discourse of the phenomenon. Thus, little professional contributions (by lawyers, criminologists, sociologists, and other social scientists) were made to the policy on vigilantism. In the twenty-first century, there has been increased scholarly research resulting in (a) the generation of information and data, and (b) the use of the available information and data in law-making and policy-making particularly on policing.

But, vigilantism affects the entire criminal justice system of each East African Community (EAC) country, not just the police. Each of the major components of criminal justice – the police, the courts, and the penal system (corrections/prisons) – affects and is affected by vigilantism in various ways. Even such sectors as the parliaments, civic societies, and the media have been reported to have had and continue to have a role to play in handling vigilantism. However, reactive responses to vigilantism appear insufficient to prevent or control vigilantism. Therefore, proactive policies and programs are needed to address the phenomenon among the EAC countries. The proactive efforts recommended for this purpose include implementation of community policing, establishment of police task forces, use of restorative justice, and the inauguration of community courts in urban as well as the rural areas of each EAC country. If fully implemented, the recommendations are expected to contribute significantly to preventing or controlling vigilantism in East Africa.

References

Abraham, H. J. (1975) *The Judicial Process*. London, England: Oxford University Press.

Abrahams, R. (1987) "Sunga Sunga: Village Vigilante Groups in Tanzania," *African Affairs*, 86 (343), pages 179-186.

Abrahams, R. (1998) *Vigilantism and the State*. Cambridge, United Kingdom: Polity Press.

Adler, F., G. O. W. Mueller, and W. S. Laufer (2010) *Criminology*. New York, NY, USA: McGraw-Hill.

African Rights (2000) *Northern Uganda: Justice in Conflict*. London, England.

Arusha Peace and Reconciliation Agreement for Burundi. Arusha, Tanzania, August 28, 2000.

Bailey, S. (2008) "Perception of Corruption in Humanitarian Assistance Among Displaced Persons in Northern Uganda." Humanitarian Policy Group Working Paper (August).

Baker, W. D. et al. (2005) "Community Policing Assessment in Northern Uganda". Report to the United States Agency for International Development (March 1-15).

BBC News, "Bribes Paid to Join Kenya Police." (Friday, December 15, 2005).

Benit-Gabafou, C., "Community Policing and Disputed Norms for Local Social Control in Informal Justice Systems of Burundi and Somalia." Geneva, Switzerland: Center for Humanitarian Affairs.

Berry, L., G. E. Curtis, and J. N. Gibbs (2003 October) *Nations Hospitable to Organized Crime*. Washington, D.C., USA: Library of Congress.

Bohannan, I. (1957) *Justice Among the Tiv*. Princeton, New Jersey, USA: Princeton University Press.

Casper, J. D. (1972a) *American Criminal Justice*. Englewood Cliffs, New Jersey, USA: Prentice Hall.

Castellano, T. C., and J. B. Gould (2007) "Neglect of Justice in Criminal Justice Theory: Causes, Consequences, and Alternative" in D. E. Duffee and E. R.

Maguire (eds.). *Criminal Justice Theory*. London, England: Routledge, pp. 71-88.

Chippendale, N. (2000) *Crimes Against Humanity*. Philadelphia, Pennsylvania, USA: Chelsea House.

Clinard, M. B. and R. F. Meier (1979) *Sociology of Deviant Behavior*. New York, NY, USA: Holt, Rinehart, and Winston.

Cocks, T. (2006) "Troubles Threaten Ugandan Hopes of Peace." News-Africa (October 12). Available at http://cc.bingj.com/cache. aspx?q=lawlessnes+in+uganda&d; Internet.

Coleman, M. (1998) *Crime Against Humanity: Analyzing the Repression of the Apartheid State*. Cape Town, South Africa: David Philip.

Daniels, N. (2009) "Militias, Gangs, and Vigilantes in Kenya: The Consequences of Abandoning the Reform Agenda," *Open Democracy*. London, England, September 2.

Dexter, T., et al. (2005) The Report on the Role of Informal Justice Systems in Fostering the Rule of Law in Post-Conflict Situations: The Case of Burundi (July).

Duffee, D. E. and E. R. Maguire (2007) *Criminal Justice Theory: Explaining the Nature and Behavior of Criminal Justice*. London, England: Routledge.

ETurboNews, "East African Community: United Nations Claims Conflict, Weak Rule of Law Leave East African Community Prey to Organized Crime" (February 5, 2009). Available at http://cc.bingj.com/cache.aspx?q=the+rule+of+law +in+east+africa&d; Internet.

Fleisher, M. (2000) "Sundusungu: State-Sponsored Village Vigilante Groups Among the Kuria of Tanzania," *Africa*, 70, 2, 209-28.

Fleisher, M. (2002) "Sungu Sungu: State-Sponsored Village Groups Among the Kuria of Tanzania," *The African*, 70 (2), pages 209-228.

Fortes, M. and E. E. Evans-Pritchard (1947) *African Political Systems*. London, England: Oxford University Press.

Gluckman, M. (1965) *Ideas in Lozi Jurisprudence*. New Haven, Connecticut, USA: Yale University Press.

Harris, B. (2001 May) "As for Violent Crime That's Our Daily Bread: Vigilantism Violence During South Africa's Period of Transition," *Violence and Transition Series* 1, pp. 1-8.

Heald, S. (2005) "State, Law, and Vigilantism in Northern Tanzania," *African Affairs*, December 33, pages 265-283.

Heald, S. (2007) "Making Law in Rural East African Community: Sungu Sungu in Kenya." Working Paper No. 12. Crisis State Research Center, London (March).

Huyse, L. (2008) "Introduction: Traditional-Based Approaches in Peacekeeping, Transitional Justice and Reconciliation Policies." Government and Social

Development Resource Center.

Independent Online News, "Policy Warn Against Vigilantism" (November 23, 2009).

IRIN, Burundi: Armed Banditry, Sexual Violence Increasing." (Monday, February 22, 2010).

IRIN, Burundi: Grappling with Repatriation, Relocation of Returnees and IDPs (2004 8 November). Available at: http://www.irnnews.org; Internet.

IRIN, "Kenya, Armed and Dangerous" (2008 February 22). Available at http://cc.bingj.com/cache.aspx?q=vigilantism+in+western+unganda&d; Internet.

Jaramogi, P. (2008) "Uganda: Police Urged to Use Data to Fight Crime," *The New Vision* (May 25).

Jeffrey, C. A. (1962) "Criminal Justice and Social Change" in F. J. Davis, et al, (eds). *Society and the Law*. New York, NY, USA: Free Press.

Johnston, L. (1996) "What is Vigilantism?" *British Journal of Criminology* 36(2) (Spring).

Jooma, M. B. (2005) "We Can't Eat the Constitution, Transformation and the Socio-Economic Reconstruction of Burundi." Occasional Paper 109 (May). Available at http://ccbingj.com/cache.aspx?=vigilantism+in+burundi&d; Internet.

Kane, M., J. Oloka-Onyango, and A. Tejan-Cole (2006) "Assessing Customary Law Systems as a Vehicle for Providing Equitable Access to Justice for the Poor." Paper presented at the Arusha Conference on New Frontiers of Social Policy, December 12-15.

Kenya Police, "Kenya Marks One Year of Community Policing." (Friday, December 11, 2009) Press Release.

Klein, M. S. G. (1984) *Law Courts and Policy*. Englewood Cliffs, New Jersey, USA: Prentice Hall.

Kyalimpa, J. (2009) "Uganda: Mob Justice Increases as Court Backlog Escalates," *All Africa.com*, December 9.

"Mafias in Africa: The Rise of Drinking Companies and Vigilante Groups in Bugisu, Uganda," *Africa*, 1986; 56, 446-67.

MacGregor, K. (2001) "Guilty and Innocent Alike Fall Victim to 'Necklace' Justice by South African Mobs," *The Independent*, March 3.

Mastrofiski, S. (2007) "Community Policing: A Skeptical View" in D. Weisburd and A. A. Braga (eds.). *Police Innovation: Contrasting Perspectives*. Cambridge, United Kingdom: Cambridge University Press, pp. 44-73.

"Mob Justice Increases as Court Backlogs Escalate," *Inter Press Services News Agency* (2010, January 11).

Morris, M. (2002) "Kangaroo Courts Demand Government Action." *Independent Online News*, January 21.

Muli, E. (2004) "Kiamas: Informal Justice Processes and Domestic Violence in Kenya." Paper presented at the Annual Meeting of the Law and Society Association, Renaissance Hotel, Chicago, Illinois, USA, May 27th.

Ndagala, D. (1991) "The Unmaking of the Datoga: Decreasing and Increasing Conflict," *Normadic Peoples* 28, pp. 71-82.

New York Times, "Side by Side, With the Guilty, After Courts Send Them Home" (January 12, 2010).

Ntambara, P. (2010) "Rwanda-Burundi to Combat Borders Crimes." *The New Times* (February 19, 2010).

Nyamu-Musembi, C. (2003) Review of Experience in Engaging With 'Non-State' Justice Systems in East African Community. Commissioned by Governance Division, Institute for Development Studies, Sussex University, United Kingdom (February).

Odongo, G. (2009) "Kenya: Post-Election Violence Suspects Must Be Brought to Justice," *Amnesty International* (November 9).

Okafọ, Nọnso (2009) *Reconstructing Law and Justice in a Postcolony*. Surrey, England and Burlington, USA: Ashgate Publishing.

Opolot, J. E. (1995) *The Crime Problem in Africa: A Wake Up Call*. Houston, Texas, USA: de Press.

Opolot, J. E. (2002) *A Discourse on Just and Unjust Legal Institutions*. Lewiston, NY, USA: Edwin Mellen Press.

Orengo, P. (2009) "TI Ranks Kenya Third Most Corrupt Sub-Saharan Country," *The Standard Online* Edition (Monday, December 14).

Ortmeier, P. J. and E. Meese (2009) *Leadership, Ethics, and Policing: Challenges for the 21st Century*. Upper Saddle River, New Jersey, USA: Prentice Hall.

Pratten, D. and A. Sen (2007) *Global Vigilantes*. London, England: Hurst.

Rackley, E. (2004) "Burundi: The Impact of Small Arms and Armed Violence on Women," *United Nations Development Program* (November), p. 4.

Refworld, "Kenya's Unfinished Democracy: A Human Rights Agenda for the New Government," United Nations High Commission for Refugees (December 12, 2002).

Rheinstein, M. (1967) *Max Weber On Law in Economy and Society*. New York, NY, USA: Clarion Books.

Safeworld (2008) "Implementing Community-Based Policing in Kenya" (February). London, England.

Schmalleger, F. and J. L. Worrall (2010) *Policing Today*. Upper Saddle River, New Jersey, USA: Prentice Hall.

Security Watch, "Kenya: Vigilantes Unleashed" (2009 June 2).

"State, Law, and Vigilantism in Northern Tanzania," *African Affairs*, 2006; 105, 419, 265-83.

Szabo, D. (1971) "Applied Criminology and Government Policy: Future Perspectives and Conditions of Collaboration," *Issue in Criminology* 6 (Winter), pp. 55-64.

The Law and Development Partnership, "Safety, Security and Access to Partnership". The National Academies Press, "Role of Extra-African Forces in Democratization" in The National Academies Press (ed.). Democratization in Africa: African Views (2009) Washington, DC., USA, pp. 60-72.

The Statesman, "Linking Judicial Inefficiency to Mob Justice, Vigilantism and Spiritual Justice?" (December 21, 2009).

Tmarsh, M. S. (2009) "Pirates Widen Range, Straining Naval Patrols." *The New York Times* (November 19, 2009). Available at http://www.nytimes.com/2009/11/20/world/africa/20pirates.html; Internet.

Tordoff, W. (2002) *Government and Politics in Africa*. Bloomington, Indiana, USA: Indiana University Press.

UN News Center, "Conflict and Weak Rule of Law Leave East African Community Prey to Organized Crime" (February 4, 2009).

United States Government, "U. S. Government Conducts Courses on Community Policing and Anti-Terrorism for Tanzanian Police." Press Release (October 11, 2007).

Vijeyarasa, R. (2009) "Traditional and Informal Justice: A Tool for Accountability, Truth and Reconciliation?" Paper presented at the International Women for Peace Conference held March 6.

Warigi, G. (2007) "The Rise of Kenya's Vigilantes," *BBC News*, October 9. See at http://news.bbc.co.uk/2/hi/africa/6995577.stm; Internet (accessed April 26, 2011).

Yakubu, J. A. (2000) *Administration of Justice in Nigeria*. Lagos, Nigeria: Malthouse Press.

Zimring, F. (2003) *The Contradictions in American Capital Punishment*. New York, NY, USA: Oxford University Press.

Part C

CRIMINAL RESPONSIBILITY, SANCTION, ENVIRONMENTAL CRIME ANALYSIS

In this Part

Chapter 11

Plea Bargain: Negotiating Guilt Away or Compounding Offenses? Another Look at "Cutting Deals" in Criminal Cases

Simon Ortuanya
University of Nigeria

Introduction

Recent developments in Nigeria's criminal justice jurisprudence have made this research imperative. The developments revolve mainly around high profile financial and political cases that were resolved through plea bargains. The most recent of these cases was that of Cecilia Ibru, then Managing Director and Chief Executive Officer of Oceanic Bank of Nigeria, PLC. The Economic and Financial Crimes Commission (EFCC) arraigned Ibru on multiple charges of fraud, money laundering, and embezzlement. She "negotiated" her charges and pleaded guilty to fraud. She was convicted and sentenced to six months imprisonment. By the "deal," she was also required to forfeit properties she had illegally acquired in Nigeria and in other countries totaling about 191 billion Naira.[1]

The second high profile case was that of the former Governor of Delta state, James Ibori. Like Ibru, the former Governor was charged on 93 counts of embezzlement of public funds while he was Governor of Delta state. He "cut a deal" with the EFCC prosecutors, pleaded guilty and was sentenced to three months in jail and made to refund the sums of money he illegally acquired. It was the same plea bargain that ensured that the former Governor of Bayelsa state, Diepreye Alamieseigha, was freed from prison. He pleaded guilty to a charge of false declaration of assets and was convicted on six out of the 33 amended charges filed against him. He was sentenced to two years imprisonment on each of the six counts while the sentences were to run concurrently. He forfeited four properties, 2.29 million Naira, 1 billion Naira worth of shares in a commercial bank, 105 million Naira, and 160,000 United States dollars to the Bayelsa state government.[2] Further, there was the case of former Inspector-General of Police, Tafa Balogun, who was charged with some seventy counts of fraud-related crimes, involving money laundering, theft, and diversion of stolen funds, but again negotiated his guilt. He pleaded guilty, was convicted and sentenced to six months imprisonment after a negotiated settlement. He was also made to refund his loot to the coffers of the federal government.

The challenge of this chapter is to resolve the apparent contradictions in the above line of cases with the penal provision under the Nigerian criminal justice system. For instance, under the *Criminal Code*, which is the operative law in the southern states of Nigeria, as well as the *Penal Code*, which applies to the northern states, compounding a felony is an offense. Therefore, it amounts to infraction of the law for parties to a crime to negotiate their guilt or for any other

---

[1] See Yusuf Alli, "N747b Fraud: Six More Ex-Bank Chiefs Opt for Plea Bargain" *The Nation*, Vol. 05, No. 1549, October 17, 2010, p. 8. It is also reported that other bank executives who are also facing trials are considering plea bargain deals. They are worried that their trials may be prolonged and protracted having regard to the slow pace of criminal justice in Nigeria. According to the bank executives, plea bargains will save them a lot of agony and psychological trauma. See also Tunji Adegboyega, "Cecilia's Greed" *Ibid*, p. 15.

[2] See Dapo Falade & Festus Ojudum, "Legal Intricacies of Alams Release" *The Tribune*, August 2, 2007, p. 19.

agent whether of the State or otherwise to aid, abet, or in any manner stand in the way of the wheel of justice. Put differently, this paper responds to the following queries: Is it unconstitutional for legislations such as the *Economic and Financial Crimes Commission Act* to provide for plea bargain deals? Does the practice of plea bargain erode the constitutional power of the Attorney-General of the Federation or of a state to institute or discontinue a legal action? This chapter takes concrete steps to resolve these constitutional issues.

At this stage of the present paper, suffice it to state as follows. It is our contention that plea bargain as an emerging trend ought to be encouraged as the advantages far outweigh the disadvantages. Since crime violates the State, it seems that returning ill-gotten wealth to the coffers of the State is one sure way of placating the State that the illegal conduct has affected. By extrapolation, even where the injured is an individual, restitution would also appear to be an adequate remedy especially in crimes relating to property. It is our further contention that this principle of restitution accords more with our traditional criminal justice system. We cannot therefore agree more with Professor Okafọ, who advocates a return to restorative justice, i.e. healing and soothing justice of restoring the victim or his relatives to their original condition as much as possible.[3] Restorative justice, which is not a new invention,[4] seems to support plea bargains.

However, even if we rely on restorative justice to apply restitution in the Nigerian criminal justice system, it should be noted that there is a strong challenge to plea bargains in general in the country. Some legal experts and commentators fervently oppose the plea bargain practice, mainly because the procedure is a latter-day phenomenon in the Nigerian criminal justice system and it seems fundamentally unjust that a criminal[5] would receive perhaps a significantly reduced sanction than what the law stipulates for the crime charged. Moreover, plea bargain is not available to all accused persons. Rather, it is typically extended only to the well-connected, high profile criminal defendants. Thus, even while recognizing the pragmatism of plea bargains, lawyers and lay Nigerians alike strongly criticize the practice. For example, in May 2011 a senior Nigerian lawyer (Senior Advocate of Nigeria – SAN) intensely opposed plea bargain because, according to him, it is a practice that commercializes the Nigerian criminal justice system. The SAN described plea bargain as alien to Nigerian law. He explained that, through the EFCC in particular, the Nigerian government promotes the practice as a means of recovering some of the money looted by accused persons who otherwise could walk away with the entire amount stolen from the public;

---

[3] Nọnso Okafọ, *Reconstructing Law and Justice in a Postcolony* (Surrey, England and Burlington, USA: Ashgate Publishing, 2009) at pp. 22-28.

[4] *Ibid*, p. 22.

[5] The accused person in a plea bargain arrangement accepts criminal responsibility on the basis of which criminal punishment is imposed, even if the crime for which he accepts responsibility differs from the original crime charged.

therefore, the Nigerian government champions plea bargain from the commercial point of view.[6]

Meaning of Plea Bargain

Black's Law Dictionary defines plea bargain as a negotiated agreement between a prosecutor and a criminal defendant whereby the defendant (accused person) pleads guilty to a lesser offense or to one of multiple charges in exchange for some concession by the prosecutor, usually a more lenient sentence or a dismissal of other charges.[7] Also, Sandefur defines plea bargain as follows: Plea bargain is a contract with the State. The criminal defendant agrees to plead guilty to a lesser charge, rather than go to trial on a more severe charge whereby he faces the possibility of a harsher sentence.[8] Describing the plea-bargaining process, Fine, an American jurist, states:

> Plea-bargaining is a nearly universal part of our nation's (United States) criminal justice system, for better or worse. In plea-bargaining the prosecution in a criminal case strikes a deal in which the prosecution agrees to charge a crime or crimes less seriously than the facts warrant, and/or reduce a charge or charges issued, and/or dismiss a charge or charges already issued and/or not issue additional charges, and/or make a sentence recommendation, all in return for a guilty or no contest plea.[9]

By way of further explanation, a plea bargain is an agreement in a criminal case by which the prosecutor and the accused person (usually through the defense lawyer) agree that the accused should plead guilty, typically to a reduced (that is, less serious) charge, or to fewer charges. Another kind of plea bargain is that which requires the accused person to plead guilty to the original charge with the prosecutor endorsing a lighter sentence than the maximum allowed by law. Yet a different type takes the shape of an agreement that the accused person should admit specified fact(s) of the case to avoid the prosecutor introducing other

---

[6] See Bertram Nwannekanma, "Plea-bargain Commercialises Our Criminal Justice System," *The Guardian*, May 17, 2011. See at: http://www.guardiannewsngr.com/index.php?option=com_content&view=article&id=48219:plea-bargain-commercialises-our-criminal-justice-ystem&catid=42:law&itemid=600; Internet (accessed May 18, 2011).

[7] Bryan A Garner, (ed.), *Black's Law Dictionary*, 8th ed. (St. Paul, Minnesota, USA: Thomson/West Publishing, 2004) p. 1190.

[8] Timothy Sandefur, "In Defence of Plea Bargaining" *The Pacific Legal Foundation*, November 4, 2003, p. 28.

[9] See D. M. Heshieh, "Plea Bargaining: Economic Costs and Benefits," http://www/diana-heshieh. com; Internet. Accessed on July 22, 2010.

damaging evidence.

Thus, a plea bargain is usually in any one of four main forms, namely:

Sentence Bargain – Sentence bargain involves an agreement by the accused person to a plea of guilty for the stated charge(s) in return for a lighter sentence usually recommended by the prosecutor to the trial judge, even though the judge is not bound by such recommendations. Nonetheless, in the spirit of the "courtroom workgroup" relationship that exists among the prosecutor, defense lawyer, and judge,[10] the trial judge usually goes along with the prosecutor's recommendation.

Charge Bargain – Charge bargain seems to be the most common form of plea negotiations. It entails a bargaining for the severity of the charges proffered against the accused. Usually in return for a plea of guilty to a lesser charge, the prosecutor dismisses the higher or other charges.

Count Bargain – In count bargain, the prosecutor and the accused person agree to a reduction of the number criminal charge counts filed against the accused. This emphasizes that although the facts of a case can give rise to several criminal counts, the prosecutor exercises discretion in deciding whether to charge on all counts. Count bargain is an effective way to avoid unnecessary repetition in charging the accused based on the same conduct.

Fact Bargain – This may be the least used form of bargaining. It entails the accused person admitting to some information stipulating to the truth and existence of provable facts, thus removing the need for the prosecutor to prove them. On his part, the prosecutor agrees not to introduce some other facts (probably more damaging to the accused) into evidence.

Overall, any form of plea bargain gives an accused person a chance to circumvent a trial with the risk of being convicted on the initial more serious charge(s).

Parties to a Plea Bargain

There are three main parties to a plea bargain: the prosecutor, the accused person/defense counsel, and the judge. However, there have been calls for the crime victim to be (more) involved in a plea bargain and some prosecutors take steps to ensure that. Thus, a plea bargain may include the following persons.

Prosecutor: The prosecutor is often referred to as the principal party in a plea negotiation and this is hinged on the fact that in most jurisdictions he has the discretion to initiate negotiations. In making plea agreements, the prosecutor is influenced by a plethora of reasons, prominent among which is the need to keep caseloads within manageable proportions. The prosecutor also considers the

---

[10] See David Neubauer, *America's Courts and the Criminal Justice System*, 10th ed. (Florence, Kentucky, USA: Cengage Learning, 2011).

strength and weakness of the evidence against the accused in reaching decisions on plea bargain agreements. Other criteria usually considered by prosecutors during the bargaining process include the seriousness of the accused person's crime(s) and his prior criminal records.

Accused Person/Defense Counsel: In plea negotiations, counsel typically represents the accused person. The defense counsel seeks to advance the interest of the accused in the bargaining process and in advancing this interest, the defense lawyer weighs the concessions offered by the prosecution against the accused person's chances of an acquittal at trial. It is also the job of the defense counsel to advise his client as to the strengths and weaknesses of the case against him, his possible defenses to the charge(s) and his chances of acquittal.

Trial Judge: Judicial participation in the actual bargaining process is rare in most jurisdictions, as judges are not permitted to take part in any implicit or explicit bargaining. However, in some jurisdictions, judges conduct in-chamber conferences and may offer to impose a specific sentence should the accused choose to plead guilty. There have been calls in some quarters in support of greater judicial participation in the negotiation process but these also raise questions as to the ability of the accused to secure a fair hearing should he choose the option of trial instead of bargaining. Finally, the onus falls on the judge to either accept or reject the plea agreement entered into by the other parties.

Victim: Crime victims have often been referred to as the forgotten persons in plea bargains; however, some prosecutors give substantial weight to the desires of the victims. Over the years, there have also been increased requests for greater victim participation in the criminal justice process by champions of a sub-specialty of criminology known as victimology. This is the branch of criminology that focuses on the socio-legal psychology of crime victims.[11]

Requirements for a Valid Plea

The United States of America has been described as "the cradle of plea bargaining".[12] In addition, the US Supreme Court has referred to plea-bargaining as "an essential part of the administration of justice" stating further that "properly administered plea bargaining is to be encouraged".[13] These statements demonstrate the important role and wide use of plea bargains in the US justice

---

[11] See generally A. C. Odinkalu and U. R. Chiemeka, "Victimology and the Criminal Justice System in Nigeria" *Journal of Human Rights and Practice*, Vol. 3, No. 1, 2, 3, December 1993.

[12] Anna Petrig, "Negotiated Justice and the Goals of International Criminal Tribunals: With a Focus on the Plea-Bargaining Practice of the ICTY and the Legal Framework of the ICC", *Chi-Kent J. Int'l & Comp. L. 1*. See at http://www.kentlaw.edu/jicl/articles/spring2008/Petrig_negotiated_justice_final.pdf; Internet (Accessed June 1, 2010).

[13] *Santobello v. New York*, 404 U.S. 257, 260 (1971). See at http://supreme.justia.com/us/404/257/case.html; Internet (Accessed May 20, 2010).

system. Thus, it is fitting for this chapter to examine the US model to help the reader understand the requirements for a valid plea agreement.

The conditions for a valid plea have been set out in a host of cases emanating from the United States Supreme Court and from statute. There are three basic requirements for a valid plea, namely: a voluntary waiver of rights; an intelligent waiver of rights; and factual basis to support the charges to which the defendant is pleading guilty. In *Brady v. United States*,[14] the US Supreme Court held as follows:

(a) A plea of guilty is not invalid merely because it is entered into to avoid the possibility of the death penalty and in this case the petitioner's plea of guilty met the standard of voluntariness, as it was made by one fully aware of the direct consequences of that plea.

(b) The petitioner's plea made after the advice by competent counsel was intelligently made. Also in this case, the Supreme Court quoted with approval the *dictum* of Judge Tuttle of the Court of Appeal for the Fifth Circuit on the standard of voluntariness of guilty plea, thus: A plea of guilty entered by one fully aware of the direct consequence, including the actual value of any committals made to him by the courts, prosecutor or his own counsel, must stand unless induced by threats (or promises to discontinue improper harassment), misrepresentation (including unfulfilled or unfulfillable promises), or perhaps by promises that are by their very nature improper as having no proper relationship to the prosecutor's business (e.g. bribe).[15] And in *Henderson v. Morgan*,[16] the US Supreme Court held that a plea may be involuntary either because the accused does not understand the nature of the constitutional protection he is waiving or because he has such an incomplete understanding of the charges that his plea cannot stand as an intelligent admission of guilt.

(c)   Finally, the third requirement for a valid guilty plea in the United States is not a creation of case law but one of statute, precisely Rule 11 (b) (3), *Federal Rules of Criminal Procedure*,[17] which states: "Before entering a judgment on a guilty plea, the court must determine that there is a factual basis for the plea."

The US Supreme Court has also given similar rulings on the requirements for a valid guilty plea in some other cases like *United States v. Jackson*,[18] and *Boykin v. Alabama*,[19] where the court held that the record must affirmatively

---

[14] 397 U.S. 742 (1970). See at http://supreme.justia.com/us/397/742/case.html; Internet (Accessed May 20, 2010).

[15] *Ibid.*

[16] 426 U.S. 637 (1976).

[17] See at http://www.law.cornell.edu/rules/frcrmp/#chapter_ii; Internet (Accessed March 14, 2011).

[18] 390 U.S. 570 (1968). See at http://www.supreme.justia.com/us/390/570/case.html; Internet (Accessed 20/5/2010).

[19] 395 U.S. 238 (1969). See at http://www.supreme.justia.com/us/395/238/case.html; Internet (Ac-

disclose that a defendant who pleaded guilty entered his plea understandingly and voluntarily.

In Nigeria, the position as to guilty plea is regulated by statute and a string of decided cases. Section 218 of the *Criminal Procedure Act*,[20] states:

> If the accused pleads guilty to any offence with which he is charged, the court shall record his plea as nearly as possible in the words used by him and if satisfied that he intends to admit the truth of all the essentials of the offence of which he has pleaded guilty, the court shall convict him of the offence and pass sentence upon or make an order against him unless there appear sufficient cause to the contrary.[21]

The above section provides for the effect of a guilty plea and the inherent duty of the courts when recording a plea of guilty. The court in this regard is required to adhere to certain procedures, which have been laid down by case law, including the following.

In *R. v. Heyes*,[22] the court held that the accused must plead guilty by himself as he cannot plead through counsel or anyone else. Also in *R. v. Ellis*,[23] the court held that if the accused pleads guilty through counsel the subsequent trial would be declared a nullity. As was held in *Onuoha v. The Police*,[24] the court must also ask sufficient questions to ensure that the accused intends to admit the charge and to plead guilty. Finally, in *Gbadamosi v. C.O.P.*,[25] it was held that the court must satisfy itself that the facts, which the accused must admit, constitute all the essential elements of the offense. The following *dictum* of Adefarasin, J. in *Ogbulare v. C.O.P.*[26] on the procedure to be followed on the entering of a guilty plea by the accused is quite instructive:

> It seems clear from the words of S. 218 of the C.P.A. that the mere fact that the accused has pleaded guilty to a charge should not be regarded as evidence of his guilt. The courts must be satisfied having regards to all the ingredients of the charge; the statements of the fact by the prosecution and the statement by the accused person in relation to the facts and ingredients

---

cessed 5/5/2010).

[20] Cap. C41, *(LFN) Supra.*

[21] Cap. C41, *Laws of the Federation of Nigeria* (LFN), 2004.

[22] (1951) 1 K.B. 29.

[23] (1973) 57 Cr. App. R. 571.

[24] (1959) NRNLR 96.

[25] (1974) 1 WNLR 172.

[26] (1974) C.C.H.C.J. 8992.

constituting the charge that the accused intended to admit the truth of all the essentials of the offence of which he has pleaded guilty. The language of the law makes it clear that the courts must be satisfied from what the accused person has said in answer to the facts relating to the charge that he intended to admit having committed the offence with which he was charged. It is therefore necessary for the courts to put all the facts which are alleged by the prosecution to the accused person and give him an opportunity of admitting or denying them before proceeding to a conviction. If the accused person admits these facts stated and the ingredients constituting the offence, it could convict. If however the facts stated do not constitute the offence, he is entitled to a plea of not guilty and notwithstanding the plea of guilty by the accused.[27]

There have also been other cases where the courts enunciated useful principles as regards a plea of guilty. In *John Ward Stevenson v. Inspector General of Police*,[28] the accused was charged with the offense of possessing Indian hemp. He pleaded guilty and neither the hemp nor a chemist's report was tendered in evidence. On appeal, the question for determination was whether it was safe to convict on such basis. The court held that when a person is charged under Section 5 (1) (b) of the *Indian Hemp Decree* No. 19, 1966, in the absence of evidence of the nature of the plants or seed or their production in court, it is unsafe to convict. The court also held the same in *Ishola v. The State*.[29] The cases give credence to the view that there must be a factual basis for a guilty plea.

Further, sometimes in criminal proceedings the circumstances of the court may be altered by events beyond human control after the accused person has pleaded guilty. When that happens, an important question is what happens to the guilty plea. In *Sanmamo v. The State*,[30] the issue for determination on appeal was whether the failure to take a new plea where there was a change in the constitution of the trial court voided proceedings for non-compliance with Section 215 of the *Criminal Procedure Act*. The court held as follows: (a) The provision of Section 215 is mandatory and the requirement of a plea is not one of mere form but of law; (b) Nothing showed that the trial judge read over the charge and explained it to the appellant; (c) Where a judge dies during a trial and a new judge takes over, there should be a *de novo* trial including a new plea; and (d) Non-compliance with Section 215 is fatal and renders the trial a nullity *ab initio*.

---

[27] *Ibid.*
[28] (1966) 2 All N.L.R 261.
[29] (1969) N.M.L.R 259.
[30] (1967) N.M.L.R 314.

In *R. v. Guest (ex-parte Anthony)*,[31] the court held that conviction must be evidenced by some overt act such as an entry in the record book under Section 245. The court was also of the opinion that in a trial on indictment in England the court has discretion to allow a plea of guilty to be withdrawn at any time before the sentence but a court of summary jurisdiction is *functus officio* once an equivocal plea of guilty has been entered.

Finally for this section, it remains to add that, as a matter of principle, in cases where the offense charged attracts capital punishment, the court enters a plea of "not guilty" even if the accused pleads "guilty". This is probably because the human life is sacred and therefore there should be adequate institutional safeguards to protect it.

Offense of Compounding Under Nigerian Law

Compounding of a criminal offense is any agreement, promise for any reward, restitution, or other consideration, to forbear to prosecute or to further prosecute an offender in respect of any offense, whether such offense shall have been committed or not.[32] This means that compounding involves both the victim of the crime and the law enforcement agent. Compounding of felonious offenses is a crime and if the punishment for the offense being compounded is death or life imprisonment, the compounding offense attracts a seven-year jail term. In any other case, the offender is liable to imprisonment for three years.[33]

The recognition that an agreement to stifle prosecution is unlawful and that it defeats the ends of justice dates back to a very early period of English history. Compounding an offense was equivalent to the common law offense of theft when the owner not only knew of the felony, but also took back his goods from the thief or took steps to protect or favor the thief or to protect him from being prosecuted and thereby provided an escape for him. The essence of compounding lies in the corrupt agreement by the person charged with the person offering consideration.

Another form which compounding of offenses can take is an advertisement for the return of stolen property where there is express or implied undertaking that no prosecution will be commenced against the offender.[34] Though the Nigerian *Criminal Code* does not specifically categorize advertising in the above manner

---

[31] (1964) 1 W.L.R. 1273.

[32] See Section 127 of the *Criminal Code CAP* C38, LFN 2004; see also E. A. Joshua, *Corruption in the Rock* (Abuja, Nigeria: John Global Ltd., 2006) p. 113.

[33] Section 127 of the *Criminal Code, Ibid*; see also B. Layi, *Criminal Law and Procedure Through the Cases* (Lagos, Nigeria: Lawbreed, 2003) p. 142.

[34] Section 129 of the *Criminal Code, Ibid*.

to be compounding of an offense, it is regarded as such in England. This could be because under the Nigerian *Criminal Code*, such an advertisement is classified as a simple offense while compounding of an offense properly so called is a felony.

Although compounding of an offense is a crime, prosecution for the crime can be discontinued by the Attorney-General and Minister of Justice in the exercise of powers conferred on him by the Constitution[35] or where such power to compound is specifically provided for by a statute.[36] In the case of amicable settlement, where a matter has already commenced in court, the fact that the parties failed to obtain leave of the court before which the case is pending does not make the parties guilty of compounding a crime, unless there is evidence that some consideration passed to the complainant to induce him to agree to the settlement.

Overall, there are two ingredients of the offense of compounding: one is the offer or agreement, while the other is the consideration of money or any valuable thing or advantage involving the accused person (standing trial for compounding an offense) or any other person in the arrangement.

Under the Criminal Code

Compounding of offenses under the Nigerian *Criminal Code* is restricted to felonies.[37] The *Criminal Code* provides:

> Any person who asks, receives, or obtains, or agrees or attempts to receive or obtain any property or benefit of any kind for himself or any other person upon any agreement or understanding that he will compound or conceal a felony, or will abstain from, discontinue, or delay a prosecution for a felony, or will withhold any evidence thereof, is guilty of an offence.[38]

Compounding is deemed complete where the accused person merely agrees to forbear to prosecute. He need not actually forbear. He is equally guilty if he offers to desist from prosecuting the offender. However, where a complainant, in a criminal offense committed against him, settles out of court in order to bring peace and harmony, such a person (complainant) cannot be said to have compounded such an offense. This is because peace and harmony cannot be interpreted to mean benefit or any advantage within the meaning of section 127

---

[35] See Section 174 of the 1999 Constitution.

[36] Example: Section 14 (2), *EFCC Act, 2004*.

[37] *Criminal Code*, op. cit., section 127; see also *C. O. Okonkwo and Naish, Criminal Law in Nigeria* 2nd ed. (Ibadan, Nigeria: Spectrum Books, 2005).

[38] *Criminal Code*, op. cit., section 127.

of the *Criminal Code*.

An offense, if not compounded before it is taken to court for trial, can amount to compounding of penal action.[39] However, in the case of settlement or attempted settlement of a case, compounding can only occur where the trial judge has not given consent or order authorizing such settlement.[40] Under the *Criminal Code*, although it is an offense to conceal or agree not to prosecute an offense, which is classified as felonious, it is not an offense to conceal or agree to desist from prosecuting a misdemeanor.

In view of the English influences on the Nigerian *Criminal Code*, an update of the law of England on compounding is in order. By virtue of the *Criminal Law Act of 1967*, which eliminated the common law classification of felonies and misdemeanors, the offense of compounding felonies does not exist any longer in the English criminal law.[41] In place of that, all arrestable offenses are recognized as being capable of being compounded.[42] The *actus reus* of the offense of compounding involves two elements: an arrestable offense must actually have been committed; and (2) the accused must have agreed to accept or have accepted consideration for not disclosing information, which he knows or believes to be material or to forbear to prosecute the offender.[43] The mental element also consists in two elements, which must be proved, thus: (1) the accused must have known or believed that an offense of the class of felony has been committed; and (2) intended to accept or to agree to accept consideration other than making good of loss or the making of reasonable commendation.[44]

Under the Penal Code

Just like the provisions of other penal legislations, the Nigerian *Penal Code* prohibits the act of compounding offenses. However, it makes no distinction between compoundable offense and non-compoundable offense *vis-à-vis* whether the offense is an indictable offense or not as is found in the *Criminal Code*. The application of the *Penal Code* is restricted to those states carved out of the northern region of Nigeria.[45] The *Penal Code* provides as follows: "Whoever,

---

[39] *Ibid.*

[40] Section 128 of the *Criminal Code*.

[41] Smith and Hogan, *Criminal Law* 10th ed. (London, England: Butterworths, 2002) p. 6.

[42] Section 5 (1) of the *Criminal Law Act, 1967*.

[43] Smith and Hogan *op. cit.*, p. 188.

[44] *Ibid.*, p. 189. It has been recommended that compounding offense will not apply to a person who refrains from giving information because he does not think it right that the offender should be prosecuted or because of a promise of reparation by the offender. It would be difficult to justify making the offense apply to those kinds of cases.

[45] C. O. Okonkwo and Naish, *Criminal Law in Nigeria* 2nd ed., (Ibadan, Nigeria: Spectrum Books, 2005).

knowing or having reason to believe that an offence has been committed by a person and accepts or attempts to accept a gratification from that other person in order to screen that other person from prosecution is guilty of an offence."[46] The implication of the words used in the provision is that there is no classification of the offenses to which the section applies. Again, nobody has the right to conceal any offense in order to receive any gratification.[47] However, such concealment will not amount to compounding of offenses if there is no element of gratification. Offenders shall be punished with imprisonment, which may extend to five years and shall also be liable to fine.[48] However, where a law provides that a particular offense is a compoundable one, no criminal charges are maintainable against any person who conceals it for material gains.[49] This crime is common in the northern region of Nigeria in cases of animal theft and is distinguished from other offenses known in Muslim law as the accepting of *Bushara* whereby restoration of stolen property is effected through payment of money.[50]

In addition to the foregoing, the inducing of the concealment of an offense through the offer of gratification by the offender or any other person is also punishable although to a greater degree (7 years).[51] Where the offense is a compoundable one, it becomes lawful to induce concealment.[52] The place of the commission of the offense makes no difference: whether in northern or southern Nigeria, provided it would be an offense in the north.[53]

Plea Bargaining in Nigeria

It is doubtful, indeed arguable, if plea bargain as a sentencing option had been in use in Nigeria prior to the enactment of the *Economic and Financial Crimes Commission (Establishment) Act*. More than anything, the EFCC Act has popularized plea bargain as a sentencing option in Nigeria. Section 13 (2) of the Act reads thus:

> Without prejudice to section 174 of the Constitution of the Federal Republic of Nigeria 1999 (which relates to the power of the Attorney-General of the Federation to institute, continue or discontinue criminal proceedings against any persons in any court

---

[46] Section 168 (1) of the *Penal Code*.

[47] S. S. Richardson, *Notes on the Penal Code Law* 3rd ed. (Zaria, Nigeria: Institute of Administration, 1986) p. 132.

[48] Section 168 (1) of the *Penal Code*.

[49] *Ibid*, section 168 (2).

[50] *Richardson, op. cit.*, p. 132.

[51] Section 169 (1) of the *Penal Code*.

[52] *Ibid*, section 169 (2).

[53] Explanatory note to section 169 of the *Penal Code*.

of law), the Commission may compound any offence punishable under this Act by accepting such sums of money as it thinks fit, not exceeding the amount of the maximum fine to which that person would have been liable if he had been convicted of that offence.[54]

For a proper understanding of the above provision, attention ought to be given to the key phrase in the second limb of the subsection. The *Black's Law Dictionary* defines compounding as, "the offence of either agreeing not to prosecute a crime that one knows has been committed or agreeing to hamper the prosecution."[55] Ordinarily, compounding is a crime in Nigeria; however, Section 13 (2) of the EFCC Act makes an exception. The Section 13 appears to be unconstitutional in that it seems to authorize the commission of a crime by a public statutory body, which is unacceptable in the Nigerian legal system.

Our position therefore is that Section 13 of the EFCC Act is similar to but not plea-bargaining. Plea-bargaining is the process whereby the defense pleads guilty to a lesser offense with the agreement of the prosecution for a lesser punishment. However, in Section 13 (2) of the EFCC Act cited above, compounding an offense simply means collecting huge sums of money allegedly stolen by the criminal defendant instead of prosecuting him. We opine that it seems similar owing to the fact that both the defense and the prosecution still agree here on the money to be returned just as in a plea bargain. Probably, in the absence of substantial evidence on the part of the prosecution to prove that the accused person committed the crime at issue, the prosecutor bargains for certainty of a conviction. But, the provision of the EFCC Act is impliedly geared towards restoration of the national treasury, to prevent public servants from looting the treasury. This position is supported by the provision of Section 13 (3) of the Act, thus: "All monies received by the Commission under the provisions of subsection (2) of this section shall be paid into the Consolidated Revenue Fund of the Federation."

---

[54] There are a number of federal legislations that have provisions that can be approximated to plea bargain as contained in the EFCC Act. For instance, Section 186 (1) of the *Customs and Excise Management Act*, Cap. C45, Laws of the Federation of Nigeria, 2004 empowers the Board to continue or discontinue criminal proceedings against any person in any Court of Law or institute proceedings against forfeited property. Also, the National Drug Law Enforcement Agency (NDLEA) has relied heavily on Section 11 (2) of the *National Drug Law Enforcement Agency Act* to cut deals with some drug barons whereby such drug barons are made to return their drug money in exchange for lighter sentences. This practice has been much criticised especially as the enabling Act provides for a minimum of 15 years imprisonment without the option of fine.

[55] Bryan Garner, *Black's Law Dictionary, op. cit*, p. 304.

Under the Economic and Financial Crimes Commission Act

The porous nature of the Nigerian criminal investigation machinery has made the various crime-fighting agencies to always look for quick ways out. The Economic and Financial Crimes Commission (EFCC) is no exception. However, unlike some other agencies, the EFCC is statutorily empowered to do so. This is its tool of compounding offenses. Subject to the power of the Attorney-General of the Federation *vis-à-vis* the prosecution of crimes, the EFCC is empowered to compound a crime under the Act by accepting from a person any money it thinks fit but not exceeding the maximum amount of which the person would have been liable if he had been convicted of that offense.[56] A further improvement on this kind of power is that money realized from compounding an offense shall be paid into the Consolidated Revenue Fund of the Federation.[57]

However, the wording of Section 13 of the Act tends to conflict with the traditional meaning of compounding of offenses. According to Kolajo, compounding an offense means[58] accepting or agreeing to accept or entering into an agreement for valuable consideration not to prosecute a person for felony or to show him favor; or for not disclosing information that might assist in convicting or prosecuting someone who has committed an indictable offense.

The EFCC has relied on the provisions of Section 13 to solve many economic crimes in Nigeria. These range from Tafa Balogun's case to that of Diepreye Alamieseigha. However, these cases do not fall squarely on the offense of compounding but rather on plea bargaining. Despite the discrepancy between the provisions on the offense of compounding and its implementation, the EFCC has maintained that it has powers to do other things to ensure the carrying out of its duties under the EFCC Act.

Plea Bargain: Comparative Perspectives

United States of America

For many years, there was no uniform or official system of plea bargaining in the United States. The system of plea bargaining in the federal system was officially recognized with the passage of the 1974 Amendment to the *Federal Rules of Criminal Procedure*. According to Fisher, plea bargaining is far more prevalent in the United States than in any other country and the use of the guilty plea accounts

---

[56] Section 13 (2) of the *EFCC Act*.

[57] *Ibid*, section 14 (3).

[58] A. A. Kolajo, Law *Dictionary* (Ibadan, Nigeria: Brighter Star) p. 113.

for 90 to 95 percent of all convictions in the United States.[59] Indeed, the United States was recently described as the "cradle of modern plea bargaining".[60] In the United States, all criminal cases can be plea-bargained irrespective of the nature of the offense or the gravity of the sentence. Another concept likened to that of plea bargaining is *nolo contendere*, which means, "I do not wish to contest". A no contest plea, while not technically a guilty plea, has the same immediate effect as a guilty plea and is often offered as a part of a plea bargain.[61]

The Supreme Court of the United States has in a string of cases endorsed the practice of plea bargaining and has also laid down condition precedents for a valid guilty plea. In *Santobello v. New York*,[62] the US Supreme Court held that plea bargaining is to be encouraged because if every criminal charge were subjected to a full scale trial, the states and the federal government would need to multiply by many times the number of judges and court facilities in order to accommodate all the cases. In *Boykin v. Alabama*,[63] the Supreme Court held that the records must disclose that the defendant voluntarily and understandingly pleaded guilty. Also, in *Strickland v. Washington*,[64] the Supreme Court defined the Sixth Amendment (to the US Constitution) guarantee of assistance to counsel to mean "effective assistance" which seems to entail a modicum of bargaining and negotiation. In *Brady v. U.S.*,[65] the court held that the voluntariness of a guilty plea was motivated by fear of a heavier sentence following trial, even though that fear was held under a statute that the courts declared unconstitutional subsequent to the guilty plea.

In the United States, a guilty plea constitutes a waiver of certain Fifth and Sixth Amendment rights, such as the right against self-incrimination, right to confront witnesses, and right to a jury trial. However, in some cases an appeal may lie against the results of a plea bargain if the accused can prove "ineffectiveness of counsel" and this occurs when the accused proves that there was a reasonable probability that but for counsel's incompetence the defendant would not have pleaded guilty and would have insisted on trial.[66] But, the rule as to the intelligent

---

[59] George Fisher, "Plea Bargaining's Triumph" 109 *Yale Law Journal*, 857, 1012-1013 (2000).

[60] Anna Petrig, "Negotiated Justice and the Goals of International Criminal Tribunals: With a Focus on the Plea-Bargaining Practice of the ICTY and the Legal Framework of the ICC", Chi-Kent J. Int'l & Comp. L. 1. See at http://www.kentlaw.edu/jicl/articles/spring2008/Petrig_negotiated_justice_final.pdf; Internet (Accessed June 1, 2010).

[61] Stephano Bibas, "Harmonizing Substantive Criminal Law Values and Criminal Procedure: The Case of Alford and Nolo Contendere Pleas", *Cornell Law Review*, Vol. 88 (No. 6) July 2003.

[62] 404 U.S. 257, 260 (1971). See at http://supreme.justia.com/us/404/257/case.html; Internet (Accessed May 20, 2010).

[63] 395 U.S. 238 (1969). See at http://www.supreme.justia.com/us/395/238/case.html; Internet (Accessed May 5, 2010).

[64] 507 U.S. 265, 266 (1973).

[65] 397 U.S. 742 (1970).

[66] See Central European and Eurasian Law Initiative, "PLEA BARGAINS: A Concept Paper" at http://www.docstoc.com/docs/51006703/Plea-Bargaining—A-Concept-Paper; Internet (Accessed

nature of a plea does not require that a plea be attacked if the defendant did not correctly assess every relevant factor before entering into the decision. In addition, a defendant is not entitled to withdraw his plea merely because he discovers long after the plea has been accepted that he guessed incorrectly the quality of the state's case or the likely penalties attached to the alternative course of action.

Italy

The need to introduce expedient forms of criminal disposition in Italy was borne out of the fact that the drafters of the Italian code felt that the former trial system was not fair and open and generally in line with the values of an open democratic society.[67] The second reason was the growing condemnation by the European Court of Human Rights for the tremendous delays defendants suffered before their cases went on trial.[68]

The Italian Code[69] allows for a limited system of plea bargaining under the section titled *"applicazione della pena su richies ta delle parti"*, which translates roughly as "the application of punishment upon request of parties". Under this system, the prosecutor and defense attorney enter an agreement on the sentence to be required and ask the judge to impose the sentence. This form of plea bargaining differs from the United States system in the sense that it does not permit "charge bargaining" where the criminal charge is reduced as part of the bargain to gain a lower sentencing range for the accused person.

Originally, Italy restricted plea bargaining to minor cases in the sense that anyone charged with a crime that might involve a sentence in excess of three years could not enter into a plea bargain. But this limitation was extended in 2003 so that no crime exceeding a sentence of 7 and half years can be plea bargained and the new code excludes certain offenses, such as organized crime, kidnapping, extortion, trafficking of drugs, and crimes of terrorism.[70]

To understand Italy's nervousness about plea bargaining, one has to appreciate how much the concept of "bargained justice" conflicts with Italy's civil law heritage. European systems of criminal justice are deeply committed to the proposition that similar defendants (meaning those with the same sentencing background) should be treated similarly under the law. This is in stark disparity

---

March 18, 2011).

[67] Mario Chiavario, *La Reformia Del Processo Penale* [The Reform of the Criminal Process] 24, 2nd Edition 1990; *Piermaria Corso*, cited in "The Battle to Establish an Adversarial Trial System in Italy", *Michigan Journal of International Law*, Vol. 25: 550.

[68] Giuseppe Di Federico, "The Crises of the Justice System and the Referendum on the Judiciary", *Italian Politics: A Review* (Corbetta eds., 1989) 382.

[69] *Codice di Procedure Penal 1988* (hereinafter referred to as C.P.P.).

[70] C.P.P, Art. 444. The provision also states that plea bargaining is not permitted for defendants who are recidivists if the final sentence would exceed two years.

with the situation in the United States where a defendant and a co-defendant who have committed the same crime may receive very different sentences. It has been posited that Italy and many other European countries have a doctrine of mandatory prosecution whereby the prosecuting authority must bring a criminal complaint against someone if they have reason to believe that the person committed a crime.[71] The Italian Constitution also enshrines this principle of mandatory prosecution.[72] This doctrine of mandatory prosecution is somewhat incompatible with plea bargaining because of the wide discretion given to the prosecutor.

The *Italian Code* also provides important safeguards for defendants against the arbitrary refusal of a public prosecutor to allow the defendant to avoid trial and receive a discounted sentence. First, a prosecutor who refuses a defendant's request for a reduced sentence must explain and justify the reasons for refusing the plea bargain sought by the defendant.[73] Second, if the public prosecutor refuses to agree to the reduced sentence, the defendant may make application to the court at the start of the trial for the discounted sentence and if the judge thinks it appropriate, the judge may agree to sentence the defendant according to the plea bargaining provisions thereby giving the defendant the reduced sentence.[74] Third, even after a full trial, if the judge concludes that the refusal of the public prosecutor to enter into a plea bargain before the trial was in error, the judge in sentencing may give the defendant the reduction in sentence allowed under the plea bargaining procedure.[75]

Further, Italian judges are not compelled to ratify any plea agreement reached between the parties. To protect the independence of the judges, the plea bargaining procedure in the code requires that before a judge accepts a plea bargain the judge must examine the evidence and see if it is possible despite the defense agreement to the bargain to enter a judgment of acquittal for the defendant.[76] If there is no possibility of acquittal, the judge must make sure that the crime fits the facts presented and that the punishment asked by the parties is adequate and fair for the offense. The code also provides that the judge should examine the defendant personally to make sure that the defendant has agreed to the disposition.[77]

---

[71] J. H. Langbien "Controlling Prosecutorial Discretion in Germany", 41 *University of Chicago Law Review,* (1994) 3.

[72] Art. 112 of the Italian Constitution.

[73] *C.P.P,* Art. 446, Sec. 6.

[74] *Ibid,* Art. 448.

[75] *Ibid,* Art. 448, Sec. 1.

[76] *Ibid,* Art. 444, Sec. 2.

[77] *Ibid,* Art. 446, Sec. 5.

England

Underlying the common law theory of evidence procedure in criminal cases is an assumption that guilt will be determined by means of a formal adversarial process in which evidence is presented to an impartial jury.[78] In England, the courts have been reluctant to acknowledge that a plea of guilty can be anything other than a full, free and voluntary decision by the criminal defendant. And, specifically, the idea of plea bargaining or the notion that pressures may be brought to bear on a defendant to induce him to plead guilty has traditionally been regarded as being repugnant to the English legal system. In *R. v. Turner*,[79] the court sought to check, if not eradicate, the development of plea bargaining. Accordingly, Lord Parker stated that a judge should never indicate the sentence which he intends to impose, unless he says that whatever happens whether the accused pleads guilty or not guilty, the sentence will or will not take a particular form, example a probation order or a fine or custodial remedy. Lord Parker went on to say that, the practice of bargaining "could be taken to be undue pressure on the accused thus depriving him of that complete freedom of choice which is essential".[80] Critics of plea bargaining in England regard it as a betrayal of the ideal of the professional construction of justice. They argue that plea negotiations operate on the premise that the right of an accused to trial is mere rhetoric.

In *Ryan*,[81] the Court of Appeal indicated that it is invariably inappropriate for counsel to approach a judge seeking an indication as to the length of the sentence he was minded to impose. Further, that it was even more undesirable when the basis of the approach was that the defendant might be prepared to plead guilty in the light of the indictment. In England, the role of judges in plea bargaining is heavily circumscribed and discouraged. Notwithstanding, the English criminal justice system effectively secures a large number of guilty pleas by means of overt negotiations.[82] The system also customarily awards a reduction in sentence in return for a guilty plea.

India

Until recently, plea bargaining was alien to the Indian criminal justice system. In March 2003, the Committee on Criminal Justice Reforms headed by Justice V. S. Malimath submitted its report recommending that a system of plea

---

[78] John Baldwin and Michael McConville, "Plea Bargaining and Plea Negotiation in England" *Law and Society Review,* Vol. 13, No. 2, Special Issue on Plea Bargaining (Winter 1979) pp. 287-307. See at http://www.jstor.org/stable/3053255; Internet (Accessed on March 18, 2011).

[79] (1970) 2 Q.B. 321.

[80] *Ibid.*

[81] Court of Appeal, Unreported 30 April, 1999. *The Times,* April 30, 1999.

[82] John Baldwin and Michael McConville, *loc. cit.*

bargaining be introduced into the criminal justice system of India to facilitate the early resolution of criminal cases and reduce the burden of the courts. Plea bargaining has now been introduced into India's criminal procedure via the *Criminal Law (Amendment) Act 2005*.[83] Some of the salient features of the Indian system of plea bargaining that should be noted are:

(1) The plea bargaining is only applicable in cases where the punishment or sentence is up to 7 years imprisonment.

(2) It does not apply to socio-economic offenses.

(3) It does not apply to offenses committed against a woman or child below 14 years of age.

(4) Once a court passes an order in such a case, no appeal shall lie to any court against that order.

(5) The accused is examined in chambers with the prosecutor, the investigating police officer, and the victim in order to work out a mutually satisfying disposition of the case.

Critics of this form of plea bargaining have leveled a host of criticisms, including the following:

a) The court's examination of the accused in chambers as opposed to open court will lead to public cynicism and distrust for the plea-bargaining system.

b) The failure of the courts to ensure that the accused understands the implications of entering into a plea bargain will inevitably lead to injustice for the accused, particularly given the likelihood that most accused persons will not be able to avoid legal advice.

c) Involving the police in the bargaining process would lead to coercion.

d) Involving the victim in the bargaining process would lead to corruption.

e) By involving the court in the bargaining process, the court's impartiality is undermined.

f) Failure to arm the court with broad discretion to reject the plea bargain will inevitably lead to injustice.

Prior to the passing of the 2005 Act, the Supreme Court of India had ruled thus: It is settled law that the court cannot dispose of a criminal case based on plea bargaining. The court has to decide it on its merits. If the accused confesses his guilt, the appropriate sentence is required to be implemented; mere acceptance or admission of guilt should not be a ground for reduction of the sentence.[84] However, in a more recent case, the court in *State of Gujarat v.*

---

[83] S. S. Ghosh, "Plea Bargaining - An Analysis of the Concept". See at http://www.legalservicesIndia.com; Internet (Accessed on March 19, 2011).

[84] *State of Uttar Predesh v. Chandrika*, 2000, Cr. L. J. 384 (386).

Natwar Harchanji Thakor[85] held: The very object of the law is to provide cheap and expeditious justice by resolution of disputes, including the trial of criminal cases. Considering the present realistic profile of the pendency and delay in disposal in the administration of law and justice, fundamental reforms are inevitable. Nothing should be static.

Thus, by the 2005 Act and subject to its limitations, plea bargaining is now a part of the Indian criminal justice system.

The International Criminal Tribunal

Globalization and interdependence have created a world where nations voluntarily relinquish aspects of their sovereignty for what they view as the communal good of the world. This has led to the formulation of such organizations and agencies as the United Nations Organization, the African Union, the European Union, and the International Criminal Court, amongst a host of others. The International Criminal Tribunal was set up in line with the Rome Statute.[86] We shall be considering specifically the International Criminal Tribunal Yugoslavia (ICTY).

The ICTY was established in line with Resolution 827 on May 25, 1993 as a response to the violation of international law and threats to peace in the former Yugoslavia. At its inception, the tribunal rejected negotiated outcomes as incompatible with its broad mandate but eventually amended its Rules of Procedure and Evidence to make provisions for plea bargaining.[87] This action by the ICTY led to widespread outcry as to the incompatibility of negotiated justice with the goals of the international criminal justice, i.e. the duty to prosecute, the principle of just desert, the establishment of a historical record, and the realization of the victim's interest.[88]

Thus, initially, the judges at the ICTY rejected a proposal of immunity to any accused who offered substantial cooperation. The United States of America had offered the proposal.[89] However, later, the appointment of a United States judge set the tone for the momentum of change at the ICTY. And in *Prosecutor v. Eredemovic*,[90] the tribunal stated as follows: The concept of the guilty plea *per se* is the peculiar product of the adversarial system of the common law, which recognizes the advantage it provides to the public in minimizing costs and in saving

---

[85] (2005) Cr. L. J. 2957.

[86] *Rome Statute on the International Criminal Court*, Art. 5, Sec. 1, U.N. Doc A/Conf.183/9.

[87] Rule 62 ICTY – *Rules of Procedure and Evidence*.

[88] Anna Petrig, *loc. cit.*

[89] Michael P. Scharf, "Trading Justice for Efficiency, Plea Bargaining and International Tribunals", *Journal of International Criminal* Justice 2 (4) (2004) 1070-1081.

[90] CASE NO. IT-96-22-A, Joint Separate Opinion of Judge McDonald and Judge Vohran 2, (Oct. 7, 1997).

of courts' time. This common law institution of the guilty plea should find in our view a ready place in an international criminal forum such as the International Tribunal confronted by cases, which by their inherent nature are very complex and necessarily require lengthy hearings.

In *Prosecutor v. Eredemovic*,[91] Eredemovic was indicted on a one-count charge of a crime against humanity and on an alternative count of a violation of the laws and customs of war. He pleaded guilty to the crimes against humanity and the courts dismissed the second count. Upon appeal by Eredemovic, the appellate division of the ICTY ruled that the plea was not informed because he did not have full knowledge of both the nature of the charge against him and the consequences of his plea before another trial chamber. A retrial was ordered and this time he pleaded guilty to violation of laws and customs of war and the other count of crimes against humanity was dropped. The tribunal in this case also stated that an admission of guilt demonstrates honesty and it is important for the International Tribunal to encourage people to come forth whether already indicted or as unknown perpetrators. Furthermore, this voluntary admission of guilt, which saved the International Tribunal the time and effort of a lengthy investigation and trial, is to be commended.

Thus, finally, plea bargaining is a part of the ICTY process. And it should be observed that Rule 62 of the ICTY's *Rules of Procedure and Evidence*, which allows for both sentence and charge bargaining reflects a unique amalgam between the adversarial and inquisitorial procedural elements.[92]

Plea Bargain: A Constitutional Question

One of the major criticisms of the concept of plea bargaining or "negotiated justice" is that the practice is unconstitutional. It has been opined by a host of scholars, writers, and analysts that plea bargaining is inconsistent with the provisions of the constitution especially as it relates to the fundamental right of fair hearing. This is because plea bargaining necessarily entails the waiver of some fair hearing rights including the right against self-incrimination, and the right to confront one's accuser and witnesses. Plea bargain also circumscribes the right of an accused person to appeal the decision of the trial court. However, it should be noted that these rights are not absolute or inalienable. The person vested with such rights can indeed waive them. The criticisms of plea bargain and the answers to them apply to Nigeria as they do to other countries.

In the Nigerian case of *Ariori v. Elemo*,[93] the issues for determination were: (1) Whether a person can waive his fundamental right conferred by the

---

[91] *Ibid.*

[92] Anna Petrig, *loc. cit.*

[93] (1983) 1 SCNLR 1.

Constitution? (2) What constitutes a waiver? (3) To what extent can a person waive rights conferred upon him by law? The court held: The concept of a waiver must be one that presupposes that the person who is to enjoy a benefit or who has the choice of two benefits is fully aware of his right to the benefit or benefits but either neglects to exercise his rights to the benefit or, where he has a choice of two, he decides to take one but not both. The exercise has to be a voluntary act. Where a right is conferred solely on an individual, there is no problem as to the extent to which he can waive such right since it is for his own benefit. A beneficiary under a statute should have full competence to waive these rights once they are conferred solely for his benefit, unless the statute forbids such waivers. If however the right conferred involves an element of public policy, i.e. are of interest to the public, the individual might not be entitled to waive them. Idigbe, J.S.C. went ahead to define a waiver thus: The intentional and voluntary surrender or relinquishment of a known privilege and or right, it therefore implies a dispensation or abandonment by the party waiving the right or privilege, upon which at his own option he could have insisted.

It is sufficiently clear from the *dictum* enunciated in *Ariori v. Elemo*[94] that the party entitled thereto can indeed waive certain rights. It is our view that the right to cross-examine and confront witnesses, the right against self-incrimination, and the right to a full trial are not rights that touch on public policy but are rights that accrue and are personal to the accused on trial and not to the public at large. As long as the accused waives such rights voluntarily and intelligently (i.e., he has the full competence to waive such rights), such waivers should be considered valid. The second issue that necessarily arises is that stated by critics of plea bargaining to the effect that a negotiated plea is inherently coercive thereby vitiating voluntariness. It has been stated as follows: Critics of plea bargaining continue to voice earlier judicial and legislative sentiments condemning the practice on the ground that the standard of voluntariness cannot be met because the practice is intrinsically coercive.[95]

The first line of argument proffered by critics is that any difference between the sentences for a guilty plea and not guilty plea constitutes an implied threat that operates to coerce the accused person to plead guilty.[96] The bargain situation facing the criminal defendant has been likened to that facing a victim of a gunman demanding the victim's money.[97] Kipnis states that the element of threat is intrinsic to a plea bargain insofar as the prosecutor, like the gunman,

---

[94] *Ibid.*

[95] Conrad Brunk, "The problem of Voluntariness and Coercion in the Negotiated Plea", *Law and Society Review,* Vol. 13, No.2, Special Issue on Plea Bargaining, (Winter, 1979) pp. 527-533. Blackwell Publishing.

[96] A. S. Blumberg. *op. cit.*

[97] Kenneth Kipnis "Criminal Justice and the Negotiated Plea," 86 *Ethics* 93 in Conrad Brunk, *loc. cit.*

"requires persons to make hard choices between a very certain smaller imposition and an uncertain greater imposition".[98] The second line of argument is as follows: Whether or not threats or other forms of duress enter into a decision to "cop a plea," the very offer of consideration in exchange for a plea constitutes an "inducement" that places a burden on the right to trial by undermining the will of the accused person to exercise it.[99] Also, whether a guilty plea is as a result of threats, false promises, or misrepresentation, or merely a proffered reduction in the sentence or charge, it is likely that the accused will feel the same pressure to plead guilty. In offering benefits or concessions to accused persons in order to secure guilty pleas, plea bargaining encourages both the guilty and innocent to plead guilty. As the concession or inducement increases, so also does the risk of causing an innocent person to plead guilty.[100]

Conrad Brunk suggests that in order to resolve these differences, one has to understand the sense of freedom at issue in answering whether a negotiated plea is voluntarily given. He tags this freedom "social freedom", which is the question of the conditions under which the choice of an action by an individual or group is free from constraints imposed by other persons or social institutions. He goes ahead to opine that a person's choice may be coerced in this sense even though it is voluntary in the psychological sense. And a person's choice may be involuntary even though it is free in the social sense ("not coerced"). Brunk goes on to ask the question: Do all inducements presented to a person influence or call into question the voluntariness of his choice? To this question, he offers an analogy: "The person who offers to buy my house at an unreasonably high price is certainly influencing my choice and in this sense is 'inducing' me to sell the house. But certainly this 'inducement' does not necessarily impinge upon my (social) freedom of choice. My freedom to act is increased by the offer, not diminished; hence I am not being coerced to sell the house."[101] He then concluded by stating as follows: "Since pure and simple offers do not infringe upon voluntariness of choice and there is no suggestion that the defendant is being 'forced' to plead guilty, what is at issue is whether 'soft' or 'hard' coercion is applied to the defendant so that his choice to plead guilty can be said to be against his own will."[102]

Brunk further opines that the question should be whether the one alternative (the guilty plea) is made preferable to the other (trial) by coercive incentives that are not themselves a part of the normal prosecutorial process or alternatively, whether the right to trial is being "burdened" with conditions not

---

[98] *Harvard Law Review*, "Comment: The Unconstitutionality of Plea Bargaining", 83 *Harvard Law Review* (1970). Cited in Conrad Brunk, *loc. cit.*

[99] Conrad Brunk, *loc. cit.*

[100] See Fergurson and Roberts "Plea Bargaining: Directions for Canadian Reforms" 52 *Canadian Bar Review* 297 in Conrad Brunk *loc. cit.*

[101] Conrad Brunk, *loc. cit.*, p. 533.

[102] *Ibid.*

"normally" present, which prod the accused person's choice in the direction of waiving the right. Hence, it is wrong to argue that since the prosecutorial process is intrinsically coercive, every choice among options within the process is also necessarily coerced. If we want to know whether or not elements of coercion that influence a defendant's choice of a trial are being introduced into a choice situation, we cannot use as evidence the rigors and risks of the normal trial, which are the very things to which the defendant has a right.

To ensure that plea negotiations and the resultant guilty plea are non-coerced, Brunk recommends the following:

(1) There must be an assurance of full due process at trial if the criminal defendant refuses a bargain and opts for trial. Direct or indirect involvement of a judge in plea bargaining gives rise to the need for this assurance. To help guard against burdening the trial and against the equally important fear of it by the defendant, it would be necessary to eliminate judicial participation, or create separate benches – one to conduct the bargaining process and the other the trial.

(2) There can be no extended pre-trial detention following the decision to go on trial. The length of detention in some jurisdictions makes a guilty plea a reasonable option even though no concessions are granted.

(3) The prosecutor or the police in a plea bargain system should not engage in "overcharging" i.e., drawing up a multiplicity of charges. If the accused is overcharged, the offer to reduce the level or number of charges in exchange for a guilty plea is again only apparently a concession and the criminal defendant is being coerced.

(4) There must be no appreciable increase in the sentence-risk faced by the accused person in the plea bargain system.

(5) Another condition protecting the voluntariness of a plea bargain concerns the nature of the information available to the accused in choosing whether to plead guilty in exchange for leniency.[103] In a related opinion, Timothy Lynch is of the view that the accused person must be given access to certain impeachment and exculpatory evidence to offer him an accurate assessment of the prosecution's case.[104]

Finally, critics of plea bargaining argue that a plea agreement circumscribes the right of the accused to appeal the decision reached after such bargaining. The accused is indeed allowed to appeal the decision but this right of appeal is limited, the limit of which was enunciated in the case of *Essien Akpan Essien v. The King*.[105] In that case, the court approved and followed the decision of the court in *Rex v.*

---

[103] *Ibid.*

[104] Timothy Lynch "An Eerie Efficiency," *Cato Supreme Court Review 2001-2002*, p. 171. See at http://www.cato.org/pubs/scr/docs/2002/lynch.pdf; Internet (Accessed March 21, 2011).

[105] 13 WACA 6.

Forde[106] as to when an appeal court could entertain an appeal in a case where the appellant had pleaded guilty. The principle of law is as follows: "[a] plea of guilty having been recorded, the court can only entertain an appeal against conviction if it appears that the appellant did not appreciate the nature of the charges or did not intend to admit he was guilty or that upon the admitted facts he could not in law have been convicted of the offence charged."

Conclusion

Compounding of felonious offenses, though outlawed by the Nigerian *Criminal* and *Penal Codes*, is now allowed by later legislations like the *National Drug Law Enforcement Agency Act* (NDLEA), the *Customs and Excise Management Act* (CEMA),[107] and the *Economic and Financial Crimes Commission Act* (EFCC). There appears to be a conflict between the outlawing of compounding of offenses by the *Criminal Code* and *Penal Code*, on the one hand, and the legalization of compounding by the EFCC, CEMA, and NDLEA Acts, on the other hand. However, this need not be. It is of common interpretation that where a specific legislation provides something contrary to a general legislation, the specific statutory provision will still be given effect.

If carried out according to the provisions of the enabling statutes, the legislations authorizing compounding in Nigeria could become veritable tools of criminal law enforcement especially in the area of economic crimes.[108] However, the legalization of compounding by the agencies of the Nigerian government could be regarded as convenient especially in view of the Nigerian society *vis-à-vis* crime fighting. Many of the cases to which the compounding provisions have been applied, several of which are cited in this chapter, raise important questions that touch on the fairness of the process and the need to apply the provisions to advance the interests of the citizens in general rather than the narrow interests of privileged accused persons.

The shrinking of the world to a global village has led to the sharing of policy and practice ideas between countries. The policy and practice distribution can have positive or negative impacts on a country. Globalization has resulted in the introduction of policies and practices of other countries sometimes through the normal legislative process and at other times through the "backdoor". For Nigeria, the practice of plea bargaining is one such practice imported through the "back door". Its uses in the United States, India, Canada, and other countries are legally

---

[106] (1923) 2 KB at 403.

[107] Section 186 (1).

[108] Economic crimes, specifically defined in the EFCC Act, embrace other statutes like the *Advance Fee Fraud Act*, the *Corrupt Practices and Other Related Offences Act*, the *Money Laundering Act*, etc. Note that the fact that the EFCC has been mandated to prosecute economic crimes does not in any way remove from the powers constitutionally vested in the Attorney-General of the Federation.

recognized. The contrary is the case in Nigeria where it has no express general legislative backing except in the few aforementioned statutes. It is obvious from the foregoing that plea bargaining as practiced in Nigeria has not been regularized in concrete terms. It is equally obvious that the statutory empowerment of compounding of offenses has not been judiciously utilized.

Finally, although the idea and practice of plea bargaining have certain incontrovertible merits, there is a need to clarify the policy and process of plea bargaining in Nigeria in light of the relevant statutes and practices in the country. Perhaps, plea bargains should be used in limited situations rather than as a general tool to dispose of criminal cases. Also, it is imperative to formulate and enforce a comprehensive policy and procedure for plea bargaining to properly guide the parties and other stakeholders in plea bargaining, and ensure that the rights and duties of the citizens are protected in the criminal justice process.

Chapter 12

On Crime and Punishment: Here is a Credible Alternative to the Death Penalty[1]

Chukwunọnso Okafọ
University of Nigeria

[1] A version of this chapter was published in the journal, *Law and Policy Review*, Volume 3 (2012).

Abstract

In sum, this chapter examines the suitability of death as a form of criminal punishment and offers a credible substitute for this sanction. Sanctions (punishments) constitute an important subject for all criminal justice systems. However, the extent to which capital punishment is accepted, if at all, varies from one society to another. The level of acceptance in each society depends in part on the people's legal history and whether they have a positive or negative view of their justice system. Often, culture plays an important role on this issue. For more recent post-colonies (including Nigeria) and older post-colonies (including USA) where the chasm between the indigenous and foreign philosophies of law remains deep, it is necessary to fashion a punishment model that recognizes and, to the extent possible, addresses the opposing views. Regarding death as a punishment type, a survey of the controversy surrounding capital punishment and the questions ensuing from its implementation show that a credible alternative is necessary. After reviewing the essential nature and character of capital punishment, this chapter offers "Life in Prison with Hard Labor and No Release Before Natural Death" – LPHLNR – as a credible substitute for the death penalty. The ingredients and rationale for the preferred alternative model are given and explained. Briefly, the LPHLNR model stipulates that a capital convict will be imprisoned for the remainder of his/her life; will work for long hours (15 hours per day, 6 days per week) in a job within the prison facility or other assigned workplace; and much of the convict's earnings will be paid to the surviving close relatives of the victim. In short, by the model, the capital convict assumes the (potential) "provider" role that previously belonged to the victim. However, if later the convict is found not guilty of the crime, he/she could be freed, which would be impossible under the existing capital punishment regime, once enforced. The LPHLNR model was the subject of a field test via a guest lecture given at a university in Virginia, USA, in February 2010. The positive responses and contributions by the audience (faculty members, students, and staff) have helped to sharpen the model. Overall, this paper makes a strong case that adopting the alternative model will do away with the several flaws in capital punishment, while properly responding to the most vicious criminals in society.

Introduction

To Punish or Not to Punish? Between Restorative Justice and the Punishment Model

Three of the most challenging issues facing criminal justice are: (a) which offenders, if any, should be punished; (b) how best to punish them; and (c) how far to go in punishment. Logically, the first issue to be determined is whether to punish a criminal. It is trite that no criminal justice system is able or capable of punishing every "criminal". No criminal justice system has the capacity, the will, or even the need to identify every criminal and to punish all. Consistent with this view, norm violations (including crimes) may be regarded as "functional" (Durkheim, 1961) or good for society. This means that violations often trigger a society's official and unofficial reactions that remind the violator as well as other members of the society of the proper behavior expectations in the society. Also, a society's reaction reinforces to the citizens that they ought not to conduct themselves as the violator has done. The consequence, then, is that not all criminals in society are punished nor should they be.

Thus, the limitations on the capacity, will, and need of a criminal justice system to identify and punish all its criminals mean that offenders that are exempted from punishment abound in every system. Discretion is real and common in law and justice. Discretion is the notion that persons and agencies charged with interpreting, applying, enforcing, and executing the law could exercise reasonable judgments in the course of carrying out their duties. The real effect of this concept in the specific field of criminal justice is that whereas a law authorizes (and perhaps *requires*) a police officer to enforce a law in full, the officer often does not fully enforce the law. Rather, the officer decides whether or not to do so, in what circumstances, against whom, to what extent, etc. Those are examples of *discretion* in criminal justice (Atkins and Pogrebin, 1981; Stojkovic, Kalinich, and Klofas, 1998). Therefore, in the absence of "full enforcement" of the laws (arrest, trial, conviction, and punishment of all criminals as stipulated by the applicable laws), a criminal justice system necessarily allows some, probably many, "criminals" to go unpunished.

Even while focusing only on those criminals that are identified, processed, and convicted, there remains a major chasm between the views for and against punishment, especially regarding the *extent* and *forms* of such punishments. For a modern society, it seems reasonable to state that most citizens would support *some* punishment or sanction for *serious* crimes, even if the citizens' philosophical foundations for supporting punishment would vary among such paradigms as retribution, deterrence, incapacitation, etc.

The varied archetypes for managing criminal offenders are divisible according to their emphases on punitiveness (Okereafọezeke, 2002). Restorative Justice, for example, deemphasizes punishment. One of the goals of restorative justice is to restore the victim (and the close relatives, community, and even the offender) to his/her position before the crime at issue occurred. Thus, negotiation and consensual resolution are central to restorative justice (Van Ness and Strong, 2010, particularly pp. 41-50). Restorative justice is not intended to depend significantly, if at all, on the formal criminal justice system, rather "restorative justice is justice that has redress to the victim as one of its primary goals, whether or not the offender has been detected, arrested or charged" (Weitekamp and Kerner, eds., 2002, p. 310).

Restorative justice focuses more on offender reform than most other sanctions models do. As stated, through restorative justice, the offender is "treated" by a mixture of strategies involving the offender, the victim, close relatives, community members, and even some public justice officials. The main aim is to put the parties back to their conditions prior to the offense, to the extent possible. Sometimes, the "treatment process" includes the offender admitting his or her crime and replacing what had been stolen, or repaying the monetary value, or giving the victim other thing of equivalent value instead.

As stated, Restorative Justice advocates *healing* the offender, rather than *punishing* him/her. Taken literally, the healing formula would require the medicalization of law and justice. The view would require the criminal justice system of a society to treat or reform every person who is identified and pronounced guilty of a crime. This is highly impractical mainly because crime victims, their relatives, communities, and the State demand and expect "tougher" State responses to crimes, especially those that threaten a community and its citizens' freedoms and rights. A more realistic view is that in a State, crimes will be sanctioned as necessary. In particular, serious crimes will be sanctioned seriously, while lesser crimes will be sanctioned mildly.

It comes to this. A society needs sanctions to demonstrate its aversion to prohibited behaviors, especially those of the serious criminal kind. Most reasonable people in society would agree that some sanctions or "punishments" are necessary particularly for serious crimes. It is true that restorative justice emphasizes more of offender healing (rehabilitation) than punishment, to restore the parties to their original positions, as much as is possible. Even then, restorative justice's healing formula takes a variety of forms, including some punitive elements. This illustrates the inevitability of sanctions (punishments) for crimes in a society.

Therefore, in the final analysis, the question rightly is not whether or not a society should punish for criminal wrongdoing. A society should so punish.

The correct question is: What is the appropriate degree (extent) of criminal punishment? A related question is: What is the best way to implement criminal punishment? These questions are answered below with the death penalty as an example of extreme punishments.

How Far Should Criminal Justice Go in Punishing a Criminal?

The death penalty is *probably* the most extreme form of punishment. It is perhaps the strongest method of disapproving of a behavior. It seems that it inflicts the greatest amount of pain or harm to the convict. At least with regard to physical pain and harm, this is true. However, punishment often takes other forms besides the infliction of physical injury or pain. Consequently, when examined in a wider context, death may not be the most extreme form of punishment. To accurately determine the most extreme form of punishment, the condition and preferences of a criminal should be taken into consideration. Thus, to a criminal, the relative value of a right or object that a punishment targets ought to be weighed.

Thus, punishment that is the most extreme to one criminal may not be so to another criminal. Whereas for Convict A life may be the most valuable thing, Convict B may regard freedom of movement as most precious, and Convict C may think that preservation of his material wealth is the most important thing. Based on his belief and preference, Convict A will regard a death sentence as the most extreme form of punishment. Alternatively, Convict B will view a sentence of life in prison as the most extreme form of punishment. For Convict C, a criminal punishment that strips him of his property ownership and use will qualify as the most extreme punishment. The foregoing perspectives mean that capital punishment should not be automatically assumed to be the most extreme form of criminal sanctions. Nonetheless, without doubt, death is one of the most extreme punishment types. Therefore, the sanctions model proposed in this paper to replace capital punishment is designed with these diverse views in mind. As such, the elements of the model in this chapter are intended to apply to all persons convicted and sentenced for otherwise capital crimes. The basis for this general application is explained among the key elements of the model in the following sections of this manuscript.

In criminal justice, death is applied in relatively few cases, yet this form of punishment evokes perhaps the greatest controversy. Capital punishment is highly controversial for a variety of reasons, including the following.

Death is an extreme form of punishment:

Without doubt, the killing of a criminal offender is an extreme way to condemn his or her conduct. However grievous the crime is, there are always questions as to whether or not the offender deserves to be done away with permanently in such a premeditated and brutal manner. Normal human sensibilities usually accommodate some moderation in disapproving others' behaviors. This allows the condemner to always remember that even a bad person has some good qualities. Thus, it seems unnecessary to "throw away the bath water with the baby" in the process of condemning or punishing an offender. Because of this general human incline, it is normal to wonder whether capital punishment is justifiable.

Capital punishment appears to be imposed and executed selectively:

One of the main knocks on capital punishment is that it tends to be applied selectively. And, the perception that death is imposed selectively derives from the actions and omissions of the various officials in criminal justice charged with the responsibilities of determining the fate of an accused capital criminal. Thus, for examples, the prosecutor's decision to seek the death penalty in charging a person with murder, along with the decision to present a type of evidence to secure conviction and sentence of death, is based on the prosecutor's discretion. Similarly, the judge's instruction to the jury (in a jury trial) or the judge's reading of the law and interpretation and application to the relevant facts (in a bench trial) depend on the judge's guided discretion. Further, the jury in a capital case has and exercises substantial discretion to convict and/or sentence an accused person to death (Lane, 1993). Thus, it is commonly used even on such crucial issues as whether or not an alleged criminal offender deserves to be killed. Discretion is widely used in the criminal justice system (Atkins and Pogrebin, 1981; Stojkovic, Kalinich, and Klofas, 1998). This is inevitable and necessary.

As such, for as long as the death penalty is a sanctions option in criminal justice, criminal justice officials' discretion will continue to play roles in determining who is condemned and executed. The exercises of discretion even on death penalty decisions are unavoidable. However, the form of discretion that I find troubling is that which amounts to selectivity. Such discriminatory practice unjustly exempts certain persons from the prescribed punishment (death) on the ground of illegitimate considerations, such as wealth, influence, star power, quality of legal representation, etc. None of these variables goes to the quality of the act or omission that would otherwise lead to capital punishment. So, why then do they play such major roles in sparring privileged accused persons from capital punishment while the less privileged are routinely executed for similar crimes? This question haunts criminal justice, and the model offered in this chapter is designed to help in resolving the issue.

Race and capital punishment decisions:

In some countries, race is a major factor in the application of capital punishment. Like the other illegitimate considerations enumerated in the preceding section, using race to decide whether a suspect should be tried for a capital crime, convicted, sentenced, and/or executed, is an unacceptable exercise of discretion in criminal justice. Thankfully, the race variable is not a prominent feature of all nations' criminal laws and justice. As should be expected, it is an important variable in those countries with diverse racial groups and extensive histories of racial discrimination and injustice. It is important to emphasize that although every country has some level of racial diversity (in the sense that every modern country has citizens/residents from all racial groups in the world), racial diversity is far more extensive in some countries than in others. However, the USA, which is one of the most diverse countries in the world, offers perhaps the most notorious examples of misuses of race in death penalty decisions.

Numerous research activities on the US criminal law and justice show that race has a huge impact on the imposition of the death penalty. Statistics show that, because of racial prejudice ("Death Penalty and Innocence", 2010), Blacks (African Americans) are more likely to be convicted for crimes. In particular, there is significant evidence of racial discrepancies in charging, sentencing, and imposing capital punishment in the USA, especially where the homicide victim is White and the accused is Black. In such a circumstance, the Black accused is several times more likely to be charged, sentenced to death, and executed than an accused person of another race, especially White ("Death Penalty and Race", 2010). Thus, in those countries, such as the USA, where race is a major determinant of capital punishment, a suspect's racial category can offer a key advantage or constitute a major burden, as the case may be. The model proposed in this article to replace capital punishment (LPHLNR) is race-neutral. As such, it is applicable to capital murder suspects of all races. If implemented, the model would go a long way to help in correcting the unacceptable use of race to decide capital punishment issues in some countries.

Death penalty is final and irreversible once it is carried out:

The irreversibility and finality of death is possibly the greatest argument against this form of criminal punishment. As a human institution, the criminal justice system of a society is imperfect. This means that errors (omissions and commissions) span the system. And the criminal justice system of a society is typically long and mystical to the average citizen. Throughout the long criminal justice process – including: criminal law enactment, commission of a crime, victim's report to the police, police investigation, collection of evidence, arrest of suspect, prosecutor's decision to prosecute, charge in court, judge's rulings on admissibility of evidence, court's interpretations of relevant laws, applications of the laws to the case facts, court verdict, sentence, execution of sentence – the system is fraught with numerous officials exercising varied forms of discretion. Every exercise of discretion risks errors that could compromise the quality of the justice done to the parties.

Ostensibly, as a response to the threats posed by such errors from exercises of discretion, the hierarchical court model is a common feature of law and justice in nearly all societies. This is designed to check and correct such errors in the justice system. Even then, the many levels of courts are sometimes unable to identify and fix every error in the system many of which result in wrongful convictions even in capital cases (see Radelet, et al., 1992; Cohen 2003; Prejean, 2005; "Death Penalty and Innocence", 2010; Graham, 2010). Thus, in many instances an outside person or body is needed to identify and alert a criminal justice system to take steps to correct errors in the system, often many, many years after the offender had been convicted and sentenced for the crime. This is precisely what gave rise to the *Innocence Project* in the USA, for instance, which has helped an appreciable number of convicts to regain their freedoms many years after being sentenced to long prison terms for crimes, which it was later discovered, they did not commit (see *Innocence Project*, 2010).

Note that the many convicts that have benefited from the *Innocence Project*'s services eventually regained their freedoms because they had received prison sentences. Had the convicts been sentenced to death and the sentences carried out, it would be impossible to restore their lives on being found Not Guilty. The impossibility of restoring a person's life once it is ended is sufficient to scare every rational human being. Faced with the errors that criminal justice officials make in the administration of criminal laws, there are real chances that these officials could execute persons who do not otherwise deserve such punishment under the system. Indeed, there have been instances of such wrongful convictions and executions (or near-executions), in several jurisdictions around the world (see examples in Adams, 2010). Again, the finality and irreversibility of capital punishment, once implemented, means that a person who is made to suffer this punishment will not be around to receive any apology or remorse from the State or its agency. In the permanent absence of an executed innocent convict, several jurisdictions resort to paying monetary compensation to assuage his or her close relatives. However, no amount of money will suffice to compensate the relatives for their extreme and invaluable loss. This means that the State is obligated to devise a credible alternative sanction to avoid wrongful capital convictions, sentences, and executions. The model presented in this chapter (LPHLNR) is designed with that goal in mind.

Great expenses are involved in the implementation of the death penalty:

The criminal justice process leading to the execution of a condemned person is long and very costly. Capital cases are known to last for decades, through trial, multiple appeals, other judicial reviews, executive reviews by political leaders in each jurisdiction (such as governor or president), long wait for execution, chance of conviction or sentence error resulting in unjustified killing, leading to State apology, embarrassment, and monetary payment to the deceased's relatives), etc. In the USA, for instance, trial, appeals, and judicial reviews often swing between federal and state jurisdictions, each jurisdiction with its various courts. The inputs by the several federal and state courts further lengthen the time before the enforcement of the final verdict. In the process, both the State and the accused person spend money stupendously to secure capital conviction or acquittal, as the case may be. Note that in some jurisdictions, such the USA, the State is legally required to provide an indigent accused person with quality (reasonable) legal representation in the process (Amendment VI to the *United States Constitution*). As should be expected, this legal obligation adds to the State's expenses in such cases. Understandably, a person at risk of receiving capital punishment will do everything possible to avoid the sanction, and for most people this includes spending everything they own. This is especially because such an accused person is confronted with the might and vast resources at the State's disposal. Therefore, for the accused, great expenses will be necessary to contest the State's case.

Capital punishment arouses high emotions and needless eruptions of sentiments for and against the penalty:

Not surprisingly, many citizens in society readily express strong views on the death penalty. Often this pits opposing parties against one another. Such discourses are passionate, again as they should be, because of what is at stake: life or death. Public arguments and demonstrations are common, especially whenever there is an execution going on or planned. Individuals and groups regard such occasions as their opportunities to state publicly their positions on this form of punishment. Although these contestations are avoidable, they are sure to continue unless a credible alternative to the death penalty is devised.

Capital punishment erodes the State's moral standing:

The State's claim of a high moral pedestal that preaches and observes the sanctity and value of every human life comes into serious question when the State presides over a variety of "dramatization of evil" (see Tannenbaum, 1938) that plans, carries out, and celebrates the deliberate killing of a human being. It should make no difference that an executed human being has committed one of the most heinous crimes known to a society. The point is that by opting to kill and deliberately planning and killing the condemned criminal, the State has assumed essentially the same position as did the criminal when he/she committed the capital crime. Add to these the fact that the State goes on to broadcast the State killing of the condemned person to the world.

Moreover, it is understandable that a close relative of a murder victim, for example, would want vengeance. And, if allowed to do so, the relative is likely to inflict the same punishment (death) upon the murderer. The relative's desire to kill the murderer seems consistent with a primordial inclination to protect a blood relative at extreme costs, if necessary. However, the State has a duty to rise above such familial relationships and desires. Rather, the State is expected to safeguard the society and protect the members in general. This means that the interests of individual members should always be considered along with the interests of the society. Thus, it may well be that even a murderer should not be killed.

For the reasons stated above, among others (see further "10 Reasons to Oppose the Death Penalty", 2010), it seems necessary for criminal justice to devise a sanctions model that appropriately punishes persons that commit the most serious crimes, such as first degree murder, and at the same time avoids unneeded controversy. This need led to the sanctions model presented below.

How Can Criminal Justice Avoid the Controversy Surrounding Capital Punishment While Ensuring that a Serious Criminal is Adequately Punished?

"Life in Prison with Hard Labor and No Release Before Natural Death"

– LPHLNR

While considering the broad and specific ingredients of the best model to replace capital punishment, I am aware of the relative popularity of the alternatives to this form of criminal punishment. The literature on alternatives to the death penalty shows the following: "The most popular alternative to the death penalty is life imprisonment without the possibility of parole plus restitution. This alternative not only costs much less than capital punishment, but also keeps the criminal in jail for the rest of his life - so he cannot return back to society" ("Alternatives to the Death Penalty" 2010, p. 1). With this in mind, the "Life in Prison with Hard Labor and No Release Before Natural Death" – LPHLNR – model is propounded here for managing persons convicted of otherwise capital crimes, such as first degree murder. I had introduced this model in Okafọ (2009). I now provide a more in-depth explanation of the paradigm's various elements and related issues. As stated earlier in this chapter, LPHLNR is a punishment, rather than healing, model. Unlike Restorative Justice's healing brand, the prototype I recommend here does not aim to change or correct capital convicts, such as first-degree murderers. Instead, this model is designed to punish such convicts because of the extreme nature of their crimes (remember that the murders were premeditated).

However, the elements of the LPHLNR model are crafted to address the legitimate arguments against capital punishment and its other alternatives.

Gauging the Reactions to the LPHLNR Model: A Field Test

Before presenting and explaining the elements of the LPHLNR model, I wish to intimate the reader that I have carried out what can be described as a field test of the model. The aim was to further enhance and strengthen the prototype before formal publication. In February 2010, I gave a guest lecture to an audience (faculty, students, and staff) at a university in the USA state of Virginia, on this sanctions model. The lecture served as a constructive avenue for gauging the model and its many elements. In the exchanges I had with the participants at the event, many useful comments, suggestions, and critical appraisals were shared. The participants received the LPHLNR model very well. As should be expected, they also offered recommendations for its improvement. To the extent necessary, those recommendations have been incorporated in the model offered in this article. Without a doubt, the ideas proffered at the event have helped to better ground and strengthen the model. Wherever appropriate in this article, specific challenges, questions, suggestions, and other ideas of the Virginia, USA audience for improving this model have been reproduced and addressed.

Key Elements of the LPHLNR Model

The key elements of the Life in Prison with Hard Labor and No Release Before Natural Death (LPHLNR) model that I offer are:

1. Life in prison, with hard labor, without the possibility of release before natural death. This form of imprisonment is really for life, meaning that by law no application for an early release of a convict sentenced accordingly will be filed or considered. Research shows that one of the reasons many citizens support the death penalty is because they fear that a convict sentenced to life in prison is invariably paroled after some years. In the USA, for example, the fear is pervasive (including among jurors). "Everybody believes that a person sentenced to life for murder will be walking the streets in seven years" Weltner, J. (Georgia State USA Supreme Court), quoted in Dieter (1993, accessed August 2010). Also, "some of the jurors were wanting to know would he get out in like seven years on good behavior .... If we were gonna put him in prison, we wanted to make sure he would stay there. But ... we didn't really feel like he would ... we really felt like we didn't have any alternative" (Juror in an interview following a death sentence, quoted in Lane, 1993). It is unsettling to know that a convict could be sentenced to

death because a jury (or judge) wishes to preempt a criminal justice system that does not require a life imprisonment term to run its full course.

Consequently, research also demonstrates that where citizens are assured that a life in prison sentence means that a convict will spend the rest of his/her life behind bars, the citizens show weakened support for the death penalty, thus strengthening their backing for alternatives to capital punishment. In the USA example, the data show that contrary to the idea that Americans unreservedly support the death penalty, more people would opt for an alternative sentence that assures both protection and punishment over the death penalty (see Dieter, 1993, accessed August 2010; Lane, 1993). The LPHLNR model presented in this paper, which requires that a convict sentenced to life in prison actually spends the remainder of his/her life behind bars, is designed to address the relevant concerns of juries, judges, and other citizens.

2. The "hard labor" ingredient of the LPHLNR model deserves to be explained. An exchange I had with a participant in the guest lecture in Virginia, USA should help to clarify the concept. The participant asked: What qualifies the incarceration in LPHLNR as "hard labor" any more than what already applies to many prison inmates? I responded thus: The fact of working does not by itself make the incarceration under LPHLNR hard labor. The hard labor quality is based on the following characteristics. (a) The LPHLNR model requires a convict to work for 15 hours per day, 6 days per week. This ensures that the convict produces/earns enough to pay for his/her incarceration, reasonable maintenance, as well as restitution to the close relatives of the victim. (b) The inmate does not receive salary or wages directly. Instead, the earnings are paid to the State, which distributes them as recommended in the model (recommended distribution guidelines are provided and explained below). (c) The convict's responsibility to work and earn money to be paid to the victim's relatives does not end until the convict dies. Therefore, "hard labor" derives from all the circumstances of the incarceration to which such a convict is subjected, to demonstrate society's strong condemnation of the extreme crime.

Further, hard labor means that the convict will be required to work in a productive profession, trade, training, and/or competence (for at least 6 days per week, no less than 15 hours per day), according to his/her education. A convict without any or much education, training, or competence can still be very productive in many work situations, such as serving as an assistant to a skilled professional (bricklayer, mover, farmer, construction engineer, etc.). Thus, lack of education or formal skills training should not prevent such a convict from working and producing under this model. In any case, the managers and personnel of the prison where such a convict is housed will be responsible for determining where a convict would be most useful and productive and the prison may reassign a convict as necessary. By the "6 days per week, no less than 15 hours per day" ingredient of LPHLNR, a convict that is made to work hard for so long will produce substantially to compensate the close relatives of his/her victim. In addition, the long, hard work will surely emphasize the society's strong disapproval of the grievous crime.

3. The convict's earnings under the LPHLNR model will be paid to the State initially, not the convict. The State, as explained here, will consider the interests of the stakeholders and distribute the convict's earnings accordingly – see Key Element 6 below.

4. The State will owe the convict no more than what is necessary for reasonable health and sustenance (a small portion of what the convict produces should be enough to satisfy the necessaries).

5. The State will determine the appropriate percentage of the convict's earnings to be applied to the convict's other custodial expenses.

6. The State will pay the balance of the convict's earnings as compensation to the surviving close relatives of the murder victim (spouse, children, parents, siblings, etc. – in the order mentioned). This sequence for the payment to the survivors seems reasonable to accommodate the relative interests of the survivors. However, with good reason, the sequence may be changed if a competent court determines that a subsequent stakeholder's interest should be accommodated before the interest of a preceding party. In any case, it is expected that a substantial portion of a convict's earnings will be paid to the survivors of a victim because the expenses to be deducted for the convict's necessaries and upkeep should form a relatively small portion of the convict's total earnings. Where a convict is sentenced under this model for two or more first-degree murders, for instance, it is recommended that the State should give up its deductions from the convict's earnings. This means that the State should absorb the costs of maintaining the convict while allowing all his/her earnings to be paid to the multiple beneficiaries resulting from the double or multiple crimes. By sacrificing its share of the convict's earnings, the State would ensure that all the affected survivors of the victims receive meaningful compensations.

7. The LPHLNR model should be mandatory. In the questions and answers phase of the Virginia, USA guest lecture I gave on this model, a participant asked me if the model I proposed would allow a convict to choose capital punishment. That is, whether the model would give a convict the option of death rather than what this model stipulates – life in prison with hard labor without the possibility of release from prison before natural death (LPHLNR). The Answer: No. Denying a convict the option of death is designed mainly to ensure that a convict does not have a chance to veto or thwart the essence of the LPHLNR model. And these three goals constitute the essence of LPHLNR:

(a) To avoid erroneous capital convictions, sentences, and executions.
(b) To restore the State's moral standing and authority as the custodian

of its citizens' lives, and do away with the State's premeditated killing of its own.

(c) To ensure that a convict does not escape from his/her important responsibility of catering to the needs of the surviving close relatives of the murder victim. Within the LPHLNR model, a convict assumes and should be made to carry out the responsibility of contributing to the upkeep and maintenance of the surviving close relatives of a murder victim.

Therefore, the criminal justice system of a society should go as far as is needed to punish its criminals. Without pretence to the contrary, it is important to emphasize that the LPHLNR model is of a punitive genre. As one participant at my Virginia, USA presentation and debate of the model intoned matter-of-factly, "So your proposed model is a punishment model." "Yes", I responded without equivocation. Consequently, the model envisions stiff but prudent punishment for the persons convicted for some of the most serious crimes in a society (otherwise known as capital crimes).

Significance of the LPHLNR Model

The following are the main advantages of the LPHLNR model. One, consistent with the widely held view that persons who commit grievous crimes should be penalized severely, the model deals sternly with persons who have committed some of the worst crimes in society (example, first-degree murder). However, the paradigm also eliminates the drama surrounding capital punishment. Two, specifically, the character of this punishment model lends it to great credibility and wide acceptance even among constituencies that otherwise oppose other alternatives to the death penalty (see Dieter, 1993, accessed August 2010; Lane, 1993; Robinson, 2001; "Alternatives to the Death Penalty" 2010). Often, those other alternatives are rejected because they are perceived as "soft" on crime. No reasonable person can accuse the LPHLNR model of being a soft response to capital crimes. The model's various elements, as explained, show that it is punitive, but with good sense.

The credibility of capital punishment depends substantially on its sensibility to the standards of the people to whom it applies. A criminal justice system that prescribes the death penalty contrary to the culture of the citizens concerned is likely to be without (sufficient) credibility among the citizens. Thus, the application of the death penalty in those societies whose cultures oppose the punishment (or at least the version prescribed by the modern State criminal justice system) is bound to be problematic. Oke (2007) demonstrates the divide on capital punishment between cultural expectation and State standard. Oke (2007) presents a Yoruba (Nigeria) belief, rationale, and philosophical argument against capital punishment. The Yoruba society, which, like most African societies, is essentially communal and humanistic, offers a strong argument against capital punishment. Although the Yoruba argument differs from the Nigerian State law authorizing capital punishment, the reasoning has "a contemporary universal relevance and applicability" (at p. 1).

Further, three, implementing the model will leave room for error correction by releasing a deserving convict where evidence subsequently shows that the conviction and/or death sentence should be overturned. The finality and irreversibility of capital punishment, once enforced, makes the recommended LPHLNR punishment model particularly attractive. Four, the LPHLNR model will make for a fairer application of serious criminal sanctions among convicts. The model will likely create a more even playing field by doing away with the *status quo* (the prosecutor's invocation of the death penalty, the court's and jury's application of the sanction, as well as the prison's and State's execution of condemned criminals), which often leads to unfair application of capital punishment against indigent accused persons. At present, the extreme nature of capital punishment, the skepticism of some of those charged with applying and implementing the sanction, and the influence of well-to-do accused capital offenders conspire to effectively minimize, if not eliminate, the likelihood that wealthy and other advantaged suspects in society will be charged, tried, convicted, and executed as capital criminals. The proposed LPHLNR model is far more likely to create an equal atmosphere among capital criminals in society regardless of the relative wealth or other advantage of these criminals.

Finally, five, in some jurisdictions, there is a visible chasm between a legal provision for capital punishment and its implementation. Whereas the law may allow the imposition of death on a convict, State officials charged with the responsibility of enforcing the law are sometimes reluctant to do so. The officials' reluctance may derive from religious beliefs, ethics, politics, or other consideration. As should be expected, the reluctance would impede the enforcement of the law. Where the reluctance extends over a long period, there is bound to be an accumulation of capital convicts, leading to prison congestion with the attendant consequences for the other inmates and the general society.

The described divide between a legal provision for capital punishment and its implementation features prominently in contemporary Nigeria. For example, many Nigerian governors, whose legal responsibility it is to sign a death warrant before an execution can be carried out, have refused to sign the warrants for some of the reasons already mentioned (religion, politics, etc.). Thus, due at least in part to cultural sensitivity, Nigerian governors essentially refuse to sign death warrants, thereby declining to authorize executions of capital convicts. The lack of enforcement of the death penalty led C. O. Okonkwo, the distinguished retired professor of law and Senior Advocate of Nigeria, SAN, to remark as follows at a roundtable on responses to kidnapping in Nigeria: "Some call for death penalty, but I always ask, which governor has ever signed a death warrant?

Capital punishment is not practicable in Nigeria" (see "Experts Proffer Solution to Kidnapping", 2010). Therefore, besides legal authority for capital punishment, the cultural, social, political, religious, etc. will to implement it is critical. Further, it is important to recognize that in the Nigerian example, the deep divide between the legal provision for capital punishment and its enforcement is not limited to the governors. The citizens have also demonstrated that they are similarly conflicted on this issue. There is a dearth of executioners in the country because there are too few Nigerians willing to work in this area (see "Death-row Prisoners and the Government", 2009). The LPHLNR model, if implemented, will eliminate these problems with capital punishment.

Additional Issues and Steps to Ensure that the LPHLNR Model Works Well

It is recognized that promulgating and implementing the LPHLNR model may require taking active steps to address the following issues. One, for each country, it may be necessary to amend the relevant laws to bring the elements of LPHLNR in line with the constitutional provisions in the country. For example, in the USA, the "cruel and unusual punishment" clause of the Eighth Amendment to the *Constitution of the United States of America* may prohibit some elements of the LPHLNR model for being "cruel and unusual". However, a constitutional amendment to permit the LPHLNR provisions would avoid the undesirable consequence of a court intervening to prevent the implementation of the LPHLNR model. Thankfully, for other countries LPHLNR may be enacted into law and implemented without a constitutional obstacle. For instance, in Nigeria, Section 34 (1) of the *Constitution of the Federal Republic of Nigeria, 1999* prohibits "forced or compulsory labor" (which could be interpreted to include the "hard labor" component of LPHLNR). However, Section 34 (2) (a) of the Constitution exempts any law promulgated to effectuate the LPHLNR elements as well as a court sentence implementing such legislation.

Two, for some jurisdictions and communities, (extensive) civic education may be necessary to enlighten the citizens on the public and private gains accruable from the implementation of the LPHLNR model. In as much as many societies and people oppose capital punishment, there are many other people that strongly support this form of punishment despite its flaws. For the supporters, any sanction less than the killing of a first-degree murderer amounts to "letting the murderer off the hook". Many of these supporters of capital punishment actively seek out opportunities to witness and otherwise involve themselves in the process for executing capital convicts. A conscious, sustained, and expensive mobilization and enlightenment campaign will be required to get these (vocal) supporters of capital punishment to accept the LPHLNR paradigm. Thus, the State through its criminal justice agency (such as the Ministry or Department of Justice), social welfare agencies, professional organizations (such as the Bar Association, Criminology and Criminal Justice Associations), private bodies, and individuals have responsibilities to advance the course of LPHLNR and make this model acceptable to the majority of the citizens.

With proper citizen education and wide publicity of its elements, the LPHLNR model is likely to enjoy extensive support in society. As shown, its elements address the core concerns of the most prominent sides to the death penalty debate. For the "pro-death penalty" citizens, LPHLNR offers stiff punishment of the capital convict by requiring that the prisoner be incarcerated for life with hard labor. Also, while behind bars for life, the convict works compulsorily, earns money, and pays for the maintenance of the victim's close relatives. Regarding the "anti-death penalty" citizens, LPHLNR assures that a convict who is subsequently found Not Guilty of the capital crime would be released from prison. If the advantages that LPHLNR affords the opposing sides to the death penalty debate are made available to the different constituencies, they are likely to support the model.

Three, to ensure that the deceased victim's close relatives derive the maximum benefits obtainable from this model, the following question, which a participant raised at my Virginia, USA guest lecture on this model, should be addressed. Question: In this model, how can we ensure that prison officials do not divert some of the inmate's earnings away from a murder victim's relatives or otherwise behave corruptly in the State's role in the administration of the proposed punishment model? Answer: As it should be, the State and its criminal justice officials will play a central role in managing convicts and their earnings under this model. Much of the State's role is particularly intrusive, and as such, it would be unwise to leave this role to private persons or even delegate it to them. Nonetheless, the existing mechanism in the internal structure of each prison facility and in the larger society's legal framework for monitoring the activities of criminal justice officials in relation to prisoners should apply in cases under this model. Consequently, the rights of convicts, victims, and other interested persons to Constitutional and other legal protections should be preserved and enforced.

Also, this model should encourage victim's relatives to periodically review the records concerning such things as a convict's earnings under this model and make sure that the records of those earnings are accurate and that the earnings are managed and distributed fairly as stipulated. Where errors are found, the relatives should challenge the officials in charge through judicial proceedings and/or other legal options. The State should ensure that victims' relatives are apprised of their rights to investigate and challenge misuse of a prisoner's earnings. Where errors are found, the State should encourage the relevant victim's relatives to proceed against the responsible officials.

The following related questions are the other posers that came up at the Virginia, USA lecture. Questions: How long should the convict's responsibility to work, earn money, and compensate the surviving close relatives of the murder victim last? Does the responsibility end or change when, for example, the victim's surviving children and/or siblings attain adulthood and/or become gainfully employed? Answer: The convict's responsibility should begin at conviction and sentence for an otherwise capital crime and continue for the rest of the convict's natural life. A change in the status of an eligible surviving close relative, such as by attaining adulthood, finding gainful employment, marriage, etc., should not affect the convict's responsibility. Note that even a surviving close relative whose status changes continues to suffer the loss of a loved close relative (the victim), which the convict caused. The enormous loss could never be replaced. The least the convict should do is to atone for his/her action by making the periodic compensatory payment in this model. However, a convict's obligation to pay to a particular qualifying survivor should end if the survivor dies before the convict. Considering the sequence of beneficiaries identified in this model, all of the convict's payment obligation will not soon end and is far more likely to remain through the remainder of his/her life. On the death of a beneficiary, the convict's payment obligation should simply transfer to the other beneficiaries.

The LPHLNR Model versus LWOP

Finally, it seems necessary to state that the model of criminal punishment proposed in this article to replace the death penalty (LPHLNR) differs from life in prison without parole (LWOP). Ordinarily, "life sentence" should mean imprisonment for the remainder of a person's natural life. However, the term is used in various other ways hence the confusion over its meaning. In fact, it includes several undetermined sentence terms that may be affected by such things as pardon, parole, or commutation. Similarly, the expression "life without parole" (LWOP) ought to mean a sentence in which parole is not possible. Such incarceration should go on for the remainder of the prisoner's natural life. In its correct sense, LWOP should be indeterminate since no one can be certain about the end point of another's natural life. Thus, sentencing a 30-year-old man to 100 years in prison, for instance, does not qualify as LWOP (an indeterminate sentence) mainly because the imprisonment term is specified. It makes no difference that the convict's natural life is unlikely to go on for a total of 130 years.

However, there is a distinction between the proper meaning of LWOP and its application. As stated in the preceding paragraph, LWOP should mean that a convict so sentenced is not to be released from incarceration before his/her life ends naturally. But, in some jurisdictions, including the USA, LWOP often means a prison term much less than life in prison. Typically, a person sentenced to a life term is incarcerated for a decade or less, and then released on parole. As should be expected, the public is dissatisfied with the situation, hence the evolutions of "sentencing guidelines, mandatory minimums, and truth-in-sentencing laws to restrict parole eligibility" (Nellis and King, 2009, p. 5; see also Dieter, 1993, accessed August 2010; Lane, 1993). Thus, in the USA for example, LWOP continues to be expanded in different states to ensure that life sentence means sentence for the remainder of the prisoner's life. Until the confusion surrounding the true meaning of "life sentence" or "life without parole" (LWOP) in many jurisdictions is resolved, those terms remain imprecise.

On the other hand, the substitute recommended in this article for the death penalty (Life in Prison with Hard Labor and No Release Before Natural Death" – LPHLNR – does not carry the burden of confused meanings that saddles LWOP and its equivalents. As explained in the section of this chapter on the elements of LPHLNR, the proposed model does not allow a prisoner to be released before the end of his/her natural life. Unlike LWOP, there is no exception to this stipulation under LPHLNR. In addition to this distinguishing characteristic, LPHLNR differs from LWOP in some other significant ways, including the following. LPHLNR is not just about a convict spending the remainder of his/her life in prison. An important feature of LPHLNR, which is absent in LWOP, is the requirement of "hard labor", which I have explained as a prisoner's obligation to work for long hours to earn money. In addition, the bulk of the prisoner's earnings will be paid as compensation (restitution) to the close survivors of the deceased crime victim. Further, the hard labor and payment will continue for the remainder of the prisoner's life, regardless of changes in a beneficiary's condition (such as attainment of adulthood, marriage, or employment). In sum, with LPHLNR, unlike LWOP, "life means life", plus hard labor, and the prisoner pays restitution to the surviving close relatives of the deceased crime victim.

Conclusion

The vexed issue of capital punishment is a major headache for criminal law and justice worldwide. Every justice system that allows the conviction, sentence, and execution of criminal offenders is bound to be dogged by a variety of contests and arguments for and against this extreme form of sanctions. For various reasons, many of which touch on the fallibility of the justice process and officials, as well as the unfairness of capital punishment and its nature as an extreme societal reaction to crime, many people within and outside each jurisdiction oppose, question, and express discomfort with this punishment. Thus, the role of the State as an entity that values all lives seems compromised by the continued resort to capital punishment. The chance of wrongful conviction and/or sentence of a capital convict remains one of the most topical issues in criminal justice. Research and common sense show that even substantial monetary compensation to the relatives of a person wrongfully executed cannot assuage the immense injustice to the victim and the relatives.

In this circumstance, then, it has become necessary to fashion a credible model for managing persons convicted for what would otherwise result in capital sentences. The literature on capital punishment shows that alternatives are available to criminal law and justice. However, each alternative has its limitations. With these in mind, I have offered "Life in Prison with Hard Labor and No Release Before Natural Death" – LPHLNR – as the best alternative to capital punishment. In this chapter, I have identified and explained the elements of LPHLNR. Key elements of the LPHLNR model include the following. One, an otherwise capital convict will serve life in prison, with hard labor, without the possibility of release before natural death. Two, the convict will work for 6 days per week and 15 hours per day to earn money. Three, the convict's earnings will be paid to the State and the State will consider the interests of the stakeholders and distribute the earnings accordingly. Four, the State will owe the convict no more than what is necessary for reasonable health, sustenance, and other custodial expenses. Five, the State will pay the balance of the convict's earnings as compensation to the surviving close relatives of the deceased victim (spouse, children, parents, siblings, etc.).

The LPHLNR model, if implemented, will punish deserving convicts who have committed some of the worst crimes in society, while eliminating the drama surrounding capital punishment. The model will also allow for error correction by releasing a deserving convict where evidence subsequently shows that the conviction and/or death sentence should be overturned. The finality and irreversibility of capital punishment, once enforced, makes the recommended punishment model particularly attractive. Finally, by balancing appropriate punishment for the worst criminals in society and error correction opportunity in the case of wrongful capital conviction and/or sentence, the LPHLNR model will enjoy significant credibility on both major sides of the capital punishment debate.

It remains to add the following. This LPHLNR model should not be read as a naïve or narrow idea. On the contrary, this model is designed to replace capital punishment broadly. Thus, in offering this model, I am cognizant of the fact that the realities in a State may cause the State to take limited steps to ensure the advancement of the State and the welfare of its citizens. In particular, the State's economic, political, and social realities are instructive. This means that in a State, such as Nigeria and some other less developed countries, where economic sabotage, corruption, and all manner of abuse of office have stalled the State's development, or even threatened the continued corporate existence of the State, temporary use of the death penalty to cleanse the State's political, economic, and social institutions should be regarded as a viable and necessary option, especially where other sanctions have failed. The Nigerian reality is such that government and corporate leaders view themselves as above the law and superior to the rest of the citizens. As such, these leaders operate with impunity. Diversion of public funds and properties, bribery, corruption, and other abuses of public positions are rife and *normal* in Nigeria. Ostensibly, the present circumstances in the country mean that prison terms and refunds of some of the stolen public funds may not suffice to reduce these crimes. Therefore, a temporary, targeted, and efficient death penalty policy to cleanse the Nigerian State of those persons that have crippled the country and its citizens seems necessary.[1] In this connection, Jerry Rawlings' Ghana offers an example of an efficient use of capital punishment in this manner. That effort became the foundation for the renewal of Ghana, which is widely adjudged to be a modern success story.

References

"10 Reasons to Oppose the Death Penalty" (2010) *Death Penalty Focus*, http://www.deathpenalty.org/article.php?list=type=24; Internet.

"Alternatives to the Death Penalty" (2010) *End the Death Penalty*, https://www.msu.edu/~millettf/DeathPenalty/alternatives.html; Internet.

Atkins, B. and M. Pogrebin (1981) *The Invisible Justice System: Discretion and the Law*. Cincinnati, Ohio, USA: Anderson.

Cohen, Stanley (2003) *The Wrong Men: America's Epidemic of Wrongful Death Row Convictions*. New York, New York, USA: Carroll & Graf Publishers.

Constitution of the Federal Republic of Nigeria, 1999.

Constitution of the United States of America.

"Death Penalty and Innocence" (2010) *Amnesty International USA*, http://www.amnestyusa.org/death-penalty/death-penalty-facts/death-penalty-and-innocence/page.do?id=1101086; Internet.

"Death Penalty and Race" (2010) *Amnesty International USA*, http://www.amnestyusa.org/death-penalty/death-penalty-facts/death-penalty-and-race/page.do?id=1101091; Internet.

"Death-row Prisoners and the Government" (2009) in *The Guardian*, http://www.ngrguardiannews.com/editorial_opinion/article01//indexn2_html?pdate=12010...; Internet.

Dieter, Richard C. (1993, accessed August 2010) "Sentencing for Life: Americans Embrace Alternatives to the Death Penalty" *Death Penalty Information Center*, http://www.deathpenaltyinfo.org/sentencing-life-americans-embrace-alternatives-death-penalty; Internet.

---

[1] See "Corruption: Yusuf Alli Canvasses Death Penalty for Corruption" *The Sun* http://www.sun-newsonline.com/article/corruption-yusuf-alli-canvasses-death-penalty-corruption; Internet (last accessed July 10, 2012), for support for this view.

Durkheim, Emile (1961) "On the Normality of Crime", in *Theories of Society: Foundations of Modern Sociological Theory*, edited by Talcott Parsons, Edward Shils, Kaspar D. Naegele, and Jesse R. Pitts. New York, New York, USA: Free Press, pp. 872-75.

"Experts Proffer Solution to Kidnapping" (2010) in *The Nation*, March 16, http://thenationonlineng.net/web2/articles/39741/1/Experts-proffer-solution-to-kidnapping/Page1.html; Internet.

Graham, David A. (2010) "Guilty Until Proven Innocent" *NEWSWEEK*, August 22, http://www.newsweek.com/photo/2010/08/19/famous-people-falsely-accused-then-exonerated.html.html; Internet.

Innocence Project (2010), http://www.innocenceproject.org/; Internet.

Lane, J. Mark (1993) "Is There Life Without Parole? A Capital Defendant's Right to a Meaningful Alternative Sentence" 26 *Loyola of Los Angeles Law Review* 327.

Nellis, Ashley and Ryan S. King (2009) "No Exit: The Expanding Use of Life Sentences in America," *The Sentencing Project: Research and Advocacy for Reform*, http://www.sentencingproject.org/doc/publications/publications/inc_noexitseptember2009.pdf; Internet.

Nonet, Philippe and Philip Selznick (2001) *Law & Society in Transition: Toward Responsive Law*. New Brunswick, USA: Transaction Publishers.

Okafọ, Nọnso (2009) *Reconstructing Law and Justice in a Postcolony*. Surrey, England and Burlington, USA: Ashgate Publishing.

Oke, Moses (2007) "An Indigenous Yoruba - African Philosophical Argument Against Capital Punishment," *The Journal of Philosophy, Science & Law*, Volume 7, July 11. See at http://www6.miami.edu/ethics/jpsl/archives/all/AfricanCapitalPunishment.pdf; Internet (Accessed March 23, 2011).

Okereafọezeke (Okafọ), Nọnso (2002) *Law and Justice in Post-British Nigeria: Conflicts and Interactions Between Native and Foreign Systems of Social Control in Igbo*. Westport, Connecticut, USA: Greenwood Press.

Prejean, Helen (2005) *The Death of Innocents: An Eyewitness Account of Wrongful Executions*. New York, New York, USA: Random House.

Radelet, Michael L., Putnam, Constance E., and Bedau, Hugo Adam (1992) *In Spite of Innocence: Erroneous Convictions in Capital Cases*. Boston, Massachusetts, USA: Northeastern University Press.

Robinson, B. A. (2001) "Alternatives to Capital Punishment", *Religious Tolerance*, http://www.religioustolerance.org/execut2.htm; Internet.

Stojkovic, Stan, David Kalinich, and John Klofas 1998) *Criminal Justice Organizations: Administration and Management*, Second Edition. Belmont, California, USA: West/Wadsworth Publishing.

Tannenbaum, Frank (1938) *Crime and the Community*. Boston, Massachusetts, USA: Ginn.

Van Ness, Daniel W. and Karen Heetderks Strong (2010) *Restoring Justice: An Introduction to Restorative Justice*, 4th edition. New Providence, New Jersey, USA: LexisNexis.

Weitekamp, Elmar G. M. and Hans-Jurgen Kerner, eds. (2002) *Restorative Justice: Theoretical Foundations*. Cullompton, Devon, United Kingdom: Willan Publishing.

Chapter 13

Green Criminology and Africa: A Case Study of Environmental Terrorism in Nigeria

Ihekwoaba D. Onwudiwe
Kingsley U. Ejiogu
Texas Southern University, USA

Abstract

This chapter examines the extent of green criminology and environmental crimes in Africa with specific emphasis on Deltaic violence in Nigeria. Using content analysis, the paper articulates the negative impacts of environmental policy, industrialization, globalization, diplomacy, laws and treaties on the African landscape. Where necessary, comparisons are made among African countries and the United States of America.

Introduction

Environmental Crime and Diplomacy in Africa

Environmental diplomacy is a budding issue and has become one of the most embracing and interesting trends circuiting international negotiating tables on green or ecological matters. We noticed that this trend gained momentum towards the fourth quarter of the last century when the Kyoto, Montreal, and Basel treaties were signed by nations around the world. These treaties became an epochal setting for major global economies that had decided to be watchdogs of their home industries and lifestyles' environmental impacts. The treaties were further affirmation that the world was no longer a congregation of insular nations and nationalities, but a welded matrix of one interconnected monolithic unit. Nothing stood firmer as proof of this new reality than the aspect of our substantive interdependence with the circular regeneration of the environment.

Further scientific arguments and studies point out that life-sustaining activity within the environment can be attenuated if we continue beyond certain thresholds of its resource exploitation in our uncontrollable search for material wealth (Benedick, 1998). The Montreal Protocol adopted and signed in 1987 during the tenure of Kofi Annan as the Secretary General of the United Nations aims to control the release of halogenated hydrocarbon and other related chemical compounds known to deplete the ozone layer, which form an ultraviolet protective shield beyond the earth's outer surface area. The phasing out of ozone-depleting compounds was mandated to be effective in 1994 (Tolba, 2008; Susskind, 1994; Benedick, 1998). However, this target appears not to have been achieved especially in nations of the developing world (Newton, 1995). Within the ambit of the United Nations Framework Convention on Climate Change (UNFCCC), the Kyoto Protocol mandates nations to reduce their green house gases or trade them as credit from less greenhouse polluting nations. The complex nature of procedural regulations required to carry out the articles of the treaty have posed major hindrances to its implementation, though it is arguable if this has been more so than its enforceability. This aspect of environmental degradation, known as global warming, has been accused by a series of scientific and political authorities as being responsible for the phenomenon of climate change, where globalization and increased consumption by rising population growth have heightened natural resource exploitation (Benedick, 1998).

The Basel Convention is considered the most comprehensive global environmental agreement on trans-boundary movement of hazardous wastes. The *Khian Sea* Waste disposal incident of 1986 in Haiti and the Koko incident of 1988 in Nigeria provided much of the impetus for the Basel accord on international hazardous material movement signed in 1989 (Lloyd, 2008). The treaty is designed to prevent the movement of such hazardous wastes into developing nations. As a result, different sections of the world have experienced and continue to witness a rise in critical activist movements and academic discourse on environmental sustainability and diplomacy.

Bargaining Environmental Diplomacy

Indeed, environmental diplomacy is a negotiating instrument and process for enacting international environmental regulations, management and sustenance (Tolba, 2008; Susskind, 1994; Benedick, 1998). In bargaining this paradigm, the world affirms an all-inclusive view of the environment as a global common. The world is drawing from one multifaceted environmental resource, which disposes human occupants of the earth to certain elements of responsibility in order to ensure the continual environmental/ecological life process of providing resources and consuming wastes. According to Susskind (1994), in his apt analysis of the problems, interests, and trends in environmental diplomacy, sustainability should be the key focus of multilateral global treaties on the environment. Susskind, however, observed that the expectation of a new environmental unity with respect to global proclivity to the enchanting and much publicized UN Earth Summit held in Rio, Brazil in 1992 has fallen far beyond expectations. Susskind further suggests that environmental treaties must ensure that they navigate the narrow path that would ensure "compliance" without hampering "sovereignty." Certain acts of environmental treatments should constitute criminality. In another excellent work, Szasz (1986) has examined the implications of the advent of organized crime, shoddy implementation, and corrupt enforcement in the criminalization, regulation and control of illegal hazardous waste disposal.

It is evident that the world in the information age has quietly embraced the ideal of environmental responsibility and sustainability, where nations may be weighed, not only according to their manner of governance, but on how they relate to the earth environment—our common patrimony. Far beyond the ground delineation of boundaries, within stratosphere, the troposphere and other equally significant spheres of atmospheric activities, environmental and its elemental units crisscross national boundaries without hindrance. But, this is only one part of a many sided polygonal reality. Ejiogu and Pautler (2008, p. 16) elaborated on the implications of modern human lifestyle on environmental sustainability, thus:

> One of the most significant fall-outs of globalization is the interrelatedness of the sustenance of human life styles and existence; how are we able to manage the Earth's resources responsibly? This understanding has heightened interest in the appreciation of global ecological studies within the past decades. Increased industrialization and subsequent urbanization has seen a leap for emissions released into the ambient environment, water bodies and land in which we live. Deforestation and other modern agricultural and mining practices have also been held accountable for these disturbances. A variety of unknown ecological change until now has arisen in such proportion to give governments and peoples all over the world a great concern. As witnesses to the direct and indirect effects of changing weather patterns on the health and survival of communities all over the world, it is no longer news that we are living in an interesting time that demands us to understand the impact of our activities on the global ecosystem as one whole unit, and that we must define ways to manage the environment sustainably.

As identified by Ejiogu and Pautler (2008), within individual nation states, pollution of surface terrestrial and aquatic habitats by industrial enterprises constitutes major environmental problems, which permeate and contaminates the underground water table across flowing river channels and transgresses atmospheric protective shields. No single part or constituent of the earth environment, including its biological species, such as humans, can claim a freedom from one aspect or the other of this encroaching contamination. While others can claim innocence when issues of informed causality are considered, South and Beirne (2006) provide multiple scholarly evidence in their seminal book *Green Criminology* to suggest that the human species today stand accused under the new era of criminalization of acts and omissions against the environment. Globally, it is estimated that critical international environmental crime issues, such as illegal dumping of hazardous waste, logging, fishing and ozone depletion, cost an astounding 20-40 billion United States dollars; which is about 5-10% the value of the global trade in drugs (Brack, 2004, p. A80), leading to a new epoch in the discipline called green or environmental criminology.

Green Criminology Paradigm

The green criminology paradigm as explained by South and Beirne (2006) is a follow-up to recent articulations and evolution of human understanding of the inherent dependency of living systems on environmental resource renewal and sustainability for continuous survival on earth. It calls for a rethinking and development of core principles of criminal offenses against the environment, the identification of actors, and enactment of relevant criminal status and strict enforcement of such laws. It tasks criminology with the requirement of understanding the irreplaceable nature of environmental resources and the need to cull them with understanding, and a mindset of sustainability. In this way, criminology would thus aim to study relevant issues to the discipline that are basic to environmental degradation within governments, corporate entities, organizations and individuals involved, such as corruption, social deviance, manslaughter, murder, conflicts, devaluation of the human person (based on race, ethnicity, class, age, gender), over exploitation of resources and so on (South and Beirne, 2006). These influences are in principle significant for any objective appraisal of why issues of environmental degradation continue unabated in many parts of the globe regardless of countless treaties by concerned world bodies to provide solutions. Paula De Prez (2006, p. 406) has noted that the trivialization of environmental offenses within regulatory and corporate sources have helped deter enforcement. To this point, Paula De Prez identified that innumerable mitigating arguments, often paraphrased to hinder and preclude regulatory enforcement, were in many cases made highly technical and filled with intentional regurgitating semantics.

The cold paradox of our uncontrolled consumptive lifestyles and industrial habits is that while it tends the business of satisfying human wants, it nevertheless denies the opportunity to derive pleasure from the purity of the earth's environment. It also drives human existence further down the road of non-existence as it claims an unconscionable portion of our well-being and health with its deleterious impact on human, animal, and plant life. This was one of the shocking realizations of the past century, that while we thought environmental resources were inelastic, we seemed to have forgotten about one of the most memorized stanzas of the then primary school science classes, "matter can neither be created nor destroyed." Aggressive human exploitation of environmental resources has given rise to the paradigm of environmental degradation and crime.

Urbinato (1994) reported that as early as 1217 in London, England, King Edward I outlawed the burning of sea coal, because it caused massive smog in the nearer earth atmosphere and evidently but uncorrelated health hazard to the cities' inhabitants. Richard III (1377-1399) and Henry V (1413-1422) further affirmed his efforts, which did not stop use of the cheap and easily available resource by Londoners. Urbinato further documented that in spite of the fact that the crime of pollution of London's atmospheric environment by burning coal was enforced with a death sentence, the inhabitants of the city did not obey the laws due to vagrant trivialization. Since then, series of laws have followed each other in a string in the twentieth century in order to control air pollution in England: the *Smog Abatement Act of 1926*; the *Clean Air Acts of 1956 and 1968*; and the *Environment Act of 1995* (Oke, 1987). Before London, during the Tang dynasty in China, the burning of tree trunks to produce ink for use by government offices also caused a great deal of environmental pollution (Epstein, 1992). Each of these ancient societies was conscious of uncontrolled environmental attrition due to the life-style and habits of their citizens. Moreover, environmental pollution increases with the growth of cities and neighborhoods (Borsos et al., 2003).

In view of the foregoing, the following questions are relevant to the subject of this chapter. Why are environmental laws often ignored or trivialized? What are the innate relationships between the human person and the environment that appeases every effort to make a focus for controlled management? What factors determine people's perception of the environment about the need to protect it, its renewal or sustainability? How indistinct is really the knowledge of the environment or none thereof with respect to relevant social control procedures necessary to assure sustainability? How and where did this conceptual realization of the impracticability of uncontrolled exploitation, and the needful enforcement of control regulations elude modern man in contrast to the glory age of English kingship for instance? How has criminal justice adjusted to the challenges of explicating environmental crimes and green offenses as violations of the criminal laws? How could criminal justice further expound these types of crimes in view of the realities of the modern society? There is a view that the overreaching interests and profits that came with the industrial revolution of the early seventeenth century (Hong et al., 1994) appears to have numbed the human senses of environmental probity with an overriding recourse to mercantilism, which suggests that individual wealth and aggrandizement are to be considered before the common good and issues of public trust (Simon, 2000).

According to Montague (2003), environmental justice is a public trust issue. Industrial production using modern chemical and solid mineral processes had created great wealth that was able to generate an equally somber list of crimes. Industrial processes release xenobiotic substances, such as Lead, Mercury, Aluminum, Cadmium, Arsenic, Chlorides, etc, into the environment (Lynch and Stretesky, 2006; Beardsley, 1994). These substances lead to illness, paralysis, stillbirth, birth defects, bronchitis and other maladies in humans (Borsos et al., 2003). Some authors have noted that viewing the environment as a public trust allows some cultures to believe, rather unconsciously, that they are in essence one with the environment (Dei, 1996; Anoliefo et al., 2003). Such cultural artifacts equally demand criminal justice illumination in the light of a future, where as a matter of policy the environment and justice would be meeting on a more regular basis.

The resistance to environmental laws could be a frontal presentation of an inner predisposition of citizens' argument that no one can grant rights to environmental use; that the environment belongs to us as a group and individually and thus cannot be legally charted. It appears people are not yet prepared to concede rights to the environment to any institutional authority. Studies have shown much of this deviant mindset is more founded within the club of enlightened big global corporate entities (Simon, 2000; Lynch and Stretesky 2006). The dynamics of these possibilities are in some respects equally potent in developing societies whose belief systems still remain factored in ancient informal social structures and unidirectional ethos, while big corporate entities could still be accused of mindless profiteering (Simon, 2000; Lynch and Stretesky 2006). The object for lower class citizens of the third world may be the flaw of exposing them to environmental crime issues in ways that are antithetical to their cultural knowledge and relationships with the *pre-existing environment*.

For instance, the existing understanding of waste management in Africa is outdated. The common belief is that wastes, when released into the environment, simply take care of themselves. But, that might have been the case in the past with significantly less human population and unadulterated agrarian economies when native biological processes took care of issues of waste management through bio-degradation. However, wastes are more varied in nature today. Many of the recalcitrant wastes from industries today resist biological degradation. These wastes from a variety of effluents, as a result of process industries, have been found to contain an assortment of metallic and non-metallic elements as businesses from the developing world angle to catch-up with the rest of the world with affordable and obsolete polluting technologies (see Saif, Midrar-ul-haq and Memon, 2005; Karunyal et al., 1994; Manivasagam, 1987).

As global thought maneuvers between the formed age of information technology and the unfolding clarion for the age of environmental sustainability and responsibility, nations would increasingly be weighed, not only according to their manner of governance, but on how they relate to the earth environment. Nations and corporate entities that ignore the call for sustainable management of the environment may increasingly find it more difficult to make friends and secure new businesses due to the implications of possible sanctions for offenses against nature. This is a hard-cold fact, which every nation on earth, irrespective of socio-economic and political exigencies, would have to face, eventually. The dilemmas of desertification, drought, and issues of climate change, extinction of biological organisms, water pollution and natural resource contamination are real (Benedick, 1998).

Indeed, we must underscore that deleterious health conditions due to industrial toxicity effects seem to be affecting adversely innocent citizens of the world. Once again, world citizens are perhaps standing on the threshold of historical moments. The future is bound to favor industrialization that would do well to adapt to this new vision by limiting the extent to which they impact the environment deleteriously. The future may demand even stricter controls, likely a more integrative approach to industrial processing. The consumption of an industry's materials and processes may no longer be done in isolation of other industries. One industry's poison would be required to automatically become another's delicacy. In effect, secrets will have to cave in, and other innovations will emerge for maintaining product patents. It is not difficult to posit that the earth environment may not for too long accommodate our continual waste discharges on its surfaces, sub-surfaces and within its core. Even with the best treatment technologies available, waste disposal for chemical industries remain a problem as environmental crimes increasingly become normative in the lexicon of law enforcement.

Indeed, nations of the developing world, which for the past half a century, have been badly undernourished by continued socio-economic stagnation of drought, desert encroachment and starvation, will certainly face greater environmental problems. The interesting paradox on issues of environmental justice in the developing world is that while many nations in Africa are in a rush to do catch-up with industrialization, they are in an uncontrolled quest for more industrial economy. Some of these countries have endeavored to set up steel industries, metal fabricating industries, aluminum extrusion industries, chemical industries, and battery manufacturing industries. Additionally, some governments are even contemplating nuclear power plants. The reality may be that the industrialized world seems to be trying to let it all go as far away from their homeland as possible in order to concentrate on less polluting and less burdensome knowledge-based enterprises. China, for example, is aggressively exploring Africa on different levels of economic pact. This situation is evident in a nation like Nigeria more than most because, with its large market, an energetic and highly mobile populace, a lot of easy rolling petrodollars to play with, a government that appears lax on enforcement of laws, all imaginable and sometimes obsolete industrial plants from all over the world, including those that are still being tested, are represented in Nigeria today. Under the stranglehold of corrupt governmental and regulatory practices, it becomes even more difficult to enact stringent laws and enforce them against polluting corporate entities.

Benedick (1998) indicates that global momentum and understanding of environmental issues seem to have shifted to climate change, plant and animal extinctions, drought and desertification, fish-kill and persistent organic pollutions. Further, one of the major environmental problems in many developing countries is how to manage the increasing amount of wastes generated by industries. Benedick insists that the inability to manage Africa's industrial environmental issues, such as crude oil pollution of fishing grounds and farmlands, has created conflicts between industrial entities and local communities in nations like Nigeria. These communes or entities accuse each other of pipeline vandalism and environmental degradation, respectively, giving fodder to the existing contentions in the field of criminal justice for definitions applicable to the concerns of environmental crimes (Ogundiya, 2005; 2009). However, some major studies in this area amongst local and international scholars have mostly focused on the conflicts (Ogundiya, 2005; 2009), not on the green nature (environmental impacts) of the problem. The environmental devastation has been generally relegated to a secondary status.

The issue of environmental justice is highly pertinent to the African situation where local cultural practices limit the appreciation of the intersection between environmental sustainability and practices that destroy it. According to Benedick (1998), the environmental problem in Africa requires a more ardent attention because of the havoc it has engendered in the arena of the economic and social conditions of the people. The problem has generated rising tides of piracy, terrorism, hostage situations, environmental crimes and a weakening of the health and well-being of the citizens.

Indeed, the knowledge management capacity of African States, which includes the limitations of criminal justice data on what constitutes an environmental crime and how to derive a foundation upon which to build enforceable laws and procedures, deserves critical attention. Due to this dysfunction in criminological understanding and enforcement, multinational corporate entities seem to have had a field day – growing profits at the expense of the global environment – as evident from several incidents in the industrial and agricultural sectors, crude oil prospecting and mining collateral damages to the environment. Governments appear ill attuned in the African context to the needs of their citizens for a healthy environment. We must underscore that this is also a perennial problem in highly industrialized societies. As we pen this article, British Petroleum (BP), the oil magnate, has advertently or inadvertently polluted the Gulf-Coast of the USA. It seems that BP had scaled through government watchful eyes in the face of various organs of the government, including an active criminal justice management, knowledge and laws.

Issues of environmental justice are often likened to social justice. This is partly correct. Environmental justice has its own distinctiveness mostly because of its direct relationship to human survival and health, not only rights and justice. However, the goal of environmental justice has been variously described in terms of the distribution of environmental good and bad practices (Schlosberg, 2007; Stephens, 2009). Generally, Africa suffers from adverse environmental practices in mining, oil exploration and agricultural applications and uncontrolled local industrial waste disposal. Benedick (1998) has advanced the idea that some of the major problems leading to mankind's modern ecological problems are overpopulation and poverty. Issues of poverty and overpopulation deserve explication in many nations in Africa under socioeconomic exigencies of industrial waste producing and ecological degrading entities. Benedick further noted that the UNCED conference imposed the relevance of environmental diplomacy on the agenda of national public policy tables around the world. Thus, he insists, it was no longer quite comfortable to hold on to the aphorism of irrelevance often assigned to environmental issues prior to this time. Environmental diplomacy in the European Union (EU) has been described as setting the framework for economic negotiations, integration and advancement within the continental body (Muller-Kraener, 1998).

Additionally, it has been deduced by other scholars that environmental diplomacy in Africa remains an infantile discourse aroused at the call of one unending crisis or the other, such as the imbroglio in Nigeria's Niger-Delta Region (Ogundiya 2005; 2009). White (2006) notes that increased state and institutional interdependence led by capitalist enhanced globalization have spread the possibility of various environmentally damaging enterprises all over the globe. Among the African nations, there appears to be a problem of association clouding most of the international treaties on the environment. For many of the countries, it appears more important to be a part of the diverse negotiations, conferences, workshops and documentations than the actual of implementation of the treaties. Some of the diplomatic initiatives are not substantive; rather, they constitute direct recourse to policy symbolism and idealism. Nigeria typifies this latent approach to core issues of environmental diplomacy in Africa. And, as noted by the Microsoft Encarta Online Encyclopedia (2004), Nigeria is a signatory to a majority of United Nations' regional and continental treaties on the environment, namely:

UN Convention on Biological Biodiversity, the Convention on Climate Change, Desertification Convention, Convention on Trade in Endangered Species of Wild Fauna and Flora, Basel Convention on the Control of Transboundary Movements of Hazardous Wastes and their Disposal, Law of the Sea Convention, Marine Dumping, Marine Life Conservation, Nuclear Test Ban, Nuclear Safety, Vienna Convention for the Protection of the Ozone Layer, Wetlands, Oil Pollution Preparedness Marine and Coastal Environment, World Cultural and Natural Heritage, Continental Shelf, Fishing and Conservation of Living Resources, Joint Regulations on Fauna and Flora, Prohibition on Poisonous Gases and Bacteriological Methods of Warfare, International Covenant on Civil and Political Rights, The African Charter on Human and Peoples' Rights, The International Covenant on Economic, Social and Cultural Rights.

However, involvement in treaty making, while it is typical of many nations in the global society today, has not resulted in dramatic reductions of the rate of environmental degradations. This necessitates new efforts by nations of the world, especially African states, to pass laws that criminalize environmental breaches. The articulation of the environmental crime paradigm is important for Africa. For instance, evidence of multiple treaty involvements by Nigeria, the supposed paragon of Africa, has not curtailed drastic environmental havocs in the country. The Microsoft Encarta Online Encyclopedia (2004) reports identified the following environmental problems in Nigeria:

> periodic droughts; soil degradation; rapid deforestation (due to uncontrolled logging); desertification; air and water pollution; oil pollution, oil spills (water, air and soil); industrial pollution, municipal waste generation and urban decay; loss of arable land; loss of flora and fauna; rapid urbanization and population pressure; erosion (coastal, marine gully, sheet erosion and land subsidence); flooding (coastal, river and urban flooding); inappropriate agricultural practices; destruction of watersheds; loss of biodiversity; soil-crust formation caused by loss of water; and climatic change/ozone layer depletion.

The environmental problems subsist in spite of the various treaties Nigeria signed to prevent or control the challenges.

For policymaking and environmental justice in Africa, it is pertinent to determine the implications of bad industrial disposal practices and other crimes against the environment. The policy leaders in the continent must understand that there seems to be a disconnection between the policy and practice of environmental regulation mainly due to unacceptable definition or lack of official protocols on environmental crimes. In Africa, research on multilateral negotiations among private corporations, communities, public and international organizations on the definition and identification of environmental crimes appear limited. Similarly, studies on environmental implications, sustainability, and control in the Africa are insufficient.

In this chapter, we find it pertinent to scrutinize some of the under-explored opportunities and relationships that await multilateral attention in order to tackle chronic and persisting issues of environmental crimes in Africa. Further, we review a scientific study on the effects of industrial effluents on some commonly grown food crops in Eastern Nigeria. Finally, using Nigeria's uncontrolled industrialization and crude oil exploration as study subjects, we examine the implications of pervasive environmental crimes, and the possibility of accessing solutions to the environmental crimes and other problems within the multilateral sphere of environmental diplomacy.

Literature Review: Do They Know that the Environment Has a Life?

Our analyses of the issues in this paper rely on collected public information in content and secondary research. We also reviewed already published work for the present treatise. Further, based on our search of the Internet, published documents, and retrieval of academic studies in the nascent discipline of environmental crimes, we observed that the idea of a living environment is still a bother to many cultures of the world. The mere mention that the environment could be protected with enforceable laws has often drawn curious attention, especially concerning trans-boundary environmental problems (Verweij, 2001). Is the environment only a mass of inanimate entities of resources just waiting to be exploited at will? This question arises as often as issues of environmental crimes are raised. However, the environment is much more than a mass of inanimate entities and resources. It equally consists of living systems and the interaction of these living systems among themselves, and their extrinsic interactions with the inanimate entities that equally interact within themselves and with others (Bychkov et al., 2007). Non-living systems may interact by non-conditional/conditioned physical and chemical processes, which may alter their constituents unchangeably/chemically, or physically in which case the chemical integrity of their constituents may remain intact. Even within the living units, innumerable alterations occur of chemical and biological nature. These are perhaps the theoretical foundations of chemo and biogenesis (Bychkov et al., 2007).

The systems could be likened to a series of intertwined superhighways of interactions hinged on countless control mechanisms that ensure regeneration while averting senescence. Control mechanisms for system integrity between the human race and the earth environment are in a sense the overriding motive of the environmental crime paradigm. Acts considered inimical to the circular restoration of the global ecological and environmental system have to be understood and sanctioned. The sanctions must, however, be understood as needful in order to avert societal quandary. This is because the nexus of green criminology and environmental crimes is still largely emergent in concept (South and Beirne, 2006), notwithstanding that crimes against the environment are age-old activities that have only raised concern as a result of global climatic changes and deleterious contaminant effects on the health and well-being of living systems. It is necessary for the disciplines of criminology, criminal justice, and law to search and properly identify their roles in this emergent riddle of human existence called environmental crimes although we must point out that many criminologists are already embarking on this aspect of criminological enterprise (see for examples, South and Beirne, 2006; Lynch and Stretesky, 2003; 2006; Benton, 2006).

A variety of the studies on the environment and environmental crimes has of recent flowered under the aegis of green criminology. Lynch and Stretesky (2006) have discussed the human health implications of uncontrolled toxic waste disposal by industrial corporate entities. Two perspectives of green criminology can be derived by politico-economic players defining individual group interests. One is the aspect of green environmentalism defined by the corporate world in a bid to position business interests with the clarion of environmental sustainability. The opposing perspectives of environmental justice emanates from environmental advocacy groups who relate the environment mostly to the social situation of race, gender and crime in the society (Lynch and Stretesky, 2003).

Some scholars have gone the extra mile of extrapolating the green criminology paradigm to specific situations, such as the protection of animal rights, as did Benton (2006) in his examination of the "rights and justice on a shared planet." Simon (2006) points to a variety of issues of regular environmental violations and policy manipulations of corporate entities. In another study, Halsey (2004) considers how best criminology could approach the problems of environmental crimes as problematic in themselves, as they generally appear theoretically ill-defined. Whatever may be the case, ill-defined or not, it is noteworthy that the green criminology paradigm is fast structuring how society would view and relate to the regulation and sanctioning of harms against the environment in the unfolding green future.

In the workings of most social relationships within modern African States, two basic class positions aligning asymmetrically to Karl Max's theories of class conflict could easily be determined. Modern social construct in Africa consists essentially of a conflict between the following two groups: (a) the upper class, which consists mainly of wealthy and better educated citizenry that took over governance from the colonialists, and (b) the lower placed, poorer and less educated group, who appear to have actually retrogressed since the end of the colonial period (African Network for Environment and Economic Justice 2004; Ejobowah, 2000; Mazrui and Wondji, 1994; Usoro, 1977). This subsisting class distinction, which was not so prominent in so many ancient African cultures, have followed the Michel Foucault's perspective (see Foucault, 1991) of the government essentially suspecting and targeting the lower class in almost every inebriant business of social control.

With the environmental crimes axis, the interesting paradox is that a majority of the more noticeable incidents, such as oil pollution and industrial effluent disposable, are total in their control and malfeasance by the upper class. Formal social control systems have of necessity found this group to be very difficult to bring under regulations because of their political clout and control of productive resources upon which societies subsist. Simon (2006) has studied the historical perspective of the impact of upper class demography in the context of environmental crimes. He concludes that informal relationships between the private company leadership and government public offices responsible for environmental regulation have played an intrinsic role in seeing that violations, such as uncontrolled industrial effluent disposal, have not been easily subjected to environmental protection laws.

It seems that a majority of the corporate entities in Africa operate on the erroneous view that the African humanity had existed without being aware of the need to account for the environment and its resources. This view can only explain the corporations' complicity in the continued denigration of the indigenous African civilizations, which have successfully subsisted on the continent for thousands of years in tandem with environmental sustainability. African cultural realities are mostly holistic ways of life within which are enshrined the spiritual, natural and physical essences of their living and survival. Within this all-forming cultural ethos, environmental management and regulations were often in-built. It is important to locate these cultures of environmental protection in the African context in order to better appreciate the patterns of informal justice procedures that have helped sustain the African environment before the inroad of industrialization in the latter half of the twentieth century.

Anoliefo, Isikhuemhen, and Ochije (2003) in their work titled *"Environmental Implications of the Erosion of Cultural Taboo Practices in Awka-South Local Government Area of Anambra State, Nigeria"* have examined this very aspect of the relationships between African culture and the environment. They note that cultural taboos and sanctions were used in the past to protect the environment from unwholesome activities and degradation. The authors emphasize that the natives have historically protected and preserved the forests. According to these authors, the law only allowed some parts of the forest fringes to be utilized for agricultural purposes and austerely permitted the felling of trees in ominous circumstances. Many of these protected forests have remained the same for centuries, and are usually typified by vast covering of green creepers and all day darkness within. Anoliefo, Isikhuemhen and Ochije (2003) believe that identification with cultural realities is analogous to acceptance of institutional practices. They enlist the view that the annulment of certain traditional cultural practices has endangered natural environmental structures in the community. They hold that unilateral implementation of modern cultural practices relevant to the environment while abandoning age-old informal controls and cultures is a major factor of increasing environmental crimes in Nigeria. However, African governments structured in dysfunctional colonial bureaucracies appear to have been unconsciously predisposed to ignore this very fact in their approach to the enforcement of environmental laws. There is a strong argument that a lot of contending criminal justice issues may have found more bearing and understanding from the ordinary citizen if knowledge and practice are presented through an axis with more bearing to their cultural reality.

Many African scholars have rejected the replacement of indigenous laws with foreign legal mandates [see Okereafọezeke (Okafọ), 2002; Okafọ, 2009]. In criminal justice practice, Wisler and Onwudiwe (2009) have pointed out that the wholesale importation of the Western community policing system into Africa without local domestication would have less chances of success. In nations like China, most foreign cultural practices and formal criminal justice procedures are made to first undergo local informal adaptations. Still using community policing for exemplification, Chinese COP System has been conceptually made subject to the country's informal culture. Thus, the situation is such that Wong (2009) can claim that in China the people are non-distinguishable from the police; in other words, the people in China are the police. Berkes et al. (1998:274) have noted that pastoralists in ancient Africa were able to condition their practices and pastoral systems to maintain ecological sustainability by using a diversity of variables, which included ecosystem evaluation processes, tracking, site management, and communal coordination.

Citing Ostrom, Walker and Gardner (1992), Beskes et al. (1998) stated that whereas the common belief is that a form of authority in charge of social control is required to enforce environmental laws, traditional users of common resources have been known to maintain sustainability. Berkes et al.'s observation may be part of the reason why cultures that are still steeped in informal traditional practices find it difficult to understand or accept that the authority figures of State should manage the environment. According to Berkes et al., pastoralists have been known to use communal land tenure systems to cull the environment responsibly without endangering its resilience and renewal. Berkes et al. also submit that nationalization of land ownership, delegitimization of traditional authority in land matters and other modern uses of land have in effect resulted in the forest steadily facing imminent dissolution.

As it were, traditional concepts of environmental and land resource management appear as if they never existed. A vast majority of policy articulations on environmental sustainability treat local communal stakeholders as if their relationships with the environment had no meaning or affiliation. Maintaining that there is no longer an incentive for managing and maintaining natural resources, Berkes et al. further examined the role of cultural rights in effecting natural resource conservation because of its flexibility and adaptability. Additionally, Behnke (1994) and Velded (1993) take a view factored on social condition and control and posit that with empowering of informal resource control privileges would arise less need for structured formal control systems. In this sense, a national legal regime that recognizes the decentralized, informal and flexible communal social control systems at the local level may be better attuned for the regulation of environmental resources.

Dei (1996) has studied the issue of utilizing the socio-cultural factors and knowledge base of indigenous people for African development. The conceptual foundations in many of these cultures have become so entrenched in their living realities that outright importation of foreign contents and knowledge base is often viewed as simply something to get through with for the sake of surviving the age. According to Dei, there is need for a form of development based on the spiritual and moral values that are founded on their linkages to the social and natural worlds. Perhaps this suggestion may be the key to understanding the flight of fancies of most imported development concepts within the African continent. For instance, United Nations' environmental development projects have, in many cases, met with little success in most of the countries in Africa (Dei, 1996). It will be interesting to understand the series of factors behind these failures; which may explain why issues of crimes against the environment are looked at with much less seriousness both from local populations and from private corporate and governmental authority figures. Conceptually, the lethargy in accepting the paradigm of environmental crimes cannot be far removed from Dei's (1996) position that international development in Africa has been disappointing, or Sachs' (1992) postulation that international development obituary in the continent may have already been written.

Thus, in Africa, there is a crisis position of weariness with a diversity of development and social control practices important to the continent. This position must be understood in order to appreciate the implications of the social reticence to the institution of environmental justice through the identification and enforcement of environmental crimes in Africa. Dei's call for the inclusion of African indigenous cultures and practices in multilateral international and local development is equally relevant to social control through the articulation of laws, law enforcement as well as the judiciary. It is probably much easier for a people cultured in the appreciation of the elemental working unities of the environment as tied to human existence through taboos and sanctions to appreciate environmental sustainability than for others that are not similarly cultured. This position articulates that the revaluation and integration of African social values with its sustainable attributes would be a much better approach towards a broadly accepted and functional development system (Dei, 1996).

The foregoing implies that our belief systems are relevant to how seriously we approach certain issues that should be of concern to us. Many in the environmental crime scholarship subscribe to the view that a healthy environment is a form of ancient right and hence a public trust (Lynch and Stretesky, 2006; White, 2006; Simon, 2000). Dei, in fact, builds an effortless case against the ecological cost of many of the intercontinental development efforts in Africa that were led by foreign entities. For one thing, he mentions the latent issues of ecologically degrading policies, which have inherently destroyed the sources of livelihood of many African citizens, creating extreme divides of poverty while facilitating the profiting of international corporate capital adventures.

In essence, the complicity of the governments and industrial entities in various parts of Africa seem to be denying the citizens a variety of their ancient long-standing rights. Examples abound throughout the continent. However, the Niger Delta Region of Nigeria illustrates this condition. Acid rain from gas flaring has already sterilized rivers and streams and destroyed the forest cover in the Niger Delta (Ogundiya, 2005; 2009). Thus, today, more than ever, it is critical for African citizens to understand the importance of enforcing their rights concerning a livable environment. They must also understand the influence of corruptive political and business processes in devouring the national resources and leaving the citizens as easy preys to the vagaries of environmental and health disasters.

Further, on the role of government in environmental sustainability, the following question deserves consideration. What is the implication of ill-defined policies on the ability of African societies to protect their environment? The role of government is to protect the common interests of the people (Garland, 1997) against undue expropriation by wealth and power. In calling for the consideration of indigenous cultures in crafting development efforts in the African context, Dei (1996) has eminently posited that indigenousness does not suggest *backwardness and lack of knowledge,* but simply a specific highway of understanding and appreciation of issues, values, phenomena, things, and technologies around them. The latent disconnect between modern socio-economic and political reality and enforcement of environmental crime issues can much more easily reconnect with the indigenous ethos and systems of environmental protection of African cultures and wellbeing.

Conflicts and Environmental Crimes

There is an obvious relationship between international development capital (both from private sources and international multilateral agencies) and environmental determination in many African states (Ifeka, 2004). The significance of this factor seems to have eluded background actors in many of these developing nations. It also points policymakers in the environmental and socio-economic diplomatic directions. This situation has also resulted in citizens of African nations paying the price for bad and faulty treaties and agreements. This is evident in the pervasiveness of poverty-related scenarios prevalent in these regions, which manifest in scores of flashes of conflicts, and uncontrolled and unsanctioned regimes of environmental crimes and disasters (Agbese, 1993;

Ejobowah, 2000; Ifeka, 2004; Ogundiya, 2005; 2009). The Deltaic turbulence in Nigeria provides a penultimate example, as we shall explain below.

The Niger Delta Region (Nigeria) problem has gained international attention in recent decades. For some time now, this area of the Nigerian landscape has been characterized by violence and kidnappings of domestic and foreign nationals in Nigeria. The dilemma rests on remonstrations about oil development and drilling in this region. While the Oil companies are amassing immense wealth with the Nigerian government engulfing the rest of the funds, the environment of the Niger Delta continues to shrivel away into oblivion. The region is characterized by episodic pollution, draconian unemployment of the citizens, land and agricultural decay, and political marginalization, despite the fact that the region has just produced its first President of Nigeria (fifty years after the country gained political independence). Fisheries and the reaches of the sea have suffered. These calamities have led to incessant militancy, the use of guns and gunboats, hostage taking, and mayhem. Indeed, the Niger Delta crisis in Nigeria has displayed the worst scenario of government profligacy, negligence and utter disregard for the citizens, and environmental degradation of indigent habitations and way of life.

The impertinence in the Niger Delta, borne out of negotiated oil exploration deals between the Nigerian State and corporate multinational entities, has thus exposed the perfidy of development efforts that are targeted solely at accrued monetary gains, but not the welfare and development of the people. The cost of this Nigerian situation to the environment of the concerned communities has led to the rise of indigent group resistance that has often deviated to various forms of criminality and dissident socio-economic terrorism (Ogundiya, 2005; 2009). Globalization has apparently forcefully broken boundaries in utter contempt and disregard for cultures and ungrounded local systems, which are thus pushed into the international political and economic stage without preparation, and safeguards (Dei, 1996).

In *Globalization of Terrorism*, Onwudiwe (2001) has developed a relevant analysis of the globalization of terrorism paradigm. It relates to the spread and institutionalization of terrorist forms around the world. From his analytical perspective, the problem of the Niger Delta could only be ameliorated if the government of Nigeria addressed the root causes of the environmental dilemmas that have direct association to the scourge of terrorism. Dei (1996) in his profound cultural and indigenous critical context believes that distortions and destructions of natural environmental resources are bound to have consequences for social relations. Such relations lead to more poignant environmental degradation by the governments, their partners, and agents, thus leading to massive conflicts primed on the tangents of the environment and socio-economic despoliation. We will illustrate with examples of the desecration of the African environment through illicit dumping of waste below.

We can infer two patterns of waste disposal problems confronting global industrial corporations this century. However, each of them has major implications for environmental justice in developing nations. One is the problem of waste disposal in the home base of these corporations in the developed north of the world where advancements in laws, public awareness and technologies are increasingly forcing the hands of governments to desist from supporting environmental criminal deviance by industrial corporations. And the other one is foreign-based waste disposal issues in weak and peripheral nations with governments much more easily maneuverable by wealth, personality and power. As Simon (2000) aptly asserts, in both of these cases, the most easily attainable goal for waste disposal has been located in developing nations through corporate manipulations of governments and international treaties. Simon (2000) narrates how Italy was compelled to take back 6,400 tons of radioactive toxic waste that was illegally dumped in Nigeria in 1988 by an international cargo vessel from Italy. Guinea-Bissau has also been involved in the business of accepting millions of US dollars from some European nations in exchange for accepting toxic wastes from these nations. In Congo, government officials reportedly struck an $84 million deal to import one million tons of industrial hazardous waste into the country.

We view this general pattern of unlawful activities as increasingly converting the African continent into one huge waste dumpsite. The ease and cost effectiveness of international trans-boundary shipment of wastes in comparison to treatment at home in part accounts for the choice of shipment abroad. While it costs about $30 million and several years of efforts to set up one toxic waste treatment facility in the mechanized world, Simon (2000) insists that it costs only about $20 to dump one ton in a developing nation (see also Cass, 1994, p. 7 cited by Simon, 2000). This unsavory profit-making attitude to such life debilitating substances like toxic waste brings to mind Simon's earlier mentioned submissions regarding minds with "institutionalized insensitivity to right and wrong." Another factor attributable to shipment of waste abroad is that strident regulations and public advocacy limit choices of dumping opportunities and sites at home. Moreover, inquest in corporate environmental responsibility has seen companies checking out each other's environmental integrity through regular audit reports as prerequisite for business engagements. So, the most obvious choice is to target nations with weak, poor and corrupt governments, who could be bought off to sell the environmental health of their nations to corporations for a fee.

These governments' (native states) oblivious attitude to the well-being of their citizens has encouraged corporations to further downgrade the citizens' interests in order to enhance the corporations' profits. Implicit in all of these is the lack of analytic, insightful and negotiating finesse in the new era of environmental diplomacy suddenly thrust on ill-prepared nation states by globalization. Simply signing countless treaties on environmental matters without critically researching, articulating and subjecting them to a broad national review has seen African governments knotting-up their nations with irrelevant and debilitating global rules and regulations. On the other hand, States that are more prudent do a better job of determining their best interests in relation to international treaties. For example, although the United States is a major player in global environmental governance, the country has been increasingly shrewd in matters of treaty ratification (see Institute for Agricultural and Trade Policy 2004). This is due, as it should be, to the various contending interests within the country. America seeks and only considers the American interests first in any global agreements or arrangements. This is a clear contrast to the non-interest-led approach by third-world diplomats.

However, the United States' behavior on this issue may be more related to its government's approach to shielding the interests of big corporations, which are considered to be the major arms of American global power and hegemony. This analysis of the vastness of the United States' power and influence is apt. It is especially so in relation to the considerably weaker (militarily, economically etc.) States of Africa. Notwithstanding, there is the need to maintain and keep core trade relationships among countries (Onwudiwe, 2001). Yet, we insist that the major players in bilateral and multilateral relationships must duly regard and accommodate the African and other weaker countries to secure the global environment. Beyond this, the environmental protection of African states is so important that the African governments, the African Union, and other related regional organizations must begin to play hardball against the antics of big corporations and their sponsoring countries for environmental survival of Africa in the next millennium.

Multinational Corporations and the African Environment

The history of modern industrial environmental degradation in Africa cannot be properly examined without an explanation of the role of foreign multinational industrial entities. Collusion of governments and private corporations has been a major determinant of Africa's political, social and economic configurations since colonial times. Even in the developed world, such collaborations have had a major role in policy decisions affecting major aspects of the lives of citizens (Caldicott, 1992). However, today, negative prospects of uncontrolled industrial pollution have made such collaborations appear increasingly perilous for many nations. Many companies, this century, have been unconscionably caught in the midst of industrial ventures and process technologies designed without due consideration of its environmental impacts. The sudden rousing of environmental advocacy, which heightened in the fourth quarter of the past century, has been the bedrock of national legislations and international treaties drafted to sanction erring corporations.

In Nigeria, for example, oil companies take advantage of government failures to address the environmental and human impact of their various operations. Incidents of oil spills are blamed on community sabotage and the government responds by utter abuses of community advocacy groups, gated communes and government aided militarization of operations (Ogundiya, 2005; Ogwu, 2009; Ikelegbe, 2001). On the other hand, in the United States state of Louisiana, as we write, the 2010 oil spill is blamed on the British Petroleum (BP) and the U.S. government has marshaled every effort to make BP to carry its own burden of "cleaning-up" the mess without blaming the citizens. We have not yet witnessed any incidents or reports of American soldiers using gunboats and military arsenals against American citizens. Indeed, the BP oil spill would have been handled differently had it occurred in Nigeria. This is because of the scant monitoring of oil companies' activities in Nigeria, even with the known negative environmental impacts they visit on the country. Also, informal relationships of official agencies with the companies may determine official action. And, scientific reports on the impact of environmental regulations are often ignored, and the government and multi-national oil giants have been blamed for human rights abuses (Ogundiya, 2005; 2009).

Despite the environmental hazards caused by oil spillage, the oil corporations prefer to use powerful public relations practices to make their activities appear erroneously environmentally friendly to the public. This practice, which is very common amongst companies in the United States, is known as "greenwashing" (Simon, 2000). The most profound pattern of corporate greenwashing in the U.S. is the practice of using lobbyists to write and define environmental regulations that are eventually passed by members in the U.S. Congress (Simon, 2000). Holcombe (2008) has identified corporate greenwashing on the Internet as one of the major challenges of environmental justice. She identified Coca Cola, Georgia Pacific and Shell in the major league of companies with *questionable* environmental characteristics and widely steep in greenwashing tactics. This scenario describes a close circuit of internecine game against the proper regulations of environmental crime with players mostly under the employ of big corporate polluting entities.

There is little hope that this practice will change as long as it is cheaper for these corporations to undermine environmental crime regulations than to ensure environmental responsibility in their operations. The best bet for African nations is to be more aggressive on issues of environmental crimes that directly affect the continent's huge socio-economic life. Also, African nations may do well to call for a renegotiation of how environmental crime issues are defined and sanctioned on broad global bases, and how corporate restorations ought to be effected. In the struggle for diminishing global resources, there would likely continue to be a conflict of interest in matters of environmental sustainability and criminality. African interests must be framed in such a way as to protect its environment while at the same time remaining firm for the improvement of quality of life of the people in the areas of poverty, military defense agendas, politics, business and industrialization.

This implies that criminologists must also be part of the intellectual enterprise through research that will propose certain policy changes for Africa in this regard. It is our duty as scholars and criminologists to do so by imposing our intellects on our African elites through research for the interest of humanity and human rights in Africa. We call for recognition of African criminologists and integration of these scholars in African institutes for policy issues and brain activities. The days are gone when anything European is better for Africa at the expense of the African intellectual. We believe, without apologies, that the African philosopher king possesses more of the African interest at heart than any imported expert or other hitherto preferred expatriate. This, in our view, will augur well for Africa.

The ideological tendency by globally renowned democracies like the United States of America towards neo-liberalism (see Garland, 1997) has almost conclusively established a new approach by governments all over the world towards corporate-public alliances. The outsourcing and privatization of government duties to private corporations has yielded government departments that run almost like private corporate entities, while at the same time receiving benefits, welfare and policy nourishments just like government departments (Simon, 2000). Government and private departments are increasingly becoming indistinct in their business approaches and areas of competence. It would have been impossible to believe by the middle of the last century that a private corporation, for instance, would administer the British immigration service. White (2006) has identified that the reach of this new public private collaboration will necessarily portend some limitations in the ability of governments to intervene in the affairs of these corporations even when they breach environmental rules.

"Privatization and commodification of nature," according to White, expose the link between public and private entities. The link places a pejorative burden on relevant legal and jurisprudential issues as they relate to governments' role for law enforcement, formulation of rules, distribution of resources and as an impartial arbiter of public affairs. Contrasting the pattern from advanced nations of the Western democratic economies, many governments in Africa are unmindful of the class conflict between owners of huge private corporations and the public. This blur between government and private duties tends to deny African citizens the rights to a healthy environment. The Koko Creek international toxic waste dumping in Nigeria in 1988 (Simon, 2000) exposed Africa's perilous position on environmental crimes. It is time that African countries began to take sole responsibilities in matters of the environment. Blaming wholly international corporations or governments is no longer tolerable. The problem is also internal; it is no longer exclusively colonial or imperial in nature. The era of blaming England, America, or other external entities is over. The African comprador bourgeoisie must take responsibility for the environment, because environmental injustice is a vital issue that demands all of our attention.

We believe that no amount of gory largesse constitutes enough reward for polluting any African child. For instance, in Nigeria, a Lagos-based market called the computer village, imported desecrated computers from all over the developed world and sold them at extraordinary rates. This type of business practice produces a growing mountain of waste dumps consisting entirely of broken down computer parts. In addition, we all know that there is virtually no element in the Periodic Table that you would not find on a computer motherboard. The Nigerian government has been known to regularly by-pass its obligation to respect and protect the environmental rights of the Nigerian people as typified by the Niger Delta region's environmental pollution debacle and conflicts (Ogundiya, 2009). White (2006), while examining the capitalist/neo-liberalist government response to environmental regulations, has noted that whereas we have witnessed a great deal of activity in the area of law-making to control environmental degradation and for sustainable management, not much force of action seems to have been applied in the area of compliance and sanctions. Citing Snider (2000), White adds that in Canada, an all-engrossing philosophy of 'compliance promotion' is the norm against government policies, which indicate 'strict compliance.'

The symbolic approach to environmental regulations is equally relevant to Africa, where the major industrial players and environmental degraders are branches of the same major Western corporate units. By far, in Africa, the greatest concern of environmental justice practitioners, law enforcement and researchers in the field of law and justice is the ease with which government agencies and institutions could be subverted to promote petty private interests. Corruption is, therefore, a major linchpin against legal conformance on issues of environmental crime. With diminishing natural resources due to environmental crimes, Dei (1996) has observed that many African households are living a diametrically unsteady existence held by the dynamics of the conflicting interests of local, national and international forces. White (2006) also reported that instead of applying government resources towards issues of compliance and sanctions for environmental degradation, governments have rather applied resources as tax waivers or as packages to lessen the bite of the business climate.

There is probably deep neo-liberalist recourse and commitment to tie-up government interests with that of large corporate entities in Africa. Such pact, if established, serves as a great barrier to corporate legal conformance to environmental regulations on the continent. The base line of administrative responsibilities for any government is usually between administering the haves as seen in formidable corporate entities, and the have-nots, as seen in a greater part of the general population. A government with less people-centric focus is more likely to fall far away from tackling the reality of the majority of its population. Such a government will pander instead to the wealthy at the expense of the downtrodden. White (2006) opines that the conversion of legal and environmental issues into social and economic matters means that governments would be beholden to a variety of political and jurisprudential issues that are relevant to corporate private interests. This phenomenon of government collusion in enhancing the ability of corporations to evade sanctions for environmental pollutions is not peculiar.

The same craft is perpetrated to seek the patronage of corporations for political reasons and the populace, who suffer the turmoil of living in contaminated and unhealthy environments. Caldicott (1992) examines the U.S. government's relationships with big corporate entities with huge political influences, and concludes that government is the chief polluter in America. Aside from the U.S. government's direct discharge of toxic contaminants through the activities of its numerous federal buildings and defense industry plants, the U.S. Environmental Protection Agency (EPA) has been accused of relaxing sanctions in order to protect huge corporate polluters (see Jensen, 1993, p. 56). The EPA has accused many U.S. companies for criminal waste dumping acts in the environment, but established relationships of patronage between these companies and the government have often made their prosecution an uphill task (Simon, 2000, pp. 178-179).

The issue of corporate-government collusion in relaxing sanctions against environmental crimes is most evident in many African nations where the line between government attitudes and corporate practices are obviously indistinct. Public-private partnership is seen literally and functionally as that which excludes the masses, treating the citizens as the outsiders (Onimode, 1983; Saro Wiwa, 1993). For instance, in a nation like Nigeria, there is an obvious disconnect between the government and people's aspirations. This factor, which transcends the social, political and economic governance, has seen government departments operating as singular sub-corporations linked to the federal government as the main arm and totally above the public. With this view in mind, it is easy to decipher why and how government decisions on environmental crimes are relatively lax when their foreign multinational collaborators, such as Shell Petroleum Development Company is involved (Ogundiya, 2005; 2009; Omeje, 2006; Ikelegbe, 2001). This is the dilemma of environmental justice in many Africa states.

Simon (2000), in analyzing *corporate environmental crimes and social inequality*, notes that certain deviant environmental practices, such as illegal waste dumping, have become established among global corporations and that the victims have always been global minorities. By way of extension, global minorities mostly denote the less powerful and peripheral nations of the developing world or most of their citizens. Although the minorities (less powerful members of each society) constitute the larger portion of each country, their poverty conditions disadvantage them from making and implementing the proper environmentally friendly policies for their respective countries. Instead, as Simon indicates, the upper-class society, consisting of the CEO's of the primary echelon of the global industrial entities, although much fewer than the majority of the population, have the means to, and do, resist laws that regulate their environmentally deviant behaviors. This is accomplished by using political muscle, social connections and wealth to negotiate economically beneficial regulations, which equally ensure conformance by the lower class.

Other authors (see Blumberg and Gottleib, 1989; Gedicks, 1993; Taylor, 1997) have supported the salient point of the role of corporations in perpetrating environmental crimes. Brandishing the concept of globalized power relations (Simon, 2000), the multinational entities are entrenched in the governments of most African nations. The attitude of criminal defiance has been described by Simon as "an institutionalized insensitivity to right and wrong," which operates in a way that permitted the invidious neglect of social and environmentally related crimes. Africans have directly and indirectly been dehumanized and communities have suffered and depopulated (Ogundiya, 2005). In Simon's depiction of these criminal corporate practices, society will likely experience more white-collar crimes perpetrated against the green atmosphere of the African continent. Nigeria, certainly, will suffer more of the environmental greenhouse gasses with its oil productions as the basis for its economic engine.

Industrial Pollution in Nigeria: A Case Study

In Lynch and Stretesky's (2006) work on corporate environmental waste victimization, they note that uncontrolled industrial waste disposal may violate environmental regulation laws and can cause moral and social harm to society. These two perspectives of how environmental crimes are perceived are important in order to appreciate the dilemma of environmental crime identification, regulation and sanctioning in the African context. Lynch and Stretesky equally focus on the important point of *responsibility and culpability* for environmental crimes. The activities of industrial entities from across the world in relation to the damage of the environment, food, economic, social and political culture of many African States is pervasive. This mindless but steady attenuation of the health and manifest physical existence of communities has seen a corollary in deaths and depopulation as citizens migrate further away from the industrial plants, leaving their ancient ancestral and cultural abodes. Those who insist on staying in their ancestral homes, as some community members do in the Niger Delta (Nigeria), where oil exploration activities hold sway, report the preponderance of a variety of uncommon diseases, such as poor vision, skin infections and coughs and cancerous growths (Ejuwa, 2005). Lynch and Stretesky have utilized scientific evidence in their study and examined how medical health evidence could be used to identify harms due to toxicity of anthropogenic or manmade emissions. Industrial wastewater pollution is a growing concern in several developing countries with limited infrastructure and regulatory framework for their control (Karunyal et al., 1994; Manivasagam, 1987).

In many cases, the most expedient approach for the disposal of the effluents has been straight discharge into storm sewers, aquatic and terrestrial environment without pretreatment. Seed germination and growth tests for toxicity due to direct physical impacts of pollutants, bioaccumulation of metals and non-metallic nutrients, and physiological/growth dysfunction, among others (Paterson et al., 1998) are being investigated to determine the effects of industrial effluents on biological systems. Chiras (1985) has noted that plants are usually very sensitive and vulnerable at the stage of germination and early seedling growth. It must be emphasized that in Nigeria, there is a noticeable impact of uncontrolled discharge of industrial effluents, leading to deterioration in the aesthetics of land and water environment across cities and the hinterland areas (Aina, 1989). Today, the once beautiful scenic natural lagoon system in the city of Lagos is polluted with all manner of dense effluents from industries to such an extent that one could literally *walk on the waters*. Furthermore, citizens of Nigeria have experienced health problems due to the nature of these discharges, because about ninety-five percent of the communities that border the national waterways are agrarian. Effluent composition often depends on the type of industry and raw materials used (Manivasagam, 1987); quality may range from harmless to toxic sludge or water (Dix, 1981). Therefore, for administrative policy decisions on breach of environmental laws as well as for proper management of disposal efforts, it is important to understand the potential impact of the pollutants on subsisting biological systems.

We will proceed, however, to buttress dangerous aspects of environmental toxicity further from the perspective of corporate environmental malpractices in local communities in Africa, with an update of a scientific study conducted in 2004 by one of the present authors. Ejiogu (2004) examined the effect of uncontrolled corporate industrial effluent discharges on local food crop agriculture in Nigeria. This simple, but elegant scientific study, demonstrated the reality of the ill effects of mindless environmental crimes against indigent communities in Nigeria by corporate industrial organizations. This investigation was originally conducted using a variety of industrial effluents in Eastern Nigeria. The methodology involved the sampling and physico-chemical analysis of effluents from industries discharged into the river Otamiri, which transects southeastern Nigeria as it flows down into the Niger Delta estuary, including industries along the Inyishi River. The effluents were investigated by comparative analysis for their germination and early seedling growth effect on bean, corn and okra, which are major local food-crops commonly grown within this area. Around the Otamiri transect-bed and the banks of river Inyishi, discharge of effluents by local industries is a regular and uncontrolled occurrence.

For the present report, we conduct our analysis from the means of growth indicator variance (ANOVA) data from the scientific study as recorded by Ejiogu (2004). The study used effluents from an aluminum extrusion industry for analysis of the banks of River Inyishi and its polluting agents. This follows standard scientific patterns of research as Foucault (1975) has noted, that just like social science research, science reports are also based on individual explanations. The data from the aluminum extrusion industry effluent study reveals very serious and damaging effects of the effluents from this aluminum industry as discharged into the Inyishi River on local food crops in Nigeria. The Aluminum effluent, sampled from point source interface with the flowing river, supported minimal germination for cultured seeds in comparison to control seeds irrigated with distilled water. The study also supported bean seed germination briefly only at 25 percent concentration. The results of mortality experiments were more drastic and recognizable as the effluent caused considerable mortality to growing seedlings and by the middle of the investigation had caused 100 percent mortality. The effluent was physico-chemically determined to contain 10.98 mg/L Aluminum.

The toxicity effect of the high concentration of Aluminum found in Ejiogu (2004) must have negated the ability of the seeds to germinate and seedlings to grow. Ma et al. (2004) corroborates this argument when they showed that aluminum toxicity reduced root length in wheat plants. In sum, the investigation conducted and analyzed under standard experimental and statistical conditions for seeds tested for virility was proof that effluent from this industry had a deleterious toxicity effect on living systems. The investigation contrasted the position of the company's leadership that their effluents had no negative effect on the environment. The effect of this effluent type on germination capacity of locally grown bean seeds is shown graphically in Figure 1. The graph shows that the effluent only supported germination up to the third day and mostly at minimal dosage levels of between zero and 25 percent; clearly indicating its deleterious impact on seedling germination capacity.

Figure 1: Graphical display of germination capacity (%) of bean seeds with time under different concentrations of aluminum effluents discharged into the Inyishi River in Imo State Southeastern Nigeria.

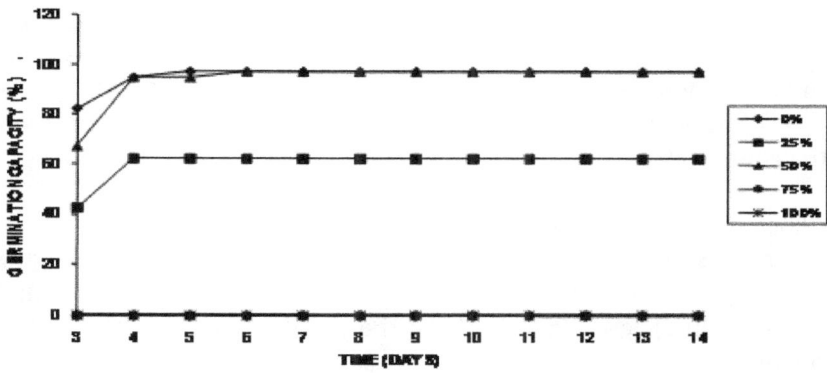

Subsequently, Figure 2 illustrates the impact of a series of industrial effluents tested (including the aluminum industry effluents) on an important seedling growth indicator (root length). It is evident that these effluents limited root growth with increasing concentration. In addition, mortality was quicker and greatest with the aluminum industry effluents deposited directly into the village Inyishi River. It is noteworthy that for the Inyishi village community, the river served the dual purpose of domestic and irrigation water supply. Generally, the different industrial effluents studied were found to reduce the water potential of the seeds. This corresponds with the report of Chatterjee and Chatterjee (2000), and Fritter and Hay (1981) that the simplest resistance mechanism of plants to toxic compounds is exclusion, which makes it impossible for water uptake. For the Aluminum industry effluent, physical effect on the seeds was also noted to have been partly corrosive.

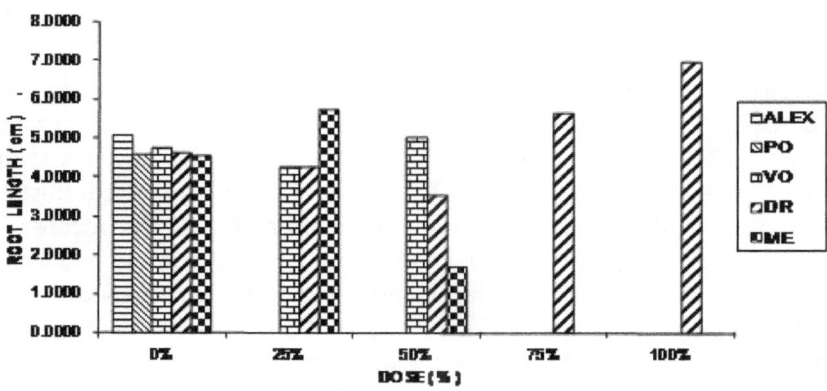

Figure 2: Graphical display of root length (cm) of Okra seedlings under different dosage levels of different effluent types (ALEX - aluminum industry; PO - palm oil mill; VO - vegetable oil industry; DR - city drain effluents; ME - mixed effluents of PO and VO) concentrations discharged into the Inyishi river in Imo State Southeastern Nigeria.

In line with previous studies, such as Paterson et al. (1998), several pertinent inferences can be drawn from the data in Ejiogu (2004) (see Figures 1 and 2). Prominent among the inferences is that the discharge of effluents in some of the rivers in Ejiogu (2004) is above the standard water quality criteria for physico-chemical constitution. Secondly, these effluents negate the growth of food crops by limiting germination and seedling growth. Finally, the one hundred percent deleterious mortality of these effluents on plant systems increased the possibility of negative health effects occurring when the contaminants are ingested by people, who depend on the river as a source of portable water. When, amid bio-accumulated amount of the substances, the plant systems are used for food, their impacts on the community could be devastating.

Further, Colborn, et al. (1997) identified the increasing dimensions of studies linking environmental toxicity to certain forms of illness. Consistent with this, Lynch and Stretesky (2006) report that while lifestyle has been associated with cancerous disease, the ever-increasing number of such cases is deserving of another level of explanation. In this sense, they factored on three perspectives to determine flagrant corporate processes that could impact the environment: evidence of the deleterious impartation of such products/substance on human health; a comparison of associated harm with other harms of significant societal stature; and a determination of source awareness of the health risks attendant to the products/substances. Citing Stretesky and Hogan (1998), Lynch and Stretesky identified a correlation between proximity to hazardous waste sites and rate of increase of cancerous disease in American underclass neighborhoods.

The situation in Nigeria is similar to that in the American underclass neighborhoods. In Nigeria, especially in the hinterlands, effluent toxicity crimes due to industrial effluent disposal are the most pervasive of environmental justice issues. Contentions, however, persist amongst the government, industrial corporations, citizen groups, and environmental health and justice advocates on a standard measure of legal redress. While examining toxic crimes, Lynch and Stretesky (2006) made this same general observation in their analysis of the legal implications of harms due to industrial waste. They assert that permissive corruption in government agencies responsible for enforcing environmental laws has mostly led to unsuccessful management of monitoring activities. This slipshod in environmental regulation has seen the dumping of various obsolete industrial polluting technologies in lower and minority communities as well as the developing societies.

We must note, however, that despite global corporate malfeasance, business environmental malpractices exhibited in nations like Nigeria are often impracticable in core states (Silverman and Lydecker, 1982; Waldo, 1985). This indicates that companies are most likely to follow the line of least resistance, not that they are unaware of the law or the need to obey its statutes, but that they are prone to disobey for as long as they can get away with it or it is cheaper to do so. On the contrary, in the wake of the BP oil pollution in the United States in 2010, the BP polluters would be better served to consider the "booth on their necks" if they rebuffed government's warning to "plug" the leaking "well." The real point in this assumption is that continued underdevelopment of policies relevant to environmental crime enforcement protocols and practices in Nigeria and Africa is injurious to the environmental wellbeing and societal health.

For the developed world especially, researches sponsored by the companies themselves sometimes contaminate and define environmental law-making (Lynch and Strestesky, 2006; Erhlich and Erhlich, 1996). Companies may be well placed to alter research results and establish conformities of both scholarship and official government sources in order to protect issues of criminal neglect in articulation of toxic products and in their general environmental transgression (Stauber and Rampton, 1995). The most worrying prospect for Nigeria is that a sizeable number of the toxic effluent producing companies are tucked away near streams, rivers and waterways in rural communities detached from the eyes of the few existing environmental monitoring agencies. The locations of these corporations have implied uncontrolled effluent discharge in aquatic, terrestrial habitats and farmlands of a monumental proportion, and an invidious positioning to get away with all manner of environmental crimes.

Conclusion and Recommendations

In view of the environmental condition in the Nigerian Niger Delta, it may be asked: how are the farmers and fishermen adapting to changes in their environment considering the activities of the oil corporations? The communities in the Niger Delta are suspicious of their contaminated waters. But these communities are powerless to hold the huge multi-national oil entities, like the Shell oil conglomerate, responsible. This situation has led to the resurgence of anti-State insurgency in the Niger Delta region. This is just a part of the dilemma of environmental justice in Nigeria. Issues of environmental justice or green criminology deserve serious and immediate attention in Nigeria to avert an imminent environmental and socio-political disaster. Many environmental advocacy groups (and there are certainly many represented in the Niger Delta) call for the government to enact enabling laws to tackle issues of environmental disaster in the Niger Delta.

Thus, the questions that arise for the criminal justice system is: What are the enabling laws to tackle issues of environmental crimes in Nigeria? Are there procedures to monitor and execute these laws? Do the victims of these crimes know that they have rights to a healthy environment? What are the implications for policy decisions on the environment? And, can corporations and their executives be held legally responsible without pecuniary caps being placed on compensations? There are environmental laws in the Nigerian justice system that touch on a variety of environmental crime issues. Pursuant to Section 20 of the *Constitution of the Federal Republic of Nigeria 1999*, the State is empowered to protect the water, air, land, wild life and forests, and to protect and improve the environment. The *Environmental Impact Assessment Act* (EIA), adopted in 1992, requires prior consideration of the environment before authorization of any project. Problems of poor administrative protocols, management and trained labor, and governmental attitudes will limit enforcement. Therefore, it is not as if the Nigerian environment is subsisting under a legal void. Environmental laws in Nigeria are pretty detailed and tap on major areas of environmental concerns as in other countries.

Nations borrow laws, procedures and protocols from other places where those laws and protocols have been known to work. In spite of this fact, the unwillingness or inability of the Nigerian government to address social issues of nationhood, such as poverty, crime, and corruption, remains a fundamental obstacle to environmental justice in the country. Administration of justice procedures for the execution of the country's environmental laws is not properly defined. So, the Nigerian environment continues to be subjected to the hold of mindless polluting corporate entities, and thus remains a major hazard to her citizens. There are laws in international environmental multilateral pacts worldwide that constrain the activities of corporations, including those that operate in Nigeria. The problem is enforcing the laws effectively, especially when and where, as in Nigeria, the people who run the businesses can frequently persuade the authorities to change the rules to suit the environmental criminals.

In Dei's (1996) analogy, the African cultural system is more prone to relating to the environment than mastering and conquering it. This appears to be the basic line of difference between the indigenous African perspective of managing the environment and the dominant approach of the international corporations. Modern global management antics foreshadow the subjugation and denigration of the environment, which is later followed with efforts at remediation. That Africans prefer(red) the proactive environmental management approach, which relates to the environment in ways that least disturbs it and ensures its renewal, does not make their approach less daring, scientific or knowledgeable. The paradox in these twin perspectives of environmental management understanding must be underscored in relation to their implications for sanctioning unwarranted degradation and destructiveness.

Going forward, it would help us to appreciate the apparent lethargy in citizen class participation on issues of environmental renewal and the encroaching pace of industrial led environmental contamination and crimes against aquatic, atmospheric and terrestrial systems in the African continent. The question in the minds of citizens mindful of their cultural relationship to the environment appears to be this: "What is this talk about the environment? It is there, it has always been there. We live with it as we live our own lives." Apparently, not many people intentionally aim at attenuating their own lives. Africans rely heavily on the local environment to supply food and basic household essentials. Modern industrial led environmental damages therefore negatively influence the livelihood, wellbeing and economies of neighboring communities. The environmental crime concourse is really that of governance and corporate practice.

A thoughtful review of the social contract between the State and the society will today be ineffectual and perhaps utterly incomplete without a composite of its relationships to environmental management. The evolution of environmental consciousness and its implication for the survival of the post-modern society is a critical open space for criminal justice administration this century. Criminal justice is a dynamic discipline, which draws on theories and research methods from across the social and human sciences. Added to its portfolio towards the last quarter of the last century is a crisis of existence, which has pitched environmental crimes (as seen in increased air pollution, water pollution, deforestation, species decline, and animal rights) against national interests and corporate globalization agendas. Damage to the environment is an increasingly occurring crime in today's world. Social research on environmental crimes in Africa appears limited by a lack of government interest and corporate pretensions. Articulating issues of corporate compliance is important to the development of a practical agenda for environmental justice in the continent.

Challenges of enforcement of environmental regulations in Africa are heightened by a high-rate of corruption amongst government officials and corporate leadership. Though a number of scientific studies have provided insight into the potential health risks of uncontrolled environmental contamination, an administrative and policy frame for law enforcement with respect to industrial effluent disposal is required urgently in the continent. This is pivotal if criminal corporate activities are to be dissuaded from turning Africa's terrestrial, inland waters and continental shelf into one huge garbage bin of toxic health debilitating substances. These forms of criminal waste dumping activities are increasingly devaluing the social, economic and environmental capital of African States. It is essential to articulate measures to reduce the opportunity for environmental crimes by examining the legal administrative structures and regulations as well as cultural and indigenous ethos involved in the identification, prevention and punishment of environmental crimes.

On a global scale, it is important to identify the relationship between global environmental changes and management of toxic waste and other anthropogenic pollutants. Acts of criminality leading to dangerous dumping of these wastes across international waters ought also to be categorized. To regularly understudy the social, cultural, economic and political phenomenon and behaviors leading to environmental crimes across international waters creates more dilemmas for the continent of Africa. It would also be important to habitually look at and be mindful of the indices for streamlining the values of society in order to be wary about the critical importance of environmental toxic pollution against global security and eco-sustainability in this post-modern era.

Policy issues attendant to corporate crimes are very sensitive for many nations, especially regarding international trade, and by extension, environmental crimes. States attempt to protect their home companies by virtue of derived national benefits. An environmental diplomacy perspective that critically examines charters and protocols of international environmental and trade issues is therefore advocated for African governments in the unfolding global industrial system, which requires the weaker nations to bear the brunt of the industrial successes or ill-conceptions of the core nations. While we have framed our thoughts for deliberate understanding of the enormity of the environmental issues, we are also mindful of the worthy projects of the corporations in terms of economic developments and government's attempts to improve the economic livelihood of the citizens in polluted areas of the various African enclaves. Nigeria, particularly, has endeavored to allocate additional resources to the Delta regions of the country through such outlets as the Niger Delta Development Commission and more recently the creation of the federal Ministry of the Niger Delta. We insist, however, that more efforts should be directed to these regions in the future. Finally, we call on African criminologists and legal researchers to embrace studies in this real and emerging criminological enterprise as American scholars have quickly embraced and propagated research in the field of terrorism and homeland security after the September 2001 terrorist havoc on the United States.

References

African Network for Environment and Economic Justice (2004) *Oil of Poverty in Niger Delta.* Retrieved December 9, 2009, from: http://www.boellnigeria. org/documents/Oil%20of%20Poverty%20in%20Niger%20Delta.pdf; Internet.

Agbese, D. (1993, January 25) "The Curse of Oil," *Newswatch*, 17(4), 8.

Aina, O. A. (1989) "Environmental Pollution Problems," *The Nigerian Business Law and Practice Journal*. Notes on Environmental Edit. No. 13 of Lagos State, Nigeria.

Anoliefo, G. O., O. S. Isikhuemhen, and N. R. Ochije (2003) "Environmental Implications of the Erosion of Cultural Taboo Practices in Awka-South Local Government Area of Anambra State, Nigeria: Forests, Trees, and Water Resource Preservation," *Journal of Agricultural and Environmental Ethics, 16*(3): 1187-7863.

Beadsley, T. (1994) "A War Not Won – Trends in Cancer Epidemiology," *Scientific American 270*, 130-138.

Behnke, R. (1994) "Natural Resource Management in Pastoral Africa," *Development Policy Review*, (12), 1:5-28.

Benedick, R. E. (1998) "Diplomacy for the Environmental," *Environmental Diplomacy Conference Report*. Paper presented at the American Institute of Contemporary German Studies, John Hopkins University, Washington, D.C., USA.

Benton, T. (2006) "Rights and Justice on a Shared Planet: More Rights or New Relations?" in N. South and P. Beirne, (Eds.) *Green Criminology*. Aldershot, England: Ashgate Publishing, pp. 1-27.

Berkes, F., C. Folke, and J. Colding (1998) *Linking Social and Ecological Systems: Management Practices and Social Mechanisms for Building Resilience*. New York, NY, USA: Cambridge University Press.

Blumberg, L. and R. Gottlieb (1989) *War on Waste: Can America Win its Battle with the Garbage?* Covelo, Colorado, USA: Island Press.

Borsos, E., L. Makra, R. Beczi, B. Vitanyi, and M. Szentpeteri (2003) "Anthropogenic Air Pollution in the Ancient Times," *Acta Climatologica Et Chorologica Universitatais Szegeiensis,* Tom. 36-37, 5-15.

Brack, D. (2004) "The Growth and Control of International Environmental Crime," *Environmental Health Perspectives*, 112 (2), p. A80. Retrieved from: http://ehp.niehs.nih.gov/docs/2004/112-2/toc.html; Internet.

Brimblecombe, P. (1987) *The Big Smoke: A History of Air Pollution in London Since Medieval Times*. London, England: Metbuen and Co.

Bychkov, A. Y., O. E. Kikvadze, V. Y. Lavrushin, and V. N. Kuleshov (2007) "Physicochemical Model for the Generation of the Isotopic Composition of the Carbonate Travertine Produced by the Tokhana Spring, Mount Elbrus Area, Northern Caucasus," Geochemistry International. *Earth and Environmental Science, 45*(3), 235-246.

Caldicott, H. (1992) *If You Love this Planet: A Plan to Heal the Earth*. New York, NY, USA: Norton.

Cass, V. (1994, November) *The International Toxic Waste Trade: Who Gets Left Holding the Toxic Trash Bag?* Paper presented at the 1994 meeting of the

American Society of Criminology, Miami, Florida, USA, November 9-12.

Chatterjee, J. and S. Chatterjee (2000) "Phytotoxicity of Cobalt, Chromium and Copper in Cauliflower," *Environ Pollut., 109*, pp. 69-74.

Chiras, D. D. (1985) *Environmental Science: A Framework for Decision Making.* New York, NY, USA: John Wiley and Sons.

Colborn, T., D. Dumanoski, and J. Myers (1997) *Our Stolen Future.* New York, NY, USA: Plume.

Constitution of the Federal Republic of Nigeria, 1999.

Dei, G. J. S. (1996) "The Relevance and Implications of Indigenousness." Paper delivered at the Learned Societies' meeting of the Canadian Association for the Study of International Development (CASID), Brock University, St. Catharine's, Ontario, May 31-June 2, 1996.

Dix, H. M. (1981) *Environmental Pollution: Atmosphere, Land, Water, and Noise.* New York, NY, USA: John Wiley and Sons.

Ejiogu, K. U. (2004) "A Comparative Study of the Effects of Some Industrial Effluents on Germination and Seedling Development of Three Plant Species." M.Sc. Thesis, Federal University of Technology Owerri, Nigeria.

Ejiogu, K. U. and M. Pautler (2008) *Calculating Ecological Footprint of Sheridan College.* Final Project Report, Environmental Control Program, School of Applied Computing and Engineering Services, Sheridan College Institute of Technology Davis Campus, Brampton, Ontario, Canada.

Ejobowah, J. B. (2000) "Who Owns the Oil?" The Politics of Ethnicity in the Niger Delta of Nigeria. *Africa Today, 47* (1), 28-49.

Ejuwa, G. A. (2005, April) "Saving the Niger Delta from Oil Pollution," *News and Trends in Africa*, 10(8). Retrieved December 17, 2009, from Alexanders Gas and Oil Connections: http://www.gasandoil.com/goc/news/nta51683.htm; Internet.

Environmental Impact Assessment Act, 1992.

Environmental Justice Research. In N. South and P. Beirne, (Eds.) *Green Criminology*. Aldershot, England: Ashgate Publishing.

Epstein, R. (1992) "Pollution and the Environment. *Vajra Bodhi Sea: A Monthly Journal of Orthodox Buddhism*. Pt. 1, v. 30, pp. 36, 12.

Erhlich, P. and A. Erhlich (1996) *Betrayal of Science and Reason*. Washington, D.C., USA: Island Press.

Foucault, M. (1975) *The Birth of the Clinic*. New York, NY, USA: Vintage.

Foucault, M. (1991) *Discipline and Punish: The Birth of the Prison*. Cambridge, Massachusetts, USA: Harvard University Press.

Fritter, A. H. and R. K. M. Hay (1981) *Environmental Physiology of Plants*. New York, NY, USA: Academic Press.

Garland, D. (1997) "Governmentality and the Problem of Crime: Foucault, Criminology, Sociology," *Theoretical Criminology*, 1(2), 173-214.

Gedicks, A. (1993) *The New Resource Wars: Native Environmental Struggles Against Multinational Corporations*. Boston, Massachusetts, USA: South End.

Halsey, M. (2004) "Against 'Green' Criminology. *The British Journal of Criminology* 44:833-853.

Holcomb, J. J. (2008) "Environmentalism and the Internet: Corporate Greenwashers and Environmental Groups," *Contemporary Justice Review, 11*(3), 203.

Hong, S., J. P. Candelone, C. C. Patterson, and C. F. Boutron (1994) "Greenland Ice Evidence of Hemispheric Lead Pollution Two Millennia Ago by Greek and Roman Civilizations," *Science 265*, 1841-1843.

Ifeka, C. (2004) "Violence, Market Forces & Militarization in the Niger Delta," *Review of African Political Economy, 31*(99).

Ikelegbe, A. (2001) "Civil Society, Oil and Conflict in the Niger Delta Region of Nigeria: Ramifications of civil Society for a Regional Resource Struggle," *The Journal of Modern African Studies, 39*(3)437-469.

Institute for Agricultural and Trade Policy, Trade and Global Governance Program (2004) "US Involvement in Global Treaties." Minneapolis, Minnesota, USA. Retrieved May 20, 2011, from: http://www.iatp.org/iatp/factsheets.cfm?accountID=451&refID=37336; Internet.

Jensen, C. (1993) *Censored: The News that Didn't Make It – and Why*. Chapel Hill, North Carolina, USA: Shelburne.

Karunyal, S., G. Renuga, and L. Paliwal (1994) "Effects of Tannery Effluents on Seed Germination, Leaf Area, Biomass and Mineral Content of Some Plants," *Bioresource Technology 47*:215-218.

Lloyd, J. (2008) "Toxic Trade: International Knowledge Networks & the Development of the Basel Convention," *International Public Policy Review*, 3(2).

Lynch, M. J. and P. B. Strestesky (2003) "The Meaning of Green: Contrasting Criminological Perspectives," *Theoretical Criminology, 7*(2), 217-238.

Lynch, M. J. and P. Stretesky (2006) "Examining Corporate Victimization of the General Public Employing Medical and Epidemiological Evidence," in N. South and P. Beirne, (Eds.) *Green Criminology*. Aldershot, England: Ashgate Publishing.

Ma, G., P. Rengasamy, and A. J. Rathjen (2004) "Phytotoxicity of Aluminum to Wheat Plants in High pH Solutions," *Australian Journal of experimental Agriculture, 43*(5) 497-501.

Manivasagam, N. (1987) *Industrial Effluent Origin, Characteristics, Effects, Analyses and Treatment*. Sakhti Publications, Combatore, pp. 79-92.

Mazrui, A. A. and C. Wondji (1994) *General History of Africa: VIII AFRICA Since 1935*. (Eds.), UNESCO International Scientific Committee for the Drafting of a General History of Africa, UNESCO, CA.

Microsoft Encarta Online Encyclopedia (2004) "Nigeria" in CBPR Database –

Nigeria Center for International Environmental Law. Retrieved from:http://encarta.msn.com/text_761557915__1/Nigeria; Internet.

Montague, P. (2003) *Government Has a Public Trust Duty to Take Precautionary Action to Achieve Environmental Justice.* Comments at a meeting convened by the South Coast Air Quality Management District, Diamond Bar, California, August 21, 2003. Retrieved December 17 2009, from: http://www.aqmd.gov/ej/events/Precautionary_Principle/Montague.pdf; Internet.

Muller-Kraener, S. (1998) *Environmental Diplomacy.* Opening Remark, Conference Report, American Institute of Contemporary German Studies, Washington, D.C., USA: Johns Hopkins University.

Newton, D. E. (1995) *The Ozone Dilemma: Contemporary World Issues.* Santa Barbara, California, USA: ABC-CLIO.

Okafọ, N. (2009) *Reconstructing Law and Justice in a Postcolony.* Surrey, England and Burlington, USA: Ashgate Publishing.

Oke, T. R. (1987) *Boundary Layer Climate* (Second Edition). London, United Kingdom: Methuen Publishing.

Okereafọezeke (Okafọ), N. (2002) *Law and Justice in Post-British Nigeria: Conflicts and Interactions Between Native and Foreign Systems of Social Control in Igbo.* Connecticut: Greenwood Press.

Ogundiya, I. S. (2005) *The Threats of Terrorism in Nigeria: Myths or Reality.* Paper Presented at the Workshop on Disaster and Emergency Management, Organized by the Office of the Secretary to the Kebbi State Government, Kebbi, Nigeria, September, 20-22.

Ogundiya, I. S. (2009) "Domestic Terrorism and Security Threats in the Niger Delta Region of Nigeria," *J. Soc Sci, 20*(1), 31-42.

Ogwu, F. A. (2009) *Petroleum Pipeline Distribution System: The Case of Oil and Gas Pipeline Network in Nigeria - An Environmental Justice Approach.* School of Architecture, Planning and Landscape, ESRC SEMINAR, PhD Research Student, Newcastle University.

Omeje, K. C. (2006) *High Stakes and Stakeholders: Oil Conflict and Security in Nigeria.* Aldershot, England: Ashgate Publishing.

Onimode, B. (1983) *Imperialism and Underdevelopment in Nigeria.* Lagos, Nigeria: Macmillan.

Onwudiwe, I. D. (2001) *Globalization of Terrorism.* Aldershot, England: Ashgate Publishing.

Ostrom, E., J. Walker, and R. Gardner (1992) "Covenants With and Without a Sword; A Self Governance is Possible," *American Political Science* 86:404-17.

Paterson, M. M., G. L. Horst, P. J. Shea, and S. D. Comfort (1998) "Germination and Seedling Development of Switch Grass and Smooth Brome Grass Exposed to 2,4,6-trinitrotoluene," *Environmental Pollution 99 Number 1*, 53-59.

Paula de Perez (2006) "Excuses, Excuses: The Ritual of Trivialisation of Environmental Prosecutions," in N. South and P. Beirne, (Eds.) *Green Criminology*. Aldershot, England: Ashgate Publishing.

Sachs, W. (1992) "Development: A Guide to the Ruins," *New Internationalist*, June: 4.

Saif, M. S. I., Midrar-ul-haq, and K. S. Memon (2005) "Heavy Metals Contamination Through Industrial Effluent to Irrigation Water and Soil in Korangi Area of Karachi, Pakistan," *International Journal of Agriculture & Biology*, 7(4), 646-648.

Saro-Wiwa, K. (1993) "These We Demand," *Newswatch*, 17 (4).

Schlosberg, D. (2007) *Defining Environmental Justice: Theories, Movements, and Nature*. New York, NY, USA: Oxford University Press.

Silverman, M., P. L. Lee, and M. Lydecker (1982) *Prescription of Death: Drugging of Third World*. Berkely, Calfornia, USA: University of California Press.

Simon, D. R. (1999) *Elite Deviance* (6th ed.). Needham Heights, Massachusetts, USA: Allyn and Bacon.

Simon, D. R. (2000) "Corporate Environmental Crimes and Social Inequality," *American Behavioural Scientist, 43,* pp.633-45.

Snider, L. (2000) "The Sociology of Corporate Crime: An Obituary: (or: Whose Knowledge Claims Have Legs?)," *Theoretical Criminology*, 4(2):169-206.

South, N. and P. Beirne (2006) *Green Criminology*. Aldershot, England: Ashgate Publishing.

Stauber, J. C. and R. Rampton (1995) *Toxic Sludge is Good For You!* Monroe, Maine, USA: Common Courage Press.

Stephens, S. (2009) "Reflections on Environmental Justice: Children as Victims and Actors," *Environmental Crimes: A Reader*. White, R.(eds.). Devon, United Kingdom: Willan Publishing.

Stretesky, P. B. and M. J. Hogan (1998) "Environmental Justice: An Analysis of Superfund Sites in Florida," *Social Problems, 45*, 268-287.

Susskind, L. E. (1994) *Environmental Diplomacy: Negotiating More Effective Global Agreements*. New York, NY, USA: Oxford University Press.

Szasz, A. (1986) "Corporations, Organized Crime, and the Disposal of Hazardous Waste: An Examination of the Making of a Criminogenic Regulatory Structure," *Criminology, 2*:27-52.

Taylor, D. E. (1997) "American Environmentalism: The Role of Race, Class and Gender in Shaping Activism, 1820-1995," *Race, Gender, and Class, 5*(1),16-62.

Tolba, M. K. (2008) *Global Environmental Diplomacy: Negotiating Environmental Agreements for the World, 1973-1992*. The MIT Press.

Urbinato, D. (1994) 'London's Historic "Pea-Soupers",' *US Environmental Protection Journal*. Retrieved December 11, from US EPA Website: http://

www.epa.gov/history/topics/perspect/london.htm; Internet.

Usoro, E. J. (1977) "Colonial Economic Development Planning in Nigeria, 1919-1939: An Appraisal," *Nigerian Journal of Economic and Social Studies,* 19, 121-136.

Velded, T. (1993) *Enabling Pastoral Institution Building in Dry Land Sahel.* Paper for Donor/Specialized Agency Consultation on Pastoral Development, New York: UNSO.

Verweij, M. (2001) *Transboundary Environmental Problems and Cultural Theory: The Protection of the Rhine and the Great Lakes.* Hampshire, England: Pelgrave Macmillan.**Marco Verweij** (Author) › Visit Amazon's Marco Verweij PageWaldo, A. (1985) "A Review of US and International Restrictions on Exports of Hazardous Substances," in J. Ives (ed.), *The Export of Hazard: Transnational Corporations and Environmental Control Issues.* Boston, Massachusetts, USA: Routledge and Kegan Paul.

White, R. (2006) "Environmental Harm and the Political Economy of Consumption," in N. South and P. Beirne, (Eds.) *Green Criminology.* Aldershot, England: Ashgate Publishing, pp. 485-505.

Wisler, D. and I. D. Onwudiwe (2009) *Community Policing: International Patterns and Comparative Perspectives.* CRC Press. London, England: Taylor and Francis.

Wong, K. C. (2009) "A Chinese Theory of Community Policing," in D. Wisler and I. D. Onwudiwe (Eds.), *Community Policing: International Patterns and Comparative Perspectives*, pp. 215-256. Boca Raton: Taylor and Francis Group.

Chapter 14

Economic Digression in Developing Countries: Implications of Poor Governance, Corruption, and Absence of Independent Judicial Systems

Sikiru Asifatu

University of Texas at Dallas, USA

Abstract

Over the past few decades, economic development and growth have been very slow in most of the developing countries, especially in Africa. Several factors have been attributed to this slow economic growth with much weight being placed on poor governance and corruption as a result of lack of independent judicial systems. While most of the economic stagnation in African and other developing countries can be attributed to internal factors, there are also external factors that have led to the aggravation of this situation. Despite considerable economic improvements and expected increase in GDP in the beginning of the twenty first century, the economic performance after 2007 slowed down and the economy is therefore incapable of dealing with the growing poverty and inequality in Africa. It is clear that today most African countries are facing the task of achieving important structural changes in their economies in order to protect hard-won economic gains of the recent years and try to achieve Africa's development goals. In most African countries, there is the need for effective economic and legal reforms directed towards improvement of the business environment and removing trade barriers, thus creating a favorable investment climate in the countries. In order to achieve the above goals, structural economic adjustments should be implemented that will try to engage the private sector in the State's developmental programs. This chapter makes the case that higher and sustained levels of economic growth by means of integration with the world and a liberalization agenda can hardly be achieved without the promotion of the private sector as a dynamic engine for growth. The paper also offers ideas for removing the serious barriers to private sector development in Africa to support overall economic growth. Both core and peripheral nations have a stake in improving the economic conditions of developing countries especially because of the social control and security implications of bad economic conditions. Tunisia is cited as an example of countries where the needed reforms have been implemented. However, the 2010-2011 mass protests in Tunisia, which led to the resignation of the country's longtime president (Ben Ali), demonstrate the inadequacies of the Tunisian reforms. The Tunisian example also provides a lesson for other African countries on the need to tailor their reforms to the specific needs of the average citizens as well as the broad national goals.

Introduction

Poor economic conditions are found in every part of the world. However, by every reasonable measure, Africa is today the poorest region in the world, both in relative and absolute terms. The 21st century has recorded a reduction in economic growth in most of the countries in Africa. Consequently, the predictions by the neoclassical theory of growth, asserting that there is a chance of poorer countries such as those in Africa to "catch up" with richer countries in terms of per capita income has become an over optimistic view that today seems almost impossible to achieve. Actually, most of the African countries have registered a decline in economic growth compared to the 1980s and 1990s. In the year 1995, most African countries (apart from South Africa) had an "average per capita income" of less than 1,045 United States dollars, articulated in "real terms purchasing power" (International Monetary Fund, 1995; Spatafora, 2005; World Economic Outlook, 1995). Between the years 1965 and 1990, Africa's real gross domestic product registered very slow growth as compared to the Pacific and East Asia.

In recognition of the crucial role of law and an enabling legal environment for economic activities, this chapter considers the present and future functions of law for economic growth. Through the examination of Tunisia's strategy for handling its social, economic, and political problems, the article demonstrates that economic adjustment is the key measure for eliminating economic setback and promoting growth and development in the developing countries. Understandably, it seems surprising that such a small North African country (Tunisia) could offer significant lessons for comprehending the nature of a momentous international problem such as widespread poor economic conditions. Yet, geographical size is not a crucial factor in reaching adjustment success. Indeed, successfully adjusting developing countries, such as Tunisia, may at some point or another be seen as the best examples of a strong economic policy for the countries on the Mediterranean (Marks, 1992, p. 2). Tunisia's economic and legal reform in its time of crisis is what makes the country a good example for the study of economic adjustment in African countries. Thus, Tunisia is offered as a model of adjustment of a conceptual framework that should be implemented in other developing countries. The presentation of the Tunisian model in this chapter is accomplished through an analysis of the critical role of State/private sector relations in Tunisia's economic and political adjustment. However, in view of the 2010-2011 mass protests by Tunisians stemming from their general socio-political and economic conditions, the Tunisian reforms should be regarded with caution. The mass demonstrations, which led to the ouster of President Ben Ali, highlight the limitations of the country's reforms.

Literature Review

This section examines the various empirical issues facing the Third World countries with regard to their economies and the citizens' well-being. Interestingly, the "factors that severally or collectively generate economic malaise – inappropriate policies, abuse of power, fraud, corruption, oppression and violence, inefficiency, embezzlement, incompetence, misappropriation of public funds, and economic and financial mismanagement – are present to some degree in all societies" (Caiden and Caiden, 1977; Gould and Amaro-Reyes, 1983; Ghartey, 1987, p. 69). However, it is rather unfortunate that the use of political power appears to be a particularly challenging issue for most people in developing countries. Statistically, over 60 percent of the entire work force in Africa is fully engaged in farming. Nonetheless, many of these countries are relatively worse off than what they were many years ago, even with regard to food sustenance. Many of the countries have launched an aggressive approach to pursue various trade reforms with core nations in an attempt to bridge the economic barrier between Africa and the more developed world. Even then, the economic conditions remain very challenging. The "world recession, indebtedness and shortage of foreign exchange, coupled with limited achievements in agricultural development, poor health and welfare, rapid population growth and crumbling infrastructures, have all contributed to the poverty in many African countries today" (Bins, 1994, p. 14).

After a long economic and political decline from the 1980s to early 1990s, Africa's economic growth prospects have improved substantially in the period of 2003 to 2007, with above 5 per cent economic growth per annum between 2000 and 2007 (IMF African Department, 2009). For the most part, the economic progress has occurred because of economic reforms introduced starting from the 1980s. A gradual drop in budget deficits and inflation rates evidenced this process of recovery. Moreover, more favorable exchange rates and real interest rates were attained in most African countries (Hope, 2002, p. 172). From that time on, however, the picture has gradually become one of economic setback instead of development and growth. Today, most African countries are suffering from global economic weakness that is further worsened by the fact that the developing countries have rather weak legal and political framework.

Also, the globalization of economic interdependence between developed and Third World countries appears to be one of the major causes of job losses. The core nations continue to oppress and deprive the peripheral nations of the opportunity to have control over their resources. Similarly, African countries turn to the core nations for their goods and services as well as financial support. While it may be true that the African countries rely heavily on these supports,

> the very institutions which in the past 25 years have contributed to the deprivation of the poor through their growth-oriented policy prescriptions are also the ones presenting themselves as champions of peasants' rights and the environment. Their renewed rhetoric, however, is designed to deflect the growing popular resistance by workers and peasants in Africa against the economic policies of the IMF and the World Bank (Cheru, 1989, p. 152).

Africa and the Global Economic Crisis

African countries are currently well integrated into the world economy. From 2003 to 2007, globalization through trade and regional cooperation has been promoted and developed in the region. Actually, before the global crisis and economic slowdown, Africa directed its efforts towards intercontinental alliances and international joint operations. As a result, its economy has finally begun to recover from prolonged economic stagnation (Lundahl, 2001). However, the global economic crisis has presented African countries with many new problems and economic setback.

The African economy is facing difficult times. For almost a decade, it was characterized by a growth rate. In 2007, however, the growth machine essentially stopped working. According to the African Development Bank Group (2009), "what is most worrying is that what took Africa a decade to build has been wiped off in a matter of months" (p. 3). A series of global shocks, notably the oil price slump and decreased commodity prices, put pressure on the economy in the region. In a very short period, oil exporting countries witnessed "a budget deficit of -7% of GDP in 2009 against a surplus of +7% of GDP in 2008 and 3.8% of GDP in 2007" (ACON Chief Economist's Office, 2009, p. iii). The IMF reports that the FDI in Africa lowered by approximately 26.7 per cent in 2009, in comparison with 2008 (Arieff et al., 2009, p. 15). The World Bank (2009) reported that in Africa, "GDP growth was expected to halve from 4.9 percent in 2008 to 2.4 percent in 2009". The considerable drop in commodity prices had strongly struck the African economy.

In general, the global crisis has several dimensions in the various African countries. Slowing or negative economic growth, serious balance of payments difficulties, considerable fiscal problems, and ineffective and underproductive agricultural performance, in addition to problems of rapid rates of population increases, are only some indicators of the economic crisis. Other dimensions of the economic crisis involve rapidly growing unemployment. Thus, for example, the United Nations Development Programme (UNDP) (2009) observed, "in the Katanga province of the Democratic Republic of Congo, 60 percent of enterprises have closed and about 300,000 people have been laid off. In South Africa, where migrants from Lesotho and Swaziland also work in the mines, more than 5,000 workers lost their jobs in February 2009 alone".

There are also considerable reductions in investments on indispensable social services and education, leading to worsening health conditions and growing child mortality. Loss of environmental resources and degradation, including such problems as desertification and deforestation, also hinder economic development. Furthermore, these conditions are worsened even more by the fact that the political and legal systems are generally characterized by corruption, inefficient policies, particularly regarding the private sector. The following section will briefly review the current profile of the private sector in Africa and the constraints experienced by the private sector.

Private Sector Development in Africa

The private sector plays an important role in the economies of African countries. In particular, it contributes to GDPs, creation of employment opportunities and foreign direct investment. The private sector encourages economic progress and development, and therefore makes important contributions to the State's poverty reduction program (see Williamson and D'Alessandro, 1999; The World Bank Group, 1999; International Monetary Fund, 1998; Department of Econ. & Soc. Affairs & United Nations Conference on Trade & Dev., 1999; Ibru, 2009; Jonah, 1995; Supporting the Private Sector for Growth, 2009).

The activity directed towards the development of the private sector, especially in the time of economic crisis, not only generates jobs, but can also be an effective mechanism of *participatory development* (Olowu and Sako, 2002; Platt, 2007). This means that it provides a vast part of the population, particularly the poor, with an opportunity to participate in the process and profits of economic development. However, a number of restrictive conditions, some of which are policy-related and others legal, hinder the process of developing the private sector in Africa. According to a well-known study by Brunetti et al. (1997), which examined and analyzed approximately 3,600 private businesses in 69 countries, African businessmen indicated that regulatory, legal, and institutional constraints were their main difficulties. Corruption was indicated as the most problematic aspect of doing business in Africa, followed by tax laws or extremely high taxes. According to Ferreira and Bayat (2005), "corruption in the government service is the major concern among foreign investors." Moreover, the authors note that according to the CPSI, "a survey of sixty-nine countries ranked corruption as the single largest obstacle to doing business with South Africa" (pp. 15-17). In Brunetti et al.'s (1997) study, ineffective structure and organization came third, in addition to inflation.

The Case of Tunisia

Tunisia is regarded as a major framework for the developing countries of Africa. The country accomplished this through an examination of the important role of State-private sector relationship and partnership in the context of economic and legal adjustments during economic crisis. The following discussion will help the reader to understand Tunisia's own success in economic adjustment and how it can be applied to most developing countries.

After decades of very poor economic performance, Tunisia launched the

Economic Recovery Programme (ERP) in 1986. The program included efficient steps towards economic strengthening, structural adjustment and process of recovering from stagnation. The main goal of the program was to improve private sector development and its relations with the State. As a result, many price incentives were introduced within the agricultural sector and there was a more efficient distribution of currency within the manufacturing sector. In addition, new regulatory fiscal and monetary policies were to be introduced, the currency was to be reduced in exchange value, and the economy was to become increasingly open, liberated and oriented towards the foreign investors.

The ERP produced many positive results. A number of important steps were taken in the right direction, and as a result, Tunisia's GDP grew in a short time. Despite the fact that the social infrastructure was not included in the ERP goals, income distribution was considerably improved because of the measures that produced improvements in farming (see Hansson, 1993; Grilli and Salvatore, 1994; Howard, 2001). Importantly, Tunisia negotiated with the IMF and as a result was granted an Extended Fund Facility (EFF) loan in 1988. It should be noted that, at the same time that Tunisia was granted the EFF, both Morocco and Algeria were denied the facility. The grant and its subsequent extension demonstrated confidence in Tunisia's economy (International Monetary Fund, 1991). In view of the ERP's success in Tunisia, observers in many international financial institutions (such as the IMF and the World Bank) on many occasions admired Tunisia's advances in economic adjustment, for instance calling it "one of the best examples of how a developing country can overcome apparently intractable difficulties" (O'Sullivan, 1992, p. 5).

One of the most important features of Tunisia's ERP has been that of legal reforms. It should be noted that economic reforms are closely interrelated with legal reforms. And, economic reforms are unlikely to bear significant fruit unless legal reforms are undertaken at the same time. The policy measures that will be employed to steer an economy are ultimately determined by the legal system that prevails. Certain laws are simply not compatible with certain economic systems, and if the new economic system is to be implemented, the legal system must be reformed as well. Perhaps the best example of this is when the legal framework in a country must be made highly liberal before it is possible to go ahead with a market-oriented policy directed towards a favorable investment climate. Thus, by the end of 2000, the Tunisian State introduced a number of laws providing the necessary legislative framework for economic reform. In particular, these included the budget law, the law on economic processes, the law on foreign direct investments, the law on foreign exchange, and the law on public businesses (see Tunisia's Commitment to an Open Economy in a Global Environment, 1996; Dorraj, 1995; Gibbon and Ponte, 2005). As a result, foreign trade has been made more liberal and price controls removed. These measures have undoubtedly contributed to the development and consolidation of the private sector in Tunisia.

However, even the best reforms can affect different segments of a society differently. Apparently, this has happened in Tunisia where high living costs among the citizens, high unemployment, and general dissatisfaction with the country's leadership resulted in irrepressible social unrest and political instability in 2010-2011. The Sidi Bouzid Revolt or Jasmine Revolution in the country was the result of despair and anger of the youth with their socio-economic and political circumstances. The unrest began on December 12, 2010, after a young man named Mohammed Bouazizi became so frustrated with his joblessness and poverty along with the contemptuous and demeaning treatment he suffered in the hands of the official police that he set himself on fire at the provincial headquarters. This led to mass protest against the Tunisian government headed by Zine El Abidine Ben Ali (Byrne, 2011). The youth, who are the majority of Tunisia's population, were experiencing a high rate of unemployment and diminishing living standards. The protests led to clashes with the government's security forces for a sustained period. Eventually, these events resulted in the Tunisian president's resignation.

Thus, despite the Tunisian reforms to diversify and liberalize economic participation, the Bouaziz's of the country ostensibly have not benefited from the expanded economic activities. The Sidi Bouzid Revolt, the subsequent mass protests, and the events that followed them show that a large portion of the Tunisian population has been left behind by the reforms. Essentially, the Tunisian elite and other privileged persons benefit from extensive economic initiatives presented to them by large multinational corporations. As should be expected, these corporations, their local sponsors, and other stakeholders maximize profits in the reformed Tunisian economy. At the same time, however, the multinationals and their collaborators push the average citizens' incomes to a minimum while further cutting labor (Liberal Ironist, 2011). In 2010-2011, the general dissatisfaction among Tunisians came to a head with Mohammed Bouazizi's case. That case served as the final straw for the citizens, especially the youth who constitute most of the country's population. The lesson for Tunisia as well as other countries, especially those in Africa, is that it is quite possible to create and implement reforms that boost economic activities in a country without a credible mechanism for ensuring that the average citizens participate in and benefit from the reforms.

The Case of Nigeria

Unlike Nigeria, some African countries have succeeded considerably in improving their macroeconomic and legal environment in the last ten years, and continue to do so. As stated in a related literature, "Nigerians view the English system of law and justice in Nigeria as ineffective and inefficient for social control in the country" (Okafọ, 2007, p. 6). The alien nature of the Nigerian laws and the overall law and justice environment is inconsistent with formulating laws and economic policies for increased participation in economic activities, especially by individual Nigerian citizens and groups. Thus, several economic issues or factors have contributed to the slack economic growth in Nigeria. The factors include poor governance, corruption, and poor infrastructure (Salim, n. d; Snider, 1996). Apparently, it is widely acknowledged that the creation and development of a sound macroeconomic and legal framework is a required condition for a quick and steady growth and development of Africa's private sector (Winiecki et al., 2004; Chui and Gai, 2005; Olowu and Wunsch, 2004; Brüntrup et al., 2006). The consequences of ineffective macroeconomic and legal framework are easily noticed in the forms of high inflation, low foreign direct investment, and slow growth, with their negative impact on the Nigerian private sector.

Empirical Issues and Solutions

This section addresses the empirical issues militating against the economic development of Africa and offers solutions to those problems. As already mentioned, developing countries have in the last decade registered a decline or slow economic growth. This fact has continued to widen the gap between the rich or developed countries and their developing counterparts. Consequently, most African countries experience pervasive economic hardships. These African and other countries face several factors or challenges that affect their economic growth and development (BBC MMX, n. d; VOA, 2003). To support this argument, this paper considers the cases of Tunisia and Nigeria. Strong win-win partnership between the private and State sectors is the major priority in the countries' economic adjustment strategies. Tunisia's legislative and regulatory framework provided enticing advantages to foreign investment that led to overall economic growth, reduction of inflation and budget deficits, as well as adjustment to growing debt services (Jere-Malanda, 2009, p. 52).

Poor Governance

The government of a country dictates its economic policies and practices. Thus, governance has a direct impact on the economic development experienced or achieved in an area. Unfortunately, poor governance characterized by pervasive corruption typifies most developing countries. Corruption refers to the abuse or misuse of public power or office with an aim of meeting personal or narrow group interests. According to World Bank's findings, corruption is the greatest obstacle to effective social and economic development of a society (World Economic Outlook, 1995). Corruption weakens development by interfering with or distorting the law, thus undermining or destabilizing the institutional foundation upon which economic development is to be built. Most of the major causes of corruption have economic implications. Thus, these causes have a direct impact on economic development in a country (Sako, 2006; Corrigan, 2009; Kilgour, 2009). Corruption in most developing countries is very rampant and this is a major challenge to these countries and their developmental efforts.

Economic development can only be achieved where good governance is achieved and corruption is rooted out. In most developing countries, governance is based on the desire to fulfill personal interests rather than the achievement of the overall good of the country. This has been a major cause of increasing corruption in developing countries. Businessmen and government officials collude in order to increase their wealth at the expense of the citizens (Baffoe-Bonnie & Khayum, 2003). Most of the economic policies formulated in developing countries are self-serving and protect only the interests of a few persons, with little or no benefit for the vast majority of the population. This has resulted in the creation of few bourgeoisies on the one hand and very poor individuals on the other hand.

Thus, most developing countries, especially in Africa, are characterized by a wide gap between the poor and the rich. Innovation and creativity among the significantly larger poor group is discouraged. In these developing countries, corruption resulting from poor governance has led to the creation of cartels and monopolies that affect free and fair competition, which is essential for economic development (Dinavo, 1995). Thus, the poor citizens end up paying more of the little they have towards the running of the government while they receive very little in return for their contribution. Wealth is distributed among the powerful politicians and prominent people while the qualified, innovative and entrepreneurial poor people are discouraged and condemned to poverty (Thirsk, 1997). In sum, rampant corruption in developing countries makes it difficult to achieve economic growth and development. In addition, poor governance is a major economic challenge among the developing countries and a hindrance to their economic development (Obasanjo, Orville & Africa Leadership Forum, 1990; Spector, 2005).

Poverty

Poverty is a major economic challenge facing developing countries. Africa is one of the poorest continents in the world. The extreme poverty in most developing countries, including those of Africa, makes it impossible for these countries to exploit the natural resources that should help in bringing about their economic development. In the 21st century, the world has recorded an increase in globalization and the use of technological modes to improve production and trade (Gries & Naudé, n. d). However, participation in the global markets is an expensive endeavor even if very rewarding in the end. Such participation requires the use of modern technology in production to ensure that goods produced meet the many quality standards set by the global market and to increase the competitive strength of a company or an industry and the country that sponsors it. Developing countries lack the financial resources to enable them participate in the global markets hence their dwindling economic conditions.

Therefore, poverty is a major challenge facing most African countries and poverty contributes to the slow economic growth being experienced by these countries. Poverty or lack of financial resources has also made it difficult for industries in developing countries to adopt the new technological means necessary for improving the production and quality of goods. The result is that many of the goods from the developing countries lack the necessary quality to enable them trade successfully in global markets. As widely recognized in previous research, poverty as an economic challenge to developing countries, has hindered economic development in these countries (see Nnadozie, 2003; Adésínà, Graham & Olukoshi, 2006).

Poor Infrastructure

One of the major contributors to a country's economic development is its infrastructure network. Infrastructure, such as roads and airports among others, ensure that goods and services are transported from those areas where the goods and services are highly concentrated to the areas of low concentration, thus enabling trade and bringing about economic development. Good infrastructure also creates avenues for mass production hence leading to the production of enough goods and services for export (international trade). Without good infrastructure, it is impossible to engage in any meaningful trade. Most developing countries, especially in Africa, are characterized by poor infrastructures that are unable to support national and international trade. These countries have poor road networks, substandard airports and inefficient railway infrastructures. This has made it difficult for the transportation of goods from the areas of production to major national and international destinations (Adhikari, Kirkpatrick & Weiss, 1992). Due to poor infrastructures in developing countries, goods and services tend to be exchanged within a locality or a small area at very low prices since almost all individuals within such an area produce similar goods and services. This has led to an increase in poverty and lack of development. Trade is a great avenue for achieving economic growth and development, but it can only be effective if there is a good infrastructural network in a society. Without such infrastructure, it is difficult to achieve national or international trade.

Another form of infrastructure that is poorly supported in the developing countries is the communication network (Frischtak, 1994). Today, in most Western and more developed countries, face-to-face communication, telephone lines/ communication, and letters have ceased to be common means of communication. For the most part, they have been replaced by Online (electronic) communication enabled by Internet services. It is estimated that over 70% of United States citizens have full access to Internet services at any given time. With increasing use of information technology, it is also possible to purchase goods and services using the Internet. This reduces transaction costs while increasing efficiency and the speed of a business deal. It is not surprising that information technology has led to tremendous increase in trade and commerce, hence increased economic development. However, this is not the case with developing countries. Less than 20% of the citizens of African countries have access to the Internet. And, Online purchasing is still a new concept, being developed in Africa (Kilgour, 2009). Therefore, poor communication infrastructure is a major hindrance to economic development in developing countries and a major challenge to the governments of these countries.

As mentioned, infrastructure is the backbone of national and international development and trade. One of the major obstacles to developing countries' participation in international markets is the lack of good infrastructure networks. To improve economic growth and development in developing countries, it is vital for the governments of these countries to commit a large portion of their budget to upgrading of infrastructures (Sarris, 1987; Isham, Kelly & Ramaswamy, 2002). Developing countries should also seek for donor aid from already developed countries. Instead of taking loans, developing countries should request for grants and donations from developed countries as well as international organizations such as the International Monetary Fund (White & Leavy, 2000; Fanelli & Squire, 2008). Grants and donations, instead of loans, will provide the developing countries with the needed financial resources to upgrade their infrastructure without burdening them with debts servicing and repayments.

Lack of Manpower and High Illiteracy Level

Most African developing countries are rich in precious minerals and stones while others have very fertile agricultural lands. Minerals and agricultural products had created avenues for economic development in some developed countries. However, this has not been the case in the African developing countries. Explanations for this include incompetent and unpatriotic national leadership, corruption, and low literacy level among the citizens. Most developing countries, such as those in Africa, have very low literacy levels. In these countries, good quality education is accessible only to the rich and influential persons. Low literacy levels have made it impossible to have the relevant manpower and experts to aid in the extraction of minerals and effective utilization of lands for the economic growth of the developing countries (Bloom & Rosovsky, 2003).

Foreign Direct Investment

An increase in globalization and technological advancement has made it vital for countries to open up their borders to foreign investors with an aim of improving their economic growth and development. Like all other countries, developing countries have in the recent past opened up their national borders and invited foreign investors to do different types of business. To make foreign investment in developing countries more attractive, the governments of these countries have reduced most of the relevant restrictions including environmental rules and regulations. In view of the negative issues it raises for the local population, Foreign Direct Investment is today one of the biggest challenges facing developing countries. Foreign investors own most of the industries in developing countries, especially in Africa. Such companies engage in various businesses including exploration and extraction of minerals, using many methods that are neither friendly to the citizens nor to the environment.

Thus, most of the foreign-owned companies exploit the workers in developing countries owing to the high levels of poverty, unemployment, and illiteracy. At the end, developing countries and their citizens do not derive substantial benefits from such foreign direct investments as all finished goods are exported back to the home country of the investors. These investors have also led to the "killing" of local industries and demoralization of local entrepreneurs (Ekeledo & Bewayo, 2009; Adams & Behrman, 1982). Environmental degradation and depletion of raw materials are some of the other effects of foreign direct investments in developing countries. In the circumstances, many of the governments of the disadvantaged developing countries have begun to channel taxpayers' funds to environmental conservation rather than economic development, thereby further undermining the economic stand of these countries (Gullberg, n. d; Batterbury & Forsyth, 1997).

Loans and Debts

Another major hindrance to economic development in African countries is the repayment of international loans and debts. In the name of "helping" developing countries, the international community gives out loans for construction of infrastructure, social amenities, etc. in the developing countries. Most of such funding has no revenue return and they carry high interest rates (Sachs & Collins, 1989). Developing countries are today burdened with loans and debts, which they are required to service for further loans to be given. As such, a lot of money that should be dedicated to economic development is used to repay loans and debts. Also, the loans come with many restrictions. For example, for a government or a developing country to be granted a loan, it may be required to retrench some of its public workers. This leads to loss of revenue in terms of taxes and an increase in poverty level. Thus, stringent and costly terms of international funding as well as increased burden of loan repayment form parts of the economic challenges confronting developing countries in their endeavor to improve their economies.

Government and Judicial Restructuring

Most of the economic challenges facing developing countries are founded on or can be attributed to poor governance and ineffective legal avenues or structures. As mentioned earlier in this chapter, corruption is one of the killers of economic development in African countries, as examples, and if these countries are to prosper, corruption needs to be addressed. Currently, most developing countries' legal systems, including the judiciary and the police, are largely continuations of the foreign systems, which the relevant colonial authorities imposed on the colonized. This situation makes it difficult for corruption perpetrators to be prosecuted at all or to the satisfaction of the general citizenry. Often, corruption and other crime suspects, especially the prominent ones among them, are the same privileged persons in society who appoint or influence the appointments of high-ranking police officers and prosecutors. Thus, the outcomes of judicial decisions are highly influenced by government and other influential persons in developing countries (Cline & Weintraub, 1981; Ross, 1991).[1]

For economic progress to be achieved in the developing countries, legal restructuring is highly important. The discharges of the judicial, the executive, and the legislative duties of government should be separated. As much as possible, the three arms of government should be kept independent of one another. The judiciary in particular should be restructured in such a manner that enables it to fully exercise its mandate without any outside or political influence. This way, cartels, monopolies and wealth accumulation by few persons via illegal conducts can be reduced (Cheema, 2005; Sahn, 1996). However, the separation of powers advocated for developing countries should go beyond mere legal or other official declaration. The arms of government should be separated in reality, demonstrated by how cases and related issues are actually handled. Also, it should be recognized that proper separation of powers includes checks and balances by which each arm of government, based on legal authority, oversees and is overseen by the other arms (see Chapter 1 on the Rule of Law, Element 8).

Legal restructuring in a developing country should incorporate transparency and accountability, especially in official government businesses. Transparency and accountability should be made mandatory for all government

---

[1] As a way of addressing the negative influence that many public officials and other privileged persons exert on efforts to fight corruption, Chapter 19 of this book advocates greater use of indigenous systems and processes to check this vice.

and public servants to root out corruption. Civic education should also be given to the citizens in developing countries (Colman & Nixson, 1986; Demirgüç-Kunt, 2006). Most of the citizens in developing countries do not know their rights or even government operations and procedures. And, elections even in the advertised democratic countries are largely carried out not on merit but on the power to influence. This needs to change and can only be achieved via rigorous civic education which would in turn ensure good governance. These changes need to be put in place for economic reforms to be implemented.

Other Recommendations for Economic, Social, and Legal Improvements

To improve the business environment in a developing African country in particular, attention needs to be focused on the areas of accountability and legal framework. These should include the following: improving the legal and judicial system and making the regulatory framework better in quality and more effective; encouraging and providing the necessities of productive work for business development; encouraging the progress of trade and foreign direct investment; speeding up the process of privatization; and stabilizing the financial area. Likewise, in the present time of global economic downturn, African countries should direct State efforts towards the development of competitive markets by supporting indigenous entrepreneurship, removing strict regulations and controls from business activities, and getting rid of barriers to entry and exit in a number of sectors.

Importantly, legal reforms should also concentrate on improving tax and customs management, together with business permissions and registration regulations. New laws for competitive labor markets are also needed to provide small businesses with more freedom in reacting to constantly transforming competition. A trustworthy and reliable legal and judicial framework in Africa that would support private economic rights is essential for private sector activity and building of transparent relations between State and private sectors.

Role of the Developed Countries

Considering that they have a significant stake in the economic degradation of African and other developing countries, the developed countries should participate in efforts to revive the economies of these developing countries. Debts and loans repayment burdens are some of the economic challenges facing developing countries, especially those in Africa. The developed countries should consider writing off such long-term debts as well as their interests to help the developing countries concentrate on improving their economies. Going forward, any loan granted to a developing country should also not have terms and conditions that contradict the wellbeing of these countries in view of their endeavors to rebuild their economy (Cooper, 1992; Killick et al., 1982). On their part, developing countries should be decisive and bold enough to refuse any grants or loans as well as investment that may hinder their economic development and growth.

Conclusion

Developing countries have been struggling with the issue of economic development for a long time. After the 1990s, the economic development gap between the developing countries and the developed world widened and this trend has persisted to date. Many of the economic challenges that developing countries face are internal and related to governance, infrastructure, law and justice. Improvement of State/private sector relations is likely to assist in creating a viable environment for economic growth. This article fully demonstrates that developing countries can substantially diversify and improve their economies even in the midst of a difficult economic climate. However, if a developing country is to achieve economic growth, law and justice reform – to go along with other aspects of economic reforms – is critical. Despite the internal efforts of developing countries to diversify and grow economic activities, developed countries should assist the developing countries to improve their economies by giving them the necessary resources, guidance and advice without interfering in the running of the developing countries. Finally, the Tunisian experience indicates that private sector development can lead to the rapid growth of a developing country's economy and the improvement of the social conditions in general. However, the 2010-2011 mass protests in Tunisia, due substantially to economic difficulties for the citizens, highlight the problems with the Tunisian reforms. The lesson from Tunisia is that for each country, reforms should be designed and implemented with a view to positively affecting the lives of the average citizens, not just the privileged few.

References

ACON Chief Economist's Office (2009) *Financial Crisis Impacts on Africa*. Retrieved on January 22, 2010 from http://docs.google.com/viewer?a=v&q=cache: tG9S5ENCEPYJ; Internet.

Adams, F. G. and J. R. Behrman (1982) *Commodity Exports and Economic Development: The Commodity Problem and Policy in Developing Countries.* ISBN 0669051454, Lexington Books.

Adésínà, J. O., Y. Graham, and A. O. Olukoshi (2006) *Africa & Development Challenges in the New Millennium.* London, England: Zed Books.

Adhikari, R., C. H. Kirkpatrick, and J. Weiss (1992) *Industrial and Trade Policy Reform in Developing Countries*. ISBN 0719035538, Manchester University Press.

African Development Bank Group (2009). *The Financial Crisis & Africa*. Retrieved January 22, 2010 from http://docs.google.com/viewer?a=v&q=cache:Bn DSHOn1lvoJ:www.afdb.org; Internet.

Arieff, A., M. A. Weiss, and V. C. Jones (2009) *The Global Economic Crisis: Impact on Sub-Saharan Africa and Global Policy Responses*. Retrieved on January 24, 2010, from http://webcache.googleusercontent.com/ search?q=cache:twWIwAdz3oQJ:www.fas.org/sgp/crs/row/R40778.pdf+ africa+oil+%22economic+crisis%22&hl=en; Internet.

Baffoe-Bonnie, J. and M. Khayum (2003) *Contemporary Economic Issues in Developing Countries*. ISBN 0275974545, Greenwood Publishing Group.

Batterbury, S. and T. Forsyth (1997) "Environmental Transformation in Developing Countries," *The Geographical Journal* (March) Royal Geographical Society. See at http://www.highbeam.com/doc/1G1-19359510.html; Internet (Accessed April 5, 2011).

BBC MMX (n. d), *What Are the Challenges Facing Africa?* Retrieved on January 21, 2010 from http://news.bbc.co.uk/2/hi/talking_point/3682523.stm; Internet.

Binns, T. (1994) *Tropical Africa*. New York, NY, USA: Routledge.

Bloom, D. E. and H. Rosovsky (2003) "Liberal Education: Why Developing Countries Should Not Neglect It," *Liberal Education*, Vol. 89, pp. 16-23.

Brunetti, A., G. Kisunko, and B. Weder (1997) "Institutional Obstacles to Doing Business: Region-by-Region Results from a Worldwide Survey of the Private Sector," *Policy Research Working Paper 1759*, World Bank, Washington D.C., USA.

Brüntrup, M., H. Melber, and I. Taylor (2006) *Africa, Regional Cooperation and the World Market: Socio-Economic Strategies in Times of Global Trade Regimes*. Uppsala: Nordiska Afrika Institutet.

Byrne, C. (2011) "Tunisia's Jasmine Revolution: A Work in Progress," *Tegbar*. See at http://tegbar.org/?cat=6&paged=5; Internet (Accessed April 4, 2011).

Caiden and Caiden (1977) (cited in J. B. Ghartey, *Crisis Accountability and Development in the Third World*. Avebury, 1987, page 69).

Cheema, G. S. (2005) *Building Democratic Institutions: Governance Reform in Developing Countries*. ISBN 1565491971. Sterling, Virginia, USA: Kumarian Press.

Cheru, P. (1989) *The Silent Revolution in Africa*. New Jersey, USA: Zed Books.

Chui, M. and P. Gai (2005) *Private Sector Involvement and International Financial Crises: An Analytical Perspective*. Oxford, England: Oxford University Press.

Cline, W. R. and S. Weintraub (1981) *Economic Stabilization in Developing Countries*. ISBN 0815714653, Brookings Institution.

Colman, D. F. and I. Nixson (1986) *Economics of Change in Less Developed Countries*.

ISBN 0860031667, Philip Allan.

Cooper, R. N. (1992) *Economic Stabilization and Debt in Developing Countries*. ISBN 0262031876, MIT Press.

Corrigan, T. (2009) "Socio-economic Problems Facing Africa: Insights from Six APRM Country Review Reports." Retrieved on January 21, 2010 from http://www.saiia.org.za/occasional-papers/saiia-occasional-paper-no.34-june-2009-english.html; Internet.

Demirgüç-Kunt, A. (2006) *Finance and Economic Development: Policy Choices for Developing Countries*. World Bank Publications, Volume 3955 of Policy Research Working Papers.

Department of Econ. & Soc. Affairs & United Nations Conference on Trade & Dev. (1999), *World Economic Situation and Prospects for 1999*.

Dinavo, J. V. (1995) *Privatization in Developing Countries: Its Impact on Economic Development and Democracy*. ISBN 0275950077, Greenwood Publishing Group.

Dorraj, M. (1995) *The Changing Political Economy of the Third World*. Boulder, Colorado, USA: Lynne Rienner.

Ekeledo, I. and E. D. Bewayo (2009) *Challenges and Opportunities Facing African Entrepreneurs and their Small Firms*. Retrieved on January 21, 2010 from, http://findarticles.com/p/articles/mi_6773/is_3_9/ai_n39236694/; Internet.

Fanelli, J. and L. Squire (2008) *Economic Reform in Developing Countries: Reach, Range, Reason*. ISBN 1847202489, Edward Elgar Publishing.

Ferreira, I.W. and M. S. Bayat (2005) Curbing Corruption in the Republic of South Africa: Learn How New Measures Put in Place Since the 1996 Constitution, Such as the Drafting of Codes of Conduct, Whistle-Blowing, and Training Initiatives, Are Making Public Officials More Aware of the Need for Ethical Conduct in Their Public Dealings. *The Public Manager 34 (2)*, 15.

Frischtak, L. (1994) *Governance Capacity and Economic Reform in Developing Countries*. ISBN 0821329626, World Bank Publications.

Ghartey, J. B. (1987) *Crisis Accountability and Development in the Third World*. Britain: Avebury.

Gibbon, P. and S. Ponte (2005) *Trading Down: Africa, Value Chains, and the Global Economy*. Philadelphia, Pennsylvania, USA: Temple University Press.

Gould and Amaro-Reyes (1983) (cited in J. B. Ghartey, *Crisis Accountability and Development in the Third World*. Avebury, 1987, page 69).

Gries, T. & Naudé, W. (n. d) *On Global Economic Growth and the Challenge Facing Africa*. Retrieved on 21st January 2010 from http://www.springerlink.com/content/mm6807553rn66356; Internet.

Grilli, E. and D. Salvatore (1994) *Economic Development*. Westport, Connecticut, USA: Greenwood Press.

Gullberg, A. T. (n. d) *The Dilemma Facing Developing Countries: Climate vs. Economic Growth*. Retrieved on January 21, 2010 from http://www.cicero.

uio.no/fulltext.asp?id=4214(=en; Internet.

Hansson, G. (1993) *Trade, Growth, and Development: The Role of Politics and Institutions*. New York, NY, USA: Routledge.

Hope, K. R. (2002) *From Crisis to Renewal: Development Policy and Management in Africa*. Boston, Massachusetts, USA: Brill.

Howard, M. (2001) *Public Sector Economics for Developing Countries*. Barbados: University Press of the West Indies.

Ibru, C. (2009) "Africa Private Sector Driving a New Dawn for Development," *African Business* 353, 41.

IMF African Department (2009) *Impact of the Global Financial Crisis on Sub-Saharan Africa*. Retrieved on February 18, 2010 from http://docs.google.com/viewer?a=v&q=cache:dz1K0EFn2WkJ:www.imf.org/external/pubs/ft/books/2009/afrglobfin/ssaglobalfin.pdf+Africa; Internet.

International Monetary Fund (1991) *Tunisia's Economic Reforms Advance*, IMF Survey, 243.

International Monetary Fund (1995) *Policy Challenges Facing Developing Countries*. Retrieved on January 21, 2010 from http://www.accessmylibrary.com/article-1G1-17197212/policy-challenges-facing-developing.html; Internet.

International Monetary Fund (1998) *World Economic Outlook*, May 1998.

Isham, J., T. Kelly, and S. Ramaswamy (2002) *Social Capital and Economic Development: Well-being in Developing Countries*. ISBN 1840646993, Edward Elgar Publishing.

Jere-Malanda, R. (2009) Looking to the Future: Regina Jere-Malanda Was in the Tunisian Capital to Witness the Launch of a New Government Economic Strategy for the Period 2009-2016. It's an Ambitious Programme and Provides Valuable Lessons for the Rest of Africa. *New African, 485*, 52.

Jonah, S. (1995) "The Role of the Private Sector," *African Business, 199*, 12.

Kilgour, D. (2009) *Challenges and Opportunities Facing Africa*. Retrieved on January 21, 2010, from http://www.david-kilgour.com/2009/Jan_30_2009_01.php; Internet.

Killick, T. et al. (1982) *Adjustment and Financing in the Developing World: The Role of the International Monetary Fund*. ISBN 0939934191, International Monetary Fund.

Liberal Ironist (2011) "Variance in Middle Eastern Uprisings," *The Liberal Ironist*. See at http://liberalironist.wordpress.com/2011/03/04/variance-in-middle-eastern-uprisings/; Internet (Accessed May 21, 2011).

Lundahl, M. (2001) *From Crisis to Growth in Africa?* London, England: Routledge.

Marks, J. (1992) "Mediterranean Tiger Emerges in Tunisia" *MEED 31*, p. 2.

Mbaku, J. M. (1994) Bureaucratic Corruption and Policy Reform in Africa. *The Journal of Social, Political, and Economic Studies, 19 (2)*, 149.

Nnadozie, E. (2003) *African Economic Development*. ISBN 0125199929, Emerald Group Publishing.

O'Sullivan, E. (1992) "Grappling With the Legacy of the Past," *MEED*, 5.

Obasanjo, O., H. Orville, and Africa Leadership Forum (1990) *Challenges of Leadership in African Development*. ISBN 0844816701, Taylor & Francis.

Okafọ, N. (2007) "Law Enforcement in Post-Colonial Africa: Interfacing Indigenous and English Policing in Nigeria," *International Executive Police Symposium*. See at http://www.ipes.info/WPS/WPS%20No%207.pdf; Internet (Retrieved April 2011).

Olowu, D. and S. Sako (2002) *Better Governance and Public Policy: Capacity Building for Democratic Renewal in Africa*. West Hartford: Kumarian Press.

Ross, A. C. (1991) *Economic Stabilization for Developing Countries*. ISBN 1852783141, E. Elgar Pub. Co.

Olowu, D. and J. S. Wunsch (2004) *Local Governance in Africa: The Challenges of Democratic Decentralization*. Boulder, Colorado, USA: Lynne Rienner.

Platt, G. (2007) "Reliance Grows on Private Sector," *Global Finance, 21 (4)*, 30.

Sachs, J. and S. M. Collins (1989) *Developing Country Debt and Economic Performance, Volume 3: Country Studies--Indonesia, Korea, Philippines, Turkey*. ISBN 0226733351, Chicago, USA: University of Chicago Press.

Sahn, D. E. (1996) *Economic Reform and the Poor in Africa*. ISBN 0198290357, Oxford University Press.

Sako, S. (2006) *Challenges Facing Africa's Regional Economic Communities in Capacity Building*. Retrieved on January 21, 2010 from http://lencd.com/data/docs/9challenges%20facing%20Africas%20regional%20economic%20communities%20in.pdf; Internet.

Salim, S. A. (n. d) *The Challenges Facing Africa in the Coming Decades*. Retrieved on January 21, 2010 from http://unpan1.un.org/intradoc/groups/public/documents/IDEP/UNPAN002468.pdf; Internet.

Sarris, A. (1987) *Agricultural Stabilization and Structural Adjustment Policies in Developing Countries*. ISBN 9251025320, Food & Agriculture Org.

Snider, L. W. (1996) *Growth, Debt, and Politics: Economic Adjustment and the Political Performance of Developing Countries*. ISBN 0813380421, Westview Press.

Spatafora, N. (2005) Chapter II: Two Current Issues Facing Developing Countries. *World Economic Outlook*. See http://www.questia.com/googleScholar.qst?docId=5010850271; Internet.

Spector, B. I. (2005) *Fighting Corruption in Developing Countries: Strategies and Analysis*. Virginia, USA: Kumarian Press.

Supporting the Private Sector for Growth: Mabousso Thiam Was Appointed Director General of the Centre for Development of Enterprise (CDE) in March 2009. Funded by the European Development Fund (EDF), the CDE Aims to Support the Development of the Private Sector in the Africa, Caribbean and Pacific (ACP) Group of Countries. *African Business. Issue, 357*. Publication Date: October 2009, 59.

The World Bank Group in Africa (1999) in Williamson, I. and S. D'Alessandro, *Law and Policy in International Business* - New Prospects for Private Sector led

Trade, Investment and Economic Development in Sub-Saharan Africa.

Thirsk, W. R. (1997) *Tax Reform in Developing Countries*. ISBN 0821339990, World Bank Publications.

Tunisia's Commitment to an Open Economy in a Global Environment. *Presidents & Prime Ministers. Volume: 5 (6)*, 1996, 6.

United Nations Development Programme (2009) *The Economic Crisis in Africa*. Retrieved on March 2, 2010 from http://www.undp.org/economic_crisis/africa.shtml; Internet.

VOA (2003) *Challenges Facing Africa*. Retrieved on January 21, 2010 from http://www.voanews.com/uspolicy/archive/2003-07/a-2003-07-25-4-1.cfm?moddate=2003-07-25; Internet.

White, H. and J. Leavy (2000) *Economic Reform and Economic Performance: Evidence from 20 Developing Countries*. Institute of Development Studies.

Williamson, I. and S. D'Alessandro (1999) "New Prospects for Private Sector Led Trade, Investment and Economic Development in Sub-Saharan Africa," *Law and Policy in International Business, 30 (4)*, 637.

Winiecki, J., V. Benacek, and M. Laki (2004) *The Private Sector After Communism: New Entrepreneurial Firms in Transition Economies*. New York, NY, USA: Routledge.

World Bank Group (1999) *The World Bank Group in Africa: An Overview*.

World Economic Outlook (1995) *Policy Challenges Facing Developing Countries*. World Economic Outlook.

Chapter 15

Life on the Atoll: Singapore Ecology as a Neglected Dimension of Social Order[1] [2]

W. Timothy Austin
Indiana University of Pennsylvania,
USA

[1] Reprinted by permission of Sage Publications from the *International Journal of Offender Therapy and Comparative Criminology*, 49(5), 2005.

[2] This project was made possible by grants from these three sources: the Fulbright-Hays program, the National Science Foundation, and a research award from Indiana University of Pennsylvania, all in the USA. Appreciation must also go to the Institute of Southeast Asian Studies for support in Singapore. And, members of the Singapore Police Force deserve appreciation for their assistance although they may not agree with all the research conclusions.

Abstract

Based on field interviews in Singapore in 1985, 1997, and 2003, this article addresses the issue of how island ecology helps explain the remarkable low rates of crime that are often attributed mainly to cultural and government policies. Understanding crime and control on this most densely populated Southeast Asian atoll must begin with how people are dispersed over the limited spatial area. Ecology also influences how styles of some crimes are defined and controlled. Several of Donald Black's propositions are given further consideration.

Keywords: Singapore; ecology; crime; Donald Black

Introduction

Earlier field research (Austin, 1987; 1989) concluded that the Republic of Singapore, in only 20 years after its independence from Malaysia in 1965, had emerged as a squeaky clean society with its citizenry living in what appeared as near-perfect social harmony. All the usual indicators revealed that this tiny Southeast Asian atoll, barely 20 miles wide and 14 miles north to south, and now with a population of 4.7 million, remains surprisingly successful economically while holding unusually high levels of social order. Measured against Americans, Singaporeans live longer, have lower infant mortality rates, less crime, lower rates of unemployment, and hold approximate annual wages.

Most would agree that life in Singapore is highly regimented. Among numerous other ordinances, residents cannot chew gum, jaywalk, pick flowers or fruit from public parks, flag taxies outside official queuing stations, own a car older than 10 years old, spit on sidewalks, or read Cosmopolitan magazine. These and numerous similar regulations persist. They formally prohibit various behaviors which, if they result in arrest, can lead to substantial fines (e.g., Singapore $350 for spitting). Of course, these more minor infractions are in addition to laws against major acts of violence and property offenses and the highly publicized anti-drug regulations (Swensen, 1999; Vreeland, 1977).

Deviations certainly do occur in Singapore in all categories; however, they are few compared to the United States and most other nations. Comparing crime rates between nations is chancy. Yet the numbers are provocative with Singapore Ecology reflecting in 2003 an index crime rate per 100,000 residents less than one half that found in rural America. Interpersonal violence is rare with murder (0.5 per 100,000) and rape (3.2 per 100,000) offenses being 10 times lower, and with a robbery rate (22.7 per 100,000) 7 times lower than in the United States. The total number of robberies in Singapore is slightly more than 900 per year. The likelihood of being a victim of burglary (27.7 per 100,000) in Singapore is 30 times less than in the United States. Motor vehicle thefts do occur, but most are of motorcycles. Automobile thefts per capita (4.5 per 100,000) are nearly 100 times less than in the United States.

A question raised in earlier reports was whether Singapore could retain its image portrayed by one news correspondent (Reiss, 1985) as a nation scrubbed clean of temptation. Would the tightly knitted society be able to maintain such low rates of deviance and crime when the rest of the world was moving at such a fast pace? Fifty percent of Singaporeans own cell phones, and computer use is strong (Central Intelligence Agency, 2002). Internet usage is high, and cybercafés, along with Starbucks, appear on the street corners and in an endless array of shopping malls. Tourism rates remain high. That also works, along with surfing the Web, to increase the mobility of ideas from the outside. Still, between 1985 and 2003, with only minor fluctuations, the overall crime rate for Singapore actually decreased. This challenges traditional criminological theory that crime rates should rise with increases in population size and density. What explanations help us understand such success in what remains one of the most crowded, urban environments of the world with 17,000 persons per square mile?

Of particular interest is whether several of Donald Black's propositions remain as convincing now as they appeared in the mid-1980s. Black's (1976; 1980; 1993) celebrated work on the behavior of law predicts many relationships between the prevalence of law, or lack of it, and other social variables. For instance, in what ways might a rise in informal or non-governmental social controls in Singapore be associated with less of a need for law and traditional police operations? Is it possible that Singapore could manage with less of a police presence while its population density has increased? Black also predicted the relationship between the necessity for law and the extent of social intimacy or social distance between people. When people reflect higher levels of social intimacy, the need for the mobilization of formal police control would be less critical (Black, 1976). Or, as the proportion of strangers rises in a region, the level of social intimacy would be reduced, and the reliance on formal police would be greater.

It is true that no single factor best explains Singapore's low crime rate. Rather, a series of variables have been addressed over the years to include government and law (Bartholomew, 1989), formal enforcement strategies (Austin, 1987), and the more indirect or strictly informal controls such as religion, education, and employment (Ling, 1989). A parliamentary democracy allows multiple political parties. However, in the years since national independence of Singapore, the People's Action Party has remained singularly dominant. Political debate is kept to a minimum, and the conflict observed in nations with more evenly competing political systems is avoided. The dominant religion of Buddhism is claimed by more than one half of the citizenry, a religion that accepts right conduct as one of the paths to enlightenment. To the extent such spiritual belief is practiced one must presume a positive impact on overall low crime rates (Ling, 1989; cf., Fenwick, 1982).

However, often overlooked is the impact that island ecology or spatial features have exerted on criminal conduct. Donald Black's predictions on the link among law, social intimacy, and styles of social control are logically couched, in part, in the broader perspective of social ecology especially at the small group level. How features of law and the violation of law pertain to the social ecology of urban locales holds a rich tradition in social science beginning with Park, Burgess, and McKenzie (1925). For more recent reviews see Martin, Mutchnick, and Austin (1990, particularly chapter 5), and Stark (1987; cf., Sacco & Kennedy, 2002).

Singapore, with its millions of citizens squeezed onto a land mass only a few times larger than Washington, D.C., USA, offers an appropriate laboratory to help fill the research void.

Procedures

This article represents a 20-year follow-up to field research conducted in 1985. Two additional field trips were made to Singapore during the summers of 1997 and 2003. Multiple, in-depth interviews were carried out with officers of the Singapore Police Force, faculty of the National University of Singapore, government workers, local business owners, tourists, students, and other locals. Friendships were rekindled with researchers at the Institute of Southeast Asian Studies (ISEAS) where the investigator held a visiting research affiliation during the three visits.

Beginning with respondents in the Singapore Police Force and with researchers at the ISEAS, a network or snowball sample was initiated (Berg, 1989; Curran & Renzetti, 1994). At least 20 respondents, most of whom must be considered expert informants, were interviewed in-depth and on multiple occasions. The data were synthesized and collapsed into themes that were then reintroduced as topics to some of the same respondents as further checks on validity. Interviews continued until a point of redundancy was reached.

Unlike the first trip to Singapore in 1985, frequent e-mail contact after subsequent field trips allowed rapid clarification and further inquiry with many of the respondents remaining in Singapore. In addition, more recent ethnographic data benefits from easily accessed Web-based Singaporean newspapers and government documents that can be scrutinized to generate further e-mail inquiry with previous interviewees. Numerous thematic patterns emerged from the in-depth interviews pertaining to life on the island with particular emphasis on crime prevention and law enforcement styles.

Findings

Island Ecology and Social Order

Life on the small island restricts movement and influences social control in three fundamental ways. First, in several instances, cooperation among citizens ultimately tends to provide positive rewards over conflict and fosters order maintenance, rather than law enforcement perspectives of police. Second, Singapore's housing problem was solved in a way that directly results in changes in police-community relations. Third, island containment modifies the way some deviance and crimes are defined and carried out. Each of these themes is considered separately.

Order maintenance perspectives

The limited space associated with diminutive island existence crowds people together and introduces a cloistering effect that can work to generate social order. Although territorial theory does suggest that competition and conflict could escalate with increasing density of population, an opposite effect can be observed with increased population size and density working to increase sociality (Sussman & Chapman, 2004). The Singapore example illustrates how order-maintenance strategies of police (Bittner, 1980; cf., Skolnick & Bayley, 1988) provide an advantage over rigid law enforcement. The data support this conclusion in a number of ways.

On a small island, where mobility is highly restricted and citizens are forced into tight community living, dispute resolution through negotiation and mediation makes more common sense than making an arrest and carrying a dispute to trial. A formal trial forces a win-lose scenario that in Singapore would be particularly problematic because the loser in a dispute could not easily leave town to save face. Literally, short of departing the country, there are fewer places to run and hide. Rather, disputing parties are typically compelled to return to the same housing block where the disagreement originated that can provoke further stigma and animosity. It is not surprising that informal controls would naturally emerge in such densely populated locales and that formal mobilization of police would be a last resort. Thus, a proactive police approach whereby an officer patrols the streets looking for lawbreakers, making an arrest and forcing a court hearing can become dysfunctional (Black & Baumgartner, 1980; Bracey, 1989; Wilson, 1968; cf., Black, 1980).

Although Singapore is well known for being strict, it appears that beneath the surface, minor illegality is dealt with without official police intervention. In fact, uniformed police and marked patrol cars are not seen on the streets in heavy numbers. For instance, rarely will one observe police interrupting the steady flow of traffic to stop an errant motorist. Rather, video cameras detect traffic infractions resulting in a citation through the mail. Taxis need to pay a toll to enter certain street zones, and violators have fines withdrawn directly from credit cards monitored through required dashboard sensors. It is well publicized that corporal punishment by a rattan cane (caning) and capital punishments do occur. Yet these punishments appear infrequent even if consistently implemented; that is, a few cases of caning are reported daily in newspapers; however, this is not exceptional in a population approaching five million.

The number of executions is not officially reported; however, interview accounts confirm the perception that they are infrequent and deter drug crimes and crimes involving firearms, both capital offenses. When passing through the customs inspection station upon entering the Changi International Airport, officers are occasionally nowhere to be seen. Especially at late hours, travelers may simply walk through with bags uninspected. At the end of the corridor, large signs warn all passersby of mandatory death to any violators of drug laws. No juries operate in Singapore.

The case of Singapore, as a small island, is analogous to shipboard justice whereby a captain can be strict but must encourage camaraderie and social harmony to keep the ship operational that requires the efforts of all. An efficient ship's captain cannot afford to imprison crewmembers in the hulk of the ship and, as with tightly controlled island life, strategies of order maintenance prove functional. This is similar to *barangay* (community) justice in individual villages and particularly out islands of the Philippines whereby village captains are quickly available though rarely proactive (Austin, 1999). Singapore police tend to be crime prevention oriented and more apt to follow a reactive format of patrol. The confines of the small island allow a very quick response time thus making the physical presence of the police on the street less necessary.

Living space and security

The ecological dilemma of housing Singapore's citizenry on the small island reflects four periods of transition since the mid-1960s. Each displays a distinctive linkage to police patrol strategies that can be viewed in the context of Donald Black's propositions on the behavior of law.

First, prior to 1963, when Singapore was part of Malaysia and under British rule, most citizens lived in metal-roofed huts (kampongs) oftentimes elevated on stilts and clustered in what appeared to be a haphazard, disorganized, and disease-ridden aggregate of villages. These villages represented Chinese, Malay, and Indian communities that likely were not as disrupted as they first appeared and, in fact, according to some early reports, reflected extended families and culturally cohesive sociopolitical neighborhoods (Chen & Ling, 1977; Hassan, 1976). Rates of crime were conjectured as being high during this kampong era though the data is sporadic. In addition, it is likely that much of the resumed social deviance during the kampong era was managed locally.

Official crime rates were low and police intervention slight even if behind the scenes high levels of hidden illegalities persisted as reflected by public perceptions and accounts of pre-independence Singapore as a seamy, pirate-infested port city (Clutterbuck, 1985; Colless, 1969). Building on Black's theory, formal mobilization of law and police would be infrequent and less needed during the kampong era when locally coalesced neighborhoods tended to manage their own affairs (Black & Baumgartner, 1980). In addition, police intervention would be less likely when the structure of Singaporean society was reflective of lower levels of the quantity of organization (Black, 1976).

A second ecological period is observed during the decades of the 1960s and 1970s when what was reputed to be the world's largest urban renewal project was implemented. The project relocated citizens from kampongs to high-rise housing blocks. This project was motivated by a desire to improve the public health of the port city as well as by a fear that the politically charged cultural enclaves might be potentially volatile. By the end of the 1980s, more than 3,000 high-rise housing blocks were spread over the landscape, each with about 1,000 residents. With the exception of the more well-to-do, who could afford individual houses, the masses of Singaporeans lived out their lives high above the city's horizon. Such an ecological transformation greatly affected police-community relations.

With the newly constructed high-rise blocks, police could more efficiently keep tabs on specific households that remained pigeon holed, layer on layer from the ground level to the top floor. With the buildings reminiscent of some prison designs, the police could now visualize precisely where everyone was located in a very structured format. As viewed from the outside, the individual flats look nearly identical in the hotel-like housing blocks that average 20 floors in height. With mathematical precision, police were able to quickly identify on a grid exactly where a particular family resided. A $5,000 fine is levied against a resident who fails to notify authorities of a change in residence. This second transition upset many residents who did not want to be moved in the first place from their culturally based yet crowded and unhygienic kampongs. The early housing block initiative was followed by a spike in official crime rates that was of great concern to government organizers. Apparently, the social cohesion earlier associated with kampong life was lost in the high-rise blocks, resulting in disenchantment among some citizens, many of whom were detached from extended families and work locations. The rise in official crime rates affirms Black's prediction that law and police control increase and become more necessary as the social distance among the citizenry increases (Black, 1976; cf., Black, 1993). A sense of social intimacy was lacking in the newly established high-rise blocks that previously in the culturally cohesive kampong villages had worked to pull people together without government intervention.

A third ecological and organizational transition is identified when the Singapore government acted to increase police efficiency and police-community relations by initiating the Japanese koban (neighborhood police office) model by strategically positioning small police stations, referred to as Neighborhood Police Posts (NPPs) at the base of selected housing blocks. A police officer's beat could be a single housing block, and a police practice known as vertical patrol was introduced. Officers rode elevators to the top of a housing block and walked each floor, passing in front of individual flats periodically and meeting personally with all residents thereby deepening police-community linkages.

Just as important as the establishment of the NPPs, the government also mandated the development of a nationwide network of citizen groups referred to as Residence Committees (RCs) elected within the housing blocks. An RC, comprising 15 to 20 members, meets to discuss neighborhood issues and problems of the housing block (e.g., sanitation, safety, recreation, security, etc.). Coincidently, this provided a location for the airing of some grievances at the most grassroots level and generally without police intervention or even their knowledge. A housing block resident could informally bring a grievance before the RC rather than to the NPP. In addition, some grievances and disputes discovered by police could now be referred to the RCs for possible resolution. Potential police matters could be nipped in the bud and without formal police intervention.

The interplay between the NPP and the RC coincided with, and possibly stimulated, a decrease in official crime rates, much to the relief of the government sponsors of the housing block program. The ecological initiatives followed by lower crime rates tend to validate Black's prediction that a mobilization of law and police would be less necessary with an increase of social intimacy between citizens. Police units in the blocks in the 1980s and 1990s worked to maintain close and positive relationships with RCs. The general rate of crime remained low.

A fourth transition was unexpectedly uncovered during a field visit in 2003. The official crime rate had been reduced even further since 1999 with a surprising change in police patrol techniques. The introduction of sophisticated electronic monitoring was beginning to replace the NPP. In the words of one police administrator, the NPPs were becoming shells of their former selves. Telephone use, and the modern personal cell phone, many now including video and global positioning systems, are highly prevalent in Singapore. Monitoring by police was apparently not disrupted by the physical absence of police officers at the base of the housing blocks. More to the point, the definition of authentic, face-to-face interaction between police and citizens was becoming blurred now that rapid contact via cell phone, or use of a video-phone box at the ground floor of the housing block, could be linked directly to a police center located nearby but outside the individual housing block. This electronic link provides the same function, in many instances, as the original NPP.

It is significant to note, in the Singapore case, electronic communication appears to provide a viable substitute to direct police contact. The crime rates within the housing blocks actually decreased at the same time that the NPPs were being replaced with sophisticated electronic systems. On several occasions, a police official offhandedly referred to the housing block residents as the collective. Arguably, housing block residents may be even more comfortable linking up with police electronically than by physically visiting a police department office. A greater sense of privacy and attentiveness may unfold between two callers on a video phone than between a police officer and patron across a desk in a crowded office. In addition, if one is in a hurry, a ringing phone might be given precedence over ongoing physical interaction even if the phone momentarily disrupts other interaction. The definition of what is so-called personal and face-to-face must be reconsidered with two-way video becoming so commonplace in Singapore. If it is true, as appears to be happening, that modern electronic communication networks can substitute for physical interaction, then Black's proposition remains true to the Singapore situation.

That is, the mobilization of law and of police can be expected to decrease, or become less necessary, with an increase in social intimacy (i.e., a decrease in social distance) provided by mobile video phones. Cellular video phones may be non-disruptive and may even enhance a sense of social intimacy between police and citizen in time of crisis or need.

Following Black's prediction, the relationship between law and social distance between people is curvilinear (Black, 1976). Thus, law was less necessary during the kampong era where citizens lived in consolidated neighborhoods, became more necessary when citizens were disrupted and disoriented in high-rise housing blocks, and again law became less necessary with the return to social cohesiveness provided by the RCs and NPPs and later by cellular phone technology.

Island containment and self-regulating activities

Some activities tend to emerge as self-regulating because to act otherwise becomes dysfunctional on a small but crowded island. The data argues for a slight modification of Black's perspective with the following proposition: The more self-regulation that exists, the less the need for law and the less need for police intervention. In this case, self-regulation is not a result of individual reliance on one's own group or neighborhood for social control, as commonly equated with self-help (Black & Baumgartner, 1980). Rather, it is an outcome of ecological advantage or situation with lesser attention given to culture and personality issues (see the discussion of situation by Bates & Harvey, 1975; cf., Garreau, 1992).

Consider the case of jaywalking as influenced by island ecology. In a rural area or even a small town, there is little need for jaywalking laws. Residents stroll at will on the streets and meander across roadways often jumping between slow-moving traffic. Jaywalking becomes more complicated and problematic in larger cities and certainly in Singapore. On the heavily used streets crisscrossing the island, the smooth movement of millions of people by motor vehicle is crucial and illustrates how the citizenry adapt to island life. Jaywalking laws have been traditionally severe in Singapore because the fast-moving, bumper-to-bumper traffic cannot be disrupted by the added problem of pedestrians dangerously scurrying across the streets to save a few moments. In recent years, where automobiles are kept moving at relatively high speeds, pedestrians jaywalk only at extreme risk to life and limb. Thus, in Singapore, jaywalking becomes self-regulating as motor vehicles speed down the multiple-lane highways with infrequent traffic lights. Traffic is kept at an uninterrupted fast pace while pedestrians are left to follow established and sometimes cumbersome walking routes; refusal to use them can result in heavy penalties (up to Singapore $350).

However, in the shopping districts where traffic often slows to a snail's pace, it is not surprising that jaywalking increases even though it remains illegal. Even so, few arrests are noted here given the large groups of shoppers, locals, and foreigners, bolting en masse between slow-moving cars. Shoppers reflected a power in numbers that seemed to stymie the Singapore police in the summer of 2003 as they looked away as large crowds of tourists cut across the streets on the side roads in the popular Orchard Boulevard district of the city even though nearby road signs disallowing such activity were in clear sight.

As well, the efficient subway system of Singapore has had an impact on jaywalking. In earlier years when buses were more prevalent, pedestrians could be observed illegally running across the street to catch a bus. Today this practice is rarely seen, likely because the rail transportation is accessible from sidewalk entrances, and waiting periods for the subway trains are no more than 10 minutes. In addition, in earlier years elderly Singaporean shoppers, mostly women, could be seen jaywalking while carrying parcels of groceries from the marketplace. Being aged and without an automobile, they chose not to climb the steep walkway bridges crossing the streets. These relatively feeble shoppers broke the law but out of necessity. The more well-to-do citizens were able to drive to markets and avoid the need to consider jaywalking. Regardless, today fewer elderly grocery shoppers are seen jaywalking on the residential streets, likely also benefiting from the rapid rail system. Jaywalking appears to have become less of a problem during the past several decades.

Public spitting as outlawed behavior in Singapore can also be seen as self-regulating because of the extreme density of the population. It makes common sense, as is publicized by the government on public billboards, that sidewalk spitting, for instance, can be unhygienic as well as irritating to the sensibilities. Ecologically, widespread spitting in the most densely populated nation in the world has immediate negative consequences for the citizenry. Spitting could spread disease and also be socially irritating. Refraining from public spitting reaps its own rewards. It is true that public spitting is illegal (technically a style of public littering); however, it is unknown how much of the control of spitting results from deterrence from a high fine or simply that the behavior is at least somewhat self-regulating.

The issue of queuing for a taxi is also a function of ecology. Finding a taxi in a densely populated locale can be a problem and even dangerous. Resulting from a government-imposed regulation, Singapore citizenry must use queuing stations where travelers methodically stand in line for transportation rather than to resorting to open competition and provoking a possible disruption to traffic. In some locales, taxi drivers can be fined for picking up passengers outside queuing stations. With military precision, all travelers are eventually accommodated at the queuing stations. Open rivalry for taxies may have immediate rewards for the few but at the certain risk of irritating the many. Getting along with one another becomes mutually beneficial.

Similarly, in the ultra-sleek subway system, one experiences conspicuous order and even unusual calm as patrons move in near lockstep to assigned ramp locations, prepared to leisurely enter the trains without pushing or shoving. This queuing scenario of collected composure is observed throughout Singapore in many everyday social activities whether on the sidewalk, streets, or in department store checkout lines, all adding to a heightened sense of orderliness and cooperation.

The confinement of island life also works to regulate the nature of more severe criminal conduct. For example, certain kinds of theft do not make common sense given the difficulty of escape. Auto theft is a good example whereby the thief is compelled to drive in circles on the island in avoidance of police, eventually an exercise in futility. Even the 10,000 taxis in Singapore can be alerted by police radio to be on the lookout for specific fugitives. Theft of motorcycles, the target of most motor vehicle theft on the island, is more logical because they can be easily hidden or quickly disassembled for illegal sale. Such situational factors are difficult to assess; however, their consequence is not in doubt.

The impact of island ecology can be extended to other kinds of conduct. For example, burglary rates, as in the case of auto theft, are low given the great advantage to police of being able to track down offenders in the confines of the small island. Only a single roadway to the north takes a fleeing offender off the island across a causeway into Malaysia. All cars can be efficiently scrutinized, and all are scanned by video cameras. The waters surrounding Singapore are continuously patrolled by a marine police unit in high-speed cruisers that travel in opposite directions around the island, scrutinizing any unusual activities and making police available at coastline locations.

In addition, from a purely spatial perspective, Singapore's high-rise housing blocks make burglary difficult to execute in the first place, with each floor posing a neighborhood watch effect and typically being situated where police can be quickly summoned. Security and crime prevention are made more efficient by high-rise block living (Newman, 1973). Windows are typically inaccessible to thieves on the upper decks, and the few main doors can be heavily bolted. Burglary becomes self-regulating in housing blocks, particularly the upper levels, due to the difficulty of successful escape by elevators or stairways by offenders.

Many housing blocks have no residences at the ground floor level, and a second floor, designated as a void deck, is reserved for recreational and other community activities. This area works to keep residents, especially children, off the streets. Even though one would think it unnecessary, security guards are seen in an increasing number of housing blocks. A desk clerk is often located at the ground floor, and in some blocks a security guard is positioned at the main entrance. In the more well-to-do blocks, a security guard post is located at the entry to the parking area.

Finally, law itself can be influenced by the spatial distribution of people on the small island. For example, any law legislated by the parliament can be immediately disseminated throughout the island. All citizens can be quickly made aware of a new law, and ignorance of new legislation is less meaningful than in nations with widely dispersed populations. In Singapore, the major news outlets are government-controlled, which only adds to the rapid dissemination.

Discussion and Conclusion

Human ecology pertains to how people adapt to their living space. As illustrated here, this can be in regards to a high-rise housing block or to adjustment of a larger population to life on a small island. This article was designed as an ethnographic study of a single island community and stands alone. Yet some may question how other similarly positioned nations may compare to Singapore. Specifically, for instance, why would Hong Kong, a nation with many parallel features, show higher crime rates than its Singapore neighbor to the south?

The data and space limitations do not allow full comparisons; however, several differences stand out. First, Hong Kong represents a densely populated nation with a much older urban history than the youthful Singapore. A brief taxi ride through Hong Kong reveals high-rise block living often in comparatively low-rent districts, reminiscent of project dwellers of working poor and frequently minority populations of some large American cities. In contrast, Singapore's high-rise blocks remain pristine and do not suggest crowdedness as foretold by the demographics. One cannot but be reminded of the broken windows perspectives of Wilson and Kelling (1982). The rougher street life in Hong Kong appears more conducive to youthful gangs that are borne out by others (Lo, 1992; cf., Choi & Lo, 2004).

Second, Singapore appears to have landed on a pragmatic and mandatory conscription process for military obligation of all male citizens that also includes an option of service with the Singapore Police Force. A further requirement of ten years of reserve duty following active police service compels many youthful male citizens who commonly reside in the housing blocks to be prepared and duty bound to cooperate with regular police and even to intervene with illegal activity if they are first to arrive on the scene.

Without question, the issues of island ecology represent only a few, although consequential, features that work to augment an already low-crime area as generated by social and cultural patterns. This article provides heretofore neglected attention to the issue of how island confinement in Singapore tends to affect, generally in a positive way, several styles of illegality, and also how police strategies are influenced.

Several of the propositions set forth by Black are shown to be useful in guiding ethnographic observations conducted in Singapore in 1997 and 2003. Order maintenance perspectives make common sense as citizens are confined to island life. Police-community relations tend toward cooperation and partnership rather than on pure law enforcement. This is observed in the Singapore case even though much attention, and possibly myth, surrounds the presumption of relentless and staunch law enforcement and punitiveness on the small island.

Deterrence and punishment persist on the surface but are underridden by substantial crime preventiveness and strong police-community relations. Community policing corresponds with the ways that the Singapore government has relocated its millions of citizens into high-rise housing blocks. Ecologically, life in high-rise flats was necessary with little room for outward migration on the small island. When people are forced into close quarters, the end effect does not necessarily lead to conflict. Social intimacy can generate less law and less need for police as suggested by Black. The nature of certain styles of illegality is shaped, at least in part, by island ecology to include, among others, jaywalking, burglary, and motor vehicle theft. The findings set the stage for future hypothesizing and invite replication and increased ethnographic detail.

References

Austin, W. T. (1987) "Crime and Custom in an Orderly Society: The Singapore Prototype," *Criminology*, 25, 279-294.

Austin, W. T. (1989) "Crime and custom," in K. S. Sandhu & P. Wheatley (Eds.), *Management of Success: The Molding of Modern Singapore* (pp. 913-927). Singapore: Institute of Southeast Asian Studies.

Austin, W. T. (1999) *Banana Justice: Field Notes on Philippine Crime and Custom*. Westport, Connecticut, USA: Praeger.

Bartholomew, G. W. (1989) "The Singapore Legal System," in K. S. Sandhu & P.

Wheatley (Eds.), *Management of Success: The Molding of Modern Singapore* (pp. 601-646). Singapore: Institute of Southeast Asian Studies.

Bates, F. L., & C. C. Harvey (1975) *The Structure of Social Systems*. New York, NY, USA: Gardner.

Berg, B. L. (1989) *Qualitative Research Methods for the Social Sciences*. Boston, Massachusetts, USA: Allyn & Bacon.

Bittner, E. (1980) *The Functions of Police in Modern Society*. Cambridge, Massachusetts, USA: Delgeschlager, Gunn, and Hain.

Black, D. (1976) *The Behavior of Law*. New York, NY, USA: Academic Press.

Black, D. (1980) *The Manners and Customs of the Police*. New York, NY, USA: Academic Press.

Black, D. (1993) *The Social Structure of Right and Wrong*. New York, NY, USA: Academic Press.

Black, D. & M. P. Baumgartner (1980) "On Self-Help in Modern Society," in D. Black (Ed.), *The Manners and Customs of the Police* (pp. 193-208). New York, NY, USA: Academic Press.

Bracey, D. H. (1989) "Policing the Peoples Republic," in R. J. Troyer, J. P. Clark, & D. G. Rojek (Eds.), *Social Control in the Peoples Republic of China* (pp. 159-166). New York, NY, USA: Praeger.

Central Intelligence Agency (2002) The World Factbook. Washington, DC., USA: U. S. GPO.

Chen, P. S. & T. C. Ling (1977) *Social Ecology of Singapore*. Singapore: Federal Publications.

Choi, A. & T. W. Lo (2004) *Fighting Youth Crime: A Comparative Study of Two Little Dragons in Asia* (2nd ed.). Singapore: Marshall Cavendish, East University Press.

Clutterbuck, R. (1985) *Conflict and Violence in Singapore and Malaysia 1945-1983*. Singapore: Graham Brach.

Colless, B. E. (1969) "The ancient history of Singapore," *Journal of Southeast Asian History*, 10, 1-11.

Curran, D. J. & C. M. Renzetti (1994) *Theories of Crime*. Boston, Massachusetts, USA: Allyn & Bacon.

Fenwick, C. R. (1982) "Crime and Justice in Japan: Implications for the United States," *International Journal of Comparative and Applied Criminal Justice*, 6(1), 61-71.

Garreau, J. (1992) *Edge City: Life on the New Frontier*. New York, NY, USA: Anchor.

Hassan, R. (1976) *Singapore: Society in Transition*. Kuala Lumpur, Malaysia: Oxford University Press.

Ling, T. (1989) "Religion," in K. S. Sandhu & P. Wheatley (Eds.), *Management of Success: The Molding of Singapore* (pp. 693-709). Singapore: Institute of Southeast Asian Studies.

Lo, T. W. (1992) "Groupwork with Youth Gangs in Hong Kong," *Groupwork*, 5, 58-71.

Martin, R., R. Mutchnick, R., & T. Austin (1990) *Criminological Thought: Pioneers Past and Present*. New York, NY, USA: Macmillan.

Newman, O. (1973) *Defensible Space: Crime Prevention Through   Enviromend Design*. New York, NY, USA: Macmillan.

Park, R. E., E. W. Burgess, & R. D. McKenzie (1925) *The City*. Chicago, Illinois, USA: University of Chicago Press.

Reiss, S. (1985) "Singapore: A Case of Growing Pains," *Newsweek: The International News Magazine*, 11, 611.

Sacco, V. F. & L. W. Kennedy (2002) *The Criminal Event: Perspectives in Space and Time*. Belmont, California, USA: Wadsworth.

Skolnick, J. & D. Bayley (1988) "Theme and Variation in Community Policing," in M. Tonry & N. Morris (Eds.), *Crime and Justice, A Review of Research* (pp. 1-38). Chicago, Illinois, USA: University of Chicago Press.

Stark, R. (1987) "Deviant Places: A Theory of the Ecology of Crime," *Criminology*, 25, 841-862.

Sussman, R. W. & A. R. Chapman (2004) *The Origins and Nature of Sociality*. New York, NY, USA: Aldine de Gruyter.

Swensen, G. (1999) *The Drug War Asian Style: A Study of Legal Measures Adopted to Combat Illegal Drug Use in Singapore and China*. Murdoch University Electronic Journal of Law, 6(1), 1-31.

Vreeland, N. (1977) *Area Handbook for Singapore*. Washington, DC: Superintendent of Documents, U.S. GPO.

Wilson, J. Q. (1968) *Varieties of Police Behavior: The Management of Law and Order in Eight Communities*. Cambridge, Massachusetts, USA: Harvard University Press.

Wilson, J. Q. & G. Kelling (1982, March) "Broken Windows: The Police and Neighborhood Safety," *Atlantic Monthly*, 249, 2938.

CASE STUDIES OF ALTERNATIVE LAW, JUSTICE, AND SOCIAL CONTROL

In this Part

Chapter 16

African Jurisprudence and the Question of Supremacy of Thoughts on Control, Justice, and Law[1]

Chukwunọnso Okafọ
University of Nigeria

---

[1] An earlier, limited version of this chapter was published as Okafọ (2006), in *African Journal of Criminology and Justice Studies*, Vol. 2, No. 1.

Abstract

African ideas, systems, and processes of control, justice, and law offer the best strategies for social control in African societies. As such, the ideas, systems, and processes should be preferred in official (governmental) as well as unofficial (non-governmental) social control and used accordingly. Many empirical reasons support this line of reasoning, including the following two. One, African control, justice, and law – along with the relevant ideas, systems, and processes – derive fundamentally from African societies, rather than foreign cultures. There is strong historical and contemporary support for the relevance, wide use, effectiveness, and efficiency of African jurisprudence. Thus, this chapter – indeed this book – offers *Grounded Law* as the appropriate name for African (and other societies' homegrown) control, justice, and law. *Grounded Law* is offered to replace *Customary Law*, *Indigenous Law*, *Native Law*, etc. in view of the negative connotations attributed to *Customary Law*, *Indigenous Law*, etc., especially in the Western legal literature. It is expected that the use of *Grounded Law* to identify African law (and other societies' homegrown laws) will divest the African and similar models of the undeserved opprobrium attached to *Customary Law*, *Indigenous Law*, etc. The *Grounded Law* label strengthens the theme of this book, particularly this chapter, as follows. For social control in a society with a major divide between indigenous and foreign laws, the indigenous law should supersede the foreign law. A recent post-colony or a post-colony that is yet to effectively and efficiently reconcile the indigenous and foreign law models is "a society with a major divide between indigenous and foreign laws". Although all continents have instances of indigenous/foreign law interactions, no continent is burdened with a greater divide between indigenous and foreign laws than Africa. Therefore, Africa features prominently in this paper, even as the article offers *Grounded Law* as the replacement name for *Customary Law*, *Indigenous Law*, etc. wherever it is found. Consistent with *Grounded Law*, African jurisprudence is superior to Euro-American jurisprudence. This means that there is no rational basis to disparage the African model *vis-à-vis* its foreign, typically European, counterpart. Two, the second reason for preferring African jurisprudence for African social control is that the continent's ideas, systems, and processes of control, justice, and law remain potent in the post-colonial era. In spite of the numerous denials, skepticism, condemnations, and manifestations of ignorance by Western administrators, policymakers, and intellectuals toward African jurisprudence, this *Grounded Law* and justice paradigm offers great capacity and potentials for managing African grievances, conflicts, and disputes as well as those of other societies. However, many post-colonial governments in Africa have denied African jurisprudence the requisite official government support for increased strength and growth. Additionally, the African tendency to defer to the West on thought, problem-solving capability, and every important element of life remains a major impediment to African ability to rely on and promote African jurisprudence.

Introduction

The Issues

What then are the qualities that justify the claim that indigenous African thoughts on control, justice, and law are pre-eminent *vis-à-vis* the European, American, and other such thoughts? The answer lies in appreciating the emphasis area of the declaration. This statement refers primarily to societal, group, and individual controls in African societies. Therefore, this article's primary population context is Africa. The paper examines the utility of African thoughts on control, justice, and law in comparison with other societies' control, justice, and law thoughts that apply to Africa. Considering the indigenous African thoughts on control, justice, and law as compared with the foreign philosophies applied to the continent allows us to properly gauge the best social control approach for Africa.

Although the primary focus of this chapter is on the proper control, justice, and law philosophy for Africa, it is important to recognize that the values of the African philosophy and themes on control, justice, and law are extensible and useable in other world societies. Indeed, the philosophies, themes, and values have in fact been so adopted and utilized in other world populations, including the more developed Western societies. Restorative Justice is replete with prominent examples of control, justice, and law ideas copied from Africa, even if the borrowers have made necessary alterations on account of the peculiar local circumstances of each borrowing society. Regardless, the crux of this article is that for the purposes of addressing issues of control, justice, and law in African societies, the indigenous African beliefs and models should be accorded a paramount position over and above their foreign counterparts (see Okafọ, 2009).

With the foregoing in mind, "control" needs to be properly defined and expanded to appropriately address the issues in this paper. Thus, "control" in this chapter includes social, cultural, religious, political, and economic control influences and restraints on the lives and activities of a person as an individual, as a member of a group or other collective, or both. However, indigenous African conceptions and theories of social, cultural, and religious controls through traditions, customs, justice, and law are emphasized here *vis-à-vis* the foreign alternatives. Although African concepts and initiatives regarding individual, group, organizational, and structural control, justice, and law vary among the continent's nations and societies, whenever possible, common themes are highlighted in this article.

And, finally on the relevant issues, this article offers *Grounded Law* as the preferred name for the body of indigenous law, custom, and tradition of a society. Hitherto, *customary*, *native*, or *indigenous law* has been used pejoratively to imply that the aboriginal law of a colonized society is inherently inferior to the law of the colonizing European or American power. For avoidance of doubt, there is no rational basis or justification for this conclusion. Therefore, to reflect the homegrown quality of the original law of a society as distinct from the foreign law applied to the society, such as those imposed on Africans by Africa's colonizers, using *Grounded Law* in place of *Customary, Native,* or *Indigenous Law* makes more sense. The use of the term *Grounded Law* should do away with the needless bickering and opprobrium that accompanies *customary law, native law,* and similar labels (see also Okafọ, 2009, pp. 7-8).

In developing the *Grounded Law* name, I was guided in part by Glaser and Strauss' (1967) "Constant Comparative Method" or "Grounded Theory", in which the authors posited a theory that develops or grows out of a scientific observation. Thus, Grounded Theory is a consequence of actual research, rather than the guiding statement that leads a research process. And so, whereas the deductive process is based on a theory offered at the beginning of a research process, the inductive process leads to a theory ("Grounded Theory") at the end of a research process. In short, Grounded Theory develops from specific data, whereas Theory (or Grand Theory) does not. Similar to "Grounded Theory", *Grounded Law* is offered as a latter-day name for the various forms of (indigenous) jurisprudence in former colonies, such as Africa, to capture and reflect the crucial element that African jurisprudence, far more than Euro-American jurisprudence, represents the historical and contemporary realities of control, justice, and law in Africa.

Explaining the Relationships Among Control, Justice, and Law in Society

It is important to point out immediately that I deliberately arranged the three central themes in the title of this chapter: control, justice, and law. The order of the layout (that is, from *control* through *justice* to *law*) is not accidental. By this order of the subjects, I wish to emphasize the African outlook on life and the complementary role each theme and its application plays in social control. The three ideas apply in different ways to the ideals of individual or self-control, conformity with group and community laws and other behavior norms, as well as formal society's controls and determination of fairness in efforts initiated to respond to breaches and alleged breaches of laws and other norms. It seems that there is great logic in the African view of the progressive relationship among control, justice, and law.

The control or lack thereof of a person or group is to be found primarily in each individual. This is appropriately named *individual control* or *self-control.* Thus, a person may or may not conform to societal expectations based on the individual's inherent or learned dispositions, convictions, and responses to the situations that confront him or her. Some inherent dispositions are a part of the biological, psychological, and other natural traits of a person, whereas other dispositions are learned. Learning (socialization) takes various forms, including observing and interacting with other members of the learner's family and community as well as understanding traditions, cultures, customs, and other societal practices. Invariably, such learning begins with what the learner derives from significant others, including parents, siblings, other family or extended family members, peers, neighbors, etc. In this circumstance, the learner gains behavioral ideas mainly informally and uses them as such, voluntarily, to control his or her behavior. This means that, unlike in *private control* (see below), the source of a behavioral idea (parent, sibling, etc.) in *self-control* does not typically take an overt step to ensure that the learner learns or uses the social control standard conveyed.

It should be pointed out that improper behavior (illegal or other abnormal behavior) is learned in much the same way that proper behavior (legal or other normal behavior) is learned. But, a learned improper behavior does not automatically translate to criminal or other deviant conduct. A person who learns improper behavior may have, with *self-control* inspired by sources other than the source of the improper behavior, sufficient restraint to overcome the learned improper behavior and comply with the relevant law or other norm.

However, invariably *self-control* is the most basic form of all controls. Where *self-control* is properly applied to comply with the law and other norms, the other forms of control (*private control, non-governmental or unofficial public control*, and *governmental public control*) become irrelevant. African societies, like many others, primarily expect individuals to control themselves, except a person is for instance mentally deficient. But even if a person cannot reasonably be assigned total responsibility for a crime or other conduct, such as where the offender is mistaken in an action or omission or otherwise does not have control of the relevant situation (example, accidental homicide), he or she is not necessarily divested of all responsibility. Instead, the liability may be lessened.

However, if *self-control* is absent or insufficient, *private control* by significant others, such as parents, guardians, siblings, peers, community leaders, cultural and religious authority figures, community institutions, and other societal structures, becomes elevated in importance. Elevating the significance of the agents of *private control* means that the named significant others (parents, guardians, siblings, etc.) take overt steps to ensure that the learner learns and uses the relevant social control standards. This is the difference between the role of significant others in *self-control* and their role in *private control*.

Further, where *self-control* and *private control* by the significant others do not or are incapable of ensuring conformity with societal expectations, *non-*

governmental or unofficial public control by others becomes relevant. The *non-governmental public control* involves community groups and organs for control but not official government institutions or personnel. The community groups and organs involved at this stage of social control include the (non-governmental) community police, watch groups, or vigilante services, community courts, and masquerades that enforce community decisions. The *non-governmental public control* is the first credible attempt to control behavior by objectively applying community behavior norms. As such, an objective body or other agent is delegated to examine the relevant issues and determine an acceptable and progressive response to them. Thus, unlike in *self-control* and *private control*, the concept of "justice" (including its requirement of objectivity) is particularly relevant in *non-governmental public control* and *governmental public control* because at either level the control process or decision in a case is likely to involve opposing parties.

And, in the absence of *self-control*, *private control*, and *non-governmental public control*, the *governmental public control* is invoked as an instrument of social control. The *governmental public control* involves the use of State (local, state, and federal) institutions and personnel to enquire into, decide, and enforce decisions on disputed issues or otherwise regulate the citizens. The actions of the State institutions and personnel in a case clarify the law and other norms for the parties as well as other citizens.

The roles of the different forms of control sometimes overlap. Moreover, an aggrieved party or disputant may not exhaust one control before embarking on another. Depending on the seriousness of the subject matter of a dispute, such as where a felony is involved, the State (by means of *governmental public control*) may step in to control the parties and the issue immediately after the *self-control* and *private control*. The bottom line is that an aggrieved person typically has a number of opportunities to control a grievance, conflict, or dispute. Where the more personal controls (*self-control* and *private control*) fail or prove insufficient, the more public controls (*non-governmental public control* and *governmental public control*) become involved.

For indigenous Africa, to do "justice" is to do right based on the totality of the applicable information and with a view to advancing the relevant society and ensuring the well being of the members *as a collective group*. Oftentimes, the collective group interest differs from and is inconsistent with the interests of the group members *as individuals*. Thus, the well-being of an individual, such as a party to a dispute, mostly assumes a secondary consideration to the community's wellbeing. Individual rights, while recognized and enforced, do not supersede the collective rights. In fact, it is doubtful that an individual right would be elevated to the same level of importance as a collective right or interest. This necessarily means that in Africa, the thought and application of "justice" takes the form of *fairness to the parties while ensuring a stronger society*, rather than *fairness to the parties as the law strictly guarantees to each individual*. Thus, the control philosophy in Africa includes a recognition that the strength of a society depends on the strength of the relationships and interactions among its members. To the extent possible, the institutions and personnel of law and justice ought to maintain and repair dislocated relationships and interactions in every case they manage. Gluckman's (1967) Barotse, Zambia example reveals this African emphasis on the collective interest rather than the interest of the individual, thus (at p. 28):

> When a case came to be argued before the judges, they conceive their task to be not only detecting who was in the wrong and who in the right, but also the readjustment of the generally disturbed social relationships, so that these might be saved and persist. They had to give a judgment on the matter in dispute, but they had also, if possible, to reconcile the parties, while maintaining the general principles of law.

Thus, in Africa "law" assumes a wide dimension (this issue is addressed further in the section of this chapter on "Features of African Thoughts on Control, Justice, and Law"). However, "law" in an indigenous African society includes the expressed commands of political sovereigns or superiors, such as the *Eze* in Igbo, the *Alafin* in Yoruba, and the *Tor* in Tiv (Nigeria), and other kings, chiefs, and titleholders in African societies. Apart from the expressed commands, there are implied dos and don'ts contained in each society's body of traditions passed down from one generation to another as well as customs in contemporary use in each society. Thus, African "customary law" (*Grounded Law*), which is largely unwritten, is no less law in both pre-colonial and post-colonial societies. Specifically, in the pre-colonial era, African laws were hardly written. However, the laws were fairly easily ascertained and properly applied to issues as necessary, mainly because of the high levels of honesty and integrity among the individuals and groups that had the duty to ascertain and apply the relevant laws, customs, and traditions.

Even with the advent of writing, "law" in post-colonial Africa should, wherever appropriate, include credible germane customs and traditions, even if they are not written. In addition, credible, indigenous-based statements of relevant customs and traditions may qualify as aspects of law in a post-colonial African society. It is necessary to emphasize that the statements of customs and traditions contemplated here are those that emanate from legitimate traditional authorities that are generally accepted and supported by the concerned citizens. Consequently, a usurper or other dictatorial leader, such as a chief imposed on the members of a community, will have no foundation to pronounce on the community's laws, customs, or traditions. The common occurrence in Nigeria whereby the official governments appoint individuals friendly to the governments to assume positions as traditional rulers and leaders, even where the appointees do not have the support of their citizens, does not qualify the appointees to pronounce on their communities' laws, customs, or traditions. In circumstances such as these, the citizens are likely to ignore the commands given by such appointees. However, many contemporary African societies, particularly the small, rural, close-knit communities, continue to place a lot of emphasis on legitimate customs, traditions, and other unwritten customary laws in their interpretations of "law".

Historical and Contemporary Divide Between African and Euro-American Jurisprudential Outlooks

The *Grounded* or indigenous African (as opposed to the Westernized or "modern") mind understands and construes the "control", "justice", and "law" themes as instruments for general societal cohesion, rather than instruments for advancing individual, factional group, or State (official government) interests. This is a major point of dissension between Africa and the West (Euro-America). Thus, whereas some aspects of the Western ideas and interpretations of the themes agree with the African meanings, the African thoughts and their Western counterparts disagree substantially because of many other characteristics. Moreover, Africa and the West disagree strongly on many of the means for achieving control, justice, and law in society. For instance, African efforts toward attaining societal control, justice, and law tend to rely more on building cohesion and securing the consent of the society's members than the Western means do. In the course of this paper, several other points of conflict between African conceptions of control, justice, and law and the Western interpretations will be identified and analyzed.

In light of numerous dissimilarities between African and Western ideas of control, justice, and law, it is illogical and perturbing that most of post-colonial Africa continues in the control, justice, and law paths imposed on Africa by the West. This is particularly problematic because the invading Western colonizers imposed their control, justice, and law ideas on the long-established, self-sustaining, well-run pre-colonial independent African nations. The African societies did not consent to the importation of Western philosophies of law and justice into Africa. So, despite the many falsehoods and manufactured "facts" that Western colonial and post-colonial officials and intellectuals have imposed on Africa over the centuries (examples: Hegel, Trevor-Roper, Frederick Lugard, Foote, etc. – see below), the undeniable truth is that African societies were well established and functioned well, albeit differently from their Western counterparts, before the

Western invasion. Therefore, a colonial or post-colonial mechanism that supplants (or attempts to supplant) an African idea or way of life cannot legitimately be counted as the genesis of the relevant African society's ability to address the issue concerned. Jurisprudence is an important area where the West made a rather audacious move to obliterate and supplant the African ideas and mechanisms of social control.

Overall, the Western (Euro-American) perception of Africa is shockingly negative, and has been so since the initial contact between Africa and the West. Whereas the specifics of the Western perception of Africa may vary from person to person, and from generation to generation, it remains condemnatory. The West disparages Africa as inherently "less than", "inferior", "dark", etc. relative to the West. Whereas Western ignorance of Africa plays some role in the West's conclusions about and attitudes to Africa, ignorance alone does not exhaustively explain the situation. In fact, it seems that substantially more of the explanation lies somewhere else: Western intolerance. It is one thing to not know Africa (as many Euro-Americans do not know Africa), but it is quite another thing to not want to know Africa (and more Euro-Americans do not want to know Africa). Both the ignorant Euro-Americans and those of them that have closed their minds against Africa are content with a strong negative view of Africa. These Euro-Americans are also armed with a ready-made reductionistic answer to everything African. The answer is that whoever or whatever it is, he, she, or it must be bad, inferior, evil, irrelevant, or otherwise not good. Therefore, the person or thing ought not to be contemplated in the "general" or "mainstream" scheme of things in the world, or even within the "modern" African society. A consideration of this wide condemnation together with Euro-American hypocrisy reveals the bad intensions of the disapproving Euro-Americans. To the extent that Africa is "bad, inferior, evil, irrelevant, or otherwise not good", Euro-America, through the enslavement, colonization, and neo-colonization of Africa, has played an eminent role in creating the situation. These astounding, debilitating events, to which Euro-America subjected Africa, have been widely documented and analyzed, and their effects on Africa subsist.

Records abound of pronouncements, policies, thoughts, and even (Christian) religious teachings by Euro-Americans in which they unabashedly and with absolute certainty condemned Africa, Africans, and everything African. The following examples are instructive. Professor Trevor-Roper (1964), an Oxford historian, in his *Rise of Christian Europe* concluded that Africa is nothing more than whatever Europe has made it or put into it, thus that Africa has nothing to contribute to the world (p. 9): "Perhaps, in the future, there will be some African history to teach. But at present, there is none: there is only the history of Europeans in Africa. The rest is darkness ... and darkness is not a subject of history." Similarly, in the presence of the American Colonization Society, Andrew

Foote (1854, p. 207) had emphatically condemned Africa, thus: "If all that Negroes of all generations have ever done were to be obliterated from recollection forever the world would lose no great truth, no profitable art, and no exemplary form of life. The loss of all that is African would offer no memorable deduction from anything but earth's BLACK catalogue of crimes." Is there a worse denunciation of an entire race in the history of humanity?

The Euro-American condemnation of Africa is by no means limited to the statements and actions of private, even if influential, Westerners. Western policymakers and administrators have exhibited equally vile attitudes towards Africa and its people. As an example, the British Lord Frederick Lugard's disparagement of Africa and its people, over whom he held colonial sway for Britain in several countries including Nigeria, is chilling. Lugard had no qualms consigning all Africans to ignominy through his vitriolic characterizations of this race. According to Lugard (1922/1926, p. 70):

> In character and temperament, the typical African of this race-type is [an] excitable person. Lacking in self control, discipline, and foresight ... full of personal vanity, with little sense of veracity.... His thoughts are concentrated on the events and feelings of the moment, and he suffers little from the apprehension for the future, or grief for the past. His mind is far nearer to the animal world than that of the European or Asiatic, and exhibits something of the animals placidity and want of desire to rise beyond the State he has reached. Through the ages the African appears to have evolved no organized religious creed, and though some tribes appear to believe in a deity, the religious sense seldom rises above pantheistic animalism and seems more often to take the form of a vague dread of the supernatural. He lacks the power of organization, and is conspicuously deficient in the management and control alike of men or business. He loves the display of power, but fails to realize its responsibility. ...he will work hard with a less incentive than most races. He has the courage of the fighting animal – an instinct rather than a moral virtue.... In brief, the virtues and defects of this race-type are those of attractive children, whose confidence when it is won is given ungrudgingly as to an older and wiser superior and without envy. Perhaps the two traits which have impressed me as those most characteristic of the African native are his lack of apprehension and his ability to visualize the future.

Startling!

Perhaps, it is better to respond to Lugard while recognizing the others (including some Africans) who support his colonialist views. A few misguided modern-day Africans have misinterpreted Lugard's statement and intensions by claiming that Lugard was correct because of the present-day leadership inadequacies in Africa (see example, Fagbenle, 2009). The leadership failures are widely known. However, it is a curious error for an honest and deliberate mind to ignore the genesis of the leadership and other problems in contemporary Africa. I would like to know how Hegel's, Lugard's, and other Euro-Americans' pure "White" race would fare if a criminal gang of colonialists invaded the West and visited upon them the same atrocities they have poured on Africa.

The pace and quality of Africa's adjustment and renewal after the colonialists' onslaught are unsatisfactory but these must remain separate issues. However, it is worthy of note that Lugard conveniently omitted from his derisive characterization of Africans that he and his British band of colonialists had left Britain and travelled to Africa, uninvited by Africans. While in Africa, the Africans for the most part welcomed and accommodated the colonialists, treating them as fellow humans. Rather than reciprocate and respect the long-existing societies the colonialists met in Africa, they, in a show of their true colors, proceeded to kill, destroy, steal, and emasculate everything they did not like, did not understand, or perceived as threatening to their quest to dominate the world. It is mindboggling that after their crimes against the colonized Africans, the colonialists could muster enough courage and hypocrisy to criticize the victims of the colonial crimes. But that is precisely what Frederick Lugard and the colonialists have done to Africa.

The source of a commentary typically throws light on the words. Therefore, we must always consider the source of a statement on the African humanity or relevance. A lawless, murderous, marauding tribe of intruders (the colonizing West in Africa) cannot be allowed to turn around and accuse their victims (Africa) of lawlessness when the colonialist tribe is responsible for instituting the bulk of Africa's post-colonial lawlessness. The inadequacies of Africa's post-colonial leaders (as well as some other citizens) should be pointed out and addressed, but not by the erstwhile colonialists who provided the idea, baseness, institutions, and mechanisms for the entrenchment of Africa's post-colonial leaders and the anguish they have inflicted on the continent. Neither Lugard nor any other revisionist of the colonization of Africa is morally fit to condemn Africans. By their comments on Africa, Lugard and his kinsmen seek to cover up their crimes against Africa and masquerade as pure-hearted humanists. The history of their conquests and plunder of Africa speaks eloquently to the contrary.

The numerous ideas and pronouncements in which influential Euro-Americans have poured scorn on and written-off Africans thoroughly color the Euro-American policies and actions towards Africa. As an example in law, the colonially instituted Repugnancy Test policy, by which the official courts in the colonized territories, such as Nigeria, will not give effect to an indigenous African law, custom, or tradition if such law, custom, or tradition contradicts an official, written law, leaves much to be desired, especially because of the manner of the policy's implementation in the post-colonial age (see Okereafọezeke, 2000). Two main reasons account for this policy's unacceptability. One, an official, written law that grew either directly or indirectly from the subjugating policies of the erstwhile colonialists of Africa should not be preferred to a homegrown law, custom, or tradition (*Grounded Law*). The indigenous law, custom, or tradition is appropriately named *Grounded Law* because, as described earlier in this chapter, it grew out of the longstanding history, culture, and practices of the relevant African people.

The second reason for rejecting the continued application of the repugnancy test as propounded by the colonialists is as follows. Even in the instances where an official, written law is purely post-colonial in the sense that it is enacted by a post-colonial government consisting of indigenous Africans, such a law may be illegitimate when one recognizes the manner of choosing the lawmakers that enacted the law. Much of post-colonial Africa is notoriously undemocratic. In the overwhelming majority of the African countries, the governments that produce such post-colonial laws are either entirely or substantially illegal or otherwise undemocratic. Each of these governments is either a civilian or a military dictatorship because it is not based on the consent, contribution, or participation of the majority of the citizens. Therefore, laws enacted by such a government either do not reflect or are not perceived as reflecting the citizens' wishes. Such illegitimate "official" laws should not be preferred to the generally accepted indigenous laws, customs, and traditions of the relevant society.

Features of African Thought on Control, Justice, and Law

In theory and in practice, the foundations of African and Western conceptions of control, justice, and law differ in important respects. As to be expected, the African and Western world views of the subjects are founded on the relevant cultures, histories, religions, practices, and other life ways of Africans on the one hand, and those of Westerners, on the other hand. Generally, the life of an African – as is that of a Westerner – is predicated on the commonly accepted tenets regarding the source of life, living, and coexistence with others in society. The African and Western thoughts on, and applications of, the control, justice, and law themes to advance each society's conditions reflect the common beliefs in that society. Africans have a wider view, interpretation, and application of law than Euro-Americans. Thus, African jurisprudence is broad, as follows:

The province of African jurisprudence is thus large enough to include divine laws, positive laws, customary laws, and any other kinds of laws, provided such laws are intended for the promotion and preservation of the vital force.... What is considered ontologically good will therefore be accounted as ethically good; and at length be assessed as juridically just (Okafor, 1984, at p. 163).

Therefore, the conception and application of control, justice, and law in Africa fundamentally reflect the African homegrown elements for managing relationships among the people. This is as it should be. Without doubt, there are always opportunities for the beliefs of one society to affect or influence the citizens of another society and their thoughts on the subjects of control, justice, and law. Nonetheless, there are many important, homegrown features of African jurisprudence. A major characteristic of African control, justice, and law is that the mechanisms are aimed primarily at peacemaking in society – between individuals and groups. The African systems are designed with the understanding that the quest for peace in a society necessarily begins with peaceful coexistence among the individual members of the society. Peace among individual members and smaller groups will add up to a peaceful society. Thus, peacemaking is the main thrust of the African systems of control, justice, and law. For instance, as Gluckman (1967) shows in a study of the Barotse of the then Northern Rhodesia (now Zambia), peacemaking is at the core of the judicial process. Accordingly, African justice systems are designed to redress wrongs, fine-tune claims, preserve norms, and prevent the break-up of interpersonal and group relationships (Nzimiro, 1972).

The following research-based conclusions further illustrate various aspects of African jurisprudence:

Gluckman (1963, p. 198) illustrates the African emphasis on achieving justice, sometimes with necessary adjustment of the justice process:

The pull and push of Barotse [Zambia] jurisprudence consists in the task of achieving justice while maintaining the general principles of law. This is clearly demonstrated in the fact that while at some time, the judges are compelled to go against their view of the moral merits of cases in order to meet the demand for certainty of law, on the other hand they try to vary the law to meet those moral merits.

Regarding the Igbo, Nigeria jurisprudence, it is essential to note the fundamental disagreement the Igbos have with legal positivism. By their sociocultural organization and republican government style, the Igbos strongly reject jurisprudence based on legal positivism. According to Okafor (1992, pp. 90-91):

> If political sovereignty is the only legitimate source of valid laws, there is no doubt that customary law, canon law, positive international law as well as other legitimate legal phenomena is[sic] in serious danger. The legal phenomena in the Igbo country are opposed to the spirit and tenet of legal positivism... They have no standing constituted legislative authority as such either. The people themselves, the *"Oha"* are the sovereign authority and the legislative authority rests on them. With the sovereign authority invested on the *"Oha"* and the legislative powers entrusted on no special group to the exclusion of other groups, the dangers of legal authoritarianism and tyranny are forestalled and eliminated.

By "the source or origin thesis", the Yoruba, Nigeria, jurisprudence shows that: "The attributes of law are not independent of moral values. In this case, also, one can be led to the tentative conclusion that law and morality are inseparable. ...Law, in this case, is founded on and intricately connected to morality" (William, 2009, p. 140). And, based on a study of Sierra Leone, Thompson (1996) illustrates the critical need that indigenous African courts serve, especially in the rural communities. In these communities – in which the vast majority of Africans reside – the indigenous courts hear and decide a wide variety of cases, civil as well as criminal:

> Regardless of the availability of statistics, it is fair to say that local courts dispose of a significant volume of *small* criminal cases involving customary law yearly throughout the country since the vast majority of Sierra Leoneans are rural people who regard themselves, and actually live their daily lives, as subjects of customary law (Thompson, 1996, p. 347).[1]

The other main elements composing the African control, justice, and law include consensus among the relevant community members. Most aspects of African control, justice, and law are rooted in the members' general consent to the principles, as well as the modes and agents for applying the principles for the greater public good. Thus, traditions, customs, and laws (*Grounded Law*) are

---

[1] Italics added for emphasis. However, the local official as well as unofficial courts in many parts of Africa hear and decide both *small* and *big* civil and criminal cases, some of which are not based on customary law. In general, the issues managed by these courts are not limited to minor matters.

usually developed and made with the consent, and to the satisfaction, of most community members. The traditions, customs, and laws cover procedural as well as substantive facets of control, justice, and law in society. Because they are involved in the making, application, and enforcement of their traditions, customs, and laws, community members generally have a greater sense of belonging in their jurisprudence than in the Euro-American alternative. Being so involved motivates the citizens to accept the homegrown social control (*Grounded Law*) as distinct from the imposed, foreign control.

As should be expected, consensus and wide acceptance are two crucial aspects of law and social control in an African society. A broadly accepted tradition, custom, or law offers a much better option for control, justice, and law in society. The situation is also likely to translate to a more secure and stable population. The democratic ideal is an effective way to achieve wide acceptance for tradition, custom, or law. Thus, indigenous African institutions and processes are typically based on democracy in which efforts are made to gain consensus on an issue before a verdict is adopted. The consensus and general acceptance are founded on Africans' faithfulness to their history. The fact that contemporary Africans continue to borrow norms, rules, regulations, and laws from previous generations manifests this faithfulness.

Perhaps, it is necessary to expatiate further on the "consensus" and "general acceptance" themes as they apply to African institutions, especially on the issues of control, justice, and law. It seems that the best way to explain the two subjects is to note that control, justice, and law in indigenous Africa are typically based on *consented, harmonious management of issues*. This, of course, does not mean that every community member consents or assents to the handling of every issue. As is common in most instances where different personalities intermingle, there are sometimes opposing views, disagreements, and conflicts. Such interpersonal and group variances, if not properly and satisfactorily checked, would grow into deep-seated disputes (consider that an issue could grow from a *grievance*, through a *conflict*, to become a *dispute* – see Nader and Todd, 1978).

Consistent with the African courts' duties of righting wrongs, adjusting claims to bring them in line with the larger societal interest, safeguarding norms, and avoiding the breaking of relationships (Nzimiro, 1972), these courts manage civil and criminal *disputes*, as well as civil and criminal *conflicts* and *grievances*. As mentioned in the preceding paragraph, a disagreement may begin as a *grievance*, then grow into a *conflict*, and finally become a *dispute*. Several characteristics differentiate among *grievance*, *conflict*, and *dispute*, thus: the seriousness of the issue, the victim's reaction to the fact of being victimized, and the open/closed nature of the disagreement. Regarding the seriousness of the issue, a serious subject of disagreement usually leads to a conflict situation rather than a grievance, and an even more serious subject is expected for a dispute. In short, the more serious the subject matter of a disagreement, the higher the form of the disagreement displayed. On the victim's reaction to being victimized, a victim reacts stronger in a conflict situation than in a grievance situation. Similarly, a victim in a dispute situation responds the strongest among the three categories of disagreement. The open/closed nature of the disagreement refers to the arena in which a disagreement takes place or is managed. The following questions are relevant to the open/closed nature of the disagreement characteristic: Does the victim in a disagreement situation express a reaction to the disagreement in a perceptible manner? Does the victim express the reaction privately or publicly? A reaction in a conflict situation is expected to be more discernible and perhaps public than a reaction in a grievance situation. Further, a reaction in a dispute situation will be even more visible and public than the reactions in a grievance and a conflict.

Thus, whereas each type of disagreement indicates the absence of harmony between the parties, a grievance is the least serious kind of disagreement, with dispute as the most serious form. A *grievance* (the first of the three kinds of disagreement) is specifically a perception of injustice, and a grievance may be expressed in the form of a moan or a gripe or it may not be expressed in any perceptible form. A *conflict* (the second of the three kinds of disagreement) refers particularly to a quarrel or discord between parties. Thus, a conflict involves more overt action and reaction by the parties than a grievance involves. A *dispute* (the third of the three kinds of disagreement) more aptly describes a situation where the parties have clashed over an issue. A dispute is the most public form of disagreement often involving complaints to significant others, such as mutual friends and the official courts.

The essence of the distinction among grievances, conflicts, and disputes in African jurisprudence is that the distinction allows judicial personnel in State as well as non-State courts to recognize that there is an opportunity to satisfactorily manage a *grievance* and avoid a situation where it could graduate through a *conflict* to a full-blown *dispute*. As expressed through its systems and processes, African jurisprudence appreciates this opportunity and uses it in the management of issues, to prevent more destabilizing situations in society. Thus, the African court recognizes a grievance as actionable, even though the Western-styled justice systems may not regard a grievance as such. As an instance, ostracism, which is not actionable under the English-styled justice system in Nigeria, is actionable in the Igbo system. Thus, ostracism and disrespect for community institutions and personnel are managed only unofficially in community tribunals (Okereafoezeke, 1996; 2002). The official, English-styled laws do not consider these issues actionable.

For Okereafoezeke (1996; 2002), I had studied a case on ostracism. The case illustrates that the African justice systems operate in a broad framework.

As pointed out, African justice is designed to create and maintain peace and harmonious interactions among the citizens of each society. The parties in the ostracism case in Okereafọezeke (1996; 2002) were members of the same Igbo ụmụnna (extended family). The "plaintiff" in the case contended before the Eze-in-Council (an unofficial, non-governmental case management body in the Igbo community) that the "defendants", who represented themselves and their ụmụnna, had ostracized him for ten years from their common ụmụnna. He wanted the defendants to explain why they had ostracized him. He also wanted them to accept him back fully into their ụmụnna. On their part, the defendants identified three main reasons why they ostracized the plaintiff. One, when the plaintiff's wife died, he shaved his own hair and took charge of the burial arrangements contrary to the customs and traditions. The defendants considered this behavior taboo because according to the customs and traditions of the community (and other parts of Igbo), the bereaved should leave the responsibilities for such things to the members of the ụmụnna and ụmụnna (village). Two, when other persons died in their ụmụnna, the plaintiff did not participate in the burial ceremonies as every able-bodied, mature, member of the ụmụnna is obligated to do. Three, for years the plaintiff had not paid his membership and other dues in the ụmụnna. In view of all these, the defendants had decided that in the best interest of their ụmụnna, the plaintiff "should stand alone and outside [their ụmụnna]" (at p. 95 of the case record).

The official government laws applicable in the community where the ostracism case occurred do not recognize ostracism per se (the basis of the plaintiff's case) as actionable. Therefore, an official, English-styled court cannot grant the remedies that the plaintiff sought in the case. An official court cannot rely on the principles of equity to order the defendants to accept and treat the plaintiff as one of their members. Such an order would be extremely difficult, if not impossible, to enforce. Considering that equity, on which an official, English-styled court in Nigeria is partly based, does not act in vain, it is very unlikely that an official court would grant the plaintiff any remedy. Only an African court, such as the Eze-in-Council in Ajalli (Igbo), can grant the remedy. This is because the Igbo justice system recognizes ostracism as actionable and justiceable. In an ostracism case, *the ostracizer's conduct towards the ostracized* (this is the subject of the ostracized person's case against the ostracizer) is typically an omission. That is, the ostracized person accuses the ostracizer of shunning, ignoring, or failing to include the ostracized in some group or activity. Although the ostracizer's conduct is an omission, it is an effective means of control and justice and its consequences for the ostracized can be devastating.

In Igbo and other African societies, ostracism is used to punish or protest a disapproved or socially reprehensible conduct. Ostracism exemplifies punishment by omission. Ostracism takes various forms, including refusing to greet an ostracized person, ignoring a greeting from the ostracized, ignoring or rejecting an invitation from the ostracized and refusing to invite him or her to an event, refusing to purchase goods or services from the ostracized, refusing to sell to him or her, etc. Also, community members may refuse to help an ostracized person who needs assistance, even to the extent of refusing to assist an ostracized person to bury a deceased close relative. Thus, an ostracized person is socially and otherwise handicapped. The Igbo proverb, "*Ofu onye siere ọra, ọra erisịa ya, mana ọra siere ofu onye, ọgaghị erisị ya*" (English translation: "If one person cooks for the public, the public eats it all, however if the public cooks for one person, he or she cannot eat it all") captures the fate of the ostracized. By way of interpretation, the Igbo maxim means that an individual who challenges the society rarely wins, particularly in a relatively close-knit, homogenous community, such as the Igbo and each of the other African societies with a "higher density of acquaintanceships" (Weisheit, et al., 1996, p. 18). The Igbo aphorism acknowledges the aggregate group's superiority over the individual.

In the ostracism case under review, the *Eze*-in-Council accepted jurisdiction, heard, and decided the matter. The English-styled courts in Nigeria would not have done so because they do not consider the *res* of the case (ostracism *per se*) actionable. The *Eze*-in-Council's handling of the case illustrates that African jurisprudence recognizes and deals with a broader array of issues than the official, Western-styled law and justice. The utility of African jurisprudence in anticipating and managing the ostracism case lies in the opportunity the judicial process provides for the early resolution of the disagreement between the parties. Such early management avoids a further deterioration of relationships among community members, thus strengthening cohesion and control in the society (see Nzimiro, 1972). The official, English-styled law and justice system in Nigeria will not get involved in an issue between parties to a case until a more overt dispute is established. The problem, however, is that by then the social control problem must have deteriorated further.

However, the genius of the African philosophy, systems, and processes of control, justice, and law is that the African model recognizes the critical need for a model to inspire the confidence of most members of the society to which it applies. Allowing the members significant roles in the relevant model effectively inspires and maintains the citizens' confidence. With the consent and general acceptance by most members of the society, the few members that unreasonably disagree with the generally consented and accepted principles are regarded as deviants. Moreover, this assures that the deviants in each society are relatively few. Thus, the society will be stable and secure because most of its members genuinely identify and agree with, and support, the consented and generally accepted principles (Okereafọezeke, 2001). Identifying and agreeing with, supporting, and consenting to the behavior norms of a society are indicators of faithfulness to the standards of the society.

Illustrations of Africans' faithfulness to their history – on the basis of which they continue to borrow norms, rules, regulations, and laws from previous generations – are common. In Igbo, Nigeria, for example, *ana*, *anị*, or *ala* (land) is a very important force in interpersonal and group relationships. A person who is faithful to the land does not disrespect it by selling it. Thus, in Igbo, as in Yoruba (see Johnson, 1921/1970, particularly p. 95), land is not sold. The Igbo, Yoruba, and other African nations have high regard for land. Thus, a person who makes a claim and swears on land without suffering negative consequences (such as death or grievous bodily harm, to the oath taker or his/her blood relative) is regarded as having told the truth. See Nzimiro (1972, particularly p. 122) which, based on a study of four Igbo communities – Abo, Oguta, Onitsha, and Osomari – describes and illustrates the settlement of a land case in Igbo by means of oath taking.

Other important characteristics of African jurisprudence include the fact that case management organs are close to the citizens. Relative to the case management organs in the Western-styled systems in Africa, the (indigenous) organs for control, justice, and law in Africa are closer to the citizens and easier to access than their Western-styled counterparts. Many members of the case management organs are either indigenous to the respective communities where they function or they must have been residing there for a long time. The other important characteristic is that the justice system has credibility with the locals. The system's credibility is derived partly from the integrity of the individuals and groups that perform various functions to achieve justice. Thus, in an African society, different individuals, groups, and organizations (including the age grades of the young and old, the women and male groups, etc.) perform different functions toward the society's goals of control, justice, and law. For example, depending on the issues involved in a situation, the young or elderly community members, as the case may be, may play a more prominent role with a view to maintaining or achieving peace for the community and addressing the parties' concerns as much as possible.

African institutions, including those on control, justice, and law, are designed to combine popular participation with ability and experience (see Isichei, 1976, p. 21). For instance, the Igbo generally respect and defer to the elderly on matters of control, justice, and law, particularly in policymaking (traditions, customs, and law making) and policy applications (trials and judgments). Thus, the Igbos usually rely on the elders and other respected members of each community to manage/settle grievances, conflicts, and disputes. Achebe's (1959) description of the prelude to a trial in Umuofia (Igbo) illustrates the elders' role in judicial proceedings in Africa. Achebe (1959, p. 83) writes: "It was clear that the ceremony was for men.... The titled men and elders sat on their stools waiting for the trials to begin". Achebe continues (at pp. 86-87) by noting that the trial procedure allows each side to present its case beginning with duly saluting and acknowledging individuals to whom the salutes and acknowledgments are due. Ottenberg's (1971, pp. 246-303) study of the Afikpo (Igbo) and Nzimiro's (1972) study of the Onitsha (Igbo) similarly find that community elders, along with the traditional ruler of each community, are the judges in judicial proceedings. Isichei (1976, pp. 21-24) exemplifies the role of the elders in case management in Owerri (Igbo). Some elders may also serve as advocates in judicial proceedings. However, the enforcement of a decision is typically the responsibility of several groups and institutions, such as the age grades of the youth and the *mmanwu* (masquerade) institution. The research findings cited here agree with the situation in many African societies, including the Barotse, Zambia, of whose judicial process Gluckman (1967) had reported.

In the Igbo, Nigeria example, the African court system typically comprises the following levels, from the lowest to the highest: *Ezi na Uno*, or "Family" Level; *umunna*, or "Extended Family" Level; *Onuma*, or "Village" Level; and *Obodo*, or "Town" Level. A case may be processed initially at the *Ezi na Uno* Level and subsequently appealed through the other higher levels. Also, in many instances a case may be processed at the indigenous court levels before being initiated in the official court system, which includes the Customary Court (Area or Native Court) and the other official courts, such as the Magistrate Court, High Court, Court of Appeal, and Supreme Court of Nigeria (Okereafoezeke, 2002). All the layers of courts in the indigenous judicial system apply customary laws and traditions (*Grounded Law*) to the cases brought before the courts. Also, sometimes, the official courts apply the indigenous laws, customs, and traditions to the cases managed officially. However, as pointed out, across Africa, regardless of the various forms of the indigenous courts, these courts can be distinguished from their Western-styled counterparts in that Africans widely regard the indigenous courts as agencies for conciliation, building and maintaining peace in society, not so much as agencies for upholding the rights of the individual. In African jurisprudence, the mechanisms of justice seek to make peace, rather than to allocate rights between disputants as under the English-styled justice system (Nzimiro, 1972).

Nzimiro's (1972) oft quoted statement about the general nature of African jurisprudence, particularly on the character of the courts, states as follows (at pp. 118-119): "[The task of African courts] is to right wrongs, to adjust claims, to defend norms, and where permanent relationships are concerned, they have to strive to prevent them from being broken". Thus, the African court strives to create and maintain harmony and cohesion among the citizens for the greater good of society. Sometimes, this means that even the wronged party will have to sacrifice his or her "rights" for the overriding general good. Contrast the Western-styled court and justice system that underscore proof at trial, determination of guilt or non-guilt in a criminal proceeding (wrong or right in a civil proceeding), the assessment of monetary equivalent of injury, and other allocation of rights between the parties to a case. In the Western-styled justice systems, as introduced into African societies through colonization, a party to a case is legally entitled to insist – and parties usually insist – on his or her rights even if those rights contradict the general good of the society.

The African courts' philosophy of redressing wrongs, modifying claims to bring them in line with the larger societal interest, preserving norms, and averting the breakup of relationships is based, in part, on the courts' appreciation that not all injuries can be corrected with money or other material. Thus, monetary or other property award as remedy for a wrongdoing may not be ideal to resolve the issue(s) in a case. Although monetary or other property award may satisfy the material needs of a party, this type of solution does little to assuage the present and future antagonisms, hostilities, and conflicts between the parties. The African courts' values reflect an effective way of ensuring that the parties to a case cool off, reflect on their circumstances and relationships, reconcile their differences, and to the extent possible coexist and relate with each other peacefully. In the final analysis, as far as African jurisprudence is concerned, the most important thing for a society is group harmony, peaceful coexistence among the citizens, individual and collective progress, and stability of the society. In the African view, a society will not achieve these ideals if the *individual rights* of the members are championed stronger than the *collective rights* of the society.

Thus, Africa and Euro-America differ in their jurisprudential outlooks. African jurisprudence varies from Euro-American jurisprudence in fundamental ways. The numerous distinguishing attributes of African control, justice, and law *vis-à-vis* those of Euro-America strongly support the view that Euro-American jurisprudence ought not to be the philosophical basis or foundation for control, justice, and law in Africa. Based on the African thought and the differences between African and Western jurisprudential viewpoints, an Okigwe, Nigeria elder who witnessed the English law and justice changes the British colonialists brought to the Igbo, Nigeria justice system, lamented as follows: "Immediately white men came, justice vanished" (Afigbo, 1972, pp. 282-283; see also Isichei, 1976, p. 140). For the elderly research participant in Afigbo (1972), in view of the justice administered by the Igbo system prior to the British colonization of Nigeria, the English system and process that Britain imposed on Nigeria took away justice in its true sense. Bear in mind that the elder, because of his advanced age, had witnessed justice in Igbo, pre- and post-colonization. Therefore, he sufficiently understood the quality of justice the Igbos derived in each era. The elderly participant's lamentation ought to be taken seriously. This is especially so when we consider that an important component of justice is the parties' and other citizens' perceptions of the quality of the judicial response to the issue(s) in a case.

However, in spite of the fundamental differences between African jurisprudence and its Euro-American counterpart, the colonial regimes in different African societies sought, through different strategies including the use of the Repugnancy Test (see Okereafoezeke, 2000), to replace or enervate the pre-existing, widely used, effective, and efficient African philosophy, systems, and processes of control, justice, and law. In many ways, the colonial regimes successfully accomplished their goal, but they were not so successful in other respects, hence the persistence and continued use of African jurisprudence, especially in non-governmental settings. Many of the post-colonial regimes in Africa have maintained, unfortunately, the official colonial philosophies, systems, and processes of control, justice, and law. The colonial ideas and practices have been continued with token changes. Despite the great variances that exist between African philosophy, systems, and processes of control, justice, and law, on the one hand, and their Euro-American counterparts, on the other hand, the most credible change made to law and justice in post-colonial African States is the replacement of the erstwhile colonial (foreign) judicial officials and other administrators with Africans. The systems in the various post-colonial African States have not changed much since the end of colonization several decades ago. Similarly, the processes for control, justice, and law have remained essentially intact from the colonial-era set-up. The laws administered and applied by the judicial officials continue to closely emulate those applied by the former colonial regimes (Onyechi, 1975, p. 270, per Gower). Even the recruitment of lawmakers, training of new lawyers, police officers, corrections (prisons) staff, etc. fail to properly acknowledge and utilize the rich African control, justice, and law philosophy, systems, and processes.

Thus, official control, justice, and law in post-colonial Africa focus too much on Euro-American jurisprudence. The official philosophies, systems, and processes in contemporary Africa give too much, undeserved credit to the Euro-American ideas. This means that the focus of official control, justice, and law in contemporary Africa is away from Africa's indigenous (*Grounded*) philosophy, systems, and processes. Instead, contemporary official social control in Africa is fixated on the foreign-styled, Western varieties of control, justice, and law. Understandably, the obsession with the Western ideal is a consequence of the imperial structures and the neo-colonial reasoning that the colonialists installed and instilled in the various African States and their leaders as well as many of the followers. This situation has further led to dual or multiple control, justice, and law philosophies, systems, and processes in each contemporary African country. In almost every instance, the colonial powers had unilaterally installed a foreign system[2] of laws as the *grundnorm* or basic system of law and justice in

---

[2] However, for some countries, such as Cameroon, two or more Western countries colonized the same African country, thus leading to the impositions of dual or multiple foreign philosophies, systems, and processes of control, justice, and law on the colonized country. Invariably, the impositions of two or more foreign models further complicate the receiving country's ability to reconcile or otherwise manage the competing foreign institutions and their indigenous counterparts (see Time, Chapter 4 of

the African State. For the most part, the post-colonial governments in the various African countries have sustained the imperial structures, systems, and processes by continuing to look outside Africa for philosophies, systems, and processes of control, justice, and law to be used for official social control in the continent. Instead of first looking inward within each African society, looking at other African societies second, and looking outside Africa last for the most effective and efficient philosophies, systems, and processes of control, justice, and law, Africa's official governments look outside Africa first (see Onyechi, 1975, p. 270 for Gower's apt and scathing criticism of Africans who unduly rely on Western legal thoughts, laws, and justice processes at the expense of the African ideas; see also Okereafǫezeke, 1998; 2000; Okafǫ, 2009). Africans would be better served if their governments' efforts were directed at strengthening and developing the relevant African philosophies, systems, and processes for improved control, justice, and law in each country.

Are African Philosophy, Systems, and Processes of Control, Justice, and Law Relevant in Modern States?

It seems necessary to answer this question by first examining the circumstances that produced the "modern States" or "countries" in Africa. There are some fifty-four countries in today's Africa. The genesis of the overwhelming majority of these countries is simply the Berlin Conference of 1885 at which the Western world converged and partitioned Africa as the circumstances suited the partitioning Western nations. By this action, the Western countries reduced Africa and its people to mere properties of the West. The division of Africa and the associated exploitation of the continent brought about Western gains against Africa. By virtue of the Trans-Atlantic Slave Trade, the West had entrenched themselves in the lives of Africans. Colonialism, which further subjugated Africans to the West, advanced the West at the expense of Africans. However, none of the three unparalleled events (Trans-Atlantic Slave Trade, the Berlin Conference that unilaterally carved up Africa, and colonization) was sufficient to obliterate African laws, traditions, customs, cultures, religions, or other indigenous institutions. Whereas the three events succeeded, in various ways, in destroying, emasculating, altering, or relegating many African institutions, systems, and processes, numerous others survived. Therefore, countless aspects of African philosophy, systems, and processes of control, justice, and law outlived slavery, and the partitioning and colonization of Africa. The surviving African legal philosophy, systems, and processes remain efficacious in today's world, even if they now operate in the

---

this book, "Legal Pluralism and Harmonization of Law: The Dilemma").

midst of confusion, disagreements, and conflicts with the colonially imposed Western ideas (Okereafoezeke, 1998; 2001; 2002; Elechi, 2006; Okafo, 2009).

Thus, the modern States in contemporary Africa represent the Western legacy in Africa. As examples, today's Kenya, Nigeria, Senegal, and South Africa are "nations" created at the convenience, and by the fiat, of the Western colonial powers. These African States usurped the positions, statuses, and authorities of the pre-colonial African nations. As should be expected, the Western impositions of Western-styled States on Africa caused significant dislocations to the various pre-existing African societies. The imperial reasoning that led the Western colonial powers to thrust sometimes widely different African societies together to create a "modern" African State or country continues to breed discontent and antagonism among members of the different African nations many years after colonization and political independence. It seems beyond argument that the discontent and antagonism among Africans is rooted in their feeling that they were not involved in the establishment of the modern States that now exercise immense powers and controls over Africans. In the Nigerian example, Nigerians – with their three hundred ethnic nations – continue to struggle with the imperial British imposition of one country on the varied peoples of Nigeria without the peoples' consent. In Nigeria, as in most African societies, the Western colonial forces gave little consideration, if any, to the pre-existing, well-established, and highly functional structures and allegiances in the pre-colonial societies.

Despite the vast powers of control exercised by post-colonial African governments in the largely imposed, artificial modern African nations, indigenous African philosophy, systems, and processes of control, justice, and law remain entrenched in the various societies, and the citizens commonly and overwhelmingly use the African model. Instances of the efficacy of the African model in contemporary African States abound throughout the continent. At the risk of over-generalizing, some examples from Kenya, Nigeria, Sierra Leone, and South Africa, among others, are cited in this chapter to illustrate the present-day utility of the African philosophy, systems, and processes of control, justice, and law. The examples demonstrate that African jurisprudence remains relevant in a modern State.

Like other aspects of control, justice, and law, there is strong evidence that the indigenous philosophy, systems, and processes for security maintenance, crime prevention, and judgment and other law enforcement remain strikingly relevant in modern Africa. Instances of indigenous-based security and law enforcement systems and organizations abound in Africa. These mostly unofficial organizations and groups remain important to their respective societies mainly because of the broadly held view that the official systems and organizations are incapable of providing the needed security and law enforcement. The other reason for the continued prominence of the unofficial security and law enforcement organizations is that most citizens regard the official organizations as imposed, irrelevant, and different in forms and procedures from the citizens' indigenous outlooks, convictions, beliefs, and practices.

There are numerous examples of indigenous-based security and law enforcement organizations throughout Africa. Some of them operate with some level of official government support (mainly finance and equipment), while others function entirely on private group or community efforts. A significant number of them derive from the customs and traditions of the relevant community or communities. In Nigeria, for example, there are the more prominent *Bakassi Boys* of the Igbo, the *Hisha* of the Hausa/Fulani, and the *Odu'a Peoples Congress (OPC)* of the Yoruba, among many other organizations. The *Hisha* is a law enforcement organization based on Islam. Each of the northern state governments in which *shari'a* (Islamic religious law) system operates officially charges the Hisha with the responsibility of enforcing the state's *shari'a*. The form of the *shari'a* that the *Hisha* is directed to enforce came into being in Nigeria approximately 2000. The *Bakassi Boys* and the *OPC* are not as religious-based as the *Hisha*.

The *Bakassi Boys* and the *OPC* are rooted in the customs and traditions of their respective ethnic groups. The two security and law enforcement organizations often use African religious beliefs and practices to secure and maintain the supernatural powers with which their members operate. However, indigenous and mob action efforts at security and law enforcement in African societies illustrate the inefficiency of the official police. The unofficial alternatives to government law enforcement are established or maintained principally because the citizens of the relevant communities recognize and accept the indigenous alternatives as more effective and efficient, and thus preferable to the official, Western-styled models. The wide acceptance and continued use of the indigenous African models strongly support the position that African systems of control, justice, and law (including law enforcement) remain relevant in the modern State.

Therefore, the African philosophy, systems, and processes of control, justice, and law are relevant in modern States. The roles of the homegrown ideas and practices go beyond merely identifying the provisions of our pre-colonial laws. The African philosophy, systems, and processes serve practical purposes. Further, the African thoughts and actions on control, justice, and law serve to broaden our understanding of jurisprudence by providing us with alternative perspectives, even for a modern State (see Elias, 1956; see also William, 2009). According to Elias (1956, p. 6),

> current legal theory has yet to take full account of the African interpretation of the juridical problems with which law must grapple in [a] given society. Thus, an intellectual adventure into African legal conceptions should enlarge our horizon, if it

does not enrich our knowledge of the function and purpose of law in the modern world.

Elias' words about the capacity of African jurisprudence to provide an important perspective for understanding juridical problems remain valid. But, Elias also hesitates on the issue of whether or not the African idea of law "enrich[es] our knowledge of the function and purpose of law in the modern world". I must add that, without question and contrary to Elias' hesitation, African law has the capacity to and does enhance our comprehension of the behavior and purpose of law in the contemporary world. It is quite reasonable to consider that at the time of Elias' statement (1956), there was dearth of research and publications on African jurisprudence, particularly by Africans. Thus, his statement would be expected in the circumstances of that era. However, about six decades after Elias' statement, we witness that numerous indigenous-based control, justice, and law functions throughout Africa, along with many research and publications, substantiate the statement that African jurisprudence enhances our comprehension of the behavior and purpose of law in the contemporary world.

Political Challenge of Implementing African Jurisprudence

Most contemporary African States continue to struggle with the legacy of legal pluralism bestowed on them by their erstwhile colonizers. As an example, Thompson (1996) analyzes the impact of legal pluralism on due process and its application in Sierra Leone, which Thompson describes as "a former British territory struggling to adapt traditional African cultural values to the modernizing demands and pressures of Western values inherited from Britain" (at p. 344). For Sierra Leone and other African States, the contradictions result from the legacies of Britain and the other former colonialists. The discrepancies are easily observed in many aspects of African lives, including the legal philosophy, system(s), and process(es) of each State. Managing the contradictions in each African State's control, justice, and law requires honest, concerted efforts to identify and properly use the relevant African philosophy, system, and process. Even though non-State (that is, individual, group, community, etc.) as well as State contributions are needed to properly manage the social control disparities that abound in the African States, there is no doubt that the official governments of the respective countries should play major roles in leading and directing these efforts. Several decades after political independence for the African States, the responsible governments have not shown the necessary efforts or commitment.

In view of the overwhelming evidence (many pieces of which I have presented in this paper) that indigenous African philosophy, systems, and processes of control, justice, and law are effective, efficient, and widely used in modern Africa, a major obstacle to the advancement of the African idea and practices is the negative attitudes by the official governments of the respective African States. In line with the contempt and ignominy with which African legal philosophy, systems, and processes are generally treated, many African States routinely enact laws that subject the indigenous laws, systems, and models to their Western-styled counterparts. Even where a government does not actively subjugate the homegrown laws, systems, and models to the Western-styled alternatives, it may acquiesce to the colonially established system. This, invariably, results in the continued subjugation of African jurisprudence to its Euro-American counterpart. Any of the forms of subjugation means that the superseding foreign system becomes or remains the standard by which the applicable indigenous African traditions, customs, and laws (*Grounded Law*) are measured to determine whether or not they should be applied. It is asinine for an independent African country to look to a European or American tradition, custom, or law to guide the African State in deciding whether to continue to apply or reject its long-practiced tradition, custom, or law. What is needed in Africa is official commitment to African jurisprudence, while recognizing that wherever necessary relevant and useful aspects of foreign philosophies, systems, and processes may be considered to supplement the African ideas and practices.

In addition to the imprudent policy that allows foreigners (through Euro-American jurisprudence) to define control, justice, and law for Africa, a major obstacle to the proper positioning and use of African jurisprudence lies in Africa's distorted political systems, processes, and leaderships. Most African leaders possess little or no credibility, and they earned this due mainly to their unwillingness to subject themselves to the law and operate by fair, reasonable, and just electoral rules. Rather, these leaders across the continent typically view themselves as the lords of the citizens. The processes for choosing the leaders of these countries constitute a major area in which these leaders showcase their arrogance and contempt toward their citizens. A strong component of instituting a credible leadership and quality followership in a country lies in a sacrosanct and respectable process for periodically choosing the country's government leaders. Also, the process should be such that the leaders understand that the sacred and reputable process that produced them is designed and quite capable of sweeping them away if they fail to cater to the needs of the general citizenry. Thus, more than any other method for selecting its leaders, a credible general (broad-based) election process is far more likely to produce leaders that will give their best to the country on various issues.

Citizen control, justice, and law, which address some of the most important concerns to the people (including citizens' legal obligations, rights, and relationships, etc.), are some of the most important issues in a society. The quality of a society's responses to the issues will go a long way in determining whether the society should be regarded as a fair and just society based on the rule of law (see Chapter 1 for a more detailed discussion of the rule of law). The absence of the rule of law in a society is traceable to the lack of a transparent and credible process for choosing and removing leaders because the absence of a transparent and credible process encourages aspiring leaders (and partisan followers alike) to live and operate above all other citizens. Unfortunately, most African countries, including Nigeria, lack the essentials of a sacrosanct and respectable election process, hence the leaders have largely operated with impunity and without regard for the citizens' needs and aspirations. Not surprisingly, these countries have made no meaningful effort to properly position and use African jurisprudence in their social control.

Isi N'Ezi Ama Mma and Defeatism

The Igbos say that: "Anaghị esi n'ezi ama mma" (literally, "Beauty is not begun outside the home"). The implication is that beauty is begun at home. For the English, "Charity begins at home". These are two ways of making the same point. The English expect kindness to be shown at home first, before being demonstrated to outsiders. On their part, the Igbos view negatively any effort that focuses primarily on foreigners or foreign ideas, while relegating the locals or indigenous ideas to the background. This Igbo view in favor of the citizens should in no way be interpreted to mean that the Igbos are hostile to foreigners. Far from it, the Igbo and other African hospitality toward, and accommodation of, foreigners are well known. If anything, the Igbos and Africans in general could be said to be rather too friendly to foreigners. There is a strong argument that Europeans would not have succeeded in enslaving and colonizing Africa if not for the legendary African hospitality toward foreigners.

However, in essence, the Igbo worldview expects a person or group responsible for formulating a policy or implementing a program to first look within the local population for the best policy or method of implementation, and to look outside the population for opportunities to enhance or strengthen the indigenous-based policy or program. Looking outside first, especially with the emphasis and certainty displayed by various African governments, is defeatist. This sort of behavior ensures that each government sabotages its citizens' history as well as their future. Thus, consistent with this African ideal (Anaghị esi n'ezi ama mma), official as well as unofficial policies and programs on control, justice, and law in Africa should focus primarily on the relevant African belief system, practices, and aspirations, before looking for complements from outside the continent. Unfortunately, official policies and programs in post-colonial African countries routinely contradict this African viewpoint because the official policies and programs emphasize, expressly or impliedly, foreign systems and ideals.

Post-colonial leaders and many of the followers in various African countries have simply not lived up to their responsibilities because these leaders and followers have adopted a defeatist or *fait acompli* attitude. They have thereby accepted the baseless notion that Euro-American ideas on control, justice, and law are superior to their African counterparts. Because of or in addition to the enslavement and colonization of Africa, post-colonial African rulers and many citizens have essentially surrendered their senses of history, imagination, and creativity on various issues to the Western ideals. This is contrary to the notion of "independence" from the West. When a post-colonial African government surrenders to the Euro-American understanding, no meaningful or positive change can be made to the colonially imposed and entrenched systems and processes in Africa. Specifically, as a consequence of this surrender by much of post-colonial Africa, no significant official effort has been made to fundamentally change the illogical, baseless, and oppressive colonial era systems and processes of control, justice, and law based on Euro-American jurisprudence.

Notwithstanding that many Westerners have denied that it exists and continue to do so, the greatest question surrounding African jurisprudence is not whether or not it exists (*Ex abundante cautela*: It exists and has existed in various forms for millennia). Similarly, the question is not whether or not African jurisprudence is effective and efficient for social control (It is). Further, the question is not whether or not African jurisprudence is transferrable or adaptable to other societies (It is, as evidenced extensively in several aspects of law and justice, including Restorative Justice and other models of law and justice). The biggest challenge or handicap for African jurisprudence is that Africans pay too much attention and give too much credit to the naysayers, Western and otherwise. Over several centuries, Western policy makers, administrators, and scholars have told Africans and the rest of the world that Africa has no "law"; that at best Africa has loose, primitive guidelines on how to relate with other members of a society; that Africa has no "law" because Africans lack discipline, order, and self-control; that if Africans want "law" to regulate them and their relationships they must look outside the African continent – to Europe and America – for "law". The disparaging statements fit and reinforce the Euro-American xenophobic profile toward Africans, as illustrated in Frederick Lugard's, Engel's, and other prominent Westerners' conclusions about Africa and Africans (cited earlier in this chapter). Africans and the rest of the world have been fed these negative opinions for so long that even some African intellectuals have accepted that African jurisprudence, if it exists at all, is merely a colonial creation.

Consider for instance William (2009, p. 130), who states: "The African jurisprudence project is, from all indications, a latecomer to the jurisprudential scene." Even if the author did not intend to do so, the statement is irrefutably predicated on the foundation that Euro-American jurisprudence constitutes the mainstream or norm for all societies of the world and that African jurisprudence is trying to prove itself in order to be accepted, to whatever extent Euro-Americans please, as a part of the mainstream. Thus, three pertinent questions arise from William's statement: One, to whose "indications" does William refer in the assertion? Certainly, the indications do not include those of credible Africans. Similarly, the indications do not accommodate non-African objective observers. As explained and illustrated in many portions of this book and in this chapter in particular, prudent and fact-based information clearly shows that African jurisprudence is a worthy and prominent contributor to control, justice, and law in Africa and other parts of the world. Moreover, the African jurisprudence's contributions predated by millennia the importation of Euro-American jurisprudence into Africa. Thus, William's "indications" are likely to be limited to foreigners (non-Africans), specifically Euro-Americans.

Two, by which and whose measure is African jurisprudence a latecomer? Again, presumably the measure belongs to the West to the exclusion of the African standard. Three, William refers to "the jurisprudential scene" to indicate the arena at which, according to him, African jurisprudence has only recently arrived. Of course, the West prepared and owns the arena. They made the rules governing the arena and its membership criteria. The qualifications for membership were put in place with zero input by Africa. All these are understandable because the arena and the object of the membership belong to the West. However, what is not understandable is that so many Africans are bent on becoming members of the Western law and justice ideal, apparently at enormous costs to African jurisprudence. Ostensibly, these Africans are willing to sacrifice or deny the essence of African jurisprudence to bring it in line with Euro-American legal thought. It makes no sense to insist on becoming members of the Western jurisprudential arena, nor does it impress a reasonable mind to complain that African jurisprudence is not recognized by the Western definitions, when *ab initio* Africa was excluded because the Western jurisprudential standard had no room for the African model.

As Taiwo (1998, p. 1) points out:

> It is only insofar as Western Philosophy has passed itself off as Universal Philosophy that we may talk of the peculiar absence [of African philosophy]. It is only insofar as we confront, or have to deal with, or inhabit a world constructed by Western Philosophy that we are forced to think of an absence and of how to make sense of it. And we must confront our absence from the history of this tradition because, no thanks to colonialism

and Christianization, we are inheritors and perpetrators of this heritage. Additionally, given that the "West" presents itself as the embodiment and inventor of the "universal," we must protest even more loudly that its universal is so peculiar and that its global is so local. That is, the West, in constructing the universal, instead of truly embracing all that there is, or at least what of it can be so embraced, has merely puffed itself up and invited the rest of humanity, or the educated segment of it, to be complicit in this historical swindle.

Taiwo's (1998) observation that Western Philosophy has passed itself off as Universal Philosophy is instructive. He rightly notes that a statement that African Philosophy (or other body of knowledge) is omitted from conversations about the relevant field of learning is predicated on a representation of Euro-American understanding as universal, and this feeds the African acceptance of the universality of the Euro-American standard as ideal. The example of philosophy as an area of knowledge in which the West has conveniently arrogated to itself all creativity and brainpower does not mean that the West has restricted its claim to this area of understanding. Following the Hegelian model of condemning Africa and assigning credit to the West for everything good in human existence (see Hegel, 1956; see also Taiwo, 1998), the West extends its claim to sole ownership of all good ideas and products of the world to all manner of knowledge, including jurisprudence, ethics, technology, morals, and science.

However, regarding the relationship between African jurisprudence and Euro-American jurisprudence, it is fitting to consider the following question. Why are we even having an argument as to whether or not African law is law, whether or not African jurisprudence exists? The truth is that fundamentally we are having this argument because we Africans insist on convincing and impressing Euro-Americans to see us as equally human, to acknowledge us as such, and accept our thought, models, and practices regarding control, justice, and law. But, the contact and relationship between Euro-Americans and Africans is replete with evidences of Euro-Americans defining and treating Africans as inferior to the West. Thus, the nature of the contact and the form of the relationship between Africa and the West contradicts the optimism that jurisprudence affords all human beings an opportunity to be fundamentally human on a unified subject (jurisprudence) (cf. William, 2006, p. 43). See also Murungi (2004, p. 525), thus:

> Each part of jurisprudence represents an attempt by human beings to tell a story about being human. Unless one discounts the humanity of others, one must admit that one has something in common with all other human beings ... what African

jurisprudence calls for is an ongoing dialogue among Africans on being human, a dialogue that of necessity leads to dialogue with other human beings. This dialogue is not an end in itself. It is a dialogue with an existential implication ....

Ordinarily, William's (2006) and Murungi's (2004) respective statements about a common humanity on jurisprudence would be noble. However, the reality is that the West does not regard Africa as sharing a common nature with the West on jurisprudence or other subject for that matter.

Finally, it is safe to state that if not for our embarrassing and inexplicable *need* to impress and be in the good books of the West, we would not be engaged in this mindless and self-debasing debate about whether or not African jurisprudence exits. Unavoidably, the debate is actually about our respective personhood and common African humanity. In the final analysis, why do we allow the West to define us, including our jurisprudential institutions and processes for control, justice, and law? Fundamentally and inherently, the Western paradigm is narrow, self-serving, and thus incapable of addressing *our* control, justice, and law issues for *us*. We have to solve those issues with *our* ideas and models.

Conclusion

In this chapter, I have made the case that for control, justice, and law in an African society, African jurisprudence is superior to Euro-American or Western jurisprudence. Consequently, law and other forms of social control in Africa ought to be predicated on and reflect the African ideals in jurisprudential thought, systems, processes, and practices. This contention is based on strong evidence, many pieces of which have been identified in this paper. At the present, however, Euro-American jurisprudence has a significant hold on control, justice, and law in Africa. This situation derives from the European colonization of the various African States. The domination of African jurisprudence by Euro-American reasoning has led Africans and non-Africans to question the efficacy and even the existence of African jurisprudence. For many Euro-American intellectuals, political leaders, and other influential persons, African jurisprudence simply does not exist because Africans had no "law" before the advent of the colonialists to Africa. However, despite the strong denials and attempts to obliterate or debase African jurisprudence, historical and contemporary evidence shows that law was and remains a fact among Africans including the indigenous populations. The fact that African law differs in substantive and procedural particulars from Euro-American "law" should not minimize African jurisprudence. Rather, the nature of African jurisprudence is such that it is equipped, more than Euro-American jurisprudence, to deal with the issues that are important to African societies, including matters that Euro-American jurisprudence does not contemplate. Therefore, based on many reasons including the following six, for control, justice, and law in an African society, African jurisprudence should be preferred to Euro-American jurisprudence.

One, African ideas and models of control, justice, and law are predicated upon, and strongly supported by, the histories, experiences, practices, beliefs, and expectations of the respective African societies. As such, African jurisprudence is grounded in Africa while Euro-American jurisprudence is not. Two, the foreign systems of control, justice, and law in Africa were imposed on Africans with little, if any, consultation with the citizens whose lives were – and continue to be – regulated by the foreign models. Thus, Africans did not consent to the adoption of the foreign, Western systems for the African societies. Three, African systems and processes of control, justice, and law are efficient and effective, even in the post-colonial State. These systems and processes continue to be widely used, even if the various official governments in Africa continue to favor the colonially imposed Euro-American models. Four, despite the many declarations to the contrary, Western colonial importations of Euro-American jurisprudence into the various African societies was self-serving. The importations were designed to further the interests of the colonialists, not Africans. Thus, when the British Lord Frederick Lugard stated in a December 1916 "Quote of the Week" that, "I have spent the best part of my life in Africa, my aim has been the betterment of the Natives for whom I have been ready to give my life", he was being untruthful and deceptive. In the area of law and justice, for example, the facts belie Lugard's claim because Africa was, and remains, replete with the consequences of the British and other Western conquests, expansionism, and subjugation of African jurisprudence to the Euro-American model. Five, the imposed Euro-American jurisprudence differs fundamentally from African jurisprudence. For instance, the undue emphasis that the English justice system puts on formal processes contradicts the spirit of African jurisprudence that emphasizes *righting wrongs as circumstances necessitate* over a specific formal structure (Nzimiro, 1972). Six, the Western systems of control, justice, and law in Africa are limited in scope. They do not anticipate or manage all the species of issues that African systems anticipate and manage (see Okereafoezeke, 1996; 2002). African control, justice, and law systems understand and accommodate the need to tackle an issue early to prevent it from escalating into a major problem that could destabilize interpersonal and inter-group relationships and, perhaps, a whole society. Therefore, over and above Euro-American jurisprudence, African jurisprudence is equipped to serve African societies.

References

Achebe, Chinua (1959) *Things Fall Apart*, New York, NY, USA: Fawcett Crest Books.

Afigbo, A. E. (1972) *The Warrant Chiefs, Indirect Rule in Southeastern Nigeria 1891 – 1929*. London, England: Longman.

Elechi, O. Oko (2006) *Doing Justice Without the State: The Afikpo (Ehugbo) Nigeria Model*. New York, NY, USA: Routledge.

Elias, Taslim O. (1956) *The Nature of African Customary Law*. Manchester: Manchester University Press.

Fagbenle, Tunde (2009) "What Lord Lugard Thought About Nigerians" in *Nigeria Village Square* (November 23), http://www.nigeriavillagesquare.com/articles/tunde-fagbenle/what-lord-lugard-thought-about-nigerians.html; Internet.

Foote, Andrew (1854) *Africa and the American Flag*. New York, NY, USA: Appleton & Co.

Glaser, Barney G. and Anselm L. Strauss (1967) *The Discovery of Grounded Theory: Strategies for Qualitative Research.* Chicago, Illinois, USA: Aldine.

Gluckman, M. (1963) *Order and Rebellion in Tribal Africa*. London, England: Cohen and West.

Gluckman, M. (1967) *Judicial Process Among the Barotse*. Manchester, England: Manchester University Press.

Hegel, Georg Wilhelm Friedrich (1956) *The Philosophy of History*, trans. J. Sibree. New York, NY, USA: Dover Publications.

Isichei, E. (1976) *A History of the Igbo People*. New York, USA: St. Martin's Press.

Isichei, E. (1978) *Igbo Worlds: An Anthology of Oral Histories and Historical Descriptions*. Philadelphia, Pennsylvania, USA: Institute for the Study of Human Issues.

Johnson, Samuel (1921/1970) *The History of the Yorubas: From the Earliest Times to the Beginning of the British Protectorate*. Westport, Connecticut, USA: Negro Universities Press.

Lugard, Frederick (Governor-General of Colonial Nigeria) (1916) "Quote of the Week".

Lugard, Frederick (1922/1926) *The Dual Mandate in British Tropical Africa*. William Blackwood and Sons.

Murungi, John (2004) "The Question of African Jurisprudence: Some Hermeneutic Reflections" in *A Companion to African Philosophy*, edited by Kwasi Wirendu. Malden, Massachusetts, USA: Blackwell Publishing, pp. 519-526.

Nader, Laura and Harry F. Todd, eds. (1978) *The Disputing Process—Law in Ten Societies*. New York, NY, USA: Columbia University Press.

Nzimiro, Ikenna (1972) *Studies in Ibo Political Systems: Chieftaincy and Politics in Four Niger States.* Berkeley, California, USA: University of California Press.

Obi, S. N. C. (1963) *The Ibo Law of Property.* London, England: Butterworths.

Okafọ, Nọnso (2006) "Relevance of African Traditional Jurisprudence on Control, Justice, and Law: A Critique of the Igbo Experience" in *African Journal of Criminology and Justice Studies*, Vol. 2, No. 1, June, pp. 36-62. Also published in *Restorative Justice Online*, at http://www.restorativejustice. org/articlesdb/authors/6084; Internet.

Okafọ, Nọnso (2009) *Reconstructing Law and Justice in a Postcolony.* Surrey, England and Burlington, USA: Ashgate Publishing.

Okafor, F. U. (1984) "Legal Positivism and the African Legal Tradition" in *International Philosophical Quarterly*, No. 2, Issue No. 94, June.

Okafor, F. U. (1992) *Igbo Philosophy of Law.* Enugu, Nigeria: Fourth Dimension.

Okereafọezeke (Okafọ), Nọnso (1996) *The Relationship Between Informal and Formal Strategies of Social Control: An Analysis of the Contemporary Methods of Dispute Processing Among the Igbos of Nigeria*, UMI Number 9638581, Ann Arbor, Michigan, USA: University Microfilms.

Okereafọezeke (Okafọ), Nọnso (1998) *"Isi N'Ezi Ama Mma*; Anomic Conditions in the Management and Utilization of Africa's Human and Natural Resources". Paper presented at the Phi Beta Delta Honor Society for International Scholars' symposium on, *Africa in the 21st Century: A Look at the Potential of the Continent's Natural and Human Resources*, Western Carolina University, Cullowhee, North Carolina, USA, December 3.

Okereafọezeke (Okafọ), Nọnso (2000) "Repugnancy Test (Policy) and the Impact of Colonially Imposed Laws on the Growth of Nigeria's Native Justice Systems", in *The Journal of African Policy Studies*, Volume 6, Number 1, pp. 55-74.

Okereafọezeke (Okafọ), Nọnso (2001) "Africa's Native Versus Foreign Crime Control Systems: A Critical Analysis." Paper presented at the Africa/Diaspora Conference, California State University at Sacramento, California, USA, May 3-5.

Okereafọezeke (Okafọ), Nọnso (2002) *Law and Justice in Post-British Nigeria: Conflicts and Interactions Between Native and Foreign Systems of Social Control in Igbo.* Westport, Connecticut, USA: Greenwood Press.

Onyechi, N. M. (1975) "A Problem of Assimilation or Dominance" in Elias, T. O., et al., eds., *African Indigenous Laws: Proceedings of Workshop (7-9 August, 1974).* Enugu, Nigeria: The Government Printer.

Ottenberg, Simon (1971) *Leadership and Authority in an African Society: The Afikpo Village-Group.* Seattle, Washington, USA: University of Washington Press.

Proclamation No. 6 of 1900 (Laws of the Federation of Nigeria).

Taiwo, O. (1998) "Exorcising Hegel's Ghost: Africa's Challenge to Philosophy" in *African Studies Quarterly*, Vol. 1, Issue 4.

Thompson, R. B. (1996) "Due Process and Legal Pluralism in Sierra Leone: The Challenge of Reconciling Contradictions in the Laws and Cultures of a Developing Nation" in *Comparative Criminal Justice: Traditional and Nontraditional Systems of Law and Control*, C. B. Fields and R. H. Moore, Jr., eds. Prospect Hills, Illinois, USA: Waveland Press.

Trevor-Roper, Hugh (1964) *Rise of Christian Europe*. London, England: Thames and Hudson.

Weisheit, R. A., D. N. Falcone, and L. E. Wells (1996) *Crime and Policing in Rural and Small-Town America*. Prospect Heights, Illinois, USA: Waveland Press.

William, Idowu (2006) "Against the *Skeptical* Argument and the *Absence* Thesis: African Jurisprudence and the Challenge of Positivist Historiography" in *The Journal of Philosophy, Science & Law*, Volume 6, pp. 34-49.

William, Idowu (2009) "Eurocentrism and the Separability-Inseparability Debate: Challenges From African Cultural Jurisprudence" in *The Journal of Pan African Studies*, Volume 2, No. 9 (March), pp. 123-150.

Chapter 17

Corruption and Governance: Dynamics, Institutional Reform, and Strategies for Controlling Leadership-Centered Crimes

Smart Otu

Ebonyi State University, Nigeria

Abstract

Corruption is generally perceived as widespread and entrenched in Nigeria, especially in the conduct of the country's public affairs. Many Nigerians and non-Nigerian observers share this view. Against this background, this chapter diagnoses and presents the dimensions of corruption, especially as it affects governance in Nigeria. In doing so, the paper considers other scholars' works on corruption while striving to build a more promising conceptual framework for a better understanding of the corruption problem in Nigeria. Further, the article develops and presents practical strategies to combat corruption and to reform the relevant institutions for addressing the problem.

Introduction

Background and Overview

Corruption is a universal phenomenon and an acknowledged significant social problem. It pervades all countries. In Nigeria today, as in most countries of the world, corruption to all intents and purposes, is apparently a most talked about social malaise. In public and private discussions, the issue of corruption is a recurring one. It is apparently one social problem that lives as vividly in the public imagination of all Nigerians and the world community. This may account for why there is a mobilized public outrage and legislative and renewed enforcement responses to the scourge in the new democratic Nigeria. It is estimated that up to 70% of the international discussions on Nigeria focus on the issue of corruption in its various ramifications. Thus, for Nigerians and non-Nigerians interested in the country's affairs, corruption is a major topic of discourse and varied solution ideas.

In line with this focus, the Transparency International has within the last decade consistently ranked Nigeria among the most corrupt countries in the world. The enormity of corruption in both public and private circles in Nigeria, and its extensive devastation of the country, is widely recognized. And as Erero and Oladoyin (2000) rightly noted, several authors have addressed the corruption pandemic from different perspectives. The extensive corruption in Nigeria has resulted in numerous calls for urgent steps to address the problem, especially by correcting government malfeasance and nonfeasance. Of course, corruption and misgovernance are connected. They are often reflected in diverse misdeeds. The calls for steps to deal with corruption in Nigeria recognize the central role of the official governments and their officials in shaping attitudes, expectations, and performance levels in society.

As with all other societies, corruption has been with Nigeria and its group activities since the country's beginning. Politicians (civilian and military), bureaucrats, economic merchants, religious leaders, artisans, as well as ordinary citizens, are looking for advantages over one another as they scramble for the nation's wealth, which is often derogatorily referred to as the "national cake". However, the pervasiveness of the corruption cankerworm among Nigerians of different social classes, and its extreme form in the society, have jolted most Nigerians and the world out of complacency into great concerns, empathy, and sympathy. As such, lack of city revenue generation, despicable service delivery, unstimulated public confidence and participation in the social engineering of Nigeria, lack of trust, immense poverty and misery among the Nigerian populace, and the general underdevelopment of Nigeria as a nation, are all attributed to the insidious corrupt practices in the country. In support of this view, the United States Agency for International Development (USAID) (2000) and the World Development Report (2005), report that corruption is the single greatest barrier to development. In sum, billions of Naira is lost each year in Nigeria because of different kinds of corrupt practices.

Corruption seems to provide the major and fastest means to amass wealth in Nigeria. For the most part, corrupt practices are supposed to be obscured or shrouded in secrecy. Most citizens would even wish to ignore it. However, corruption in Nigeria is uniquely phenomenal in many respects. It is often operated openly and with impunity due mainly to the ineffectiveness of the responsible law and justice officials. In many instances, the law and justice officials are themselves compromised. Corruption in the country has regrettably assumed the dimension of expected behavior. The behavior is widely seen as normal – as the people's way of life. To refuse to participate in the ring of corrupt practices that pervade every facet of the Nigerian socio-political, economic, and religious life is like stigmatizing oneself and assuming a deviant status in a society where corruption is "normal". Unlike in most countries across the world where local (grassroots) governments seem particularly susceptible to corrupt practices, the story is different in the Nigerian context. In Nigeria, all the levels of government – Federal, State, and Local – are susceptible and deeply enmeshed in corruption. In the circumstances, it is difficult to identify a particular government level as being more or less corrupt than the others are. Thus, there is not really a credible level or agency of government that holds the other levels and agencies accountable. To compound the situation, most Nigerians only speak out against or express interest in corruption when, for instance, the amount of money involved is particularly large, perhaps involving hundreds of millions of Naira.

Corruption is, to say the least, institutionalized in Nigeria. In the country, most contracts are over-inflated, over-invoiced and sadly, usually unexecuted. In addition, inept individuals are wantonly recruited into positions that they do not qualify to occupy while corrupt government officials dubiously and expressly approve substandard goods and services for the public. Such is the scenario that today corruption in Nigeria is the subject of both private and public scrutiny. The challenge now is how to convince so many people that have participated in or witnessed so many corrupt acts and omissions to deviate from the vice.

Like all other crimes, corruption reported to the police is very different from the reality on the ground. For example, a statistical summary of bribery and corruption reported to the police between 1988 and 1990 stood at 823 cases. This figure indeed makes nonsense of the perceived pervasiveness of the offense as can be mentally conjured and gleaned from various media reports and personal experiences. The principal reason for this gross underreporting is that corruption smears so many Nigerians that most citizens do not feel a sense of moral obligation to report the crime. The second reason is the widespread perception that the police are the most corrupt institution in the country and therefore the least morally qualified to receive reports of corrupt behaviors and to act upon them.

Defining Corruption

Several authors have bared their minds on what corruption means. The different viewpoints so far expressed have thus produced different kinds of corruption. Smith (1995) defines corruption as wrongful acts on the part of public office holders. According to Theodore Lewi and others, there is Big Corruption and Little Corruption (cf. de Leon, 1993). Dolive and Potter (2000) see corruption as the use of public office for private gain. This definition fits well with the conventional definition shared by many writers who broadly define corruption as the misuse of office for personal gain (see for examples, Lipset and Lenz, 2000, pp. 112-114; Sen, 1999; and USAID, 2000).

Corruption can occur in the form of an act (example, receiving inducement to give an advantage to the giver or his designee which advantage is not legally and/or ethically deserved) or omission (example, the occupier of an office deliberately refuses to use the authority and power of the office to perform his duties). In this paper, corruption is defined as an action or omission that violates the legal, moral, or ethical rules of public office, aimed at achieving a personal gain, and which directly or indirectly undermines efforts to augment the living conditions of the public. This is the viewpoint on which Osoba (1996) defines corruption, especially as it relates to the Nigerian context. In simple terms, corruption denotes the subversion of the code of conduct governing the occupancy of a public office, for personal aggrandizement. Corrupt behaviors include levying an illicit price for a service rendered or using the power of an office to further illicit aims. Corruption is about violating the code of conduct of an institutional office predicated on honesty, confidentiality, loyalty, accountability, and neutrality, among others.

A democratic culture, healthy competition, credible system of control, and a guaranteed and enforced right to public information tend to dissuade corruption. Indeed, corruption is largely a result of a monopolistic tendency to power where officials have unchecked discretion. Thus, the following formula has been offered for corruption, that is: C = M + D − A. Put differently, corruption (C) equals monopoly of power (M) plus unchecked discretion (D) minus accountability (A) (see Klitgaard, Maclean-Abaroa, and Parris (2000, p. 26). The logic of this formula is that if someone has monopoly over a good or service, and has the discretion to decide who gets what and how much a person receives, and there is no accountability enabling others to glean what and how the power holder is deciding, then, corruption is likely to take place. This argument applies to the public and private sectors, as well as the poor and rich societies.

Corruption is basically a utilitarian crime; it is a crime of calculation, not of passion or biology. Corruption goes beyond an immoral individual violating the law and a trust. It is rather about a system that is more or less susceptible to various illegal activities. Like other crimes, people tend to engage in corruption when the risk of apprehension and punishment is low, the penalty is mild, and the accruing benefit is great. Drawing from the above corruption formula, as the monopoly of power increases, the rewards increase. There is an aspect of corruption that is paradoxical. It is interesting that persons who are corrupt may hold complicated mixed feelings about it, thus the corrupt may loathe corruption and wish it to be eradicated, while at the same time they participate in it or allow it to occur.

Why Is Corruption Such a Salient Issue in Nigeria?

In many countries, the issue of corruption is gaining wide currency not only among government officials, but also among the civil population. More and more individuals, groups, and non-profits organizations are expressing genuine concerns on the need to tackle the menace of corruption. Nigeria is not an exception in this regard; the same concerns are expressed with regard to the country. The question is, why this heightened interest in corruption? Several factors could explain this. Of course, the explanations vary from one country to another.

For Nigeria, a plausible explanation is that corruption has suddenly increased, leading to a wave of outrage and some resolve to address it. However, it is difficult to determine whether corruption is increasing or decreasing in the country. There is paucity of information about corruption in Nigeria, and any information on it could be misleading. Notwithstanding the spate of newspaper and other media publications about the crusades by the Economic and Financial Crimes Commission (EFCC) and the Independent Corrupt Practices and Other Related Offences Commission (ICPC) against corruption, it may be that the incidence of corruption in Nigeria today has not increased beyond what it was pre-EFCC and ICPC. Indeed, it could be that Nigeria's political will and institutional capabilities to fight corruption are becoming stronger. Taken at face value, however, the impression one readily derives is that, as with all social malaise which blossomed when unchecked, corruption in Nigeria has deepened and become more common, especially as the country has grown both in functional complexity and interdependence. But, this initial impression may not be accurate.

Another possible explanation for the renewed interest in corruption in Nigeria is that the citizens' awareness and tolerance of the problem has changed much more than the offense itself. More than ever before, Nigerians can now gauge more accurately the cost of corruption on their well-beings, especially now that economic reforms and multiparty politics are back in the national discourse following years of military rule. Or, perhaps, it may be as Klitgaard, Maclean-Abaroa, and Parris (2000, p. 9) put it, because political liberalization has allowed new freedoms to record and protest corruption, Nigerians and non-Nigerians are made more aware of it. Even though there is so much yet to be addressed with respect to freedom of the press and access to information in present day Nigeria, the post-military political dispensation ensures that Nigerians enjoy a freer press and more international exchange of information than in the past. The increased freedom facilitates the work of the press in this regard, thus making it easier for the press to report on corruption.

One interesting aspect of the hype about corruption in Nigeria is what I regard as the "defense or excuse strategy". The tendency among reform (capitalist) apologists is to whip up the evil of corruption as a scapegoat that is blamed for their failure to live up to the expectations of the much talked about free market and democratic reforms. Thus, with the International Monetary Fund and World Bank-backed reforms not yielding the desired results, what these financial bodies and their United States and Western backed nations do is to criticize Nigeria's corrupt implementation of the reforms. In the circumstances, the advertised corruption in Nigeria is used as a defense or excuse for the failures of the internationally designed and sometimes imposed reforms.

The following is a final point as to why the issue of corruption has become a major source of concern and a common topic of discussion for many individuals, groups, and organizations inside and outside Nigeria. The degree of corruption with which a particular country is associated has become a major factor in determining the standard for the country's moral judgment, respect, and international economic and political co-operation with the other countries of the world. Nigerian leaders and the generality of the citizens are mindful of the fact that both the country and the people have experienced international condemnation, opprobrium, and isolation as a result of being perceived as corrupt. After years of isolation because of military dictatorship and corruption, for Nigeria to earn the confidence of the world community, be readmitted into the comity of nations, and attract the much sought after economic investment, Nigerian leaders needed to fight the evil of corruption headlong. Indeed, to gain both national and international legitimacy, the Obasanjo-led government (1999-2007) seemed to understand that the sensitive issue of corruption must be addressed, hence his government established the EFCC and the ICPC. The high profile actions have further emphasized and advertised corruption as a common feature of life in Nigeria.

Positive Effects of Corruption

Corruption has both positive and negative effects. This might sound astonishing to the average person or a person not schooled in the art of the social sciences. However, as the French foremost sociologist, Emile Durkheim (1858-1917), noted decades ago, crime, including corruption, is not only dysfunctional but also functional in its own respect. Crime, Durkheim observed, strengthens group solidarity, ensuring that the value of society is well guarded and sustained. A violation of the society's value elicits reaction from the other members of the society, thus reminding the wrongdoer and everyone else of how not to behave and the consequences of deviating from the group norm. As such, the initial violation serves to bind the members of the society or to strengthen the bond among them.

The positive effects of corruption can be summarized as follows:

(a) Corruption helps to spur economic development, national integration, and administrative capacity, and in so doing, it is beneficial to political development or political modernization. This is the lofty argument of Pye (1965) and Nye (1967). The argument is that politics and economy are strongly related so that what happens in either of these two institutions affects the other directly or indirectly. Scandals arising from the political realm may awaken the consciousness of the economic class who may wish to redirect funds in a more guarded and restrained manner. Such scandals may also have the effect of strengthening the value system of society as a whole (see Gluckman, 1955). Political modernization means growth in the capacity of society's structures and complex process to maintain their legitimacy over time, especially in time of social change. The examples of Ghana and Nigeria readily come to mind. It was the scandals associated with the rapacious looting of the countries' treasuries and the human rights violations in both countries that gave each of the two nations food for thought and reason to institute reforms. Because of the reforms in Ghana, today democratic ideals and principles have been put in place and they continue to grow. Nigeria is farther behind Ghana on the needed reforms. The key essentials of democracy and the rule of law (free, fair, and credible elections and obedience to the relevant laws) are yet to take root in Nigeria. However, despite the governance shortcomings, both Nigeria and Ghana are preoccupied with the issue of strengthening the nations' important government structures to avoid slipping back to the dark days of rights violations and impunity by dictators.

(b) Corruption has also been determined to be capable of facilitating the transition from traditional life to modern political life, which may not immediately carry everyone along. Such transition often creates tension and suspicion between the literate officials and their illiterate peasants. Corruption, the argument goes, may help reduce the tension and suspicion and bridge the gap between the officials and the peasants. This can occur when the illiterate peasants approach the officials bearing traditional gifts or (corrupt) money equivalent. According to Shils (1962), in such a situation, corruption can humanize government and make it less awesome. This observation is not far-fetched in Nigeria where communities are often in the habit of paying political visits to their governors, commissioners, and other political office holders, the president inclusive. These visits typically involve gifts of cows, wine, and even huge sums of money made to each office holder to get the official to attend to the visiting community's needs.

(c) Further, corruption may help to redistribute wealth and open up opportunity to some people. When money or gifts are exchanged as gratis to influence an office holder in the performance of his responsibilities, a kind of redistribution of wealth has taken place. For instance, when a political office seeker gives money to an election official in order to help the office seeker to influence the outcome of an election, a kind of redistribution of wealth may have taken place especially if the office seeker is in a better financial position than the election official is. In addition, there are many citizens who, if they followed the socially approved means to success, would remain at the bottom of the social ladder. However, by some means of corruption, these individuals have broken through and improved their circumstances and those of their dependents.

The positive effects of corruption identified here are real components of the Nigerian society, even if one does not approve of them.

Negative Effects of Corruption

In corruption discourses among criminologists and sociologists alike, the negative consequences of the social problem are usually of greater interest than its positive consequences. Thus, despite the good things that may be said about corruption, the numerous destructive effects are significant and attract wide scholarly attention. These negative consequences are both pervasive and damning in the developing countries such as Nigeria. The following are some of these results.

(a) Major negative effects of corruption include the following: corruption stifles and kills skill, it undermines quality, and it reduces productivity. Corruption promotes incompetence as unsuitable and wrong persons are often put in undeserved positions to perform important tasks. In the process, quality of services is compromised, cost is increased, and overall productivity is reduced. Corruption is one major reason among others why productivity in the public sector has typically been low. In the private sector, corruption compromises quality as companies cut corners to increase profit margin.

(b) Corruption affects the investment level and the overall socioeconomic development of a country. The dominance of corruption means that nothing works unless the palm is greased. It increases bureaucratic bottlenecks and redtapeism, which are obstacles to innovation and due process. Many potential investors are scared of being caught in the intractable web of corrupt practices. The investors rightly fear that corruption will surely increase their cost of doing business thereby reducing their targeted profit. They therefore seek an alternative environment where they can invest and recoup their money as quickly as possible. This is more so in the highly competitive modern capital market system. For Nigeria, corruption is seen as the major reason that investment – by Nigerians as well as foreigners – has remained low in the country even after military dictatorship and the country's return to civilian leadership.

(c) Corruption has the capacity to cause political instability, leading to social revolution and eventual military incursion into the body polity. Most coups in the less developed world have been rationalized on the ground of corruption. In Latin America, Asia, and Africa where, for extended periods, coups and countercoups reigned, each group of successful coupists claimed that it took over State power by force of arms because of the need to tackle the hydra headed corruption in the country. In Nigeria, for example, beginning from the first *coup d'etat* of 1966 down the long list to the last Sani Abacha palace coup of 1993, the need to fight the corruption perpetrated by the officers and personnel of the overthrown junta was always a key reason given by the successful coupists for each forceful take-over of the Nigerian government.

(d) Corruption can exacerbate inequality and poverty in society. This is the leading argument regarding the negative consequences of corruption. Again, in most poor nations of the world, the major cause of the pervasive poverty has been identified as the high rate of corruption in these countries. The Nigerian *Daily Trust* newspaper (July 9, 2002) rightly observed thus: "the price of corruption is poverty". Corruption leads to poverty by encouraging the government to divert its spending to areas in which government officials can easily collect bribe. For instance, corrupt governments often embark upon contracts for all manner of supplies and phony mega projects, such as the construction of airports and highways, because it is easier to receive kickbacks and personal cuts in these types of contract awards. The diversion of public funds through kickbacks and personal cuts results in the availability of fewer funds for other important State responsibilities, thus forcing the government to spend less in the other sectors.

When, as a result of dwindling resources caused by corruption, the government spends less than what is needed in a particular sector, the multiplier effect is usually increased misery and poverty of the ordinary citizens.

(e) Corruption and the efforts to control it also waste resources and further limit the capacity of government to render the needed services to the citizens. If a country dominated by corruption is to make significant progress to develop and improve the circumstances of the generality of its citizens, it must commit a significant amount of time, money, and other resources to fighting corruption. In fact, fighting corruption requires mobilizing all structures and institutions at the government's disposal. The analysis of the means employed to deal with corruption in Hong Kong by Klitgaard, Abaroa, and Parris (2000) clearly illustrates the fact that fighting corruption requires huge sums of money and vested time. The Nigerian President Obasanjo's anti-corruption crusade gulped substantial amounts of money and other resources that came from government purse and donors. During the Obasanjo presidency (1999-2007) and since, the two key institutions charged with anti-corruption efforts – the ICPC and EFCC – have spent a considerable sum of money and other resources to investigate, arrest, and prosecute relevant crime suspects.

(f) Corruption dents the image of a country and its citizens. Corruption demeans their dignity and social standing, at home and abroad. Corruption casts doubt on the citizens' integrity, honesty, and honor. As examples, Ghana in the era of the military juntas especially in the 1970s suffered a negative image stemming from the perception that the country and its citizens were corrupt. That negative image has since been changed to a positive image with the transformation of the country through the institution of the rule of law. Similarly, Nigeria suffered a negative international image during the country's corrupt military era. Unfortunately, this image persists even years after the military returned the Nigerian government to civilians. The continuing negative image for Nigeria and the citizens is predicated mainly on the belief that the country's post-military civilian leaders are as corrupt as the departed military or, at a minimum the civilians are indifferent to the widespread corruption in the country. Other countries, such as Bangladesh, Pakistan, and Colombia are often viewed with suspicion and disdain in all major international arenas. To be sure, corruption is found in every country. The difference between the notoriously corrupt countries and those not so labeled lies in whether or not proper and credible State institutions and processes are put in place and applied to control and reduce corruption to such an extent that it does not become the norm of the society.

(g) Finally, corruption brings about ineffective government policies; corruption breeds nepotism and favoritism. Corruption distorts information, casts doubt on the proper moral standard, and discourages hard work and innovation.

Typology of Corruption

Various authors have identified several categories of corruption. In this paper, I have chosen to recognize and separate corruption types according to the mechanisms by which corruption is perpetrated. The following are the identified categories.

Systemic Corruption

Systemic corruption is the most cited or alluded to type of corruption in the literature on this problem (see Dolive and Potter, 2000; Erero and Oladoyin, 2000; Klitgaard, Maclean-Abaroa and Parris, 2000). In the sense it is often used, systemic corruption emphasizes the scale, level, or degree of corruption associated with a particular society. When corruption becomes a way of life of the people, or as it is often sociologically explained, culturally endemic, it is regarded as systemic. Some authors such as Johnson (1986), MacDougall (1988), and Murobushi (1981) use the term "structural corruption" to describe widespread and endemic corruption in a society. Indeed, systemic corruption pervades the political, bureaucratic, and economic sphere of any nation embroiled in it. Regrettably, this type of corruption is found in several nations around the world, particularly the less developed countries. Because of the deep corruption, the development of these countries remains stagnated.

Free-Lance Corruption

This is the type of corruption that takes place when an individual or group in an official position takes or attempts to take advantage of their monopoly of power to generate bribes. In other words, free-lance corruption is more or less opportunistic corruption. While occupying a public position and enjoying a monopoly of power over policy-making or implementation, a person or group involved in free-lance corruption uses the unquestioned control at their disposal to obtain or accept bribes and other advantages. In view of the strategic position occupied by the person or group involved in free-lance corruption, this form of subornment is particularly difficult to uproot or control.

Political Corruption

Political corruption takes place at all levels of political authority. It is the type of corruption associated with the politicians and the privileged political decision makers who are saddled with the responsibility of formulating, establishing, and implementing the laws on behalf of the people. Political corruption involves formulating policy, taking action, or making omission that benefits only, or substantially, the politicians, their immediate families, and cronies. Political subornment takes the form of manipulating government institutions and machinery and distorting the process of government for selfish or narrow advantages. In the circumstances, the general interest of the citizens is given little or no consideration. Instead, the interest of the politically influential few dominates the formulation of public policies and their implementation. Relatedly, the political corruption players regard and treat the citizens as inconsequential and with impunity. This is because the ordinary citizens essentially lack the power to compel the politicians and their cronies to comply with the rule of law and to govern in ways that respond to the best interests of the general citizenry. To be sure, the ordinary citizens' lack of power is due mainly to absent or limited resources, and lack of judicial and other institutional unwillingness or inability to subject the political leaders to the law.

Political corruption is pervasive in many societies, but it appears to be in its acme in Nigeria. In this country, from councilors at the local government level, to state legislators, on to federal legislators, as well as their executive arm counterparts (local government chairmen, state governors, and the president and his cabinet), political corruption is a dominant problem. With so many strategic political office holders involved in this type of corruption, it is equipped to frustrate efforts to install transparency in the country. For example, for more than a decade, attempts to pass a Freedom of Information Bill – one of the most strategic instruments for fighting corruption – were thwarted by legislators in the Nigerian House of Representatives and the Senate. However, finally in early 2011, a version of the Bill was passed, even if the original provisions had been watered down because of the selfish and corrupt challenges to the original Bill.

Political corruption also takes the form of intimidation and muzzling of opponents and dissenting views. Again, unfortunately, Nigeria presents an illustration of countries where this sub-type of corruption is rife. Indeed, assassinations and other violence against political rivals in Nigeria is a recurring problem. To compound the situation, most of the assassinations and other crimes against political rivals remain unsolved.

Electoral Corruption

Nigeria remains a prime example of countries in which large scale electoral corruption is perpetrated, routinely, with impunity and utter disregard for the law and the citizens. Electoral corruption (appropriately termed "election rigging") is eminently manifested in the various actions and omissions that characterize elections in Nigeria. The actions and omissions include vote-buying, stuffing of ballot boxes in favor of specific candidates, writing and announcing fictitious results in place of actual votes, intimidation of the opposition and their supporters, intimidating and compromising election officials, and subverting election rules by employing "consensus" candidacy rather than transparent and credible nomination of candidates. In view of the consistent and widespread electoral corruption in Nigeria, the citizens generally regard the government that results from an elections exercise as dishonest and illegal.

It should be obvious that, wherever it occurs, electoral corruption has far reaching implications. The citizens' right to vote freely and choose their leaders is one of the most critical rights in a society. Electoral corruption is the antithesis of the realization of that right. Electoral corruption discounts the citizens in this very important element of citizenship and humanity (the citizens' right to choose their leaders). A country that is unable to provide credible institutions and an electoral process that allows the citizens to freely and periodically choose their leaders is unlikely to rein in corruption. And, a society dominated by corruption has little chance of significant progress and development.

Bureaucratic Corruption

This form of corruption is commonly found in the administration of public institutions, agencies, and organizations. The corruption type typically involves illegal or otherwise illegitimate solicitation or exchange of money, goods, services, or other benefits to prevent or influence the delivery of a public service. Bureaucratic corruption undermines, interferes with, and stalls the processes and results that citizens should expect from public entities. The effects of bureaucratic corruption are especially noticeable with regard to institutions charged with responsibilities for providing specialized services. A corruption of the process laid out for such an institution runs counter to the citizens' expectation of high effectiveness and efficiency levels in the delivery of the relevant services.

Bureaucratic corruption is pervasive in Nigeria and occurs at all levels of public administration. In police stations (departments), court offices, ministerial offices, hospitals, schools, local licensing offices, tax offices, immigration offices, custom services offices, and similar agencies, Nigerians daily encounter bureaucratic corruption. This corruption, which occurs mainly at the implementation end of public policies, is a major obstacle to carrying out good public policy to improve the lives of the average citizen.

Organized versus Unorganized Corruption

Corruption can also be described as either organized or unorganized. In the former case, corruption is perpetrated by a ring or a network of people organized in a structural and hierarchical manner to help facilitate the corruption activities.

This is a standing group of people joined with the purpose or major purpose of engaging in corruption for the benefit or interest of the organization. In this type of corruption, there is usually a systematic arrangement involving several strata or layers of individuals and/or groups connected to the corruption enterprise. It is a cartel through which, by conviction, intimidation, physical violence, payoff, or otherwise, persons or groups who are considered vital in facilitating a corrupt deal are co-opted into the corruption-ridden activity. In typical fashion, organized corruption is clinically executed and is often instrumental in facilitating other criminal activities, such as drug trafficking, prostitution, and money laundering.

For unorganized corruption, individuals and groups engage in corruption as the opportunity presents itself without recourse to a standing group organization, coordination, effective and systematic planning, execution, and disposal. Unorganized corruption is simply an opportunistic corruption where an individual or group may get involved because the opportunity presents itself and the participants have avoided or can avoid criminal sanctions that would have otherwise discouraged the partakers from engaging in the corrupt behavior. In most instances, unorganized corruption is executed perfunctorily with little, if any, consideration for the society's norm being violated and the negative impact of the violation on the immediate victims as well as the general population.

Big versus Small Corruption

Finally, classes of corruption may be Big and Small. This particular way of categorizing corruption has been associated with Theodore Lewi and others, and cited in de Leon (1993, pp. 19-20). The categories of corruption as Big and Small are consistent with the USAID's view of corruption as capable of being either petty or grand. As their names suggest, big corruption is the corruption that involves substantial loss, either of money or other property to the public and which impact is likely to be felt by a significant portion of the population. On the other hand, small corruption refers to corruption that involves either a small amount of money or property with an impact that is of little significance to the psyche of the generality of people. However, a big corruption may be regarded as small if its impact on most of the citizens is minor, while a small corruption can be viewed as big if the amount of money or property involved is small but the impact is great on most of the people. In Nigeria, the widespread and shameless police practice of extorting twenty Naira from each motorist along the highways, although small corruption with regard to the amount involved, is big because it is so omnipresent and threatening to the average Nigerian road user. Each instance of the extortion reminds the citizen of his vulnerability to the police.

Techniques of Corruption in Nigeria

This section of the paper addresses the various, overt and covert, ways by which corruption participants in Nigeria perpetrate their corrupt practices. In some authors' views, these means of corruption also constitute the typology of corruption. However, in this article, we choose to treat the following as the *modus operandi* of corruption as distinct from the typology.

Bribery

Bribery is the giving, offering, soliciting, or receiving of money or other valuable thing in order to induce or influence the execution of a legal or official responsibility, or to refrain from doing so. Bayart, et al. (1999, p. 11) defines bribery as the payment either in money or kind that is taken or given in a corrupt relationship. By this definition, inducing someone either with money or any other kind of gratification, and/or receiving such money or gratification, amounts to corruption. Therefore, both the giver and the receiver are participants in corruption. Bribery includes kickback, pay-off, greasing of palms or as has literally come to be known in the Nigerian lexicography "settlement". These forms of bribery are fairly common in Nigeria, some more so than the others. Kickbacks, for example, dominate dealings with the various local, state, and federal governments and their agencies. Thus, it is expected that a person who seeks or receives a contract with the government has to make allowance in the contract amount for the financial inducement of the government official(s) responsible for awarding the contract or making payment on it.

The "kickback" is the amount or percentage of the contract sum that the contract winner is expected to turn over to the official(s) as a part of the understanding among the parties. Failure to "kickback" the said money effectively forecloses all future opportunities for business with that government official(s). In fact, in most cases, the official(s), not willing to take a risk of the contract winner absconding with the entire contract sum, refuse to approve payment to him until he first pays the sum agreed upon to the official(s). This means that the contract winner will find money from another source to pay the official(s) before the contractor is able to access the contract funds. "Pay-off" can be used to refer to "kickback". In particular, "settlement" is commonly used in Nigeria to capture the illegal exchange of money, goods, or services to compromise the receiver (usually an office holder or a person in authority) into performing or abstaining from performing a duty.

Fraud

Fraud presents another *modus operandi* of corruption in Nigeria. Fraud is a kind of deceit that creates a false impression about an imaginary gain to lure the victim into parting with his or her possession, such as money or other material, for the perpetrator's gain. Fraud involves obtaining money, property, or other benefit by pretence. Trickery, swindle and deceit, counterfeiting, racketing, smuggling, and forgery are typically implicated in fraud (Bayart, et al., 1999). This corrupt behavior has gained wide currency in contemporary Nigeria spanning both government and non-government circles. Thus, fraud is not just a means of corruption by people holding government positions; it is also popular among many unemployed and semi-employed Nigerian youths whose Advance Fee Fraud scheme (popularly called "419") has become a global phenomenon (see Schoenmakers, et al., 2009). The Nigerian society, with its very high unemployment, is a fertile ground for fraudulent behaviors. In addition, the fact that the officials of the various local, state, and federal governments of Nigeria conduct themselves with such impunity and contempt for the citizens further fuels the fraud perpetrators in their behaviors. As such, the prevailing general mentality favors gaining wealth or other advantage by all available means, because that is consistent with the manner in which most Nigerian government officials behave (see Durkheim, 1897/1951/1997; Merton, 1938-10, for the role of "anomie" in crime and deviance).

Embezzlement

This remains by far the most viable means by which public office holders in Nigeria engage in corrupt practices. Embezzlement is stealing from the public coffers by public office holders. This occurs whenever someone steals public money and/or property entrusted to his or her care by virtue of being the occupier and custodian of such office and resources. Embezzlement is widespread among public office holders in Nigeria. Community, national, as well as international newspapers and other news outlets are awash with confounding and very disturbing news of numerous acts of embezzlement at the local, state, and federal levels of the governments in the country. Unfortunately, the official Nigerian environment seems to encourage this corrupt behavior. Apart from the widespread nature of corruption in general and embezzlement in particular, in Nigeria, the official responses to these crimes is muted, at best. In many instances, embezzlers get away with their loot and are left to enjoy the fruit of their crimes. Understandably, this official attitude feeds the desire for more embezzlement and facilitates future corruption by the same and other offenders. Where an embezzler is officially challenged at all (through the criminal justice system), the offender typically receives an insignificant punishment, often wrapped in the cloak of "plea bargain." This is especially the situation with regard to influential or high profile crime suspects. In most cases, the plea bargain arrangement means that the offender receives far less penalty than he deserves (see Chapter 11 for more detailed analysis of plea bargain). In these circumstances, there is little in the form of law or other public policy, its application, and enforcement to discourage an embezzler from engaging in this corruption.

Favoritism

Favoritism is a mechanism of power abuse in which the distribution of the scarce resources of a given group, organization, or society is carried out in a biased manner. Favoritism plays out most commonly in a highly conscious, polarized, and less developed plural society in which there is excess loyalty to racial, ethnic, religious, or other divisive variable. Favoritism involves undue display of affection or deference towards a person or section of society at the expense of the others, which display negates the principle of fairness and consistency expected of a public authority. Admittedly, it is a natural human proclivity to favor relatives, friends, close and trusted others. However, the challenge of a modern society is to ensure that its citizens are treated fairly and consistently relative to acceptable laws and ethics. In many ways, Nigeria, as an example, is yet to meet this challenge because favoritism based on ethnicity, religion, and other related variables features prominently in public affairs in the country.

Extortion

Extortion indeed constitutes one of the most effective means of perpetuating corruption in Nigeria. Extortion refers to extracting money or other resource from a person or group by means of coercion, violence, or threat of force. In Nigeria, most public service providers and/or institutions are often found to engage in this means of corruption. They include essentially the police, customs, power holdings, and immigration and customs. The powers that the officials of these agencies enjoy enable them to essentially impose their will on their victims. For example, a group of police officers who man a checkpoint on a highway is positioned and equipped to impose the officers' will on motorists. Although most of the motorists know and understand that they are not legally obligated to "settle" the officers with say 20 Naira, the citizens are forced to do so in order to be allowed to continue on their trip. Failure to part with the money demanded by the police is sure to lead to undue delay for the non-complying motorist. Moreover, there is no telling how far the police officers may go to inconvenience or punish the stubborn motorist. There have been instances of "accidental discharges" in which the police shot and killed innocent citizens, allegedly because the gun went off accidentally. Nigerians generally regard these shootings as intentional acts, which the responsible police officers attempt to cover up with the "accidental discharge" claim. There have also been other examples of the police framing innocent but stubborn motorists for crimes they did not commit, to make clear to the defaulting motorists and others that they should comply. Without question, these circumstances amount to extortion.

Nepotism

Nepotism is a special kind of favoritism. It occurs when an office holder or a privileged member of the public uses his or her position to secure undue advantage for a family member or a member of his/her kinfolk. The beneficiary is given undue preference in the allocation of scarce resources. Typically, the beneficiary is exempted from the application of the relevant laws, regulations, and due process. This amounts to unjustified, special treatment for the beneficiary because of his or her relationship to the office holder. Nepotism is widespread in Nigeria, especially in government ministries, departments, and agencies. Consequently, nepotism generates the ineptitude and inefficiency that characterize many Nigerian public services.

Causes of Corruption in Nigeria

The causes of corruption vary in much the same way as the forms of the vice. Also, the causes of corruption tend to be rooted in the specific circumstances of each organization, community, or country. As different societies have differences in their polity, economy, and culture, so also are variations in the factors that can cause or exacerbate corruption. Factors such as social diversity (heterogeneity), ethno-linguistic fractionalization, and the proportion of a country's population that adheres to different religious beliefs relate to the specific causes of corruption in a society (see Lipset and Lenz, 2000). Other factors, such as lack of democracy, excessive patrimony, kleptocracy, prebendary, poor leadership, low level of conscientization, etc., are capable of instigating or promoting corruption. In sum, the following are various fundamental causes of corruption. In explaining each factor, effort is made to clarify it by relating it to the Nigerian environment.

Income Inequality

Income inequality refers to a skewed distribution of wealth, which typically favors a small portion of the population at the expense of the vast majority of the people. In most developing economies and especially those of Africa, the large gap between the rich and the poor is largely responsible for the widespread crime, including corruption, witnessed in those countries. There is a strong reason to believe that, in a number of ways, income inequality feeds the temptation to engage in one corrupt practice or the other to narrow the earnings gap. Also, taking illegal steps to bridge the income inequality is likely to be found in situations where rewards are not commensurate with either educational attainment or job performance. In fact, a person who takes such a step may claim to be grabbing what he has actually earned through high educational qualification or high job performance, as the case may be.

Consistent with the "income inequality thesis," low income earners are more likely to engage in corruption than high-income earners. However, offering income inequality to explain corruption raises the following important question. If corruption is precipitated by high income inequality, why then is *big corruption* (corruption that involves substantial loss, either of money or other property to the public and which impact is likely to be felt by a significant portion of the population) perpetrated mostly by those whose incomes are significantly higher than that of the average person? Apparently, income inequality is capable of explaining some corruption but not all, hence the need to recognize other relevant points of view.

Political Offices as Means to Wealth

Political offices are recognized as important means of illegally gaining and maintaining wealth in many parts of the world. Such offices serve as vehicles for pursuing and satisfying the narrow interests of the office holders rather than the interests of the generality of the citizens. Lobbying, acquisition of power, controlling and allocating scarce resources are critical aspects of politics. Money is a centerpiece of a political process. Money, thus invested, has to be recouped. Often, recovering the invested funds involves circumventing the law and regulations to satisfy the specific interests of the funders. Dolive and Potter (2000, p. 19) have clearly elucidated how, through constitutional reforms, the Italian and Japanese formal political systems served to foster corruption in each of the countries. This situation, according to the two authors, created a group of leaders and policy makers subjected to lobbying by private sector interests. In turn, the leaders and policy makers depended on the largesse of the lobbyists to fund the political activities necessary to stay in power.

Indeed, it may be argued that the most devastating acts of corruption in a society are perpetuated or tacitly aided and abetted by political office holders. At the very minimum, political office holders conveniently ignore the corruption. This is especially true in those developing countries, including Nigeria, where the rule of law is weak and the institutions needed to prevent and control corruption are unstable and inconsistent, if they exist at all. In the circumstances, the politicians regard political offices as officially sanctioned and easy means to wealth. Further complicating the issues, in some countries such as Nigeria, certain political office holders are constitutionally immune from prosecution while in office. As such, the office occupants are often at liberty to do almost as they wish with State resources for as long as they remain in offices. And, in most of these countries, politics are played with such lack of consideration for others that the winner takes all and the looser loses all. In such a system, corruption thrives.

Changing/Conflicting Morals

Nigerians and foreign observers of public affairs in Nigeria generally agree that morals and ethics are overwhelmingly relaxed in the country. In fact, on some issues, the general attitude in Nigeria is that of abandonment or replacement of the moral standard (norm) or ethics. The abandonment, replacement, or relaxation frequently leads to a confused or anomic condition in which the hitherto behavior standard no longer applies, often without a legitimate, if any, substitute, thus resulting in a condition of normlessness (see Durkheim, 1897/1951/1997; Merton, 1938-10). An important aspect of this abandonment, replacement, or relaxation concerns the pursuit of money and material wealth. Many Nigerians appear to have abandoned the morals and ethics regulating money and wealth pursuit. In many instances, these Nigerians are confronted with conflicting moral codes as the citizens struggle to attain the society's expectation of success measured in monetary and material terms.

Ordinarily, ethics and morals both direct and regulate the way we practice and pursue our values and goals. The importance of morals and ethics in the pursuit of public as well as personal goals and the conduct of other affairs in society cannot be over-emphasized. Even positive law – to be fully and satisfactorily interpreted, applied, and enforced in the best interest of society – requires law and justice personnel to be moral and ethical in the exercise of their duties. Otherwise, the law may become an abstract code with little connection with the human subjects it is designed to serve. Therefore, the use of law in society to define and regulate relationships and allocate rights and responsibilities should be predicated on proper ethics and morals (see Chapter 1 on The Rule of Law). Specifically, the justice system owes a duty to ensure accountability for the applicable morals and ethics. Wherever and to the extent appropriate, the system should hold individuals and groups pursuing money and wealth accountable to the applicable morals and ethics even while upholding the relevant law.

Weak Law Application and Enforcement

A strong and consistent argument in the literature on corruption in Nigeria is that although Nigeria has an abundance of laws and regulations against corruption, these laws and regulations are feebly enforced and implemented. Against this backdrop, the argument is that the Nigeria Police Force and other investigation authorities, prosecutors, judges, and public officials entrusted with the responsibility of dealing with corrupt practices are simply weak, or at best, largely indifferent to corruption. Indeed, the Nigerian law enforcement and application agencies are caught up in the seemingly inescapable garment of corruption in the country. Consequently, there is a strong motivation for corrupt officials and other persons to proceed with their misbehavior with the expectation that they will get away with the misconduct. Thus, sadly, there is a general notion in Nigeria that only those Nigerians (and they are few) who cannot bribe their way out in the event of an arrest on corruption charges will be prosecuted, and fewer still will be convicted.

Ineffectual Public Policies

A notorious characteristic of successive Nigerian governments is the formulation and imposition of inappropriate and rudimentary policies with negligible impact on the country's development. When a policy is made that stifles the individuals' wellbeing or interferes with their access to means of livelihood, such a policy is bound to create disaffection, disenchantment, poverty, and corruption-imbued minds. Take for instance, the Nigerian government policy that bans the importation of fairly used motor vehicles that are more than ten years old (from the date of manufacture).[1] Note that Nigeria does not manufacture many motor vehicles, certainly not to a level that would make an appreciable contribution to addressing the country's consumer needs. For a few years now, there has been at least one indigenous manufacturer in the country. However, this company's products are insignificant relative to Nigerians' motor vehicle needs. Even the previously established local vehicle assembly plants have drastically declined due mainly to lack of needed infrastructure, especially steady and affordable power. The assembly plants also suffer from the absence of meaningful government support.

Thus, Nigerians rely almost exclusively on foreign made (and assembled) motor vehicles for the citizens' transportation needs. In the circumstances, the vast majority of Nigerians who cannot afford new motor vehicles or vehicles aged ten years or less are likely to resort to illegal ways (including corruption) to meet

---

[1] The policy on 10-year age limit was formulated in 2010. Previously, the maximum age of importable vehicles was 5 years.

their needs and aspirations. Similarly, motor vehicle dealers whose livelihood depends on the ability to import as many motor vehicles as possible are likely to devise or follow illegal methods to bring in the banned vehicles. The crimes resulting from the Nigerian government policy on the importation of motor vehicles is likely to include bribery and corruption of customs personnel to ensure that they allow the bringing in of motor vehicles that are older than the maximum ten years allowed.

Actually, a more sensible and impressive policy concerning motor vehicles in Nigeria should be aimed at developing an indigenous Nigerian motor manufacturing industry. Over the decades, there have been commendable efforts and innovations by several Nigerians along this line. Unfortunately, as often happens in Nigeria, the various inventions died in their infancy or were forgotten, mainly because successive Nigerian governments have lacked the necessary vision, dedication, patriotic zeal, and commitment for nation-building. Rather, the leaders and officials of these governments prefer to let Nigeria remain essentially a mere consumer nation without the capacity to produce anything of significance. A policy aimed at developing indigenous motor vehicle manufacturing in Nigeria would allow importation of a reasonable number of vehicles to meet current needs, but would put more emphasis on initiating and sustaining efforts by both private and public entrepreneurs to develop and expand indigenous motor manufacturing. Anything less, will surely continue to stifle indigenous efforts on this issue.

Lack of Opportunity Structure

Based on the theoretical perspective offered by Robert Merton,[2] lack of access to legitimate means to success induces individuals to devise other means to achieving the central goal. One of these means is "innovation" which denotes holding dear to the goal while devising one's own means to achieving it (see also Lipset and Lenze, 2000, pp. 112-117). This means that the *socially accepted means*, which is supposed to be equally regarded and followed as the *socially accepted goal*, is abandoned. In place of the means, the "innovator" devises a more convenient – even if criminal – way for achieving the goal. Many Nigerians' experiences reflect blocked opportunities due to such factors as limited openings for employment, lack of education, lack of skilled training, absence of capital, and even ethnic and religious considerations. Thus, access to legitimate means to success is highly restricted to few Nigerians. As such, the vast majority of the citizens turn to illegitimate means, which typically involve corruption. Overall, it is reasonable to hypothesize that the lack of sufficient opportunities for the vast majority of Nigerians accounts for the high level of corruption associated with the

---

[2] *Op. cit.*

ordinary citizens.

Level of Development

Corruption is as old as mankind and no society is insulated from it. However, corruption seems to be linked to a society's level of development. The developmental stage found in a country appears to inform the amount and forms of corruption found in that country. This is because development is associated with changing values. As such, the process of development includes continuous adjustments in the material and non-material things available to the citizens, as well as the citizens' perceptions, interpretations, and responses to those things and the general environment. The actions and reactions by the citizens to the material and non-material things, along with the citizens' interactions with one another, mirrow the society's developmental level. Therefore, the specific level and forms of corruption that occurs in the circumstances cannot differ from the prevailing stage of development in the society. For Nigeria, ongoing development means that the vast majority of the citizens have developed a new form of taste and values that need to be satisfied. Flamboyance, greed, avarice, and selfishness are some of the offshoots of the Western-style development, which dominates contemporary Nigeria. For many citizens, nourishing these new behavioral traits usually requires devising or adopting the unapproved means and mechanisms for success.

Theoretical Clarification of Corruption in Nigeria

A more comprehensive understanding and explanation of the widespread corruption in Nigeria necessitates the application of relevant theories of crime. Each of the crime theories offers a promise to understanding corruption in Nigeria from a specific paradigm. This means that a theory only provides opportunity for a limited view on corruption and the processes leading to it. Consequently, a more promising theory of corruption in Nigeria can be achieved by integrating the unique qualities of some of the conventional criminological theories, namely: differential association, social learning, control, and political economy theories. For this analysis, we elect to refer to the emerging integrated theory of corruption in Nigeria as the *Alliance-Contagion Theory* of corruption. The Alliance-Contagion theory is premised on the fact that the constituent theories generally agree on the relevant corruption variables. Also, the component theories agree that corrupt practices are both corrosive and contagious. On this issue, Loftin's (1984) contagion theory is relevant. Loftin (1984), while explaining gun prevalence and use among gang members in the United States, observes that when violence/crime occurs, it draws multiple people into conflict through the network, potentially involving every member of the community in the clash. Similarly, once corruption is perpetrated by a family member, friend, colleague, peer, or leader, other related persons often involve themselves, and thus corruption becomes increasingly a part of society's way of life.

Before further considering the Alliance-Contagion theory, let us examine the individual contribution and relevance of each of the identified theories. Thereafter, we shall attempt a fusion of the models.

Differential Association Theory, also Differential Association-Reinforcement Theory

Differential Association theory holds the view that crime, including corruption, is learned in interactions with other persons in a process of communication within intimate personal groups (see Sutherland, 1939; Matza, 1969; Sutherland and Cressey, 1970; Sutherland, 1973; Beirne and Messerschmidt, 2006, particularly pp. 331-334; Adler, Mueller, and Laufer, 2010, particularly pp. 121-123; Vito and Maahs, 2012). Sutherland's Differential Association theory was extended to produce the Differential Association-Reinforcement theory. For Differential Association-Reinforcement theory, the endurance of criminal behavior depends on whether or not the behavior is punished or rewarded; and the most meaningful punishments and rewards are those provided by persons and groups that are significant in a person's life, including family members, peers, schoolteachers, and religious leaders (Adler, Mueller, and Laufer, 2010, p. 94). Thus, a person is more likely to become a criminal (corrupt) if he is exposed to a preponderance of persons favorable to law violations (corruption) relative to those unfavorable to such violations. As an example, substantial evidence exists showing the effects of delinquent peers on a person's delinquent behavior during adolescence (see Agnew, 1991; Benda and Whiteside, 1995), and these impacts have been found to also extend to adult criminals such as those engaged in corruption.

Social Learning Theory

Closely related to Differential Association Theory is Social Learning Theory, which emphasizes that criminal behavior is learned through reinforcement of behavior (Burgess and Akers, 1966; Bandura, 1973; 1977; Akers, 1977; Akers, et al., 1979; Beirne and Messerschmidt, 2006; Adler, Mueller, and Laufer, 2010; Vito and Maahs, 2012). It follows from the Learning Theory that corruption is primarily learned in those groups or contexts that comprise the individual's major source of reinforcement. Thus, most Nigerians engage in corruption because groups or individuals who give tacit, overt, and covert approvals to the behavior surround them. The perpetrators are motivated to continue in the corrupt behaviors because they are rewarded (eulogized, worshiped, and extolled) by those around them, rather than being sanctioned (disdained, ostracized, reprimanded, and subjected to the criminal justice process). Nigerians who become enriched through corruption are often extolled as "new arrivals", "big men", "blessed", "achievers", and "on-high seas" by family members, friends, colleagues, and other members of the public. The praises bestowed on the corrupt are forms of Thio's (1998) reinforcement in social learning.

Control Theory

The Control Theory also holds a key to understanding the wanton and pervasive corruption in contemporary Nigeria. Control theory generally recognizes that outlawed behavior tends to be attractive to many people. Consequently, it is reasoned, the focus should not be on what motivates people to commit crime, rather the focus ought to be on why they do not commit crime. Put differently, why, in spite of the attractions of criminal behavior (including corruption), do some people not commit crime? Applied to the Nigerian context, therefore, the concern is not about what motivates so many Nigerians to engage in corruption, rather the interest pertains to why some Nigerians conform to non-corrupt behavior. Of all the social control theories, Travis Hirschi's (1969) Social Bond Theory is perhaps the most quoted and supported by data. The theory argues that the choice of behavior is considerably affected by the strength of a person's bond to conventional role models, institutions, and activities, which epitomize the moral order of the society.

More specifically, Hirschi (1969; see also Beirne and Messerschmidt, 2006; Adler, Mueller, and Laufer, 2010; Vito and Maahs, 2012) identifies four elements of the social bond, which can either insulate or predispose an individual to choose the path of either pro-social or antisocial behavior. The four elements are: (1) *Attachment* – This refers to the respect, honor, and emotion that an individual has towards his significant others, with parents being the most important. According to the Social Bond Theory, the stronger a person's attachment to the significant others, the less likely he is to commit crime. (2) *Commitment* – Commitment deals with the actual or anticipated investment one has in conventional activities, such as acquiring a reputation for virtue, building a business, or getting an education. The more committed a person is, the less likely he is to risk his commitment by engaging in criminal behavior. (3) *Involvement* – Involvement concerns the amount of time one invests in doing conventional activities, such as participating in family or community meetings, assemblies, celebrations, and other events. The more a person invests with conventional groups or in conventional activities, the less likely he is to commit crime. (4) *Belief* – Finally, belief captures an individual's dedication to the central value system of his society, including respect for the rule of law, sense of justice, sharing, and respect for the rights of others. A strong belief in the values of one's society tends to lessen the likelihood of involvement in crime.

Political Economy Theory

There is also the Political Economy dimension to explaining the current scourge of corruption in Nigeria. The political economy approach relates to the Conflict-Marxist theory. The political economy reasoning identifies capitalism and its operation as responsible for many of the crimes in society, including corruption. Therefore, the type of economic order operated in Nigeria holds the key to explaining the intractable corrupt practices in the country. In supporting this view, Ake (1981), Odekunle (1991), and Iwarimie-Jaja (2003) allude to the fact that the organization of the Nigerian economy puts the people in an inescapable network of unfair competition and struggle to survive, which has the tendency to induce people to behave corruptly.

The economy of Nigeria, especially in the public sphere, can be best described as unproductive, parasitic, and consumer-oriented. The near-absence of proper institutional and infrastructural support for productivity in the country essentially renders innovation, entrepreneurship, creativity, and foresight nugatory. Rather, the economy rewards only those people who are well connected to the government in power, thus allowing them to buy and sell various "licenses" (including oil, supply, and other contract permits) and make fortunes in the process. The Nigerian economy provides little incentive or opportunity for the vast majority of Nigerians. Therefore, given that there is no strong economic base for most citizens, economic and other crimes involving corruption are widely committed as a source of survival. In sum, within the adopted capitalist mode in Nigeria, several elements encourage many citizens to engage in corruption. These factors include high taste, greed and inordinate ambition, poor reward system, unhealthy competition (unequal access to opportunity), ineffective laws and other policies, and weak criminal justice and other public institutions.

Having presented the contributions of the relevant theories, the following section examines the framework and application of the resultant Alliance-Contagion Theory.

Alliance-Contagion Theory of Corruption

The Alliance-Contagion Theory of corruption seeks to synthesize the most strongly supported propositions of the political economy theory, social learning theory, differential association theory, and social bond theory. The Alliance-Contagion Theory is consistent with renewed efforts to develop an integrated theory in criminology. It hypothesizes that corrupt behavior among Nigerians is a learned behavior from various socializing agents, including the family, schools, religions, workplaces, peer groups, clubs and organizations, and community institutions. The strong ties developed between the individual and the socializing agents that harbor and encourage corruption facilitate this learning. Learning also entails gaining knowledge of the skills, motives, rationalization and all other mechanisms of carrying out the corrupt practices, either within an intimate personal group, or non-intimate group. The theory is, thus, about contagion-learning-bond-differential association-context interaction.

The Alliance-Contagion Theory also presupposes that participating in corruption in Nigeria involves learning or socializing through various processes. The processes include understanding the following components that facilitate the commission of corruption crimes: (a) the relevant methods (such as creating phony projects), (b) the needed skills (such as tampering with and manipulating official figures), and (c) rationalization techniques (expressed in any of the following phrases, "public wealth is the national cake", "it is nobody's money", "there can be no success without an element of crime", etc.). Theoretically, corrupt behavior is learned principally in those groups and contexts that involve four possible constructs similar to what Huang, et al. (2001, p. 77) identified. These are (1) opportunity to be involved in activities and interactions with others; (2) sustained degree of involvement in the activities and interactions; (3) skill to participate in the activities and interactions; and (4) reinforcement for performance in the activities and interactions. The groups and contexts, which now serve as agents of corrupt socialization, are ubiquitous and found in families, schools, workplaces, unions and clubs, religious and other community institutions, as well as similar locations in Nigeria.

Corruption is contagious, persistent, and pervasive in Nigeria because it is generally deemed beneficial. Furthermore, by and large, those who engage in corruption incur little negative consequences. The Nigerian situation highlights the social learning theory's reinforcement/punishment calculation as it concerns corruption (see Burgess and Akers, 1966; Bandura, 1973; 1977; Akers, 1977; Akers, et al., 1979). Reinforcement occurs by extolling, worshipping, and glamorizing individuals and groups that corruptly enriched themselves. The corrupt are typically honored, accorded prestige and respect, and in a unique Nigerian fashion, awarded the highest traditional titles and even honorary university degrees that ordinarily should be bestowed to epitomize honesty, hard work, and service to mankind. The result is that in Nigeria, corruption is widely associated with pleasure. Punishments for corruption are few, enfeebled, and inconsistent. Not surprisingly, many people find it profitable to engage in corruption. It is reasonable to state that Nigeria has a *corrupt culture*, which has offered a congenial milieu to all vulnerable persons to be easily socialized into corrupt behavior. By Sutherland's argument, therefore, it appears that in Nigeria there is an excess of factors favorable to corrupt practices than those unfavorable to such conduct.

Social bond can have positive or negative impact, as the case may be, on behavior. Based on the analysis already given, when opportunities and skills are available, and participation in corrupt behavior is rewarded (such as by worshipping persons who succeed by means of corruption), other citizens feel justified to avail themselves of the opportunity to partake in a deviant behavior that they have thus deemed right and appropriate. Employing Hirschi's social bond argument, we can capture and present corruption as a way of life in Nigeria. Thus, when opportunity and performance are commensurate and corrupt behavior is rewarded or reinforced – as is common in Nigeria – a sort of social bond develops between the individual and the socializing agents so that there are territorial, reciprocal, and escalating reasons for corrupt individuals and the socializing agents to fail in their responsibilities for proper social control. Rather, by ignoring their duties as agents for socializing individuals against corrupt conducts, the socializing agents encourage and facilitate corruption.

Therefore, instead of the strong bonds insulating the citizens from corrupt practices as envisaged by Hirschi, the bonds have a promotional effect on corruption, which typically brings about quick pleasure and huge returns. Another aspect of this is that many Nigerians, sometimes with little or no consideration for the consequences of their behaviors, engage in various corrupt conducts, which represent the standards and norms of those persons and groups to whom they are bonded. The participants follow the bond standards and norms because the bond may be threatened if its expected behavior is violated (see for a similar argument, Krohn and Massey, 1980; Brook, et al., 1986; Brook, et al., 1990; Kempf, 1993). Like its cousins, social learning and differential association theories, our reconstructed Alliance-Contagion Theory of corruption hypothesizes that an individual's behavior is either pro-social or antisocial depending on the predominant behavior, norm, and value held by those to whom the individual is bonded.

The context of Alliance-Contagion Theory is to be understood from the perspective of the political economy of Nigeria. From the Marxian point of view, socio-economic formation is the aggregate of the economic structure and the noneconomic structure (politics, religion/belief, law, and ideology) of a society. The socio-economic outlook of a society is of significance in understanding diverse behaviors – pro-social and antisocial – of such a society.

It follows that the environment provides the context in which corrupt behavior emerges and thrives in a society. Nigeria's socio-economic formation is predicated on the capitalist mode of production, which emphasizes capital accumulation. Often, this capitalism tolerates, even encourages, primitive accumulation of money and material wealth. Besides its notoriety for providing unequal opportunity for the citizens, the capitalism is also imbued with crude and excessive greed for material wealth, power, and prestige. As other scholars (see Ake, 1981; Odekunle, 1991; Iwarimie-Jaja, 2003; Otu, 2003) have at different times noted, Nigeria's socio-economic system is such that almost everyone scrambles and aspires to ride the best cars, build the best houses (sometimes, these houses remain uninhabited long after their construction), dress in the best apparels that money can purchase, and donate huge sums of money on occasions with little or no regulations on how such donations are made. The consequence is that people engage in all manners of illegal activities, mostly involving corruption, to achieve the much vaunted success goal of the society. This partly explains why corruption is not only a problem of the people in high social classes but also that of all strata of the Nigerian society. Thus, the nature of the social and economic environment of contemporary Nigeria is such that it accurately predicts the widespread corruption witnessed in the country.

Tackling Corruption in Nigeria: A Historical Account

Although corruption has often been cited as the major reason for most political changes (especially *coups d'etat*) that have occurred in Nigeria, the first few post-independence governments did little or nothing to checkmate corruption in the country. It was the General Murtala Mohammed military regime (1975-1976) that first, in the true manner of things, prominently challenged the problem of corruption in the country. At the time, corruption had become endemic in the lives of many Nigerians, especially the office-holders. Over the years, some other Nigerian leaders and governments have spoken against corruption and taken some measures to address the syndrome in the country. Some of the programs and steps employed by different governments to deal with corruption in Nigeria are discussed as follows. The anti-corruption efforts produced various degrees of success.

Forfeiture of Assets and Mass Purge

One of the first major initiatives of the General Murtala Mohammed regime on assuming office in 1975 was to investigate the sources of wealth of all the governors in the overthrown General Yakubu Gowon regime. The Gowon administration included civilian as well as military governors. Under the Mohammed government, civilian governors of the Gowon era who were determined to have acquired wealth illegitimately were forced to forfeit the ill-gotten riches. Former military governors found to have gained wealth in similar fashion were, in addition to the forfeiture, dismissed from the armed forces. A second major effort in tackling corruption by the Mohammed-led government was to engage in national mass purge of public officers on various grounds, including corruption (the most prominent basis for dismissal), misappropriation of public funds, divided loyalty, and abuse of office. Erero and Oladoyin (2000, p. 282) estimate that about eleven thousand officers were involved in the purge. The regime also put in place some institutional measures to deal with the challenge of corruption. Some of the measures were *ad hoc*, while others were eventually enshrined in the Constitution of Nigeria 1979. They include the Code of Conduct Bureau, Code of Conduct Tribunal, Public Complaints Commission, and the Public Account Committee. These agencies are retained in the *Constitution of the Federal Republic of Nigeria, 1999*.

Ethical Revolution

The Ethical Revolution was the brainchild of the President Shehu Shagari-led government (1979-1983). The program seemed to be a response to the success achieved by the Murtala Mohamed-Olusegun Obasanjo governments (1975-1979) and the popular mood of the Nigerian public. As presented to Nigerians by the Shagari government, Ethical Revolution was designed to fight corruption in the country. However, in general, analysts and average Nigerians have described the endeavor as merely existing on the pages of newspapers, public radios, television stations, and other media outlets. Maximizing its stranglehold on the Nigerian media, the Shagari regime took various steps to portray itself as a warrior against corruption. But the evidence in the country strongly supported the contrary view. There were numerous instances of the government, the ruling National Party of Nigeria (NPN), and several law enforcement and other justice agencies and personnel working to fleece Nigeria and protect crime suspects. Outrageous, over-inflated, and abandoned contracts were common at all levels of government throughout the country. The ruling party's (National Party of Nigeria) loyalists and their cronies were mostly the beneficiaries under the contracts. However, the Shagari government's unwillingness to yield power and its insistence on continuing to rule regardless of the Nigerian voters' preference led to the mess the regime made of the 1983 general elections in the country. The pervasive corruption over which the regime presided and its conscienceless rigging of the 1983 elections in particular culminated in the military overthrow of the Shagari government on

December 31, 1983.

War Against Indiscipline

The War Against Indiscipline (WAI) was a widely acknowledged program established by the General Muhammadu Buhari regime (December 31, 1983-August 27, 1985). The WAI was aimed at combating corruption and correcting all other forms of indiscipline among Nigerians. As part of efforts to achieve the goal of WAI, the Buhari government created a Special Military Tribunal to recover illegitimately acquired properties and funds, particularly from public office holders who had corruptly enriched themselves or others. Even though the regime recorded success in the areas of recovering public funds and re-orienting Nigerians towards the path of discipline, the administration's anti-corruption and anti-indiscipline program became enmeshed in abuses of human rights. The consequence was that many Nigerians grew dissatisfied with the program, but especially with the manner of its implementation. Numerous Nigerians and international groups condemned the highhanded actions of the regime in its fight against corruption and indiscipline. On August 27, 1985, the regime was overthrown by another military *junta*, which cited the disregard for citizens' rights as one of its justifications for the *coup d'etat*.

War Against Indiscipline and Corruption

When the late General Sani Abacha's *junta* (1993-1998) unilaterally took over the Nigerian leadership from the enfeebled Ernest Shonekan Interim Government, Abacha made fighting corruption his regime's priority. Ostensibly, General Abacha professed to fight corruption to win public sympathy especially in view of the overwhelming condemnation of his regime on seizing the Nigerian leadership shortly after a widely adjudged free and fair presidential election. M. K. O. Abiola won the election, but General Ibrahim Babangida annulled it, thus paving the way for Abacha to seize power. However, by making anti-corruption campaign a prominent thrust of his regime, Abacha seemed to be signaling that he would oppose the policies and style of the regime of his close associate, General Babangida (1985-1993), who was widely believed to have legitimized and entrenched corruption in Nigeria with his "settlement" method. Babangida and his lieutenants operated the "settlement" technique by using public appointments, titles, money, and other resources to compromise the regime's critics and those identified as potential troublemakers.

Apparently, in an effort to present a regime that would be perceived differently from Babangida's, Abacha expanded General Buhari's War Against Indiscipline (WAI) to include specifically the word "Corruption", hence Abacha's

WAIC. To boost his war against corruption, Abacha reconstituted the National Orientation Agency to carry the campaign against the malaise of corruption to all parts of Nigeria. However, of particular significance in the regime's fight against corruption was the institution of several probe panels to investigate the many moribund and underperforming government parastatals, such as the Nigeria Telecommunications (NITEL), Nigeria Airways, and Customs. Abacha also established the Failed Bank Tribunal to try the executives of failed banks and their collaborators. Many of the bank officials spent years in detention before being released. Again, Abacha's touted war against corruption was largely a smokescreen as his government and he were in fact enmeshed in grand corruption. The extent of Abacha's vast and astonishing corruption (involving himself, his family, and regime) became known after his unexpected death in 1998.

Independent Corrupt Practices and Other Related Offences Commission (ICPC)

Economic and Financial Crimes Commission (EFCC)

The ICPC and the EFCC constitute the main thrust of official anti-corruption efforts in contemporary Nigeria. Established under the leadership of President Olusegun Obasanjo (1999-2007), the Commissions, especially the EFCC, quickly became popular among Nigerians and outside observers committed to tackling corruption and economic and financial crimes in Nigeria. Soon after it was established, the EFCC under its founding Chairman, Nuhu Ribadu, took the bull by the horn in its fight against corruption, economic, and financial crimes. In doing so, the EFCC won the admiration of many Nigerians and foreigners. Overall, the agency seemed to be committed to its assignment and to carry it out with zeal and focus on justice. Since the establishment of ICPC and EFCC, illegally acquired money and other properties worth tens of billions of Naira has been recovered, some accused persons prosecuted, and a few convicted.[3] There is, however, a credibility problem for both the ICPC and EFCC. In particular, the EFCC is perceived in some quarters as a tool for personal vendetta against political and other enemies of the government and the ruling party (PDP) leadership. As an example, the role of the EFCC in declaring some political opponents unfit to vie for elective offices in the 2007 general elections is not lost on Nigerians. Many people wondered why

---

[3] As explained and illustrated in Chapter 11 (on Plea Bargain), beyond the convictions, note that several offenders, especially those of the well-connected, high-profile variety, have typically been treated with kid gloves, such that these privileged criminals get away with extremely light sentences as results of negotiations with prosecutors.

a non-partisan agency would join in political attacks against certain politicians especially without judicial pronouncements to ground the EFCC declarations.

Fighting Corruption in Nigeria: Essential Features

As demonstrated in the historical outline of anti-corruption policies and programs in Nigeria, various degrees of success have been achieved, while several shortcomings and areas of improvement are identified. The lessons learned from the historical and contemporary endeavors at controlling corruption in Nigeria show that an effective, efficient, and credible policy/program to check this behavior has to include some key characteristics, including the following.

(a) A general feature of anti-corruption in Nigeria is the lack of continuity of an established policy or program between governments. Each government insists on devising and running its anti-corruption policy and program, even if simply by renaming an existing endeavor and making other cosmetic changes. Considering that the governments have been mostly without guaranteed duration of office and short-lived, each program or policy is typically applied for only a short period before it is replaced by the succeeding administration. For a sustained national strategy against corruption, retaining and strengthening an existing policy and program seems important to avoid wasteful deployment of limited resources and confusing the citizens about the focus of the government.

(b) In addressing corruption at each level of administration in the country, someone or some official body should be put in charge of the anti-corruption campaign, and the responsible person or body has to have the political will and authority in the eye of the public as well as possess the requisite personal accountability. Since there is no one agency that can do everything in the fight against corruption, a coordinated effort is required among the agencies responsible for fighting corruption, including the police, EFCC, ICPC, prosecutors, courts, and the ministry of justice. Such coordination is expected to produce a better result than isolated efforts by each agency. However, among the coordinated agencies, there is the need for an official body to serve as the facilitator of the joint action. The facilitating body (or coordinator) has to be a mobilizer of the resources of many agencies of government. The facilitating agency should ensure that the various anti-corruption arms and activities, including crime (corruption) investigation, are properly managed to derive, preserve, and present the best evidence at the trial of an accused person. The agency should also ensure that the citizens are given every reasonable opportunity to participate in the anti-corruption efforts. This would help to increase public confidence in the anti-corruption work. Along this line, a community relations office is desirable, to establish and maintain smooth access between the citizens and the agencies and personnel of the criminal justice system (see Klitgaard, Abaroa, and Parris, 2000, p. 69). It follows that the facilitating agency should be provided with sufficient budget and other resources to hire and maintain excellent staff, such as lawyers, accountants, economists, criminologists, management experts, and systems analysts.

(c) Also, in formulating and implementing a credible anti-corruption policy/program, it is important to do what Klitgaard, Abaroa, and Parris (2000) describe as *picking low-hanging fruit*. By this, they mean that a comprehensive analysis of all relevant issues and questions about corruption in a society should be done, and then the type of corruption on which visible progress could be made in a relatively short period, without too great a cost, should be selected. This advice runs counter to the conventional view that all forms of corruption should be fought at once. The bottom line is that it seems more prudent to tackle the kind(s) of corruption with the best cost-benefit prospect and the best chance to make significant progress in corruption reduction or control.

(d) Further, an effective, efficient, and credible anti-corruption policy/ program must shatter the cloak of impunity. In the Nigerian example, there is a general perception that corrupt persons, especially those responsible for the most damage to the country, are above the law. They are seen as operating with the assurance and protection of powerful public officials. Thus, it is unrealistic to expect that such corrupt persons would be subjected to the law. A meaningful fight against corruption must remove the assurances and protections enjoyed by the powerful and connected criminals so that they could be held to account for their behaviors under the law. To achieve this, it is essential to deal with the leaders and most prominent corrupt persons as a way of setting examples for all others. It is important to identify, arrest, try, convict, and punish big corrupt actors so that cynical citizens would have reason to believe that an anti-corruption drive is more than mere rhetoric. More specifically, for greater citizen confidence in an anti-corruption policy/program, it seems advisable to set an example by professionally investigating, prosecuting, and convicting a corrupt prominent member of the ruling political party. If the rule of law is applied, this strategy would bolster the citizens' confidence in the anti-corruption policy/program applied to them. However, effort should be made to separate campaign against corruption from that of creating political advantages or campaigning against the opposition.

Conclusion

Corruption is the misuse of official position for unofficial ends. There is a wide variety of corruption, including systemic, political, economic, organized, unorganized, big and small/petty corruption. Corruption is a deep-rooted social problem in Nigeria. It pervades all levels of government in the country. Different social classes perpetrate it. Corrupt behaviors are carried out through a variety of means, such as bribery, fraud, favoritism, nepotism, and embezzlement. Although corruption is often seen as government-based misbehavior, it also exists in the private sector. Nonetheless, most corrupt behaviors (especially the ones with the greatest impact on society) tend to result from the actions and omissions of government officials and from partnerships and other relationships between unscrupulous government officials and their private counterparts. It is, however, necessary to point out that the primary responsibility for preventing corruption and devising strategies for dealing with the behavior in a society lies with the government, its agencies, and personnel. After all, the government controls the laws, State institutions, and other resources necessary for fighting corruption.

Corruption is particularly tempting when the anticipated gain is significant, the chance of apprehension and subjection to the criminal justice system is small, and the penalty is inconsiderable, as illustrated by Nigeria. The Nigerian example shows the influence of the characteristics in enticing many people to engage in corrupt behavior. Thus, in Nigeria, corruption is pervasive, in public as well as private organizations and transactions. Even then, corrupt behaviors are grossly under-reported because, it seems, corruption is generally accepted or conceded as a way of life. Other than those Nigerians who engage in corrupt behavior, many other responsible citizens engaged in legitimate enterprises and lines of work have apparently concluded that they have to acquiesce to corruption (as either perpetrators or victims) if they are to succeed in their legitimate endeavors. In essence, the responsible citizens have been compelled to operate in a corrupt environment and they are making the best of the situation.

It is important to stress that the government of a society bears the primary duty to check corruption in its jurisdiction. However, to achieve an effective, efficient, and credible anti-corruption policy/program, a comprehensive approach involving government and private ideas and efforts is required. In the daunting circumstances of widespread corruption, such as the Nigerian situation presents, fighting corruption requires a systematic, methodical, organized, and coordinated approach involving public and private partners. In addition, combating corruption necessitates the participation of many professionals, including lawyers, investigators, accountants, management consultants, as well as the general public. There is also the need to employ the services of undercover agents, wiretaps, and covert surveillance. Finally, ill-conceived policies and legislations are not the panacea for corruption.

References

Adler, F., G. O. W. Mueller, and W. S. Laufer (2010) *Criminology*. New York, NY, USA: McGraw Hill.

Agnew, R. (1991) "The Interactive Effects of Peer Variables on Delinquency," *Criminology*, 29: 47-72.

Ake, C. (1981) *The Political Economy of Africa*. Lagos, Nigeria: Longman.

Akers, R. L. (1977) *Deviant Behaviour: A Social Learning Approach* (2nd ed.). Belmont, California, USA: Wadsworth.

Akers, R. L., M. D. Krohn, L. Lanza-Kaduce, and M. Radosevich (1979) "Social Learning and Deviant Behaviour: A Specific Test of a General Theory," *American Sociological Review*, 44: 636-655.

Bandura, A. (1973) *Aggression: A Social Learning Analysis*. Englewood Cliffs, New Jersey, USA: Prentice Hall.

Bandura, A. (1977) "Self-Efficacy: Toward a Unifying Theory of Behavioural Change," *Psychological Review* 84:191-215.

Bayart, Jean-Francois, Stephen Ellis, and Beatrice Hibou (1999) *The Criminalization of the State of Africa*. Oxford, England: James Curry.

Beirne, P. and J. W. Messerschmidt (2006) *Criminology*. Los Angeles, California, USA: Roxbury Publishing.

Benda, B. and L. Whiteside (1995) "Testing an Integrated Model of Delinquency Using LISREL," *Journal of Social Service Research*, 21: 1-32.

Brook, J. S., A. S. Gordon, M. Whiteman, and P. Cohen (1986) "Some Models and Mechanisms for Explaining the Impact of Maternal and Adolescent Characteristics on Adolescent Stage of Drug Use," *Developmental Psychology*, 22: 460-467.

Brook, J. S., D. W. Brook, A. S. Gordon, M. Whiteman, and P. Cohen (1990) "The Psychosocial Etiology of Drug Use: A Family of Interactional Approach," *Genetic, Social, and General Psychology Monographs* 116 (Number 2).

Burgess, R. L. and R. L. Akers (1966) "A Differential Association-Reinforcement Theory of Criminal Behaviour," *Social Problems*, 4:128-147.

Daily Trust Newspaper (Nigeria) (2002, July 9) "The Evil of Corruption".

Dike, V. (2004) "Corruption in Nigeria. A New Paradigm for Effective Control," see at www.nigerdeltalcongress.com; Internet (accessed June 24, 2010).

Dolive, Linda and David Potter (2000) "Electoral Corruption in Italy and Japan," in Delbert Rounds (ed.) *International Criminal Justice: Issues in a Global Perspective*. Boston, Massachusetts, USA: Allyn and Bacon.

Durkheim, Emile (1897/1951/1997) *Suicide: A Study in Sociology*. New York, NY, USA: The Free Press.

Erero, John and Tony Oladoyin (2000) "Tackling Corruption in Nigeria," in Kempe Ronald Hope and Burnwell Chikulo (eds.). *Corruption and Development in Africa: Lessons from Country Studies*. New York, NY, USA: Palgrave.

Gluckman, Max (1955) *Custom and Conflict in Africa*. Oxford, England: Basil

Blackwell.

Hirschi, T. (1969) "Causes of Delinquency: A Partial Replication and Extension," *Social Problems*, 20: 471-483.

Huang, B, R. Korsterman, R. Catalano, J. D. Hawkins, and R. D. Abbott (2001) "Modeling Mediation in the Etiology of Violent Behaviour in Adolescence: A Test of the Social Development Model," *Criminology*, Vol. 39, Number 1, 75-107.

Iwarimie-Jaja, D. (2003) *Criminology: The Study of Crime* (3rd ed.). Owerri, Nigeria: Springfield.

Johnson, C. (1986) "Structural Corruption and the Advent of Machine Politics in Japan," *Journal of Japanese Studies*, 12 (Winter), 1-28.

Kempf, K. (1993) "The Empirical Status of Hirsch's Control Theory," in Adler, F. and W. S. Laufer, (eds.). *New Direction in Criminological Theory: Advances in Criminological Theory*, Vol. 4. New Brunswick, New Jersey, USA: Transaction.

Klitgaard, Robert, Ronald MacLean-Abaroa, and H. Lindsey Parris (2000) *Corrupt Cities: A Practical Guide to Cure and Prevention*. Richmond, California, USA: Institute for Contemporary Studies Press.

Krohn, K. and J. L. Massey (1980) "Social Control and Delinquent Behaviour: An Examination of the Elements of the Social Bond," *Sociological Quarterly*, 21: 529-543.

de Leon, P. (1993) *Thinking About Political Corruption*. Armonk, New York, NY, USA: M. E. Sharpe.

Lipset, Seymour Martin and Gabriel Salman Lenz (2000) "Corruption, Culture, and Markets," in Lawrence Harrison and Samuel P. Huntington (eds.) *Culture Matters: How Values Shape Human Progress*. New York, NY, USA: Basic Books, p. 112.

Loftin, C. (1984) "Assaultive Violence as a Contagious Social Process," *Bulletin of the New York Academy of Medicine*, 62 Number 5:559-555.

MacDougall, T. (1988) "The Lockheed Scandal and the High Cost of Politics in Japan," in A. S. Markovits and M. Silverstein (eds.). *The Politics of Scandal*. New York, NY, USA: Holmes and Meier.

Matza, D. (1969) *Becoming Deviant*. Englewood Cliffs, New Jersy, USA: Prentice Hall.

Merton, Robert K. (1938-10) "Social Structure and Anomie," *American Sociological Review* 3 (5): 672-682.

Murobushi, T. (1981) *Structure of Corruption*. Tokyo, Japan: Iwanami Shoten.

Nye, J. S. (1967) "Corruption and Political Development: A Case-Benefit Analysis," *The American Political Science Review*, 417-427.

Odekunle, F. (1991) "Illustrations of Types, Patterns and Avenues of Corruption in Nigeria," in P. B. Ajibola (ed.), *Perspectives on Corruption and Other Economic Crimes in Nigeria*. Lagos, Nigeria: The Federal Ministry of Justice.

Osoba, S. O. (1996) "Corruption in Nigeria: Historical Perspective," *A Review of African Political Economy*, No.69; 371-86.

Otu, S. E. (2003) "Armed Robbery in the Southeastern States of Contemporary Nigeria. A Criminological Analysis". Unpublished D. Litt. & Phil. Dissertation. Department of Criminology, University of South Africa, Pretoria, South Africa.

Pye, Lucian (1965) "The Concept of Political Development," *The Annals*, 358, March:1-19.

Schoenmakers, Y. M. M., Edo de Vries Robbe, and Anton Ph. Van Wijk (2009) *Mountains of Gold: An Exploratory Research on 419 Fraud*. Amsterdam, Netherlands: SWP Publishers.

Sen, A. (1999) *Development as Freedom,* New York, NY, USA: Anchor Books.

Shils, Edward (1962) "Political Development in New States," *The Hague*, 385.

Smith, T. (1995) "Political Sleaze in Britain: Causes, Concerns and Cures," *Parliamentary Affair*, 48,551-561.

Sutherland, E. (1939) *Principles of Criminology*. Philadelphia, Pennsylvania, USA: Lippincott.

Sutherland, E. (1973) "Development of the Theory," in K. F. Schuessler, (ed.). *Edwin Sutherland on Analyzing Crime*. Chicago, Illinois, USA: University of Chicago Press.

Sutherland, E. H. and D. R. Cressey (1970) *Criminology* (9th ed.). Philadelphia, Pennsylvania, USA: Lippincott.

United States Agency for International Development (USAID) (2000) "Anti-Corruption Resources: What is Corruption?"

Vito, Gennaro F. and Jeffrey R. Maahs (2012) *Criminology: Theory, Research, and Policy*. Sudbury, Massachussetts, USA: Jones & Bartlett Learning.

World Development Reports (2005) "A Better Investment Climate for Everyone," see at http://web.worldbank.org; Internet (accessed July 10, 2010).

Chapter 18

The Cameroonian Woman and the Law

Caroline Time
Buea, Cameroon

Introduction

Female victimization in Cameroon continues to be entrenched even though women are steadfastly asserting their rights by challenging institutions, both customary and formal/legal, that fail to protect such rights. To say that there are no laws in Cameroon guaranteeing the rights of women will be an overstatement. However, the following questions are relevant. Are the laws adequate and are they implemented when and where necessary? What is the role of customary laws on the rights of Cameroonian women? How do these laws affect the socio-legal status of the women and what is the way forward? This chapter answers these questions. Using court cases, referring to customary and statutory laws, as well as decided cases, the chapter delineates forms of female suppression in Cameroon. The chapter also offers recommendations on how the rights of women can be preserved.

Cameroon is used here as a case study because the author is a practicing attorney in the country. She specializes among other things in women's and children's issues. This chapter is structured in five sections. Section one explains Cameroonian laws that adequately address the rights of women and children. Section two explains the biased and poorly drafted laws, while section three deals with the influence of customary laws and the role of the custodians of customs. Section four hinges on the influence of the judge's gender in dispensing justice, and finally, chapter five provides recommendations on how the law should equitably apply to all.

Good/Equitable Laws

Various provisions of the *Constitution of Cameroon*, *Labor Code of Cameroon*, and *Penal Code* stipulate rights and protections for females, as follows. The preamble of the Constitution provides that "human beings, without distinction of race, religion, sex, belief, possess inalienable and sacred rights." Article 1 (2) of the Constitution ensures the equality of all citizens before the law. In politics, the Cameroonian woman was accorded the right to vote at independence. However, this is a right that the woman herself has not effectively exercised until recently (1990), with the birth of multiparty politics.

Section 61 (2) of the *Labor Code of Cameroon* provides that workers of the same type and same level of proficiency shall be entitled to the same remuneration irrespective of their sex. Section 84 (1) of the Labor Code provides that once it is determined that a woman is pregnant, she may stop work and will not be liable to dismissal and will still receive pay. Sub-section 2 provides that she is entitled to fourteen weeks of maternity leave with pay, and such leave may be extended for six more weeks in cases where complications arise during or after delivery. Section 85 of the Labor Code provides for one hour of breast feeding break. Such break may be taken without prior notice.

Section 27 (2) of the *Penal Code* states: "no woman who is with child or who has been recently delivered may begin to serve her sentence until six weeks after delivery." Sub-section 3 states "a woman with child already in custody pending trial shall continue until the expiry of the said period to be in custody as if awaiting trial." Section 22 (3) of the Code states: "no woman with child may be executed until after her delivery."

In addition to the *Constitution of Cameroon*, *Labor Code of Cameroon*, and *Penal Code*, the *Civil Status Registration Ordinance* of June 1981 – which regulates the status of persons in Cameroon – contains many important provisions that guarantee legal protections for Cameroonian women. The following provisions of the Ordinance are important. The Ordinance provides as follows in Article 74 (1): "a woman may exercise a trade different from that of her husband." Article 75 (1) of the 1981 Ordinance provides, "where a woman exercises a trade separate from that of the husband, she may open a separate account in her own name and make deposits or withdrawals as she sees fit." Article 76 (1) of the 1981 Ordinance provides that "a wife who has been deserted by her husband may obtain alimony for both the children left under her care and herself." A woman has the right to consent to her marriage as provided in Article 52 (4) of the 1981 Ordinance. The 1981 Ordinance forbids parents from objecting to the marriage of the girl child on grounds of non-payment of Bride Price. Article 61 (2) states: "any objection based on the existence, payments or terms of payment of customary dowry, even if agreed to in advance shall be inadmissible and against public policy." Article 77 (2) of the 1981 Ordinance provides, "in the event of the death of the husband, his heirs have no right over the widow or over her freedom or share of property belonging to her---." This Article goes further to state that she has a choice to either stay single or remarry any man of her choice after a period of 180 days of mourning without any one laying claim whatsoever to any compensation or material benefit for dowry or otherwise, received either at the time of engagement, during marriage or after marriage.

In the case of succession where a man dies intestate, the English law, which is in force in Anglophone Cameroon, is applied. The *Administration of Estates Act* of 1925, section 46 (1) states: where a man dies intestate whether he is survived by a parent or brother or sister, the beneficiaries to his estate shall be the surviving spouse and their issues. This was applied in the case of *Nforba Aloysius, Bougyisi Elizabeth vs. Nchari Mary Kinyui* (ex parte Luanga Nforba Nchari, Administrator of the estate of Nchari Anthony Nforba, deceased), AE/06/96/1M/96. See also Ngassa and Time (1999).

Biased Laws

While the laws cited above exist and guarantee the rights of women, there are some statutory laws that from their plain language discriminate against women. Here are some examples, identified by subjects.

Marriage and Cameroonian Citizenship: The *Nationality Code* of Cameroon provides that a Cameroonian man married to a foreigner can confer nationality on the wife but a Cameroonian woman married to a foreigner cannot confer nationality on the husband and children. A 1972 law on prostitution requires that all single women in the township who cannot not be identified with any particular job have to go back to the villages, and that a woman cannot go to a leisure spot without a male companion. Even though the implementation of this law has not been very active in recent years, it is worth noting that the law has not been repealed, which means that it is still in force.

Polygamous Relationships: Article 49 of the *Civil Status Registration Ordinance*, 1981 recognizes polygamy. The provision of polygamy as an option in marriage lowers the status of a woman. Article 43 (1) of the 1981 Ordinance provides for a father to recognize a child born out of wedlock, while Article 46 (3) of the same Ordinance provides thus: "under pain of foreclosure, action in search of the real father shall be taken by the mother within two years from the date of delivery or when the father ceases to maintain the child." The woman is given a limited time to search for the father of her child but the man has no time limitation. Not only is the woman given a limited time within which to bring an action for the search of the real father, sub-section 2 of Article 46 states: "however, any action in search of the real father shall be rejected if during the legal period of conception, the mother led a loose life or had intercourse with another man or if the alleged father was physically unfit to be the father." It remains an open question whether a scientific test is required before an action in search of the real father can be rejected.

Marriage and Careers of Spouses: Article 74 (1) of the 1981 Ordinance provides that, a woman may exercise a trade different from her husband's, but sub-section 2 states: "the husband may object to the exercise of such a trade in the interest of the marriage and children." Sub-section 3 goes further to make such action free of charge. The danger of this provision is that some spiteful men may use it to frustrate the careers of their wives.

Marriage Age: Article 52 of the 1981 Ordinance sets the age of marriage for girls at 15 years and that of boys at 18 years. Also, section 356 (3) of the *Penal Code* makes it a criminal offense to give away a boy under the age of 16 years for marriage. For a girl, the minimum age for marriage is 14 years. The age difference between boys and girls places the girl child at a disadvantage.

Adultery: Section 361 (1) of the *Penal Code* provides as follows: "any married woman having sexual intercourse with any man other than her husband shall be punished with imprisonment from six months and with a fine of twenty-five thousand to one hundred thousand francs CFA". Sub-section 2 provides, "any man having intercourse in the matrimonial home, or habitually having sexual intercourse elsewhere, with a woman other than his wife or wives, shall be punished in like manner." The catch here is a man can only be charged for adultery if the act took place in the matrimonial home, or if it is habitual. For a woman it takes just one isolated act. The question is, how often does a man take his mistress to the matrimonial home? Or, in the case of a polygamist, how does one differentiate between the mistress and the wife, since a polygamous marriage is a customary marriage?

Rape and the Law of Evidence: The rule of corroboration of evidence in rape cases has helped to keep rape cases out of court to the detriment of the victim (woman). The law of evidence requires the evidence of the victim in rape cases to be corroborated by "independent evidence in every material particular." The question is how often is rape committed with an eyewitness? Because there is hardly any witness to a rape, rape victims end up keeping quiet about the crime and never bother to bring action against the perpetrator. These laws, which are actually in force, are some of the reasons for the very slow pace of the elevation of the socio-legal status of women in Cameroon.

Poorly Drafted Laws

Many Cameroonian laws are discriminatory in their provisions. Additionally, some of these laws are obscure in the manner in which they are drafted. For example, section 344 (1) of the *Penal Code* punishes the corruption of youth. The English translation of sub-section 1 provides, "whoever, in order to satisfy the desires of another person, habitually excites, encourages or facilitates the debauch or corruption of any person under eighteen years of age shall be punished with imprisonment for from one to five years and with a fine of from twenty to one million francs." The French version states that anyone who excites, encourages or facilitates the debauch or corruption of any person under the age of twenty-one years shall be punished with imprisonment for a period ranging from one to five years and with a fine of twenty thousand to one million CFA francs. There are unsettling gaps in the versions of the law.

The conflicting ages in the French and English versions make the law wanting in substance and difficult to apply. Sub-section 2 of the French version states that the penalty will be doubled if the victim is below 16 years of age. There is no corresponding section in the English version. Rather, sub-section 2 of the English version is sub-section 3 in the French version. The sub-section 3 states, "upon conviction, the court may order the forfeitures described in section 30 of the *Penal Code* and deprive the offender for the same period of parental power and disqualify him from being guardian or curator of any minor." Sub-section 1 does not categorize who the person is; it merely states *any person*. On the state of this law, Ngassa (1999) observes as follows: "The meaning of section 344 is completely obscure." She adds that, "it has been very difficult to prosecute and convict anyone under the above section in the Anglophone Cameroon." She cited the case of *Lyonga Ndive v. The people* (CASWP/13C/90), where after the victim had gone through a long period of trial and was convicted, the conviction was quashed on appeal. The appeal court held that the corruption was done to satisfy the accuser's own desires and so quashed the conviction by the court below.

Absence of Laws on Gender Sensitive Issues

For some time now, gender equality has driven the activities of women's groups and nations around the world. The relevant gender issues are present in Cameroon as in many other countries. In Cameroon, despite the struggle by and on behalf of women, equality seems to be farfetched mainly because the laws needed to regulate touchy issues pertaining to the status of women are non-existent. One of the areas where the necessary law is absent is sexual harassment. This issue affects the rights of women, yet Cameroonian laws are silent on the matter. There is no official law that specifically sanctions sexual harassment. Sexual harassment takes place at homes, in schools, at workplaces, and sadly in the churches and other religious places of worship, among other avenues. Thus, a sexual harassment incident can occur in a wide variety of private as well as public settings. Notwithstanding its wide reach, transgressors harass their victims with impunity mainly because there is no specific law that proscribes sexual harassment. Sexual harassment takes different forms, including touching the victim inappropriately, making unsolicited visits, or calling the victim some offensive pet names. Women victims – and sexual harassment victims are mostly women – end up abandoning school, quitting their jobs, leaving their homes, and even switching church, or suffering in silence because the present legal environment in Cameroon discourages the victims from complaining or being heard. It is time for Cameroon to pass a law that makes sexual harassment an offense.

Domestic violence is another important issue that is not specifically addressed in the *Penal Code* or other law. A domestic violence victim – usually a woman – can seek protection under the country's general assault law, but this law does not sufficiently address the specific needs of domestic violence victims. In Cameroon, wife beating has been accepted as a part of the culture. This attitude sometimes influences the statutory courts to the extent that a judge may decide that a man has a right to chastise his wife. Most often, women victims run to the police for protection and assistance. However, the police tend to treat the issue as a family problem and ask the women to return to their homes. There are no structures that can help to facilitate justice on this issue. Consequently, many women are hesitant to complain. For one thing, they think nobody is going to listen to them; secondly, they do not want to be stigmatized by society. The victims are not encouraged to report the victimization they have suffered. Most often, the courts learn of violence in the home only during divorce proceedings. At that stage, the assault is no longer given the attention it should receive. As Ngassa (1999) notes, even the hospitals where the victims run to, never keep statistics and are not empowered to make reports on behalf of the victims. In the case of *Ndenno c/ Mme Guamgne Alphonsine* (no. 36 of 27th June 1996), the Baffoussam Court of Appeal dismissed the wife's claims that her husband used to strangle her until she succumbed to unnatural acts of sexual intercourse. The court held that the woman's assertions were not proved since there was no witness. It should be noted that domestic violence takes the form of physical violence, but it can also take the form of emotional or economic violence (FIDA Cameroon "Women, Children and the LAW" 1996).

Influence of Customary Laws and the Role of the Custodians of Customs

The creation of Customary and Alkali courts in Anglophone Cameroon pursuant to law number 79 - 4 of 29th June 1979 has given strength to customary laws and practices. Also, decree number 69/DF/544 of 19th December 1969, on the organization of traditional courts in Francophone Cameroon, has strengthened traditional laws. The law and the decree both insist that the courts shall apply the customs of the parties if the customs are not contrary to written law and public policy. Similarly, section 27 (1) of the *Southern Cameroons High Court Law* of 1955 provides: "the high court shall observe and enforce observance of every native law and custom which is not repugnant to natural justice equity and good conscience nor incompatible with any law for the time being in force, and nothing in this law shall deprive any person of the benefit of any such native law or custom."

However, in defiance of statutory laws, customary courts treat bride price as the *sine qua non* for the celebration of marriage. Article 70 (1) of the *Civil Status Registration Ordinance* of June 1981 states as follows: "the total or partial payment or non-payment of dowry, the total or partial execution, or non-execution of any marriage agreement, shall have no effect on the validity of the marriage." On the other hand, customary law does not recognize any marriage where bride price has not been paid. What makes it worse is the effect this customary practice has even on the statutory courts. In *Maya Ikome v. Manga Ekenason* (CASWP/ CC76/85 (unreported), a woman had been married for thirty years. After her death, her family sued her husband to claim her property on the ground that she was not lawfully married because the full amount of her bride price was not paid. The customary court dismissed the claim. On appeal, the court of appeal allowed the appeal, stating that a marriage certificate "is only *prima facie* evidence of marriage", that since bride price was not paid the marriage certificate "did not perfect what was already an imperfect union." The man was thus disinherited. Thus, the payment of bride price is so deeply rooted in the different ethnic cultures in Cameroon that it has gained the force of law in the country.

Levirate marriage is a customary law practice that can lead to abuse and cause a woman to be treated as mere property. Levirate marriage is a kind of marriage whereby a widow is forced to marry her deceased husband's brother, uncle, nephew, or even son because her bride price was paid. She is thus considered the property of the family and since the bride price was never refunded, even after the death of her husband, she is still bound to his family. In some cases, this is the only way she can inherit her deceased husband's property, by getting married to her in-law. This practice is contrary to Article 77 (1) of the 1981 Ordinance, which is to the effect that in the event of the death of one spouse, the marriage shall be dissolved. Further, Sub section (2) states that in the event of the death of the husband, his heirs shall have no right over the widow, and the heirs shall have no right over the widow's freedom, nor shall they share the property belonging to her. She is at liberty to remarry whosoever she chooses without anyone laying a claim to any compensation, material, or dowry received either at the time of engagement, during or after the marriage. The practice of levirate marriage can so disadvantage the widow that she may seek redress in an official court. In the case of *Kong Dione Agnes v. Melong Akola Boniface* (HCK/38/96, unreported) the widow, Kong Dione Agnes from the Bakossi ethnic group, sued her levirate husband who had taken all her deceased husband's property and after one child with her, proceeded to abandon her (Ngassa, 1999).

The widowhood rites tradition is another customary practice that has also gained the force of law. By this practice, the widow is forced to carry out rituals after the death of her husband with one of the reasons being "to prove that she did not kill her husband." These kinds of rituals are carried out only by widows and not by widowers. A woman who refuses to perform the widowhood rites rituals is almost certain to be banished or suffer disinheritance. For a woman who depended heavily on her husband, and now (after her husband's death) needs his family relations to survive, banishment or disinheritance is sure to be devastating. Therefore, she is highly unlikely to muster sufficient courage to challenge the tradition. That the widowhood rites custom assumes that the widow is responsible for her husband's death is reason enough to condemn it. Additionally, however, the application of the practice to widows – while excluding widowers – is another illustration of the biased nature of this practice.

The property right of a woman is another area where customary law has gained force in Cameroon. In customary law, the woman has no right to inheritance because she is considered the property of her husband. This practice was aptly illustrated in the case of *Rose Ndollo Achu vs. Richard Achu* (BCA/62/86 of 20th June, 1988). In that case, the court held that "the customary law does not countenance the sharing of property especially landed property between husband and wife on divorce. The wife is still regarded as part of her husband's property. That conception is underscored by the payment of dowry upon marriage and on the refund of same on divorce" (see also Ngassa, 1999). Thus, in Cameroon, the statutory courts, as well as the customary courts, apply those customary laws that should be considered repugnant.

Role of the Custodians of Customs

In every society, the role of the custodians of the customs of the people is very important. The custodians perform a very important function in the lives of their subjects. This is the situation in Cameroon. The traditional rulers of the various communities in Cameroon constitute a critical group of these custodians. The traditional rulers serve as customary judges and counselors. They also serve as mediators between their subjects and the State. Further, the traditional rulers ensure the safety of their communities through the formulation, application, and enforcement of a variety of measures to promote security, law enforcement, and general social control among the citizens. In short, traditional rulers have a duty to maintain stable, peaceful, and progressive communities.

In their efforts to achieve stable, peaceful, and progressive communities, the traditional rulers in the various Cameroonian communities have to decide or oversee decisions that affect the rights of citizens on diverse issues. In particular, in the performance of their duties, the traditional rulers frequently deal with the effects of various customary practices on the rights of women. These rulers sit and approve or disapprove the enforcements of customary practices that may be repugnant, and the effects of such practices on women. Therefore, the role of traditional rulers *vis-à-vis* the customary practices that affect women is very important. In the circumstances of most women in Cameroon, a woman is bound to comply with a traditional ruler's decision. She has very little, if any, leeway to oppose the ruler.

Role of Gender in Judicial Decisions

In years past, male judges were the most dominant in Cameroonian courts and in many cases, their judgments tended to cater to their gender. In some respects, this trend continues in the country. It would be an overstatement to generalize that male judges pass judgments that are biased against the opposite sex. However, there are instances where the presiding judges have given decisions that gratify the dominant male view, especially regarding customary law. For an example, in a case on the *Estate of Nchari* (Suit Number AE/06/11/96), the deceased woman, married, left an estate. On her death, the deceased wife's family claimed the estate. Without proper legal justification in our view (Ngassa and Time, 1999), the presiding judge, His Lordship Epuli M. A., took sides with the family of the deceased wife. As well, in *Florence Agwe Nyang v. Emmanuel Agwe Nyang* (No. CASWP/CC/08/91), His Lordship Epuli M.A., in another apparent solidarity with male domination, held that the appellant (wife) could not refund the previously paid bride price or dowry at divorce (see also Ngassa and Time, 1999). Further, Justice Monekosso also held in the case of *Buma v. Buma* (BCA/20/81), that a woman cannot return bride price after so many years of marriage (see as well, Ngassa, 1999).

In line with the above cases, in the case of *Ngnietedem Etienne v. Tashi Lydia Sinaga* (BCA/46/86), Justice O. M. Inglis held that a customary court has no jurisdiction to share property especially landed property upon divorce and that no equity could apply in the circumstances. He set aside the order of the customary court that had awarded a house to the woman in the case. The judge (O. M. Inglis) is the same male judge that stated in another case that a woman is a property and cannot inherit property [see *Achu v. Achu* (supra); see also Ngassa, 1999].

All the above decisions were handed down by male judges. Each of the verdicts is an unreasonable limitation on the rights of women in Cameroon.

Like cases on such issues as the devolution of property and other property rights, marriage cases often throw up gender (of the judge as well as the parties) as an important variable for understanding many judicial decisions in Cameroon. The phrase "according to native laws and customs" that some civil status clerks insert in marriage certificates has led some judges to interpret the concerned marriages as polygamous even where the relevant marriage certificates state that the unions are monogamous. Thus, in the case of *Kumbongsi v. Kumbongsi* (CASWP/4/84, Unreported) as well as in *Tufon v. Tufon* (HCB/59/MC/83, Unreported), the court in each case held that even though the parties opted for monogamy the marriage was polygamous because of the phrase. Further, in *Lyonga Christina v. Andrew Lyonga* (CASWP/5/94), His Lordship Bawack Benson Bonny did not only hold that the marriage was polygamous, he went on to say that it was superfluous to mention monogamy in customary marriage. Sometimes, the imputation of polygamy even in clearly monogamous marriages is particularly absurd. Thus, in *Temple Cole v. Temple Cole*, the marriage at issue was purely a monogamous marriage and the marriage certificate did not carry the phrase "according to native laws and customs", yet the Buea Court of Appeal declared that the marriage was polygamous because the bride price was not paid (see also Ngassa, 1999).

In recent years with the influx of female lawyers and judges in Cameroon, the positions of the country's courts on many issues affecting women have changed. It is conceivable that these changes reflect the gender redistribution of judicial and other legal positions in the country. A survey of decided cases seems to bear out the suggestion that the current trend is in favor of more women-friendly judicial decisions due to an increase in the number of women judicial and other legal officials across Cameroon. The following cases serve to illustrate the current movement.

In the case of *Nganso Tchakounte N. Isabelle v. Nganso Apollinaire* (CSWP/CC/95), the parties were married under the native laws and customs of the Bamileke people. The parties also registered the marriage at the civil status registry; further, they had the matrimony blessed in church. In dissolving the marriage, the customary court held that the marriage was polygamous. On appeal, Her Lordship H. N. Najeme, in setting aside the customary court judgment, held that the fact that the parties went to the civil status registry (to register) and the church (to bless) their marriage showed that they intended the marriage to be monogamous. Thus, the appeal court held, the customary court does not have jurisdiction over the marriage (see also Ngassa, 1999). Whereas the customary court judge was male, the appeal court judge was female. In view of the subject under consideration (that is, the role of gender in judicial decisions), it is interesting that the lower and appellate judges differ as widely as they do on the clearly established facts.

In essence, *Nganso Tchakounte N. Isabelle v. Nganso Apollinaire* shows how multiple ceremonies may be performed to celebrate the union of a couple (one marriage). In this case, any one of the three locations where a marriage ceremony was performed for the couple (that is, under the native laws and customs, civil status registry, and the church) should suffice to establish that the parties were married. However, the parties went on to celebrate their union rather superfluously by doing so under three sets of laws. Indeed, the trend of redundant celebrations of one marriage is unfortunately common in Cameroon, Nigeria, and other postcolonies. The consequence is that parties who put themselves through these double or multiple ceremonies for one marriage end up creating conflicts among the laws regulating the different marriage forms.

Other cases that support the view that female judges tend to be more sympathetic to other women's issues in Cameroon include the following. In the case of *Che Maabo v. Che Maboo* (HCF/7MC/97/2M/98), Justice Ngassa ruled that the marriage at issue was monogamous even though it carried the phrase "according to native laws and customs" (see also Ngassa, 1999). And in *Kang Nsume v. Kang Nsume* (HCF/38/96) her Lordship, Mba Acha, in rendering judgment, took into consideration the wife's contribution and ordered that the lone house be sold and the proceeds shared between the parties. Unlike Justice O. M. Inglis who took the stand of the customary law and considered women as "property" who cannot inherit property, his female counterpart, Justice Florence Rita Arrey, in the case of *Alice Fodge v. Ndangsi Kette* (BCA/45/1986), awarded landed property to the woman in the dispute even though she was married under customary law.

At this juncture, this chapter has demonstrated that the biased laws, the absence of laws on gender sensitive issues, the influence of customary laws, the role played by the custodians of customs, as well as the gender of the judge before whom the parties appear, are factors that determine the fate of the woman in a Cameroonian court of law. The elevation of the socio-legal status of the Cameroonian woman will depend largely on the laws in place, on how the laws are interpreted and applied, and on when women will garner the fortitude to stand up for their rights. Thus, the following section of this article discusses the next step for the Cameroonian woman and the law.

The Way Forward

The Constitution of Cameroon provides that all citizens are equal before the law. To protect female – as well as male – citizens within the country's laws, this provision should be implemented to the letter. Also, section 27 (1) of the *Southern Cameroon High Court Law*, which is still in force, makes it clear that customs that contravene equity, good conscience, and public policy should be disregarded. Similarly, the provisions of the High Court Law should be applied to deny enforcement to customs that fail to uphold equal protection for women. Thus, there are some very good laws in the books to advance women's interests in Cameroon. However, these laws should be strengthened and applied to cases. And, wherever appropriate and in line with *stare decisis*, judges should follow previous judgments that create gender balance. Further, traditional rulers should be able to eradicate those repugnant customs that are adversely affecting the rights and status of women.

Aside from the opportunities that local laws, policies, and practices provide for protecting Cameroonian women, international law bestows several prospects for improving the circumstances of Cameroonian women, in Cameroon. Thus, regarding those women's rights issues on which Cameroon's local laws are silent, it should be noted that Cameroon is a signatory to many international treaties, which can and should be evoked as applicable to further the protection of women in Cameroon. The international treaties to which Cameroon is a signatory include the *Universal Declaration of Human Rights*, the *Convention on the Elimination of all forms of Discrimination Against Women* (ratified 23rd August 1994), the *Convention Against Torture and Inhuman Treatment* (ratified 1986), the *International Convention on the Elimination of all Forms of Racial Discrimination* (ratified 1971), and the *African Charter on Human Rights*. These treaties, which

Cameroon has ratified, are therefore parts of the country's laws. The laws cover various aspects of human rights, and as such, the laws should be applied in the country as and when needed. For example, in areas where the law is silent on domestic violence and sexual harassment, lawyers can invoke the provisions of the convention against torture, cruel, degrading, or inhuman treatment.

As another example, Cameroon's nationality law that confers citizenship only on a foreign woman married to a Cameroonian man but not on a foreign man married to a Cameroonian woman discriminates against women. The law ought to be changed to confer equal privileges on both genders. While the law remains in force, the woman can avail herself of the relevant international laws on human rights and equal protection. The question is how the international laws become applicable in local courts. In Cameroon, international conventions become part of domestic law as soon as the conventions are ratified. By Article 43 of 1996 Constitution of Cameroon, the President of the Republic of Cameroon ratifies these conventions by Article 45 of the same Constitution. Once ratified, these conventions take precedence over national laws, with the exception of the conventions that carry criminal sanctions. The conventions that carry criminal sanctions have to be passed into local laws and adopted by parliament before they become applicable in Cameroon.

Availing herself of the international laws on human rights and equal protection to which Cameroon is a signatory requires that a Cameroonian woman, whose foreign husband or the children she has with such husband are refused Cameroonian nationality, should take legal action asking the court to invoke the relevant international conventions, just like a Botswanan lady did in the following case. The citizenship case of *Attorney General of Botswana v. Unity Dow* (Botswana Supreme Court, 1992) is a resource guide for litigating international law in domestic courts. In this case, the *Botswana Citizenship Act* of 1984 based on Tswana Customary Law was challenged in court. The 1984 Act effectively prevented a woman citizen of Botswana from transmitting Botswanan citizenship to her foreign husband or children. The Act was challenged because its restriction did not apply to Botswanan men married to foreigners.

In *Attorney General of Botswana v. Unity Dow*, Unity Dow, a native of Botswana, was married to a foreigner. Her husband and children were denied Botswanan citizenship. A local women's NGO took up the case invoking international conventions. According to the NGO, the *Botswana Citizenship Act* contradicts the country's Constitution that provides equal rights for all Botswanans irrespective of race, sex, and religion. The Supreme Court held that the Act discriminated against women and violated human rights. Consequently, the Citizenship Act was amended. It is instructive that the *Unity Dow* case guided the judgment in the following Zimbabwean case: *Rattigan and Ors v. Chief Immigration Officer* (1994), where the Supreme Court of Zimbabwe cited and applied the reasoning in the *Unity Dow* case. Similarly, Zimbabwe's Constitution was amended in 1996 to reflect equal immigration status for the spouses and offsprings of Zimbabwean women as well as men. The Cameroonian courts are urged to follow the decision and reasoning demonstrated by the Botswanan and Zimbabwean courts on immigration issues.

Conclusion

This chapter has presented and analyzed the legal circumstances of Cameroonian women. Based on many constitutional and legal provisions on a wide variety of issues of concern to the women, the article scrutinizes the hurdles confronting the Cameroonian woman. Some of these obstacles derive from customs and traditions, while others are built into more formal laws of the modern Cameroonian State. Thus, whereas the absence of appropriate laws on many issues militates against the rights and welfare of the Cameroonian woman, on some other matters, the difficulty facing the Cameroonian woman stems from lack of proper interpretation, application, and enforcement of existing laws. On account of the analysis in this chapter, and in line with the recommendations already offered in the paper, the following is a summary of the steps needed to further the legal conditions of the Cameroonian woman.

The Cameroonian legislature should treat the task of rectifying the several discrepancies in the country's laws as an urgent responsibility. Accordingly, the same age for marriage should be set for both males and females. The legislature should enact laws that specifically define domestic violence and sexual harassment as offenses. Further, generally, the legislature should repeal the archaic and biased laws in the country. Traditional rulers should be educated on those customs that contravene statutory laws, are repugnant, or violate public policy. Such customs should be eradicated. Apart from the legislative changes, judicial and law enforcement officials (judges and police officers in particular) must adjust their official attitudes in favor of enthroning equality of the sexes, in the interpretation and enforcement of the country's laws. Finally, it is necessary to point out that a fair system of law and justice that protects its citizens regardless of gender differences is essential for peaceful co-existence among the citizens and for the progress of the country. Thus, Cameroon should strive to build a balanced society by ensuring equality between males and females.

References

Administration of Estates Act, 1925.
African Charter on Human Rights (African Union).
Alice Fodge v. Ndangsi Kette (Suit No. BCA/45/1986, Cameroon, unreported).

Attorney-General of Botswana v. Unity Dow (Botswana Supreme Court, 1992).

Botswana Citizenship Act, 1984.

Buma v. Buma (Suit No. BCA/20/81, Cameroon, unreported).

Che Maabo v. Che Maboo (Suit No. HCF/7MC/97/2M/98, Cameroon, unreported).

Civil Status Registration Ordinance, 1981 (Cameroon).

Constitution of Cameroon, 1996.

Convention Against Torture and Inhuman Treatment (ratified by Cameroon in 1986).

Convention on the Elimination of all forms of Discrimination Against Women (ratified by Cameroon on 23rd August 1994).

Estate of Nchari (Suit No. AE/06/11/96, Cameroon, unreported).

Florence Agwe Nyang v. Emmanuel Agwe Nyang (Suit No. CASWP/CC/08/91, Cameroon, unreported).

International Convention on the Elimination of all Forms of Racial Discrimination (ratified by Cameroon in 1971).

Kang Nsume v. Kang Nsume (Suit No. HCF/38/96, Cameroon, unreported).

Kong Dione Agnes v. Melong Akola Boniface (Suit No. HCK/38/96, Cameroon, unreported).

Kumbongsi v. Kumbongsi (Suit No. CASWP/4/84, Cameroon, unreported).

Labor Code of Cameroon.

Lyonga Christina v. Andrew Lyonga (Suit No. CASWP/5/94, Cameroon, unreported).

Lyonga Ndive v. The people (Suit No. CASWP/13C/90, Cameroon).

Maya Ikome v. Manga Ekenason (Suit No. CASWP/CC76/85, Cameroon, unreported).

Nationality Code of Cameroon.

Ndenno c/ Mme Guamgne Alphonsine (Suit No. 36 of 27th June 1996, Cameroon).

Nforba Aloysius, Bougyisi Elizabeth vs. Nchari Mary Kinyui (ex parte Luanga Nforba Nchari Administrator of the Estate of Nchari Anthony Nforba deceased) (Suit No. AE/06/96/1M/96).

Nganso Tchakounte N. Isabelle v. Nganso Apollinaire (Suit No. CSWP/CC/95, Cameroon, unreported).

Ngassa, V. (1999) *Gender Approach to Court Action.* Editions Saagraph and Friedrich-Ebert-Stiftung.

Ngassa, V. and Time C. (1999) *Gender Law Report*, volume 1. Editions Saagraph and Friedrich-Ebert-Stiftung.

Ngnietedem Etienne v. Tashi Lydia Sinaga (Suit No. BCA/46/86, Cameroon, unreported).

Penal Code of Cameroon.

Rattigan and Ors v. Chief Immigration Officer (Supreme Court of Zimbabwe,

1994).

Rose Ndollo Achu vs. Richard Achu (Suit No. BCA/62/86 of 20th June, 1988, Cameroon, unreported).

Southern Cameroon High Court Law, 1955.

Temple Cole v. Temple Cole (Suit No. caswp/cc/1/99, Cameroon, unreported).

Tufon v. Tufon (Suit No. HCB/59/MC/83, Cameroon, unreported).

Universal Declaration of Human Rights (United Nations Organization).

"Women Children and the Law" (1996) *FIDA Cameroon*. Tencam Press.

Chapter 19

Role of Indigenous Institutions and Processes in Curbing Corruption

O. Oko Elechi

Prairie View A & M University, USA

Introduction

A person familiar with Nigeria's history is likely to agree with the view that corruption is one of the country's most intractable problems. The assertion that corruption is endemic and that there is hardly any government agency or institution that is free of corruption is a truism with which many Nigerians are likely to agree. Corruption is said to occur when a public official takes advantage of his or her office to solicit, accept, or extort money or other property from someone to circumvent the law or rules for the public official's profit or another person's benefit. Corruption is an unethical and illegal behavior that takes place in both the public and private sectors.

Corruption is known to undermine a country's economic development and denigrate its social and political institutions. Also, corruption hampers a government's capacity to govern effectively. Corruption weakens democratic and human rights institutions and undercuts the people's ability to participate in decision-making. There is a strong correlation between corruption and poverty in a country. For Nigeria, it seems accurate to state that the political and legal reforms undertaken by successive governments to eradicate corruption have failed.

Consequently, this chapter makes a case for the employment of Nigerian indigenous institutions and processes of social control to complement the efforts of State institutions and processes in the fight against corruption. The motivation for this paper came after I witnessed the success recorded by the indigenous government of Afikpo community, Nigeria, in enforcing relevant electoral laws better than the State courts. During the 2011 Nigerian national elections, some politicians from Afikpo had employed violence and bribery in attempts to manipulate the elections in their favor. The offending individuals were prosecuted at the indigenous courts, convicted, and fined. And the trial was carried out openly, transparently, and speedily.

What is Corruption?

Corruption is a deviant behavior motivated by economic interests or desire for other advantages. Corruption is committed mainly by people with power and status in the course of their occupations. It involves rarely reported crimes because victims of corruption are sometimes, perhaps often, actively involved in the behavior. Also, the society as a whole, not just the participants in corruption, suffers tremendously. As Aubert (1952) notes, corruption damages social relations, lowers morale, and is capable of producing social disorganization. Corruption occurs when a public official negates the legal and ethical standards of his or her office by carrying out functions or failing to do so for personal gains. Ceesay's (1979, p. 8) definition of corruption will suffice for our purposes here. According to him,

corruption includes all the circumstances in which the

public office holder sacrifices or sells all or part of his judgment on matters within his official purview in return for personal gain. Corruption thus defined includes a direct or tacit agreement between the official and the person requesting action that would benefit the official in exchange for official action.

Corruption is a deviant act that results from both personal and institutional failures. In a country like Nigeria where it is fair to argue that corruption is widespread, the blame for corruption should be placed more on institutional failures than on personal disappointments. A public official in contemporary Nigeria who refuses bribe or fails to take advantage of his or her office to amass wealth risks being viewed as a deviant.[1] However, few would contest the characterization that corruption is pervasive in Nigeria and that the bureaucracy, rather than isolated government officials, bears the greater responsibility. In view of the generally corrupt national environment, can one appropriately describe a Nigerian government official accused or arrested for corrupt practices as a deviant? Along this line of reasoning, Summer (as cited in Kameir & Kursany, 1985, p. 9) ponders:

> If everyone commits a crime, what's left of the concept of the criminal personality? If what counts as crime is much dependent upon the political power to criminalize and the financial power to bribe the police, what is left of the concepts of crime and criminal behavior? What relevance for scientific work would official criminal statistics have? How could one take a sample of prisoners as a sample of criminals?

Despite the all-encompassing nature of corruption in Nigeria, it is pertinent to delineate two categories of corrupt officials in the country. One is the corrupt officials who aggressively solicit kickbacks before they can render the services they are paid to perform. Another category of corrupt officials is made up of those who accept monetary or other valuable gifts from people who require their services. Even in the deviant world, it is interesting to note that there are still standards that guide the practices of public servants. Nigerians can tell apart a good or bad corrupt official.

Insidious corruption makes it difficult for a government to be effective and earn the confidence of the people. According to the Parliamentary Centre, Canada (2000, p. 29), "corruption undermines good governance, distorting policy, leading to poorer public services and infrastructure, reduced spending on health

---

[1] This is not to imply that all Nigerian public officials are corrupt. A significant percentage of those officials still perform their duties as legally, ethically, and morally mandated.

and education, and serious budgetary problems." Again, corruption according to the Parliamentary Centre, Canada, reinforces the culture of corruption. It also can further lead to the social and economic marginalization of the poor. Widespread corruption in a country discourages both local and foreign investors. And, such high level of corruption makes it difficult for a developing country to attract international development aid.

There are many forms of corruption. However, the most common types of corruption in Nigeria include bribery, nepotism, extortion, theft of State assets, diversion of State revenues, mobilization fee racket, contract inflation, over-invoicing, favoritism, and payment of salaries to ghost workers.

Causes of Corruption

To understand the causes of corruption in Nigeria, an appreciation of the nation's political, legal, and social history is imperative. It is particularly difficult to effectively control corruption without a full understanding of what causes it. It is the position of this chapter that the forces that cause corruption in Nigeria are the same powers that impede its prosecution and control. The primary perpetrator of corruption in Nigeria is the Nigerian State. The successive Nigerian governments (both civilian and military) have not been democratic. They do not have the citizens' support. Therefore, the governments lack legitimacy. To sustain themselves in power, they typically resort to intimidation, force, and threat of force to neutralize and remove their opponents. Alternatively, these governments use money, land, and political appointments to bribe and win support among the people. The quest to gain support for the illegitimate regimes extends to indigenous institutions. Thus, the various Nigerian governments have intimidated, shunned, excluded, bribed, and used violence against community leaders, influential community members, religious leaders, as well as political and human rights activists.

It is noteworthy that the post-colonial Nigerian State inherited this strategy of governance from the colonial authorities. The colonial governments of Nigeria were authoritarian. The regimes were not accountable to the people. Those governments did not have the Nigerian people's mandate to govern them. Thus, Nigerians deeply resented the colonial regimes. A key element of the colonial domination was that the indigenous system of government was subordinated to the colonial governments. This trend has continued under the post-colonial governments of Nigeria. Moreover, as the undemocratic Nigerian State shows, corruption is rampant in governmental systems where there are no checks and balances. When a government is involved in breaking its own laws, it emboldens other people to violate the law with impunity.

Other causes of corruption in Nigeria include the lack of political will by the governments to enforce the laws. In addition, the governments lack the moral authority to enforce laws, especially the laws against elite crimes. Further undermining the governments' ability to enforce the laws is the public's skepticism about government agents with authority to enforce laws. Many Nigerians are doubtful that a corrupt agent of government has the commitment, capacity, and moral authority to regulate the activities of other agents or individuals accused of malfeasance. Ordinarily, a criminal prosecution should start with a victim or witness filing a complaint to that effect. However, people are reluctant to file complaints against corrupt government officials because the people do not trust the police. The citizens are widely skeptical that the police or other government agencies with authority to enforce laws are interested or even capable of enforcing the laws.

Earlier in this chapter, I stated that the Nigerian State is the primary source of corruption in the country. That statement (already explained) extends to the fact that the central government of Nigeria dominates the society and holds a stranglehold on all the citizens and the federating units. This means that the federal government of Nigeria is too powerful and it controls all other divisions and sectors of the society in spite of the claim that Nigeria is a federation. This type of domineering relationship is found in Nigeria and perhaps in other parts of the world as well. According to the Parliamentary Centre, Canada (2000, p. 12), "state institutions are large and powerful in relationship to those of civil society and the marketplace, both of which are relatively small and underdeveloped. Within the state, the executive dominates both the legislature and the judiciary and central institutions dominate regional and local governments." Other branches of government in Nigeria, such as the Legislature and the Judiciary, that are supposed to act as sources of checks and balances against executive domination and abuse are marginalized and ineffective. Furthermore, the civil society and the media are relatively weak and dependent on the State for their survival and therefore unable to play their watchdog role against executive abuse. As the Parliamentary Centre, Canada (2000, p. 14) notes,

> the weaknesses in state institutions are often compounded by the weaknesses of civil society and the media. Instead of vigorous, independent spheres of influence able to hold government accountable, civil society organizations are often dependent on or closely allied with government. Like watchdog agencies, media is often dependent on if not under the direct control of the executive.

Assessing the Nigerian State and Its Efforts to Control Corruption

A key point of this chapter is that the political and legal reforms put in place so far to eradicate corruption in Nigeria have failed to achieve their objectives because such measures failed to recognize the strategic importance of African indigenous institutions of social control in the fight against corruption. Judicial reforms, for example, have been a top down approach with minimal impact upon the behavior or attitudes of Nigerian elites who have the greatest opportunity to engage in corruption. The position of this chapter is that African indigenous institutions of social control remain relevant and viable even for corruption control. It is obvious that, contrary to the suggestion by some of the extant literature on the subject, the indigenous institutions of social control have not withered away nor have Western-inspired State institutions of social control replaced them. For example, Baade & Everett (1963, p. 1) raise concerns about whether the indigenous laws and Western-inspired legal systems can co-exist and again, if the indigenous laws are suitable for resolving conflicts in modern industrial and heterogeneous societies. They ponder (1) "whether a modern society can long remain viable if it has an interpersonal conflict of laws system" and (2) "whether a revealed divine law is or can be rendered sufficiently adaptable for the purposes of resolving the typical conflicts of an industrial society." Baade & Everett's (1963) questions notwithstanding, for Nigeria as well as other African and non-African countries, there is abundant literature verifying the continued importance and viability of indigenous institutions and processes (*Grounded Law*) in the social control of a modern State (see examples, Okereafọezeke, 1996; Austin, 1999; Okereafọezeke, 2002; Elechi, 2006; Okafo, 2009).

Therefore, this chapter contends that indigenous institutions of social control remain viable and effective in justice delivery, and as a bulwark against corruption and oppression, especially by the most and least influential in a modern State. As Christie (1993) has suggested, the two most difficult classes of people to regulate are the upper and under classes. This is because the upper class is part of the ruling class and can use their massive influence to manipulate the political process to their advantage. They are also able to emasculate the legal processes to serve their parochial interests. Moreover, it is apparent that the dominant class operates on a different moral standard from the rest of society. Corruption is primarily a crime of the dominant class. The underclass, according to Christie, is also difficult to control as they have nothing to lose. Loss of reputation and even freedom, as important as it may seem, is not a priority concern for someone that is marginalized economically, socially, and politically. Thus, Christie (1993, p. 61) notes:

a basic tenet of social control is that those who own very much and those who own nothing are the two extremes that are most difficult to govern. This is so because those who own much also have much power, and those with little, have nothing to lose. They have no stocks in life, no property, may be not even a social network and thus not even honor.

The political and legal reforms put in place in Nigeria to control corruption are largely ineffective. The conventional division of powers enshrined in the country's Constitution to provide checks and balances and prohibit abuse and domination by one agent of government, and make government more accountable to the people, is also not working. In support of the view that checks and balances in government are often absent or insufficient, Diamond, et al. (1988, p. 65) note: "I posit based on my experience that the integrity of the legislature and executive is so suspect, and that the pressures for abuse so powerful, that some wholly new type of institutional check is necessary." This statement accurately captures the situation in Nigeria. Furthermore, the political and legal reforms to control corruption have left the existing dysfunctional social structure intact. As Falola & Ihonvbere (1985, p. 230) observe, "the structures, institutions, class and production relations, external linkages and class contradictions and struggles remain the same."

Therefore, for an effective and efficient check on corruption in Nigeria, the indigenous institutions and processes must be incorporated into governance and State social control. The relegation of the indigenous institutions and processes to the background is at the country's peril. The African indigenous system of justice is open and accessible to all, and the processes are transparent. As Ekeh (1975) has eloquently argued, even African elites remain loyal and respectful of African indigenous political and social institutions. According to Eke, this is because of the immense tangible and intangible benefits they derive from the indigenous institutions. The benefits include both social and psychological security, which they do not get from State institutions. This accounts for why African elites are likely to make sometimes even personal costly sacrifices to support and nurture the indigenous institutions. Besides, Africans are socialized to appreciate and respect the morality, transparency, and accountability values inherent in these institutions. The moral linkage to the private realm is very strong unlike that of the civic public. The average African does not have a bad conscience exploiting and undermining State institutions. As Ekeh (1975, p. 100) has observed, the African elite is caught between these two moral dichotomies, namely the "simultaneous adaptation to two mentally contraposing orders. One solution to this problem formulated by the educated African is to define one of these orders in moral terms and the other in amoral terms."

To clarify Ekeh's (1975) postulation, a brief account of how the State emerged in Africa is imperative. It is instructive that European countries as part of their colonization of African countries imposed the European political, legal, religious, social, and educational systems on African societies. This development, according to Eke, created two publics in Africa – the primordial and civic publics. In the primordial public, priority is accorded primary relationships such as peers, family, and kingship groupings. The civic public, on the other hand, is as represented by State institutions such as the military, police, and the bureaucracy. These institutions are alien to Africa as they were foisted on Africa by the colonial authorities. These developments have implications for democracy, rule of law, and accountability in governance. To demonstrate further the significance of this historical account and its implications for the behavior of African States, a brief comparison with how the State emerged to become the dominant agent of modernization in Europe is essential.

The State in Europe evolved over several centuries following a protracted struggle for supremacy amongst the dominant power groups, such as the Feudal Lords, the Aristocracy, the Church, and the Mercantile powers. The constellation of power and authority under the State was the ensuing compromise. For our purposes here, the resultant effect was one public with the Judeo-Christian belief systems as the underlying moral foundation. According to Eke, despite the fact that the private and public realms are easily distinguishable in the Western countries, their moral foundations derive primarily from the Judeo-Christian belief systems. Westerners therefore have no difficulties identifying with the State institutions and their functions in the citizens' social, cultural, religious, and political lives.

Another important factor to be taken into consideration is that pre-colonial African indigenous governments had effective checks and balances such that leaders that were corrupt and abused their powers were easily removed from office. African traditional leaders did not have monopoly over the instrument of violence unlike the present African governments that can use violence and threats of violence to sustain themselves in power against the will of the people. To govern effectively and ensure proper social control of the citizens, African leaders must be seen as legitimate and must have goodwill. Christie (1981) opines that any power wielder that does not see himself or herself as vulnerable has the potential to abuse that power. The most effective means of checking corruption and abuse of power is through the ordinary people who are directly impacted by the exercise of power. Pre-colonial African leaders were (and most post-colonial traditional leaders remain) vulnerable and therefore sensitive and accountable to the people. According to Christie (1981, p. 85), for a leader to be vulnerable, the following factors must be present: "vulnerability might be established in several ways. Three are particularly important. These are vulnerability through equality in status, through equality in qualifications, and through close and available physical proximity." The factors are present and a lot easier to identify in African indigenous governments and societies than in a modern State.

At a minimum, the African indigenous justice system is a viable supplement to the State institutions of social control. As Elechi (2006, p. xvi) has noted,

> the [indigenous justice] system is flexible, dynamic, and allows for the democratic participation of villagers. Group interest and social solidarity are the goals of the justice process. Victims, offenders, their families, as well as the general community, are involved in defining harm and repairing harm, and resolutions of conflict are arrived at through rigorous discussions of all stakeholders. Judgments are based on consensus and derive from available evidence and the [reasoned] opinions of participants.

In support of Elechi's (2006, p. xvi) statement, Simon Ottenberg, a renowned Africanist scholar, in the foreword to Elechi's book, states as follows:

> The present system of state and federal government justice in Nigeria is a farce; it is rarely fair, it seldom works well and it often leaves one or both sides involved in a case financially in ruin from the pressure of having to bribe the police, and even a judge, in order to have a hearing, no less a fair one. Professor Elechi's writings contribute to a broader move among Nigerians today to rethink governance in the country ....

To be sure, the African indigenous justice system is not perfect or incorruptible. However, it is more responsive to the needs of the people and, as Okafọ (2009) has demonstrated, it can be redesigned (or "reconstructed") to improve its functioning and capacity to meet the peoples' expectations of governance and social control. And as the Parliamentary Centre, Canada (2000, p. 10), observes,

> accountability flourishes when a healthy balance of power exists between state, civil society, the marketplace and the global village, with no one institutional sphere being in absolute control. The same principle of balance applies within the state to relations between the executive, legislative and judicial branches, and between levels of government from the national to the local. In this model, extreme imbalances of power are seen as dangerous if not fatal for good governance.

In short, Nigerian and other African indigenous governments and processes have strong relevance in the lives of the people and must be part of the balanced ecology of governance for an accountable, transparent and participatory democracy to flourish.

Necessary State Actions for Corruption Control

For corruption control efforts to produce the desired result, a variety of techniques is required. As the Parliamentary Centre, Canada (2000) observes, for corruption control to be effective, it must entail a multi-dimensional and holistic approach. The control efforts must recognize that corruption stems more from systemic failures than individual problems. The emphasis must therefore be on system changes rather than individual changes. Such changes must include political, legal, administrative, and economic reforms. The civil society must also be integrated into the crime control mechanism. In this respect, the media and other Non-Governmental Organizations must be involved in the campaign to raise public awareness about the effects of corruption. They must also play active role in monitoring and controlling corruption.

In recognition of the critical role of the State agencies of law and justice in controlling corruption, the United Nations Organization (UN) recently collaborated with various Nigerian law and justice agencies to produce a comprehensive report on the specific steps that the Nigerian government should take to control corruption in the country. Following meetings between them on July 6 and 7, 2010, the UN Office on Drugs and Crime and the Nigerian National Judicial Institute (involving the following government agencies – the Federal High Court; the High Court of the Federal Capital Territory; the Lagos State High Court; Senior prosecutors and investigators of the Code of Conduct Bureau, the Economic and Financial Crimes Commission, and the Independent Corrupt Practices and Other Related Offenses Commission) issued a Communiqué regarding corruption control in Nigeria. The Communiqué contains the following recommendations to the Nigerian Attorney-General and Minister of Justice:

1. As an immediate action, review and re-introduce the Non-Conviction-Based-Asset-Forfeiture Bill;

2. Develop a witness protection bill in line with the requirements of the United Nations Convention against Corruption;

3. Introduce a whistleblower protection bill, as an executive bill, drawing on already existing legislative proposals

and international good practices;

4. Review and re-introduce the bill for the amendment of the Evidence Act, in order to ensure the admissibility of electronic and digital evidence;

5. Limit the right to interlocutory appeals, in particular as relates to cases handled by the EFCC and the ICPC, including the consideration of a constitutional amendment;

6. Introduce other amendments to the Criminal and Penal Procedure Acts, as appropriate, aimed to facilitate the handling of cases of corruption, economic and financial crimes (including the regulation of plea bargaining) drawing from examples already adopted at State levels, in particular the administration of Criminal Justice Law of Lagos State;

7. Introduce amendments to the EFCC and ICPC Acts, allowing for cases of corruption, economic, and financial crimes, in particular as they relate to politically exposed persons (PEPs), to be tried in jurisdictions, other than the one of the locus of the crimes.

(Reproduced from the United Nations Office on Drugs and Crime (UNODC) and National Judicial Institute, Abuja, July 6-7, 2010).

If Nigeria implements the recommendations outlined in the Communiqué, corruption would be significantly curtailed in the country.

However, for farther reaching, more enduring, and more effective corruption control, indigenous institutions and processes must be involved.

Further Analysis of Indigenous Institutions and Processes and the Control of Corruption

This chapter recommends that the indigenous governments of Nigeria be integrated into the social control network of the State. What happened during the 2011 Nigerian national elections demonstrates that the indigenous governments can be effective in the control of corruption, especially electoral corruption. Since independence, the official governments in power in Nigeria have typically manipulated elections. The election rigging takes different forms, including sales of ballot papers to the highest bidder, substitution of ballot boxes, invalidation of genuine ballot papers, disappearance of polling officials on the day of the poll, double counting of ballot papers, use of money or violence to intimidate opponents and the electorate, and the general subjugation of laws and policies guiding the election. As a specific instance, all modern elections in the Afikpo North Local Government Area of the country's Ebonyi State have been rigged through the means listed above.

Determined to check the political crimes and excesses in their domain during the 2011 national elections, the Afikpo community resolved to call the politicians to order through the exercise of the indigenous government's authority. The community demonstrated its determination to ensure that elections in the area were as free and fair as possible. They invited some local politicians who had employed violence against political opponents to one of the indigenous government's tribunals. The tribunal tried the politicians. Some of them were found guilty of corrupting the electoral process. The guilty persons were made to pay fines. They were also required to apologize to the community, which they did. It should be pointed out that the process of determining guilt in this and other indigenous tribunals is open and transparent. Also, conflicts are speedily resolved in the tribunals. The indigenous government in Afikpo community seized the opportunity presented by the electoral issues to call a meeting of the political class in the area. The government issued a strong warning to the politicians that the community would not tolerate electoral corruption of any kind.

It is important to emphasize that the state governments and the indigenous governments in Nigeria have interacted since the creation of the country's thirty-six states. Actually, many of the cases handled at the Afikpo community indigenous tribunals were delegated from the state courts. Moreover, the state courts generally take into evidence decisions reached at the indigenous courts. However, the 2011 Afikpo community initiative to check electoral corruption is the first time in the history of the relationship between state institutions and the indigenous institutions that the indigenous institutions are playing a major role in defining the terms of the relationship. It is tantamount to an indigenous court taking it upon itself to enforce state laws. It is not really that the indigenous institutions are dictating to the state institutions. Rather, the indigenous institutions are exercising the power they have over the residents of their community.

It so happened that the political gladiators in the 2011 national elections were competing to represent the Afikpo community in state institutions. The position of the community elders was (and remains) that if the actions of the political actors in the community interfere with the quality of life of the people, that the elders cannot sit by and let things continue in that way. Furthermore, the elders insist that the 2011 elections and future elections must reflect the will of the people.

To better appreciate the Afikpo community leaders' knowledge of the relevant issues, authority, and appeal to the generality of the citizens, it is important to note the demographic shift in the community. The elders who preside over the indigenous institutions are today mostly highly educated professionals, including retired judges, professors, lawyers, teachers, civil servants, and other professionals of note. They have mastery of the laws and policies guiding the operations of State institutions and the relationship between the indigenous and State institutions. Obviously, the State actors in the community do not intimidate such highly qualified community elders. Additionally, it is appropriate to observe here that these grassroots institutions are good places to start public education and enlightenment about the dangers of corruption and authoritarian governance. The credibility that the institutions enjoy among the people is likely to encourage more citizens to accept the anti-corruption and anti-authoritarian campaigns.

It is pertinent to describe the two main tribunals in Afikpo community that convened to examine the allegations of violence leveled against some members of the political class. In Afikpo, as in most other human communities, numerous grievances, conflicts, and disputes arise that require informal or formal management. In this community, there are therefore understandably many institutions established to address the many cases that arise in the daily interactions among the people. The institutions for conflict resolution in the community include the Age-grade system, the village groupings, the Matrilineal groupings, the Patrilineal groupings, the Family groupings, the Elders Ad-hoc tribunal, the Village-group traditional courts, the Chiefs-in-Council, etc. (cf. similar institutions in Okereafo̟ezeke, 1996; 2002; Okafọ, 2009). The advantages these institutions of conflict resolution have over the State courts are that "in these institutions, justice-making is cost-free, participatory, and effective. Disputes receive immediate attention and resolution" (Elechi, 2006, p. 117).

One of the indigenous tribunals where the cases against the politicians in the 2011 national elections were heard is an Elders Ad-hoc tribunal. The tribunal belongs to one of the villages where electoral violence took place. This tribunal is not permanent and can be constituted when needed to deal with any conflict that may arise. Ottenberg (1971) notes that the elders' special court, such as the Elders Ad-hoc tribunal, is not part of the regular administrative or legal structure of the community. As its name suggests, the court is created and dissolved after the particular matter that it is invoked to deal with is addressed. Typically, the court is convened to deal with emergencies. As in other tribunals in the community, participants are free to express their opinions and decisions are reached based on the evidence presented and the reasoned opinion of participants. Those found guilty are made to pay a fine. The fine is determined based on the seriousness of the matter. The guilty party must also apologize to the community for the conduct that breached its peace and harmony.

Those cases that the tribunal does not resolve may be appealed to the Village-Group Traditional Courts. The courts sit at the central market square (cf. Austin's, 1999, "banana justice"). There are two components of these courts operated by the indigenous government of Afikpo. One of the courts is presided over by the junior elders in their fifties and early sixties age bracket. The second court is administered by the senior elders in their mid-sixties and older. The two courts sit concurrently every market day – which is every four days. The courts both have legislative and judicial functions. They make laws governing the administration of the community; also all the elders present arbitrate cases brought to the attention of the courts. The guilty party in each case resolved is asked to pay a fine.

One of the electoral corruption cases earlier resolved at the Elders Ad-hoc council of one of the villages in Afikpo was also brought to the Village-Group traditional court. This is unusual, as the case had been settled in one of the community's recognized tribunals. However, the elders reasoned that issues bordering on electoral violence and corruption were serious matters that needed the adjudication of the entire community. Accordingly, the elders heard and decided the case. The party found at fault was made to pay a fine and apologize to the entire community for the misbehavior. The significance of this matter is that the traditional justice system seemed more effective in enforcing the state laws than the state courts. The nature of the indigenous courts is such that it is much more difficult for politicians to manipulate the courts through such tactics as legal technicalities and unreasonable delays. Again, justice is speedily, openly, and transparently done in the indigenous courts.

The genesis of the forms of corruption in Nigeria and the various justice institutions given the responsibility of curbing the vice should shed more light on the successes and failures that these institutions have endured. The prevailing attitude in numerous African communities, including those of Nigeria, is that government property is nobody's property. This way of behaving is a colonial legacy. State institutions, processes, and property are generally viewed as alien. The institutions, etc. came with colonialism. Regarding institutions in particular, the colonial authorities made no effort to integrate the governmental institutions with the pre-existing indigenous institutions. Furthermore, the colonial institutions were not democratic. Nigerians, like other Africans, opposed those institutions. One way of coping with the alien and oppressive institutions was to undermine them. Stealing from the State was not discouraged and even sometimes perceived as a heroic act. African elites working with the colonial governments were expected to exploit the State for the benefit of the people. Unfortunately, this attitude has remained despite the fact that Africans now operate the State institutions. On the other hand, Africans are raised to recognize the important role of the indigenous institutions in their everyday lives and well-being. The Africans therefore view the indigenous institutions as legitimate and worthy of support and protection.

In the post-colonial era, Nigerians, like other post-colonial peoples, can be socialized to appreciate the danger corruption poses to their well-being. However, in doing so, efforts should be made to integrate State and indigenous institutions of social control. The indigenous institutions are or ought to be recognized as extensions of the peoples' lives (Okafọ, 2009). The citizens broadly regard the indigenous institutions as legitimate. As Ekeh (1975) has noted, Nigerian people derive immense tangible and intangible benefits from the indigenous institutions. The people therefore view the indigenous institutions as fair and legitimate. Moreover, the people have access to and actively participate in the institutions' processes. As the indigenous institutions have grassroots support and are accountable to the people, it is easier to mobilize the people through these institutions to defend democracy and promote probity and accountability in the State institutions.

A system based on egalitarian and democratic foundation and principles has a higher chance of meeting its community's needs and expectations (Christie, 1993). Due to the close proximity the leaders of such a community have with the ordinary people, the citizens are in a strong position to resist any attempt at high handedness and abuse by the leaders of the institutions. By contrast, citizens of a restricted and autocratic society lack the opportunity and means to challenge abuses by their leaders. The leaders of the egalitarian and democratic institutions, unlike those of the restricted and autocratic establishments, count on their goodwill for survival rather than rely on their power and ability to mobilize instruments of violence to sustain them in power. In short, participatory democracy is incompatible with authoritarian and corrupt governance. Therefore, the enthronement of democratic values and ethos and their sustenance are higher when the ordinary people – those at the receiving end of policies – are actively involved in articulating and developing the policies.

However, experience has also shown that powerful interest groups can and do influence decisions even in an egalitarian system like the African indigenous institutions of social control. Determined interest groups can mobilize their supporters and push their positions to such an extent that they can overwhelm other stakeholders. For example, in Afikpo community, there have been times when wealthy and politically connected individuals lobbied powerful speakers and opinion leaders in the community to influence the decision-making processes. This type of influence can lead to injustice. However, the good thing about the indigenous justice system is that a matter can be revisited if people realize that a mistake has been made and a petition for a re-examination of the particular matter is submitted.

The Afikpo community example shows how indigenous justice can be used to fight corruption in a modern State. At a minimum, the community efforts can complement those of the State agencies. The ingredients of the indigenous justice, including speed, openness, transparency, and credibility, endear it to the citizens. Thus, it is not surprising that the people widely perceive the indigenous courts as legitimate. The legitimacy derives from the economic, social, and other benefits the community members derive from the indigenous system. Furthermore, the courts' legitimacy derives from the fact that they are broadly inclusive. For example, the only requirement for participation in the Afikpo Community courts' proceedings is age. Thus, being a gerontocratic system, every male of age has the opportunity to participate in the judicial process. It should be pointed out that females have analogous institutions for conflict resolution. However, the male institutions address all conflicts that emanate in the community, while the female institutions of conflict resolution deal with conflicts amongst the women in the community.

In addition to their role as avenues for resolving cases, the community courts are major agents of socialization and re-socialization. Issues concerning the welfare of the community are reviewed in the courts and judgments pronounced. The broadly inclusive deliberations, judgments, and post-verdict enforcement efforts serve as invaluable avenues and tools for socializing and re-socializing the citizens on the proper standard of behavior in the community. A party at fault is sanctioned as necessary. However, he or she is given another chance to modify the impugned behavior and bring it in line with the community's standard.

It is important however to point out that despite the popularity and power of the indigenous courts, litigants who are not satisfied with the judgments of the courts can appeal the judgments to state courts. State courts have power and authority over the indigenous courts. Even then, the influence of the indigenous courts over the life of community members cannot be overemphasized.

Conclusion

Corruption, like other deviant behaviors, is learned. Corruption is often complex. It involves crimes perpetrated by people with power and influence. Efforts to control corruption in Nigeria through political, legal, and administrative reforms have failed. This is partly because corruption results more from systemic issues than individual failings. Besides, the people profiting from corruption are typically those with the power to make or enforce the laws and other policies regulating corruption. These people are therefore able to circumvent the system and render the laws and policies ineffective. The position of this chapter is that it is important that the Nigerian governments at the various levels should give serious attention to properly balancing State and community (local) corruption control efforts. Accordingly, the indigenous institutions of social control should be included in the ecology of governance. It is clear that the indigenous institutions are not withering away; they remain relevant in the affairs of the people. Moreover, the caliber of people governing these institutions is comparable to those of State institutions. In fact, the personnel of the indigenous institutions tend to be more matured and have a higher appreciation for stability and community survival.

Regarding the judicial process in the indigenous institutions, participation in the courts is voluntary. Notwithstanding, most of the citizens in many communities participate directly or indirectly in the process. The people participate because they care about the community well-being, especially considering that there is no remuneration for participation. Again, the arbitration process is open, transparent, and allows for the active participation of the community members. It is therefore much more difficult to manipulate the process, unlike the situation among the State institutions.

Finally, the indigenous institutions of social control described in this study are for illustrative purposes only. For greater participation of Nigerian indigenous institutions in corruption control, every community can search within itself for the institutions that can be mobilized to enthrone democratic values and ethos, rule of law, and accountability in the society and its government. A fundamental point remains that the active participation of the people in their governance is a key element of a comprehensive approach for curbing corruption. The State alone cannot control the vice. It is therefore the recommendation of this chapter that the fight against corruption in Nigeria is more likely to succeed if the official Local, State, and Federal governments see value in strengthening and integrating the indigenous institutions into governance, and initiate and implement policies accordingly.

References

Aubert, V. (1952) "White-Collar Crime and Social Structure," *American Journal of Sociology*, pp. 263-271.

Austin, Timothy (1999) *Banana Justice*. Westport, Connecticut, USA: Greenwood Publishing Group.

Baade, H. W. & R. O. Everett, (eds.) (1963) *African Law – New Law for New Nations*. New York, NY, USA: Oceana Publications.

Ceesay, M. M. M. (1979) "White-Collar Crime in the Gambia," *Institutt for Kriminologi Stensilserie N. 34*, Universitetet i Oslo.

Christie, N. (1981) *Limits to Pain*. Oslo, Norway: Universitetet Forlaget.

Christie, N. (1993) *Crime Control as Industry*. London, England: Routledge.

Diamond, L., J. J. Linz, & S. M. Lipset (eds.) (1988) *Democracy in Developing Countries – Africa*. London, England: Adamantine Press.

Eke, P. P. (1975) "Colonialism and the Two Publics in Africa: A Theoretical Statement," *Comparative Studies in Society and History*, Vol. 17.

Elechi, O. O. (2005) "African Indigenous Justice System," *Encyclopedia of Criminology*, by Richard A. Wright and J. Mitchell Miller (eds.). New York, NY, USA: Routledge Publishers, Taylor and Francis Group, pp. 18-22.

Elechi, O. O. (2005) "Nigeria, Corruption" Encyclopedia of Criminology, by Richard A. Wright and J. Mitchell Miller (eds.). New York, NY, USA: Routledge Publishers, Taylor and Francis Group, pp. 1043-1047.

Elechi, O. O. (2006) *Doing Justice Without the State: The Afikpo (Ehugbo) Nigeria Model*. New York, NY, USA: Routledge (Taylor and Francis Group Publishers).

Falola, T. & J. Ihonvbere (1985) *The Rise and Fall of Nigeria's Second Republic*. London, England: Zed Books.

Kameir, E. & I. Kursany (1985) "Corruption as the 'Fifth' Factor of Production in the Sudan." Research Report No. 72. Scandinavian Institute of African Studies, Uppsala.

Okafọ, Nọnso (2009) *Reconstructing Law and Justice in a Postcolony*. Surrey, England and Burlington, USA: Ashgate Publishing.

Okereafọezeke (Okafọ), Nọnso (1996) *The Relationship Between Informal and Formal Strategies of Social Control: An Analysis of the Contemporary Methods of Dispute Processing Among the Igbos of Nigeria*, UMI Number 9638581, Ann Arbor, Michigan, USA: University Microfilms.

Okereafọezeke (Okafọ), Nọnso (2002) *Law and Justice in Post-British Nigeria: Conflicts and Interactions Between Native and Foreign Systems of Social Control in Igbo*. Westport, Connecticut, USA: Greenwood Press.

Ottenberg, S. (1971) *Leadership and Authority in an African Society: The Afikpo Village-Group*. Seattle, Washington, USA: University of Washington Press.

The Parliamentary Centre, Canada (2000) *Controlling Corruption: A Parliamentarian's Handbook* (2nd Edition). In Partnership with the World Bank Institute and Support from the Canadian International Development Agency (see www.parlcent.ca).

Punch, M. (2009) *Police Corruption: Deviance, Accountability and Reform in Policing*. Portland, Oregon, USA: Willan Publishing.

UNODC/NJI (2010) Corruption Casework Policy Roundtable.

Chapter 20

Coping With Payola: Field Ventures From Mindanao, Philippines[1] [2]

W. Timothy Austin
Indiana University of Pennsylvania, USA

---

[1] Reprinted by permission of the Society for Applied Anthropology from *Human Organization*, v. 67, n. 2.

[2] This project was supported by a grant from the United States Institute of Peace and a Senate Foundation grant from Indiana University of Pennsylvania, Pennsylvania, USA. Some of the findings reflect earlier awards from the Fulbright program and the National Science Foundation (both of the USA). Special thanks must go to Edilberto M. and Trinidad Mugot, and also Elizabeth M. Austin for conceptual derivations and translations of *Tagalog* and *Cebuano* terms. Portions of this paper were presented at the conferences of the American Society of Criminology in Los Angeles, California, in 2006 and the Academy of Criminal Justice Sciences in Cincinnati, Ohio, in 2008.

Abstract

Based on on-site observations and field interviews in the northwest coastal region of Mindanao of the southern Philippines, this chapter presents a typology of bribery and extortion. The manner in which payola is paid under-the-table in the routine life of locals is discussed along with how such activity appears to be approaching normality. Of concern is how a payola abundant landscape affects the field worker. Several of Donald Black's propositions are given further clarification.

Key Words: Bribery; Extortion; Philippines; Mindanao; Donald Black

Introduction

The Issue

In earlier years while conducting fieldwork on the northwestern coast of Mindanao, it did not occur to me that as an outside researcher I would be forced to come to grips with the constant barrage of briberous and extortionate relationships that pervade the marketplace, public utility companies, government operations, and elsewhere.[1] Giving and receiving some sort of payola is second nature to locals and many would find such near normalized activity rather odd as an object of study. Certainly, payola has flourished for a long time and not just in the Philippines. Bribery and extortion are cited in the most ancient documents, including the Codes of Hammurabi, the Old Testament, and the earliest of Egyptian, Aztec, Greek, and Roman texts (Lasswell, 1963, p. 690).

The following observations were penned while on a brief research venture during the summer of 2006 and reflect cross-referencing of side comments and anecdotes made in field notes about bribery and extortion over the past twenty years in the southern Philippines (see Austin, 1999).

What is Payola?

Actually, the word payola is not commonly used in the research setting. Rather, the term *hip-hip* (meaning "to hide" or to "secretly put something away") is widespread in the Visayan language at the research site. The term *hip-hip* may have originated with a reference to placing a hand on the hip near the wallet to suggest money hidden away in the back pocket. The term *"lagay"* (literally meaning "to put") is more typical in the national language of Tagalog. *Lagay* can

---

[1] Perhaps the bigger issue was that my primary research focus during earlier field trips emphasized other themes such as "Muslim-Christian conflict" or "Informal dispute resolution." The prevalence of bribery and extortion appeared serendipitously and opened the door to new avenues of inquiry. Yet, the ubiquitous nature of such activity proved disconcerting and something to which I quickly learned I would have to adapt.

mean to put something (i.e., cash) under-the-table as in a bribe. Also, *lagay* is sometimes used at the research site as street slang for male genitalia that, as with payola, occasionally pertains to covert deviance so the context of word usage becomes important.

In the southern Philippines, one does not necessarily think of payola in the strict legal sense. That is, technically, offering something of value to influence a public official is referred to as bribery and is generally a felony in most nations. Yet, at the research setting, one may try to influence others to gain some advantage and/or be intimidated to the point where they give payola outside the strict legal definition—for instance, not involving public officials. Also, the flip side of bribery is when a public official intimidates or coerces a person to the point where a person feels compelled to make available something of value (payola) out of fear of some kind of reprisal (i.e., extortion). Both bribery and extortion are outlawed behaviors in the Philippines though rarely prosecuted. These two activities may be seen at opposite ends of a continuum and tend to morph into each other at the center so that it is difficult to see whether one has freely offered a bribe or has been extorted. In northwest Mindanao, many forms of payola concern what might best be categorized as social deviance rather than unlawful behavior, although any form irritates the field researcher who likely will find it impossible to escape its impact.[2]

An Avoided Area of Study

Research on bribery and extortion has been surprisingly sparse. Myrdal suggested the topics of bribery and extortion may have been avoided by researchers in favor of less sensitive issues of study (1968, pp. 937-951). Surely, gaining permission to enter another nation to study the extent and character of its corruption could be challenging. As well, in recent times, receiving the blessing of rigorous "institutional review boards" (IRBs) could also prove problematic, particularly if the researcher would be identifying, even if unintentional, actual occurrences of illegal behavior (see, for example, Berg, Austin, and Zuern, 1992, cf., Seiber, 1992).[3]

---

[2] Even though field workers typically remain as outsiders, they still can feel the impact of the very deviant or illegal behaviors they may be scrutinizing. Occasionally I was approached by extorters and at times found that the only way to efficiently carry on among locals was to behave as a local by offering favors (pesos) under-the-table for needed goods or services. This can be an annoyance if not an irritation.

[3] When a researcher returns to the field on multiple occasions, it is likely that he or she is aware of certain unsavory, deviant, or even illegal practices the researcher may encounter. A decision must be made as to just how much an IRB needs to know, particularly if the researcher wants to ultimately gain permission. A delicate balance must be found between the researcher and the IRB to insure ethi-

Setting and Procedures

This paper draws upon field research in the southern Philippines over the past several decades that allowed for the establishment of a long-term network of informants (Austin, 1987; 1989; 1991; 1995; 2003). However, during the summer of 2006, a visit to the province of Lanao del Norte specifically addressed the issues of bribery and extortion with particular focus on their impact on outsiders. At least forty in-depth interviews were conducted in and around the province's only city of Iligan. Frequent side-trips to the rural inland region and to the small coastal towns south of the city rounded out the interviews to include professionals (physicians, lawyers, educators, government officials) as well as farm laborers, retirees, and students. Although the research emphasizes Iligan City and the adjacent region on the northwest shoreline of Mindanao, similar findings will predictably be found in the northern cities of Cebu and Manila.

Theoretical Undercurrents

As so often happens with fieldwork, this paper did not originate with any explicit attempt to test theory or specific hypotheses. Rather, this discussion of bribery and extortion happened after the fact. That is, while living at the research setting and collecting field notes on other issues, it became apparent that as a field worker, I was immersed in the middle of a wide variety of bribing and extortionate relationships from which I could not disentangle myself. Notes were taken and laid aside for future pondering. It also became clear, after the fact, that Donald Black's work on the relationship between behavior and law (1976) and the social structure of "right and wrong" (1993) could dove-tail with the field notes on bribery and payola as observed in Mindanao. The field observations could work to add clarification to a few of Black's propositions as they may apply to bribery and extortion. It should be pointed out that the observations here apply to examples of bribery or extortion as performed by individuals. Yet, the individuals described do link to larger group behaviors that allows for a more appropriate link to Black's analysis of how various forms of behavior – deviance and illegality – pertain to the larger social structure. Specific connections to several of Black's propositions will be set forth in the Discussion and Theoretical Overview section of this paper.

Shades of Payola

Whether one is talking about bribery or extortion, the issue involves a transfer of things of value often against one's will. At least eight examples impact on fieldwork in Mindanao and deserve clarification. Most, but not all involve

---

cal conduct while at the same time only disclosing what is specifically asked for by the IRB.

cash.

The Case of Beggars

Consider the issue of street beggars. I recall being in Iligan City in the southern Philippines a few years ago and being confronted with throngs of children following me for blocks paparazzi style shouting peso, peso, peso! My first instinct was to hand over some loose change. After all, the exchange rate for a Philippine peso to United States dollar was only two cents in 2006. A Filipino companion suggested I best ignore them. He warned that a few cents was not much but then other needy children will be around the corner and may not be content with only a peso. Manila, for example, claims as many as 100,000 street children (Arquiza, 1997, p. 15). I envisioned a feeding frenzy against my limited government budget that did not include payola. Technically speaking, this is not extortion in the legal sense because the beggars were not public employees. Yet, if the field worker acquiesces and hands over a peso to shake off a stalking beggar, extortive behavior has taken place. One feels obliged to hand over something of value to ward off some perceived impairment of freedom or harm in the immediate future even if just down the street. Some well-to-do locals have been observed tossing coins out the window of their vehicles in order to appease street dwellers before the dwellers get a chance to antagonize the locals for handouts when they exit their vehicle.

Offering money willingly to keep someone off your back can also be viewed as approaching bribery.[4] Coin tossing from the vehicle window can be occasionally observed as vehicle passengers pass through the many military or police checkpoints in the rural regions that were known to be hideouts for religious or communist extremists. The assumption was that a few coins from passing vehicles might appease the checkpoint guards who were known to receive low pay or infrequent paychecks. Yet, this act can be viewed either as latent extortion or mild bribery depending on the motive for offering cash.

---

[4] Without question, experiencing the begging from the perspective of the one being pursued is a learning experience that can only be fully understood from the inside. Consequently, as a researcher with some loose change, I occasionally welcomed the experience if only to be able to gain heightened subjective understanding of what was going on. One astute manuscript reviewer was concerned if begging should, in fact, be seen as extortion. The point is that from a social psychological perspective the behavior is extortive, or one feels they have been extorted, even though it may not involve a public official demanding payoffs from a citizen. The complex behavior of "tipping" for service rendered, as in a restaurant, is relevant to this discussion. If one feels compelled to offer a tip in order to avoid poor service in the future, one can logically conclude that one is being extorted even if mildly so. If a tip is given only to assist a struggling waiter, or a pizza-delivery person, then it would not be a result of extortion.

Bantay Boys

A more intricate example of extortion is seen in the case of the *"bantay"* boys (meaning watch or guard). Once, I drove a jeep to the local market in the center of town. A cluster of boys surrounded the jeep yelling *"bantay, bantay!"* They were volunteering to watch my jeep while I was in the market place. If I say yes, they will protect it for me. If I say no, when I return, the jeep may be missing a part or two, doubtlessly taken by the *bantay* boys. Most drivers say "yes" and accept the extortion, even if mild. After all, if you are driving a vehicle, you must be wealthy in the eyes of the *bantay* boys. You have been coerced to provide money even if against your will. Actually, the *bantay* boys appear rather highly organized and will often "watch" or pretend to watch numerous vehicles simultaneously, sometimes with an adult in the distance regulating and supervising their game and taking a cut of the profits reminiscent of Oliver Twist.[5] Both the begging and *Bantay* boys are appropriate examples of individual interaction but with an understanding of organized group activity behind the scenes supporting the specific person with whom the researcher may come into contact.

Strangers at the Gate

Extortion does not have to be in the form of cash. For many decades, the research area has held a deserved reputation as an unstable region with regard to conflict of Muslim-Christian extremists and political rivals. Rebel troops have been known to band together as mercenaries and although local life goes on, a low level of intimidation persists that can be particularly disconcerting to outsiders and field workers alike. A form of coercion or threat well-known in the region involves door-to-door soliciting of items of value to support religious or political ideologies. The approach of a stranger at the front gate results in furious dog barking. Longtime residents, and the researcher, would instantly peek through the shutters to scrutinize the disturbance. Whether or not the person at the gate

---

[5] This practice predictably exists in many urban areas worldwide. Downtown Chicago was notorious for the number of young men who would appear in traffic and squirt one's windshield with water and then expect money after a few wipes of a paper towel. Many undoubtedly felt intimidated and would pay. The city outlawed such street antics although such activity persists in some areas (see Erlenbusch, 2006; cf. Smith, 2005). The *Bantay* boys are tolerated, and generally not feared, though their practice adds another style of extortion to the research setting. Personal conversation with Professor Gustav Lundberg of Duquesne University (Pittsburgh) revealed that *bantay*-type activity exists today in Miami, USA. Dr. Victoria Time, Old Dominion University and Professor Nọnso Okafọ, Norfolk State University, state that similar activity flourishes in the cities of Cameroon and Nigeria (reported at the American Society of Criminology Conference, Los Angeles, California, USA, 2006). Begging activity is widely covered in the literature although not commonly in criminological outlets. For a few extensive reports, see Gmelch and Gmelch (1978) regarding Dublin, Ireland; Kudriavtseva (2001) regarding Russia; and Lu (2005) regarding China.

was an unfamiliar person, street person, or rag-tag mercenary, a decision had to be made quickly if a handout should be given. Typically, a small plastic bag of uncooked rice was taken to the gate. Appeasing such disturbers is often considered a better approach than dismissing them outright. Part of the rationale is simply that it is likely best to remain on the friendly side of all parties. Regardless, the household and the researcher were begrudging but willing victims of extortion. Locals argued that some poverty-stricken extremists tagged households to let others know of sympathizers or at least those not antagonistic toward them. In recent years, it is likely that most of the visitors at the gate seeking handouts are indigent and not hostile. It is only that the resident can never be certain.

Land Squatting

Another non-cash form of extortion is quite prevalent in the research area but likely only indirectly impacts fieldworkers. That is land or house "squatting" on another's property. The sprawling bamboo cottage where the researcher stayed for multiple field ventures was also home to a number of tenants. The landlord had the constant worry that a tenant might refuse to pay rent and make the argument that he or she (the tenant), in fact, owned the property. It would then become the difficult task of the landlord to prove, sometimes in court, that the landlord was the true owner of the property. Such cases are common, and because written records decay quickly in the equatorial climate the necessary paperwork is not always easy to reconstruct decades after land has been purchased. Local judges or other officials sometimes become entangled with family or ethnic allegiances on one side or the other of the dispute.

At the research site, and immediately down the road from the researcher, one beach-front squatter neighborhood led to multiple others and soon a village emerged that ultimately was given official recognition with its own elected representatives. With in-depth interviewing and participant observation, it is likely that informants, acquaintances, or even long-term friends of the researcher will be involved with land squatting events, either as victims or offenders. The longer a researcher remains in the field in Mindanao the more likely that some ties with such common disputes involving informants or acquaintances will arise. Everyone has a story of land squatting and it remains one of the more intractable social problems in Mindanao. The researcher must be careful during field interviews when topics turn to sensitive issues of property ownership. For more complete and early coverage of land squatting in Third World countries, see Abrams (1964), Payne (1977), and Neuwirth (2004).

Written Endorsements

Another style of non-cash extortion pertains to a request for written endorsements. This is similar to beggar activity but in this case, a signature is requested as a type of promissory note of favors to come at a later date to the asker. It is surprising that such activity would actually result in a total stranger offering up a signature. This appears comparable to email spam messages requesting that one voluntarily enter into some sort of mysterious financial enterprise, which will reap huge financial benefits down the road (popularly called "419" in Nigeria and other parts of the world). At the research site, it has been common for total strangers to select well-heeled outsiders, typically including foreign researchers, at the marketplace, on the street, or other public places and insist that if only a piece of paper be read it will become clear why a signature should be offered. This is most often for some sort of backing for a job, entry to an educational institution, sponsorship to emigrate the country, or other investment involving the needy person. Because the petitioner is face-to-face and can persistently pursue the outsider, this qualifies as a type of extortive behavior.

A more complex and troubling kind of extortion involving written endorsements occurs when an employee is coerced by a boss to falsify records. One interviewee reported that he was retiring after decades of government service. His superior remarked that he would sign the necessary paperwork for the employee to receive his retirement bonus only if the employee would rig some papers before retirement to benefit the boss. The employee handled financial matters of the business. The employee refused the extortionate boss and retired with no retirement bonus. This kind of deceit by a supervisor often occurs with no official record and attempts to resolve such extortion commonly require complex and timely informal dispute strategies rather than official court action. Locals interviewed in government positions were well aware of such behind-the-scenes maneuvering involving workers nearing retirement. Comments such as "be very careful with your government boss, after all you know you are getting close to retirement" were common among locals. For discussion of dispute settlement strategies to resolve such problems, see Austin (1999).

Palo-apon

In some cases, the need to offer payola (a bribe) can confront the field worker. The research site has been well-known for its slowness in completing transactions for various public utilities, home repair requests, and virtually any government or private business transaction. Low salaried workers depend on a little *hip-hip* to make ends meet. Originally, and even in recent times, reliance on hand-written paperwork and manual typewriters leads to a need to return the following day on multiple revisits to continue the transaction. This is referred to as *palo-apon* (literally to "follow upon" or to "follow up") in the research area. For locals and field researchers alike, the problem arises when a business appears to drum up a pseudo need for a "follow-up" just to aggravate the customer to a point where, out of frustration, an offer of some *hip-hip* is made under-the-table. Longtime residents will often build the extra cost of *hip-hip* into the daily transaction.

The "follow-up" practice became so rampant in the past few years that a new occupational position emerged – the *tig* (literally meaning "to go" or "to stand" in place of another). Today, it is possible that a local Filipino or field researcher could hire for a few dollars a *tig* (pronounced "*teeg*") who will manage the *hip-hip* for you. Without question, some *tigs* are more likely to transact *hip-hip* than others. A *tig* qualifies for what might be called a deviant occupation although some are surely legitimate. The *tig* appears closely related, for example, to an ex-police officer who may open a private detective agency and is willing to provide some services that might be considered unsavory or improper if performed by a regular police agency (Inciardi and Dee, 1987).

Companion Enigma

Reciprocal gift exchange can take many forms. Although a style not commonly discussed in the literature, giving gifts is sometimes replaced in the research area with providing assistance to another with the expectation that another will then be obligated to come to your aid, if called upon. This can be seen in a positive light as when neighbors can rely upon each other in time of need. Such practice is referred to in the Visayan language as *utang kabubut-on*, meaning "inner debt." As a field researcher, it was common for one of my longtime informants to shout at me in the morning as I was departing the house "don't get any *utang kabubut-on* from anyone." It took me some time to appreciate what was meant. Many locals will go out of their way to offer their help. Many will want to be a "companion" or guide. It is considered unusual for one to walk alone and having a companion certainly reaps benefits. However, a few, not all, are more interested in some long-range profit they may gain by building up credits in the form of favors provided. They might, for instance, return at a later date and ask for a loan of money or endorsement with a subtle understanding that they have assisted you in the past in some manner. This qualifies as a most delicate kind of extortive behavior. For earlier discussions of reciprocal gift exchange, see Gouldner (1960); cf. Sahlins (1965); Mauss (1990).

Extorted Personal Space

Finally, extortion may not involve payola at all in the usual sense. Instead, one's own personal space or territory can be encroached upon and stolen and in such cases, one suffers an unusual type of extortion. This has been quite distinctive at the research site. Wealthy or other very influential citizens, including heads of local religious or political factions, can be seen arriving at banks or other public gathering places in their vans with darkened windshields and side windows. Sometimes an entourage of armed bodyguards and other followers accompanying the high status individual will clear a path by pushing the lower-status citizens out of the way to allow immediate and special service for the luminary. Such a line-butting scenario is likely common in all highly stratified societies and reflects a fundamental form of extortive behavior. Should the encroaching entourage reveal weapons, even if partially hidden with pistols in holsters, a sense of unease or fear prevails. On these occasions, the researcher would also stand aside.

Sometime later, it became embarrassingly obvious that the field researcher, as an American outsider, could also be the cause of locals stepping aside to give up their space or to offer a chair in a crowded room. It took some time and concerted effort to convince persons in near poverty circumstances that it was not necessary to forgo their place in line. Yet, for the researcher to turn down an opportunity to go to the front of a bank or restaurant line to be served directly, rather than to stand in long queues, was never really understood or accepted by many locals (see Lyman and Scott, 1970, for an interesting outline of types of personal and public territoriality).

An ultimate form of territorial encroachment and extorted personal space applies when a prominent individual, usually including outside researchers, must manage a continuous apprehension of being kidnapped. Although, in a statistical sense, this is remote, locals are fearful for the outsider who is pressured, generally against his or her will, to alter a daily routine in order to thwart any would-be kidnappers. As an outside researcher, I was constantly reminded not to take my usual daybreak walk to the corner bakery for *"init pan de sal"* (hot rolls) because such a daily routine could be a signal to kidnappers of a predictable and thus potential prey. Having to modify my behavior qualifies as extortion of my personal and social space.

Discussion and Theoretical Overview

This paper necessitates some discussion of the theoretical implications of bribery and extortion. A few comments are in order in regards to how local citizens in the research setting of the southern Philippines respond to acts of payola whether cash or favors offered willingly or compelled by others through intimidation. Donald Black argues in *The Social Structure of Right and Wrong* (1993, cf., 1976) that crime may be seen as a type of social control and that such may reflect a variety of styles. Thus, the motivations of offenders may vary widely. Also, the motivations of victims may take numerous forms in response to wrongs and controls directed toward them. Black presents four basic styles or rationales for response to crime: penal, compensatory, therapeutic, and conciliatory. The examples of bribery and extortion presented here are more precisely conceptualized through Black's themes and at the same time, the Philippine scenarios allow for a further clarification of several of his theoretical predictions.[6]

In Lanao del Norte, motivations for intimidation and how persons respond to intimidation include all of the four styles as predicted by Black, some occurring more often than others and some in unexpected ways. Penal and compensatory rationales apply when relationships are accusatory. Therapeutic and conciliatory rationales involve remedial relationships (see Black, 1993, pp. 6-9; cf., Austin, 1999, pp. 111-114).

Table 1 reflects all styles of extortion discussed here with a designation of whether the style was met by a response of anger (penal), a desire to reimburse or pay off (compensatory), a desire to offer help (therapeutic), or a desire to simply resolve a difference or dispute (conciliatory). Based upon a subjective consensus of informant accounts, a response to extortion by a victim was calculated as frequent, occasional or rare. For instance, regarding confrontation by street beggars (particularly in the case of children), a response would most likely be "therapeutic" (frequent). It would not be surprising that one would feel sympathy for impoverished street children and offer a few centavos. In such cases, a penal or punitive response would be rare. On the other hand, being confronted with an intimidating stranger at the front gate asking for a handout would more likely be met with a frequent response of compensation (i.e., give them some rice and they will go away) and occasionally by a therapeutic response, but rarely with an angry or punitive response.

Table 1. Rationale for Victim Responses to Extortion

Extortion Type	Rationale for Response			
	Penal	Compensatory	Therapeutic	Conciliatory
Beggars	rare	rare	frequent	occasional
***Bantay* boys**	rare	occasional	frequent	occasional
Strangers at gate	rare	occasional	occasional	frequent
Land squatting	frequent	rare	rare	occasional
Written endorsements	frequent	rare	rare	rare

---

[6] These findings do not reflect pure examples of "case studies" but are "quick snapshots" of bribing and extortionate issues. Space limitations disallow fully detailed and rich descriptions of the examples of bribery and extortion.

Extortion Type	Rationale for Response			
	Penal	Compensatory	Therapeutic	Conciliatory
Palo-apon	occasional	frequent	rare	frequent
Companion enigma	rare	frequent	frequent	rare
Extorted space	occasional	rare	rare	frequent

When one is coerced by another to offer a written endorsement, it is more likely that the victim may respond with anger and any other reaction would be rather rare. On the other hand, if a companion secretly wishes to take advantage of an outsider by asking favors, the response would less likely be anger and more toward offering assistance (therapeutic) or more toward reimbursing the extorting companion for his or her time (compensatory). The typology of eight styles of extortion/bribery presented here allows for further analysis beyond the issue of the rationale of the victim in response to intimidation. For instance, Donald Black also argues that the mobilization of law varies with the stratification of a society, or segments of the society, and also that law varies depending on the direction of the deviant act, whether against a lower status or higher status person (1976, pp. 13-17). Although these data do not allow absolute test of this proposition, several examples of payola are noteworthy. For example, street beggars and *bantay* children are, by definition, of low status, and they are extorting higher status persons. Following Black, the control is actually in the hands of the higher status individual. In this case, the person being extorted by beggars can simply walk away and ignore the beggars. Also, the vehicle owner can also ignore the *bantay* children. Theoretically, the higher status individuals could organize the legal system to ban beggars and *bantay* children from the streets as sometimes happens in urban areas as in the Chicago, USA, example noted earlier.

As pointed out by Black, when the deviant or illegal act is actually between persons of similar position and rank, the case becomes more complicated (1976, pp. 41-42). The person being extorted is not in immediate control. This can be seen in the case of the boss who refused to sign for the employee to receive his terminal leave bonus. Both were actually of similar social status (i.e., college graduates and longtime government supervisors) even though one had authority over clearing the other employee for retirement. Black claims that in such cases the relationship can become most contentious and litigious with lawsuits being brought against the other. The example of the employee who retired without his bonus pay dragged on for years with various third-party mediators introduced to try to resolve the case.

Also, in the example of the "companion enigma," both parties are of similar social status. Extortion by the friend is rather latent and only at a later date does the companion return to ask for favors thus extorting the accompanying person who may feel obligated to return favors. These kinds of cases are also complex and it is difficult for the party being extorted to simply walk away without some guilt. This kind of social deviance involves intricate maneuvers to escape from what was first thought a friendship but turns out to be more of a scheme by one party to extract favors from the other by engendering a sense of obligation between companions. These cases can also extend for years.

Black also predicts that law varies with the relational distance or social intimacy between individuals. Table 2 shows how the diverse styles of extortion vary according to social intimacy between extorter and victim and also with the complexity and severity of the deviant act. Thus, for instance, the relational distance between street beggars and tourists is high (non-intimate and fleeting) and perhaps without eye contact. In such cases, the complexity and severity of the payola is low. In the case of "strangers at the gate," the relational distance is designated as medium because the extorter must be addressed at the home site and the brief face-to-face conversation that commonly ensues is somewhat more involved than with a street beggar. The complexity and severity of the extortion is designated as medium in that this scenario includes a greater degree of fear and distrust as one's home space is encroached upon.

Table 2. Relationship between the Style, Complexity and Severity of Extortion by the Relational Distance between Offenders and Victims

Complexity/Severity of Extortion	Relational Distance between Offenders and Victims		
	Low	Medium	High
Low		*bantay* boys	street beggars
Medium	companion enigma	palo apon & extorted space	strangers
High	written endorsements	land squatting	

Table 2 shows that in the extortion case of land squatting and written endorsements, the complexity and severity of the deviant or illegal act is designated as high. These cases can extend for years, involve large sums of money, and can even turn violent. Interestingly, however, in these cases the relational distance is low or "closer" and less fleeting. Such extortive relationships are less transitory and often require frequent interactions. Consequently, following Black's proposition, some cases reveal that as the relational distance increases between persons or groups (i.e., a reduction in social intimacy), we see the dispute or extortive act as less complex and less severe and a reduced need to mobilize the legal system. And, the opposite is true, that extortive cases involving close associates can be most troublesome and require multiple attempts toward some sort of resolution.

Conclusion and Directions for Future Research

Some issues that are suggested by the data must become the basis for future hypothesizing and can only be noted here. These include at least three categories or directions. First, how do the various styles of extortion/bribery differ in regards to role complexity? That is, do styles of intimidation vary with the number of persons involved in the extortionate or bribing scenario or in the intricacy of the roles making up such relationships? Thus, when a boss intimidates a subordinate by refusing to sign papers allowing smooth retirement, is this more complex than the relationship between beggar and victim? Why would this be so?

Second, in what ways do role duration and role direction come into play in the styles of extortion and bribery? For instance, some styles of extortion appear to continue on for years and others are more short-lived. Also, some styles appear to move in one direction from extorter to victim (begging) and other styles appear to involve long-range reciprocal relationships with planned retaliation by the victim, as in land squatting. Third, other than the few comments made here, it appears likely that the social class of the offender and victim must be better understood in regards to the styles of extortion and bribery. Stated differently, extortion apparently develops with some styles of extortion being based strongly on the social status of the victim. Surely, beggars and the *bantay* boys will target the more well-to-do. In other styles of extortion, such as land squatting and extortion of personal space, the relationship may not be as clear. The nature and extent of poverty in Mindanao rather obviously must have direct relationship with the prevalence of extortion and bribery. This issue and perhaps how such styles of social deviance could or should be resolved remain unanswered.

In the research area of northwest Mindanao, bribery and extortion appear to take on nearly normalized action that is much more subtle and complex than simply handing over cash to a police officer. To the field worker, such activities can make life cumbersome and sometimes frustrating. Yet, such forms of inappropriate and oftentimes illegal activity highlight a subject matter (begging) to be further explored.

References

Abrams, Charles (1964) *Man's Struggle for Shelter in an Urbanizing World.* Cambridge, Massachusetts, USA: The MIT Press.

Arquiza, Rey (1997) "Number of Street Children on the Rise". *The Philippine Star* (April 22).

Austin, Timothy (1987) "Conceptual Confusion Among Rural Filipinos in Adapting to Modern Procedures of Amicable Settlement," *International Journal of Comparative and Applied Criminal Justice*, 11 (2): 241-250.

Austin, Timothy (1989) "Living on the Edge: The Impact of Terrorism upon Philippine Villagers," *International Journal of Offender Therapy and Comparative Criminology*, 33 (1): 103-119.

Austin, Timothy (1991) "Toward a Theory on the Impact of Terrorism: The Philippine Scenario," *International Journal of Comparative and Applied Criminal Justice*, 15 (1): 33-48.

Austin, Timothy (1995) "Filipino Self-help and Peacemaking Strategies: A View from the Mindanao Hinterland," *Human Organization*, 54 (1): 10-19.

Austin, Timothy (1999) *Banana Justice.* Westport, Connecticut, USA: Greenwood Publishing Group.

Austin, Timothy (2003) "Tenting Amidst Terrorists: The Upside of Central Mindanao Field Work," *Practicing Anthropology*, 25 (2): 43-47l.

Berg, B. L., Austin, W. T., and Zuern, G. A. (1992) "Institutional Review Boards: Virtue Machines or Villains?" *Criminal Justice Policy Review*, Vol. 6 (2): 87-102.

Black, Donald (1976) *The Behavior of Law.* New York, NY, USA: Academic Press.

Black, Donald (1993) *The Structure of Right and Wrong.* New York, NY, USA: Academic Press.

Erlenbusch, Robert (2006) "A Dream Denied: The Criminalization of Homelessness in U. S. Cities". *A Report by the National Coalition for the Homeless and the National Law Center on Homelessness & Poverty.* Washington, D.C., USA.

Gmelch, George and Sharon Bohn Gmelch (1978) "Begging in Dublin: The Strategies of a Marginal Urban Occupation," *Journal of Contemporary Ethnography*, 6: 439-454.

Gouldner, Alvin W. (1960) "The Norm of Reciprocity: A Preliminary Statement," *American Sociological Review*, 25: 161-178.

Inciardi, James A. and Juliet L. Dee. (1987) "From the Keystone Cops to Miami Vice: Images of Policing in American Popular Culture," *Journal of Popular Culture*, 21 (Fall): 84-102.

Kudriavtseva, M. (2001) "The Dramaturgy of Begging: A Description of an Everyday Practice," *Journal of Sociology and Social Anthropology*, 4 (3): 37-48.

Laswell, H. D. (1963) "Bribery," *The Encyclopedia of the Social Sciences*. New York, NY, USA: McMillan.

Lu, Hanchao (2005) *Street Criers: A Cultural History of Chinese Beggars*. Palo Alto, California, USA: Stanford University Press.

Lyman, S. M. and M. B. Scott (1967) "Territoriality: A Neglected Sociological Dimension," *Social Problems*, 15:236-249.

Mauss, Marcel (1990) *The Gift: The Form and Reason for Exchange in Archaic Societies*. (Translated by W. D. Halls). London, England: Routledge.

Myrdal, Gunnassr (1968) *Asian Drama: An Enquiry into the Poverty of Nations*. Vol. II. (937-951). New York, NY, USA: Twentieth Century Publications.

Neuwirth, Robert (2004) *Shadow Cities: A Billion Squatters, A New Urban World*. London, England: Routledge.

Offer, Avner (1995) "Between the Gift and the Market: The Economy of Regard," *Economic History Review*, L (3):450-476.

Payne, Geoffrey K. (1977) *Urban Housing in the Third World*. London, England: Leonard Hill.

Rush, George E. (1986) *The Dictionary of Criminal Justice* (2nd Edition). Guilford, Connecticut, USA: Dushkin Publishing Group.

Sahlins, Marshall D. (1965) "On the Sociology of Primitive Exchange," *The Relevance of Models for Social Anthropology*, Michael Banton (ed). London, England: Tavistock.

Seiber, J. E. (1990) *Planning Ethnically Responsible Research: A Guide for Students and Internal Review Boards*. Thousand Oaks, California, USA: Sage Publications.

Smith, Patricia K. (2005) "The Economics of Anti-begging Regulations," *The American Journal of Economics and Sociology*, 64 (2): 549-577.

Postscript

In this book's title, *GROUNDED LAW*, the word *Grounded* is used to capture the law that emanates from and reflects the society to which it applies. This law represents the direct and indirect experiences, history, and expectations of the citizens whose affairs the law regulates. Thus, Igbo *Grounded Law*, Yoruba *Grounded Law*, Hausa *Grounded Law*, or Nigerian *Grounded Law*, emanates from and reflects the Nigerian society, in much the same way that English (*Grounded*) Law, French (*Grounded*) Law, American (USA) (*Grounded*) Law, German (*Grounded*) Law, and each of the other Western laws emanates from and reflects its home culture. Similarly, each of the Kenyan, Chinese, South African, Japanese, and Singaporean *Grounded Law* is expected to be entrenched in and reflect the society from which it developed. There are thus inevitable differences among the laws of different societies. Consequently, wherever necessary in this book, the law, justice, and social control of one society are compared to those of another or others to better explain and illustrate the issues.

It is trite that foreign interventions are responsible for the present divide between homegrown and foreign laws in most societies. Colonization is arguably the most prominent form of the foreign interventions that produced many of the modern States and their laws. Colonization and other interventions have brought about the need for *Grounded Law* as a means of re-ordering the law of a society. Although the legacies of colonization are present in every postcolonial State, it should be obvious that the need for *Grounded Law* is felt far more in Africa than in other parts of the world. This derives from the rather extreme nature of the African experience in the hands of various Euro-American powers, through Enslavement and Colonization. Both epochal events, particularly Colonization, were based on "Substitutive Interaction" (Okereafoezeke, 2002, pp. 18-20), to the advantage of the West but at Africa's expense. Decades after political independence by the African States, they fundamentally remain enmeshed in colonially created and sustained laws and other expectations. And, there is no evidence that this condition will be changed anytime soon, if at all.

Thus, the colonial domination of substantive and procedural aspects of life in postcolonial Africa, in particular, is highly visible in the area of law and justice. However, this upper hand extends far beyond jurisprudence. A cursory examination of every area of knowledge, learning, or other human endeavor will demonstrate the extent to which Africans – at individual, group, and State levels –

rely on the Western idea. For example, as I pointed out in Chapter 16, the field of Philosophy has little or no acknowledgement for African Philosophy. The so-called mainstream Philosophy is in fact Western Philosophy, which has been positioned, sometimes with the acquiescence of African philosophers and intellectuals, as the Universal Philosophy. And so, Africans are expected and required to adjust to and adopt the Western philosophical idea, if they are to be regarded as a part of the modern world. Again, this attitude is not confined to law and justice, and philosophy. In the field of Psychology, the paradigms and practices of the West are typically offered as the universal model. Further, in the areas of science, medicine, and pharmacy, is it not wondrous that Western drug researchers and manufacturers remove natural herbal ingredients from the tropics (mainly Africa), process the ingredients, and offer the finished products to Africans and the rest of the world while declaring the products to be Western? African medical scientists and pharmacy schools scramble to learn and adopt the Western manufacture, often at Western schools, when these could be more conveniently achieved in African institutions.

In conclusion, the fundamental points of this book are threefold. One, considering the crucial, extensive, and long-established roles that indigenous, customary, native, etc. law (more appropriately, *Grounded Law*) plays in managing grievances, conflicts, and disputes, and in social control in general in a modern State, continuing to deny this original law of a society the "law" label is illogical and indefensible. It is time to recognize the original law of a society as "law" especially because the argument for limiting "law" to essentially Euro-American models is Western. Where appropriate in this book (particularly in Chapter 16), I have argued that based on historical evidence, the West lacks the credibility to judge the law, justice, and other systems of other societies that differ from the Western view, such as those of Africa. Two, *Grounded Law* is a far more appropriate name for the original law of a society. Thus, *Grounded Law* should be adopted to replace the string of names (including, *customary law*, *native law*, *aboriginal law*, *indigenous law*, *traditional law*, etc.) that have been used to disparage the homegrown laws of a society, particularly a postcolony. Three, in law and justice, as well as other areas of human relationships and endeavors, African and other postcolonial societies should seek primarily to address their problems from within, relying on their homegrown systems and other resources. Of course, foreign models should always be considered to determine their capacity and suitability for augmenting the homemade models.

Index

About the Author

Chukwunọnso Okafọ, Ph.D., is a Professor of Law at the University of Nigeria. Prior to joining the University of Nigeria academic staff, he was a tenured Professor in the Postgraduate Program in Criminal Justice, Norfolk State University, USA, 2003-2011. Before he arrived Norfolk State University in 2003, Professor Okafọ taught at Western Carolina University, USA, 1996-2003. Having been called to the Nigerian Bar in 1989, Professor Okafọ earned a Ph.D. from the Indiana University of Pennsylvania, USA in 1996. He is a member of the International Bar Association (along with membership of the Association's Anti-Corruption Committee of the Public and Professional Interest Division). Professor Okafọ is the author of *Reconstructing Law and Justice in a Postcolony*, Ashgate Publishing. The book scrutinizes the challenges, considerations, and model for rebuilding the law, justice, and social control of a former colony, such as Nigeria. He also published *Law and Justice in Post-British Nigeria: Conflicts and Interactions Between Native and Foreign Systems of Social Control in Igbo*, Greenwood Press. This book, which is on the plurality of Nigerian law, justice, and social control, delineates formal and informal law and justice, and creates a model for testing the formality or informality of a law and justice process. Further, Professor Okafọ is the author of numerous peer-reviewed, professional articles as well as other essays on law, justice, and social control. He has presented abundant professional papers at local, national, and international conferences. Professor Okafọ is the Associate Editor of the *Journal of Law and Conflict Resolution*. And, he serves on the Editorial Boards of other international professional journals, including *Law and Policy Review*; *Race and Justice: An International Journal*; and *African Journal of Criminology and Justice Studies*. Professor Okafọ currently teaches international criminal law (postgraduate), criminology, and jurisprudence.

Professor Okafọ can be reached by e-mail at:
ChukwunonsoOkafo@lawyer.com or NonsoOkafo@yahoo.com
Website: www.LawPracticeandJusticeResearch.com

Contributors

Sikiru Asifatu is a Ph.D. Candidate, Criminology, at the University of Texas at Dallas, United States of America.

W. Timothy Austin, Ph.D., is a Professor, Criminology, at Indiana University of Pennsylvania, United States of America.

Kingsley Ejiogu is a Ph.D. Candidate, Administration of Justice, at Texas Southern University, United States of America.

O. Oko Elechi, Ph.D., is an Associate Professor, Justice Studies, at Prairie View A&M University, United States of America.

Ihekwoaba D. Onwudiwe, Ph.D., is a Professor and Chairman, Administration of Justice, at Texas Southern University, United States of America.

James Opolot, Ph.D., is a Professor, Administration of Justice, at Texas Southern University, United States of America.

Simon Ortuanya, SJD, Senior Lecturer, Faculty of Law, at the University of Nigeria (UNN), and Executive Director of Nigeria HIV/AIDS Law Project (NIHALP). Dr. Ortuanya, on leave of absence from UNN, is currently the Commissioner for Education, Enugu State.

Smart Otu, Ph.D., is a Senior Lecturer, Criminology, at Ebonyi State University, Nigeria.

Susan Smith-Cunnien, Ph.D., is a Professor, Sociology and Criminal Justice, at the University of St. Thomas, United States of America.

Caroline Time, LL.B., is a Legal Practitioner, a member of the Cameroon Bar Association as well as the International Federation of Women Lawyers.

Victoria Time, Ph.D., is an Associate Professor and University Professor, Criminal Justice, at Old Dominion University, United States of America.